Business Communication
Developing Leaders for a Networked World

Fourth Edition

Peter W. Cardon
University of Southern California

BUSINESS COMMUNICATION: DEVELOPING LEADERS FOR A NETWORKED WORLD, FOURTH EDITION

Published by McGraw-Hill Education, 2 Penn Plaza, New York, NY 10121. Copyright © 2021 by McGraw-Hill Education. All rights reserved. Printed in the United States of America. Previous edition © 2018, 2016, and 2014. No part of this publication may be reproduced or distributed in any form or by any means, or stored in a database or retrieval system, without the prior written consent of McGraw-Hill Education, including, but not limited to, in any network or other electronic storage or transmission, or broadcast for distance learning.

Some ancillaries, including electronic and print components, may not be available to customers outside the United States.

This book is printed on acid-free paper.

2 3 4 5 6 7 8 9 LWI 24 23 22 21 20

ISBN 978-1-260-08834-2 (bound edition)
MHID 1-260-08834-0 (bound edition)
ISBN 978-1-264-10910-4 (loose-leaf edition)
MHID 1-26410910-5 (loose-leaf edition)

Portfolio Manager: *Peter Jurmu*
Senior Product Developer: *Anne Leung*
Marketing Manager: *Gabe Fedota*
Lead Content Project Manager: *Christine Vaughan*
Senior Content Project Manager: *Bruce Gin*
Senior Buyer: *Susan K. Culbertson*
Designer: *Egzon Shaqiri*
Senior Content Licensing Specialist: *Brianna Kirschbaum*
Cover Image: *©Vitalex/Shutterstock*
Compositor: *Aptara®, Inc.*

All credits appearing on page or at the end of the book are considered to be an extension of the copyright page.

Library of Congress Cataloging-in-Publication Data

Names: Cardon, Peter W., author.
Title: Business communication : developing leaders for a networked world /
    Peter W. Cardon.
Description: Fourth edition. | New York, NY : McGraw-Hill Education, 2021.
    | Includes index.
Identifiers: LCCN 2019040775 | ISBN 9781260088342 (hardcover)
Subjects: LCSH: Business communication. | Business enterprises—Computer
    networks. | Business communication—Computer network resources.
Classification: LCC HF5718 .C267 2021 | DDC 658.4/5—dc23
LC record available at https://lccn.loc.gov/2019040775

The Internet addresses listed in the text were accurate at the time of publication. The inclusion of a website does not indicate an endorsement by the authors or McGraw-Hill Education, and McGraw-Hill Education does not guarantee the accuracy of the information presented at these sites.

mheducation.com/highered

Dedication

To my daughters: Camilla Jean and Audrey Mei. Your mom and I love spending every day with you. You make me the happiest dad in the world!

—Peter W. Cardon

About the Author

Courtesy of Peter Cardon

Peter W. Cardon, MBA, PhD, is a professor in the Department of Business Communication at the University of Southern California. He also serves as Academic Director for the MBA for Professionals and Managers program. He teaches a variety of courses in the MBA and undergraduate business programs, including management communication, intercultural communication, and new media and communication. With approximately 75 refereed articles, Pete is an active contributor to the latest research in intercultural communication, social networking, team collaboration, and leadership communication. He is proud to engage in a discipline that helps so many business professionals and students reach career and personal goals.

Pete is an active member of the Association for Business Communication (ABC), for which he previously served as president. He currently serves as an Editorial Review Board member for the *International Journal of Business Communication (IJBC)* and *Business and Professional Communication Quarterly (BPCQ)*.

Prior to joining higher education, Pete worked as a marketing director at an international tourism company that focused on the markets of Brazil, South Korea, Japan, and Taiwan. Before that position, he was an account manager in a manufacturing company.

Pete is a strong advocate of global business ties. Having worked in China for three years and consulted in and traveled to roughly 70 countries, he has worked extensively with clients, customers, colleagues, and other partners across the world. To help students develop global leadership skills, he has led student groups on company tours and humanitarian projects to mainland China, Hong Kong, Macao, Taiwan, South Korea, Mexico, and the Dominican Republic. He is an active member of Rotary International, a global service organization committed to promoting peace, fighting disease, providing educational opportunities, and growing local economies.

Brief Contents

Bonus Content Mc Graw Hill create   Mc Graw Hill connect

Available only at www.mcgrawhillcreate.com/cardon or in the e-book within McGraw-Hill Connect®.

(Developing Leaders for a Networked World)

Welcome to the fourth edition of *Business Communication: Developing Leaders for a Networked World*. Taking Peter Cardon's **practitioner and case-based approach**, this text helps students develop an understanding of how course content applies to the business world. Maintaining a central theme of **credibility**, the fourth edition communicates why **credibility** is essential to effective communication in today's rapidly changing business environment. Cardon's text, integrated with *Connect for Business Communication*, provides a contemporary yet traditional view into the business communication field, empowering students to learn bedrock communication principles while also staying up to date with cultural and **technological** changes in the business world—transforming them into leaders for a networked world.

©Vitalex/Shutterstock

Credibility

Since professional success often depends on engendering trust within professional relationships, this text begins with a discussion of credibility and refers to it throughout. Principles of relationship-building such as personal credibility, emotional intelligence, and listening hold a prominent role throughout the text.

Effective Writing Builds Relationships

Effective writing in the workplace is essential to building connections and a professional brand. Cardon's three-stage writing process drives excellence in critical thinking, collaboration, and productivity in work relationships. With additional examples of internal messages, Cardon develops the skills used early in a career.

Enhanced Coverage of Technology

This text adopts a visionary view of communication technologies. Cardon's text takes a view of social media use that includes team communication and communication with external partners. The need for students to develop an online professional persona that builds credibility is also addressed. This prepares students for communication in the evolving workplace.

Business Focus

The case-based approach helps students learn how communication can build rich and productive relationships between professionals. Each chapter opens with a short business case, and weaves examples from the case throughout the chapter and into the model documents, engaging readers in the story behind each business message.

Forward-Looking Vision Built on Tradition

While the text stays true to core business communication principles established over many decades, it also goes beyond traditional coverage with inclusion of the latest communication practices facilitated by communication technologies and its enhanced coverage of increasingly important business communication topics such as:

Interpersonal communication (Chapters 2, 3, and 4), social media and technology (Chapters 7 and 8), crisis communication and public relations (Bonus Chapter), oral communication (throughout the text), and business plans and business proposals (Bonus Appendix).

Why Does This Matter?

Each chapter begins with a section that explains why the content is crucial to career success. A URL located at the beginning of these sections direct students to view a short video clip of the author reinforcing this message.

Chapter Takeaways

With graphics and lists, the chapter takeaways engage students with key chapter content, and serve as a reference for applying the principles to their oral and written communication.

Learning Exercises

Each chapter contains engaging learning exercises. These exercises are organized into discussion exercises, evaluation exercises, application exercises, and language and mechanics checks to help students develop expertise in business communication.

McGraw Hill connect®

You're in the driver's seat.

Want to build your own course? No problem. Prefer to use our turnkey, prebuilt course? Easy. Want to make changes throughout the semester? Sure. And you'll save time with Connect's auto-grading too.

65%
Less Time Grading

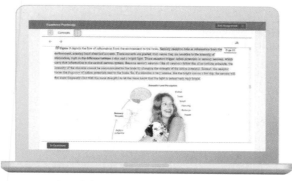
Laptop: McGraw-Hill; Woman/dog: George Doyle/Getty Images

They'll thank you for it.

Adaptive study resources like SmartBook® 2.0 help your students be better prepared in less time. You can transform your class time from dull definitions to dynamic debates. Find out more about the powerful personalized learning experience available in SmartBook 2.0 at **www.mheducation.com/highered/connect/smartbook**

Make it simple, make it affordable.

Connect makes it easy with seamless integration using any of the major Learning Management Systems— Blackboard®, Canvas, and D2L, among others—to let you organize your course in one convenient location. Give your students access to digital materials at a discount with our inclusive access program. Ask your McGraw-Hill representative for more information.

Padlock: Jobalou/Getty Images

Solutions for your challenges.

A product isn't a solution. Real solutions are affordable, reliable, and come with training and ongoing support when you need it and how you want it. Our Customer Experience Group can also help you troubleshoot tech problems— although Connect's 99% uptime means you might not need to call them. See for yourself at **status.mheducation.com**

Checkmark: Jobalou/Getty Images

FOR STUDENTS

Effective, efficient studying.

Connect helps you be more productive with your study time and get better grades using tools like SmartBook 2.0, which highlights key concepts and creates a personalized study plan. Connect sets you up for success, so you walk into class with confidence and walk out with better grades.

Study anytime, anywhere.

Download the free ReadAnywhere app and access your online eBook or SmartBook 2.0 assignments when it's convenient, even if you're offline. And since the app automatically syncs with your eBook and SmartBook 2.0 assignments in Connect, all of your work is available every time you open it. Find out more at
www.mheducation.com/readanywhere

"I really liked this app—it made it easy to study when you don't have your text-book in front of you."

- Jordan Cunningham,
Eastern Washington University

Calendar: owattaphotos/Getty Images

No surprises.

The Connect Calendar and Reports tools keep you on track with the work you need to get done and your assignment scores. Life gets busy; Connect tools help you keep learning through it all.

Learning for everyone.

McGraw-Hill works directly with Accessibility Services Departments and faculty to meet the learning needs of all students. Please contact your Accessibility Services office and ask them to email accessibility@mheducation.com, or visit
www.mheducation.com/about/accessibility
for more information.

Grammar and Mechanics

LearnSmart Achieve

Put responsible writing into practice. LearnSmart Achieve develops and improves editing and business writing skills. This adaptive learning system helps students learn faster, study more efficiently, and retain more knowledge for greater success. Visit **bit.ly/meetLSAchieve** for a walkthrough.

Grammar Quizzes

Students may not think grammar and mechanics are the most exciting topics, but they need to master the basics. Our grammar quizzes within Connect assess students' grammar and mechanics. With a total of 150 auto-graded questions, these are great to use as pre- and post-tests in your courses.

Application

Tegrity: Lectures 24/7

Tegrity in Connect is a tool that makes class time available 24/7 by automatically capturing every lecture. With a simple one-click start-and-stop process, you capture all computer screens and corresponding audio in a format that is easy to search, frame by frame. Students can replay any part of any class with easy-to-use, browser-based viewing on a PC, Mac, iPod, or other mobile device.

Educators know that the more students can see, hear, and experience class resources, the better they learn. In fact, studies prove it. Tegrity's unique search feature helps students efficiently find what they need, when they need it, across an entire semester of class recordings. Help turn your students' study time into learning moments immediately supported by your lecture. With Tegrity, you also increase intent listening and class participation by easing students' concerns about note-taking. Using Tegrity in Connect will make it more likely you will see students' faces, not the tops of their heads.

Test Builder in Connect

Available within Connect, Test Builder is a cloud-based tool that enables instructors to format tests that can be printed or administered within an LMS. Test Builder offers a modern, streamlined interface for easy content configuration that matches course needs, without requiring a download.

Test Builder allows you to:

- access all test bank content from a particular title.
- easily pinpoint the most relevant content through robust filtering options.
- manipulate the order of questions or scramble questions and/or answers.
- pin questions to a specific location within a test.
- determine your preferred treatment of algorithmic questions.
- choose the layout and spacing.
- add instructions and configure default settings.

Test Builder provides a secure interface for better protection of content and allows for just-in-time updates to flow directly into assessments.

Exercises

Each chapter contains exercises that allow students to:

- apply concepts to real-world video cases.
- analyze a case and apply chapter concepts.
- quiz knowledge on grammar and usage.
- demonstrate problem-solving skills through complex examples and diagrams.
- assess students' values, skills, and interests via self-assessments.
- demonstrate knowledge about business models and processes.

Students receive immediate feedback and can track their progress in their own report. Detailed results let instructors see at a glance how each student performs and easily track the progress of every student in their course.

Keeping Up with What's New

The fourth edition of *Business Communication: Developing Leaders for a Networked World* continues to provide results-driven, technology-focused, case-based, and forward-looking content to help business students develop professional credibility for the workplace of tomorrow.

In an increasingly networked world, students will need better interpersonal skills than ever before; they will need better team skills than ever before; they will need better writing skills, especially adapted to new technologies; and they will need stronger presentation skills. This fourth edition contains the following changes to help students succeed:

Chapter 1 (Credibility)
- A new tech tip about developing credibility on LinkedIn.
- A new feature, called Ideas in Action, which appears in each chapter, highlighting a business leader's views on credibility.

Chapters 2, 3, and 4 (Interpersonal, Team, and Global Communication)
- New content about perspective getting and responding to gossip and complaining.
- New content about groupthink.
- Updated information about global etiquette.
- New tech tips and Ideas in Action features.

Chapters 5 and 6 (The Writing Process)
- Half the examples are new and the other half are updated.
- New tech tips and Ideas in Action features.

Chapters 7 and 8 (Technology and Communication)
- Additional content about team messaging.
- Half the examples are new and the other half are updated.
- New tech tips and Ideas in Action features.

Chapters 9, 10, and 11 (Business Messages: Routine, Persuasive, and Bad-News Messages)
- Half the examples are new and the other half are updated.
- Additional exercises are added at the end of each chapter.
- New tech tips and Ideas in Action features.

Chapters 12 and 13 (Business Reports and Proposals)
- Half the examples are new and the other half are updated.
- Additional exercises are added at the end of each chapter.
- New tech tips and Ideas in Action features.

Chapters 14 and 15 (Presentations)
- Half the examples are new and the other half are updated.
- Additional exercises are added at the end of each chapter.
- New tech tips and Ideas in Action features.

Chapter 16 (Employment Communication)
- A new section on professional networking has been added.
- Examples of résumés are updated.
- Additional exercises are added at the end of the chapter.
- New tech tips and Ideas in Action feature.

[Appreciation]

Thank you to all the reviewers and other business communication instructors who gave advice for the fourth edition. I've made dozens of changes and updates to meet the needs of today's business students based on the recommendations of these reviewers and advisory board members. Each of these instructors is at the forefront of best practices in business communication. Again, I express my appreciation for their advice and time to help improve this learning program. A special thank you to Jennifer Loney and Suzanne Buck for their ongoing support.

Reviewers and Advisory Board Members Supporting Development of the Fourth Edition

Kathryn R. Archard, University of Massachusetts–Boston

Heather Bisalski, Dalton State College

Audrey Blume, Wilmington University

Edward David Brown, Alabama State University

Shanti Bruce, Nova Southeastern University

Suzanne Buck, University of Houston

Barbara Chambers, Texas Tech University

Donna Chlopak, Montclair State University

Corey Ann Clem, Texas Tech University

Barbara Cox, Saddleback College

Jeanne Craig, Indiana Wesleyan University

Karen Cristiano, Drexel University

Jacquelin Joy Curry, California State University–Fresno

Gretchen Skok DiSanto, Lakeland Community College

Sandra Ehrlich-Mathiesen, University of Alaska–Anchorage

Megan Lee Endres, Eastern Michigan University

Elizabeth Goins, McCombs School of Business

Connie Golden, Lakeland Community College

Elizabeth Guerrero, Texas State University

Matari Gunter, Texas State University

Patricia L. Hanna-Garlitz, Bowling Green State University

Carolyn Jensen, University of Oklahoma

Sue Joiner, Tarleton State University

Doranne Jung, Santa Monica College

Jennifer Loney, Portland State University

Terry R. Lowe, Illinois State University

Marla Mahar, Oklahoma State University–Stillwater

Gene Manhart, Central Community College

Daniel McRoberts, Northcentral Technical College

Steve Merriam, San Diego State University

Elizabeth Metzger, University of South Florida

Christina J. Moore, Texas State University

Jenny Morse, Colorado State University

Anita Pandey, Morgan State University

Iswari P. Pandey, California State University–Northridge

Telicia Palmer, Georgia Piedmont Technical College

Melinda Phillabaum, Indiana University–Purdue University Indianapolis

Teeanna Rizkallah, California State University–Fullerton

Cassie Rockwell, Santa Monica College

Juli Rosenbaum, Baylor University

Sherri Shade, Kennesaw State University

Rachel V. Smydra, Oakland University

Jason L. Snyder, Central Connecticut State University

Stephen Soucy, Santa Monica College

Lisa Tyler, Sinclair Community College

Carol Watson, Indiana University–Bloomington

McClain Watson, University of Texas at Dallas

Susan Hall Webb, University of West Georgia

Theresa Wernimont, Colorado State University

Gail L. Yosh, Montclair State University

Reviewers and Event Participants Supporting the Development of Previous Editions

I extend my deepest thanks to the many business leaders and professionals, business communication scholars and instructors, and colleagues and friends who have contributed their valuable ideas. I especially appreciate the efforts of reviewers and other colleagues who reviewed iterations of the previous editions of this product. With each round of reviews, reviewers provided excellent and influential feedback to improve and refine the content. Thank you to each of the following experts in the business communication field who have contributed to the development of this learning program!

Nicky Adams, University of Dayton

Laura L. Alderson, University of Memphis

Angel Alexander, Piedmont Technical College

Melody Alexander, Ball State University

Dianne Anderson, Texas Tech University

Delia Anderson-Osteen, Texas Tech University

Kathryn R. Archard, University of Massachusetts–Boston

Eve Ash, Oklahoma State University–Stillwater

Carolyn Ashe, University of Houston–Downtown

Traci L. Austin, Sam Houston State University

Beverly Augustine, Elgin Community College

Kathie Bahnson, Boise State University

Lisa Bailey, University of South Carolina

Melissa Bakeman-Daly, California State University–San Bernardino

Rod Barker, Mount Hood Community College

Fiona Barnes, University of Florida

Mary Barton, California State University–Chico

Jim Beard, University of Arkansas–Fort Smith

Judith Haywood Bello, Lander University

Roxanne Bengelink, Kalamazoo Valley Community College

Cynthia Bennett, Albany State University

Magdalena Berry, Missouri State University

Shavawn Berry, Arizona State University

Danielle Blesi, Hudson Valley Community College

Erin Blocher, University of Missouri–Kansas City

Yvonne Block, College of Lake County

Julie E. Boto, Liberty University

Pamela Bourjaily, University of Iowa

Mary Bowers, Northern Arizona University

Sandy Braathen, University of North Dakota

Sheryl Broedel, University of North Dakota

Paula E. Brown, Northern Illinois University

Shanti Bruce, Nova Southeastern University

Suzanne Buck, University of Houston

Michael Buckman, University of Texas at Arlington

Debra Burleson, Baylor University

Amy Burton, Northwest Vista College

Dana Burton, The University of Alabama in Huntsville

Cheryl Byrne, Washtenaw Community College

Kim Campbell, Sydow University of Alabama

Kevin Michael Caporicci, University of Southern California

Donna Carlon, University of Central Oklahoma

Deborah Casanova, California State University–Dominguez Hills

Marilyn Chalupa, Ball State University

Barbara Chambers, Texas Tech University

Elizabeth Christensen, Sinclair Community College

G. Jay Christensen, California State University–Northridge

Miriam Coleman, Western Michigan University

Maria Colman, University of Southern California

Debbie Cook, Utah State University

Anthony M. Corte, University of Illinois at Chicago

Jan Robin Costello, Georgia State University

David Covington, North Carolina State University

Barbara Cox, Saddleback College

C. Brad Cox, Midlands Technical College

Jeanne Craig, Indiana Wesleyan University

Rosemarie Cramer, Community College of Baltimore

Tena Crews, University of South Carolina

Karen Cristiano, Drexel University

Brittany T. Cuenin, Lander University

Jacquelin Joy Curry, California State University–Fresno

Jennifer D'Alessandro, Niagara County Community College

Michelle Dawson, Missouri Southern State University

Andrea Deacon, University of Wisconsin–Stout

Sandra Dean, Jacksonville University

Patrick Delana, Boise State University

Linda Didesidero, University of Maryland–University College

Nicole Dilts, Angelo State University

Gretchen Skok DiSanto, Lakeland Community College

Jack Doo, California State University

Lucía Durá, The University of Texas at El Paso

Heidi Eaton, Elgin Community College

Sandra Ehrlich-Mathiesen, University of Alaska–Anchorage

Daniel Emery, University of Oklahoma

Megan Lee Endres, Eastern Michigan University

Donna R. Everett, Morehead State University

Stevina Evuleocha, California State University–East Bay

Joyce Anne Ezrow, Arundel Community College

Jodie Ferise, University of Indianapolis

Anne Finestone, Santa Monica College

Melissa Fish, American River College

Kathe Kenny Fradkin, Portland State University

Marla Fowler, Albany Technical College

Heidi Fuller, American River College

Jan Gabel-Goes, Western Michigan University

David Gadish, California State University

Anthony Gatling, University of Nevada–Las Vegas

Melissa Gavin, University of Wisconsin–Platteville

Jorge Gaytan, North Carolina A&T State University

Elizabeth Goins, McCombs School of Business

Robert Goldberg, Prince George's Community College

Connie Golden, Lakeland Community College

Terri Gonzales-Kreisman, Delgado Community College

Debra Gosh, Cleveland State University

Douglas Gray, Columbus State Community College

Germaine Gray, Texas Southern University

Diana J. Green, Weber State University

Kenneth Green, University of South Dakota

Mary Groves, University of Nevada–Reno

Kari Guedea, Edmonds Community College

Elizabeth Guerrero, Texas State University

Karen Gulbrandsen, University of Massachusetts–Dartmouth

Matari Gunter, Texas State University

Lynda Haas, University of California–Irvine

Frances Hale, Columbus State Community College

Melissa Hancock, Texas Tech University

Patricia L. Hanna-Garlitz, Bowling Green State University

Jeanette Heidewald, Indiana University–Bloomington

K. Virginia Hemby, Middle Tennessee State University

Ronda G. Henderson, Middle Tennessee State University

Candy Henry, Westmoreland County Community College

Melanie A. Hicks, Liberty University

Nancy Hicks, Central Michigan University

Kathy Hill, Sam Houston State University

Dini M. Homsey, University of Central Oklahoma

Matthew Houseworth, University of Central Missouri

Sally Humphries, Georgia College & State University

Sandie Idziak, The University of Texas at Arlington

Christina Iluzada, Baylor University

Sandra Jackson, California State University–Northridge

Jack Janosik, Cleveland State University

Elaine Jansky, Northwest Vista College

Carolyn Jensen, University of Oklahoma

Norma Johansen, Scottsdale Community College

Sue Joiner, Tarleton State University

Kenneth E. Jones Jr., Northeastern State University–Broken Arrow

Susan M. Jones, Utah State University

William T. Jones, State University of New York at Canton

Marguerite P. Joyce, Belhaven University

Doranne Jung, Santa Monica College

Brian Keliher, Grossmont College

Kayla Kelly, Tarleton State University

Stephanie Kelly, North Carolina A&T State University

Beth Kilbane, Lorain County Community College

Erin Kilbride-Vincent, Indiana University

Mary Catherine Kiliany, Robert Morris University

Stephen Kirk, East Carolina University

Jack Kleban, Barry University, Miami Shores, Florida Atlantic University

Lisa Kleiman, Boise State University

David Koehler, DePaul University

Erin Kramer, Owens Community College

Melinda G. Kramer, Prince George's Community College

Gary Lacefield, University of Texas at Arlington

Linda LaMarca, Tarleton State University

Robert Lambdin, University of South Carolina–Columbia

Elizabeth A. Lariviere, University of Akron

Marianna Larsen, Utah State University

Newton Lassiter, Florida Atlantic University

Cheryl Law, Tarrant County College

Janet L. Lear, University of Nebraska at Kearney

Lisa D. Lenoir, Stephens College

Paula Lentz, University of Wisconsin–Eau Claire

Jeffrey S. Lewis, Metropolitan State College of Denver

Jere Littlejohn, University of Mississippi

Jennifer Loney, Portland State University

Susan Long, Portland Community College

Joyce Lopez, Missouri State University

Terry R. Lowe, Illinois State University

Jo Mackiewicz, Iowa State University

Eunice Madison, Purdue University Calumet

Marla Mahar, Oklahoma State University–Stillwater

Anna Maheshwari, Schoolcraft College

Becky Mahr, Western Illinois University

Gene Manhart, Central Community College

Joan Mansfield, University of Central Missouri

Kenneth R. Mayer, Cleveland State University

Molly Mayer, University of Cincinnati

Elaine McCullough, Ferris State University

Sheryl McGough, Iowa State University

David A. McMurrey, Austin Community College

Daniel McRoberts, Northcentral Technical College

John Meis, Thomas University

Jacqueline Meisel, California State University–Northridge

Steve Merriam, San Diego State University

Marcia Metcalf, Northern Arizona University

Elizabeth Metzger, University of South Florida

Michelle Meyer, Joliet Junior College

Annie Laurie I. Meyers, Northampton Community College

Jack Miao, Southern Methodist University

Julianne Michalenko, Robert Morris University

Angelina Misaghi, California State University–Northridge

Karl Mitchell, Queens College–CUNY

Shawna Moffitt, University of South Carolina

Kathaleena Edward Monds, Albany State University

Gregory H. Morin, University of Nebraska–Omaha

Rodger Morrison, Troy University

Jenny Morse, Colorado State University

Farrokh Moshiri, University of California, Riverside

Gwen Moultrie, Midlands Technical College

Bill Moylan, Shidler College of Business, University of Hawaii–Manoa

Elwin Myers, Texas A&M University–Corpus Christi

Chynette Nealy, University of Houston–Downtown

Ashley Keller Nelson, Tulane University

Christina Anne Nelson, Indiana University–Purdue University Indianapolis

Darryl Neher, Indiana University–Bloomington

Grace Noyes, Texas Tech University

Keith Nyquist, Northern Illinois University

Ephraim Okoro, Howard University

Lisa O'Laughlin, Delta College

Lori Oldham, San Diego City College

Cathy Onion, Western Illinois University

Jo Ann Oravec, University of Wisconsin–Whitewater

Delia (Joy) O'Steen, Texas Tech University

Mary Padula, Borough of Manhattan Community College

Ranu Paik, Santa Monica College

Telicia Palmer, Georgia Piedmont Technical College

Anita Pandey, Morgan State University

Iswari P. Pandey, California State University–Northridge

Audrey Parajon, Wilmington University

Robyn E. Parker, Plymouth State University

Beverly Payne, Missouri Western State University

Michael Pennell, University of Kentucky

Delissa Perez, Northwest Vista College

Debra Ann Petrizzo-Wilkins, Franklin University

Melinda Phillabaum, Indiana University–Purdue University Indianapolis

Evelyn Pitre, University of North Texas

Greg Rapp, Portland Community College

Rob Rector, Delaware Technical and Community College

Phyllis Annette Reed, University of Texas at San Antonio

Teeanna Rizkallah, California State University–Fullerton

Betty Robbins, University of Oklahoma

Sherry J. Roberts, Middle Tennessee State University

Cassie Rockwell, Santa Monica College

Wayne Rollins, Middle Tennessee State University

Kara Romance, Indiana University of Pennsylvania

Juli Rosenbaum, Baylor University

Sia Rose-Robinson, George Mason University

Sharon Rouse, The University of Southern Mississippi

Tim Rowe, State University of New York Fredonia

David Russell, Iowa State University

Joyce Russell, Rockingham Community College

Terry Sanders, Macon State College

Ronit Sarig, California State University–Northridge

Anita Satterlee, Liberty University

Allyson D. Saunders, Weber State University

Danielle Scane, Orange Coast College

Juliann C. Scholl, Texas Tech University

Nicola S. Scott, George Mason University

Steven Sedky, Santa Monica College

Sherri Shade, Kennesaw State University

Mary Shannon, California State University–Northridge

Mike Shaw, Montana State University–Bozeman

Nelda Shelton, Tarrant County College

Michael Shurman, University of South Florida

Lucia Sigmar, Sam Houston State University

Joyce Monroe Simmons, Florida State University

Jeanetta Sims, University of Central Oklahoma

Jean Smith, Kentucky State University

Patricia Smith, Northcentral Technical College

Rachel V. Smydra, Oakland University

Kipp Snow, Anne Arundel Community College

Kim Snyder, South Texas College

Stephen Soucy, Santa Monica College

Rita Soza, MiraCosta College

Bob Sprague, California State University–Chico

Nicole St. Germaine, Angelo State University

Kathy Standen, Fullerton College

Jo Ann Starkweather, Northeastern State University

Jan Starnes, University of Texas at Austin

Erica Steakley, California State University–Northridge

Susan Stehlik, New York University

Natalie Stillman-Webb, University of Utah

Thomas Stoffer, Ferris State University

Kevin Swafford, Bradley University

Stephen Takach, University of Texas at San Antonio

Cecil V. Tarrant III, Western Illinois University

Elvira Teller, California State University–Dominguez Hills

Sandra Thompson, University of West Georgia

Susan Timm, Elgin Community College

Erik Timmerman, University of Wisconsin–Milwaukee

Anne Tippett, Monroe Community College

Elizabeth Tomlinson, West Virginia University

Emil Towner, Saint Cloud State University

Allen D. Truell, Ball State University

Lisa Tyler, Sinclair Community College

Kathleen L. Voge, University of Alaska–Anchorage

Angelika L. Walker, University of Nebraska at Omaha

Linda Blake Walsh, University of Tennessee

Jie Wang, University of Illinois at Chicago

Melvin Washington, Howard University

Carol Watson, Indiana University–Bloomington

Kristin Watson, Metropolitan State University of Denver

McClain Watson, University of Texas at Dallas

Susan Hall Webb, University of West Georgia

Marlea Welton, Santa Monica College

Juli White, Arizona State University

Raholanda White, Middle Tennessee State University

Leigh Ann Whittle, Elon University/Liberty University

Elisabeth C. Wicker, Bossier Parish Community College

Jo Wiley, Western Michigan University

Karin A. Wilking, Northwest Vista College

Anita Williams, Oklahoma City Community College

Linda S. Williams, North Georgia College & State University

Tom Williams, University of Houston, Victoria

Linda Willis, Georgia State University

Kadi Wills, Northwest Vista College

Bennie J. Wilson, University of Texas at San Antonio

Donald J. Wood, Winston-Salem State University

Doris N. Wright, Troy University

Robert Yale, University of Dallas

Caroline Yarbrough, Delgado Community College

Gail L. Yosh, Montclair State University

Diane Youngblood, Greenville Technical College

Lydia Yznaga, Northwest Vista College

Ann Zeman, Bellarmine University

Jensen Zhao, Ball State University

I also recognize the entire editorial and marketing teams at McGraw-Hill that have made this book possible: Anne Leung, Peter Jurmu, Gabe Fedota, Kelly Pekelder, Anke Weekes, Christine Vaughan, Bruce Gin, Brianna Kirschbaum, Egzon Shaqiri, and all of the talented McGraw-Hill publisher's representatives. It has been such a pleasure to work with these incredibly talented and skilled professionals who have shaped the content and design of this textbook and consulted with instructors around the globe. When I signed with McGraw-Hill, I was proud to be aligned with such a well-respected publisher. After working for nearly a decade with these talented and quality-driven professionals, my respect has grown. I can see the focus they place on producing learning materials that have real impact on the lives of students.

I want to thank my family. My wife, Natalie, is a beautiful and inspired person. She and I are on a wonderful journey together, and she has embraced this book as part of our journey. My daughters energize me in so many ways. Camilla inspires me by her eye for beauty, her sense of wonderment, and her joy in building things. Audrey inspires me by her spontaneous expressions of happiness, her sense of fun, and her love of people. I'm also blessed to have the best parents. They understand and support me. I love them and hope to be like them.

Finally, I'd like to thank several people who have been instrumental in influencing my career direction and success. First, I recognize the influence of my dissertation advisor, James Calvert Scott. He contributed decades of research and teaching to the business communication field and selflessly devoted thousands of hours to my development. Without his influence, I would not have become part of the business communication community. Second, I want to thank Pat Moody, former dean of the College of Hospitality, Retail, and Sport Management at the University of South Carolina; Lucy Lee, former director of the Center for Management Communication at the University of Southern California; Marion Philadelphia, current director of the Department of Business Communication at the University of Southern California; and Suh-Pyng Ku, vice dean of Graduate Programs at the University of Southern California. These four women are the most inspiring and caring leaders I've worked for. They have had a lasting influence on my work.

Peter W. Cardon
Academic Director, MBA.PM Program
Professor, Department of Business Communication
Marshall School of Business
University of Southern California
Twitter: @petercardon
Pinterest: pinterest.com/cardonbcom
LinkedIn: www.linkedin.com/in/petercardon

Association for Business Communication

An international, interdisciplinary organization committed to advancing business communication research, education, and practice.

Benefits of The Association for Business Communication
- Annual international and regional conferences
- Award & grant opportunities for you and your students
- Access to decades of online archives
- Over 25 Committees and Special Interest Groups (SIGs)
- Two journals: *Business and Professional Communication Quarterly & International Journal of Business Communication*

Visit www.businesscommunication.org
Learn about ABC; join our community with its affordable membership levels, including special graduate student rates.

For assistance, contact: **abcoffice@businesscommunication.org**

Contents

Part 4   Types of Business Messages

9   Routine Business Messages 266

WHY DOES THIS MATTER? 267

Chapter Case: Routine Emails at Smith & Smith Advertising 267

Developing Routine Messages 269

Making Requests 270

Setting Expectations 272

Providing Directions 274

Responding to Inquiries 276

Creating Announcements 276

Making Claims 277

Showing Appreciation 280

Congratulations and Celebrations 282

Making Apologies 283

Expressing Sympathy 285

TECHNOLOGY TIPS: USING APPS TO CREATE A ROUTINE OF APPRECIATION AND CELEBRATION 285

IDEAS IN ACTION: SHOWING GRATITUDE 286

10   Persuasive Messages 294

WHY DOES THIS MATTER? 295

Chapter Case: Shifting Course at Better Horizons Credit Union 295

The Importance of Credibility in an Era of Mistrust and Skepticism 297

Applying the AIM Planning Process to Persuasive Messages 297

Understand Your Audience 297
Gather the Right Information 300
Set Up the Message 300

Getting the Tone and Style Right for Persuasive Messages 302

Apply the Personal Touch 302
Use Action-Oriented and Lively Language 305
Write with Confidence 305
Offer Choice 305
Show Positivity 307

Creating Internal Persuasive Messages 309

Influencing a Superior 309
Influencing Employees 310
Taking Initiative, Showing Persistence, and Adapting to Various Decision-Making Styles 310

Constructing External Persuasive Messages 314

Composing Mass Sales Messages 318

TECHNOLOGY TIPS: ARTIFICIAL INTELLIGENCE (AI) TOOLS AND PERSUASION 319

Reviewing Persuasive Messages 322

Get Feedback and Reread 324
Apply the FAIR Test 324

IDEAS IN ACTION: PERSUADING BY UNDERSTANDING OTHERS ON A PERSONAL LEVEL 325

11   Bad-News Messages 334

WHY DOES THIS MATTER? 335

Chapter Case: Bad News at Marble Home Makeovers 335

Maintaining Credibility When Delivering Bad News 337

Applying the AIM Planning Process for Bad-News Messages 338

Understand How the Bad News Will Affect Your Audience 338

PART 5 Reports and Presentations

Appendixes

Mc Graw Hill **create**   Mc Graw Hill **connect**

Bonus Content

Available only at www.mcgrawhillcreate.com/cardon or in the e-book within McGraw-Hill Connect®.

Introduction to Business Communication

Chapter 1 —— Establishing Credibility

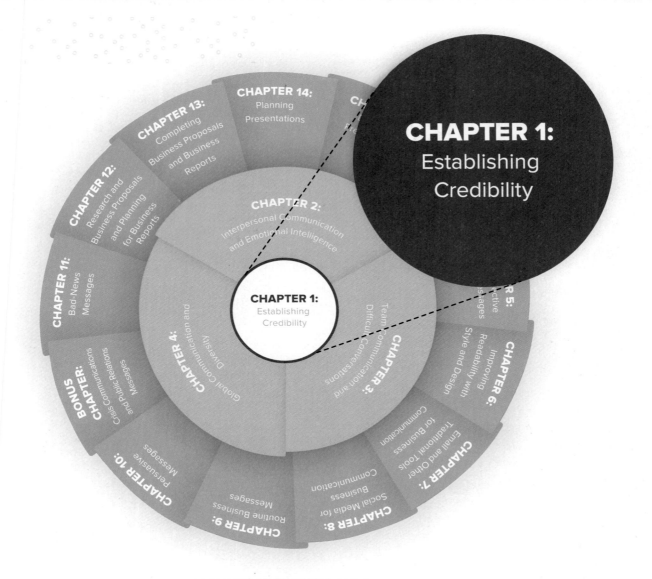

PART ONE

CHAPTER 1:
Establishing
Credibility

**ESTABLISHING
CREDIBILITY**

**PRINCIPLES OF INTERPERSONAL
COMMUNICATION**

**PRINCIPLES FOR & TYPES OF
BUSINESS MESSAGES**

LEARNING OBJECTIVES

After studying this chapter, you should be able to do the following:

LO1.1 Explain the importance of establishing credibility for business communications.

LO1.2 Describe how competence, caring, and character affect your credibility as a communicator.

LO1.3 Define and explain business ethics, corporate values, and personal values.

LO1.4 Explain the FAIR approach to ethical business communications.

In most business situations, others make judgments about what you say, write, and do based on your credibility. **Credibility** is your reputation for being trustworthy—trustworthy to perform your work with excellence; to care about those you work with and for; to live by high ethical, corporate, and personal values; and to deliver on your promises. In short, your credibility is the degree to which others believe or trust in you. In this book, we often use the terms *trust* and *credibility* interchangeably.

Business communications occur in the context of working relationships, all of which depend on trust.[1] Credibility has always been important to business relationships, yet its importance has grown in recent years with an increasingly interdependent, knowledge-based workplace.[2] As one of the foremost thinkers on trust in the workplace, Stephen M. R. Covey made this observation:

> Contrary to what most people believe, trust is not some soft, illusive quality that you either have or you don't; rather, trust is a pragmatic, tangible, actionable asset that you can create—much faster than you probably think possible. . . . It is the key leadership competency of the new global economy.[3]

In this chapter, we discuss the ways that business executives and the business community establish trust. Then, we focus on three components of credibility: competence, caring, and character.[4] First, however, you will read a short scenario about choosing a mentor. Each potential mentor has credibility but for different reasons.

Hear Pete Cardon explain why this matters.
bit.ly/cardon1

LO1.1 Explain the importance of establishing credibility for business communications.

CHAPTER CASE   WHOM DO YOU TRUST AS YOUR MENTOR?

WHO'S INVOLVED

Luis Sally Tom

Assume you were hired about a month ago. Your company has a practice of assigning a mentor to new employees during their first six months. You've been told that mentors can have a major impact on your opportunities: your team assignments, your projects, and your overall career development. You've gotten to know some of your new colleagues, and your boss has asked you which one you would like to be your mentor. Read through your impressions of your colleagues below, and consider who would make the best mentor for you.

THE SITUATION

LUIS

Luis has worked at your company for one year. Everyone enjoys working with him. He is always cheerful and happy to see those around him. He consistently finds out what his colleagues need and goes out of his way to help out. Everyone thinks Luis is fun. He likes to go out for a drink after work and gets everyone laughing. Luis is well known for being well connected within your company. One thing that every colleague says about him is that he's honest. He continues to make some rookie mistakes, however, and he has done sloppy work several times when he was up against tight deadlines.

SALLY

Sally has worked at your company for three years. She has a reputation of being a star performer. In fact, she's generally assigned the most important projects for that reason. Colleagues know that when she promises something, she makes it happen. A lot of colleagues think she's excessively critical of others when they fall short of her expectations. A colleague complained to one of the managers, "Sally never gives me a chance to develop my skills. She just takes over the project."

TOM

Tom has worked at your company for four years. He consistently receives excellent ratings on his quarterly performance reviews. He is intensely loyal to his team members, and he does everything he can to make sure they succeed. Recently, one of his team members lost a client because she missed several deadlines. When Tom's boss asked why they lost the client, Tom protected his teammate by saying that the client preferred the services of a competitor.

TASK

Luis, Sally, and Tom are like most people—they have some strengths and some weaknesses. As you read this chapter, you will find that each of them lacks complete credibility but for different reasons. Now, choose your mentor. Whom do you trust to help you succeed in your new position?

The Role of Trust in the Post-Trust Era

Do you operate from a position of trust or credibility? That is one of the first things you should consider as you communicate. In the business world, you often start from a deficit of trust. As a result, one of your first goals should be to gain trust or credibility from colleagues, clients, customers, and other contacts.[5]

Given the major business scandals and high-profile misdeeds in recent years (i.e., Enron, Volkswagen, United Airlines, Wells Fargo), trust in businesses and business executives has dropped to all-time lows. As depicted in Figure 1.1, the trust extended by the general public to business executives is far lower than the trust extended to members of other selected professions.[6]

The public also increasingly views companies and other institutions with less trust. One of the most well-known and publicized trust indexes is developed by Edelman, a prominent communications firm. Edelman experts measure trust in institutions, including business, nongovernmental organizations (NGOs), government, and media in 28 countries. In 2018, public trust in institutions dropped more in the United States than in any other country. Historically, United States was labeled a "trust" country but is now labeled a "distrust" country.[7]

A deficit of trust also exists within companies. In a global study of nearly 10,000 full-time employees, just 49 percent said they trusted their bosses and those working with them.[8] Furthermore, approximately 76 percent of employees have seen illegal or

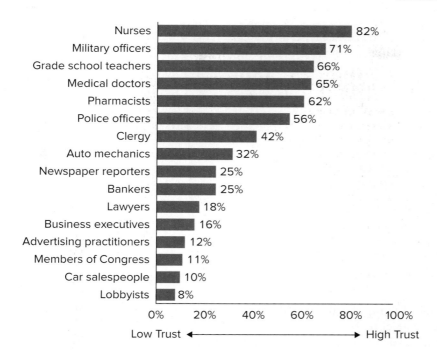

Nurses	82%
Military officers	71%
Grade school teachers	66%
Medical doctors	65%
Pharmacists	62%
Police officers	56%
Clergy	42%
Auto mechanics	32%
Newspaper reporters	25%
Bankers	25%
Lawyers	18%
Business executives	16%
Advertising practitioners	12%
Members of Congress	11%
Car salespeople	10%
Lobbyists	8%

0%   20%   40%   60%   80%   100%

Low Trust ◄──────► High Trust

FIGURE 1.1

How Will You Overcome Public Perceptions to Build Credibility?

A Look at Trust in Various Professions

Source: Gallup, Inc.

Note: Based on the percentage of American adults who considered members of these occupations "very high" or "high" in honesty and ethical standards in a November 2017 Gallup poll. Available at news.gallup.com/poll/224639/nurses-keep-healthy-lead-honest-ethical-profession.aspx.

unethical conduct in the past 12 months at their jobs.[9] As future business managers and leaders, you will often find yourself in charge of employees who are accustomed to not trusting those in leadership positions.

A strong predictor of cheating in the workplace is cheating in school. Sadly, recent research has found that cheating is so pervasive that some use the label a *global cheating culture*. Among high school students, 80 percent of high-performing students admit to having cheated, and 50 percent do not believe cheating is wrong. Other research about high school students found that more than 70 percent had engaged in serious cheating, and 50 percent had plagiarized assignments from the Internet. In a study of more than 50,000 undergraduate students in the United States, more than 70 percent admitted to serious cheating. Nearly 80 percent stated that Internet plagiarism was not a serious offense.[10]

Perhaps most concerning is that business students are among the worst offenders. When asked in anonymous surveys if they had cheated to get into graduate school, many students admitted to having done so: 43 percent of liberal arts students, 52 percent of education students, 63 percent of medical students, 63 percent of law students, and 75 percent of business students. Think about that! Three-quarters of graduate-level business students admitted to some form of cheating to get into their programs. In another study involving hypothetical ethical dilemmas, convicts in minimum-security prisons scored as high on unethical behavior as MBA students.[11] In yet another study of 6,226 undergraduate business students in 36 countries, American business students viewed cheating no differently than did students from countries considered high in corruption.[12]

Michael Maslansky, a leading corporate communications expert, and his colleagues have labeled this the post-trust era. In the **post-trust era**, the public overwhelmingly views businesses as operating against the public's best interests, and the majority of employees view their leaders and colleagues skeptically. Regarding the post-trust era, Maslansky and his colleagues said, "Just a few years ago, salespeople, corporate leaders, marketing departments, and communicators like me had it pretty easy. We looked at communication as a relatively linear process. . . . But trust disappeared, things changed."[13]

FIGURE 1.2

The Three Components of Credibility

Most of these perceptions about business leaders as untrustworthy are not necessarily fair. Daniel Janssen, former chairman of the board of directors of Solvay (a Belgian chemicals company operating in more than 50 countries), explained the dilemma:

> Executives of large companies today are generally perceived as efficient and competent, but also self-interested and ungenerous. However, I think that people who form this opinion are underestimating something of which they lack knowledge. Many executives, in top management and also at other levels, are incredibly generous and not at all self-interested. They do their job and they do it with respect for the common interest. But it is true that capitalism is too often marked by its dark and greedy side.[14]

You will often find yourself needing to establish credibility in this post-trust era. As a future manager and executive, you can control your reputation as a credible communicator by focusing on three well-established factors: competence, caring, and character. Research has shown that these three factors almost entirely account for whether a person is considered credible in professional situations. As depicted in Figure 1.2, credibility is like a three-legged stool. Without any one element, it is compromised.

The Role of Competence in Establishing Credibility

LO1.2 Describe how competence, caring, and character affect your credibility as a communicator.

Visit http://connect. mheducation.com for an exercise on this topic.

Competence refers to the knowledge and skills needed to accomplish business tasks, approach business problems, and get a job done. Most people will judge your competence based on your track record of success and achievement.

In her memoir, Meg Whitman, former CEO of HP and eBay, explains how as a young professional she gained credibility and displayed competence within her organization: "I just focused on delivering results," she said. "You have to excel at the tasks you're given and you have to add value to every single project, every conversation where someone seeks your input."[15]

People develop competence in many ways: through study, observation, and, most important, practice and real-world work experiences. Your entire business program is likely centered on developing competence in a certain business discipline and/or industry. You may already have significant business experience. If you're a novice, seeking internships and jobs related to your discipline will help you develop competence.

How you communicate directly affects the perceptions others have of your competence. Throughout this book, you will find an emphasis on two traits associated with competence: a focus on action and an emphasis on results.

A *focus on action* implies that you seize business opportunities. Meg Whitman emphasized this action-oriented approach to work: "The way I usually put it is, the price of inaction is far greater than the cost of making a mistake. You do not have to be perfect to be an effective leader, but you cannot be timid."[16] She also described an *emphasis on results:*

> I don't believe that all a company needs to do is declare that it has values and then say, "Trust us, we know what's best." To be a success, you must identify a goal with a measurable outcome, and you must hit that goal—every day, every month, every year. Trying is important. But trying is not the same as achieving success. . . . [Some] people expect to advance in their careers regardless of results and are surprised when it doesn't happen. They feel entitled. Their attitude is: "Because I'm here, because I'm me, you owe me."[17]

Former HP and eBay CEO Meg Whitman frequently shares advice with young professionals about how to develop professional credibility.
Dave Kotinsky/Getty Images

In the opening scenario in which you chose a mentor, Luis is weakest in competence. While he is strong at caring for others and displaying good character, many people will question his ability to accomplish tasks well. He has less experience than his colleagues and sometimes performs sloppy work. Yet, many people would choose him as their mentor because they trust his ability to find out about their career needs and trust he knows how to connect them to others in the company.

In summary, you demonstrate competence by taking an active role in your business and by getting results. How you communicate your plan of action and the results of those actions will determine how others perceive your competence and your credibility.

The Role of Caring in Establishing Credibility

Your colleagues, clients, and even your customers will trust you far more if they know you care about them. When asked about what makes a great leader, Lt. Gen. Nadja Y. West, the Army surgeon general, replied, "One characteristic that stands out in all the leaders I've seen is empathy. You don't have to be like everyone else, but you can try to connect with other people. People can tell if you care about them or not."[18] In the business world, **caring** implies understanding the interests of others, cultivating a sense of community, and giving to others and showing generosity. In the past, caring was seldom discussed as integral to business. Now, it is among the most important abilities for business leaders and managers. In fact, a recent study of business managers found that caring is considered among the top 3 skills or abilities (from a list of 18 skills or abilities) for managers of nearly any business discipline.[19]

Understanding the Interests of Others

Your ability to gain credibility strongly depends on your ability to show that you care for the needs of others. Furthermore, your ability to show you care puts you in a rare position as a business leader. After all, less than half (42 percent) of employees believe their managers care about them. Even worse, less than one-third (29 percent) of employees believe their managers care about whether they develop skills.[20]

Effective communicators gain trust by connecting with others—that is, seeking to understand others' needs, wants, opinions, feelings, and

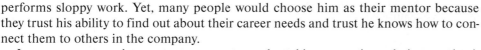

Lt. Gen. Nadja Y. West often talks about how leaders must genuinely care for others.
Source: U.S. Department of Defense

aspirations. Virtually every aspect of communication you will focus on in this book relies on this other-orientation.

Cultivating a Sense of Community

The most effective business leaders in today's corporate environment have generally risen to their positions because of their sense of community and teamwork. Meredith Ashby and Stephen Miles recently interviewed hundreds of prominent and accomplished business leaders to answer questions such as *What are the burning issues for corporate leaders today?* and *How do companies identify, attract, develop, and retain the best and brightest people in the workplace?* Here is what they learned from these CEOs:

> Most defined their main responsibility as chief executive to be that of inspiring, influencing, setting the direction for, facilitating, coaching, mentoring, and developing their employees. The word "control" was rarely used; instead, they spoke emphatically about the importance of a strong team orientation. Their role was to identify and empower a team, not command it. Indeed, many of them characteristically used the term "we" rather than "I" in discussing success within the organization. Instead of thinking in terms of individual accomplishment, most tended to think in terms of what their management teams had achieved.[21]

Throughout this textbook, you will see techniques for communicating your "we" and "you" orientation rather than a "me" orientation. Speaking about "our needs" or "your needs" as opposed to "my needs" engenders trust and helps you come up with solutions that achieve mutual benefit.

Giving to Others and Showing Generosity

Recent research has shown that most professionals can broadly be characterized as *givers* and *takers*. Givers are those professionals who go out of their way to help colleagues, respond to their requests and needs, and generously support others in the workplace. Takers are those professionals who frequently ask for favors from colleagues yet infrequently volunteer to help their peers in return.

Dozens of studies in recent years show that organizations with more generous and giving employees perform better. Companies with higher percentages of givers achieve higher profitability, higher productivity, and higher customer satisfaction. In addition, these companies experience lower employee turnover rates. These studies also show that givers are more likely than takers to be rated as top performers. (However, givers are also more likely than takers to be rated the lowest-performing employees. In Chapter 2, you'll learn more about strategies to be a giver *and* maintain top performance.)[22] Particularly early in your career, you'll find that gaining a reputation for helping your colleagues will open up many professional opportunities and enhance your professional credibility.

In the opening scenario, Sally is weakest in caring. While she is strong at getting the job done and communicating honestly, she often does not seem to act in the best interests of others. She may even be indifferent to the growth of her colleagues. Yet, many people would choose her as a mentor because they could learn from the best and likely participate in the most important projects.

The Role of Character in Establishing Credibility

Warren Buffett, the legendary investor and CEO of Berkshire Hathaway, was recently asked about how he hires people. He responded, "You look for three qualities: integrity, intelligence, and energy."[23] Like Buffett, most people look first and foremost at traits such as integrity and honesty when evaluating the character of others. **Character** refers to a reputation for staying true to commitments made to stakeholders and adhering to high moral and ethical values.

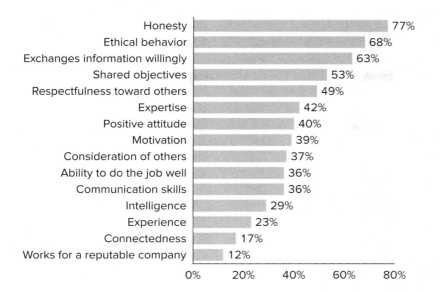

Honesty	77%
Ethical behavior	68%
Exchanges information willingly	63%
Shared objectives	53%
Respectfulness toward others	49%
Expertise	42%
Positive attitude	40%
Motivation	39%
Consideration of others	37%
Ability to do the job well	36%
Communication skills	36%
Intelligence	29%
Experience	23%
Connectedness	17%
Works for a reputable company	12%

0%   20%   40%   60%   80%

FIGURE 1.3

What Determines Trust in Individuals in the Workplace?

For Collaboration on Workplace Projects

Source: Economist Intelligence Unit.

Character is central in creating trust. Consider the recent research, depicted in Figure 1.3.[24] Business executives were asked what the most important determinants of trust in workplace projects were. Overwhelmingly, character-based traits—that is, honesty, ethical behavior, and willingness to exchange information—ranked at the top.

In the following sections, we focus on several topics closely related to character: business ethics, corporate and personal values, open and honest communication, a stakeholder view of accountability, and fairness in business communications.

Business Ethics

Business ethics are the commonly accepted beliefs and principles in the business community for acceptable behavior. At a minimum, business ethics involve adhering to laws; safeguarding confidential or proprietary information; avoiding conflicts of interest and misuse of company assets; and refraining from accepting or providing inappropriate gifts, gratuities, and entertainment.[25]

As far as corporate communications, the dominant business ethic in recent years is transparency. **Transparency** involves sharing all relevant information and decision rationale with stakeholders. You will soon be in leadership positions within your organization. You can create a transparent workplace by being accessible, acknowledging the concerns of others, and following through when you don't have immediate answers. Trust-building behaviors include extending trust, sharing information, telling it straight, providing opportunities, admitting mistakes, and setting a good example by following rules.[26]

You likely will need to analyze ethical dilemmas in your business program, while training for your job, and once you are on the job. You probably recognize that "making the right choice" is not always obvious. In such situations, where the law and ethical principles do not provide a clear answer, transparency is key: Decision making needs to be open, documented, and based on the collective conscience of your work team and affected stakeholders.

Often, employees fail to speak up when they observe potentially unethical behavior. Business professionals remain silent for four basic reasons: (1) They assume it's standard practice, (2) they rationalize that it's not a big deal, (3) they say to themselves it's not their responsibility, or (4) they want to be loyal.

Warren Buffett often talks about the importance of character.

Bill Pugliano/Getty Images

LO1.3  Define and explain business ethics, corporate values, and personal values.

Visit http://connect. mheducation.com for an exercise on this topic.

Prepare now to speak up constructively when you observe unethical behavior. It's part of your job. You can challenge rationalizations with questions such as these:

If this is standard, why is there a policy against it?
If it is expected, are we comfortable being public about it?
I may be new here, so I might not understand our policy clearly. But, shouldn't we . . . ?[27]

When you frame your concerns in terms of benefits to your team or organization, your colleagues and other contacts will often respond appropriately. Over the long run, you will be rewarded for having a reputation of speaking up when ethical dilemmas arise.[28]

Corporate and Personal Values

Corporate values are the stated and lived values of a company. Most organizations create a **code of conduct** or code of ethics to state their most important values and norms of conduct. Publicly traded companies are required by the Sarbanes-Oxley Act of 2002 to have a code of ethics available to all employees and to ensure that it is enacted. Google's code of conduct espouses values such as "respect for our users," "integrity," "deliver great products and services," and a "supportive work environment." It addresses issues related to harassment, discrimination, bullying, drugs and alcohol, a safe workplace, and even a dog policy. It describes what constitutes conflicts of interest and confidentiality. (See Google's code of conduct at abc.xyz/investor/other/google-code-of-conduct/.) It concludes:

> Google aspires to be a different kind of company. It's impossible to spell out every possible ethical scenario we might face. Instead, we rely on one another's good judgment to uphold a high standard of integrity for ourselves and our company. We expect all Googlers to be guided by both the letter and the spirit of this Code. Sometimes, identifying the right thing to do isn't an easy call. If you aren't sure, don't be afraid to ask questions of your manager, Legal or Ethics & Compliance.[29]
>
> And remember . . . don't be evil, and if you see something that you think isn't right – speak up!

Aligning **personal values**—those values that individuals prioritize and adhere to—with corporate values is an important element of character. After all, if one is living corporate values that do not match one's personal values, then there is a lack of integrity. Paul Polman, CEO of Unilever, was recently interviewed about the importance of corporate values:

> One thing I've learned over the course of my career is that if your values—your personal values—are aligned with the company's values, you're probably going to be more successful in the long term than if they are not. Because if they aren't, it requires you to be an actor when you go to work or to have a split personality.[30]

Open and Honest Communication

In Tamar Frankel's excellent book on the role of honesty in American business culture, she chronicles the increasing abuses of honesty, including health care fraud, insurance fraud, check fraud, consumer fraud, identity theft, and student cheating, to name a few. She concludes her work with an appeal for more honesty:

> The goal of honesty is not to reduce competitive ardor but to channel it in less destructive ways. Honesty encourages competition on the merits and prohibits competition by cheating. Honesty brings better quality of products and services and less shoddy products and fake services. If businesses do not compete on fraud, they can be more successful in gaining and retaining customers.[31]

Frankel's point about honesty at an institutional level also applies on a personal level. By staying honest in all situations and avoiding cutting corners in any manner, you allow yourself to perform based solely on merit. Over the long run, complete honesty not only forges your character, it helps you develop and maximize your competencies.

Nothing short of complete honesty is demanded in business for several reasons. First, the price of dishonesty on financial performance can be devastating. Over her corporate career, Meg Whitman became adept at identifying when executives were avoiding reality: "At some companies, board meetings are mainly a mind-numbing series of *happy PowerPoints.* From the agenda and the demeanor of the CEO, you would think that all is sweetness, light, and ice cream."[32] Her comment points to three important issues. First, by avoiding open and honest communication of business problems, employees doom a business to poor financial performance. Second, dishonesty is among the primary reasons for lower employee morale. Nearly six in ten employees say that they've left an organization because of lack of trust—the key reasons being lack of communication and dishonesty.[33] Finally, dishonesty can be reason for dismissal. In some cases, dishonesty can destroy careers and even result in criminal charges.

Some business executives and managers view slight deviations from the truth in small matters as inconsequential. Often, they feel, these small lies are expressed with no ill will and without much impact on important business matters. Yet, experienced executives and management consultants have observed how damaging even minor dishonesty can be. Drs. Dennis S. Reina and Michelle L. Reina focus on this point in their book *Trust and Betrayal in the Workplace:*

> There was a time, many years ago, when we too assumed that what broke the delicate fiber of trust in relationships were large acts that had significant impact. However, our research and work over the last fifteen years have taught us differently. What gradually erodes trust and creates a climate of betrayal in our workplaces today are small, subtle acts that accumulate over time. When we don't do what we say we will do, when we gossip about others behind their backs, when we renege on decisions we agreed to, when we hide our agenda and work it behind the scenes, and when we spin the truth rather than tell it, we break trust and damage relationships.[34]

Today, most organizational cultures are moving to flatter, more open communication structures. However, you will also find yourself in many situations where confidentiality is mandated. Companies often direct employees to maintain confidentiality about information that can harm profitability, productivity, and employees within the organization if it is disclosed. In some cases, confidentiality is required by legal considerations, such as laws regarding medical records, disclosure of insider information, or copyrights. In other cases, you may need to protect intellectual property. When Apple rolled out the iPhone, employees underwent a code of silence for months when they could not even talk about their work to family members. In fact, until the release of the iPhone, many Apple employees could not even speak about certain iPhone features to Apple employees in other divisions.[35]

A Stakeholder View of Accountability

A sense of accountability implies an *obligation* to meet the needs and wants of others. It also involves an *enlarged vision* of those affected by your business activities. It takes a **stakeholder** view that includes all groups in society affected by your business.

In a commencement speech to business students at UCLA, Robert Eckert, then CEO of Mattel, spoke about trust and, in particular, the sense of accountability that is needed among business executives and managers. He concluded his speech this way:

> You are the future leaders of business. And when it comes to trust, your leadership style affects those you are leading. . . . As you go to work, your top responsibility should be to build trust. To perform every day at the highest standards. Not just for yourself, but for your team, for your supervisor, for the consumer, for the company's shareholders, for the rest of us in business. . . . It's day one of the next chapter of your life, and I'm putting my trust in each of you.[36]

Thus, a sense of accountability involves a feeling of responsibility to stakeholders and a duty to other employees and customers. By placing a rationale for accountability in your communications, you will generate substantial trust and goodwill from others.

LO1.4 Explain the FAIR
approach to
ethical business
communications.

**Visit http://connect.
mheducation.com** for
an exercise on this topic.

Fairness in Business Communications

Generally, others' perceptions of your character—your unquestioned adherence to personal and corporate values—are largely determined by your communications. Moreover, your colleagues, clients, and customers will gauge your communications based on a judgment of how fair they are.

Thus, in all your communications, you should consider whether you are being fair to others. For routine communications, you make this calculation quickly. For important, less straightforward, and perhaps even controversial communications, you should spend a significant amount of time evaluating the best way to be fair. You might consider talking to your supervisor, peers, and other trusted individuals to appraise the situation. Meg Whitman explained this principle based on her experience at eBay:

> Ultimately the character of a company, like the character of a person, is an accumulation of many, many moments when the choices are not necessarily clear and we make the best decisions we can. But over time the logic and reasoning that we use to make those decisions, the moral compass to follow in making those decisions, is the essence of our authentic self, our character.[37]

One way to evaluate your communications is to use the *FAIR test* (see Figure 1.4). The FAIR test helps you examine how well you have provided the *facts*; how well you have granted *access* to your motives, reasoning, and information; how well you have examined *impacts* on stakeholders; and how well you have shown *respect*. As you respond to questions such as those posed in Figure 1.4, you ensure that your communications are fair to yourself and others.

Applying the FAIR test is especially important for high-stakes messages. Consider how Tim Cook, CEO of Apple, responded to a February 2016 court order to force Apple to bypass the security functions of the iPhone of one of the San Bernardino terrorists. Explaining that Apple should focus on the privacy and security of its customers, he resisted the court order and wrote a letter to Apple customers and spoke repeatedly to the media to defend Apple's position.[38]

This was clearly a polarizing and divisive situation, with roughly 51 percent of Americans thinking Apple should follow the court order and unlock the iPhone while about 38 percent thought Apple should resist the order to unlock the iPhone.[39] Most tech companies and advocacy groups, such as the American Civil Liberties Union (ACLU) and the Reform Government Alliance, lined up behind Apple. Yet, government agencies and law enforcement groups tended to oppose Apple's position. The top two members of the Senate Intelligence Committee, one a Republican and the other a Democrat, sided with the FBI.[40]

Accurately portraying the *facts* in such a complex situation is challenging. Tim Cook, in an open letter to customers and in media interviews, explained Apple's position that it should protect customers' privacy and security and provided what he viewed as the technical and legal facts of the case. Cook suggested that to comply with the court order, Apple would have to create a backdoor that could be used to violate the privacy and security of any iPhone user. He explained that Apple's position of protecting customers was the moral high ground. Some questioned whether Apple was accurately portraying the government's request. For example, Bill Gates and other experts suggested that the government's request was for a particular case (helping unlock a single phone) rather than creating a solution that would make all other phones vulnerable or less secure. In other words, some experts thought Tim Cook was exaggerating the nature of the FBI's request.[41]

Providing *access* to your real motivations and explaining how you made your decisions can also prove challenging in complicated and emotionally charged situations. Cook explained to customers and the media that Apple's motivation was to protect its customers' privacy and security. Most people viewed Cook as a sincere champion of digital privacy. Yet, some questioned Apple's stated motivations. For example, a *Los Angeles Times* journalist noted that Apple's defiant approach in the United States differed markedly from its approach in China, where it complied with a variety of government requests that made iPhone users' data less secure. The journalist noted that Apple's primary motivation could be profitability. In North America and Europe,

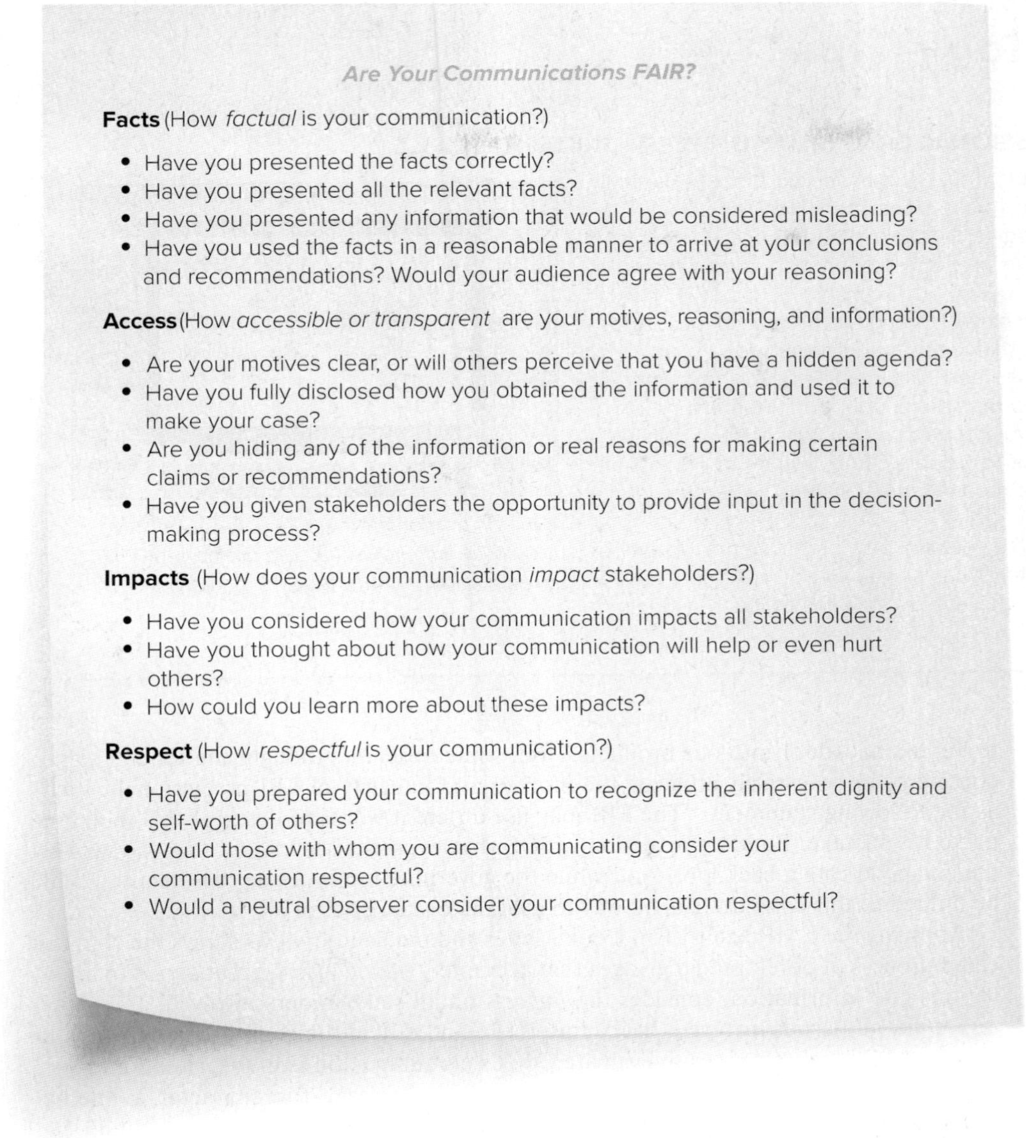

FIGURE 1.4

The FAIR Test of
Ethical Business
Communication

Are Your Communications FAIR?

Facts (How *factual* is your communication?)

- Have you presented the facts correctly?
- Have you presented all the relevant facts?
- Have you presented any information that would be considered misleading?
- Have you used the facts in a reasonable manner to arrive at your conclusions and recommendations? Would your audience agree with your reasoning?

Access (How *accessible or transparent* are your motives, reasoning, and information?)

- Are your motives clear, or will others perceive that you have a hidden agenda?
- Have you fully disclosed how you obtained the information and used it to make your case?
- Are you hiding any of the information or real reasons for making certain claims or recommendations?
- Have you given stakeholders the opportunity to provide input in the decision-making process?

Impacts (How does your communication *impact* stakeholders?)

- Have you considered how your communication impacts all stakeholders?
- Have you thought about how your communication will help or even hurt others?
- How could you learn more about these impacts?

Respect (How *respectful* is your communication?)

- Have you prepared your communication to recognize the inherent dignity and self-worth of others?
- Would those with whom you are communicating consider your communication respectful?
- Would a neutral observer consider your communication respectful?

where Apple had relatively flat sales, defying the government was less risky politically and financially. On the other hand, Apple's top market for iPhones was China and sales in China were booming. Taking a strong position in China would be much riskier to Apple. Some observers noted that Apple was unwilling to so defiantly stand on principle in the Chinese market.[42]

Evaluating *impacts* requires a stakeholder view. Tim Cook argued that resisting the court order served the privacy and security interests of its customers and the public at large. Yet, some people felt Cook was not taking national security concerns seriously enough and wasn't paying enough attention to the needs of victims. A group of victims of the crime joined a collective lawsuit to force Apple to help unlock the iPhone of one of the terrorists.[43] The FBI director specifically stated that the FBI's primary goal was to get justice for the victims of this crime and was not seeking to create a precedent to force tech companies to reduce privacy.[44]

With such a divisive issue, showing *respect* to those with different views is particularly important. In Cook's open letter to customers, he attempted to show respect for the FBI and those with similar views to the FBI. He used phrases such as "We have great respect for the professionals at the FBI, and we believe their intentions are good" and "While we believe the FBI's intentions are good, it would be wrong for the government to force us

Technology Tips

PROJECTING PROFESSIONAL CREDIBILITY ON YOUR LINKEDIN PROFILE

You likely have a LinkedIn profile, but have you thought carefully about how well you project professional credibility?

Thinking about strategies to show competence, caring, and character in your LinkedIn profile will enhance your professional credibility.

Your *competence* is displayed through clear descriptions of your professional and school achievements and skills.

Your *caring* is demonstrated with qualities such as customer orientation, teamwork, and passion for your organizations.

You can demonstrate your *character* with traits such as reliability, honesty, and commitment to values. Often, you can demonstrate these traits by getting the recommendations and endorsements of others.

Your challenge: Evaluate your LinkedIn page in terms of competence, caring, and character. What is one way you can improve your LinkedIn profile and LinkedIn activity for each of these aspects of credibility?

You can demonstrate your professional credibility with your LinkedIn profile.

M4OS Photos/Alamy Stock Photo

to build a backdoor into our products." Yet, some observers thought the tone of some comments unnecessarily attacked the motives and integrity of FBI professionals, such as the following statement: "The FBI may use different words to describe this tool, but make no mistake: Building a version of iOS that bypasses security in this way would undeniably create a backdoor. And while the government may argue that its use would be limited to this case, there is no way to guarantee such control."[45]

Applying the FAIR test to Tim Cook's letter and media interviews shows the complicated process of developing messages that accurately provide *facts*, grant *access* to motivations and information, consider the *impacts* on all stakeholders involved, and show *respect* for all parties involved. In Exercises 1.16 and 1.17 at the end of the chapter, you can see additional resources to evaluate Cook's communications in this situation.

Returning to the opening chapter scenario, Tom is weakest in character. While he performs at a high level and displays commitment and interest in those around him, he is not always honest. Many professionals will find it hard to consider him credible for this reason. Yet, some people would choose him as a mentor because they believe he will act in their interests and he can help secure important projects.

How You Can Improve Your Communication Skills

Establishing credibility will help you build high-trust relationships and communicate more effectively. In high-trust relationships, since individuals willingly and freely give the benefit of the doubt, communication is simpler, easier, quicker, and more effective.[46] As Dr. Stephen R. Covey, among the most respected management writers of the past three decades, stated regarding trust:

> It simply makes no difference how good the rhetoric is or even how good the intentions are; if there is little or no trust, there is no foundation for permanent success. . . . What we are communicates far more eloquently than anything we say or do. We all know it. There are people we trust absolutely because we know their character. Whether they're eloquent or not, whether they have the human relations techniques or not, we trust them, and we work successfully with them.[47]

This textbook is designed to help you improve your skills in a variety of professional settings so that you can become a credible and trusted communicator. Overall, you may feel that you excel at some communication skills but not others. For example, you may feel more confident in your presentation skills than your writing skills, or vice versa. Regardless of your present skill level, this textbook gives you opportunities to deliberately and consciously elevate your communication skill set. It also gives you tools to continue developing your communication abilities over the course of your career.

Figure 1.5 provides an overview of the topics we will cover in this textbook. Chapter 1 focused on the credibility of the communicator, since at the core of all communication

FIGURE 1.5

Overview of Book

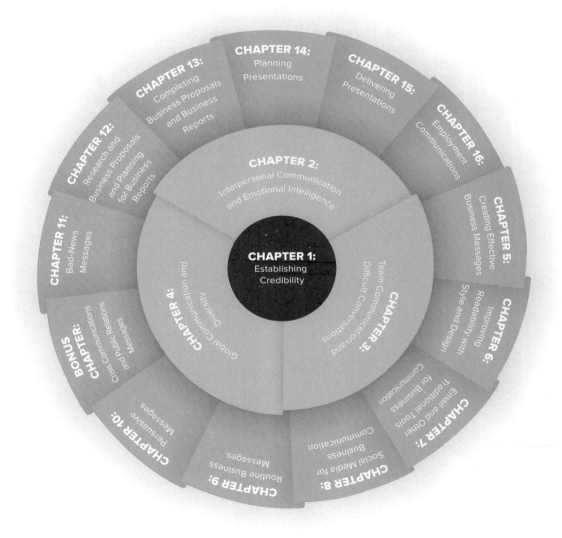

 **ESTABLISHING CREDIBILITY**    **PRINCIPLES OF INTERPERSONAL COMMUNICATION**    **PRINCIPLES FOR & TYPES OF BUSINESS MESSAGES**

is the issue of trust (explored further in the Ideas in Action feature with Mary Barra of GM). The techniques and skills covered in the rest of this textbook are of little use if you are not considered credible.

Once you have established yourself as a credible communicator, the techniques and skills in other chapters can greatly increase your communication effectiveness and career opportunities. Thus, later chapters focus on core principles, such as the interpersonal communication process, emotional intelligence, active listening, teamwork, and intercultural communication (the middle ring in Figure 1.5). These chapters lay out principles that also are important for written communication. For example, we discuss the listening-centered approach to communication, which is critical to effective writing.

You will also find chapters about planning and preparing written messages: routine messages, persuasive messages, email messages, and bad-news messages. And you will learn about conducting business research, writing business reports, and delivering presentations. You will work at developing résumés and preparing for job interviews.

As you read this book, you will be invited often to reflect about what you are reading. Try to apply what you read to your current challenges and your past experiences. Envision what you want to accomplish in your career. Imagine yourself communicating in business situations. Mentally evaluate your strengths and weaknesses. Turn off your phone and television. Reflect. You will be rewarded often during your career for staying aware of your communication skills and striving for consistent progress.[48]

IDEAS IN ACTION

LEADING WITH CREDIBILITY

Mary Barra of GM

Mary Barra joined General Motors (GM) as an intern when she was 18 years old. Roughly 35 years later she became the CEO. Within a few days of becoming CEO, GM faced one of its most serious crises in its history with widespread safety concerns about GM vehicles. Faulty ignition switches had caused at least 50 deaths. Within her first year as CEO, GM initiated 84 safety recalls for over 30 million vehicles. GM faced a major deficit of trust with the public. She is credited with rapidly shifting the GM culture and using her personal credibility to rebuild GM's reputation.

Tribune Content Agency LLC/Alamy Stock Photo

Barra often speaks about the importance of various aspects of credibility. Regarding character, she constantly promotes transparency, honesty, and high values. She refers to core values as "your North Star." She maintains that leaders demonstrate real integrity during rough times: "It's really easy to live your values when things are going well; it's more difficult when the going gets tough. It's important for colleagues and employees to trust that you will make the right decision, no matter the circumstance." She tells aspiring leaders, "If your values are little more than words on a page, they won't mean much to you or the people on your team. But when you do what you say you are going to do—in both results and behaviors—that's when you begin to build trust and earn respect."

Regarding caring, Barra frequently encourages professionals to focus on the needs of others and to build meaningful, long-term relationships. She explains, "I follow the words of Theodore Roosevelt: 'Nobody cares how much you know, until they know how much you care.' There's no shortcut to earning respect. Your relationship with your team is like any other relationship—you can't build it the moment you need it. You build it over time." She further describes the role relationships play in business: "At the end of the day, all businesses are about people first—because the only way we can build genuinely successful businesses is to build lasting relationships inside and outside the company."

Regarding competence, Barra is known for her business and technical abilities. A problem solver by nature, she is known for a track record of results. As a leader, she is constantly urging GM employees to develop their skills and create innovative, forward-looking solutions.

Mary Barra has infused credibility into GM's culture with an emphasis on integrity, transparency, collaboration and teamwork, innovation, and accountability. She is counting on these values to help GM become widely known as a tech company that makes the electric and autonomous vehicles of the future.

Sources: Barra, M. (2018, March 26). *The importance of integrity, feedback and mentoring.* Retrieved from www.linkedin.com/pulse/importance-integrity-feedback-mentoring-mary-barra/; CNN Library. (2018, October 3). General Motors fast facts. *CNN.* Retrieved from www.cnn.com/2014/04/08/us/general-motors-fast-facts/index.html; Glassdoor Team. (2016, March 24). CEO spotlight: Great advice from GM's Mary Barra. *Glassdoor CEO spotlight.* Retrieved from www.glassdoor.com/blog/ceo-spotlight-gm-mary-barra/; Lynch, S. (2016, June 30). Mary Barra: What every B-school graduate should know. Retrieved from www.gsb.stanford.edu/insights/mary-barra-what-every-b-school-graduate-should-know; Markowitz, J. (2017, May 31). *MBA alumni spotlight: General Motors CEO Mary Barra.* Retrieved from www.metromba.com/2017/05/stanford-mba-gm-ceo-mary-barra/; Thibodeau, I. (2018, October 29). CEO Mary Barra wants people to think of GM as a tech company. *The Detroit News.* Retrieved from www.detroitnews.com/story/business/autos/general-motors/2018/10/29/ceo-mary-barra-wants-people-think-gm-tech-company/1808690002/; Zacks Equity Research. (2015, January 5). *General Motors (GM): Safety recalls add up to 84 in 2014.* Retrieved from www.zacks.com/stock/news/159304/general-motors-gm-safety-recalls-add-up-to-84-in-2014.

Chapter Takeaway for *Establishing Credibility*

LO1.1 Explain the importance of establishing credibility for business communications.

You often operate from a deficit of trust when conducting business. In the **post-trust era**, skepticism is high. By establishing credibility, your colleagues, clients, customers, and other contacts will respond far more favorably to your communications.

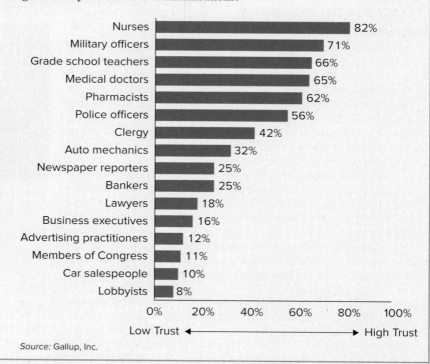

Nurses	82%
Military officers	71%
Grade school teachers	66%
Medical doctors	65%
Pharmacists	62%
Police officers	56%
Clergy	42%
Auto mechanics	32%
Newspaper reporters	25%
Bankers	25%
Lawyers	18%
Business executives	16%
Advertising practitioners	12%
Members of Congress	11%
Car salespeople	10%
Lobbyists	8%

Low Trust ◄————► High Trust

Source: Gallup, Inc.

LO1.2 Describe how competence, caring, and character affect your credibility as a communicator.

At the heart of effective business communication is **credibility**. It is a reflection of your competence, caring, and character.

Competence relates to your proven set of skills and knowledge to accomplish business tasks. Others will judge you by your track record of success.

Caring shows that you will act in the interests of others, cultivate a sense of community, and demonstrate accountability to others.

Character shows that you will adhere to high personal, corporate, and business values. You can be counted on to do the right thing.

LO1.3 Define and explain business ethics, corporate values, and personal values.

Business ethics are the commonly accepted beliefs and principles in the business community for acceptable behavior. **Corporate values** are those values that are the stated and lived values of a company. They are often provided in a formal code of conduct. **Personal values** are those values prioritized and adhered to by individuals.

LO1.4 Explain the FAIR approach to ethical business communications.

FAIR TEST

Facts: How *factual* is your communication?
Access: How *accessible* or *transparent* are your motives, reasoning, and information?
Impacts: How does your communication *impact* stakeholders?
Respect: How *respectful* is your communication?

See *example questions for the FAIR test* in Figure 1.4.

Key Terms

business ethics, 9

caring, 7

character, 8

code of conduct, 10

competence, 6

corporate values, 10

credibility, 3

personal values, 10

post-trust era, 5

stakeholder, 11

transparency, 9

Discussion Exercises

Note: Check with your instructor to see how she or he would like you to approach these exercises. Sometimes, you will work individually; other times, you'll work in teams.

1.1 Chapter Review Questions (LO1.1, LO1.2, LO1.3, LO1.4)

Answer each of the following questions with one to three paragraphs:

A. Explain the importance of establishing credibility in business communications.

B. Explain the three components of credibility: competence, caring, and character. How do they interrelate?

C. Define and explain business ethics, corporate values, and the relationship between them.

D. Explain the FAIR approach to evaluating ethical business communications.

E. Describe how credibility impacts communication efficiency and effectiveness.

1.2 Ideas in Action (LO1.1, LO1.2, LO1.3, LO1.4)

Read the Ideas in Action with Mary Barra of GM, and write a one- or two-paragraph response to each of the following questions:

A. What points does Mary Barra make about the impact of competence in establishing credibility?

B. What points does she make about the impact of caring in establishing credibility?

C. What points does she make about the impact of character in establishing credibility?

D. Which of her comments or experiences do you view as particularly insightful or helpful? Why that one?

1.3 Character and Rules (LO1.2)

As a former chair of the U.S. Federal Reserve once said, "Rules cannot take the place of character." In two to three paragraphs, explain what you think he meant by this statement.

1.4 Transparency (LO1.3)

As Drs. Dennis S. Reina and Michelle L. Reina explained in their book *Trust and Betrayal in the Workplace,* "Some leaders assume that . . . they are obligated to tell employees only what they specifically need to do their job. This couldn't be further from the truth."[49] In three to five paragraphs, explain the meaning of this statement. Why might leaders provide information about their activities and decision making, even when employees may not be directly affected?

1.5 Gather Information from Websites about Ethics in Business (LO1.3)

Read at least three blogs or articles about trust and/or ethics from a reputable organization or other source. Choose an issue that interests you, and in four to five paragraphs, summarize key findings related to that issue. Consider the following options for gathering information:

- Ethics and Compliance Initiative (www.ethics.org)
- Institute of Business Ethics (www.ibe.org.uk)
- Society of Corporate Compliance and Ethics (www.corporatecompliance.org)
- *Business Ethics* magazine (http://business-ethics.com)
- International Business Ethics Institute (www.business-ethics.org)
- Edelman website about trust (www.edelman.com/trust-barometer)

1.6 Watch Interviews with Business Executives about Credibility and Corporate Values (LO1.2, LO1.3)

Watch at least three videos of interviews with executives talking about corporate values. In four to five paragraphs, summarize what you learned. Consider the following options for gathering information:

- Go to CNBC's website (www.cnbc.com) and search with terms such as *ethics, integrity, character, credibility, values,* and/or *corporate values;* then, apply the filter for video content and search for CEO interviews about corporate values or corporate culture.
- Go to YouTube and search with terms such as *business ethics, corporate values, core values,* and *corporate culture.* Select videos of business executives and managers speaking about corporate values. Choose videos that are five minutes or longer.

1.7 Learn about Corporate Citizenship (LO1.3)

In recent years, companies have increasingly focused on their social responsibility. Many companies refer to the actions they take to help or give back to society as *corporate citizenship.* Learn about corporate citizenship from at least three reliable organizations or sources. In four to five paragraphs, summarize what you've learned. Consider the following options for gathering information:

- Boston College Center for Corporate Citizenship (www.bcccc.net/index.cfm?pageId=2053)
- *Forbes* Special Section on America's best corporate citizens (www.forbes.com/just-companies/)
- World Economic Forum special section on corporate global citizenship (http://web.worldbank.org/archive/website00818/WEB/OTHER/GLOBAL-3.HTM)
- Santa Clara University Markkula Center for Applied Ethics (www.scu.edu/ethics/)

1.8 Identify Specific Approaches to Corporate Citizenship (LO1.3)

Choose a company and analyze its corporate citizenship measures. In four to five paragraphs, explain the company's major corporate citizenship initiatives and how they reflect its core values. Generally, you can find a corporate citizenship page at a company's website by navigating within sections with titles such as "About Us," "Company Overview," "Public Relations," "Media," and so on. If you are unsure which company you would like to learn about, consider the following:

- Boeing (www.boeing.com/companyoffices/aboutus/community/)
- Citigroup (https://www.citigroup.com/citi/about/citizenship/)
- Accenture (www.accenture.com/us-en/company/citizenship/Pages/index.aspx)
- IBM (www.ibm.com/ibm/responsibility/initiatives.html)

1.9 Business Ethics and Changing Values (LO1.3)

David Pottruck, former president and co-CEO of the Charles Schwab Corporation, explained the following regarding ethics and law:

> At Schwab, we are constantly looking for new ways to express our values without compromising them. For example, we built the company on the principle of "no conflict of interest." For many years, we defined that principle as "we will not give investment advice," because we equated advice with the old-line practice of selling hot stocks to maximize brokerage commissions. When we found that our customers were demanding advice from us, we realized that our business model, one that did not compensate brokers for sales, made it possible for us to give advice and continue to avoid conflict. We changed our practice to give the customers what they wanted, expert advice that is "objective, uncomplicated and not driven by commission," and at the same time we strengthened our commitment to our values. We feel that was a highly responsible change.[50]

In three to five paragraphs, discuss whether you think corporate and personal values can and/or should change over time. Specifically discuss Pottruck's statements.

1.10 Watch Ted Talks about Credibility and Trust

Watch a TED Talk about credibility and trust. You might consider one of the following:

- "How to Build and Rebuild Trust" by Frances Frei (www.ted.com/talks/frances_frei_how_to_build_and_rebuild_trust)
- "We've Stopped Trusting Institutions and Started Trusting Strangers" by Rachel Botsman (https://www.ted.com/talks/rachel_botsman_we_ve_stopped_trusting_institutions_and_started_trusting_strangers?language=en)
- "What We Don't Understand about Trust" by Onora O'Neill (https://www.ted.com/talks/onora_o_neill_what_we_don_t_understand_about_trust)
- "What Really Motivates People to Be Honest in Business" by Alexander Wagner (www.ted.com/talks/alexander_wagner_what_really_motivates_people_to_be_honest_in_business)
- "How to Spot a Liar" by Pamela Meyer (www.ted.com/talks/pamela_meyer_how_to_spot_a_liar)

Write three to five paragraphs about the following:

1. A brief summary (four to five sentences) of the talk.
2. Two or three insights about credibility.
3. Two or three related recommendations for how professionals can act with higher credibility.

Evaluation Exercises

1.11 Compare Two Individuals' Credibility (LO1.1, LO1.2)

Think about two people—one whom you trust implicitly and another whom you do not trust. Ideally, these should be two people you currently work with or have worked with in the past. Compare them in the following ways: (a) competence, (b) caring, (c) character, (d) openness of communication, and (e) ease of communication. Write four to five paragraphs. Conclude with several general statements about the impact of credibility on communication efficiency and effectiveness.

1.12 Assess Credibility (LO1.1, LO1.2)

Think about four people: (a) a person who lacks complete credibility because he or she lacks competence, (b) a person who lacks credibility because he or she lacks caring, (c) a person who lacks credibility because he or she lacks character, and (d) a person with complete credibility. Compare and contrast these four individuals in terms of communication effectiveness in the workplace.

1.13 Evaluate a Communication Event (LO1.1, LO1.2)

Choose two communication events (conversations, email exchanges, and so on) that you were involved in—one in which you had credibility from the perspective of others and one in which you did not. If possible, choose communication events that occurred in the workplace or at your university. Respond to the following items about these two events:

A. Provide an overview of each communication event.
B. Explain the results of each event in terms of ease of communication and accomplishment of workplace objectives.

C. Explain why in one situation others granted you credibility but not in the other.
D. For the situation in which you had less perceived credibility, think about how you might have better established trust. Write down three ways you could have done so before the communication event occurred.

1.14 Examine Personal Credibility (LO1.2)

Think about a specific professional context, and respond to each of the following questions. For the context, you can use a current or previous job. Or you could use a professional or student activity in which you participated. Ideally, you will select a context with challenging cooperation issues.

A. How much do/did others trust you in this situation?
B. How credible are/were you in terms of competency, caring, and character (from the perceptions of others)?
C. Do you think you are/were being perceived inaccurately in any ways? Why?
D. Have you done/did you do anything that may have broken trust in any way?
E. Have you kept/did you keep all your agreements? Explain.
F. List three things you need to do or should have done to better establish credibility.

1.15 Apply the FAIR Test (LO1.4)

Choose a recent communication event (conversation, email exchange, and so on) that you were involved in, observed, or heard about. If possible, choose a communication event that occurred in the workplace and that involved a challenging ethical problem. Analyze the communication event with the FAIR test of ethical business communication. Devote at least one paragraph to each aspect of the test: (a) **facts** (how *factual* was the communication?); (b) **access** (how *accessible* or *transparent* were the motives, reasoning, and information?); (c) **impacts** (how did the communication *impact* stakeholders?); (d) **respect** (how *respectful* was the communication?). See Figure 1.4 for more information about the FAIR test.

1.16 Apply the FAIR Test to a Customer Letter (LO1.4)

Using the FAIR test, evaluate Tim Cook's open letter to customers (published as "A Message to Our Customers" on February 16, 2016, on the Apple website: www.apple.com/customer-letter/). Address each aspect of the FAIR test: (a) **facts** (how *factual* was the communication?); (b) **access** (how *accessible* or *transparent* were the motives, reasoning, and information?); (c) **impacts** (how did the communication *impact* stakeholders?); (d) **respect** (how *respectful* was the communication?). See Figure 1.4 for more information about the FAIR test.

Consider using other sources to help you evaluate Cook's letter. You can find a variety of online information. Some online articles you might consider include the following:

- **Examples of various views of Apple's position:** "Apple v. Washington over Encryption" in *The New York Times*, available at http://www.nytimes.com/2016/02/19/opinion/apple-vs-washington-over-encryption.html?_r=0
- **The view of an editorial board:** "Why Apple Is Right to Challenge an Order to Help the F.B.I." by *The New York Times* Editorial Board, *The New York Times*, available at www.nytimes.com/2016/02/19/opinion/why-apple-is-right-to-challenge-an-order-to-help-the-fbi.html
- **The international complications of the issue:** "While It Defies U.S. Government, Apple Abides by China's Orders—and Reaps Big Rewards" by David Pierson in the *Los Angeles Times*, available at http://www.latimes.com/business/technology/la-fi-apple-china-20160226-story.html
- **Public opinion polls:** "More Support for Justice Department Than for Apple in Dispute over Unlocking iPhone," by the Pew Research Center, available at www.people-press.org/2016/02/22/more-support-for-justice-department-than-for-apple-in-dispute-over-unlocking-iphone/
- **The views of other tech companies:** "Bill Gates Says Apple-FBI Fight Is Not Black and White," by Charles Riley in *CNNMoney*, available at money.cnn.com/2016/02/23/technology/bill-gates-apple-fbi-encryption/
- **The Apple approach to privacy:** "The Most Personal Technology Must Also Be the Most Private," available at http://www.apple.com/privacy/approach-to-privacy/
- **A public relations perspective of Apple's actions:** "The Optics of Apple's Encryption Fight," by Kaveh Wadell in *The Atlantic* (online), available at http://www.theatlantic.com/technology/archive/2016/02/why-apple-is-fighting-the-fbi/463260/
- **Reactions by victims of the terrorism:** "Anger, Praise, for Apple for Rebuffing FBI over San Bernardino's Killer's Phone" by Greg Botelho, Lorenza Brascia, and Michael Martinez on the *CNN* website, available at http://www.cnn.com/2016/02/18/us/san-bernardino-shooter-phone-apple-reaction/index.html

1.17 Apply the FAIR Test to a Media Interview (LO1.4)

Using the FAIR test, evaluate a *Wall Street Journal* interview with Tim Cook ("Tim Cook Defends Apple's Encryption Policy") on YouTube (https://www.youtube.com/watch?v=BZmeZyDGkQ0) about resistance to a U.S. court order to help unlock a terrorist's iPhone. Address each aspect of the FAIR test: (a) **facts** (how *factual* was the communication?); (b) **access** (how *accessible* or *transparent* were the motives, reasoning, and information?); (c) **impacts** (how did the communication *impact* stakeholders?); (d) **respect** (how *respectful* was the communication?). See Figure 1.4 for more information about the FAIR test. Use other online materials as needed to help you evaluate the fairness of the interview (you might consider some of the options listed in Exercise 1.16).

Application Exercises

1.18 Personal Mission Statement and Code of Conduct (LO1.3)

Write your own mission statement, including a code of conduct. Consider the following steps as you create the statement:

- Find several companies you admire. Use their code of conduct statements to help you craft your personal statement. Make sure you've personalized the statement to capture your deepest values and goals.
- Go to a career development website. These websites often contain articles and blogs about creating personal statements. For example, see the following:
  - "The Five-Step Plan for Creating Personal Mission Statements" by Randall S. Hansen (www.quintcareers.com/creating_personal_mission_statements.html)
  - "Writing a Personal Mission Statement" by Rodger Constandse (www.timethoughts.com/goalsetting/mission-statements.htm)
  - "How to Write a Personal Mission Statement" (www.daveramsey.com/blog/mission-statement-101)
- Go to a consultant website specializing in mission statements. Usually, these websites provide free resources for developing your own statement. In some cases, you will be required to create a username and password, but the online assistance is free. For example, see FranklinCovey's step-by-step guide (www.franklincovey.com/msb/).

1.19 Statement of Career Aspirations (LO1.3)

When asked "What's your career advice for young people?" Vineet Nayar, former CEO of HCL Technologies, a $5 billion IT services company centered in India, said the following:

When you come out of college, you're raw. You have energy. You want to experiment. You want to learn. You have hopes. You have aspirations. You want to be Oprah Winfrey. You want to be

Steve Jobs. You want to be Bill Gates. You want to be all that. Slowly, over time, you lose it. And by looking in the mirror every day as you get older, you fool yourself that you're OK. There has to be another way of looking in the mirror and revisiting what you really want to do. So I would say, maybe at the end of college, write it down honestly, in 100 words or whatever it is, and put it in a box. I call it the magic box. Revisit it once a year or once every two years and say, how honest are you to that? Don't let anybody run your life. That, in my mind, is very, very important. You should be in control of your life.[51]

Think about what Nayar's comments mean for you. In approximately 100 to 200 words, describe your deepest career aspirations. Include several statements about your guiding philosophy and the core personal values that drive your ambitions. Explain who you want to be in the future. Write the statement assuming that you will return to it in five, ten, or more years to see what progress you have made with your self-determined career aims.

Language Mechanics Check

1.20 Review the comma rules C1 through C4 in Appendix A. Then, rewrite each sentence to add commas where needed.

A. Financial advisors who have CFA certification can provide better advice.

B. Janice and Jim Atkinson who are certified financial advisors pay attention to your unique investment situation.

C. Janice received her CFA certification at the same time that I did.

D. Janice Atkinson president of Atkinson Financial will speak at the next Chamber of Commerce event.

E. Level 1 of the CFA exam focuses on ethical standards and Level 2 focuses on security valuation and portfolio management.

F. Janice spent almost three months preparing on her own for the CFA exam but still didn't pass it on her first try.

G. As a result she took a workshop in portfolio management from one of the top local experts.

H. Janice received her CFA certification last year the same time that I did.

I. Janice specializes in retirement planning and Jim specializes in tax preparation.

J. Jim not Janice prepares all their slide decks.

Endnotes

1. Reina, D. S., & Reina, M. L. (2006). *Trust and betrayal in the workplace.* San Francisco: Berrett-Koehler Publishers.

2. Covey, S. M. R. (2006). *The speed of trust.* New York: Free Press.

3. Covey, S. M. R. (2006). *The speed of trust.* New York: Free Press, 2.

4. These categories capture the dimensions of trust/credibility established by various scholars and experts. Various terms used in the scholarly literature include competence, benevolence, integrity, and intent. For sample works, see the following: Abrams, L. C., Cross, R., Lesser, E., & Levin, D. Z. (2003). Nurturing interpersonal trust in knowledge-sharing networks. *Academy of Management Executive, 17*(4), 64–77; Greenberg, P. S., Greenberg, R. H., & Antonucci, Y. L. (2007). Creating and sustaining trust in virtual teams. *Business Horizons, 50,* 325–333; Covey, S. M. R. (2006). *The speed of trust.* New York: Free Press; Reina, D. S., & Reina, M. L. (2006). *Trust and betrayal in the workplace.* San Francisco: Berrett-Koehler Publishers.

5. Reina, D. S., & Reina, M. L. (2006). *Trust and betrayal in the workplace.* San Francisco: Berrett-Koehler Publishers.

6. Brenan, M. (2017, December 26). Nurses keep healthy lead as most honest, ethical profession. *Gallup News.* Retrieved from news.gallup.com/poll/224639/nurses-keep-healthy-lead-honest-ethical-profession.aspx.

7. Ries, T. E., Bersoff, D. M., Armstrong, C., Adkins, S., & Bruening, J. (2018). *2018 Edelman trust barometer.* Chicago: Edelman. Retrieved from www.edelman.com/sites/g/files/aatuss191/files/2018-10/2018_Edelman_Trust_Barometer_Global_Report_FEB.pdf.

8. Fessler, L. (2017, October 30). A new study shows how managers can double employee satisfaction and trust. *Quartz at Work.* Retrieved from

https://qz.com/work/1108444/employee-satisfaction-and-trust-is-tightly-linked-to-manager-support/. Another survey showed that more than 58 percent of employees trust strangers more than their own bosses! See Sturt, D., & Nordstrom, T. (2018, March 8). 10 shocking workplace stats you need to know. *Forbes.* Retrieved from www.forbes.com/sites/davidsturt/2018/03/08/10-shocking-workplace-stats-you-need-to-know/.

9. Covey, S. M. R. (2006). *The speed of trust.* New York: Free Press.

10. Crittenden, V. L., Hanna, R. C., & Peterson, R. A. (2009). The cheating culture: A global societal phenomenon. *Business Horizons, 52,* 337–346; McCabe, D. (1996). Classroom cheating among natural science and engineering majors. *Science and Engineering Ethics, 3*(4), 433–445; McCabe, D. (2005). *Levels of cheating and plagiarism remain high.* Clemson, SC: Center for Academic Integrity; Callahan, D. (2004). *The cheating culture: Why more Americans are doing wrong to get ahead.* New York: Harcourt.

11. Covey, S. M. R. (2006). *The speed of trust.* New York: Free Press.

12. Crittenden, V. L., Hanna, R. C., & Peterson, R. A. (2009). The cheating culture: A global societal phenomenon. *Business Horizons, 52,* 337–346; McCabe, D. (1996). Classroom cheating among natural science and engineering majors. *Science and Engineering Ethics, 3*(4), 433–445; McCabe, D. (2005). *Levels of cheating and plagiarism remain high.* Clemson, SC: Center for Academic Integrity; Callahan, D. (2004). *The cheating culture: Why more Americans are doing wrong to get ahead.* New York: Harcourt.

13. Maslansky, M., West, S., DeMoss, G., & Saylor, D. (2010). *The language of trust: Selling ideas in a world of skeptics.* New York: Prentice Hall, 6.

14. de Cambourg, P. (2006). *Corporate accountability and trust: Thoughts from 12 top managers.* Paris: Economica, 37.

15. Whitman, M., & Hamilton, J. O'C. (2010). *The power of many: Values for success in business and in life.* New York: Crown Publishers, 81, 85.

16. Whitman, M., & Hamilton, J. O'C. (2010). *The power of many: Values for success in business and in life.* New York: Crown Publishers, 45–46.

17. Whitman, M., & Hamilton, J. O'C. (2010). *The power of many: Values for success in business and in life.* New York: Crown Publishers, 132.

18. Bryant, A. (2017, June 30). Lt. Gen. Nadja Y. West on the power of empathy. *The New York Times.* Retrieved from www.nytimes.com/2017/06/30/business/nadja-y-west-power-of-empathy.html.

19. Caring was listed as *conscientiousness* in a survey of important skills and abilities for business managers in the following study: Graduate Management Admission Council. (2014). *Alumni perspectives survey: 2014 survey report.* Reston, VA: Author.

20. Covey, S. M. R. (2006). *The speed of trust.* New York: Free Press.

21. Ashby, M. D., & Miles, S. A. (2002). *Leaders talk leadership: Top executives speak their minds.* New York: Oxford University Press, 5.

22. Grant, A. (2013, April). In the company of givers and takers. *Harvard Business Review,* 90–97.

23. Schwantes, M. (2018, February 13). Warren Buffett says integrity is the most important trait to hire for. Ask these 12 questions to find it. *Inc.* Retrieved from www.inc.com/marcel-schwantes/first-90-days-warren-buffetts-advice-for-hiring-based-on-3-traits.html.

24. Economist Intelligence Unit. (2008). *The role of trust in business collaboration.* London: The Economist and Cisco Systems.

25. Society for Human Resource Management. (2018). Code of ethics and business conduct. Retrieved from www.shrm.org/resourcesandtools/tools-and-samples/policies/pages/cms_014093.aspx.

26. Transparency International. What is "transparency"? Retrieved June 24, 2010, from www.transparency.org/news_room/faq/corruption_faq.

27. Gentile, M. C. (2010, March). Keeping your colleagues honest. *Harvard Business Review,* 116.

28. Gentile, M. C. (2010, March). Keeping your colleagues honest. *Harvard Business Review,* 114–117.

29. Google Code of Conduct, Alphabet Inc., July 31, 2018.

30. Bird, A. (2009). McKinsey conversations with global leaders: Paul Polman of Unilever. Retrieved July 15, 2012, from www.mckinsey-quarterly.com/McKinsey_conversations_with_global_leaders_Paul_Polman_of_Unilever_2456.

31. Frankel, T. (2006). *Trust and honesty: America's business culture at a crossroad.* Oxford: Oxford University Press, 206.

32. Whitman, M., & Hamilton, J. O'C. (2010). *The power of many: Values for success in business and in life.* New York: Crown Publishers, 92.

33. Ken Blanchard Companies. (2010). *Building Trust.* Escondido, CA: Author.

34. Reina, D. S., & Reina, M. L. (2006). *Trust and betrayal in the workplace.* San Francisco: Berrett-Koehler Publishers, 7.

35. Sussman, L. (2008). Disclosure, leaks, and slips: Issues and strategies for prohibiting employee communication. *Business Horizons, 51,* 331–339.

36. UCLA Anderson School of Management. (2004, June 18). Robert Eckert of Mattel shares insight with class of 2004 commencement address. Retrieved June 5, 2010, from www.anderson.ucla.edu/x3704.xml.

37. Whitman, M., & Hamilton, J. O'C. (2010). *The power of many: Values for success in business and in life.* New York: Crown Publishers, 99.

38. Lichtblau, E., & Benner, K. (2016, February 17). Apple fights order to unlock San Bernadino gunman's iPhone. *The New York Times.* Retrieved from www.nytimes.com/2016/02/18/technology/apple-timothy-cook-fbi-san-bernardino.html.

39. Pew Research Center. (2016, February 22). More support for Justice Department than for Apple in dispute over unlocking iPhone. Retrieved from www.people-press.org/2016/02/22/more-support-for-justice-department-than-for-apple-in-dispute-over-unlocking-iphone/.

40. Riley, C. (2016, February 23). Bill Gates says Apple-FBI fight is not black and white. *CNNMoney.* Retrieved from money.cnn.com/2016/02/23/technology/bill-gates-apple-fbi-encryption/.

41. Riley, C. (2016, February 23). Bill Gates says Apple-FBI fight is not black and white. *CNNMoney.* Retrieved from money.cnn.com/2016/02/23/technology/bill-gates-apple-fbi-encryption/; Rago, J. (2016, February 19). The FBI vs. Apple. *The Wall Street Journal.* Retrieved from www.wsj.com/articles/the-fbi-vs-apple-1455840721.

42. Pierson, D. (2016, February 26). While it defies U.S. government, Apple abides by China's orders and reaps big rewards. *Los Angeles Times.* Retrieved from http://www.latimes.com/business/technology/la-fi-apple-china-20160226-story.html.

43. Levine, D. (2016, February 21). San Bernardino victims to oppose Apple on iPhone encryption. Reuters. Retrieved from www.reuters.com/article/us-apple-encryption-victims-exclusive-idUSKCN0VV00B.

44. Ungureanu, H. (2016, February 23). San Bernardino victims side with government, legally opposing Apple in encryption debacle. *Tech Times.* Retrieved from www.techtimes.com/articles/135562/20160223/san-bernardino-victims-side-with-government-legally-opposing-apple-in-encryption-debacle.htm.

45. Tim Cook, "A Message to Our Customers," February 16, 2016, Apple website, www.apple.com/customer-letter/.

46. Covey, S. M. R. (2006). *The speed of trust.* New York: Free Press.

47. Covey, S. R. (1989). *The 7 habits of highly effective people: Restoring the character ethic.* New York: Simon and Schuster, 22–23.

48. Friedman, S. D. (2008, April). Be a better leader, have a richer life. *Harvard Business Review,* 1–13; Drucker, P. F. (2005, January). Managing oneself. *Harvard Business Review,* 16–28.

49. Reina, D. S., & Reina, M. L. (2006). *Trust and betrayal in the workplace.* San Francisco: Berrett-Koehler Publishers, 37.

50. Ashby, M. D., & Miles, S. A. (2002). *Leaders talk leadership: Top executives speak their minds.* New York: Oxford University Press, 53.

51. Bryant, A. (2010, February 13). He's not Bill Gates, or Fred Astaire. *Corner Office* (blog), *The New York Times.* Retrieved from www.nytimes.com/2010/02/14/business/14cornerweb.html.

Principles of Interpersonal Communication

PART TWO

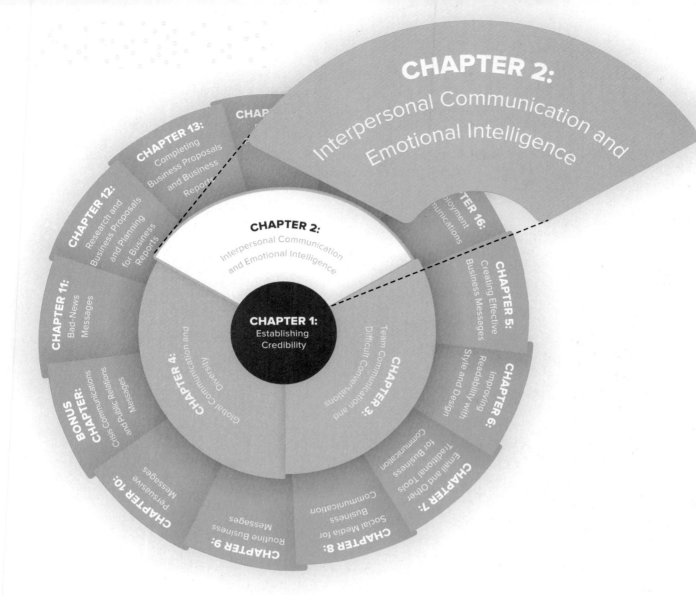

CHAPTER 2:
Interpersonal Communication and Emotional Intelligence

CHAPTER 1:
Establishing Credibility

CHAPTER 2:
Interpersonal Communication and Emotional Intelligence

ESTABLISHING CREDIBILITY

PRINCIPLES OF INTERPERSONAL COMMUNICATION

PRINCIPLES FOR & TYPES OF BUSINESS MESSAGES

LEARNING OBJECTIVES

After studying this chapter, you should be able to do the following:

LO2.1 Describe the interpersonal communication process and barriers to effective communication.

LO2.2 Explain how emotional hijacking can hinder effective interpersonal communication.

LO2.3 Explain how self-awareness impacts the communication process.

LO2.4 Describe how self-management impacts the communication process.

LO2.5 Explain and evaluate the process of active listening.

LO2.6 Describe and demonstrate effective questions for enhancing listening and learning.

LO2.7 Explain strategies to sight-read the nonverbal communication of others.

LO2.8 Identify common communication preferences based on motivational values.

LO2.9 Explain how extroversion-introversion impacts interpersonal communication.

LO2.10 Explain the role of civility in effective interpersonal communication and the common types of incivility in the workplace.

26

? WHY DOES THIS MATTER?

In nearly any poll of skills needed for career success, employees identify interpersonal skills as the most important. For example, in a 2017 survey, business recruiters identified the most important skills among a list of 20 skills. The top two skills were the following: (1) oral communication and (2) listening. These interpersonal skills were much more sought after than technical and analytical skills, core business knowledge, and a host of other skills.[1]

Consider also the remarks of Linda Hudson, former president and CEO of BAE Systems:

> *I find new business school graduates come in here thinking that, first of all, they're going to run the company overnight. Many of them are convinced they've never made a mistake. They're not accustomed to encountering the kinds of roadblocks or disappointments that often come with the way decisions get made in a corporate environment, and they have almost no people skills. So I think an important part of teaching business ought to be focused more on realistic expectations and the people-skill part of business. . . . We give them all the book smarts, but we don't tend to give them the other skills that go along with business.[2]*

In this chapter, we provide an overview of the interpersonal communication process, including an explanation of emotional intelligence, which is a foundation of effective interpersonal communication.

Read the following short case about budget cuts at Eastmond Networking. Throughout the chapter, you'll find effective and ineffective examples of interpersonal communication that are based on this case.

> **Hear Pete Cardon explain why this matters.**
>
> **bit.ly/cardon2**

CHAPTER CASE HARD DECISIONS AT EASTMOND NETWORKING

WHO'S INVOLVED

Latisha Jackson

Summer Intern
- Hired for a summer internship to develop human resource policies
- Double majoring in human resource management and family development

Jeff Brody

HR Director
- Has worked as the head of HR at Eastmond Networking for the past five years

Lisa Johnson

Finance Manager
- Has held current position for three years
- Specializes in developing budgets and financial forecasts

Steve Choi

Summer Intern
- Hired for a summer internship
- Majoring in human resource management

Jeff Brody recently hired Latisha Jackson as a summer intern to help develop new HR policies. During Latisha's interview, Jeff explained that he had seen a recent segment on a business network about how generous parental leave policies can improve retention. He said, "Our company president is asking us to identify some options to retain our younger employees and attract new employees. So if we can see what some of the other tech companies are doing and provide some fairly low-cost policies that make us comparable to other tech companies, that would be great."

Latisha was excited about the opportunity. As a dual major in human resource management and family development, this internship exactly matched her interests.

She accepted the internship at minimum wage. She had been offered another summer internship in sales that offered $15 per hour plus commissions and bonuses. But she turned down the sales position to focus on her real passion: promoting family-friendly policies in the workplace. She thought she was making the right choice, but she had believed the same thing for an internship the previous summer. That internship turned out to be a disaster; the company was disorganized and provided her with few of the exciting professional opportunities that were promised.

During Latisha's first week of work, the company president informed Jeff that he would need to make 10 to 15 percent cuts in his department budget immediately. Furthermore, the company president told him to avoid any *nonessential* work functions or initiatives.

Just after receiving this news, Jeff saw Latisha enter her office down the hall. He knew how excited she was about developing new family-friendly policies. Yet he knew that if anything could be classified as nonessential, it would be her projects. He dreaded what he was about to do—tell her that they had to postpone any work on new policies that might increase costs and that she would be reassigned to other tasks.

Jeff went to Latisha's office and said, "Latisha, can I have a minute with you?"

"Sure," she responded. "Come on in." Jeff hoped the conversation would go well.

Eastmond Networking holds performance reviews for employees once per year. Jeff sees the results of the company's internal, anonymous employee survey each year. Each year, he notices that employees do not like the performance reviews. They think the evaluations are not fair and do not help them improve. Jeff has talked to several human resource (HR) directors and learned that many companies now use continuous performance reviews with a lot of success. To help transition to continuous performance reviews, he has asked the following employees to help out: Lisa Johnson, finance manager; Steve Choi, intern; and Latisha Jackson, intern.

TASK

1 Overcome barriers to communication.

2 Manage emotions to engage in constructive communication.

Understanding the Interpersonal Communication Process

For the most part, we engage in interpersonal communication instinctively. By the time we are adults, we have engaged in hundreds of thousands of interpersonal interactions. We often take the interpersonal communication process for granted, rarely thinking about its building blocks and how they influence the quality of our communications. However, consciously becoming aware of these basic elements can help you improve your interpersonal communication skills and work more effectively with others. The **interpersonal communication process**, depicted in Figure 2.1, is the process of sending and receiving verbal and nonverbal messages between two or more people. It involves the exchange of simultaneous and mutual messages to share and negotiate meaning between those involved.[3]

Each person involved in interpersonal communication is both encoding and decoding meaning. **Meaning** refers to the thoughts and feelings that people *intend* to communicate to one another. **Encoding** is the process of converting meaning into messages composed of words and nonverbal signals. **Decoding** is the process of interpreting messages from others into meaning.

In the interpersonal communication process, communicators encode and send messages at the same time that they also receive and decode messages. When Communicator A wants to express an idea, she encodes it as a verbal (i.e., language) and nonverbal (i.e., gestures, expressions) message. Communicator B simultaneously decodes the verbal and nonverbal message and ascribes meaning to it. Whereas the verbal communication process typically involves turn-taking, with Communicator A and Communicator B alternating between sending messages, the nonverbal communication in face-to-face communication is typically constant. Furthermore, the processing of messages in the

LO2.1 Describe the interpersonal communication process and barriers to effective communication.

Mc Graw Hill **connect**

Visit **http://connect. mheducation.com** for an exercise on this topic.

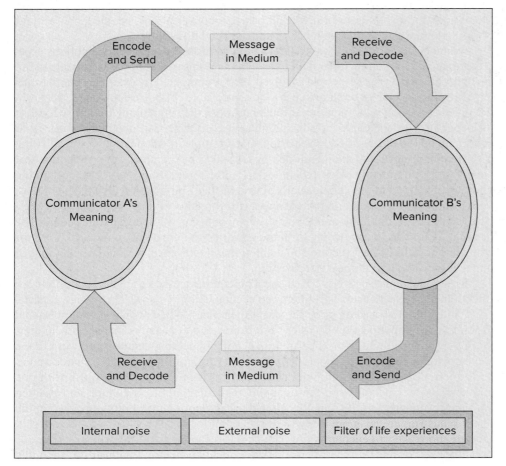

FIGURE 2.1

The Interpersonal Communication Process

form of encoding and decoding occurs continuously. One goal of interpersonal communication is to arrive at **shared meaning**—a situation in which people involved in interpersonal communication attain the same understanding about ideas, thoughts, and feelings. In practice, many barriers interfere with achieving shared meaning, including external noise, internal noise, and lifetime experiences.

Noise causes distortion to or interruption of messages. Four types of noise affect the quality of message delivery: physical noise, physiological noise, semantic noise, and psychological noise. **Physical noise** is external noise that makes a message difficult to hear or otherwise receive. Examples include loud sounds nearby that interrupt verbal signals or physical barriers that prevent communicators from observing nonverbal signals. Physical noise can also be a function of the medium used. A poor signal for a phone conversation or blurry video feed for a teleconference are examples of physical noise. The other three types of noise are distortions or interruptions of messages that are caused by *internal* characteristics of communicators.

Physiological noise refers to disruption due to physiological factors. Examples include hearing problems, illness, memory loss, and so on. Conversely, a communicator may have a difficult time sending a message due to physiological constraints such as stuttering, sickness, or other temporary or permanent impairments.

Semantic noise occurs when communicators apply different meanings to the same words or phrases. For example, two people may have different ideas about what an *acceptable profit margin* means. One manager may have a figure in mind, such as 10 percent. Another may think of a range between 20 and 30 percent. Semantic noise can be most difficult to overcome when strong emotions are attached to words or phrases. For example, a term such as *downsize* may invoke positive emotions for a manager who associates this term with frugality and wise cash management. However, another manager may view this term with negative emotions and associate it with callousness and disloyalty on the part of the corporation. In nearly all business conversations, people throw around words and phrases that they understand and interpret differently.

Psychological noise refers to interference due to attitudes, ideas, and emotions experienced during an interpersonal interaction. In many cases, this noise occurs due to the current conversation—the people involved or the content. For example, people may have preexisting feelings or stereotypes ("he's unreliable," "she's calculating," "they will not defend us in front of management") about those they are talking to. Those feelings influence how they encode and decode messages. People also may react strongly to comments made during the conversation. For example, a listener can't stop thinking about an inaccurate statistic mentioned by a speaker or the upside of a potential deal being discussed. In many cases, psychological noise comes from sources other than the interpersonal interaction. People nearly always begin a conversation affected by moods. Perhaps they are stressed and preoccupied with thoughts of upcoming deadlines. Perhaps a person is unhappy about a lost client and has a lingering sour mood. The demanding impacts of day-to-day business activities can create psychological noise for many reasons. In the next section about emotional intelligence, we focus on methods of managing psychological noise effectively.

All outgoing messages are encoded and all incoming messages are decoded through a **filter of lifetime experiences**. This filter is an accumulation of knowledge, values, expectations, and attitudes based on prior personal experiences. When people have more shared experiences, communication is easier.[4] For example, two business managers who grew up in the same community at the same time, got engineering degrees, and work in the same company likely share enough common background in the form of shared values and experiences that they can quite easily sort through noise as they speak with one another. However, people who grew up in different communities or cultures and at different times, who have far different educational backgrounds, and who have worked in different industries are far more likely to filter incoming messages differently. As a result, they are more likely to encounter noise and are less equipped to deal with the noise.

The short conversation between Jeff and Latisha in Figure 2.2 illustrates the interpersonal communication process. Notice the sender's intended messages and how they

FIGURE 2.2

The Interpersonal Communication Process in a Short Conversation

Jeff Brody sat down, shifted uncomfortably, and sighed. Latisha turned down the radio volume, but Jeff could still hear the weather report.

"Latisha, you've done a great job for us." Shrugging his shoulders, he continued, "My hands are tied, though, and we need to abandon the development of new HR policies. I'm being forced to cut our budget immediately. There's simply no room for new projects that cost additional money."

Latisha looked stunned. "I thought we went through this already. These new policies, such as new parental leave policies, can increase morale and retention and attract better employees. Doesn't the company care about that?"

"Hey," Jeff said. "Don't overreact. Look, it's not about caring. It's about surviving so we can try not to lay anyone off."

"Are you saying I don't have an internship anymore?"

"Of course you have an internship," he said, exasperated. "We'll find some other great projects for you to work on. I'm going to schedule a time this afternoon with Jenn and you. We can all talk about some new tasks for you."

"Okay," Latisha said, "well, whatever you want. I'll see you this afternoon then."

As Jeff got up, Latisha couldn't hide a look of displeasure. And, Jeff couldn't hide his frustration that Latisha didn't understand his predicament.

Jeff encodes: Thanks for your great work. Unfortunately, you will need to work on a different project.

Latisha decodes: Jeff thinks other projects are more important. This is an excuse.

Latisha encodes: Parental leave policies will help our employees and increase retention. Don't *you* care?

Jeff decodes: Latisha thinks I don't care about her projects.

Jeff encodes: Of course I care. This is the reality of business. I'm doing my best to keep everyone's job.

Latisha decodes: Jeff thinks he has to fire people to save money.

Latisha encodes: Is my job safe?

Jeff decodes: She doesn't trust me.

Jeff encodes: You have great talents, and we want you to help on an important project.

Latisha decodes: Jeff probably wants to help but has no idea of what I can do for the company.

Latisha encodes: I'll do whatever you want me to.

Jeff decodes: Latisha doesn't want to work on other projects.

Physical noise: Radio weather report is on.

Psychological noise: Jeff is worried about budget cuts in his department. He is also worried about disappointing Latisha. Latisha becomes disappointed and feels like she's in another dead-end internship.

Physiological noise: Jeff is physically tired from lack of sleep. He is also physically stressed from work.

Semantic noise: Jeff views the word *surviving* neutrally. He views it as a normal process that companies go through from time to time. Latisha perceives *surviving* as a panic word. She also views it as an excuse word to justify giving bad news.

Filter of lifetime experiences: Latisha has been disappointed by a lot of supervisors. For example, in her last internship, her supervisors repeatedly promised great opportunities and projects. She ended up doing menial database entry of personnel records. Jeff has been through ups and downs for companies. He has always tried to protect his employees during downturns and has always figured out how to do it. He has found that in each crisis, he is more effective by avoiding rash decisions.

are encoded and decoded. Also notice the noise factors and filters and consider how they interfere with achieving shared meaning. Consider that this short conversation is between two well-meaning people who are both caught up in a frustrating but relatively straightforward situation. Both want to help the other. Yet, as you read the conversation, you will notice they do not understand one another completely and become agitated. Many business conversations are far more challenging than this one.

Emotional Hijacking

LO2.2 Explain how emotional hijacking can hinder effective interpersonal communication.

Visit http://connect. mheducation.com for an exercise on this topic.

The ability to manage effective interpersonal communication depends on emotional intelligence. **Emotional intelligence** involves understanding emotions, managing emotions to serve goals, empathizing with others, and effectively handling relationships with others.[5] Business managers with high emotional intelligence are more effective at influencing others, overcoming conflict, showing leadership, collaborating in teams, and managing change.[6] Furthermore, research has shown emotional intelligence leads to better outcomes in business reasoning and strategic thinking.[7] You may see emotional intelligence referred to as **EQ**, which stands for *emotional quotient,* a play on the term *IQ, intelligence quotient.* We use both terms in this book.

Recently, EQ has been shown to be the single best predictor of workplace performance. About 90 percent of high performers in the workplace are high in EQ, whereas only 20 percent of low performers are high in EQ. On average, people with high EQs make $29,000 more per year than those with low EQs.[8]

Emotional intelligence comes into play in many business circumstances. It is especially important during moments of stress. Roughly 80 percent of Americans say they experience significant stress at work (the highest percentage in a study of eight countries).[9] Emotional intelligence contributes to one's ability to communicate clearly and constructively, overcome nerves before a presentation, gain the courage to talk to someone about bad news, respond well to disappointment and failure, motivate team members to move toward a common goal, and many other situations. In short, emotional intelligence allows business managers and executives to think clearly about business objectives without letting their emotions get the best of them.

Business leaders increasingly emphasize the need for emotional intelligence in today's demanding business environment. Richard Anderson, former CEO of Delta Air Lines, described the kind of qualities he looks for in employees:

> I think this communication point is getting more and more important. People really have to be able to handle the written and spoken word. . . . You've got to have not just the business skills, you've got to have the emotional intelligence. . . . You have to have the emotional intelligence to understand what's right culturally, both in your company and outside your company.[10]

In the upcoming pages, you will learn strategies for developing your emotional intelligence. In general, emotional intelligence is developed through conscious effort and attention to your feelings and interactions with others. Common approaches to improving emotional intelligence include practicing mindfulness, reflecting on emotions and behavior, keeping a journal, and practicing interpersonal skills in social situations.[11]

In this section, we first focus on emotional hijacking. Then, we discuss four domains of emotional intelligence—self-awareness, self-management, empathy, and relationship management. Finally, we'll suggest strategies for improving your emotional intelligence in each of these domains to achieve more effective interpersonal communication in the workplace.

Some people might wonder why emotional intelligence is so critical for business managers and executives, especially those in finance, accounting, and quantitatively driven disciplines and positions. After all, competence in many types of business decision making is primarily based on logic and reason. The primary reason that emotional intelligence is so critical is physiological: People are hardwired to experience emotions before reason. All signals to the brain first go through the limbic system, where emotions are produced, before going to the rational area of the brain (see Figure 2.3).[12]

In other words, you feel all your incoming messages before you reason about them. Furthermore, one function of the limbic system is protection. This part of the brain creates a fight-or-flight response when incoming messages appear as threats. For example, people may experience **emotional hijacking**, a situation in which emotions control our behavior, causing us to react without thinking. The impacts of emotions last long after they've subsided.[13]

Emotional hijacking prevents you from engaging in effective interpersonal communication. It can lead to unwanted behaviors: You may misrepresent your ideas, confuse the facts, say things to others that you later regret, display frustration or anger, remain silent when you would prefer to be heard, fail to listen to others, or disengage from working relationships that are in your best interest.

In the conversation between Jeff and Latisha (see Figure 2.2), both are in danger of emotional hijacking. Latisha is living the experience in the context of past disappointments with supervisors. She further panics when she perceives that her job may be in danger. All her thoughts are influenced by the emotions generated in the limbic system. Jeff similarly is at risk of emotional hijacking. He easily becomes agitated because he thinks Latisha does not trust him or understand his motives. Furthermore, he still has lingering stress from his conversation just minutes earlier with the company president, who informed him that he needed to cut nonessential work activities.

Self-Awareness

The most-used EQ test for business professionals shows that emotional intelligence can be divided into four domains: self-awareness, self-management, empathy, and relationship management. Throughout this section, we refer to statistics based on this particular measure of EQ.[14]

Self-awareness is the foundation for emotional intelligence. It involves accurately understanding your emotions as they occur and how they affect you. One prominent researcher defines self-awareness as "ongoing attention to one's internal states."[15] People high in self-awareness understand their emotions well, what satisfies them, and what irritates them. Understanding your emotions as they occur is not always easy. In fact, one study showed that just 36 percent of people can accurately identify their emotions as they occur.[16] A more recent, five-year study of the workplace showed that 95 percent of professionals think they're self-aware, yet only 10 to 15 percent actually are.[17]

Self-awareness is particularly important for stressful and unpleasant situations. People high in self-awareness have the ability to be self-reflective when they experience strong or even distressful emotions. Often, this involves the ability to explicitly identify feelings as they occur. For example, a person who becomes angry with a colleague can simultaneously think, "I'm feeling anger right now."[18]

High self-awareness includes the ability to manage events that stir strong—often fight-or-flight—responses. Events that cause strong emotional reactions are called **triggers**.[19] As you become more aware of your triggers or tendencies, you can adjust your interpersonal communication to avoid dysfunctional behaviors caused by emotional hijacking, such as blaming others as a defense mechanism or not speaking up when you're nervous.

Adele Lynn, one of the foremost experts on the role of emotional intelligence in workplace performance, explained the benefit of emotional intelligence:

> I'm sure you know people who go through life and never seem to learn from their mistakes, or they don't see how one experience is connected to another. Self-awareness will help

FIGURE 2.3

Neuropathways of Signals Entering the Brain

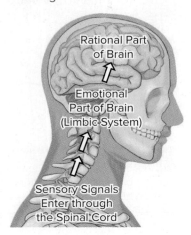

LO2.3 Explain how self-awareness impacts the communication process.

Visit http://connect. mheducation.com for an exercise on this topic.

TABLE 2.1

Low versus High Self-Awareness Thoughts

Low Self-Awareness Thoughts	High Self-Awareness Thoughts
Jeff: Latisha needs to learn how to trust people. She's not being fair to me and she needs to understand the constraints I'm facing.	**Jeff:** I'm bothered that she doesn't trust my motives. Typically, I feel disrespected when others don't trust my motives. Sometimes, I lash out in these circumstances.
Jeff ignores and deflects his feelings to focus on what he perceives as Latisha's misperceptions.	Jeff recognizes that he feels distrusted and disrespected by what Latisha said. He also recognizes that he often says things he later regrets in these situations.
Latisha: This is ridiculous. Jeff promised me that I'd be working on family-friendly HR policies. How can he go back on his word so quickly?	**Latisha:** I feel afraid and confused. Jeff doesn't seem to care if I have challenging work. I've felt this way before at other jobs. I wonder how my past experiences are impacting how I'm judging Jeff.
Latisha overreacts to Jeff's words and actions because she is not aware of how past disappointments are affecting how she is judging Jeff.	Latisha notices that how she feels about Jeff is affected by previous, similar events. She knows she should be careful not to let those events make her rush to judgment.

prevent this from happening to you, but only if you keep building on your lessons. This linking of life experiences into ever-increasing lessons is the foundation of wisdom. It is the quintessential difference in living one year of experiences thirty times versus thirty years of experience.[20]

In the conversation between Jeff and Latisha, more self-awareness would help both of them manage their feelings and thoughts. If Jeff is self-aware, he says to himself, "I'm feeling bothered that she doesn't trust me and thinks I don't care." Similarly, Latisha is self-aware if in the moment she says to herself, "I feel afraid and confused. Jeff doesn't seem to care if I have challenging work. I've felt this way before at other jobs. I wonder how my past experiences are impacting how I'm judging Jeff." Table 2.1 shows differences in low versus high self-awareness in the encounter between Jeff and Latisha.

Also, read through Table 2.2 to learn more about self-awareness and strategies for developing it. You'll notice that this table also contains information about self-management, empathy, and relationship management. After reading about each element of EQ, consider going back to the table for additional information about these dimensions of EQ.

Self-Management

LO2.4 Describe how self-management impacts the communication process.

Mc Graw Hill connect

Visit http://connect. mheducation.com for an exercise on this topic.

Self-management is the "ability to use awareness of your emotions to stay flexible and to direct your behavior positively."[21] It involves the discipline to hold off on current urges to meet long-term intentions. Excellent self-managers know how to use both positive and negative emotions to meet personal and business goals.[22]

Most strong emotions can impair rational communication and behavior. For example, anger is an intense emotion tied to a physical sense of endangerment. Most people have impulses to verbally attack or defend themselves during a rush of intense emotion. While intense emotions often last just moments, their impacts last far longer. For example, when you experience anger, the resulting adrenal and cortical excitation creates less intense reactions to this sense of endangerment that can last hours

TABLE 2.2

Emotional Intelligence Dimensions, Related Impacts on Interpersonal Communication, and Strategies for Improvement

EQ Dimension	Impact on Interpersonal Communication	Strategies for Improvement
Self-awareness	**Low self-awareness** • Unaware of own emotional states and related impacts on communication. • Unaware of triggers that lead to emotional hijacking and making judgmental, rash, or unfair comments. • Unaware of strengths and weaknesses of own communication abilities. **High self-awareness** • Aware of own emotional states and related impacts on communication. • Aware of triggers and related tendencies to say the wrong thing. • Aware of strongest communication skills.	• Constantly evaluate your feelings and moods; attempt to understand your feelings as they occur. • Think about your last reactions to the following experiences: joy, anger, self-doubt, frustration. • Ask yourself how certain emotions alter or distort your thinking. • Identify your triggers and make plans to handle them effectively. • Reflect on personal strengths, weaknesses, and values.
Self-management	**Low self-management** • Unable to control impulses. • Frequently vent frustrations without a constructive work purpose. • Spend a higher percentage of work conversations on small talk, gossip, and non-work-related issues. • React defensively and with a me-first attitude when threats are perceived. **High self-management** • Control emotional impulses that are not aligned with work and relationship goals. • Discuss frustrations in the context of solving problems and improving relationships. • Spend a higher percentage of work conversations on work-related topics with a focus on solutions. • When threats are perceived, seek to de-escalate interpersonal tensions and resolve issues at hand.	• Engage in relaxation techniques to clear your mind. • Examine strategies for overcoming impulses that compete with achieving your long-range goals. • Focus on how to improve for your next effort rather than dwelling on disappointments of the current failure. • Practice expressing positive emotions more frequently and in situations where you normally do not. • Talk to a trusted colleague who is an effective self-manager. • Sleep on it. • Practice self-talk and visualize yourself responding effectively to challenging interpersonal issues.
Empathy	**Low empathy** • Fail to listen carefully to others. • Direct conversations to topics that are important to self. • Avoid volunteering to help others with their work assignments. • Engage in a me-first approach to work with colleagues. **High empathy** • Attempt to understand the feelings, perspectives, and needs of others. • Direct conversations to topics that focus on the needs of others and self. • Volunteer advice or help to others as appropriate. • Show a sincere interest in others: their efforts, their ideas, and their successes.	• Always attempt to place yourself in the position of others: think about the emotions and thoughts others are experiencing. • Anticipate how others will react during business conversations and meetings. • Listen to others, even when you disagree, without interrupting or judging. • Pay attention to nonverbal behavior. • Practice asking good questions. • Think about group dynamics and the related impacts on each team member. • Give others your undivided attention and time. • Get to know others.

TABLE 2.2

(Continued)

EQ Dimension	Impact on Interpersonal Communication	Strategies for Improvement
Relationship management	**Low relationship management** • Focus exclusively on the task at hand without paying attention to rapport-building. • Remain silent to avoid discussions about differences of opinions, or attempt to silence the dissenting opinions of others. • Provide indirect and vague feedback and ideas to others. • Disregard feedback and constructive criticism. • Discourage dissent. • Respond to others only when it's convenient. **High relationship management** • Build rapport with others to focus on collaboration. • Speak out constructively about differences of opinion. • Provide direct and constructive feedback to others. • Accept and even welcome feedback and constructive criticism. • Encourage contrarian views. • Respond to others when it's convenient for them.	• Attend work-related social outings. • Keep records of people in your network and keep track of their skills, interests, hobbies, birthdays, and other important dates. • Maintain regular contact with colleagues and others in your work network. • Devote time to conversations on a range of topics. • Greet others by name. • Live up to your promises. • Collaborate more effectively with others. • Build up the courage to have a difficult conversation. • Speak up in meetings or work conversations when you ordinarily do not; or, encourage others who rarely speak up to voice their thoughts and feelings.

and days. An individual may ignore this less intense reaction yet still feel a sour mood for a period of time. Furthermore, research shows that anger builds on anger. Thus, people are more vulnerable to being provoked to anger during this period. Strong self-managers realize that they are still vulnerable for several days following feelings of anger and learn to heighten their levels of self-awareness during these time periods.[23]

People can quickly control moderate negative emotions. For example, an individual who tries to understand **mitigating information** can short-circuit moderate anger almost immediately. Mitigating information involves favorable explanations for why others have behaved in a certain way. See Table 2.3 for examples of low and high self-management and the use of mitigating information.

A common misperception of many business professionals is that venting negative feelings helps people cope with anger. Study after study has shown that venting is temporarily satisfying—but it rarely makes anger go away, especially when the venting is intended as retaliation. Physiologically, venting continues to arouse the brain with feelings of anger. Thus, venting is considered one of the least effective strategies for de-escalating anger.[24]

Typically, other strategies should be pursued to deal with intense anger. These strategies include removing oneself temporarily from the anger-inducing situation, going on a walk, breathing deeply, or enjoying some entertainment (e.g., TV, movies, reading). Also, writing about the feelings of frustration, anger, and hostility can help you articulate your feelings, review the events rationally, and challenge and reappraise the feelings. Typically, excellent self-managers experiment with ways of cooling down so that they find tried-and-true solutions to overcoming intense emotions. Generally, however, this cooling down is typically not effective when the time is used to relive the anger-inducing events.[25]

TABLE 2.3

Low versus High Self-Management Thoughts and the Use of Mitigating Information

Low Self-Management Thoughts	High Self-Management Thoughts
Jeff: If Latisha is going to treat me like I'm the bad guy, then maybe I should just turn her over to someone else so I don't have to worry about her.	**Jeff:** Latisha is probably reacting this way because she cares so much about family-friendly policies, which helps the employees of this company. She is eager to contribute.
Jeff assumes the worst about Latisha's comments, thus allowing his frustration with her to grow. He considers an action that is extreme.	Jeff assumes a positive explanation for Latisha's actions *(mitigating information)*, thus short-circuiting his feelings of frustration and perhaps moderating anger.
Latisha: There's no way I can change anything. Jeff will assign me to another project and that's that. I'm stuck in another dead-end internship.	**Latisha:** I want to express to Jeff my desire to work on a meaningful project. We can discuss how my approach to employee-friendly policies and quality-of-life issues could be applied to another project. And we could discuss how I can still spend some time working on options for better parental leave policies in a way that does not require cash commitments during this budget crunch.
This thought process reflects *pessimism*. Latisha neither thinks of other options available to her for working on parental leave policies nor assumes that other work tasks will provide her with rewarding challenges.	This thought process reflects *optimism*. Latisha considers how she can approach Jeff and constructively discuss options that are good for her and the company.

Self-management involves far more than corralling anger. It involves responding productively and creatively to feelings of self-doubt, worry, frustration, disappointment, and nervousness. It also includes tempering oneself when experiencing excitement and elation. In short, self-management helps you avoid knee-jerk reactions that may compromise your ability to meet your business and career objectives.[26]

A major distinction between those high in self-management and those low in self-management is **optimism** versus **pessimism**. Optimists view failures as events that can be changed in the future. They view these failures as temporary setbacks and learning experiences. Pessimists, by contrast, view failures as indications of their own incompetence or inability. They dwell on the past rather than looking to the future. Under duress or disappointment, optimists form a plan of action, whereas pessimists focus on the permanence of their situation and their inability to overcome the disappointment. One study showed that among insurance sales workers, optimists outperformed pessimists by 37 percent in sales. Furthermore, pessimists were twice as likely as optimists to quit.[27]

Empathy

Whereas the first two dimensions of emotional intelligence primarily deal with identifying and managing one's own emotions, the final two dimensions—empathy and relationship management—involve understanding others and managing your interactions with them effectively. **Empathy** is the "ability to accurately pick up on emotions in other people and understand what is really going on with them."[28] Empathy also includes the desire to help others develop in their work responsibilities and career objectives.[29] In this chapter, we focus on two communication skills that will help you develop your empathy: listening and sight-reading nonverbal communication. In nearly each chapter thereafter, we discuss types of business communication with a constant focus on understanding and relating to the needs of others (empathy).

Active Listening

LO2.5   Explain and
evaluate the
process of active
listening.

Visit http://connect.
mheducation.com for an
exercise on this topic.

Dozens of studies have shown that listening is ranked among the most important communication skills.[30] For example, corporate recruiters were recently asked which skills were most important for managers (see Table 2.4). They ranked listening skills second in a list of 25 important skills. They valued listening skills more highly than presentation skills, writing skills, and other types of communication skills.[31]

Listening requires hard work. And it requires more than simply hearing. It requires one's full attention and all senses. In fact, great listeners respond physically to others. Research indicates that brain activity in excellent listeners mimics that of the speakers. In some cases, the listener's brain shows activity before that of the speaker. In other words, the best listeners anticipate how a speaker thinks and feels.[32]

In recent years, management and communication scholars have increasingly emphasized this notion with the term **active listening**. Michael Hoppe of the Center for Creative Leadership has defined active listening as "a person's willingness and ability to hear and understand. At its core, active listening is a state of mind. . . . It involves bringing about and finding common ground, connecting to each other, and opening up new possibilities."[33] Hoppe breaks down active listening into six skills: (1) paying attention, (2) holding judgment, (3) reflecting, (4) clarifying, (5) summarizing, and (6) sharing.

Paying Attention   This first step involves devoting your whole attention to others and allowing them enough comfort and time to express themselves completely. As others speak to you, try to understand everything they say from *their* perspective. Michael Mathieu, CEO of the video advertising company YuMe, recommended that business managers pay better attention to those with whom they interact:

> Be connected, and have conversations with people. Don't be distracted, and the little nuances of life will show up, and you will hear things. I'm not immune. I have to do a lot of

TABLE 2.4

Most Important Skills for Managers

Top 15 Skills According to Corporate Recruiters (2017)

Skills	Category
1. Oral communication	Communication
2. Listening skills	**Communication**
3. Adaptability	Teamwork
4. Written communication	Communication
5. Presentation skills	Communication
6. Value opinions of others	Teamwork
7. Integrity	Leadership
8. Follow a leader	Teamwork
9. Drive	Leadership
10. Cross-cultural sensitivity	Teamwork
11. Quantitative analysis	Technical
12. Qualitative analysis	Technical
13. Innovation and creativity	Leadership
14. Core business knowledge	Technical
15. Ability to inspire others	Leadership

Source: Graduate Management Admission Council. (2017). *Corporate recruiters survey report 2017.* Reston, VA: GMAC.

Note: Survey included 25 important communication, leadership, technical, teamwork, and management skills. The top 15 skills are listed here.

things, and I try to slow down sometimes. I try to be present so I can enjoy the richness and quality of interactions with people. Most people can't multitask without losing something in each of those tasks.[34]

Paying attention requires active nonverbal communication. Your body language, including appropriate eye contact, should show you are eager to understand the other person. Lean forward. Keep an open body position. Sit up straight. Nod to show you are listening. Smile as appropriate. Pay attention to the speaker's nonverbal behaviors. Avoid any distractions, such as taking calls or checking your phone. Become comfortable with silence. To hear people out inevitably requires a few breaks in the flow of the conversation.[35] In the section "Sight-Reading Nonverbal Communication and Building Rapport" you will focus more on your ability to recognize the nonverbal communication of others.

Monkey Business Images/Shutterstock

Holding Judgment   People will share their ideas and feelings with you only if they feel safe. Holding judgment is particularly important in tense and emotionally charged situations. One of the best ways to make others feel comfortable expressing themselves fully is to demonstrate a learner mind-set rather than a judger mind-set.

In a **learner mind-set**, you show eagerness to hear others' ideas and perspectives and listen with an open mind. You do not have your mind made up before listening fully. When you disagree, you stay open to the possibility of finding common ground and mutually beneficial solutions. Under the learner mind-set, difference of opinion is considered normal, even healthy, and potentially solution-producing.[36]

In a **judger mind-set**, people have their minds made up before listening carefully to others' ideas, perspective, and experiences. Judgers view disagreement rigidly, with little possibility of finding common ground unless the other person changes his or her views. Judging often involves punishing others for disagreement. At its extreme, the judger mind-set involves ascribing negative traits to others and labeling them in undesirable terms. For example, judgers often enter conversations with thoughts such as "she's not creative" or "he's unreliable." Not surprisingly, the judger mind-set stifles conversation.[37]

Holding judgment does not mean that you agree with everything you hear. It also does not mean you avoid critiquing the ideas of others. Rather, it's a commitment to hearing the entire version of others' ideas and experiences. It's a commitment to listen fully before reacting. And, it's a mind-set of rewarding others for opening up, especially when you disagree with them. Niki Leondakis, former chief operating officer of the Kimpton Hotels, explained how she moved away from a judger mind-set to a learner mind-set over the course of her career:

> When I was a younger manager, my anxiety about what wasn't right drove me to confront things quickly. The faster I confronted it, the more quickly it could get fixed . . . and while that's a good thing, the manner in which I did it frequently left people feeling defensive. So by listening first and trying to understand how we got here and their story, I think it allows them to then hear my point of view. And then we can move into solutions. When people feel judged right out of the gate, it's hard for them to open up and listen and improve.[38]

You can create an environment in which others open up and you can listen more effectively with **learner statements**, which show your commitment to hearing people out. In effective learner statements, you explicitly state your desire to hear differing opinions with statements such as "I have a different perspective, so I want to understand how you see this." By contrast, people who make **judger statements**, which show they are closed off to hearing people out, shut down honest conversations.[39]

Active-Listening Components
• Paying attention
• Holding judgment
• Reflecting
• Clarifying
• Summarizing
• Sharing

TABLE 2.5

Judger Statements versus Learner Statements

Judger Statements	Learner Statements
Lisa: You're basing your conclusions on just a few people you've talked to. Why aren't you concerned about finding out more about the costs?	**Lisa:** I don't know much about continuous feedback systems. What have you learned from the people you've talked to?
This statement implies Jeff is not concerned about costs and isn't open to learning more. This will likely lead to defensiveness.	This statement is neutral and shows a desire to learn about Jeff's experiences and thoughts. This positions Lisa well to ask tough questions later on in a constructive manner.
Jeff: I spend a lot of time talking to HR directors and know which ones are best at helping their employees stay engaged and productive. Don't you think HR professionals would know more about this than people with a finance background?	**Jeff:** I've learned several things from HR directors about continuous feedback systems. . . . I need to learn more about the financial implications. Based on what I've told you, what are your thoughts about the cost-effectiveness?
This statement begins with an *I'm right, you're wrong* message. It directly calls into question the competence of the listener. Many listeners would become defensive.	This statement reflects a learning stance and shows a cooperative approach moving forward.

Recall Jeff Brody, the HR director from the opening case. He is hoping to transition from annual performance reviews to continuous performance reviews. Throughout this section on listening, you will see parts of a conversation between Jeff and Lisa Johnson, the finance manager. Lisa is skeptical that continuous performance reviews are cost-effective and practical. Notice the distinctions between judger statements and learner statements in this conversation in Table 2.5.

Reflecting   Active listening requires that you reflect on the ideas and emotions of others. To make sure you really understand others, you should frequently paraphrase what you're hearing. As Table 2.6 shows, good reflecting statements begin with phrases such as "It sounds like you think . . ."; "So, you're not happy with . . ."; or "Let me make sure I understand . . ."[40]

TABLE 2.6

Reflecting Statements

Types of Effective Reflecting Statements	Example
It sounds to me like . . .	*Lisa:* It sounds to me like you think we should replace annual performance reviews with continuous performance reviews because continuous reviews improve employee performance and morale.
So, you're not happy with . . .	*Jeff:* So, you're not happy with this transition unless we carefully evaluate all of the costs, is that right?
Is it fair to say that you think . . .	*Lisa:* Is it fair to say that you think we should make this change even if we don't know all the costs?
Let me make sure I understand . . .	*Jeff:* Let me make sure I understand your view. Are you saying that we can understand the costs better by . . . ?

TABLE 2.7

Clarifying Statements

Types of Effective Clarifying Statements	Example
What are your thoughts on . . . ?	*Lisa:* What are your thoughts on considering other ways of conducting annual reviews more effectively?
Could you repeat that?	*Jeff:* Could you repeat what you just said about evaluating the costs of continuous reviews?
I'm not sure I understand . . .	*Lisa:* I'm not sure I understand why the problems with our current annual review process mean that we should move away from annual reviews. Do you know of companies that are using annual reviews more effectively than we are?
Could you explain how . . . ?	*Jeff:* Could you explain how you would calculate the costs of a continuous review system?
What might be your role in . . . ?	*Lisa:* What roles will Steve and Lisa have in helping us understand what employees think of the current review process?

Clarifying   Clarifying involves making sure you have a clear understanding of what others mean. It includes double-checking that you understand the perspectives of others *and* asking them to elaborate and qualify their thoughts. It is more than simply paraphrasing. It involves trying to connect the thoughts of others so you can better understand how they are making conclusions. As Table 2.7 shows, good clarifying questions are open-ended and start with learner-oriented phrases such as, "What are your thoughts on . . . ?" or "Could you explain how . . . ?"[41]

Summarizing   The goal of summarizing is to restate major themes so that you can make sense of the *big issues* from the perspective of the other person. Ideally, you can show that you understand the major direction of the conversation. You can summarize with statements that begin with phrases such as "So, your main concern is . . ." or "It sounds like your key points are . . . ," as shown in Table 2.8.[42]

Sharing   Active listening also involves expressing your own perspectives and feelings. If you do not share your own ideas completely, your colleagues do not know what you

TABLE 2.8

Summarizing Statements

Types of Effective Summarizing Statements	Example
So, your main concern is . . .	*Jeff:* So, your two main concerns are that moving to a continuous review process will be costly and impractical. The software and time needed in the process will cost far more than what we invest in an annual review process. Also, it may be difficult to get all employees to participate often in this process. Is that right?
It sounds like your key points are . . .	*Lisa:* It sounds like you have a few key points. Continuous feedback systems improve morale and performance at each of the companies you've learned about. Also, your contacts at these companies think evaluating the costs of the software is easy, but evaluating the costs of time invested by employees is not possible. Is that correct?

really think. This is not fair to them or to you. It is even arguably dishonest. Michael Hoppe of the Center for Creative Leadership explains:

> Being an active listener doesn't mean being a sponge, passively soaking up the information coming your way. You are an active party to the conversation with your own thoughts and feelings. Yet active listening is first about understanding the other person, then about being understood.[43]

As a related point, business leaders often use the term *silence is agreement*. In other words, many organizational cultures expect all employees to state their ideas. If they don't say anything, they are presumed to agree. Because it can be so challenging to give others enough comfort and space to express themselves fully, some listeners avoid talking and inadvertently send signals that they agree. One key to active listening is allowing others to open up completely with their work-related ideas and then also to foster dialogue, which includes providing your respectful views.

Recognizing Barriers to Effective Listening

Active listening is not easy, especially in certain corporate cultures and in the face of time constraints.[44] As you read about the following barriers to listening, consider which are most challenging to you.

Lack of Time   Not surprisingly, pressing deadlines give most managers the sense that they do not have time for listening. Furthermore, when talking to others, managers are often preoccupied with thoughts of other projects. In other words, managers may feel overwhelmed with internal noise. However, the best managers understand that listening pays strong dividends over time and that they need to schedule time for listening to others each day.

Lack of Patience and Attention Span   Some people simply do not have long attention spans or for other reasons feel impatient. Patience and attention span can be improved with conscious, consistent effort. Highly self-aware communicators frequently ask themselves questions such as the following: *Did I allow others enough time to express themselves? In which situations or with which people (triggers) do I feel most impatient? What strategies help me focus my attention when I'm feeling impatient?*

Image of Leadership   Some executives and managers think that listening too much shows indecisiveness and thus threatens their authority. To preserve a command-and-control approach to leading, they speak more and listen less. This view of listening is rarely effective, especially in today's increasingly flat organizations. Yet, the image of strong leaders who do most of the talking is difficult to overcome for some business professionals.

Communication Technology   Technology continues to create new and better opportunities for people to communicate with one another. However, most communication technologies make listening more difficult due to fewer and less rich visual and nonverbal cues. Typically, using communication tools such as mobile phones and email can facilitate a listening-centered approach to communication, supplemented with significant face-to-face, rich communication. On the other hand, relying too heavily on communication technology can reduce effective listening.

Fear of Bad News or Uncomfortable Information   Once bad news and other forms of unpleasant information are out in the open, managers are generally responsible for creating solutions and responding to the morale needs of fellow employees. Listening fully to the feedback, concerns, and perspectives of colleagues and clients can make work more complicated. Astute business executives and managers recognize that they *need* information—even bad or unpleasant news—to lead an organization to its best potential performance. Conversely, when you do not listen, you may inadvertently encourage others to cover mistakes and weaknesses that harm the organization.[45]

In addition to barriers that prevent listening from occurring in the first place, other behaviors can disrupt a conversation and prevent real learning. **Nonlistening behaviors** are those actions that prematurely deflect attention from speakers or prevent them from completely expressing their ideas and feelings. Such behaviors may display lack of caring and signal that the conversation is not equitable and reciprocal. Some common nonlistening behaviors in the workplace are defending, "me too" statements, giving advice, and judging.[46]

Defending Instinctively, all of us engage in self-protective behaviors. Often, the comments of others in the workplace call into question our credibility, including our performance, competence, concern for others, or even ability to honor our commitments. When we feel threatened, we often become defensive. In other words, we are emotionally hijacked. Defensive comments end listening for several reasons. First, others often perceive them as threats or escalations. Thus, they may lead to self-protectiveness from all parties involved in a conversation and reduce trust and goodwill. These cycles of escalation close conversations off from complete and honest exchange of information. In some cases, people even attack others in an effort to protect themselves. Second, they shift attention away from the speaker to the listener—meaning the person who has made the defensive comment. This premature shift in focus is a *me-centered* maneuver that disrupts the listening process.

Figure 2.4 displays defensive and nondefensive replies to a potentially upsetting comment. Avoiding defensiveness requires a high level of self-awareness and self-management. It requires understanding the triggers that make you feel threatened in a professional environment. It also requires understanding how to manage these emotions so that you can maintain your roles as an active listener and a problem solver.

"Me Too" Statements As you listen to other people share their ideas and experiences—their stories—you often think about similar ideas and experiences of your own—your stories. This often leads to "me too" comments. We take the other

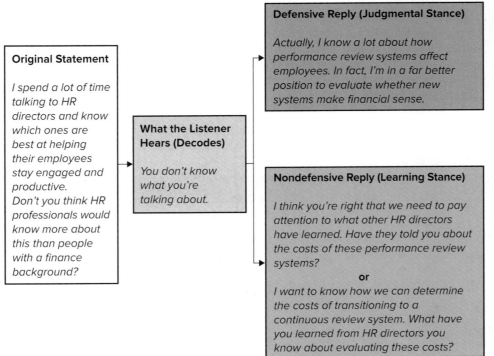

FIGURE 2.4

Defensive and Nondefensive Replies

person's story and respond with our story, in an effort to empathize and share. Sometimes, however, this shifts attention away from their story to your story. To listen effectively, be careful about prematurely drawing attention away from the stories of others.

Giving Advice   In leadership roles, your job is often to tell others what to do and how to do it. Also, many of your bosses and colleagues will give you advice. Giving advice to others in a competitive work environment is inevitable and often desirable. However, during conversations, premature or heavy-handed advice can abruptly end dialogue and result in resistance. When you provide advice too soon, you give the impression of wanting to end the conversation. When you provide excessive advice, you challenge the autonomy and decision making of others and make them feel *micromanaged*. To avoid giving advice that cuts off listening, give others enough time to fully explain themselves. Once you talk about options and solutions, make sure that it is a "we" conversation rather than just your ideas for what others should do.

LO2.6 Describe and demonstrate effective questions for enhancing listening and learning.

Judging   Judging is one of the worst nonlistening behaviors. It not only ends listening for the current conversation, but often leaves lingering animosity. Once people have displayed a judger mind-set, others may be unwilling to open up to them in the future. People who feel that their leaders are judgers might say, "He's really not interested in what I have to say," or "She's already made up her mind."[47]

Asking the Right Questions

Listening involves a cluster of communication skills. A crucial one is the ability to ask the right questions. In a recent survey of 2,181 accountants, the most sought-after interpersonal skill was *listening,* ranked 4.51 on a scale from 1 (not important) to 5 (essential). Following *listening* were closely related skills: *asks appropriate questions when talking with customers* (4.22) and *asks appropriate questions when talking with supervisors* (3.97). Next on the list of 14 skills was a cluster of presentation skills, such as *organizes presentations effectively* (3.86), *establishes rapport with audience* (3.59), and *maintains eye contact* (3.58). In other words, the ability to ask questions was valued more highly than presentation skills.[48]

Mc Graw Hill connect

Visit http://connect. mheducation.com for an exercise on this topic.

On the most fundamental level, good questions reflect the learner mind-set, and poor questions reflect a judger mind-set. The ability to ask good questions creates a culture of learning. Good questions are not good in and of themselves, however. Unless you truly listen to the answers and even encourage other perspectives and dissent, you may not achieve learning. Notice examples of questions in Table 2.9 that reflect judger and learner mind-sets.[49]

TABLE 2.9

Questions That Reflect the Judger Mind-Set and the Learner Mind-Set

Judger Mind-Set	Learner Mind-Set
How come this doesn't work?	How is this useful or beneficial?
Who is responsible for this mess?	What can we do about this?
Why can't you get it right?	Going forward, what can we learn from this?
Can't you try a better approach?	What are you trying to accomplish?
Why don't you focus on helping customers?	How will customers react?
Are you sure this approach will really meet your goals and objectives?	How well does this approach meet your goals and objectives?

TABLE 2.10

Types of Effective Questions

Types of Questions	Examples
Rapport-building	How was your trip to the human resource conference? What did you learn about at the last Chamber of Commerce event? These questions, when asked sincerely, provide an opportunity for asker and listener to bond through understanding one another. They also break the ice for a substantive conversation about the business issues at hand.
Funnel	So, how do you think we should go about researching what our employees think about performance reviews? → How do you think we can capture the employees' perspectives about continuous review systems? → What types of survey questions will help us understand their thoughts about continuous review systems? → Could you give me a word-by-word example of how you'd capture that in a survey question? These questions progressively break down a problem into manageable pieces, starting with a large, open-ended question and moving to increasingly specific and tactical questions. Once broken into smaller pieces, the asker and listener are more likely to achieve shared meaning and move toward finding solutions.
Probing	How often do you receive complaints about the annual performance review process? What concerns do supervisors have? What ideas do employees have for making the review process fairer? Do you ever hear supervisors or employees talk about how to make the process more goal-oriented? Other than the frequency of reviews, what are some other explanations for why employees make these complaints? These iterations of questions about the causes, consequences, and scope of group guest complaints attempt to look at the problem from every angle. This approach is effective at identifying root causes and best solutions.
Solution-oriented	How can we find out which software vendors offer the most attractive performance review features? What are your ideas for ensuring that employees provide continuous feedback to one another? What are some best practices in making performance reviews candid and honest yet also rewarding and productive? These questions form the basis for identifying options about how to move forward. Ideally, solution-oriented questions are open, we-oriented, and offer help to others.

To ask questions that facilitate the most learning, frame and structure your questions carefully. Generally speaking, most good questions are open-ended. In contrast, closed questions require simple responses such as *yes* or *no*. Some basic types of learning-centered questions include rapport-building questions, funnel questions, probing questions, and solution-oriented questions. See Table 2.10 for examples of each type of question.[50]

Rapport-building questions are intended to create bonds between people. They can break the ice and gradually ease people into conversations about shared business interests. They tend to be casual and social and steer clear of divisive or offensive topics. Questions about current work projects, interests, and experiences are generally appropriate. As you will notice in the team communication section in the next chapter, however, time devoted to building rapport should be limited. Too much time spent on this purpose can be counterproductive.

Funnel questions move from general to specific. They are intended to increasingly deconstruct a business issue so that a team can tackle or approach it in pieces. This approach involves starting with broad and open questions and moving to more specific and closed ones.

Probing questions are intended to analyze a business problem from every angle to uncover its root causes. Such questions can ensure that no explanation is overlooked, thus leading to a reliable understanding. The classic, institutionalized example of probing questions is the *Five Whys* approach at Toyota, in which employees were

TABLE 2.11

Types of Counterproductive Questions

Types of Questions	Examples
Leading	Wouldn't you agree that employee engagement and productivity should be our priorities? I'm sure you think it's a good idea to keep costs under control, right?
	These questions are meant to lead the listener to agree with or adopt the perspective of the asker. Many listeners will resent feeling pressured into the views of others. Also, this approach will not lead to a learning conversation.
Disguised statements	Why do you insist on focusing on costs instead of benefits? Don't you think you're jumping to conclusions by paying attention to the opinions of only a few of your close contacts?
	These are not real questions. They are statements that say you are close-minded on this issue. This flaw-finding approach will cause many listeners to become defensive and/or avoid sharing their real thoughts. Many listeners will view disguised statements as underhanded and manipulative because they are often attempts to get the listeners to acknowledge their own faults.
Cross-examination	Just now, you said annual reviews don't work because they don't happen often enough. Yet, last week, you said the real reason our annual reviews fail is not because of how often they occur but because they don't involve setting goals. So, what's the real reason annual reviews don't work?
	This cross-examination question will put most listeners on the defensive. It may score points for the asker, but it will move the conversation away from learning and toward a battle of messages.

encouraged to ask at least five iterations of questions to understand manufacturing quality issues. Ultimately, this approach led to world-class quality standards that businesses around the world have studied.

Solution-oriented questions focus on how to overcome business problems. They focus on what *should* be done to accomplish business objectives. Solution-oriented questions are among the most difficult ones in which to maintain a learner mind-set. Nearly all of us have strong preconceptions about what *should* be done. Staying flexible and open to mutually developed solutions begins with open, solution-oriented questions.

Avoiding the Wrong Questions

Not all questions are good ones. Most poor questions fall into the category of the judgmental mind-set and can actually lead to less listening. Poor questions include leading questions, disguised statements, and cross-examination questions. Table 2.11 provides examples.

Leading questions are intended to guide people to your way of thinking. These questions are often perceived as dishonest or manipulative. Business professionals are notorious for asking leading questions in sales. In fact, some sales training programs even recommend using leading questions to build desire for products and services. However, recent research indicates that even for sales, the best questions are open ones that focus on learning customers' real wants and needs.[51]

Disguised statements are opinions presented in question form. Disguised statements almost always end a learning conversation when they are used to point out flaws.

Cross-examination questions are intended to find contradictions in what others have said or done. Like disguised statements, they can abruptly end learning conversations when they repeatedly call into question the credibility of others.

Perspective-Getting and Note-Taking

One major goal of listening and asking the right questions is **perspective-getting**, which is accurately understanding the views of others.[52] Perspective-getting is a challenging process because people sometimes hide their real views, sometimes hold self-contradictory views, and sometimes change views. It is also challenging because your memory is limited.

Most effective perspective-getters are note-takers. Note-taking allows you to hold better conversations, help you recall conversations, and prepare for future conversations. You should experiment with note-taking to find a style that works for you. Here is one approach that works for many effective perspective-getters:[53]

Denis Ismagilov/123RF

In the body of your notes, write their comments and points of view. Be selective in what you write down. You can't possibly write down everything, so choose the most important thoughts.

In the margins of your notes, write your reactions, your ideas, and your questions. Consider using this space to consider themes, test assumptions, and even observe what's not being said.

Document shortly after the end of your conversation. Once you're by yourself, reflect on the conversation and use your notes to summarize the conversation.

This process of note-taking will help you understand the views of others much better and help you prepare for future conversations.

Avoiding the Traps of Empathy

In Chapter 1, you learned about the distinction between *givers* and *takers*. Givers frequently help others out in the workplace, whereas takers often accept help but infrequently reciprocate. The highest performers are most often givers. Yet, the weakest performers are also most often givers. In other words, some givers manage their generosity in a way that improves their own performance and those around them while other givers help others at the expense of their individual performance.

Givers are generally motivated by empathy. They perform best when they address three potential barriers to performance associated with empathy: *timidity, availability,* and *emotional concern for others.* Givers are often timid or less assertive about asking for help because they don't want to impose on others. By learning to frame their own requests as acts on the behalf of others, givers can be more assertive with their requests. Many givers make themselves available to all requests, often at the expense of getting their own work done. Givers should learn to set boundaries on when and what they choose to help others with. Due to a strong emotional concern for others, givers often say "yes" to takers. Givers can avoid being manipulated by takers by spending more time analyzing the needs of all parties involved. By staying self-aware about your natural impulses for timidity, availability, and/or emotional concern for others, you can manage your empathy in a way that most helps others *and* yourself.[54]

Sight-Reading Nonverbal Communication and Building Rapport

By various estimates, nonverbal communication accounts for 60 to 80 percent of meaning in various face-to-face business situations, including in conversations, meetings, and negotiations.[55] Gestures, expressions, tone, and other nonverbal signals convey seriousness or sarcasm, enthusiasm or disinterest, caring or lack of concern, attentiveness or boredom, and many other messages. Compared to verbal communication, however, the meaning of nonverbal communication is less precise. It is almost entirely understood on a subconscious level and developed instinctively. Rarely, if ever, do people consciously attempt to improve their ability to understand the nonverbal communication of others.

LO2.7 Explain strategies to sight-read the nonverbal communication of others.

Mc Graw Hill **connect**

Visit **http://connect. mheducation.com** for an exercise on this topic.

Among the foremost authorities on nonverbal communication in the workplace is David Givens of the Center for Nonverbal Studies. He has spent decades examining nonverbal behavior in the workplace. He has observed, "Perhaps even more than written memos, text messages, and e-mail, nonverbal signs have the power to inspire or intimidate, to arouse sympathy, allegiance, anger, or fear."[56] He further explains that people can learn **sight-reading**, which he defines as "intelligent observation [of nonverbal communications] . . . it is the act of anticipating intentions and moods through the perceptive examination of nonverbal cues."[57]

Throughout this section, we focus on meaning that can be conveyed through various nonverbal signals. As you read through this section, focus on how you can listen to others better in two ways: (1) by understanding the meanings of others' nonverbal signals and (2) by helping others feel more comfortable sharing their perspectives and feelings with you because of the welcoming nonverbal signals that you send to them.

Learning to Sight-Read   Research clearly shows that people are not good at masking their feelings—nearly all people reveal their real emotions through nonverbal behavior. However, research also shows that most people are not consistently effective at decoding the nonverbal signals of others. In other words, nonverbal signals are always present and important in face-to-face communications, but few people can reliably interpret them.[58]

Recently, Malcom Gladwell, in his book *Blink: The Power of Thinking without Thinking*, revealed much of the research about how expert sight-readers can quickly understand the impacts of nonverbal communication. For example, in a study of physicians and patients, researchers videotaped hundreds of interactions. They found that with just 40-second video clips, they could reliably predict whether doctors got sued simply by the intonation and pitch of the doctors' voices. Whether the doctors made mistakes or what they said was not predictive of who got sued. Rather, how the doctors spoke to the patients did impact who got sued. Those doctors whose voice displayed dominance, hostility, and indifference got sued.[59]

Generally, you should pay close attention to nonverbal signals and attempt to decode their meanings. Yet, always make sure to suspend a certain level of judgment and avoid rigid conclusions. Consider the following guidelines as you develop your sight-reading:[60]

- *Consciously practice each day.* Consider taking 15 minutes each day to watch people's nonverbal behaviors. Learn to understand the meaning of various nonverbal signals from those you interact with frequently.

- *Pay attention to congruence.* Nonverbal messages are most important when they are not congruent, or consistent, with verbal messages. Listeners instinctively place more value on nonverbal messages when nonverbal messages are incongruent with verbal messages.

- *Sight-read in clusters, not in isolation.* You can easily misinterpret nonverbal signals if you are simply looking at single behaviors. For example, arms crossed on the chest, crossing legs, clenching fists, and pointing fingers are signs of defensiveness. However, in isolation, these signals may have other meanings. Arms crossed on the chest may mean someone is cold or crossing legs may be nothing more than a comfortable sitting position. Taken together, various nonverbal signals help you more reliably decode the message.

- *Sight-read in context.* Use the situation at hand to help understand nonverbal signals. Pointing fingers during an argument likely indicates blaming, whereas pointing fingers at others during a sales presentation more than likely indicates a desire to get input from others.

Paying Attention to Nonverbal Cues   Sight-reading is the process of decoding the nonverbal signals that others send as you communicate with them. To engage in active listening and dialogue, it's also important for you to send the right nonverbal signals. Ideally, you can send nonverbal signals that show sincerity, interest, affirmation, and other traits that show your esteem and respect for others.

One key to effective nonverbal communication to make others more comfortable talking to you is to synchronize your body language with theirs. **Synchronizing** body language involves adopting some of your counterpart's body language to make the conversation more natural for them and to show empathy to them. You'll often find that others are more expressive nonverbally than you are. In these cases, you may need to be more expressive than usual to match your counterpart's preferred communication style. Or, you may find that they are less expressive nonverbally. In these cases, you may want to tone down your nonverbal communication. In any case, keeping your body language in sync with others creates a more natural conversation for you and your conversation partners. The primary goal of synchronizing is to not overwhelm or underwhelm others with your nonverbal language.[61]

As you synchronize, attempt to convey emotions appropriate to the conversation. For most business situations, you should try to express positive or neutral emotions. In some situations, you may express sad or disappointing expressions to show empathy for the setbacks others have experienced. Keep in mind that people naturally mimic one another's emotions and that the emotions you express can impact others. For example, researchers have shown that people who view a smiling face often mimic that mood with changes in their own facial muscles. Conversely, when people view angry faces, they often reflect that mood with slight changes in their own facial muscles that exhibit some signs of anger. Dr. Daniel Goleman calls this natural synchronizing of nonverbal signals the *coordination of moods*. He further stated, "Coordination of moods is the essence of rapport."[62]

In the remainder of this section, we will focus on the nonverbal signals sent by various body parts and actions. As you read these sections, think about the related nonverbal signals that you send or how you could try to understand others better by looking for certain types of body language.

Rob Daly/AGE Fotostock

Eyes Among the most influential body parts in sending nonverbal signals are the eyes. Eyes can reveal a lot about the feelings of others. This is one reason many of the best poker players wear sunglasses, aware that they may involuntarily send signals about the strength of their poker hands as well as their intentions.

Typically, people who achieve eye contact build emotional connections to one another. They are more likely to build rapport and empathy. In most situations, the more eye contact, the better. Of course, intense stares and deep gazes can make others uncomfortable. So, you should be aware of what others would consider visual intrusiveness. Most people are far better at resolving differences when making eye contact during face-to-face conversations.[63]

The eyes make many involuntary movements that are associated with various feelings. For example, large, dilated pupils show emotional excitement. By contrast, small, constricted pupils show little emotional engagement. Thus, dilated pupils can show interest and approval, whereas constricted pupils can show disinterest and boredom. Of course, extremely dilated pupils are not necessarily positive—they can also indicate extreme emotions such as anger.[64]

Another involuntary eye movement is CLEM (conjugate lateral eye movement). **CLEM** is a rapid sideward shift of the eye. It shows that a person is giving your ideas careful consideration and is thus generally positive. It indicates processing and reflection. Whereas CLEM is a rapid sideways movement of the eyes, longer sideways glances are often associated with discomfort. Your ability to distinguish between the rapid sideways glances (CLEM) and longer sideways glances can provide insight into how engaged and comfortable other people are with your ideas.[65]

You can often notice discomfort in others by observing their blinking rates. The average blinking rate is around 20 blinks per minute. Faster-than-normal blinking often indicates emotional distress. Thus, you may be able to observe the comfort level of others based on how much eye contact they give to you or others. Avoiding eye contact sometimes indicates insecurity, nervousness, and even deception. Closely related, squinting slightly is often associated with skepticism and suspicion.[66]

You should generally avoid using your eyes to show disapproval, especially when your goal is to hear people out. When people abruptly look away to indicate disapproval or disinterest, this sends a message of strong displeasure with others and their ideas. This action, called **visual cutoff**, can quickly end dialogue, especially when a superior visually cuts off subordinates. Visual cutoff is especially harsh when accompanied with sideways head movements and sighs. Similarly, intense glares to show displeasure with others and their ideas can be intimidating.[67]

Image Source/Getty Images

As you sight-read the eyes of others, make sure to do so flexibly. Be particularly careful about judging the truthfulness of what others say based solely on the eyes. A frequently perpetuated myth is that liars can't look you straight in the eye. In actuality, pathological liars can look people in the eyes and lie. There are also other explanations, including nervousness, personality, and cultural differences.[68]

Smiles and Nods Generally, you should attempt to be lively, smile a lot, and look interested. As you nod to show interest and sometimes agreement, you signal that you are interested and welcome the thoughts of others.[69] Sincere, genuine smiles are an excellent way to help others trust your intentions. Research has shown that positive emotional expressions such as smiles cause customers to have more positive feelings about transactions, be more satisfied with the products and services, and even feel more loyal to companies.[70] However, unless smiles are genuine and sincere, they may not generate goodwill. Smiles can convey many meanings, including sarcasm and mocking. They can also be displayed in moments of fear, embarrassment, and forced compliance.[71]

Hands and Arms Among the most symbolic shows of friendship, camaraderie, shared purpose, openness, hospitality, and greeting in the business world is the handshake. In introductions, handshakes can create emotional connections between people and help people build rapport quickly. Typically, handshakes should last for two to three seconds. Make the handshake firm but avoid bone-crushing or limp handshakes. Make sure that as you shake hands, you have eye contact to strengthen the emotional bond you build through handshakes.

As you shake hands, remember that holding your hand straight up and down is a show of equality. Handshakes can show dominance when the palm faces down. One study of 350 business executives found that 88 percent of male executives attempted the dominant position (compared to 31 percent of women executives). Attempt to use the handshake as a show of respect and equality to others.[72]

Hands and arms can be used as gestures to create an open and inviting atmosphere for discussion in a variety of ways. Extended and opened palms send the same positive and inviting messages as handshakes. Also, open and extended hands reduce the physical distance between people, thus increasing emotional connection. As nonverbal communication expert David Givens stated, "In business those who reach out with hands have an advantage over those who keep hands to themselves, concealed in pockets, folded in laps, or hiding beneath desks."[73]

Hands and arms sometimes contribute to an unwelcome and unfriendly atmosphere for dialogue. Typically, palms-down gestures are less inviting to others. Table pounding is an extreme version of a palms-down gesture that is used for emphasis. It emphasizes speaking points and shows confidence and conviction. However, when done too frequently, it can make others

Caia Images/Glow Images

uncomfortable and less open about their true thoughts and feelings. One of the most serious gestures is the halt hand, which involves holding the palm straight up toward others. It sends a strong message of *stop*. Withholding hand gestures, especially for people who typically use them, may suggest deceit.[74]

Hands often signal discomfort or nervousness. Placing the hands behind the head often shows uncertainty or conflicted feelings. Most self-touching gestures (i.e., playing with hair, touching the face, biting nails, rubbing or pinching skin) are displays of anxiety, confusion, or uncertainty. These self-touching gestures comfort the body as it copes with fight-or-flight impulses. Other self-touching gestures such as holding or hugging oneself are signs of deeper distress.[75]

Hands may also communicate defensiveness. Hands in pockets, fistlike gestures, pointing fingers, and other fidgeting often are part of strong self-protective urges. Placing the hands on the hips with elbows pointing away from the body is often a show of extreme defensiveness, even aggressiveness. Kids generally know they're in trouble when they see their parents do this. This nonverbal display is usually associated with annoyance, disagreement, or anger. In some cases, it is perceived positively in the workplace. For example, it may display an eagerness to move forward on a project. However, since this stance is so often perceived negatively, be careful about placing your hands on your hips because of the way others may decode your messages.[76]

Interestingly, research has shown that how well hands are groomed impacts how accurately others decode nonverbal signals. Research in board meetings has shown that executives are less able to correctly interpret gestures of meeting participants when they have "physically distressed" hands, which includes scars, dryness, dry cuticles, unkempt nails, roughness, or dirtiness. In other words, well-groomed hands allow people to better understand gestures, whereas poorly groomed hands hinder others' ability to correctly interpret your nonverbal signals.[77]

Touch Touching others, including with handshakes, can create an instant bond and establish rapport. It can build loyalty between strangers and even increase honest exchange of information. Touch has been explored extensively in customer service interaction. For example, one such study showed that servers who touch customers on the hand or elbow receive between 22 and 36 percent more in tips. Another recent experiment examined how touch impacts truthfulness. In the study, money was purposefully left in a public location. When people found the money, the researchers, acting like strangers, approached the people to ask if they'd seen any money. Without any physical touch in these interactions, people who found the money admitted to having found the money and returned it 23 percent of the time. When the researchers touched the people on the arm for a few seconds while asking, people who found the money returned the money 68 percent of the time. Of course, in this same experiment, touching for more than three seconds resulted in a more negative reaction.[78] North American culture is typically considered a nontouch culture compared to other cultures around the world. However, even in this nontouch environment, it makes sense to use brief touch such as handshakes to make connections with others.[79]

Relationship Management

Relationship management is the "ability to use your awareness of emotions and those of others to manage interactions successfully."[80] In this chapter we introduce the following principles for managing relationships effectively: adapting communication to the preferred styles of others and ensuring civility in the workplace. In each subsequent chapter, we discuss many ways of expressing your ideas to manage your work relationships effectively.

Adapting Communication to the Preferred Styles of Others

LO2.8 Identify common communication preferences based on motivational values.

Visit connect.mheducation. com for an exercise on this topic.

People have many preferences for communicating. You can benefit from constantly learning about the many ways people differ in preferences. In this section, you will learn about just a few aspects of personality—motivational values and level of extroversion-introversion—that impact communication preferences in the workplace. While there are many other ways of examining differences in communication styles, understanding motivational values and level of extroversion-introversion can dramatically improve your ability to recognize the communication preferences of others and adapt accordingly.

Differences in Communication Preferences Based on Motivational Values
Many communication styles can be traced to motives and values. Relationship Awareness Theory[81] explains how professionals often act and communicate differently from one another based on a fairly constant set of motives and values. People have a blend of three primary motives: nurturing (identified as *blue* in this model), directing (identified as *red*), and autonomizing (identified as *green*). A person's **motivational value system (MVS)** is a blend of these primary motives and refers to the frequency with which these values guide their actions. (These MVSs can be depicted on a triangle. For example, see Figure 3.4 in Chapter 3.)

Professionals with a **blue MVS** are most often guided by motives to protect others, help others grow, and act in the best interests of others. About 30 percent of business managers are strongly aligned with blue motivations. Professionals with a **red MVS** are most often guided by concerns about organizing people, time, money, and other resources to accomplish results. About 46 percent of business managers are strongly aligned with red motivations. Professionals with a **green MVS** are most often concerned about making sure business activities have been thought out carefully and that the right processes are put into place to accomplish things. About 16 percent of business managers are strongly aligned with green motivations. **Hubs** are professionals who are guided almost equally by all three of these MVSs. Among business professionals, roughly 43 percent are hubs.[82]

An important premise of Relationship Awareness Theory is that each of the primary values—nurturing, directing, and autonomizing—can be expressed by strengths. People gain a sense of self-worth by acting in ways consistent with their blend of values. While each person's motivational values generally lead to strengths, these strengths may be perceived by others as weaknesses when overdone or misapplied.

TABLE 2.12

Motivational Value Systems

	Blues (Altruistic and Nurturing)	Reds (Assertive and Directing)	Greens (Analytical and Autonomizing)	Hubs (Flexible and Cohering)
Primary concerns	Protection, growth, and welfare of others	Task accomplishment; use of time, money, and any other resources to achieve desired results	Assurance that things have been properly thought out; meaningful order being established; self-reliance and self-dependence	Flexibility; welfare of the group; sense of belonging in the group`
Preferred work environment	Open, friendly, helpful, considerate; being needed and appreciated; ensuring others reach their potential	Fast-moving, competitive, creative, progressive, innovative, verbally stimulating; potential for personal advancement and development	Clarity, logic, precision, efficiency, organized; focus on self-reliance and effective use of resources; time to explore options	Friendly, flexible, social, fun; consensus-building; encouraging interaction
People feel best when . . .	Helping others in a way that benefits them	Providing leadership and direction to others	Pursuing their own interests without needing to rely on others	Coordinating efforts with others in a common undertaking
People feel most rewarded when . . .	Being a warm and friendly person who is deserving of appreciation for giving help	Acting with strength and ambition, achieving excellence, and leading and directing others	Working with others in a fair, clear, logical, and rational manner	Being a good team member who can be loyal, direct when necessary, and knows when to follow rules
People want to avoid being perceived as . . .	Selfish, cold, unfeeling	Gullible, indecisive, unable to act	Overly emotional, exploitive of others	Subservient to others, domineering, isolated
Triggers of conflict	When others compete and take advantage; are cold and unfriendly; are slow to recognize helpful efforts on their behalf	When others are too forgiving and don't fight back; don't provide clear expectations about rewards	When others don't take issues seriously; push their help on them; do not weigh all the facts when making a decision	When others are not willing to consider alternatives; insist on one way of doing things; restrict ability to stay flexible and open to options
Overdone strengths	**Strength** **Overdone** Trusting Gullible Devoted Subservient Caring Submissive	**Strength** **Overdone** Confident Arrogant Persuasive Abrasive Competitive Combative	**Strength** **Overdone** Fair Unfeeling Analytical Nit-picking Methodical Rigid	**Strength** **Overdone** Flexible Wishy-washy Option-oriented Indecisive Tolerant Uncaring

Sources: Porter, E. (2014). Strength deployment inventory. Carlsbad, CA: Personal Strengths Publishing; Scudder, T., & LaCroix, D. (2013). Working with SDI: How to build effective relationships with the strength deployment inventory. Carlsbad, CA: Personal Strengths Publishing. You can learn more about this inventory at personalstrengths.com.

In Table 2.12, you can see how blues, reds, greens, and hubs differ in various ways. Take several minutes to view this table and see how people with these MVSs differ as far as what they prefer in work environments, what makes them feel satisfied and rewarded, what triggers conflict for them, and how their overdone strengths may be perceived as weaknesses. Think about which style best matches you. You might also think about

TABLE 2.13

Words and Phrases That Resonate with Professionals of Various MVSs

MVS	Verbs	Nouns	Modifiers	Phrases
Blues	Feel, appreciate, care, help, thank, include, support	Satisfaction, well-being, people, cooperation	Thoughtful, loyal, sincere, respectful, maybe	Serve everyone's best interests, look out for everyone
Reds	Compete, win, lead, challenge, dominate	Achievement, results, success, performance, goals, advantage	Challenging, rewarding, passionate, definitely, quickly	Make it happen, take charge, go for it
Greens	Think, analyze, evaluate, identify, organize	Process, principles, standard, schedules, accountability, details	Fair, careful, accurate, objective, correct, efficient, risky	Take our time, get it right, make sure it's fair
Hubs	Brainstorm, decide together, play, experiment, meet	Options, flexibility, teamwork, fun, consensus, compromise	Balanced, open, flexible, friendly, inclusive, committed	Let's work together, let's try this out

which style you might clash with the most. In Table 2.13, you can see some of the words that resonate most with various MVSs. Of course, all people use these words at times. But, you will often be able to recognize others' motivational values by noting *how often* they use these and synonymous words and phrases.

In Figures 2.5 and 2.6, you will notice two brief conversations. These conversations, which are somewhat simplified due to space, demonstrate some common differences

FIGURE 2.5

A Conversation between a Hub and a Green

Jeff explained, "Lisa, I'd like you, Steve, and Latisha to help work with me to implement a continuous performance review system. Our current system of annual performance reviews is really outdated."

Lisa was silent for several seconds. "I think we need to step back and really make sure we're making the right decision here. Have you taken the time to carefully compare annual reviews and continuous reviews? Can you share some of that information with me?"

Jeff was surprised Lisa wasn't enthusiastic. After all, it was Lisa who always loved data, and continuous feedback provided more information to everyone. "Well, I think it's a no-brainer. I've talked to quite a few HR directors who've had a lot of success with continuous performance reviews—never heard a bad thing yet. I guess we could gather some more information to make sure we're doing the right thing. Maybe we could do an employee survey, or we could find some industry surveys of how companies are implementing performance reviews, or maybe we could even attend a conference about performance reviews and talk to people there to figure out how we should go about this. What do you think we should do at this point?"

Lisa responded, "All those ideas might help. Let's think first about our objectives for the new system and then think about some ways of gathering information to decide whether the new system meets those objectives more so than annual reviews . . ."

Jeff encodes: Let's work as a team to improve our performance feedback system.

Lisa decodes: Jeff is rushing to a decision too quickly and thinks I'm on board.

Lisa encodes: This might be a good idea but let's weigh our options first.

Jeff decodes: Lisa doesn't like this idea. I wonder what's wrong.

Jeff encodes: I want to work with you and figure out how to move forward. Here are some additional ways of learning our options. I want your input.

Lisa decodes: Jeff doesn't really know what he wants to accomplish.

Lisa encodes: Let's be really thorough about this decision.

Jeff decodes: This approach is time-consuming and far too cautious.

FIGURE 2.6

A Conversation between a Red and a Blue

Steve: We should aim to get the survey done within the next few days. Jeff and Lisa will be really impressed if we get the results quickly. As soon as you get the questions ready and send out the link to employees, I can take over and do the statistics.

Steve encodes: Let's get results quickly.

Latisha decodes: Steve is being bossy and isn't thinking about how to include the employees.

Latisha: I feel like we should include the employees first to find out what kinds of questions we should ask in the survey. Maybe we could hold a few focus groups. If the employees see us do this, they'll feel included in the process and become more committed to our efforts.

Latisha encodes: First, let's think about how to include the employees in the process.

Steve decodes: Latisha needs to just take charge. That will take too long.

Steve: You don't need to worry so much about what the employees think about us. Sending them a survey shows we're interested in their input. If you're not comfortable doing the questions, I can do that part of the project.

Steve encodes: Let's just make this happen and not complicate the task.

Latisha decodes: Steve is too assertive. He doesn't understand you have to win people's hearts to make changes.

Latisha: Steve, it's in everyone's best interests to involve the employees more in this process. They need to feel like partners with us as we gather the information.

Latisha encodes: We REALLY need to involve everyone more.

Steve decodes: Latisha probably doesn't know how to create the survey questions on her own.

among reds, blues, greens, and hubs. In the first conversation, Jeff, a hub, talks with Lisa, a green. Jeff talks with Lisa about transitioning from annual performance reviews to continuous performance reviews. One of Jeff's strengths as a hub is flexibility. Yet, Lisa views him as wishy-washy and indecisive in this case because he appears too flexible in making a decision. One of Lisa's strengths as a green is her careful analysis and caution. Yet, Jeff perceives her as nit-picking and rigid when he presents an idea he's enthusiastic about.

In the next conversation (Figure 2.6), Latisha and Steve talk about setting up an online survey to get input from employees about performance review systems. One of Latisha's strengths as a blue is her ability to think about the needs and feelings of others. Yet, in this case, Steve views her as lacking in initiative and subservient to others. Two of Steve's strengths as a red are his focus on action and his desire to lead positive change. Yet, in this case, Latisha perceives him as combative and bossy.

Differences in Communication Preferences Based on Extroversion-Introversion
One element of personality that plays a major role in workplace communication is professionals' level of extroversion-introversion. Generally, **introverts** tend to get much of their stimulation and energy from their own thoughts, feelings, and moods. **Extroverts** tend to get much of their stimulation and energy from external sources such as social interaction. Whereas most introverts need time to recharge after social interactions, extroverts thrive on social interactions and feel more energized. Introverts are often more quiet, reserved, and thoughtful, whereas extroverts

LO2.9 Explain how extroversion-introversion impacts interpersonal communication.

are often more outspoken, charismatic, and spontaneous. Introverts often feel less comfortable around unfamiliar people and situations, whereas extroverts often relish meeting new people and entering unfamiliar environments. Similarly, introverts are more likely to feel discomfort in public speaking and speaking up in meetings, whereas extroverts are more likely to enjoy engaging with an audience while public speaking and making frequent comments in meetings. Introverts typically prefer one-to-one or small group conversations, whereas extroverts typically prefer conversations in larger groups and social events. Introverts tend to speak only once they have clarified their own thoughts privately, whereas extroverts often want to think out loud, using speech as a way of refining their ideas. Introverts usually dislike small talk and prefer extended, deep conversations, whereas extroverts usually prefer lively and varied conversations that include small talk. Introverts are more likely to want to do much of their work alone, whereas extroverts are more likely to want to do much of their work in groups.[83]

Recently, Susan Cain drew attention to the evolving research about extroversion and introversion in the workplace in her best-selling book *Quiet: The Power of Introverts in a World That Can't Stop Talking.* She documented the "Extroversion Ideal," in which the workplace tends to be structured to favor extroverts, especially in North America.[84] In the past, extroverts have been perceived as better leaders and received more promotions and opportunities. In fact, one study showed that roughly 96 percent of managers and leaders display extroverted personalities. In many workplaces, there has been bias against introverts. For example, roughly ten years ago, research showed that 65 percent of executives thought introversion was a barrier to effective leadership.[85] One of the major barriers of businesses drawing from the skills and talents of introverts is the common misunderstanding that extroversion is prosocial and introversion is antisocial. Rather, introverts and extroverts are each social in different ways. One expert characterized introverts as "social in quieter ways."[86]

In the past ten years, a variety of research has debunked the idea that introverts are less effective at leading. This research has shown that extroverts and introverts each possess many leadership qualities and essential professional traits. For companies to succeed in today's increasingly collaborative work environment, they must find ways to tap into the strengths of extroverts and introverts, especially since estimates suggest that roughly one-third to one-half of professionals are introverts. Take several minutes to review Tables 2.14 and 2.15. The first table shows some of the strengths of introverts and extroverts. Consider how people can accomplish much more by uniting these strengths. The next table gives advice for how introverts can work more effectively with extroverts and vice versa.

TABLE 2.14

Strengths of Introverted and Extroverted Professionals

Strengths of Introverted Professionals	Strengths of Extroverted Professionals
• Asking thoughtful and important questions • Listening to the ideas of others • Giving people space to innovate • Developing insights to deal with uncertain situations • Improving the listening environment in meetings • Networking among close-knit professional groups • Making lasting impressions in social tasks that require persistence • Taking time to reflect carefully • Providing objective analysis and advice • Excelling in situations requiring discipline	• Stating views directly and charismatically • Gaining the support of others • Organizing people to innovate • Inspiring confidence in uncertain situations • Driving important conversations at meetings • Networking at large social events with potential clients and other contacts • Making strong first impressions that often lead to future partnerships • Acting quickly to gain advantages • Acting pragmatically in the absence of reliable information • Excelling in competitive situations

TABLE 2.15

Working Effectively with Introverts and Extroverts

Introverts can work more effectively with extroverts by . . .	Extroverts can work more effectively with introverts by . . .
• Making sure their extroverted colleagues have enough time to interact with team members. • Engaging in small talk and light topics during conversations. • Speaking up more quickly than feels natural. • Offering personal information more often. • Expressing their preference to respond to questions later on. • Giving them more opportunities to interact with others. • Shortening their emails. • Telling people they're shy or uncomfortable speaking up; requesting that others ask or call on them to speak up. • Appreciating extroverts for their many strengths. • Teaming up with extroverts to complement one another's strengths.	• Making sure their introverted colleagues have enough time to prepare for presentations or meetings. • Allowing conversations to have fewer and more in-depth topics. • Pausing more often and allowing longer periods of silence. • Spending less time talking about personal interests. • Expressing their preference to discuss things immediately. • Giving them more opportunities to be alone and recharge. • Lengthening their emails. • Telling people they have a hard time not sharing their views; requesting that others signal them when they're talking too much. • Appreciating introverts for their many strengths. • Teaming up with introverts to complement one another's strengths.

ⓘ Technology Tips

DIGITAL NOTE-TAKING

Many professionals and students use laptops and tablets to type notes during meetings and classes. All the key smacking can distract others. And, research has shown taking notes by hand with a pen or pencil helps professionals capture key ideas better and more effectively retain information than typing notes on a computer.*

In the past few years, however, more natural and less distracting forms of digital note-taking in meetings have become available. Most of your devices allow you to use a stylus or your finger to take notes in words and diagrams. Many apps help you take digital notes, including Microsoft OneNote, Google Keep, Evernote, Quip, Simplenote, and others.

Your challenge: Try out two digital note-taking apps. Describe your experiences using each app. What features of these apps help you take effective notes? What features are missing that would be helpful? What strategies will help you become a better digital note-taker?

Aggapom Poomitud/Shutterstock

*Doubek, J. (2016, April 17). Attention, students: Put your laptops away. *NPR*. Retrieved from https://www.npr.org/2016/04/17/474525392/attention-students-put-your-laptops-away.

Maintaining Civility and Avoiding Gossip

An outgrowth of emotional intelligence for interpersonal business communication is the notion of civility. Civility is a show of respect for the dignity and importance of others. It includes an orientation toward achieving honest, open, and respectful dialogues and validating the worth of others and their work efforts. In every instance, you should find ways to maintain civil communication in the workplace, especially for situations in which you disagree with others. Even when others treat

LO2.10 Explain the role of civility in effective interpersonal communication and the common types of incivility in the workplace.

Visit http://connect.mheducation.com for an exercise on this topic.

you poorly—which will undoubtedly occur—responding civilly potentially de-escalates an ugly situation and shows your character and caring.

By contrast, incivility is "rudeness and disregard for others in a manner that violates norms for respect."[87] Unfortunately, incivility seems to be on the rise in the workplace.[88] In this section about civility, we first focus on the prominence and consequences of incivility. Then, we discuss common types and causes of incivility in the workplace. We conclude with strategies for maintaining civility.

Incivility in Society and the Workplace

Many Americans perceive society as increasingly rude and disrespectful. A recent survey of more than 2,000 people in the United States illustrated the extent to which they perceive rudeness in society.[89] Consider the following findings from this research:

- Seventy-nine percent of respondents felt that a lack of respect is a serious problem for our society and that we should try to address it.
- Eighty-eight percent of respondents said that they often or sometimes come across people who are rude and disrespectful.
- Seventy-three percent believe that Americans treated each other with more respect in the past.
- Thirty-seven percent say they are so affected by rudeness that they have thought about moving to another community.

One place respondents cite for lack of respect is retail stores. For example, 46 percent of respondents claim to have gotten such bad service sometime during the past year that they left the store. Among those making $75,000 or more (those from whom stores might lose the most business), 57 percent had received such bad service sometime during the past year that they left the store. Nearly four out of five respondents (77 percent) agreed that it is all too common to see employees act as if the customer is not even there. One danger for stores is that customers who feel disrespected may never say anything. Approximately 65 percent of respondents stated they hardly ever complained when getting bad service. On the other hand, 74 percent of respondents agreed that they often saw customers being rude or disrespectful to retail employees or customer service representatives.[90]

In the interactions among colleagues in the workplace, incivility is also common. Nearly four in ten respondents (39 percent) said they have colleagues who are rude or disrespectful. More than three in ten respondents (31 percent) said that their workplace supervisors are rude or disrespectful. About 30 percent of respondents said they *often* experienced rudeness at the workplace, and another 38 percent said they *sometimes* experienced rudeness in the workplace. The majority of respondents admitted that they are rude themselves; 61 percent agreed with the statement, "I'm so busy and pressed for time that I'm not as polite as I should be, and I feel sorry about it later on."[91] As the researchers of this study concluded, "Few people can count on being consistently treated with respect and courtesy as they go about their daily lives. The cumulative social costs—in terms of mistrust, anger, and even rage—are all too real to ignore."[92]

Perhaps the foremost experts on workplace incivility are Christine Pearson and Christine Porath. They have examined the nature and consequences of incivility in hundreds of organizations in North America over the past decade, finding that roughly one-quarter to one-half of employees experience incivility on a *weekly* basis. Furthermore, the consequences are devastating to organizational performance. Incivility erodes organizational culture and can escalate into conflict. It lowers individuals' productivity, performance, motivation, creativity, and helping behaviors. It also leads to declines in job satisfaction, organizational loyalty, and leadership impact.[93] Employees who are targets of incivility respond in the following ways:

- Half lose work time worrying about future interactions with instigators of incivility.
- Half contemplate changing jobs.

- One-fourth intentionally cut back work efforts.
- Approximately 70 percent tell friends, family, and colleagues about their dissatisfaction.
- About one in eight leave their jobs: turnover expense per job is estimated at $50,000.

The cost to companies is not always easy to quantify. However, some companies have started civility initiatives that include cost estimates of incivility. For example, Cisco started a Global Civility Program. The company estimated its annual loss due to incivility was $71 million, based on lost productivity, turnover, and absenteeism.[94]

You will soon find yourself in business leadership positions. One primary cost of incivility is business leaders' time. By one estimate, business executives spend 13 percent of their time, or what amounts to seven weeks per year, managing the fallout of disputes among employees.[95]

Types and Causes of Workplace Incivility

People show disrespect and rudeness to others in almost limitless ways. Table 2.16 includes common types of workplace incivility.[96] This list is by no means exhaustive, but it does contain broad categories. Generally, incivility occurs when a person ignores others, fails to display basic courtesies, fails to recognize the efforts of others, fails to respect the time and privacy of others, and fails to recognize the basic worth and dignity of others. As you read through the list, think about whether you have witnessed or engaged in some of these types of incivility. These actions make people feel undervalued and unwelcome. They also lead to less collegiality and cooperation among co-workers.

The final category in Table 2.16—disrespecting the dignity and worth of others—is among the most serious types of incivility. Many of these actions involve direct attacks on the identity and inherent worth of others. Verbal insults or even nonverbal expressions such as glares can send strong messages that show you do not value or respect others. Even without mean intentions, jokes about traits such as gender, ethnicity, or sexual orientation can create a hostile working environment for colleagues.

Of course, people of different personalities and cultures vary in their level of sensitivity to the behaviors listed in Table 2.16. Instigators of incivility are sometimes unaware of how much they impact others. Your responsibility, however, is to be sensitive to how others perceive your behaviors.

The world is increasingly interconnected. This is especially the case in the business world. Ironically, an increasingly interconnected world may be a force that removes many people from enduring, fairly permanent communities and creates a new kind of anonymity. P. M. Forni, founder of The Civility Initiative, highlighted the relationship between anonymity and incivility:

> Every day we encounter legions of strangers who will remain strangers. Soulless extras in our life stories, they hardly seem to warrant a nod of acknowledgment—let alone a kind word. In fact, we can easily get away with being rude to them. Gone are the days when the fear of being ostracized was an incentive to be civil: The cohesive social texture which allowed that motivation disappeared long ago. Anonymity gives us the feeling we can act with impunity.[97]

Responding to Gossip and Complaining

One of the most common forms of incivility is **gossip**, which involves talking about others behind their backs. Generally, gossip conversations can be damaging because they erode trust among colleagues and are often influenced by confirmation bias. **Confirmation bias** involves the tendency to look for support of our beliefs and opinions from others. Most people engage in gossip conversations with others who share similar viewpoints. In short, gossip can lead to biased views without giving much needed feedback to others. When you are part of a gossip conversation, you can take several actions. Name what you're doing as *gossip* and then focus on a solution. The

TABLE 2.16

Common Types of Incivility

Common Types of Incivility in the Workplace

Ignoring others
- Not responding to calls or emails in a timely manner
- Taking credit for the work of others
- Not responding when others greet you
- Withholding important information from colleagues
- Not inviting colleagues to participate in important decisions
- Overruling the decisions of others without providing any reasons
- Not acknowledging the presence of others
- Leaving some colleagues out of work social functions

Treating others without courtesy
- Not using basic terms of courtesy such as *please* and *thank you*
- Using a bossy or domineering tone, expression, or words
- Copying the boss on emails as a power play
- Interrupting others frequently
- Not using titles such as *Mr.* and *Ms.* as appropriate

Disrespecting the efforts of others
- Diminishing the ideas or efforts of others
- Providing vague and ambiguous feedback
- Blaming others unfairly

Disrespecting the time of others
- Disrupting a meeting
- Interrupting meetings or demanding an immediate meeting
- Setting deadlines without sufficient notice
- Sending too much email
- Flagging all email as important
- Calling colleagues on weekends or after work hours

Disrespecting the privacy of others
- Taking up too much space or being messy in shared space
- Being too noisy (especially in cubicles/shared work spaces)
- Telling offensive jokes
- Asking intrusive questions about the personal lives of others
- Forwarding private or sensitive emails

Disrespecting the dignity and worth of others
- Not greeting others warmly
- Delivering bad news by email
- Talking behind the backs of others and gossiping
- Criticizing or reprimanding a person in front of others
- Making condescending or demeaning comments to others
- Attacking the character of others
- Attacking others based on political, religious, or other beliefs
- Giving others a dirty look or the silent treatment
- Insulting or yelling at others
- Insulting others due to gender, ethnicity, or sexual orientation
- Harassing others

solution should usually involve talking directly to the person who you're discussing. Also, orient the conversation to your own contributions to the problem to ensure accountability.[98]

Another common and often related situation when civility is important is responding to colleagues who complain. In workplace settings, colleagues often mix complaints with gossip. When colleagues complain, you can take several actions to support them while not getting caught into a negativity trap. First, reserve judgment and give your colleagues the benefit of the doubt. Second, tactfully provide **counter-narratives**, which are alternative and generally positive explanations for events. For example, let's say you have a colleague who constantly complains about your manager not giving fair performance evaluations. You might suggest, "She's following the criteria the company has created." Third, focus on solutions. Let's say your colleague repeatedly complains about her team's performance. You can ask questions such as "What can you do to help your teammates do better?" or "Are there ways for you to give helpful feedback?" to reframe the conversation in a solutions-oriented direction. In all your responses to colleagues who complain, stay positive, but also be direct and candid.[99]

Maintaining Civil Communications

Forni, one of the leading voices on improving civility in society and the workplace, recommended eight guiding principles:[100]

1. Slow down and be present in life.
2. Listen to the voice of empathy.
3. Keep a positive attitude.
4. Respect others and grant them plenty of validation.
5. Disagree graciously and refrain from arguing.
6. Get to know people around you.
7. Pay attention to small things.
8. Ask, don't tell.

You may already use these strategies in your everyday life. The workplace, however, presents additional challenges. Intense competition and deadlines create pressures that make many of these strategies more difficult. Also, as you advance into higher leadership positions, these pressures can increase rapidly. Making a conscious effort to build emotional intelligence will help you maintain respectful communications even under moments of intense pressure.

One of the best ways of keeping your emotional intelligence high and maintaining the habit of communicating respectfully is to get to know people around you and humanize your work. While this approach may seem time-consuming, it will help you develop the types of work relationships that make communication easier, even for difficult conversations. Consider the comments of Joseph Plumeri, former chairman and CEO of the insurance broker Willis Group:

> I spend 25 percent to 30 percent of my time calling my associates—whether they had a family problem or pulled off a great deal and brought in a new client, or saved a client. Two-minute phone call, or handwritten note. I can't begin to tell you how important that stuff is.[101]

In the opening case, Jeff and Latisha are each confronted with an uncomfortable situation. In the sections about the interpersonal process and emotional intelligence, you read examples of how they could have confronted this uncomfortable situation in less effective and more effective ways. If Jeff and Latisha make personal commitments to stay civil at all times, they are each more likely to communicate effectively and productively. Furthermore, a commitment to civility will help each of them build their emotional intelligence.

IDEAS IN ACTION

BUILDING RELATIONSHIPS ONE CONVERSATION AT A TIME

Melanie Whelan of SoulCycle

Melanie Whelan is the CEO of SoulCycle, a chain of fitness studios in North America. She has helped the company rapidly grow from 7 locations to 88 locations. Whelan says the most exciting moment in her career came when the chain's Washington, DC, location opened and then—first lady Michelle Obama came to take a class.

Whelan credits much of her success to building relationships one conversation at a time. She encourages professionals to prepare for each conversation: "Be really clear about what you want to get out of the conversation that you're having, and make sure that you own that narrative." She adds, "Have your information, have your facts, have your numbers, have your point of view."

Yet, Whelan also recommends bringing a listening orientation to all conversations: "Great leaders are great listeners." She believes the key to active listening is asking questions: "You have to ask a lot of questions and you have to really listen to the answers. Don't be thinking about the next question, and don't be thinking about what you're having for lunch. Really listen, because in every answer there are at least three more questions you want to be asking."

Gary Gershoff/WireImage/Getty Images

Whelan points out that when asking questions, you have to be comfortable with silence. People often need time to collect their thoughts before responding. If you are uncomfortable with silence after asking a question, you may start talking too soon and inadvertently miss the opportunity to hear what others are thinking.

Like Melanie Whelan, you can build relationships and achieve your goals by seeking frequent meaningful conversations. Prepare for conversations carefully by formulating your own goals and ideas while also focusing on the needs of others and maintaining a listener orientation.

Sources: Bryant, A. (2015, December 17). Melanie Whelan of SoulCycle: Find the questions in every answer. *The New York Times* (online). Retrieved from https://www.nytimes.com/2015/12/20/business/melanie-whelan-of-soulcycle-find-the-questions-in-every-answer.html; Bryant, A. (2018, May 14). SoulCycle CEO on her college wake-up call and the No. 1 thing women can do to get ahead. *CNBC.* Retrieved from www.cnbc.com/2018/05/14/soulcycle-ceo-melanie-whelan-the-no-1-thing-women-can-do-to-succeed.html; Gagne, Y. (2018, October 22). SoulCycle CEO Melanie Whelan talks expanding abroad and online. *Fast Company*. Retrieved from www.fastcompany.com/90254913/soulcycle-ceo-melanie-whelan-talks-expanding-abroad-and-online; Hutcheson, S. (2017, June 2). How I became a CEO: Melanie Whelan of SoulCycle. *USA Today*. Retrieved from http://college.usatoday.com/2017/06/02/how-i-became-a-ceo-melanie-whelan-of-soulcycle.

Chapter Takeaway for *Interpersonal Communication and Emotional Intelligence*

LO2.1 Describe the interpersonal communication process and barriers to effective communication.

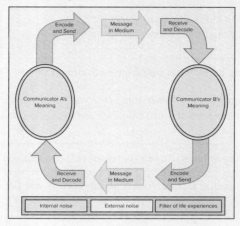

See an *example of the interpersonal communication process* in Figure 2.2.

LO2.2 Explain how emotional hijacking can hinder effective interpersonal communication.

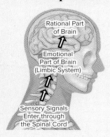

People are hardwired to experience emotions before reason. All signals to the brain first go through the limbic system, where emotions are produced, before going to the rational area of the brain. **Emotional hijacking** occurs when emotions control our behavior, causing us to react without thinking. During emotional hijacking, we often make statements that are rash, unintentional, and nonanalytical.

LO2.3 Explain how self-awareness impacts the communication process.

See *examples of low versus high self-awareness thoughts* in Table 2.1, a *summary of EQ impacts on communication* in Table 2.2, and *strategies for improving EQ* in Table 2.2.

LO2.4 Describe how self-management impacts the communication process.

See *examples of low versus high self-awareness thoughts* in Table 2.3.

LO2.5 Explain and evaluate the process of active listening.

Barriers to Active Listening	
• Lack of time	• Image of leadership
• Lack of patience and attention span	• Communication technology
	• Fear of bad news

Nonlistening Behaviors
• Defending
• "Me too" statements
• Giving advice
• Judging

See an *example of defensive and non-defensive replies* in Figure 2.4.

LO2.6 Describe and demonstrate effective questions for enhancing listening and learning.

Types of Good Questions
• Rapport-building
• Funnel
• Probing
• Solution-oriented

Types of Poor Questions
• Leading questions
• Disguised statements
• Cross-examination questions

See *examples of good questions* in Table 2.10 and *poor questions* in Table 2.11.

LO2.7 Explain strategies to sight-read the nonverbal communication of others.

Strategies for Developing Abilities in Sight-Reading
• Consciously practice each day.
• Pay attention to congruence.
• Sight-read in clusters, not in isolation.
• Sight-read in context.

LO2.8 Identify common communication preferences based on motivational values.

See a *summary of concerns, preferred work environments, and other preferences for each MVS* in Table 2.12. See *words and phrases that resonate with professionals of each MVS* in Table 2.13. See *examples of conversations between professionals of different MVSs* in Figures 2.5 and 2.6.

LO2.9 Explain how extroversion-introversion impacts interpersonal communication.

LO2.10 Explain the role of civility in effective interpersonal communication and the common types of incivility in the workplace.

Guiding principles: (1) Slow down and be present in life; (2) listen to the voice of empathy; (3) keep a positive attitude; (4) respect others and grant them plenty of validation; (5) disagree graciously and refrain from arguing; (6) get to know people around you; (7) pay attention to small things; (8) ask, don't tell. (*Source:* Forni, P. M. (2008). *The civility solution: What to do when people are rude*. New York: St. Martin's Press.)

See *examples of incivility* in Table 2.16.

Key Terms

active listening, 38
blue MVS, 52
CLEM, 49
confirmation bias, 59
counter-narrative, 61
cross-examination questions, 46
decoding, 29
disguised statements, 46
emotional hijacking, 33
emotional intelligence (EQ), 32
empathy, 37
encoding, 29
extrovert, 55
filter of lifetime experiences, 30
funnel questions, 45
gossip, 59
green MVS, 52

hub, 52
interpersonal communication
   process, 29
introvert, 55
judger mind-set, 39
judger statements, 39
leading questions, 46
learner mind-set, 39
learner statements, 39
meaning, 29
mitigating information, 36
motivational value system (MVS), 52
noise, 30
nonlistening behaviors, 43
optimism, 37
perspective-getting, 46
pessimism, 37

physical noise, 30
physiological noise, 30
probing questions, 45
psychological noise, 30
rapport-building questions, 45
red MVS, 52
relationship management, 52
self-awareness, 33
self-management, 34
semantic noise, 30
shared meaning, 30
sight-reading, 48
solution-oriented questions, 46
synchronizing, 49
triggers, 33
visual cutoff, 50

Discussion Exercises

2.1 Chapter Review Questions (LO2.1, LO2.2, LO2.3, LO2.4, LO2.5, LO2.6, LO2.7, LO2.8, LO2.9, LO2.10)

A. What barriers are there to achieving shared meaning? Explain these barriers in terms of the interpersonal communication model.

B. List ten words that could easily be perceived differently. Choose words that create semantic noise because of generational differences, occupational differences, cultural differences, or other kinds of differences.

C. Why is emotional intelligence so important in logical business tasks?

D. What are the four domains of emotional intelligence? Describe three related communication competencies for each domain (see Table 2.2).

E. What do you think are the five best strategies for developing emotional intelligence? Explain your rationale. (See Table 2.2 for help.)

F. Explain how optimism and pessimism affect self-management.

G. What are some concrete examples of people using a message-centered approach to conversations compared to people using a listening-centered approach?

H. What are some signs of a judger mentality in conversations? How about a learner mentality?

I. The active listening process contains six steps. What steps do you think are most critical? Explain.

J. How can image of leadership be a barrier to active listening? Provide some concrete examples.

K. Do you think fear of bad news is a common barrier to active listening among supervisors? Explain your viewpoint and provide some examples.

L. A common statement in classrooms is *there's no such thing as a bad question*. In the context of the workplace, in what ways would you agree and disagree with this statement? How would you qualify this statement?

M. What is meant by perspective-getting? How does note-taking improve perspective-getting?

N. What strategies can professionals use to interpret the nonverbal communication of others? How reliable do you think interpretations of nonverbal communication can be? Explain.

O. What are the motivational value systems (MVSs) explained in this chapter? What do you view as the two most important strengths and one most significant weakness of each style? Explain.

P. Which strategies do you think are most important for extroverts to work effectively with introverts? Which strategies do you think are most important for introverts to work effectively with extroverts? Explain.

Q. Consider the common types of incivility shown in Table 2.16. Which five types of incivility do you think are most common? Most serious? Name five other behaviors you view as common forms of incivility in the workplace, school, or society.

R. In what ways can gossip and complaining be uncivil? What are some ways you can constructively re-frame gossip conversations?

S. What are three things you can do to create a culture of civility and candor in the workplace? Explain.

2.2 Ideas in Action Discussion Questions (LO2.2, LO2.3, LO2.4, LO2.5)

Read the *Ideas in Action* feature in this chapter. For each question, write a one- or two-paragraph answer.

A. Melanie Whelan suggests you should come prepared for every professional conversation. What are three ways you can effectively prepare for these conversations?

B. Whelan says you should start each conversation with a point of view. What do you think this means? How can this help you? In what ways should you be careful with this approach?

C. Whelan says that when you listen to an answer to a question, it will raise at least three more questions. What do you think this means? In what ways can you improve your ability to ask a series of appropriate questions?

2.3 The Personal Part of Employees (LO2.2, LO2.3, LO2.4, LO2.10)

In response to the question "How do you hire?" Kasper Rorsted, CEO of Henkel, a consumer and industrial products company based in Düsseldorf, Germany, had this to say:

> I want to know who you are, who you've worked for, what kind of successes you've had, what are the failures or missteps in your career. But what I try to spend a lot of time on is trying to understand the person I'm speaking to. Did you work in an ice cream parlor when you were young? Do you have sisters? Do you have brothers? Why are you now living here? I'm trying to figure out who's actually behind the person, and what are the value sets that drive you as a person.
>
> Then I always ask the question, what would you do if you won 10 million bucks? Would you leave? Would you retire? Do you want to do charity work? Will you stay?
>
> I never look at grades from university. I look at what they've done, but I look very much at what they've done outside work. How do they spend their time? Who do they relate to? Have they moved? Have they been put in situations in their personal and professional lives that were not very straightforward?
>
> I'm concerned about people who have come through their career with "A" grades throughout their entire life, and have never really had any setbacks and have always been in environments where they knew the environment.
>
> Also, do they say goodbye and hello to the person who stands in front of the building, and do they say hello to the person who sweeps the floor? How do they act as a person? The personal part is, for me, equally important to the professional part. Because I think you can get a lot of people who are professionally very good, but I think the personal part and the value part are the difference between a good manager or leader and a great leader.[102]

Respond to the following questions:

A. When Rorsted says he is looking to find out about the *personal part*, not just the professional part, of a job applicant, what does he mean?

B. How does what Rorsted describes as the personal part of an employee relate to emotional intelligence? How about civility?

C. Rorsted explains that he wants to know how people have responded to setbacks. How does this relate to emotional intelligence?

D. He distinguishes between a good manager and a good leader. In two or three paragraphs, describe some characteristics that would distinguish a good leader from a good manager in terms of interpersonal communication, emotional intelligence, and/ or civility.

2.4 Listening and Caring (LO2.5, LO2.6)

Tachi Yamada, formerly of the Bill & Melinda Gates Foundation, stated the following:

> A second key lesson was from a doctor named Marcel Tuchman. He was the most compassionate person I have ever met in my life—I mean, full of human kindness. And every time he met somebody, you had the sense that he cared more about them than anything else in the world. So what I learned from him is that when you actually are with somebody, you've got to make that person feel like nobody else in the world matters. I think that's critical. So, for example, I don't have a mobile phone turned on because I'm talking to you. I don't want the outside world to impinge on the conversation we're having. I don't carry a BlackBerry. I do my e-mails regularly, but I do it when I have the time on a computer. I don't want to be sitting here thinking that I've got an e-mail message coming here and I'd better look at that while I'm talking to you. Every moment counts, and that moment is lost if you're not in that moment 100 percent.[103]

Based on Yamada's comments and your own experiences, answer the following questions:

A. What do you think Yamada means by the statement, "*that moment is lost if you're not in that moment 100 percent*"? How does this relate to listening? Do you think this is a reasonable expectation in the workplace?

B. What kinds of electronic gadgets and communication tools can take focus away from a conversation? What are some principles for making sure these gadgets and tools are not distracting?

C. Do you believe kindness is an important principle of listening and communicating in business? Can kindness be developed? If so, how?

2.5 Civility and Assertiveness (LO2.1, LO2.2, LO2.3, LO2.4, LO2.10)

Think of three business (or school) situations that require assertiveness. Describe how you can be assertive and also civil at the same time.

Evaluation Exercises

2.6 Describe a Miscommunication from a Movie or TV Episode (LO2.1)

Think about a recent movie or TV episode you observed. Select a scene that involved a miscommunication. Ideally, it should include a conversation that might occur in a workplace. Based on this conversation, do the following:

A. Summarize the conversation in one paragraph.

B. Analyze the conversation in terms of the following components of the interpersonal communication process: encoding, decoding, physical noise, physiological noise, psychological noise, semantic noise, and filter of lifetime experiences.

C. Describe at least three strategies the characters in the conversation could have adopted to increase shared meaning and avoid miscommunication. Describe these strategies in terms of reducing noise and adapting to the filters of others.

2.7 Assess a Recent Miscommunication (LO2.1)

Think about a recent miscommunication you had with someone. Ideally, select an in-depth conversation that occurred in the workplace or at school. Based on this conversation, do the following:

A. Summarize the conversation in one paragraph.

B. Analyze the conversation in terms of the following components of the interpersonal communication process: encoding, decoding, physical noise, physiological noise, psychological noise, semantic noise, and filter of lifetime experiences.

C. Describe at least three strategies you could have adopted to increase shared meaning and avoid miscommunication.

Describe these strategies in terms of reducing noise and adapting to your and your counterpart's unique filters.

2.8 Analyze a Case of Emotional Hijacking at School or Work (LO2.2)

Think about a recent situation at school or work in which you observed a serious instance of emotional hijacking. Based on this situation, do the following:

A. Briefly explain what happened. Who was involved and what were they doing? You can write about yourself and/or others.

B. Explain the cause and nature of the emotional hijacking. For example, explain what the emotions were and what caused them.

C. Explain the impacts of the emotional hijacking. How did it affect an interaction? How did it affect performance?

D. Describe how the emotional hijacking could have been avoided or lessened.

E. Write a set of self-awareness and self-management thoughts that would be considered effective and ineffective in this situation (see Tables 2.1 and 2.3).

2.9 Identify Your Triggers (LO2.2)

In three to five paragraphs, describe three triggers that could lead to emotional hijacking for you. For each trigger, explain one or two strategies you can use to calm down and communicate constructively.

2.10 Assess Your Emotional Intelligence (LO2.3, LO2.4, LO2.5, LO2.6, LO2.7, LO2.8, LO2.9)

Respond to the items below as you assess your emotional intelligence and develop a plan to raise your EQ. Ideally, choose situations from work or school. You may want to use Table 2.2 from the chapter as a guide.

A. Identify one strength and one weakness you have in terms of self-awareness. Describe a situation in which you showed low self-awareness and a situation in which you showed high self-awareness. Choose two strategies for improving your self-awareness.

B. Identify one strength and one weakness you have in terms of self-management. Describe a situation in which you showed low self-management and a situation in which you showed high self-management. Choose two strategies for improving your self-management.

C. Identify one strength and one weakness you have in terms of empathy. Describe a situation in which you showed low empathy and a situation in which you showed high empathy. Choose two strategies for improving your empathy.

D. Identify one strength and one weakness you have in terms of relationship management. Describe a situation in which you showed low relationship management and a situation in which you showed high relationship management. Choose two strategies for improving your relationship management skills.

2.11 Describe the Communication Skills of a Person with High EQ (LO2.3, LO2.4, LO2.5, LO2.6, LO2.7, LO2.8, LO2.9)

Think of someone you have worked with extensively and who you think has high emotional intelligence. Describe at least two communication skills this person has that demonstrate each of the four EQ domains: self-awareness, self-management, empathy, and relationship management. Also, in two or three paragraphs, describe one challenging interpersonal situation this person handled effectively due to high EQ.

2.12 Describe the Listening Skills of an Excellent Listener and a Poor Listener (LO2.5, LO2.6)

Think of two people with whom you have worked at school or work–one an excellent listener and the other a poor listener. Describe and contrast these two individuals in terms of their ability to actively listen: paying attention, holding judgment, reflecting, clarifying, and sharing. Explain how each person made you feel as he or she listened, or didn't listen, to you. Explain two or three ways in which you want to emulate the excellent listener in the workplace.

2.13 Assess Your Active Listening Skills (LO2.5, LO2.6)

Think about how well you listen in *high-pressure* environments or when you're busy. Explain how well you do at each of the following active listening skills: paying attention, holding judgment, reflecting, clarifying, and sharing. For each skill, take approximately two paragraphs to explain how well you do these skills and think of strategies to help you improve.

2.14 Write a Listening Journal (LO2.5, LO2.6)

For a length of time specified by your instructor (one week, two weeks, one month), write daily in a journal about your listening skills. Each day, describe one interaction you had and discuss whether you actively listened. Explain how well you did at each of the following active listening skills: paying attention, holding judgment, reflecting, clarifying, and sharing. For each of these

interactions, describe the nonverbal behavior of others and the nonverbal behavior you exhibited to show your interest. Also, analyze how effectively you asked questions. Conclude your daily journal with a summary of lessons you have learned and five goals for improving your active listening.

2.15 Evaluate the Nonverbal Actions of Others (LO2.7)

For a length of time specified by your instructor (one week, two weeks, one month), write observations about nonverbal communications during one conversation each day. For each of these conversations, explain your observations of nonverbal communication from the following: eye contact and movement, smiles and nods, other facial expressions, gestures, posture, and touch. Conclude your daily journal with a summary of lessons you have learned and five goals for improving your sight-reading.

2.16 Describe Nonverbal Behavior from a Movie or TV Episode (LO2.7)

Think about a recent movie or TV episode you watched. Select a scene that involves interesting nonverbal communication–ideally, one that might occur in the workplace. Based on this scene, do the following:

A. Summarize the scene in approximately a paragraph.

B. Analyze the nonverbal communication. Explain how various body parts sent signals, including the eyes, mouth, shoulders, arms, and hands.

C. Describe how you can mimic or avoid three aspects of this nonverbal behavior in the workplace and why you would want to do so.

2.17 Evaluate the Motivational Value Systems of Yourself and Others (LO2.8)

Explain which MVS best matches you. Then, identify three others (could be family members, friends, colleagues, classmates, or others) who match the other three MVSs described in this chapter. Explain the characteristics that lead you to believe these MVSs match you and these others. Then, explain how knowing these differences will help you communicate more effectively with each of these three people.

2.18 Analyze an Episode of Incivility at Work (LO2.10)

Think of a situation you have observed at work or at school that was uncivil. In one or two paragraphs, describe the event. Then, in two or three paragraphs, explain how each person involved in the encounter contributed to the uncivil event. Analyze the event in terms of noise, filters, and emotional intelligence. In two paragraphs, explain how the person who was most responsible for the incivility could have behaved to make the situation productive for everyone.

2.19 Assess Your Civility (LO2.10)

Look at Table 2.16 in the chapter and think about various types of incivility: ignoring others, treating others without courtesy, disrespecting the time of others, disrespecting the privacy of others, and disrespecting the dignity and worth of others. Read through examples of behaviors associated with each type of incivility. In three or four paragraphs, describe three aspects of civility you will exemplify in your professional life and how you will avoid inadvertently communicating disrespectfully to others.

Application Exercises

2.20 Create a Presentation about Avoiding Miscommunication in the Workplace (LO2.1)

Individually or in teams, develop a five- to ten-minute presentation about how to avoid miscommunication in the workplace. Use terms such as *noise*, *filter*, *encoding*, and *decoding* to explain miscommunication. Provide several specific scenarios that have happened or could happen in the workplace. Provide a simple set of recommendations that your audience will find compelling, insightful, and easy to remember.

2.21 Create a Presentation about EQ as a Basis for Effective Interpersonal Communication (LO2.2, LO2.3, LO2.4, LO2.5, LO2.6, LO2.7, LO2.8, LO2.9)

Individually or in teams, develop a five- to ten-minute presentation about the importance of EQ for effective communication in the workplace. Describe each of the four dimensions of emotional intelligence. Provide several specific scenarios that have happened or could happen in the workplace. Provide a simple set of recommendations that your audience will find compelling, insightful, and easy to remember.

2.22 Listening Exercise (LO2.5, LO2.6)

Form groups of three. You will complete this exercise three times, with each person rotating roles each time. The roles are asker, listener, and observer. Choose a time period (two minutes, three minutes, or five minutes) to complete the exercise. The asker will choose a topic to learn about from the listener (e.g., professional interests, reasons for choosing major, challenges at work or in school right now). The asker will devote the time to learning about the other person through asking questions. The observer will take notes about how effective the asker's asking, listening, and nonverbal communication skills are. Once the exercise is complete, the observer will facilitate a three- to five-minute debriefing by explaining his/her observations and asking both the asker and the listener about their observations.

2.23 Create a Presentation about Civility in Today's Workplace (LO2.10)

Individually or in teams, develop a five- to ten-minute presentation about maintaining civil communications in the workplace. Provide several scenarios that have happened or could happen in the workplace. Provide a simple set of recommendations that your audience will find compelling, insightful, and easy to remember.

Language Mechanics Check

2.24 Review the comma rules C5 through C7 in Appendix A. Then, rewrite each sentence to add commas where needed.

A. To utilize big data companies should hire data scientists.

B. You should consider hiring professionals trained in statistics social media analytics and management theory.

C. She is the first competent data scientist we've hired since starting this important expensive initiative.

D. Under her leadership our company has increased revenue because of our focus on big data.

E. By hiring the right data scientists companies can make better use of marketing resources and target the right customers.

F. Using this software will help us identify expertise among employees evaluate which employees require training and predict which employees are likely to leave the firm within two years and take their knowledge with them.

G. The business school now offers a valuable exciting major in data analytics.

H. To qualify for the program you must hold a 3.0 GPA.

I. You must hold a 3.0 GPA to qualify for the program.

J. Under the leadership of a new dean the program grew rapidly.

Endnotes

1. Graduate Management Admissions Council. (2017). *Corporate recruiters survey: 2017 report.* Reston, VA: Author.

2. Bryant, A. (2009, September 19). Fitting in, and rising to the top. *The New York Times.* Retrieved from www.nytimes.com/2009/09/20/business/20corner.html.

3. This model is based on the transactional model of communication: Watzlawick, P., Beavin, J. H., & Jackson, D. D. (1967) *Pragmatics of human communication: A study of international patterns, pathologies, and paradoxes.* New York: Norton; Barnland, D. C. (1970). A transactional model of communication. In K. K. Sereno and C. D. Mortensen (Eds.), *Foundations of communication theory.* New York: Harper & Row, 83–102; Narula, U. (2006). *Handbook of communication: Models, perspectives, strategies.* New Delhi, India: Atlantic Publishers; West, R. &

Turner, L. H. (2009). *Understanding interpersonal communication: Making choices in changing times* (2nd ed.). Boston: Wadsworth Cengage Learning.

4. West, R., & Turner, L. H. (2009). *Understanding interpersonal communication: Making choices in changing times* (2nd ed.). Boston: Wadsworth Cengage Learning.

5. Most discussion in this section, including this definition, comes from the following sources: Goleman, D. (2006). *Working with emotional intelligence.* New York: Bantam Dell; Goleman, D. (1995). *Emotional intelligence: Why it can matter more than IQ.* New York: Bantam Books; Lynn, A. B. (2005). *The EQ difference: A powerful plan for putting emotional intelligence to work.* New York: AMACOM; Bradberry, T., & Greaves, J. (2009). *Emotional intelligence 2.0.* San Diego, CA: TalentSmart.

6. Clark, S. C., Callister, R., & Wallace, R. (2003). Undergraduate management skills courses and students' emotional intelligence. *Journal of Management Education, 27*(1), 3–23.

7. Gilkey, R., Caceda, R., & Kilts, C. (2010, September). When emotional reasoning trumps IQ. *Harvard Business Review, 27;* Kelley, R., & Caplan, J. (1993, July/August). How Bell Labs creates star performers. *Harvard Business Review,* 128–139.

8. Bradberry, T., & Greaves, J. (2009). *Emotional intelligence 2.0.* San Diego, CA: TalentSmart.

9. Saras, H. (2018, May 2). *Shocking statistics of workplace stress you never knew.* Retrieved from www.harishsaras.com/stress-management/shocking-statistics-of-workplace-stress/.

10. Bryant, A. (2009, April 25). He wants subjects, verbs and objects. *The New York Times.* Retrieved from www.nytimes.com/2009/04/26/business/26corner.html.

11. Clark, S. C., Callister, R., & Wallace, R. (2003). Undergraduate management skills courses and students' emotional intelligence. *Journal of Management Education, 27*(1), 3–23; Healey, T., & Roberts, J. (2015, December 24). Don't let frustration make you say the wrong thing. *Harvard Business Review.* Retrieved from hbr.org/2015/12/dont-let-frustration-make-you-say-the-wrong-thing.

12. Bradberry, T., & Greaves, J. (2009). *Emotional intelligence 2.0.* San Diego, CA: TalentSmart.

13. Ariely, D. (2010). The long-term effects of short-term emotions. *Harvard Business Review, 38;* Goleman, D. (1995). *Emotional intelligence: Why it can matter more than IQ.* New York: Bantam Books; Lynn, A. B. (2005). *The EQ difference: A powerful plan for putting emotional intelligence to work.* New York: AMACOM.

14. Bradberry, T., & Greaves, J. (2009). *Emotional intelligence 2.0.* San Diego, CA: TalentSmart.

15. Goleman, D. (1995). *Emotional intelligence: Why it can matter more than IQ.* New York: Bantam Books, p. 46.

16. Eurich, T. (2018, October 19). Working with people who aren't self-aware. *Harvard Business Review.* Retrieved from hbr.org/2018/10/working-with-people-who-arent-self-aware.

17. Eurich, T. (2018, October 19). Working with people who aren't self-aware. *Harvard Business Review.* Retrieved from hbr.org/2018/10/working-with-people-who-arent-self-aware.

18. Goleman, D. (1995). *Emotional intelligence: Why it can matter more than IQ.* New York: Bantam Books.

19. Bradberry, T. & Greaves, J. (2009). *Emotional intelligence 2.0.* San Diego, CA: TalentSmart.

20. Lynn, A. B. (2004). *The EQ difference: A powerful plan for putting emotional intelligence to work.* New York: AMACOM, 46.

21. Bradberry, T. & Greaves, J. (2009). *Emotional intelligence 2.0.* San Diego, CA: TalentSmart, p. 32.

22. Lynn, A. B. (2005). *The EQ difference: A powerful plan for putting emotional intelligence to work.* New York: AMACOM.

23. Goleman, D. (1995). *Emotional intelligence: Why it can matter more than IQ.* New York: Bantam Books.

24. Goleman, D. (1995). *Emotional intelligence: Why it can matter more than IQ.* New York: Bantam Books.

25. Goleman, D. (1995). *Emotional intelligence: Why it can matter more than IQ.* New York: Bantam Books.

26. Lynn, A. B. (2005). *The EQ difference: A powerful plan for putting emotional intelligence to work.* New York: AMACOM.

27. Goleman, D. (1995). *Emotional intelligence: Why it can matter more than IQ.* New York: Bantam Books.

28. Bradberry, T., & Greaves, J. (2009). *Emotional intelligence 2.0.* San Diego, CA: TalentSmart.

29. Goleman, D. (1995). *Emotional intelligence: Why it can matter more than IQ.* New York: Bantam Books.

30. Purdy, M., & Borisoff, D. (1997). *Listening in everyday life: A personal and professional approach.* Lanham, MD: University Press of America.

31. Graduate Management Admission Council. (2017). *Corporate recruiters survey report 2017.* Reston, VA: GMAC.

32. Hasson, U. (2010, December). I can make your brain look like mine. *Harvard Business Review,* 32–33.

33. Hoppe, M. H. (2006). *Active listening: Improve your ability to listen and lead.* Greensboro, NC: Center for Creative Leadership, 6, 12.

34. Bryant, A. (2010, June 19). Want the job? Tell him the meaning of life. *The New York Times.* Retrieved from www.nytimes.com/2010/06/20/business/20corner.html.

35. Hoppe, M. H. (2006). *Active listening: Improve your ability to listen and lead.* Greensboro, NC: Center for Creative Leadership.

36. Marquardt, M. (2005). *Leading with questions: How leaders find the right solutions by knowing what to ask.* San Francisco: Jossey-Bass, 77–78.

37. Adams, M. (2004). *Change your questions, change your life: 7 powerful tools for life and work.* San Francisco: Berrett-Koehler; Marquardt, M. (2005). *Leading with questions: How leaders find the right solutions by knowing what to ask.* San Francisco: Jossey-Bass.

38. Bryant, A. (2010, June 12). O.K., newbies, bring out the hula hoops. *The New York Times.* Retrieved from www.nytimes.com/2010/06/13/business/13corner.html.

39. Hoppe, M. H. (2006). *Active listening: Improve your ability to listen and lead.* Greensboro, NC: Center for Creative Leadership.

40. Hoppe, M. H. (2006). *Active listening: Improve your ability to listen and lead.* Greensboro, NC: Center for Creative Leadership.

41. Hoppe, M. H. (2006). *Active listening: Improve your ability to listen and lead.* Greensboro, NC: Center for Creative Leadership.

42. Hoppe, M. H. (2006). *Active listening: Improve your ability to listen and lead.* Greensboro, NC: Center for Creative Leadership.

43. Hoppe, M. H. (2006). *Active listening: Improve your ability to listen and lead.* Greensboro, NC: Center for Creative Leadership, 18.

44. Donoghue, P. J., & Siegel, M. E. (2005). *Are you really listening? Keys to successful communication.* Notre Dame, IN: Ave Maria Press; Hoppe, M. H. (2006). *Active listening: Improve your ability to listen and lead.* Greensboro, NC: Center for Creative Leadership.

45. Donoghue, P. J., & Siegel, M. E. (2005). *Are you really listening? Keys to successful communication.* Notre Dame, IN: Ave Maria Press.

46. Donoghue, P. J., & Siegel, M. E. (2005). *Are you really listening? Keys to successful communication.* Notre Dame, IN: Ave Maria Press.

47. Hoppe, M. H. (2006). *Active listening: Improve your ability to listen and lead.* Greensboro, NC: Center for Creative Leadership.

48. Christensen, D. S., & Rees, D. (2002). An analysis of the business communication skills needed by entry-level accountants. *Proceedings of the 2002 Mountain Plains Management Conference.* Retrieved from www.mountainplains.org/articles/2002/general/Communication%20Skills4_MPJ_.pdf.

49. Baldoni, J. (2003, March). Are you asking the right questions? *Harvard Management Communication Letter,* 3–4.

50. Baldoni, J. (2003, March). Are you asking the right questions? *Harvard Management Communication Letter,* 3–4; Stone, D., Patton, B., & Heen, S. (2000). *Difficult conversations: How to discuss what matters most.* New York: Penguin; Marquardt, M. (2005). *Leading with questions: How leaders find the right solutions by knowing what to ask.* San Francisco: Jossey-Bass.

51. Brendel, D. (2015, September 17). Asking open-ended questions helps new managers build trust. *Harvard Business Review.* Retrieved from hbr.org/2015/09/asking-open-ended-questions-helps-new-managers-build-trust.

52. Eyal, T., Steffel, M., & Epley, N. (2018). Research: Perspective-taking doesn't help you understand what others want. *Harvard Business Review.* Retrieved from hbr.org/2018/10/research-perspective-taking-doesnt-help-you-understand-what-others-want.

53. Brendel, D. (2015, September 17). Asking open-ended questions helps new managers build trust. *Harvard Business Review.* Retrieved from hbr.org/2015/09/asking-open-ended-questions-helps-new-managers-build-trust.

54. Grant, A. (2013, April). In the company of givers and takers. *Harvard Business Review,* 90–97.

55. Pease, A., & Pease, B. (2006). *The definitive book of body language.* New York: Bantam Dell; Kandola, P. (2006). *The psychology of effective business communications in geographically dispersed teams.* San Jose, CA: Cisco.

56. Givens, D. (2010). *Your body at work: A guide to sight-reading the body language of business, bosses, and boardrooms.* New York: St. Martin's Griffin, xvi.

57. Givens, D. (2010). *Your body at work: A guide to sight-reading the body language of business, bosses, and boardrooms.* New York: St. Martin's Griffin, 2.

58. Morgan, N. (2002, August). The truth behind the smile and other myths: Reading body language is important, but the clues may be misleading. *Harvard Management Communication Letter,* 4.

59. Gladwell, M. (2007). *Blink: The power of thinking without thinking.* New York: Barclay Books.

60. Pease, A., & Pease, B. (2006). *The definitive book of body language.* New York: Bantam Dell.

61. Givens, D. (2010). *Your body at work: A guide to sight-reading the body language of business, bosses, and boardrooms.* New York: St. Martin's Griffin; Langford, B. (2005). *The etiquette edge: The unspoken rules for business success.* New York: American Management Association.

62. Goleman, D. (1995). *Emotional intelligence: Why it can matter more than IQ.* New York: Bantam Books, 117.

63. Morgan, N. (2003). Are you standing in the way of your own success? *Harvard Management Communication Letter,* 3.

64. Givens, D. (2010). *Your body at work: A guide to sight-reading the body language of business, bosses, and boardrooms.* New York: St. Martin's Griffin.

65. Givens, D. (2010). *Your body at work: A guide to sight-reading the body language of business, bosses, and boardrooms.* New York: St. Martin's Griffin.

66. Givens, D. (2010). *Your body at work: A guide to sight-reading the body language of business, bosses, and boardrooms.* New York: St. Martin's Griffin.

67. Givens, D. (2010). *Your body at work: A guide to sight-reading the body language of business, bosses, and boardrooms.* New York: St. Martin's Griffin.

68. Morgan, N. (2002, August). The truth behind the smile and other myths: Reading body language is important, but the clues may be misleading. *Harvard Management Communication Letter,* 4.

69. Morgan, N. (2003). Are you standing in the way of your own success? *Harvard Management Communication Letter,* 3.

70. Pugh, S. D. (2001). Service with a smile: Emotional contagion in the service encounter. *Academy of Management Journal, 44*(5), 1018–1027.

71. Morgan, N. (2002, August). The truth behind the smile and other myths: Reading body language is important, but the clues may be misleading. *Harvard Management Communication Letter,* 4.

72. Pease, A., & Pease, B. (2006). *The definitive book of body language.* New York: Bantam Dell.

73. Givens, D. (2010). *Your body at work: A guide to sight-reading the body language of business, bosses, and boardrooms.* New York: St. Martin's Griffin, 52.

74. Givens, D. (2010). *Your body at work: A guide to sight-reading the body language of business, bosses, and boardrooms.* New York: St. Martin's Griffin.

75. Givens, D. (2010). *Your body at work: A guide to sight-reading the body language of business, bosses, and boardrooms.* New York: St. Martin's Griffin.

76. Givens, D. (2010). *Your body at work: A guide to sight-reading the body language of business, bosses, and boardrooms.* New York: St. Martin's Griffin.

77. Givens, D. (2010). *Your body at work: A guide to sight-reading the body language of business, bosses, and boardrooms.* New York: St. Martin's Griffin.

78. Pease, A., & Pease, B. (2006). *The definitive book of body language.* New York: Bantam Dell.

79. Morgan, N. (2003). Are you standing in the way of your own success? *Harvard Management Communication Letter,* 3.

80. Bradberry, T., & Greaves, J. (2009). *Emotional intelligence 2.0.* San Diego, CA: TalentSmart, 44.

81. Relationship Awareness Theory was developed by the psychologist Elias H. Porter. There are many other psychological assessments and tools for assessing differences in communication styles. Each assessment has various advantages. Nearly all of these assessments can help professionals and students develop emotional intelligence to work more effectively with others. I chose this tool because it contains the following advantages: (1) The assessment has 96 percent face validity: in other words, people who use the instrument believe it explains their relating styles extremely well; (2) it is a comparatively simple and practical tool; and (3) it distinguishes between situations where things are going well and situations involving conflict and discomfort.

82. These figures are based on my administration of the Strengths Deployment Inventory (SDI) to full-time working professionals enrolled in part-time MBA programs at the University of Southern California. Among roughly 750 SDI tests of these managers, the breakdown is as follows: hubs, 43 percent; blue-reds, 22 percent; red, 17 percent; red-greens, 7 percent; blue-greens, 6 percent; greens, 3 percent; and blues, 2 percent. These figures are similar to those provided by Personal Strengths for all professionals: hubs, 39 percent; blues, 17 percent; blue-reds, 13 percent; blue-greens, 13 percent; reds, 10 percent; red-greens, 4 percent; and greens, 6 percent.

83. Cain, S. (2012). *Quiet: The power of introverts in a world that can't stop talking.* New York: Crown Publishers; Ancowitz, N. (2009). *Self-promotion for introverts: The quiet guide to getting ahead.* New York: McGraw-Hill, 2009; Conant, D. R. (2011, April 4). Are you an

introverted boss? *Harvard Business Review.* Retrieved from http://blogs.hbr.org/2011/04/are-you-an-introverted-boss/; Grant, A. M., Gino, F., & Hofmann, D. A. (2010, July). The hidden advantages of quiet bosses. *Harvard Business Review, 28.*

84. Cain, S. (2012). *Quiet: The power of introverts in a world that can't stop talking.* New York: Crown Publishers.

85. Grant, A. M., Gino, F., & Hofmann, D. A. (2010, July). The hidden advantages of quiet bosses. *Harvard Business Review, 28.*

86. HBR IdeaCast. (2014, April 4). The power of the introvert in your office. Retrieved April 4, 2014, from http://blogs.hbr.org/2012/07/the-power-of-the-introvert-in/.

87. Pearson, C. M., & Porath, C. L. (2005). On the nature, consequences and remedies of workplace incivility: No time for "nice"? Think again. *Academy of Management Executive, 19*(1), 8.

88. Alsop, R. J. (2011, January). Social disgraces. *Workforce Management, 34.*

89. Farkas, S., Johnson, J., Duffett, A., & Collins, K. (2009, November 25). *Aggravating circumstances: A status report on rudeness in America.* New York: Public Agenda.

90. Farkas, S., Johnson, J., Duffett, A., & Collins, K. (2009, November 25). *Aggravating circumstances: A status report on rudeness in America.* New York: Public Agenda.

91. Farkas, S., Johnson, J., Duffett, A., & Collins, K. (2002, November 25). *Aggravating circumstances: A status report on rudeness in America.* New York: Public Agenda, 31.

92. Farkas, S., Johnson, J., Duffett, A., & Collins, K. (2002, November 25). *Aggravating circumstances: A status report on rudeness in America.* New York: Public Agenda, 24.

93. Pearson, C. M., & Porath, C. L. (2005). On the nature, consequences and remedies of workplace incivility: No time for "nice"? think again. *Academy of Management Executive, 19*(1), 7–18.

94. Pearson, C. M., & Porath, C. L. (2009). *The cost of bad behavior: How incivility is damaging your business and what to do about it.* New York: Penguin Group.

95. Pearson, C. M., & Porath, C. L. (2009). *The cost of bad behavior: How incivility is damaging your business and what to do about it.* New York: Penguin Group.

96. These types of workplace incivility are adopted and modified from a variety of sources, including the following: Pearson, C. M., & Porath, C. L. (2009). *The cost of bad behavior: How incivility is damaging your business and what to do about it.* New York: Penguin Group; Forni, P. M. (2008). *The civility solution: What to do when people are rude.* New York: St. Martin's Press; Krajewski, L. A. (2010, October 27). Workplace incivility: A research study. Presentation at the 2010 Annual Convention of the Association for Business Communication. Chicago, IL.

97. Forni, P. M. (2008). *The civility solution: What to do when people are rude.* New York: St. Martin's Press, 24.

98. Kurland, N. B., & Pelled, L. H. (2000). Passing the word: Toward a model of gossip and power in the workplace. *Academy of Management Review, 25*(2), 428, 438; Riegel, D. G. (2018, October 12). Stop complaining about your colleagues behind their backs. *Harvard Business Review.* Retrieved from hbr.org/2018/10/stop-complaining-about-your-colleagues-behind-their-backs.

99. Knight, R. (2018, October 29). Working with a colleague who feels that the world is against them. *Harvard Business Review.* Retrieved from hbr.org/2018/10/working-with-a-colleague-who-feels-that-the-world-is-against-them.

100. Forni, P. M. (2008). *The civility solution: What to do when people are rude.* New York: St. Martin's Press.

101. Bryant, A. (2009, December 5). On passion and playing in traffic. *Corner Office* (blog). *The New York Times.* Retrieved from www.nytimes.com/2009/12/06/business/06corner.html.

102. Bryant, A. (2010, August 28). No need to hit the "send" key. Just talk to me. *The New York Times.* Retrieved from www.nytimes.com/2010/08/29/business/29corner.html.

103. Bryant, A. (2010, February 27). Talk to me. I'll turn off my phone. *The New York Times.* Retrieved from www.nytimes.com/2010/02/28/business/28corner.html.

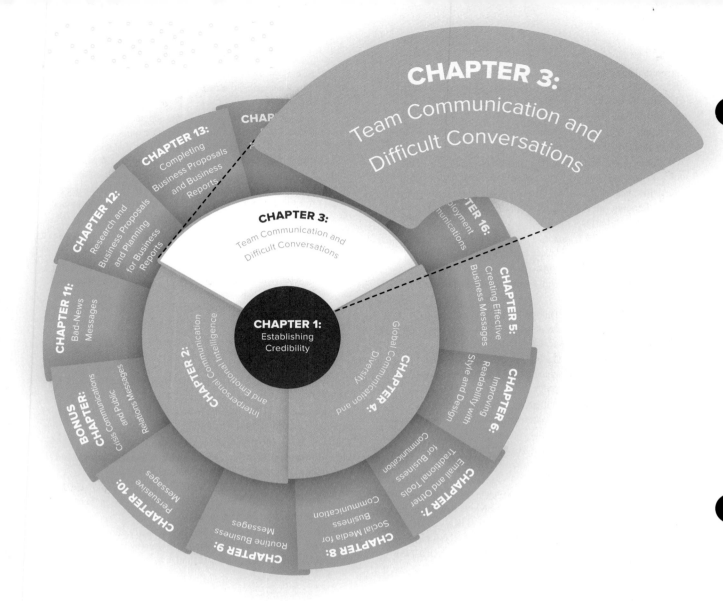

CHAPTER 3:
Team Communication and
Difficult Conversations

ESTABLISHING CREDIBILITY

PRINCIPLES OF INTERPERSONAL COMMUNICATION

PRINCIPLES FOR & TYPES OF BUSINESS MESSAGES

 LEARNING OBJECTIVES

After studying this chapter, you should be able to do the following:

LO3.1 Explain the principles of team communication in high-performing teams.

LO3.2 Describe and demonstrate approaches to planning, running, and following up on meetings.

LO3.3 Explain the principles of effective virtual team communication.

LO3.4 Describe strategies for effective group writing.

LO3.5 Explain basic principles for handling difficult conversations.

WHY DOES THIS MATTER?

Organizations of all types have increasingly recognized that teams deliver more innovation and better business results. You can expect that in your career you will spend a significant amount of your time in teams. In fact, about 54 percent of professionals spend about one-third of their work time in a team setting. Another 34 percent say they spend about half of their work time in a team setting. Yet, just 3 percent of these professionals say they've been trained to work in teams.[1]

Your ability to contribute to and lead teams will provide you with many career opportunities. In fact, excellent team players are often fast-tracked for better positions. Aside from the many career benefits of teams, working in teams can be energizing. It allows you to bond with your colleagues, learn from others, share your ideas, and celebrate together when your team hits big milestones. Working in teams isn't always easy. It requires that you give up some of your independence. It can be discouraging when team members don't work together well. However, with an understanding of principles for effective teamwork, discipline, and hard work, you're well positioned to succeed in teams. As you read this chapter, think about how you can improve your team communication skills and facilitate productive teamwork.

> **Hear Pete Cardon explain why this matters.**
> **bit.ly/cardon3**

CHAPTER CASE COLLABORATING IN TEAMS AT AICASUS TOURS

Nancy Jeffreys

Kip Yamada

WHO'S INVOLVED

The Marketing Team Prepares for a Meeting
The marketing team is about to hold its biweekly meeting. Team members intend to evaluate their team's performance over the past quarter, discuss plans for upcoming market research, and identify new product and service ideas for cultural history tours.

SITUATION 1

Nancy and Kip Hold Grudges from a Prior Disagreement

SITUATION 2

Nancy and Kip have ignored one another as much as possible in recent months. Problems started when Kip authorized discounts to clients on several group tours. The clients complained they didn't get to see all the sites listed in promotional materials.

Nancy was furious when she found out that Kip had given the refunds without first checking with her. She called him into her office and scolded him for not speaking to

(Nancy Jeffreys character): Photodisc/Getty Images; (Kip Yamada character): John A Rizzo/Pixtal/SuperStock her first. Kip abruptly said, "So much for our famous customer service," and left her office. Since then, Nancy has complained to co-workers that Kip didn't understand the business side of running tours. Kip complained that Nancy didn't relate to clients' expectations and that the company was losing repeat business because of it.

TASK

1

How will the marketing team work together effectively to implement a cohesive marketing approach? (See the team communication section.)

2

How will Nancy and Kip discuss their differences and work productively together again? (See the chapter section on difficult conversations.)

Principles of Effective Team Communication

LO3.1 Explain the principles of team communication in high-performing teams.

Visit http://connect. mheducation.com for an exercise on this topic.

Teams can take many forms. Some teams are formally and permanently organized and titled (such as the *marketing team*). Other teams are temporarily formed for completing a project or an activity (i.e., project team, committee). You will work on dozens of teams over your career.

In a recent survey, business professionals cited ineffective communication (66 percent) as the biggest barrier to team effectiveness. Other major barriers included lack of effective chartering and goal setting (56 percent), lack of clarity and understanding of roles (47 percent), low morale (44 percent), low productivity (42 percent), and lack of trust (36 percent). Similarly, when ranking the most frustrating aspects of being part of a team, business professionals cite the following: ineffective use of meeting time (54 percent), ineffective communication among team members (50 percent), lack of accountability (47 percent), individuals who don't complete assignments (44 percent), and lack of preparation in meetings (41 percent).[2] All of these factors in turn relate to communication competencies.

Your teams will perform far better if they follow the basic principles of team communication. Work in teams is among the most researched aspects of work performance, and hundreds of studies have supported each of the following principles:

Teams should focus first and foremost on performance. The most basic ingredient of excellent teams is a focus on high performance. Make sure that your team has a sense of urgency and direction to achieve excellence.[3] One signal that teams are sufficiently focused on performance is how often teams talk directly about work priorities. Out of every 100 comments team members in high-performing groups make, 60 to 70 directly relate to work—goals, coordination, roles, task clarification, and other project-related issues. Of the 100 comments, team members make about 15 to 20 supportive statements, intended to show goodwill and encouragement. And, they make 10 to 15 statements that are primarily social.[4] By contrast, team members in lower-performing groups make far fewer work-related and supportive statements. They typically replace these statements with social statements that may help team members bond socially but not around work issues.

One way teams can stay focused on performance is to use solution-oriented priming statements.[5] **Priming statements** trigger a mind-set that affects subsequent behavior. Solution-oriented priming statements trigger a focus on performance. For example, "Let's get together to work on this project" does not focus on problem solving and solutions. By contrast, "Let's figure out our options to create new customized tour options" is a solution-oriented priming statement. Effective teams often use these solution-oriented priming statements to maintain focus on high performance.

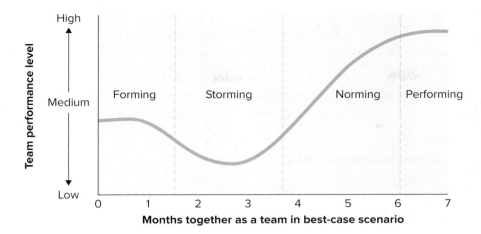

FIGURE 3.1

Stages of Development in High-Performance Teams

Source: Adapted from Wheelan, S. A. (1999). *Creating effective teams: A guide for members and leaders.* Thousand Oaks, CA: Sage, which examines hundreds of scholarly studies on teamwork.

Teams go through four natural stages to reach high performance.[6] Nearly all high-performing teams go through four stages before they maximize their performance. In best-case scenarios, work teams take roughly six to seven months to reach this level (see Figure 3.1).[7] Typically, leaders become less directive and more consultative as the team progresses through the stages:

1. *Forming* (months 1 and 2). In the **forming** stage, team members focus on gaining acceptance and avoiding conflict. In some ways, this stage is a honeymoon period in which team members get to know one another.

2. *Storming* (months 2 and 3). In the **storming** stage, team members open up with their competing ideas about how the team should approach work. This stage is typically the least productive, since team members are attempting to make sense of uncertain roles, goals, and accountabilities.

3. *Norming* (months 4 and 5). In the **norming** stage, the team arrives at a work plan, including the roles, goals, and accountabilities.

4. *Performing* (months 6 and 7). In the **performing** stage, teams operate efficiently toward accomplishing their goals. They have evolved to a level where they can transform disagreement and conflict into consensus for future action.

Effective teams build a work culture around values, norms, and goals. Organizations and teams constantly attempt to foster unity and high performance. **Team culture** refers to a set of shared perceptions and commitment to collective values, norms, roles, responsibilities, and goals.[8] Typically, teams rapidly develop such shared perceptions and commitment during the norming stage. Only at the performing stage do these shared perceptions and commitments lead to high productivity.

High-performing teams avoid simply going with the flow. Rather, they frequently, explicitly, and openly discuss the set of values, norms, and goals they share. This process is critical, since team members often attach different meanings to the same goals. Open discussion helps team members avoid misinterpreting each other's motivations and actions.

One way that high-performing teams ensure they develop and live up to shared values, norms, and goals is to create a team charter. The team charter provides direction to the team in how it functions to meet shared objectives. Common elements of team charters include purpose or mission statements, values, goals, team member roles (including leadership), tasks, ground rules, communication protocol, meeting protocol, decision-making rules, conflict resolution, and feedback mechanisms. For short-term teams and groups, such as those that operate for school projects, you should make sure your charter also includes contact information for each team member as well as deadlines for task completion.[9]

In Figure 3.2, you can see an abbreviated team charter created by the Aicasus Tours marketing team. It contains many features common to team charters. As you develop

FIGURE 3.2

Team Charter for the
Aicasus Tours
Marketing Team

Aicasus Tours Marketing Team Charter

Mission Statement: We provide marketing for Aicasus Tours that matches its mission of delivering once-in-a-lifetime tours, creating authentic and sustainable connections between tourists and host communities, and ensuring strong financial results.

Values: Excellence in all work, creativity, honesty, sharing, collaboration, professional growth.

Goals: (a) To be recognized as a leader in developing cutting-edge, interactive tours; (b) to increase revenue annually by 12 percent; and (c) to maintain 95 percent satisfaction among our clients.

Team Member Roles/Responsibilities

Team Member	Position	Responsibilities
Andrea Garcia	Director of marketing	Oversee all marketing initiatives.
Nancy Jeffreys	Director of market research	Lead all market research.
Barbara Brookshire	Director of marketing operations	Lead all marketing campaigns.
Kip Yamada	Group tours associate	Oversee custom group tours.
Jeff Anderton	Market research associate	Conduct market research and analytics.
Kailey Chang	Marketing assistant	Create concepts and graphics for campaigns.

Communication Protocol

- We will post project updates, recommendations, and relevant experiences to Slack. Team members should post roughly twice per week.
- We will respond to direct messages to one another (team messaging, emails, phone calls) within four hours.
- We recognize the value of each team member's ideas. We will discuss differences of opinions with one another directly and respectfully.

Meetings

- We will hold meetings on the first and third Wednesdays of each month at 8:30 a.m.
- We will rotate facilitators for each meeting. The facilitator will ensure agenda items are covered with the input of all team members.
- The facilitator should create the agenda. By the Monday preceding each meeting, the facilitator should make a call for agenda items. The facilitator should distribute the final agenda on Slack by Tuesday at noon on the day before each meeting.
- We will rotate note-takers for each meeting.
- The note-taker should post minutes to Slack by the end of the day on Tuesday. The note-taker will create calendar entries for all action items.

Decision Making: We aim for consensus. If we do not achieve consensus, decisions will be based on a majority vote of the director of marketing, the director of market research, and the director of marketing operations.

Feedback

- After each major marketing initiative, we will evaluate each team member's performance.
- In June and December, we will evaluate team performance and communication.
- We are dedicated to professional growth. We will constantly help one another reach our professional goals.

---

team charters, you should view this as an important agreement with your team members. From time to time, your team should evaluate the team charter itself and modify it to better meet the needs of your team.

Effective teams meet often. Most groups underperform because they do not spend enough time meeting. Frequent meetings are necessary to establish shared perceptions of roles, goals, and accountabilities. (See the next section on managing meetings.) Also, meetings force team members to meet deadlines. Teams that do not meet often may never reach the performing stage. Or they regress from the performing stage to an even less productive stage. Similarly, effective teams prioritize first meetings and actions.

They recognize that the initial series of meetings often set the tone and build a foundation for high performance for an entire project.

Effective teams focus on psychological safety and ensure all voices are heard. Over a two-year period, Google conducted an extensive study of teams to learn the key dynamics in successful teams. Google researchers conducted over 200 interviews and observed over 180 teams. They found that the most important predictor of team success was **psychological safety**, which is defined as "team members feel safe to take risks and be vulnerable in front of one another." Two particular team norms contribute most to psychological safety. First, all team members spend roughly the same amount of time speaking during their conversations. Second, team members are empathetic and understand one another's feelings.[10]

Effective teams recognize and actively seek to avoid groupthink. Teams often fall victim to groupthink. **Groupthink** is when groups verbally or nonverbally agree to ideas without gathering enough information and exhaustively evaluating their options. Groupthink often leads to poor decision making. As we discuss groupthink, we'll work through an example of the Aicasus marketing team. It is seeking innovative services for its international tours. The team has decided to invest in virtual reality (VR) headsets and software to add to the experience of clients in group tours. It is convinced these VR headsets will make tours more adventurous and educational.

Effective teams seek to avoid the following symptoms of groupthink:[11]

Collective rationalization is when group members convince themselves a solution is the best one even when faced with conflicting information. They tend to explain away or dismiss the conflicting information. For example, the Aicasus marketing team gets survey results from past clients that they wouldn't use VR headsets while on a tour. Various team members take turns saying the survey results are meaningless because "our clients don't know anything about something they haven't tried."

Moral high ground is when group members assume they're morally correct and as a result dismiss competing ideas or alternate solutions. For example, the marketing team believes tours should simulate history and help clients get a factual rendition. By using the VR headsets, they can provide programming that avoids the inconsistencies of tour guides. The team members make this argument in various forms of the following: "It's the right thing to do so our clients have an accurate understanding and appreciation of history."

Self-censorship is when group members don't voice their opinions for the sake of harmony. Jeff, in particular, doesn't like conflict. He also doesn't like to challenge authority. When he hears Andrea and Nancy argue for the VR headsets, he decides not to share several reasons why he is skeptical that clients will want to use them during tours.

Illusion of unanimity is when no one speaks out against the majority view and, as a result, everyone assumes there is agreement. For example, when the marketing team dismisses the results of the client survey, Kip considers saying, "I think we should pay attention to these results. Even though our clients haven't tried this technology, they understand very well what they want on a tour." But, he never says anything. The rest of the team members assume everyone, including Kip, agrees with their stated perspective.

FIGURE 3.3

Teams Often Suffer from Groupthink Because of Self-Censorship and the Illusion of Unanimity.

Source: Clavien, J. (2016). What do I need to know about groupthink? *42hire.*

Peer pressure is when the majority of group members pressure or even penalize a member with dissenting views. For example, when the marketing team talks about why VR headsets are the "right way to learn history," Kailey disagrees. She says, "Actually, I think we should worry about trying to give our clients a standard version of history. They learn much more by hearing local tour guides give nuanced views of history." Several team members immediately say variations of the following statement: "Kailey, we don't have time for this. We've already agreed that a more standardized presentation is better for our clients."

Illusion of invulnerability is when team members are overly optimistic in their ideas and don't consider the risks or drawbacks of their ideas. **Complacency** is when a group has experienced quite a few successes and begins to assume it will automatically make good decisions. For example, the marketing team has introduced a series of successful innovations over the past three years. As a result, it is extremely confident the VR headsets will improve the attractiveness of tours.

Mindguards are team members who purposely filter information so there is not dissent or threat to the team leader. For example, Barbara has read some research that most companies underestimate the expenses of developing content for VR headsets. She doesn't think the research is credible, so she chooses not to share this information with the team. She is concerned some team members will use the research to argue against an investment in VR technologies.

Stereotyping is when group members see outsiders as morally inferior or less competent. Let's say the finance team has sent an analysis to the marketing team. The finance team suggests an investment in VR headsets is a major financial risk. The marketing team members speak to one another making arguments such as the following: "The finance team never gets it right with new products and services. Basically, it just likes to play it safe."

Many of these groupthink patterns can be amplified through cascades.[12] **Cascades** are when the initial ideas in a discussion excessively influence the ultimate decisions. Research shows that the first point of view in a discussion is most likely to gain momentum, especially if a counterview is not offered.[13]

Effective teams embrace diversity. High-performing teams embrace conflict. They see differences of opinion as natural and as a path to creativity and innovation. So, they encourage one another to share their ideas, even when those ideas differ from their own.

One way teams can welcome new ideas is to embrace diversity. Increasingly, research shows that diversity brings better business returns. Diversity comes in two forms: inherent and acquired. **Inherent diversity** involves traits such as age, gender, ethnicity, and sexual orientation. **Acquired diversity** involves traits you acquire through experience, such as customer service experience, retail experience, or engineering experience. Having both types of diversity is called **2-D diversity**. Companies with 2-D diversity are about 45 percent more likely to report a growth in market share during the past year and about 70 percent more likely to have captured a new market. The following behaviors help drive acquired diversity: (1) making sure everyone is heard, (2) making it safe to let team members express novel ideas, (3) giving team members decision-making authority, (4) sharing credit, (5) giving useful feedback, and (6) putting feedback into action. In short, these behaviors drive an innovative, "speak-up culture."[14]

To understand a team's diversity, team members must take time to evaluate one another's backgrounds and experiences. They should question one another about their strengths and weaknesses, passions, achievements, and past school and work experiences.[15]

One particularly effective approach for developing excellent team communication is for all team members to take assessments of personality and communication styles. After taking the assessments, team members typically share their results with one another. The major value of these types of assessments is to create explicit conversations about styles and preferences.

In the last chapter, you learned about the motivational value system (MVS). You learned how individuals with blue MVSs tend to focus most on nurturing, those with red MVSs focus most on directing, those with green MVSs focus most on autonomiz-ing, and those with hub MVSs focus equally on these motivational values. In this model, the colors are also connected with approaches to conflict. Blue is associated with an *accommodating* approach in which meeting the needs of others is the first concern. These individuals tend to avoid conflict if possible. Red is associated with *asserting* one's viewpoints and interests. These individuals tend to embrace conflict and enjoy trying to win an argument. Green is associated with taking a step back and cautiously *analyzing* the situation. These individuals tend to want to discuss differences of opinion after having time to carefully think through their positions. Each approach to conflict is valid. However, team members with different approaches to conflict can easily misinter-pret the motives and intentions of one another.[16]

Team members who take this assessment can plot their personalities and approaches to conflict on a triangle. The dot depicts the MVS in routine situations, whereas the arrow depicts approaches to conflict. By taking the assessment, the Aicasus team can rapidly see how their values and preferred communication styles in routine and conflict situations compare to one another (see Figure 3.4). A variety of personality assess-ments are available to help you and your team members share your preferences of com-municating in routine interactions and in conflict situations.

Effective teams solve problems and generate creative solutions by going through cycles of divergence and convergence. Ensuring that teams are innovative requires discipline because team cultures can easily develop groupthink. In the past decade, businesses have increasingly encouraged teamwork and developed open-space environments where team members stay together for longer periods. However, for teams to function well, most team members need periods of time to work independently and without interrup-tion. The most innovative teams balance time in teams with time for independent work to capture a diversity of strong ideas.[17] Teams that go through cycles of divergence and

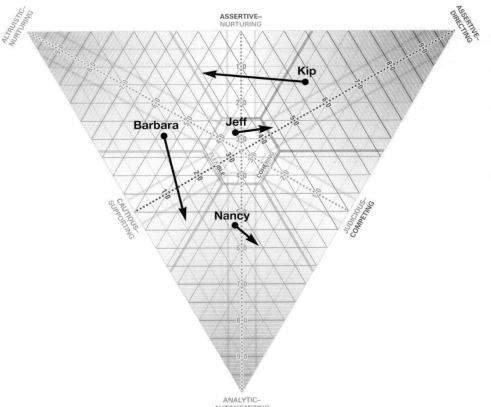

FIGURE 3.4

The Strengths Deployment Inventory Triangle Displaying Motivational Value Systems convergence generate the best solutions. Typically, when team members work independently, they diverge. When they work together, they tend to converge.[18]

Divergence involves considering as many solutions as possible. During the divergence stage, working independently can increase the number of ideas and solutions generated. One effective practice is to give each person on the team the basic problem and the criteria by which the solution will be evaluated. After team members generate ideas independently, they meet to discuss each person's ideas. Debate about the ideas is healthy at this stage. When there is high psychological safety, team members do not feel threatened as the team talks about the strengths and weaknesses of their ideas:[19]

Convergence involves evaluating the proposed ideas and solutions and narrowing them to a small set of feasible solutions to address the problem. This part of problem solving is highly collaborative and generally involves refining the best ideas with contributions from all team members.[20]

Effective teams provide a lot of positive feedback and evaluate their performance often. High-performing teams consistently provide feedback, most of which should be positive. A study of leadership of 60 leadership teams found that the primary differentiator between low-performing and high-performing teams was the ratio of positive-to-negative comments. The ratio in successful teams was 5.6 positive comments for every negative comment. Comparatively, there were roughly 1.9 positive comments for each negative comment in medium-performing teams. In low-performing teams, there were three negative comments for every positive comment! Examples of positive comments are phrases such as "I agree that . . ." or "that's a great idea." Negative comments may include "I don't agree . . ." or "That's not a good idea."[21]

While most feedback is positive in high-performing teams, they also frequently evaluate their performance and ensure they give one another direct and candid suggestions for improvement. They may evaluate performance for projects or initiatives or for certain periods of time. Many teams take time at each meeting to briefly evaluate their performance. Several keys to effective evaluation include the following: (1) the process should be primarily positive and goal-driven and rarely punitive, (2) the process should involve clear expectations, and (3) all team members should participate.[22]

You will notice that in the Aicasus marketing team's charter (see Figure 3.2) there are several ways of providing feedback to one another. One way they do this is by completing a team assessment several times per year. In Figure 3.5, you can see an

FIGURE 3.5

Sample Team Assessment for the Aicasus Marketing Team

Marketing Team Assessment

Assess your team on a scale from 1 (never) to 5 (always).

Our team . . .	1 (Never)	2 (Rarely)	3 (Sometimes)	4 (Usually)	5 (Always)
Focuses on high performance.	1	2	3	4	5
Sets high goals and standards.					
Follows the team charter.					
Gives each team member a chance to participate.					
Engages in open and candid conversation.					
Holds high-value meetings.					
Handles differences of opinion constructively.					
Develops creative solutions together.					
Helps team members grow professionally.					
Has developed trust among members.					

abbreviated example of this team assessment. Common areas of emphasis on team assessments are a focus on results, communication climate (including conflict resolution), accountability, commitment, and trust.

Effective teams feel a common sense of purpose and bond socially. This sense of purpose feeds the team's morale, dedication, and ability to negotiate roles and accountabilities. Thus, high-performing teams frequently discuss their purposes. They also commit to bonding socially and showing concern for one another. Little things, even listening to upbeat music together and eating out, have been shown to build social bonding and sense of a common purpose.[23]

Developing Quick Trust and Working in Short-Term Teams

Many teams are created to accomplish projects in short periods of time, often in just a few weeks up to a few months. Short-term teams face unique challenges. They are often comprised of people who don't know each other well. They must quickly coordinate their efforts to meet pressing deadlines. They need to reach a high level of performance rapidly. Developing trust is particularly challenging given the short duration of these teams. As a result, developing quick trust is critical.

Get to know each other. Most short-term teams are so focused on accomplishing the tasks at hand that they don't take enough time to get to know one another. This is a mistake. Investing 30 minutes to an hour getting to know one another in a social but professional manner helps build the trust the team needs to effectively coordinate its efforts.

One of the fastest ways to increase trust, particularly among teammates who don't know one another, is through self-disclosure. **Self-disclosure** is sharing information about yourself, such as your goals, aspirations, views and values, and experiences. Teammates often bond emotionally and learn about one another's strengths by opening up or self-disclosing to each other. Yet, too much self-disclosure and the wrong types of self-disclosure in professional settings can often backfire.[24] See Exercise 3.10 in the end-of-chapter exercises for ideas about getting to know each other quickly.

Hold an effective launch meeting. Short-term teams rely on a well-organized, thorough launch meeting. One of the primary barriers to success for short-term teams is not exploring all options. Because the team is under pressure to meet quick deadlines, team members often feel rushed to decide on a direction, create a plan, and start making progress. By spending an extra hour or two in the launch meeting to explore all options carefully, short-term teams generally choose a better direction from the start of a project and ultimately save time by better coordinating their efforts on a strong choice of direction.

Commit to working together and separately. Team members on high-performing teams do a lot of work together and independently. Short-term teams often quickly delegate independent work and then attempt to tie the individual pieces together near the end of the project. By setting up a regular meeting schedule, short-term teams can ensure they spend enough time together to produce excellent work.

Set up a deliverable schedule and evaluate performance regularly. Short-term teams often produce poor or mediocre work because the first time they produce shared work is close to final deadlines. Forward-looking short-term teams set up internal deadlines for deliverables across a project so they can evaluate and improve their joint work.

Managing Meetings

Meetings are one of the primary forums for teams to share and listen to one another's ideas. Because of the increasing importance of teams in the workplace, employees increasingly participate in project and interdepartmental teams. Meetings are an opportunity for teams to coordinate their efforts and increase productivity. Done well, they can be invigorating and produce new insights.[25]

At their best, problem-solving meetings provide incredible return on investment. For example, NorTel evaluated its return on investment on a series of 12 two-day meetings with the express purpose of reducing manufacturing costs. Altogether, the company invested $500,000, but calculations indicated that it saved $91 million due to solutions developed during the meetings.[26]

Yet, meetings have many trade-offs. The biggest drawback is that they take a lot of time. Many managers spend up to 50 percent of their time in meetings.[27] Furthermore, when meetings are run poorly, they can create animosity, lower morale, and decrease productivity.[28]

Managers who run effective meetings help their teams work more productively and have better career opportunities.[29] As you prepare to lead and participate in meetings, consider all phases of successful meetings: preparing for them, running them, and following up afterward.

Planning for Meetings

As with other communication responsibilities, running effective meetings starts with planning. For routine meetings, you should spend 30 to 60 minutes preparing.[30] For especially important and nonroutine meetings, you may need to spend at least several hours or days planning.

Essential Questions   Planning for meetings requires strategy, scheduling, and coordination. At a minimum, you should answer the following questions in your preparations:[31]

- What is the purpose of the meeting? What outcomes do I expect?
- Who should attend?
- When should the meeting be scheduled?
- What roles and responsibilities should people at the meeting have?
- What will be the agenda?
- What materials should I distribute prior to the meeting?
- When and how should I invite others?
- What logistical issues do I need to take care of (reserving rooms, getting equipment, printing materials)?

As you answer these questions, keep in mind your purpose and ensure that your plans focus on productive outcomes. Also, think about how scheduling will impact productivity. Generally, you should avoid meetings, especially brainstorming meetings, during the least productive times of the day (usually the afternoon). Typically, most employees are at their best performance in the morning (see Figure 3.6).[32] As far as timing during the week, Tuesdays are overwhelmingly considered the most productive days. By contrast, Fridays are the least productive days.

In addition, think about the materials you should send ahead of time. Often, you will make requests of various meeting participants before the meeting to help them prepare. Plan to send materials sufficiently far in advance to give people enough time to do required preparation.

As you plan, consider the type of meeting you want. Meetings can be broadly categorized as coordination meetings or problem-solving meetings. **Coordination meetings** primarily focus on discussing roles, goals, and accountabilities. **Problem-solving meetings** typically involve brainstorming about how to address and solve a particular work problem. In actuality, nearly all meetings involve both coordination and problem solving. However, coordination meetings typically include many agenda items with a reasonable expectation of accomplishing each item in the allocated time. Problem-solving meetings, by contrast, involve more fluid issues that are less easily classified as discrete agenda items and that are less easily given time allotments. For especially difficult

LO3.2 Describe and demonstrate approaches to planning, running, and following up on meetings.

Visit http://connect. mheducation.com for an exercise on this topic.

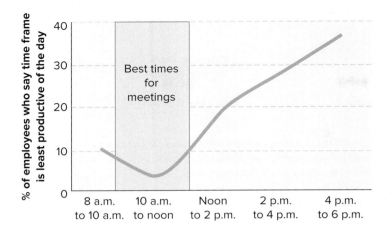

FIGURE 3.6

Least Productive Parts
of the Workday

Source: Adapted from Perrotte, K.
(2018, August 18). Accountemps
survey: Employee output is
weakest late in the day. Retrieved
from www.newswire.ca/news-
releases/accountemps-survey-
employee-output-is-weakest-late-
in-the-day-545226522.html.

issues (i.e., periods of transition such as with mergers), some teams commit to meeting at the same time each day and without a preset agenda until they clearly define the issues at hand.[33]

Creating and Distributing the Agenda

Agendas provide structure for meetings. For most meetings, preparing and distributing an agenda ahead of time allows each meeting participant to form expectations and prepare.[34]

Most agendas should include items to be covered, time frames, goals and/or expected outcomes, roles, and materials needed. You can foster more effective meetings by getting others involved in the agenda-creation process. For example, at least several days in advance, ask meeting participants for agenda items they want included. Typically, you should send out the final agenda at least one day in advance. Sending out the agenda ahead of time and inviting team members to provide agenda items increases buy-in from meeting participants. You can also consider assigning roles. For example, you might assign someone as a facilitator, a note-taker (minutes), a timer, and so on.[35]

As you develop the agenda, pay attention to the ordering of items so that it flows much like you would expect other written communications to flow from point to point. Also, consider placing those agenda items of most importance near the beginning. This way, if items take longer than expected and you are forced to shelve some items, you have addressed the highest-priority items.[36] See Figure 3.7 for an agenda for the Aicasus Tours marketing team.

Running Effective Meetings

If you've planned and prepared well for the meeting, you are in a great position to carry out your meeting objectives. Ideally, you've provided clear expectations for meeting participants—what they should have done before the meeting and what they can expect in terms of content and length of the meeting. Once the meeting arrives, you have several options for achieving productive outcomes.

Create Tradition, Culture, and Variety

Most meetings at Starbucks Coffee start with a customer story.[37] Many manufacturing companies start meetings with safety stories. You can create traditions that take only moments or minutes but that reinforce the core values of your organization. These types of traditions create a common sense of purpose (one of the key ingredients of effective teamwork) and are a light way to open people up at the start of meetings.[38]

Set Expectations and Follow the Agenda

Take a few moments to explain the purpose of the meeting and what you hope to accomplish. You may also want to set some ground rules, such as your expectations for others to participate, how much time

**Agenda
Components**

- Agenda items
- Time frames*
- Goals/expected
  outcomes
- Roles
- Materials needed

*optional

FIGURE 3.7

Sample Meeting
Agenda

Marketing Team
Meeting Agenda

Date: November 9   **Start Time:** 8:30 a.m.   **End Time:** 10:00 a.m.

Purposes
 1. Discuss the latest research and infromation about VR headsets.
 2. Evaluate client satisfaction on our homestay tours.
 3. Explore new options for cultural history tours.

To Do Before Meeting (stored in #MarketResearch channel in Slack)
 1. Read the finance team's ROI estimates (labeled "VR-Headset-Projections.xlsx")
 2. Study our client survey with attiudes toward VR (labeled "VR-Client-Survey.pdf")
 3. Prepare three new tour or service ideas with a focus on cultural history tours

Desired Outcome: Create action items to complete within the next month (by December 15). At our
December 15 meeting retreat, we will develop our annual marketing plan, which will include
priorities for new tours and services.

Agenda Item 1: *VR Headsets* **(25 minutes)**
 • Summary of financial projections from finance team (Jeff)   5 min.
 • Summary of client survey about VR (Barbara)   5 min.
 • Group discussion of findings and options   10 min.
 • Develop action items   5 min.

Agenda Item 2: *Client Satisfaction on Homestay Tours* **(20 minutes)**
 • Summary of findings from client satisfaction survey (Jeff)   5 min.
 • Group discussion of findings and options   10 min.
 • Develop action items   5 min.

Agenda Item 3: *New Options for Cultural History Tours* **(40 minutes)**
 • Each person presents three ideas for new tours or services   30 min.
 • Group reactions to the new ideas   10 min.

Summarize Action Items   5 min.

Participants: Andrea Garcia, Nancy Jeffreys, Barbara Brookshire, **Kip Yamada (note-taker)**,
           Jeff Anderton, Kailey Chang

---

to take with comments, or how to deal with differences of opinion. Part of the ground rules may involve assigning the roles of facilitator, timer, and note-taker. They may include protocol for use of mobile phones and other potentially disruptive electronic equipment. You may also point out whether certain issues are considered confidential and shouldn't be discussed outside the meeting.[39]

For most meetings, keep the discussion focused on agenda items and stick to allotted times. Some meeting participants may become uninterested or annoyed if they perceive the meeting as unstructured or off schedule.[40]

Encourage Participation and Expression of Ideas   Each meeting should have a facilitator. The **facilitator** acts from a neutral position to get each person to participate in the conversation and ensure that each agenda item is properly discussed. Facilitators should acknowledge, check for understanding, paraphrase and summarize, not judge, ask for elaboration, and get everyone involved. Sometimes, this may require using explicit phrases such as "I'd like each person to take two minutes to . . ." For routine meetings, the facilitator is often the organizer.[41]

The issue of neutrality for facilitating is critical. If others view the facilitator as predisposed toward certain positions or perspectives, they are less likely to express their real thoughts. This is especially the case when the facilitator is a person of higher authority.

Making your meetings "safe" for each team member requires conscious effort. After all, in surveys of nearly 2.5 million employees, just 15 percent of respondents agreed that *work teams function in a safe, "win-win" work environment,* and just 17 percent agreed that *work teams have mutual understanding and creative dialogue.*[42] As a meeting leader, encourage debate but defuse any comments that are perceived as noncollegial. The art of encouraging discussion but avoiding arguments takes time. In meetings, it requires that you initially foster disassociation but end with association. Research has shown that teams that have more dissent during meetings reach higher-quality decisions. By opening discussion to all available information and options, teams tend to adopt the best options more often and become more committed to the decisions.[43]

In problem-solving meetings, the leader must establish a pattern for discussion and debate. Generally, the first focus is getting agreement on the definition of the problem. Then, the focus switches to the history of the problem and its current impacts. Third, participants consider the causes and future consequences if the problem is not solved. Finally, the group is ready to brainstorm options for addressing the problem.[44]

Build Consensus and a Plan of Action   The primary purpose of meetings is to create a plan of action. When all the ideas have been stated, the team must evaluate the alternatives and create an action plan. For important decisions, the group should attempt to build consensus around a decision-making approach that prioritizes factors such as timelines, financial resources, and so on. You may find it difficult to build consensus on the bigger issues. Start by building consensus on smaller ones.[45]

Closing the Meeting   One priority should be to end the meeting on time. Before ending the meeting, summarize what you have accomplished. In just a few minutes, you can recap action items that the team has agreed on. Make sure the roles and assignments are clear for each of these action items, to establish accountabilities for follow-up.[46]

After a meeting ends (even for those you do not lead), you should mentally evaluate your performance. Consider these questions:[47]

- How much information, analysis, and interpretation did I provide?
- Did I communicate my ideas even if they conflicted with someone else's?
- Did I participate in the implementation of the timeline? Did I meet deadlines?
- Did I facilitate the decision-making process? Or did I just go with the flow?

Dealing with Difficult People   Inevitably, you will work on teams with disruptive members. They may consistently display a negative attitude, refuse to participate, interrupt others, make irrelevant comments, make condescending remarks about other participants or their ideas, or dominate with excessively lengthy comments. One of the best ways to prevent such behaviors is to provide strong leadership with a clear agenda, goals, and roles. If the problem persists, pull that team member aside. Talk about the disruptive behaviors, and explain how the behavior impacts group performance. Consider making specific and polite but firm requests such as the following: "At the next meeting, please give people more time to explain themselves."[48]

Following Up after Meetings

Follow up by distributing the minutes of the meeting as soon as possible (as a memo, in an email, in a meetings folder on the corporate intranet, or as part of a team blog or wiki). Minutes of the meeting should include the date and time, team members present,

---

Meeting Follow-Up/Minutes Components

- Date and time
- Team members present
- Meeting roles
- Key decisions
- Key discussion points (optional)
- Open issues (optional)
- Action items and deadlines

decisions, key discussion points, open issues, and action items and related deadlines. You can also include names of people who were invited but were absent and the assigned roles (i.e., note-taker). The minutes serve as a record of what your team accomplished. Figure 3.8 provides an example of meeting minutes.

If you are the team leader, make sure your team members follow through on action items. Follow up as soon as possible on those issues you were not able to resolve during the meeting. If each participant knows you will follow up, he or she will perceive the meeting as important. If you do not follow up, team members are more likely to view the meeting as a waste of time.

Also, as a team leader, you will likely hold online meetings from time to time. Online meetings have become increasingly popular with improved technology and more dispersed teams. Principles of face-to-face meetings apply well to online meetings. However, online meetings present other challenges and benefits, the topic we discuss in the Technology Tips box.

FIGURE 3.8

Sample Meeting Minutes

Marketing Team
November 9 Meeting Minutes

Date: November 9 **Start Time:** 8:30 a.m. **End Time:** 10:00 a.m.

Agenda Item 1: *VR Headsets*

Discussion: Jeff and Barbara presented research projections and survey findings about VR technologies to supplement group tours. The group agreed that we don't understand market demand for VR services enough to make any concrete investment plans.

Action Items	Responsibility	Completion Time
• Plan a set of nonintrusive field tests with VR headsets	Barbara, Jeff	December 15
• Work with VR vendors and software developers to plan small-scale field tests	Barbara	December 15

Agenda Item 2: *Client Satisfaction on Homestay Tours*

Discussion: Jeff presented client satisfaction surveys from homestay tours. The group concluded we need to improve our homestay services for the Japan, Indonesia, and Peru tours.

Action Items	Responsibility	Completion Time
• Develop plans to identify more suitable homestay families	Kip	December 15
• Develop plans for improving communication with homestay families.	Nancy, Barbara, Kip	December 15

Agenda Item 3: *New Options for Cultural History Tours*

Discussion: Team members shared their ideas for cultural history tours. We selected five tours for further exploration: (a) DNA-related family history; (b) musical performances at famous cathedrals; (c) Silicon Valley (for the Chinese market); (d) history of Chinese food; and (e) Egyptian archeology.

Action Items	Responsibility	Completion Time
• Develop ideas for DNA-related family history and muscial performances at famous cathedrals tours	Kip, Barbara	December 15
• Develop ideas for Silicon Valley tour	Andrea, Kailey	December 15
• Develop ideas for history of Chinese food and Egyptian archeology tours	Nancy, Kailey	December 15

Participants: Andrea Garcia, Nancy Jeffreys, Barbara Brookshire, **Kip Yamada (note-taker)**, Jeff Anderton, Kailey Chang

⏻ Technology Tips

ONLINE MEETINGS

Business professionals increasingly use online meetings for many purposes: to bring together work teams that have members in different locations, allow marketers and account representatives to show their products and services to customers and clients, provide training to employees, give manufacturers and suppliers a forum to work out quality issues from a distance, and deliver many other opportunities.

Steve Cole/Getty Images

Online meetings allow you to conduct a meeting in a true, multimedia format. Typically, they are appropriate when people are far away, when the group is large (25 or more), when you feel too emotional or nervous for a face-to-face meeting, when you've already established trust with meeting participants, or when the agenda is fairly routine. Consider face-to-face meetings if possible when trust is not yet established or when discussing sensitive topics such as bad news or big changes.

Learn about the many functions of meeting software and its limitations. There are many software platforms for online meetings, including commercial options such as Zoom, Skype, WebEx, and GoToMeeting, as well as platforms developed in-house. These software platforms include many functions, such as video calling, picture and drawing windows, screen sharing, virtual breakout rooms, instant polls, email, chats, slide shows, electronic whiteboards, discussion boards, shared folders, and a variety of online resources. Learn about each of these tools, experiment with them, and make sure you use them to accomplish the key objectives of your meetings.

Although online meetings provide an increasingly rich communication environment, they rarely attain the connection that face-to-face meetings do. You often encounter a lack of visual cues and thus are less able to develop trust and rapport. Also, participants can easily detach from the meeting and focus on other things going on in their own offices. So, you confront more difficulty directing or monitoring the behavior of meeting participants. Another limitation is that many meeting participants may not know how to use the meeting software well. Similarly, you may encounter technology failures. Most of these limitations can be overcome by using the many features of meeting software. Your job is to know how to use these features naturally so that you can employ them while orchestrating an effective meeting.

Prepare. Typically, you should follow roughly the same process for online meetings as face-to-face meetings: preparing an agenda, encouraging everyone to express their ideas, creating action items, and so on (see the discussion of effective meetings in the team communication section). However, since you are using meeting software with participants in many locations, you need extra time to plan how you will coordinate and keep people engaged. Consider assigning roles such as producer and moderator. Also, you should rehearse for important meetings and make sure technical details are functioning correctly before the meeting.

Discuss ways of documenting and distributing the discussion. Typically, face-to-face meetings are fairly straightforward to document: One person records the action items and/or minutes. This written document can be distributed to everyone on the team in a single format and serves as a reminder of important goals and action items and eventually a standard for follow-up. By contrast, online meetings generally involve many types of media. Plan how you will document the meeting and make it available to meeting participants later. A variety of software applications are available to document decisions, to-do items, and deadlines.

Your challenge: Hold a virtual meeting with a student team. Take notes immediately following the meeting about how effective the meeting was. How could you have improved the meeting? How could you have prepared better? How could you have facilitated better decision making? How will you follow up?

Working in Virtual Teams

LO3.3 Explain the principles of effective virtual team communication.

Visit **http://connect. mheducation.com** for an exercise on this topic.

Organizations increasingly rely on virtual teams to complete projects, initiatives, and a variety of other tasks. These virtual teams generally consist of team members located at various offices (including home offices) and rely almost entirely on virtual technologies to work with one another. One survey showed that about 80 percent of professionals in multinational companies report working on a team that is located in different locations. In fact, 64 percent of these professionals work with team members located in other countries. Of those in virtual teams, roughly 46 percent have never met their teammates in person, and another 30 percent meet in person about once per year.[49] In practice, nearly all teams, including teams located in the same office, rely on virtual technologies for a substantial amount of their communication.

Virtual teams are often created because they cost less, are more convenient, and help assemble experts who are not located in the same office. Many times, virtual teams can be more productive and effective than co-located, in-person teams (we'll call these *traditional teams*). However, virtual teams present a variety of unique challenges. Compared to professionals in traditional teams, virtual team members are more likely to experience the following challenges: feeling isolated, not feeling connected to team members, not being able to read nonverbal cues, managing conflict, making decisions, and expressing opinions (introverts generally feel more comfortable expressing opinions in virtual teams; extroverts generally feel more comfortable expressing opinions in traditional teams). Virtual teamwork is further complicated by issues such as time zone differences, language differences, and communication technologies.[50] In addition to the principles for working effectively in traditional teams, consider the following tips when working in virtual teams.[51]

Focus on Building Trust at Each Stage of Your Virtual Team

Compared to traditional teams, virtual teams typically find it more challenging to maintain trust over the duration of their work together. One way of ensuring trust within the team is living up to the characteristics most sought after in virtual teammates. Professionals in virtual teams rank the following characteristics as most important among virtual teammates: willingly sharing information, being proactively engaged, and collaborating.[52] Typically, you can take actions across the entire life cycle of a virtual team that bolster your credibility and help establish trust within your virtual team with a focus on competence, caring, and character (compared to traditional teams, research has shown that virtual teams far less often go through the storming stage).[53] In Table 3.1, you can see various strategies for displaying competence, caring, and character at each stage of virtual teamwork to build and maintain trust within the team.[54]

Meet in Person If Possible

The most effective, long-term virtual teams meet in person at the beginning of projects to help the team members build rapport. These kickoffs for virtual teams help team members do the tricky work of forming and norming. Not only are these stages of teamwork more natural for most professionals to accomplish in person, these meetings generally force team members to take enough time together to clearly articulate goals and objectives, values, responsibilities, communication protocol, and other elements of a team charter.

Get to Know One Another

For all teams, this is important. For virtual teams, this is even more important. Especially in the early stages, forming and norming, virtual team members should schedule plenty of time to bond with one another. This social cement pays off later on with stronger and more aligned teamwork. Throughout the duration of projects, virtual teams

TABLE 3.1

Maintaining Trust over the Life of a Virtual Team Project

Stage of Project	Elements of Trust	Key Actions to Foster Trust
Forming	Competence	• Asking and responding to questions about one another's professional accomplishments, strengths, and weaknesses
	Caring	• Showing interest in teammates • Expressing a desire to work with teammates
	Character	• Making commitments to high team performance • Discussing shared values for a team charter
Norming	Competence	• Demonstrating strong performance in early deliverables • Preparing well for initial meetings
	Caring	• Sharing information, offering to help teammates, and staying accessible to teammates • Responding promptly to the requests of teammates
	Character	• Living up to commitments in the team charter
Performing	Competence	• Completing all tasks with excellence
	Caring	• Encouraging and supporting teammates to complete tasks near final deadlines when the pressure is highest
	Character	• Ensuring all team outcomes are fair to team members and stakeholders

should find ways to communicate spontaneously and even socialize in virtual environments. Colleagues who work in the same location often rely on informal, *watercooler* conversations to get to know each other better and discuss emerging opportunities in a relaxed environment. Effective virtual teams find ways to establish *virtual watercoolers*, where teammates regularly and spontaneously interact. Many tools exist to help virtual teams do this (we discuss some of these tools in Chapter 8 about social media for business communication).

Use Collaborative Technologies

Over the past 25 years, virtual teams have relied primarily on phone calls, teleconferences, and email to communicate with one another. Some, but not most, virtual teams have also used videoconferences. In the past 5 years, however, there are far more social collaboration tools that allow virtual team members to communicate and collaborate more efficiently (we discuss some of these tools in Chapter 8 about social media for business communication). However, the many collaboration technologies available create a challenge for many professionals. In fact, 43 percent of virtual team members feel "confused and overwhelmed" by the many choices.[55] Virtual team members should schedule time to agree about which communication technologies to use and ensure team members who are less confident with these tools get training.

Choose an Active Team Leader

The primary obstacle to virtual team performance is the lack of regular communication. Team leaders should ensure frequent contact and communication to keep the team moving toward its goals. One strategy many virtual teams use is to periodically rotate team leaders. This helps energize the team and keeps team leaders from burning out. This strategy also helps develop leadership skills of team members.

Run Effective Virtual Meetings

Professionals in virtual teams report that the primary challenge of virtual team meetings is not enough time to build relationships (90 percent). They also cite the following major challenges: the need to make decisions too quickly (80 percent); differing leadership styles (77 percent), unclear decision-making rules (76 percent), and lack of participation (75 percent).[56] Consider the following tips to make your virtual meetings more productive:[57]

- *Start the meeting with social chat.* One long-time expert and observer of virtual teams, Keith Ferrazzi, recommends the "Take 5" strategy—for the first five minutes of the meeting, each person takes a turn to share how he or she is doing.
- *Start with a contentious question.* Opening meetings with energetic and lively conversation causes virtual team members to embrace the meeting.
- *Ask "what do you think about" questions.* Virtual teams—perhaps more than traditional teams—are able to profit from diversity. Make sure your team is capturing the perspectives of all team members.
- *Make sure each team member is involved.* Some team members are more comfortable and outspoken using virtual technologies. Make sure all team members get opportunities to share their views. You might even consider protocols for taking turns in your discussions.
- *Articulate views precisely.* Most virtual teams focus on efficiency in meetings. This forces you to prepare carefully ahead of time and state your views precisely when you have the chance.
- *Take minutes in real time.* In real-time virtual meetings, you can take minutes—particularly those related to decisions—in real time so that meeting participants can comment on and correct information during the meeting. This practice often leads to more accurate recollections of the meeting, more buy-in from team members, and a higher likelihood that action items get accomplished.
- *Focus on your teammates and avoid multitasking.* Up to 90 percent of virtual team members admit they multitask during virtual team meetings.[58] Many new collaboration tools allow teammates to participate in several conversations at a time during an online meeting. Also, most virtual teams report heavily using instant messaging (IM) and texting during virtual team meetings. In many cases, this allows side conversations that help the meeting operate more efficiently. However, there are several risks. First, this may distract focus from participating in the larger meeting. Second, it can lead to cliquish subgroups.[59] Make sure you focus sufficiently on your teammates.
- *Use video when possible.* Using video has many benefits. First and foremost, it allows virtual team members to better interpret one another's verbal and nonverbal cues. Also, this real-time conversation generally leads to faster decision making. Finally, an important but often unintended consequence of videoconferences is that virtual team members are less likely to multitask. Most virtual team members think video communication makes the most sense but rarely actually do it. One recent survey of professionals in virtual teams showed that 72 percent believed video would make team communication more effective. Yet, only 34 percent of virtual team members used video to communicate with one another.[60]

Group Writing

LO3.4 Describe strategies for effective group writing.

You will undoubtedly have many opportunities to co-create or co-author business reports and other documents during your career. The emphasis on teams in today's workplace is one reason group writing is becoming more prevalent. Many new technologies make this process easier and more efficient than at any time in the past. Yet, creating a strong, precise, and coherent document with many writers is challenging. As you write with teams or other groups, consider applying the following tips.

Start Right Away

One of the major obstacles to nearly all good writing is not starting soon enough. Developing ideas well near a deadline is rarely successful. This is even more problematic when many members of a team have competing views about the direction of a writing project close to a deadline.

Work Together at the Planning Stage

In Chapter 5, we will discuss the three stages of developing business messages: planning, writing, and reviewing. For all strong writing, planning is the most important stage—it's the stage where you carefully think about audiences and their needs, develop compelling ideas that are well-reasoned, and think about how to frame your message for the most impact. Planning is even more important for group writing. As the group plans together, it should develop clear and specific purposes and goals, clarify and define the basic problems and issues together, prioritize finding certain pieces of information, identify subject-matter experts, and delegate roles for researching and writing. Generally, you should spend a significant amount of time together (*at least* one to two hours for student team writing projects) before delegating independent work. When team members work independently during the planning stage, they often waste time and energy working with different purposes, goals, and expectations.

Make Sure Your Roles and Contributions Are Fair

Early in the process, your group should clearly discuss the roles and expectations you have for one another—make sure part of this conversation involves splitting up contributions and time commitments equally. You might consider placing this in a team charter.

Stay Flexible and Open

As a group, it's important to remain open to change during the course of a writing project. As you start gathering information and drafting initial findings and conclusions, you may recognize that earlier decisions about purpose, direction, major points, and roles aren't strong or practical. Instead of staying silent and forging ahead with the writing project, groups should constantly reevaluate whether they need to modify their original plans.

Meet in Real Time Consistently and Ensure the Writing Reflects the Views of the Group

You can accomplish a lot of coordinated writing working separately. However, you'll inevitably need to make some hard decisions as the writing project evolves. These tough decisions are often difficult to manage without holding real-time conversations about the direction and content of your project.

Discuss How You Will Edit the Document Together

Make sure all team members discuss and agree about the technologies you'll use as you write your document. Some people prefer sharing offline word processing files (in programs such as Microsoft Word) with one another. Some people prefer cloud-based documents (such as those on Google Drive) that can be edited in real time by all members of the group. Pay attention to version control (so that some members aren't simultaneously editing different versions of the same document). Discuss how your team will use comments and track changes within the document. Also, be clear about rules for overwriting one another's work. Most programs allow backtracking to find former versions of the document. However, overwriting the work of others, without talking to them first, can lead to frustration.

Finally, make sure your group is clear about the purposes of each round of revisions. Generally, you should first revise with a focus on the strength of your ideas and how well these ideas match the needs of your audience. Then, you should focus on how smoothly the various sections of your paper flow together. Next, you should consider issues such as formatting, ease of reading, and language mechanics.

Consider a Single Group Member to Polish the Final Version and Ensure a Consistent Voice

Many groups use this strategy effectively. Make sure you choose the right person for this role. Also, avoid viewing this as a single person's work. Consider having the whole group together for this process so that as your designated writer polishes the document, each group member is present to offer input and confirmation.

Managing Difficult Conversations

LO3.5 Explain basic principles for handling difficult conversations.

Mc Graw Hill connect

Visit http://connect. mheducation.com for an exercise on this topic.

Business professionals routinely—often on a daily basis—encounter difficult conversations, especially when working in teams and collaborating with others. Difficult conversations are approached with apprehension, nervousness, anxiety, and even fear. Douglas Stone, Bruce Patton, and Sheila Heen of the Harvard Negotiation Project have spent three decades training business professionals to confront difficult conversations. They define difficult conversations as follows:

> Any time we feel vulnerable or our self-esteem is implicated, when the issues at stake are important and the outcome is uncertain, when we care deeply about what is being discussed or about the people with whom we are discussing it, there is potential for us to experience the conversation as difficult.[61]

Difficult conversations often center on disagreements, conflict, and bad news. Common types of difficult conversations for entry-level business professionals include receiving a bad performance review, having ideas rejected, critiquing a colleague, giving feedback to a boss, correcting someone, approaching rule breakers about their behavior, talking to a slacker on a group project, and dealing with office politics.[62]

Many people prefer to avoid difficult conversations because they want to avoid hurting the feelings of others, want to avoid conflict, or for other reasons. Many business professionals believe that honesty during moments of conflict may backfire and hurt their careers. However, this is not necessarily the case. Those business managers and executives who approach difficult conversations in a timely, honest, and caring manner typically accomplish much more professionally. After working with corporate clients for nearly three decades, one research team concluded that the most influential people are those who can effectively handle difficult conversations:[63]

> As it turns out, you don't have to choose between being honest and being effective. You don't have to choose between candor and your career. People who routinely hold crucial conversations and hold them well are able to express controversial and even risky opinions in a way that gets heard. Their bosses, peers, and direct reports listen without becoming defensive or angry.[64]

In this section, we briefly present basic, tried-and-true principles for handling difficult conversations in the workplace. You will notice that these principles rely on active listening with a learner mind-set. You can see several examples of how to put these principles into practice (see Table 3.2 and Figure 3.9). These examples relate to Kip and Nancy from the opening case. Kip and Nancy hold strong grievances toward one other because of a past disagreement about issuing refunds to business travelers. They avoid one another when possible. Their poor working relationship hinders productivity and makes work less pleasant for them and their team.

Embrace Difficult Conversations and Assume the Best in Others

Most people back away from uncomfortable or unpleasant conversations. This is particularly the case when we feel we have a lot to gain but risk heavy losses if it doesn't go right.

TABLE 3.2

Ineffective and Effective Approaches to Difficult Conversations

Approaches	Ineffective Examples	Effective Examples
Initiating the conversation Photodisc/Getty Images John A Rizzo/ Pixtal/SuperStock	**Nancy:** I want to go over your mishandling of the refunds several months ago. I have some ideas for how we can avoid this kind of problem in the future. This approach starts with blame. Worse yet, it frames the conversation as Nancy's story.	**Nancy:** Kip, let's talk about how the refunds were handled for several group tours a few months ago. First off, I want to apologize for speaking so harshly without hearing your side first. Since then, I feel like we haven't worked as well together. I think we can figure out a better way to make sure we're on the same page, and I also think we can figure out ways to avoid misleading our clients. When you authorized the discounts, I never heard all the details. Do you mind telling me about some of the clients who were upset and what you did to address their concerns? This approach is effective for several reasons. Nancy apologizes for her harsh words. She declares her intent: to work together better and come up with solutions. Nancy expresses her intent of discussing solutions that take into account both hers and Kip's perspectives (shared story). She invites Kip to tell his story.
Disagreeing diplomatically	**Nancy:** Look, you clearly overstepped your authority. You know there's language in the promotional materials that itineraries change, and you know we're not responsible when changes happen. You're clearly not acting in the company's interests when you give refunds when we're not at fault. Nancy does not recognize Kip's explanation or feelings as having any merit, which places Kip on the defensive and could lead him to resentment. Nancy projects a tone of blame by consistently using you-statements.	**Nancy:** Thanks for telling me how you felt. I agree that at the time I should not have snapped at you. I do want to explain why I thought you should have consulted with me prior to making the refunds. We have clear language in our promotional materials that the itineraries may change slightly. In my view, this doesn't require us to give discounts. We also have policies that require you to consult me before making any major refunds. Now, I understand your perspective. I also know that you were acting with the best interests of our clients and our company in mind. Nancy validates Kip's perspective by understanding how he *felt*. She explains why she thinks he overstepped his authority with a variety of I-statements.
Avoiding exaggeration and either/or approaches	**Kip:** I can never approach you with client issues. You're always fixated on following the small print in the promotional materials to a tee, even when you know clients don't read that. You never try to understand the client's perspective. Your approach is not working, and it's losing us money. Kip repeatedly exaggerates the frequency of Nancy's actions with words such as *never* and *always*. He takes an either/or approach by saying Nancy's approach doesn't work.	**Kip:** I'm hesitant to bring up client issues with you. I think sometimes you take a tough approach to clients, even when they have legitimate complaints. I can think of several cases when top clients started booking different tours after you denied their requests for partial refunds. In each case, I agreed with their reasoning and understood why they were upset. In the end, I think we end up losing revenue when we deny partial refunds to our clients who don't receive the tour stops and tour experiences we promised. Kip states his real feelings of frustration and explains his point of view. By using phrases such as *sometimes* and *I think*, he avoids a right-versus-wrong comparison between his and Nancy's approaches.

FIGURE 3.9

Sample Approach to a Difficult Conversation

Nancy: Kip, let's talk about how the refunds were handled for several group tours a few months ago. First off, I want to apologize for speaking so harshly without hearing your side first. Since then, I feel like we haven't worked as well together. I think we can figure out a better way to make sure we're on the same page, and I also think we can figure out ways to avoid misleading our clients.

When you authorized the discounts, I never heard all the details. Do you mind telling me about some of the clients who were upset and what you did to address their concerns?

Kip: Well, I guess I think you overreacted. You were upset that I didn't get your permission before issuing the refunds. But I thought I was acting within my authority. The clients were upset we didn't include several stops listed in the brochures we sent them.

So, I didn't see a need to get your permission. We had clients who did not receive what we promised in the promotional material. I thought giving the refunds was the right thing to do. And, I felt that you didn't even give me time to explain myself.

But, it's more than that. I'm hesitant to bring up client issues with you. I think sometimes you take a tough approach to clients, even when they have legitimate complaints. I can think of several cases when top clients started booking different tours after you denied their requests for partial refunds. In each case, I agreed with their reasoning and understood why they were upset. In the end, I think we end up losing revenue when we deny partial refunds to our clients who don't receive the tour stops and tour experiences we promised.

Nancy: Thanks for telling me how you felt. I agree that at the time I should not have snapped at you. I do want to explain why I thought you should have consulted with me prior to making the refunds. We have clear language in our promotional materials that the itineraries may change slightly. In my view, this doesn't require us to give discounts. We also have policies that require you to consult me before making any major refunds. Now, I understand your perspective. I also know that you were acting with the best interests of our clients and our company in mind.

Kip: So, I think you're saying that you felt I shouldn't have made the refunds because I should clear it with you first and clients should understand itineraries may change slightly. Is that right?

Nancy: That's right. It sounds to me like there are several issues. First, we need to make sure we always hear one another out immediately instead of letting hard feelings fester. I think this issue would have been resolved right away if I had listened to you right away. Second, I think we should discuss the process for handling complaints. Finally, but I think most importantly, we should re-evaluate what we believe constitutes a reasonable complaint and under what circumstances we provide refunds. I think it's safe to say that we view this differently. Kip, do you have suggestions for how we should manage these types of situations in the future?

Kip: Well, I think there are several basic cases where we should refund our guests. For example . . .

---------- *Nancy and Kip continue to talk about shared approaches and solutions.* ----------

| Nancy initiates difficult conversation |

| Kip's story |

| Nancy's story |

| Nancy and Kip's shared story |

For these reasons, difficult conversations are often emotionally challenging.[65] Successful people in the workplace do not evade difficult conversations. Those who regularly tackle them with skill and tact improve work performance for themselves and others.

One way to embrace difficult conversations is to view conflict as an opportunity.[66] That is, the exchange of perspectives and competing ideas reflects open and honest communication. If there is no conflict, employees are likely not voicing their true perspectives. Generally, colleagues tend to respect one another more when they know they can safely disagree.

To make a difficult conversation safe, follow the advice of Jacqueline Kosecoff, CEO of Prescription Solutions:

> Assume positive intent. It's one of the ways to . . . keep communication on the high road. Perhaps somebody was misunderstood, or they misheard something. You have to go back and ask for the context, and it's very likely to be simply a misunderstanding. And if you listen, it can be resolved. And it tends to, I think, breed a lot more trust and respect among us.[67]

Adopt a Learning Stance and Commit to Hearing Everyone's Story

Earlier in the chapter, we distinguished between the judger and learner mind-sets. In emotionally charged, high-stakes conversations, approaching the conversation with a learner mind-set will often lead to productive outcomes. You can do this by avoiding the message-delivery stance.[68] Because difficult conversations typically involve unresolved problems, each person should participate in a joint process of understanding the problems and creating solutions. The message-delivery stance implies that you have nothing to learn from the other person involved in the conversation. In sensitive situations, others will resist your attempts to impose solutions.

The learning stance involves a commitment to understanding others' **stories**—their retrospective versions of interpersonal interactions or their explanations of business successes and failures. In difficult conversations, invite others to describe their views and feelings of disputed events. When people have the opportunity to share their stories, they are often less resistant to change and more accommodating of the views of others. Sharing stories with one another can lead to shared interpretations of events, empathy, and new ways of viewing workplace relationships and business possibilities.[69]

One major benefit of allowing all people involved in a difficult conversation to share their views is buy-in. Research has shown that when everyone involved shares their ideas, they tend to be more committed to the ultimate decision of the group, even when their ideas are not adopted. When they remain silent, they tend not to commit to the decision of the group.[70]

Stay Calm and Overcome Noise

Few business professionals prepare for difficult conversations. And because emotions run high during such conversations, they often do not go well. Participants face a lot of internal noise, and this muddies rational thinking: They are nervous about the outcome of the encounter for themselves and others, and they often feel incapable of constructively expressing all their thoughts and emotions.

During these difficult encounters, high emotional intelligence is crucial. Self-awareness is the foundation. When you feel angry or defensive, you need to ask yourself, "What do I really want?" and "How is what I'm feeling affecting how I'm responding?" By consciously asking yourself these questions, you are redirecting activity to the rational part of your brain. This de-escalates physical threats and allows you to respond more rationally.

While you should pay a lot of attention to your own emotions, intentions, and goals, you must also focus on those with whom you are speaking. They are likely experiencing similar emotions. Apply your active listening skills to feel and show empathy. If someone gets angry, view this as an opportunity. Do not return the anger, but rather help the other person channel the anger appropriately and rationally. Consider asking your conversational

---

Principles of Difficult Conversations

- Embrace difficult conversations.
- Assume the best in others.
- Adopt a learning stance.
- Stay calm/ overcome noise.
- Find common ground.
- Disagree diplomatically.
- Avoid exaggeration and either/or approaches.

Components of Difficult Conversations

Steps
1. Start well/declare your intent.
2. Listen to their story.
3. Tell your story.
4. Create a shared story.

partner to sit down or offer a drink. As you summarize his or her thoughts and feelings, you defuse strong emotions and make the conversation constructive and rational.[71]

Find Common Ground

Finding common ground seems like obvious advice, but it's not easy to do during emotionally charged moments when you feel attacked. Finding common ground will help you and others accomplish two things. Emotionally, it lessens the perceived distance between you, and it may even lead to bonding. Rationally, it helps you analyze the issues at hand in a way that will likely lead to mutually acceptable solutions. You can find common ground in a number of areas, including facts, conclusions, feelings, goals, and values.

Disagree Diplomatically

Difficult conversations involve different perspectives. To create a learning conversation rather than a defensive and judgmental one, find ways to disagree diplomatically. By disagreeing well, you lessen the resistance that others have to you and your views. Typically, you can disagree diplomatically by validating the views and feelings of others and using I-statements. **Validating** others means that you recognize their perspectives and feelings as credible or legitimate. It does not necessarily mean that you agree. **I-statements** begin with phrases such as *I think*, *I feel*, or *I believe.* During disagreements or difficult conversations, I-statements soften comments to sound more conciliatory and flexible and less blaming and accusatory (see examples in Table 3.2).

Avoid Exaggeration and Either/Or Approaches

As you navigate difficult conversations, avoid making them overly simplistic. Usually, you are encountering complex business and relationship issues. Also, by simplifying your story, you often inadvertently cause others to become defensive because you are in effect disputing their story or challenging their identity.

Two ways of oversimplifying your approach to difficult conversations is by exaggerating and by applying either/or approaches. If you find yourself using superlatives such as *always*, *never*, *most*, or *worst*, you might be exaggerating. By choosing other words, you're more likely to present your story accurately and also validate others. Applying an either/or approach to most business communication is ineffective. For difficult conversations, it usually translates into a right-versus-wrong approach. Approaching a difficult conversation with an *I'm right, you're wrong* approach inevitably dooms the conversation. See examples of exaggeration and either/or approaches in Table 3.2.

Initiate the Conversation, Share Stories, and Focus on Solutions

Initiating a difficult conversation is stressful. You may have avoided bringing up the issue because you are nervous about how the conversation will affect your working relationships with others, or you are worried about costs to your career. Starting well is crucial. The opening moments of a difficult conversation offer a great opportunity to frame or orient the conversation for problem solving. In the opening moments, consider declaring your intent—your sincere desire to understand and find a solution that works for each of you. One obstacle to holding difficult conversations is that one or more people involved tend to judge the motives of others unfairly. Declaring your intent can reduce the likelihood of unfairly judging motives. See Table 3.2 for examples of initiating a conversation.[72]

When you initiate a difficult conversation, a common learning stance is to listen to the story of others first, then share your story, and then create a shared story.[73] When you invite others to share their perspectives and versions of events first, they recognize your sincere interest in understanding and cooperating with them. By telling your story, you allow others to see another version of reality and empathize with you. Finally, together you create a shared story. A **shared story** involves combining yours and others' experiences, perspectives, and goals into a shared approach to work. The *their story-your story-shared story* process requires a substantial time commitment, but it is well worth it. Figure 3.9 presents a simplified example of this process.

IDEAS IN ACTION

MAKING MEETINGS FUN, OPEN, AND INCLUSIVE

Tony Hsieh of Zappos

Tony Hsieh (pronounced *shay*) is the CEO of the popular online retailer Zappos, which he sold to Amazon in 2009 for $1.2 billion but continues to operate independently. Although he's a multimillionaire, he lives in an Airstream in a trailer park to stay grounded and creative. "I just love it," he says, "because there's so many random, amazing things that happen around the campfire at night."

Tannen Maury/EPA/Shutterstock

Hsieh is recognized for creating a unique culture with a focus on delighting customers and making work enjoyable. Zappos has promoted concepts such as *self-organized teams* of *radical transparency*. The core values for the company were crowdsourced from employees and include "deliver WOW through service," "create fun and a little weirdness," "build a positive team," and "build open and honest relationships with communication." To make sure employees literally run into each other, enabling candid and creative conversations, Zappos offices have about 100 square feet per employee compared to an average of 300 in most workplaces.

Meetings at Zappos are candid; a trained facilitator ensures that everyone is open and honest. Hsieh maintains, "The main thing is that everyone's voice is heard." In fact, anyone can set the agenda for meetings. Throughout your career—whether it's in an entry-level role or in a senior leader's role—you'll open many opportunities for yourself and others as you contribute to candid conversations and make meetings fun, open, and inclusive.

Sources: De Smet, A., & Gagnon, C. (2017, October). Safe enough to try: An interview with Zappos CEO Tony Hsieh. *McKinsey Quarterly*. Retrieved from https://www.mckinsey.com/business-functions/organization/our-insights/safe-enough-to-try-an-interview-with-zappos-ceo-tony-hsieh; Gelles, D. (2015, July 17). At Zappos, pushing shoes and a vision. *The New York Times*. Retrieved from https://www.nytimes.com/2015/07/19/business/at-zappos-selling-shoes-and-a-vision.html; Martin, E. (2017, May 18). Why multi-millionaire Zappos CEO Tony Hsieh chooses to live in a trailer park. *CNBC*. Retrieved from https://www.cnbc.com/2017/05/08/why-multi-millionaire-zappos-ceo-tony-hsieh-lives-in-a-trailer-park.html; Zappos 10 core values. (n.d.). Retrieved April 25, 2018, from https://www.zapposinsights.com/about/core-values.

Chapter Takeaway for *Team Communication and Difficult Conversations*

LO3.1 Explain the principles of team communication in high-performing teams.

Characteristics of High-Performing Teams

- Teams should focus first and foremost on performance.
- Teams go through natural stages to reach high performance.
- Effective teams build a work culture around values, norms, and goals.
- Effective teams meet often.
- Effective teams focus on psychological safety and ensure all voices are heard.
- Effective teams recognize and actively seek to avoid groupthink.
- Effective teams embrace diversity.
- Effective teams solve problems and generate creative solutions by going through cycles of divergence and convergence.
- Effective teams provide a lot of positive feedback and evaluate their performance often.
- Effective teams feel a common sense of purpose.

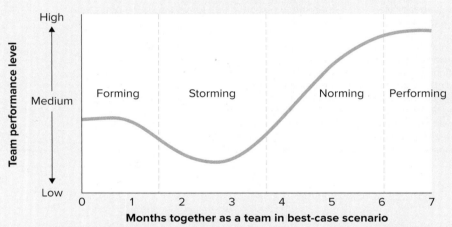

Source: Adapted from Wheelan, S. A. (1999); *Creating effective teams: A guide for members and leaders.* Thousand Oaks, CA: Sage, which examines hundreds of scholarly studies on teamwork.

LO3.2 Describe and demonstrate approaches to planning, running, and following up on meetings.

Items in an Agenda	Items in Minutes
• Agenda items • Time frames* • Expected outcomes • Roles • Materials needed *optional	• Date and time • Team members present • Meeting roles • Key decisions • Key discussion points* • Open issues* • Action items and deadlines *optional

See *examples of an agenda* in Figure 3.7 and *minutes* in Figure 3.8.

LO3.3 Explain the principles of effective virtual team communication.

Principles for Virtual Team Communication
• Focus on building trust at each stage of your virtual team.
• Meet in person if possible.
• Get to know one another.
• Use collaborative technologies.
• Choose an active team leader.
• Run effective virtual meetings.

LO3.4 Describe strategies for effective group writing.

Tips for Group Writing
• Start right away.
• Work together at the planning stage.
• Make sure your roles and contributions are fair.
• Stay flexible and open.
• Meet in real time consistently and ensure the writing reflects the views of the group.
• Discuss how you will edit the document together.
• Consider a single group member to polish the final version and ensure a consistent voice.

LO3.5 Explain basic principles for handling difficult conversations.

Principles for Difficult Conversations	Steps in Difficult Conversations
• Embrace difficult conversations.	1. Start well.
• Assume the best in others.	2. Listen to their story.
• Adopt a learning stance.	3. Tell your story.
• Stay calm/overcome noise.	4. Create a shared story.
• Find common ground.	
• Disagree diplomatically.	
• Avoid exaggeration and either/or approaches.	

See *examples of less effective and more effective statements in difficult conversations* in Table 3.2. See an *example of a difficult conversation* in Figure 3.9.

Key Terms

Discussion Exercises

3.1 Chapter Review Questions (LO3.1, LO3.2, LO3.3, LO3.4, LO3.5)

A. Research shows that under ideal conditions, most teams reach high performance in six to seven months. How can a student team that must complete a project in a few weeks to a few months go through the stages of team development more quickly and reach peak performance?

B. What is psychological safety? What do you think are the best ways to achieve it in teams?

C. Which three symptoms of groupthink do you think are most common in student teams? Explain your reasons for each symptom of groupthink.

D. In what ways can teams form a common sense of purpose? Provide examples from your experience.

E. Explain how creating and following an agenda is beneficial. Are there situations in which an agenda is not beneficial? Explain.

F. Explain the three strategies of virtual teams that you think are most important.

G. Explain the three strategies of effective group writing that you think are most important.

H. Explain what is meant by concluding a difficult conversation with a shared story.

3.2 Ideas in Action Questions (LO3.1, LO3.2)

A. Tony Hsieh says meeting should be candid, open, and honest. What are three key ways to make this happen?

B. Hsieh suggests professionals should "create fun with a little weirdness." What do you think he means by this? What does this imply for teams?

C. How does Hsieh stay creative and innovative? What habits or routines can bring out your creativity?

D. What is the value of using trained facilitators for meetings?

3.3 Speaking Up in Meetings (LO3.1, LO3.2, LO3.5)

Barbara J. Krumsiek of the Calvert Group recently talked about the style of meetings that take place in her organization:

> I think it can be a little jarring actually for people who are used to perhaps a little more civility. I think we're civil, but we're direct. I don't like meetings if my direct reports leave the room and turn to somebody and say, "Can you believe someone said that?" And so I try to explain to them by example that if you find yourself doing that when you leave the room, or shaking your head, or kicking yourself for not having said something, or thinking that there were real problems with what somebody said, next time you have to say it in the room. You have to, or you will not be the most impactful member of this team. When I first got to Calvert, there was a lot of that. And I had one of my direct reports send me an email, complaining about something somebody else said. I just got back to them and said, "I'm not going to read this because I don't see the person you're talking about CC'd on it. So if you CC them on it and send it back to me, I will deal with it." Well, I never had to get it back, because once the person really dealt with it, it was fine.[74]

Based on Krumsiek's comments, answer the following:

A. What types of expectations are there for meetings at the Calvert Group?

B. What does Krumsiek say about the nature of directness and civility at meetings? Does this imply the meetings are not civil?

C. How does Krumsiek deal with complaints about other team members?

D. What are three principles from Krumsiek's comments that you can apply to how you approach team communication?

3.4 Brainstorming at Meetings (LO3.1, LO3.2, LO3.5)

Susan Docherty, former president and managing director of General Motors, described how she and her team communicate at meetings:

> I love to brainstorm with my team around the table in my office. I like to use a big whiteboard for ideas, because when you make things visual, you encourage the team to get up there at the whiteboard and put their thoughts out there. It's one thing to say that you're inclusive, but it's a whole other thing to be inclusive. And when people come into my office, they feel welcome. My door is open. They can bring ideas. They begin to understand that, as a leader, I want to be collaborative. I don't have all the answers or all the best ideas, nor do I want to. The whiteboard also keeps great ideas in front of us, not buried in an email and not buried in a stack of papers on our desks. And it enables everybody to own what we've got to get done. People will grab a marker and put up there that we're going to do a deep dive to figure something out, and they put their name beside it. And there are lots of times where we put something on the board, and it requires a couple of people to get together to go work on it.[75]

Based on Docherty's comments and your own experiences, answer the following:

A. What strategies can you use for making meetings more visual? What are the benefits of making meetings visual?

B. What strategies can you use to make meetings more inclusive?

C. What does it mean for "everybody to own what we've got to get done"? What are a few approaches you can take to help make this happen for work teams?

3.5 *Being Friendly* **versus** *Being Friends* **for Difficult Conversations** (LO3.5)

Kasper Rorsted, CEO of Henkel, a consumer and industrial products company based in Düsseldorf, Germany, recently talked about the first time he had to be someone else's boss:

[I first became someone else's boss] in 1989, right when I got promoted from being a sales rep in the Digital Equipment Corporation to being a sales manager at the age of 27. I had about 20 people at that point in time. All but two of them were older than I was. When you're 27, you're inexperienced, so you don't know what to fear. I didn't know what I probably should have known. The first time I realized it was serious was when, after about six months, I had to lay somebody off. And then suddenly you move from the sunny side of the deal to the real deal. I remember I was sleeping very poorly for almost a week. He had a family.

So one of the lessons I learned from that, which I've been very aware of since, is to be friendly, but not a friend. I had grown up in the company and I knew everybody, so I was more a friend. But then I had to start having honest conversations with people about how they performed, and that taught me a lesson. I've always been friendly but never been friends anymore. When we have parties, I'm the one who will leave early.[76]

Based on Rorsted's comments, answer the following questions:

A. What do you think Rorsted means that he could "be friendly, but not a friend" once he became a boss and had to have difficult conversations with others?

B. Do you agree with his perspective about being friendly versus being friends? Do you think being friends makes having honest conversations in the workplace more difficult? Explain.

C. How can a person prepare for the difficult conversations necessary as one becomes a boss or supervisor?

Evaluation Exercises

3.6 Evaluating a Prior Team's Performance (LO3.1, LO3.2, LO3.3, LO3.5)

Think about a recent team or group project you were part of. Evaluate your team's performance in the following ways:

How well did your team set goals up front?

How well did your team establish norms, values, roles, and accountabilities?

To what degree did your team move through various stages of team development (forming, norming, storming, and performing)?

How effective were your meetings? Explain.

How well did all team members participate? Explain reasons for participation and nonparticipation.

How well did your team handle differences of opinion?

If you were to start the project over again, what three pieces of advice would you give to your team to drive higher performance?

3.7 Evaluating a Prior Group Writing Project (LO3.1, LO3.2, LO3.3, LO3.4, LO3.5)

Think about a recent team or group project you were part of. Evaluate your team's performance in the following ways:

A. How well did your team set goals and purposes for your writing project up front?

B. How did your team establish roles for the project? Was the rationale for these roles appropriate?

C. Did your team ever change direction during the project? Did you not change direction but wanted to? Explain how flexible your team was over the course of the project.

D. How effective were your meetings? Explain.

E. How well did all team members participate? Explain reasons for participation and nonparticipation.

F. How well did your team handle differences of opinion?

G. If you were to start the project over again, what three pieces of advice would you give to your team to create a better final report?

3.8 Describe a Difficult Conversation from a Movie or TV Episode (LO3.5)

Think about a recent movie or TV episode you watched. Select a scene that involves an interesting but difficult conversation. Ideally, select one that might occur in the workplace. Based on this scene, do the following:

A. Summarize the scene in one paragraph.

B. Analyze the difficult conversation. Explain how well the characters involved applied effective principles for communicating.

C. Describe how you can apply two strategies from the scene as you approach difficult conversations in the workplace.

3.9 Assess a Recent Difficult Conversation (LO3.5)

Think about a recent difficult conversation you had. Ideally, select a conversation that occurred in the workplace or at school. Based on this conversation, do the following:

A. Summarize the conversation in one paragraph.

B. Evaluate your and others' performance in terms of assuming the best in one another, staying calm, finding common ground, disagreeing diplomatically, avoiding exaggeration and either/or approaches, and sharing all stories (including a shared story).

C. Describe three ways you would approach the conversation differently if you did it over again.

D. Assuming you had the conversation again, what are three questions you would ask to invite a learning stance?

Application Exercises

3.10 Getting to Know Each Other (LO3.1)

In your newly formed short-term team, share responses to questions about your personal, academic, and professional backgrounds and goals. Take turns responding to questions such as the following:

Personal background and interests:

Who is a person you admire and would most want to meet? Why would you want to meet this person? What would you ask this person?

What's your favorite movie? Why?

What are some of your hobbies?

What place do you want to travel to the most? Why?

What's the craziest thing you've ever done? What is your biggest pet peeve? What's your idea of fun?

Where were you born? What is unique about that city?

Academic background:

What's the favorite class you've taken? What did you enjoy about it?

What electives would you recommend? Why?

What's your major? Why did you choose it?

Professional background and goals:

What's the best job you've had? What did you enjoy about it?

What was the best team you've worked on? Why was this team so successful?

What was the worst team you've worked on? Why was this team unsuccessful?

What companies or organizations would you want to work at? Why? What's your ideal job? Why?

3.11 Create a Team Charter (LO3.1)

For a team project you're currently working on, create a team charter. Consider using categories such as the following: purpose or mission statements, values, goals, team member roles (including leadership), tasks, ground rules, communication protocol, meeting protocol, decision-making rules, conflict resolution, and feedback mechanisms. Feel free to add your own categories as you and your team deem appropriate.

3.12 Create a Team Assessment (LO3.1)

For a team project you're currently working on, create a team assessment. You can use ratings and/or open-ended questions. Consider including items such as the following: focus on results, communication climate (including conflict resolution), accountability, commitment, and trust. Feel free to add other categories as you and your team deem appropriate.

3.13 Create an Agenda (LO3.2)

Create an agenda for a recent meeting you had or a meeting that you will have soon (it could be a work or school agenda). Feel free to make up details if necessary. Prepare the agenda with agenda items, time frames, goals, roles, and materials needed.

Language Mechanics Check

3.14 Review the comma rules C8 through C10 in Appendix A. Then, rewrite each sentence to add or remove commas where needed.

A. You must apply for this credit card offer by July 1.

B. You must apply for this credit card offer by July 1 2020.

C. You must apply for this credit card offer by July 1 2020 in order to be eligible.

D. You can apply for the credit card anytime between July 1 and July 31.

E. Please come to my office on Tuesday July 5.

F. In 2020 22 of our engineers will visit our China branch.

G. The president, of our university, was a successful entrepreneur.

H. The president of our university, a successful entrepreneur, will lead, the delegation.

I. The president, owner of three companies, believes that entrepreneurship is the key, to success.

J. The president, went out to dinner, after giving the keynote address.

Endnotes

1. Ken Blanchard Companies. (2006). *The critical role of teams.* Escondido, CA: Author.

2. Ken Blanchard Companies. (2006). *The critical role of teams.* Escondido, CA: Author.

3. Katzenbach, J. R., & Smith, D. K. (2003). The wisdom of teams: Creating the high-performance organization. New York: HarperCollins; Katzenbach, J. R., & Smith, D. K. (2005, July/August). The discipline of teams. *Harvard Business Review,* 162–171.

4. Wheelan, S. A. (1999). *Creating effective teams: A guide for members and leaders.* Thousand Oaks, CA: Sage.

5. Sunstein, C. R., & Hastie, R. (2015). *Wiser: Getting beyond groupthink to make groups smarter.* Boston. Harvard Business Press.

6. Wheelan, S. A. (1999). *Creating effective teams: A guide for members and leaders.* Thousand Oaks, CA: Sage; Tuckman, B. (1965). Developmental sequence in small groups. *Psychological Bulletin, 63*(6), 384–399. The terms *forming, storming, norming,* and *performing* are among the

most commonly used terms for stages in team development. They are used in close approximation to Susan Wheelan's stages of dependency and inclusion, counterdependency and fight, trust and structure, and work.

7. Wheelan, S. A. (1999). *Creating effective teams: A guide for members and leaders.* Thousand Oaks, CA: Sage.

8. Wheelan, S. A. (1999). *Creating effective teams: A guide for members and leaders.* Thousand Oaks, CA: Sage.

9. Byrd, J. T., & Luthy, M. R. (2010). Improving group dynamics: Creating a team charter. *Academy of Educational Leadership Journal, 14*(1), 13–26; Hillier, J., & Dunn-Jensen, L. M. (2012). Groups meet . . . teams improve: Building teams that learn. *Journal of Management Education, 37*(5), 704–733.

10. Duhigg, C. (2016, February 25). What Google learned from its quest to build the perfect team. *The New York Times Magazine.* Retrieved from www.nytimes.com/2016/02/28/magazine/what-google-learned-from-its-quest-to-build-the-perfect-team.html; Rozovsky, J. (2015, November 17). The five keys to a successful Google team. Google website. Retrieved from rework.withgoogle.com/blog/five-keys-to-a-successful-google-team/.

11. Janis, I. L. (1972). *Victims of groupthink.* Boston, MA: Houghton Mifflin; Janis, I. L. (1982). *Groupthink: Psychological studies of policy decisions and fiascoes.* Boston: Houghton Mifflin.

12. Sunstein, C. R., & Hastie, R. (2015). *Wiser: Getting beyond groupthink to make groups smarter.* Boston. Harvard Business Press.

13. Cadsby, T. (2014, July 4). The hidden enemy of productive conversations. *Harvard Business Review.* Retrieved from hbr.org/2014/07/the-hidden-enemy-of-productive-conversations.

14. Hewlett, S. A., Marshall, M., & Sherbin, L. (2013, December). How diversity can drive innovation. *Harvard Business Review, 30.*

15. Govindarajan, V., & Terwilliger, J. (2012, July 25). Yes, you can brainstorm without groupthink. *Harvard Business Review.* Retrieved from hbr.org/2012/07/yes-you-can-brainstorm-without; Harvard Business Review Staff. (2015, May 21). Measure your team's intellectual diversity. *Harvard Business Review.* Retrieved from hbr.org/2015/05/measure-your-teams-intellectual-diversity.

16. Porter, E. (2014). *Strength deployment inventory.* Carlsbad, CA: Personal Strengths Publishing; Scudder, T., & LaCroix, D. (2013). *Working with SDI: How to build effective relationships with the strength deployment inventory.* Carlsbad, CA: Personal Strengths Publishing, 7.

17. Cain, S. (2012). *Quiet: The power of introverts in a world that can't stop talking.* New York: Crown Publishers; Cain, S. (2012, January 13). The rise of the new groupthink. *The New York Times.* Retrieved from www.nytimes.com/2012/01/15/opinion/sunday/the-rise-of-the-new-groupthink.html.

18. Markman, A. (2015, November 25). The problem-solving process that prevents groupthink. *Harvard Business Review.* Retrieved from hbr.org/2015/11/the-problem-solving-process-that-prevents-groupthink.

19. Cadsby, T. (2014, July 4). The hidden enemy of productive conversations. *Harvard Business Review.* Retrieved from hbr.org/2014/07/the-hidden-enemy-of-productive-conversations; Harvard Business Review Staff. (2015, May 21). Measure your team's intellectual diversity. *Harvard Business Review.* Retrieved from hbr.org/2015/05/measure-your-teams-intellectual-diversity; Markman, A. (2015, November 25). The problem-solving process that prevents groupthink. *Harvard Business Review.* Retrieved from hbr.org/2015/11/the-problem-solving-process-that-prevents-groupthink; Sunstein, C. R., & Hastie, R.

20. Markman, A. (2015, November 25). The problem-solving process that prevents groupthink. *Harvard Business Review.* Retrieved from hbr.org/2015/11/the-problem-solving-process-that-prevents-groupthink.

21. Losada, M., & Heaphy, E. (2004). The role of positivity and connectivity in the performance of business teams: A nonlinear dynamics model. *American Behavioral Scientist, 47*(6), 740–765; Zenger, J., & Folkman, J. (2013, March 15). The ideal praise-to-criticism ratio. *Harvard Business Review.* Retrieved from hbr.org/2013/03/the-ideal-praise-to-criticism.

22. Hillier, J., & Dunn-Jensen, L. M. (2012). Groups meet . . . teams improve: Building teams that learn. *Journal of Management Education, 37*(5), 704–733.

23. Benson-Armer, B., & Hsieh, T. Y. (1997). Teamwork across time and space. *McKinsey Quarterly, 4*; Kniffin, K. (2016, August 30). Upbeat music can make employees more cooperative. *Harvard Business Review.* Retrieved from hbr.org/2016/08/upbeat-music-can-make-employees-more-cooperative.

24. Offermann, L., & Rosh, L. (2012, June 13). Building trust through skillful self-disclosure. *Harvard Business Review.* Retrieved from https://hbr.org/2012/06/instantaneous-intimacy-skillfu/.

25. Krattenmaker, T. (2003, May 3). How to make every meeting matter. *Harvard Management Communication Letter, 3–5.*

26. Watson, R. T., & Saunders, C. (2005). Managing insight velocity: The design of problem solving meetings. *Business Horizons, 48*(4), 285–295.

27. Source: Dockweiler, S. (2017). How much time do we spend in meetings? (Hint: It's scary). *The Muse.* Retrieved from www.themuse.com/advice/how-much-time-do-we-spend-in-meetings-hint-its-scary.

28. Perlow, L. A., Hadley, C. N., & Eun, E. (2017, July/August). Stop the meeting madness. *Harvard Business Review.* Retrieved from hbr.org/2017/07/stop-the-meeting-madness.

29. Ribbink, K. (2002). Run a meeting to fast-track your career. *Harvard Management Communication Letter, 3–4.*

30. Krattenmaker, T. (2003, May 3). How to make every meeting matter. *Harvard Management Communication Letter, 3–5.*

31. Ribbink, K. (2002). Run a meeting to fast-track your career. *Harvard Management Communication Letter, 3–4.*

32. Perrotte, K. (2018, August 18). Accountemps survey: Employee output is weakest late in the day. Retrieved from www.newswire.ca/news-releases/accountemps-survey-employee-output-is-weakest-late-in-the-day-545226522.html.

33. Linsky, M. (2006). The morning meeting: Best-practice communication for executive teams. *Harvard Management Communication Letter, 3–5.*

34. *New York Times Corner Office* (blog). Meetings. Retrieved June 15, 2010, from http://projects.nytimes.com/corner-office/Meetings.

35. Bielaszka-DuVernay, C. (2004). Is your company as dull and unproductive as its meetings? *Harvard Management Communication Letter, 3–5.*

36. Streibel, B. J. (2003). *The manager's guide to effective meetings.* New York: McGraw-Hill.

37. Gargiulo, T. L. (2006). *Stories at work: Using stories to improve communication and build relationships.* Westport, CT: Praeger.

38. Bixler, S., & Dugan, L. S. (2001). *How to project confidence, competence, and credibility at work: 5 steps to professional presence.* Avon, MA: Adams Media.

39. Streibel, B. J. (2003). *The manager's guide to effective meetings.* New York: McGraw-Hill.

40. Bixler, S., & Dugan, L. S. (2001). *How to project confidence, competence, and credibility at work: 5 steps to professional presence.* Avon, MA: Adams Media.

41. Ribbink, K. (2002). Run a meeting to fast-track your career. *Harvard Management Communication Letter,* 3–4; Obuchowski, J. (2005, Spring). Your meeting: Who's in charge? *Harvard Management Communication Letter,* 3–5.

42. Covey, S. R. (2004). *The 8th habit: From effectiveness to greatness.* New York: Free Press.

43. Schulz-Hardt, S., Brodbeck, F. C., Mojzisch, A., Kerschreiter, R., & Frey, D. (2006). Group decision making in hidden profile situations: Dissent as a facilitator for decision quality. *Journal of Personality and Social Psychology, 91*(6), 1080–1093.

44. Bielaszka-DuVernay. (2004). *Is your company as dull and unproductive as its meetings?* Boston: Harvard Business Review Press.

45. Ribbink, K. (2002). Run a meeting to fast-track your career. *Harvard Management Communication Letter,* 3–4; Krattenmaker, T. (2003, May 3). How to make every meeting matter. *Harvard Management Communication Letter,* 3–5; Bielaszka-DuVernay. (2004). *Is your company as dull and unproductive as its meetings?* Boston: Harvard Business Review Press.

46. Streibel, B. J. (2003). *The manager's guide to effective meetings.* New York: McGraw-Hill.

47. Snyder, L. G. (2009). Teaching teams about teamwork: Preparation, practice, and performance review. *Business Communication Quarterly, 72*(1), 77–78.

48. Obuchowski, J. (2005). *Your meeting: Who's in charge?* Boston: Harvard Business Press.

49. RW[3]. (2010). *The challenge of working in virtual teams: Virtual teams report–2010.* New York: Author.

50. Majchrzak, A., Malhotra, A., Stamps, J., & Lipnack, J. (2004). Can absence make a team grow stronger? *Harvard Business Review, 82*(5), 131–137; Greenberg, S., Greenberg, R. H., & Antonucci, Y. L. (2007). Creating and sustaining trust in virtual teams. *Business Horizons, 50,* 325–333; RW[3]. (2010). *The challenge of working in virtual teams: Virtual teams report–2010.* New York: Author; Ferrazzi, K. (2012, May 3). Five ways to run better virtual meetings. *Harvard Business Review.* Retrieved from hbr.org/2012/05/the-right-way-to-run-a-virtual.

51. Majchrzak, A., Malhotra, A., Stamps, J., & Lipnack, J. (2004). Can absence make a team grow stronger? *Harvard Business Review, 82*(5), 131–137; Watkins, M. (2013, June 27). Making virtual teams work: Ten basic principles. *Harvard Business Review.* Retrieved from hbr.org/2013/06/making-virtual-teams-work-ten; Berry, G. R. (2011). Enhancing effectiveness on virtual teams: Understanding why traditional skills are insufficient. *Journal of Business Communication, 48,* 186–206.

52. RW[3]. (2010). *The challenge of working in virtual teams: Virtual teams report–2010.* New York: Author.

53. Berry, G. R. (2011). Enhancing effectiveness on virtual teams: Understanding why traditional skills are insufficient. *Journal of Business Communication, 48,* 186–206.

54. The table is inspired by the work of Greenberg, P. S., Greenberg, R. H., & Antonucci, Y. L. (2007). Creating and sustaining trust in virtual teams. *Business Horizons, 50,* 325–333.

55. Majchrzak, A., Malhotra, A., Stamps, J., & Lipnack, J. (2004). Can absence make a team grow stronger? *Harvard Business Review, 82*(5), 131–137.

56. RW[3]. (2010). *The challenge of working in virtual teams: Virtual teams report–2010.* New York: Author.

57. Majchrzak, A., Malhotra, A., Stamps, J., & Lipnack, J. (2004). Can absence make a team grow stronger? *Harvard Business Review, 82*(5), 131–137; RW[3]. (2010). *The challenge of working in virtual teams: Virtual teams report–2010.* New York: Author; Ferrazzi, K. (2012, May 3). Five ways to run better virtual meetings. *Harvard Business Review.* Retrieved from hbr.org/2012/05/the-right-way-to-run-a-virtual.

58. Majchrzak, A., Malhotra, A., Stamps, J., & Lipnack, J. (2004). Can absence make a team grow stronger? *Harvard Business Review, 82*(5), 131–137.

59. Majchrzak, A., Malhotra, A., Stamps, J., & Lipnack, J. (2004). Can absence make a team grow stronger? *Harvard Business Review, 82*(5), 131–137.

60. Ferrazzi, K. (2014, January 31). How virtual teams can create human connections despite distance. *Harvard Business Review.* Retrieved from hbr.org/2014/01/how-virtual-teams-can-create-human-connections-despite-distance.

61. Stone, D., Patton, B., & Heen, S. (2000). *Difficult conversations: How to discuss what matters most.* New York: Penguin, xv.

62. Patterson, K., Grenny, J., McMillan, R., & Switzler, A. (2002). *Crucial conversations: Tools for talking when stakes are high.* New York: McGraw-Hill; Myers, L. L., & Larson, R. S. (2005). Preparing students for early work conflicts. *Business Communication Quarterly, 68*(3), 306–317.

63. Patterson, K., Grenny, J., McMillan, R., & Switzler, A. (2002). *Crucial conversations: Tools for talking when stakes are high.* New York: McGraw-Hill.

64. Patterson, K., Grenny, J., McMillan, R., & Switzler, A. (2002). *Crucial conversations: Tools for talking when stakes are high.* New York: McGraw-Hill.

65. Patterson, K., Grenny, J., McMillan, R., & Switzler, A. (2002). *Crucial conversations: Tools for talking when stakes are high.* New York: McGraw-Hill.

66. Evenson, R. (2009). Effective solutions for team conflict. *Toastmasters.* Retrieved from www.toastmasters.org/ToastmastersMagazine/ToastmasterArchive/2009/July/EffectiveSolutions.aspx.

67. Bryant, A. (2009, June 20). The divine, too, is in the details. *The New York Times.* Retrieved from www.nytimes.com/2009/06/21/business/21corner.html.

68. Stone, D., Patton, B., & Heen, S. (2000). *Difficult conversations: How to discuss what matters most.* New York: Penguin.

69. Baker, A. C. (2010). *Catalytic conversations: Organizational communication and innovation.* Armonk, NY: M. E. Sharpe.

70. Patterson, K., Grenny, J., McMillan, R., & Switzler, A. (2002). *Crucial conversations: Tools for talking when stakes are high.* New York: McGraw-Hill.

71. Patterson, K., Grenny, J., McMillan, R., & Switzler, A. (2002). *Crucial conversations: Tools for talking when stakes are high.* New

York: McGraw-Hill; Evenson, R. (2009). Effective solutions for team conflict. *Toastmasters.* Retrieved from www.toastmasters.org/ ToastmastersMagazine/ToastmasterArchive/2009/July/EffectiveSolutions. aspx; Bierck, R. (2001, November). Managing anger. *Harvard Management Communication Letter,* 4–5.

72. Covey, S. M. R. (2006). *The speed of trust.* New York: Free Press.

73. Evenson, R. (2009). Effective solutions for team conflict. *Toastmasters.* Retrieved from www.toastmasters.org/ToastmastersMagazine/ ToastmasterArchive/2009/July/EffectiveSolutions.aspx.

74. Bryant, A. (2010, May 22). It's not a career ladder, it's an obstacle course. *The New York Times.* Retrieved from www.nytimes.com/2010/ 05/13/business/23corner.html.

75. Bryant, A. (2010, February 6). Now, put yourself in my shoes. *The New York Times.* Retrieved from www.nytimes.com/2010/02/07/business/ 07corner.html.

76. Bryant, A. (2010, August 28). No need to hit the "send" key. *The New York Times.* Retrieved from www.nytimes.com/2010/08/29/ business/29corner.html.

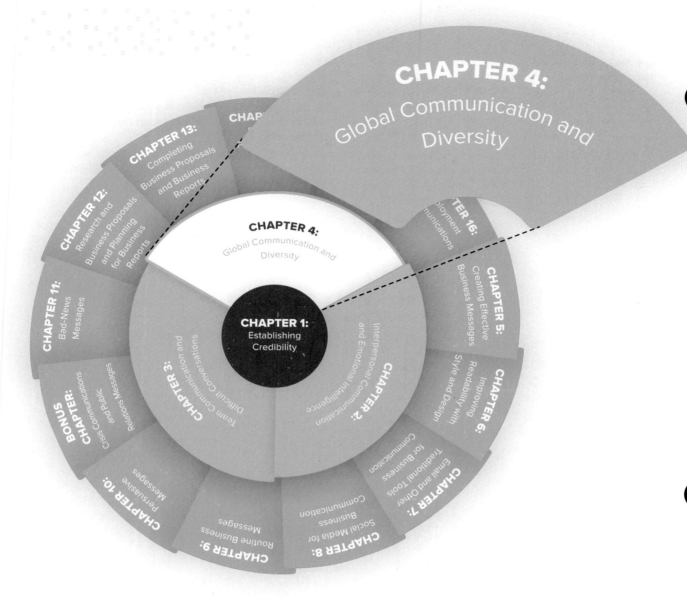

CHAPTER 4:
Global Communication and Diversity

CHAPTER 4:
Global Communication and Diversity

CHAPTER 1:
Establishing Credibility

CHAPTER 2: Interpersonal Communication and Emotional Intelligence

CHAPTER 3: Team Communication and Difficult Conversations

CHAPTER 5: Creating Effective Business Messages

CHAPTER 6: Improving Readability with Style and Design

CHAPTER 7: Email and Other Traditional Tools for Business Communication

CHAPTER 8: Social Media for Business Communication

CHAPTER 9: Routine Business Messages

CHAPTER 10: Persuasive Messages

CHAPTER 11: Bad-News Messages

BONUS CHAPTER: Crisis Communications and Public Relations Messages

CHAPTER 12: Research and Business Proposals and Planning for Business Reports

CHAPTER 13: Completing Business Proposals and Business Reports

CHAPTER 16: Employment Communications

 ESTABLISHING CREDIBILITY

 **PRINCIPLES OF INTERPERSONAL COMMUNICATION**

 PRINCIPLES FOR & TYPES OF BUSINESS MESSAGES

LEARNING OBJECTIVES

After studying this chapter, you should be able to do the following:

LO4.1 Describe characteristics of cultural intelligence, its importance for global business leaders, and approaches to developing it.

LO4.2 Explain the major cultural dimensions and related communication practices.

LO4.3 Name and describe key categories of business etiquette in the intercultural communication process.

LO4.4 Identify how generational, gender, and other aspects of diversity affect workplace communication.

WHY DOES THIS MATTER?

You are living in one of the most exciting times because of opportunities to work and interact with people from across the globe. Only a few decades ago, few businesspeople worked closely with members of other cultures. Now, however, global business connections have increased rapidly, and you will undoubtedly work across cultures throughout your career. For example, you will probably have some chances to travel internationally for work assignments. More frequently, however, you are likely to work across cultures by collaborating with work teams in India, videoconferencing or emailing with customers or suppliers in China, or working in a culturally diverse office in your hometown. The possibilities are immense!

Throughout this chapter, you will see a variety of national cultures compared. The countries selected for this chapter are among the most important trading partners for the United States. In terms of trade volume, countries such as China, Mexico, Canada, Japan, Germany, South Korea, and the United Kingdom dominate. (See Table 4.1 for the most important trading partners of the United States.) Of course, you will likely work with business professionals, clients, or customers from many other national backgrounds. Your business discipline, company, and industry will factor into the national cultures with which you most frequently interact. At the end of the chapter, you'll also read about how generation, gender, and other aspects of diversity affect communication in ways similar to culture.

Hear Pete Cardon explain why this matters.

bit.ly/cardon4

TABLE 4.1

Top Trading Partners of the United States

Country	Total Trade (billions of U.S. dollars)	Percentage of Total Trade
China	$61.4	16.0%
Mexico	56.6	14.8
Canada	54.2	14.1
Japan	19.3	5.0
Germany	15.9	4.1
South Korea	12.6	3.3
United Kingdom	11.5	3.0
France	8.5	2.2
India	8.2	2.1
Netherlands	7.5	1.9
Italy	7.2	1.9
Taiwan	7.1	1.9
Brazil	7.1	1.8
Switzerland	6.2	1.6

Note: Based on October 2018 trade figures from the U.S. Census Bureau.

You'll work with people of many cultures and of diverse backgrounds throughout your career. Understanding cultures and diversity will help you develop meaningful professional relationships and improve business outcomes.

CHAPTER CASE ERIC GOES ON HIS FIRST OVERSEAS BUSINESS TRIP

Eric Exum

Engineering Associate

WHO'S INVOLVED

THE SITUATION

Eric Exum was on his first overseas business trip, waiting in the lobby of his Seoul, Korea, hotel for Jae Kim to pick him up for meetings. Eric and Jae had emailed back and forth for the past few weeks, but Eric was worried. He had specifically notified Jae in their emails that he needed an "accessible" hotel room, yet the room Jae had reserved was a standard one. Would Jae arrive with a vehicle that could hold his wheelchair and comfortably accommodate him?

A Korean man strolled over to Eric. He appeared to be around 40 and was dressed in a stylish suit and perfectly polished shoes. He gave a slight bow and said, "Good morning! Welcome to Korea! You must be Mr. Exum."

"Oh, yes, that's right. Hello, Jae!"

Jae appeared slightly confused. "I thought you would be older, Mr. Exum. You must only be in your 20s or 30s. How old are you?"

Jason was surprised to get a question about his age. "Well, actually, I'm 28 years old. Jae, can you tell me where we'll hold our meetings today and how we'll get there?"

Jae responded, "We have a full day ahead of us. We'll start with a tour of one of our new facilities. Then, we'll get some Korean BBQ. You'll meet our president and his team at lunch. Then, we'll drive for a view from the mountains. Next, we'll go to our offices to meet with some of the engineers. This evening, we'll hold a banquet with some other members of the team. We have prepared everything for you."

Eric watched Jae summon a beautiful Mercedes-Benz sedan, which did not look like it could accommodate his wheelchair. In addition to his concerns about the hotel room and the car, Eric also wondered why Jae seemed so formal and stuffy. Were all Koreans like that? And he felt the day's agenda seemed overwhelming and likely uncomfortable. *Why wasn't Jae concerned about his comfort after a long trip?*

QUESTIONS TO CONSIDER AS YOU READ

- What types of attitudes do business professionals need to communicate effectively across cultures?
- How can business students learn about and prepare to work with members of other cultures?
- How can understanding cultural dimensions help business professionals work cross-culturally?
- What advantages accrue to companies with a global mentality?
- What is the value of global leaders?
- How do generational, gender, and other group identities affect business communication?

Developing Cultural Intelligence

Companies depend on business professionals who can manage across cultures. Companies such as Coca-Cola sell more products abroad than they do locally. In fact, Coca-Cola sells more drinks in Japan alone than in the United States. In Chapter 2, you read about emotional intelligence (EQ), your ability to manage emotions in interpersonal situations. Similarly, **cultural intelligence (CQ)** is a measure of your ability to work with and adapt to members of other cultures. Like EQ (but unlike IQ), CQ can be developed and improved over time with training, experience, and conscious effort.[1]

Business professionals with high CQ understand differences and similarities between and among cultures. **Culture** includes the shared values, norms, rules, and behaviors of an identifiable group of people who share a common history and communication system. There are many types of culture, such as national, organizational, and team. We discuss principles of intercultural communication in this chapter primarily in the context of national cultures, which tend to be more permanent and enduring than other types of culture. The norms and values of national cultures are instilled in young members through a shared language, shared history and traditions, school systems, and political and economic systems. At the end of the chapter, we also briefly discuss norms and values associated with generations, gender, and other groups.

When working with members of other cultures at the home office or abroad, business professionals with high CQ are skilled at forming goals, discussing and succeeding on joint projects, resolving differences, and negotiating mutually beneficial outcomes. They understand new markets and can develop global plans for marketing and supply chain management. When people with high CQ encounter unfamiliar situations, they implement a variety of the skills displayed in Table 4.2 and discussed throughout the chapter.[2]

Developing cultural intelligence is more than possessing favorable attitudes toward members of other groups. It also requires developing skills and knowledge. In this section, we focus briefly on several characteristics of cultural intelligence.

Respect, Recognize, and Appreciate Cultural Differences

Cultural intelligence is built on attitudes of respect and recognition of other cultures. This means that you view other cultures as holding legitimate and valid views of and approaches to managing business and workplace relationships. In recent years, many public and educational campaigns have focused on embracing diversity. In this book, we refer to **diversity** as the presence of many cultural groups in the workplace. Business professionals with high cultural intelligence embrace diversity as a moral imperative and as a means to achieve higher performance. A great deal of research has examined the role of cultural diversity in the workplace. These studies have shown that a mix of cultural groups in terms of national culture, ethnicity, age, and gender leads to better decision making.[3]

LO4.1 Describe characteristics of cultural intelligence, its importance for global business leaders, and approaches to developing it.

Mc Graw Hill connect

Visit http://connect.mheducation.com for an exercise on this topic.

TABLE 4.2

Cultural Intelligence in the Workplace

Characteristics of High Cultural Intelligence
• Respect, recognize, and appreciate cultural differences.
• Possess curiosity about and interest in other cultures.
• Avoid inappropriate stereotypes.
• Adjust conceptions of time and show patience.
• Manage language differences to achieve shared meaning.
• Understand cultural dimensions.
• Establish trust and show empathy across cultures.
• Approach cross-cultural work relationships with a learner mind-set.
• Build a co-culture of cooperation and innovation.

Be Curious about Other Cultures

As a college student, you are in a stage of life that gives you unique opportunities to acquire cross-cultural experiences. Consider the following options: studying abroad, learning a language, developing friendships with international students on campus, and taking an interest in and learning about a particular culture.[4]

Study Abroad   Living in another culture is perhaps the best approach to learning about one. It allows you to immerse yourself in another way of living—to observe and experience up close how members of another cultural group communicate, work in groups, manage relationships, celebrate successes, and deal with disappointments. When asked "What's your best career advice to young graduates?" Quintin E. Primo III, co-founder and chief executive of Capri Capital Partners, responded in the following way:

> Leave the country. Get out of here. That's what I tell everybody—just go. I don't care where you go, just go. Because the world is changing. It is no longer acceptable to speak only English if you are 25 and younger. . . . You have little chance of being successful if you speak only one language. If you don't understand Islam, you're in trouble because Islam comprises somewhere between 1.6 billion and 1.8 billion people, and there are markets that are untapped that need to be tapped. So you've got to get out of your front door, get out of the comfort and quiet of your home, and your safety zone, and step into a pool of risk where you have no idea what the outcome is going to be. Out of it all, you will have a much broader understanding of the world's cultures, and you will have a much clearer idea of how the world perceives our culture, and all the value, and the benefits, and the beauty of our culture. There is nothing more important. I don't care where you went to business school. I don't care whether your grades were good or bad. You have to leave the country.[5]

As freshmen, most university students express a desire to study abroad and even believe that they will have an opportunity to do so before they graduate. However, just 3 to 5 percent of university students actually do.[6] So, if you want to study abroad, make it a priority. Plan for it now. Furthermore, consider choosing locations and programs that are most important for your career. Typically, business recruiters value study-abroad programs that are at least one semester long, involve the development of business skills, and include language study. Also, business recruiters are more impressed with study-abroad programs located in countries that are considered strategically important business partners. Whereas most students choose locations in Western Europe and Australia, recruiters see more value in countries such as China, Japan, Brazil, Mexico, or India. Of course, this varies by discipline and industry. For example, if you are going into the fashion design industry, experience in Italy or France would be extremely valuable.

Studying abroad is one of the best ways to develop global communication skills.

Andresr/Getty Images

When you study abroad, learn all you can about adapting to the culture. However, avoid developing strong preconceptions and remain flexible. When you arrive in your chosen destination, open yourself completely to the experience. Generally, students who choose more immersive experiences, such as living with homestay families or in dormitories with students from many countries, learn much more about the cultures.

Learn a Language   Although English is considered the global business language and business managers in other parts of the world increasingly speak it well, you can benefit from learning another language for a variety of reasons. It gives you many insights into how people of other cultures think. It helps you appreciate the richness of other cultures. It fosters tremendous goodwill with others. And you may find yourself in situations where your language ability allows smoother communication than relying on English.

Develop Friendships with International Students on Your Campus Your university likely has hundreds or even thousands of international students. This presents you with a rare opportunity to experience the world. You can learn more about other cultures by befriending international students than you can by taking a group tour of another country. Also, you can help these students feel at home. One reason you can learn so much from international students is that they are experiencing the challenges of living in and adapting to a new culture. During your career, you are most likely to interact with business professionals who are the current generation of international students.

Take an Interest in a Culture and Routinely Learn about It Each culture has its own complexity. Ideally, you should seek an in-depth understanding of one culture. Once you've done this, you can more quickly adapt to and learn other cultures. One of the best ways to gain an in-depth understanding is to take an inquisitive approach—asking questions and seeking the answers to how other cultures view knowledge; how they reason and approach problems; how they work, worship, and view the world; how they view time; and so on.[7] You can routinely learn about cultures of interest in some of the following ways:[8]

- *Watch films, television, documentaries, news, and other video of the culture.* It's increasingly easy to access video of other cultures. This allows you to observe many aspects of the culture in context with visual and auditory cues.
- *Follow the business culture of a country.* Many websites contain global business news sections with both text and videos. For example, consider the following: *Bloomberg Businessweek*, CNBC, *Time*, Foreign Exchange, and CIBERweb.
- *Take courses and attend events related to particular cultures.* Your university offers numerous opportunities, including taking courses about international and intercultural topics and attending symposia that feature international speakers.
- *Make friends with people who live in other cultures and communicate online.* You might try to make friends abroad and communicate frequently via email, chat, and online calls. One of the most common means of communicating internationally is via online call services such as Zoom, Hangouts, or Skype. Read the Technology Tips box about online calls later in the chapter.

Avoid Inappropriate Stereotypes

We naturally develop stereotypes, or generalizations, to try to understand the attitudes and behavior of people we do not know, especially those of different cultures. It is an attempt by the brain to group and categorize in complex situations. Stereotypes can make interactions less complicated since they serve as a starting point for understanding the motives and values of others. For example, people may have a stereotype of tax accountants as credible, professional, competent, helpful, and detail-oriented. This stereotype allows people to go to a tax accountant's office with the assumption that the professional will help them and provide excellent service. Similarly, people who work across cultures often form stereotypes of how members of that culture communicate and approach work problems. These stereotypes can be productive as long as they are only a starting point, they are flexible, and they are primarily positive.[9]

Stereotyping about cultures can also be dysfunctional, counterproductive, and even hurtful. People tend to form two types of stereotypes when interacting with members of other cultures: *projected cognitive similarity* and *outgroup homogeneity effect*.[10] **Projected cognitive similarity** is the tendency to assume others have the same norms and values as your own cultural group. This occurs when people project their own cultural norms and values to explain the behaviors they see in others. Take the case of an American interviewing a Japanese man for a new position. The Japanese man might downplay his own achievements and give credit to the teams he has worked on. The American interviewer, based on the American cultural lens, may think the man lacks self-confidence and independence or initiative. The Japanese applicant, by contrast, is most likely displaying Japanese norms and values associated with modesty, politeness, and collectivism.

Outgroup homogeneity effect is the tendency to think members of other groups are all the same. Psychologically, this approach minimizes the mental effort needed to get to know people of other groups. Practically speaking, it is counterproductive to developing effective working relationships with members of other cultures. The reality is that all cultures contain a lot of diversity—individuals of many backgrounds, worldviews, interests, and approaches to life. In the "Individualism and Collectivism" section in this chapter, we will illustrate more about the nature of diversity.

Negative stereotyping can easily emerge from popular culture. Research has shown that television depictions of particular cultural groups as criminal, cruel, backward, or dishonest affect the stereotypes viewers have of those cultures.[11] Similarly, viewing members of other cultures through a political lens based on news stories about the political relations between countries often leads to unjustified negative stereotyping.

While you should be careful about forming negative or rigid stereotypes of members of other cultures, you should also be aware of stereotypes that others may have of you. Many people you interact with will have already formed some impressions of your cultural background and what to expect from you. Members of other cultures often form stereotypes of Americans based on news stories as well as popular culture (i.e., films, television shows, music). Typically, most people around the world hold mixed views of Americans (see Table 4.3). Even in countries where the majority of adults view Americans as dishonest or greedy, they also view Americans as hardworking and inventive.[12]

Adjust Your Conceptions of Time

One frustration that most people experience when communicating and working across cultures is dealing with time. This is because people have a lifetime of experiences,

TABLE 4.3

Perceptions That Members of Various Cultures Have about Americans

	Percentage of Respondents Who Associate Americans with Various Traits				
	Optimistic	Hardworking	Tolerant	Arrogant	Greedy
Canada	65	76	39	55	57
China	45	39	29	60	49
France	72	81	42	58	43
Germany	74	60	52	48	45
Greece	78	73	37	72	68
India	50	56	42	42	36
Italy	77	70	51	47	21
Japan	70	26	59	50	45
Sweden	80	57	38	52	55
UK	71	75	39	64	56

Source: Pew Research Center Global Trends & Attitudes.
Note: *Red* font indicates a majority of adults in a country have a negative view. *Green* font indicates a majority of adults in a country have a positive view.

related to their particular culture, that form their expectations for when things should happen during any given process.

People high in CQ show patience. They understand that most tasks take longer when working across cultures because more time is needed to understand one another and cooperate effectively. Furthermore, many cross-cultural work projects are conducted across great distances. Naturally, this requires additional time due to the communication tools and organizational decision-making processes.

Guy McLeod, former president of Airbus China, explained why business managers arriving in China need to adapt their pace: "When people have just arrived, they want to change things. But making quick moves in the wrong way isn't the right thing to do. You need to have patience, patience, patience. It is one of the clichés you hear in China, but it is true. You need to make a long-term strategy and stick to it."[13]

Also, people of various cultures conceptualize time differently. What seems *fast* in one culture may seem *slow* in another. One recent study ranked pace of life in various cultures by measuring walking speed over a distance of 60 feet, the average time for a postal worker to complete one request, and the accuracy of clocks in public. Countries such as Germany, Japan, and Italy were considered fast-paced cultures, whereas countries such as China, Brazil, and Mexico were considered slow-paced ones (see Figure 4.1).[14] The point is that cultures establish expectations about what is considered timely, late, rushed, and hectic. Cultures also differ in their priorities related to focusing on the present versus focusing on the future (as discussed in the "Future Orientation" section in the upcoming pages). As you can see, you will need to adjust your sense of time to coordinate effectively with members of other cultures.

Manage Language Differences

English is increasingly considered the global business language. Many global companies such as Nissan, which are composed primarily of non-native English-speaking business professionals, have adopted policies of conducting meetings in English. Yet, even with the strong push for English as a business language, many professionals around the business world speak limited English. Also, many forms of English exist—that of the United Kingdom, Australia, Singapore, and India, to name just a few places. Thus, standard English is a matter of interpretation. As you conduct business across cultures with those who have limited English ability, consider the following advice:[15]

- *Avoid quickly judging that others have limited communication proficiency.* Many non-native English speakers take time to warm up. The first moments—or in some cases days or weeks—of your interactions with them are not representative of their real language abilities. Many business professionals have studied English for years yet infrequently have opportunities to speak it in an authentic encounter.

- *Articulate clearly and slow down.* Many Americans inadvertently run their words together. Make sure you pronounce each word distinctly and slow your pace slightly.

- *Avoid slang and jargon.* Slang and jargon can be particularly confusing to members of other cultures. For example, Americans are well known for using sports slang in business (e.g., striking out, throwing a curve ball, hitting a home run). Use as much literal language as you can.

- *Give others time to express themselves.* Allow those with limited English ability enough time to process their thoughts into English. You will often find that non-native English speakers, given time, express their thoughts with a more precise, creative, and even accurate use of English words than native English speakers.

- *Use interpreters as necessary.* In some situations, you will rely on interpreters. Spend some time in advance getting to know the interpreter's abilities and preferences for facilitating an exchange. During interpretation, focus on the person you are communicating with rather than the interpreter. That is, focus on the person with whom you are trying to build rapport.

FIGURE 4.1

Pace of Life across Cultures

Faster Pace of Life

Germany
Japan
Italy
UK
Netherlands
Hong Kong
France
USA
Canada
S Korea
China
Brazil
Mexico

Slower Pace of Life

In the opening case, Eric shows a lack of cultural intelligence in several ways. When Eric wonders whether all Koreans act a certain way, he commits a blunder common when working across cultures: *outgroup homogeneity effect*, which is the tendency to think members of other cultures are all the same. He fails to understand that terms like *accessible* are not easy to understand across cultures. He would be more successful by using more specific and clear language, such as the following: "I'm in a wheelchair. Can you help arrange a hotel room that supports my needs? Can you make sure we use a vehicle that can hold my wheelchair?"

Understanding Cultural Dimensions

LO4.2 Explain the major cultural dimensions and related communication practices.

Visit http://connect. mheducation.com for an exercise on this topic.

FIGURE 4.2

Individualism and Collectivism across Cultures

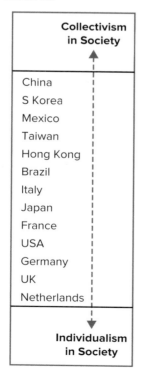

In this section, we describe recent research on cultural norms and values among businesspeople throughout the world. This research, conducted by the GLOBE group (which includes dozens of business researchers around the world), is based on surveys and interviews of about 20,000 business leaders and managers in 62 countries.[16]

The GLOBE group found that cultures can be grouped into eight dimensions. **Cultural dimensions** are fairly permanent and enduring sets of related norms and values and are classified as (1) individualism and collectivism, (2) egalitarianism and hierarchy, (3) performance orientation, (4) future orientation, (5) assertiveness, (6) humane orientation, (7) uncertainty avoidance, and (8) gender egalitarianism. By understanding these eight dimensions, you can get a good sense of the underlying motivations and goals that impact acceptable behaviors within a culture.

Although cultures constantly evolve, usually over decades or generations, the cultural dimension that changes most rapidly is individualism and collectivism. As prosperity and economic development rise, individualism typically increases as well.

We describe each of the eight cultural dimensions, along with related communication practices, focusing on norms, meaning the range of expected and acceptable behaviors in each culture. You will notice that rankings are provided for each cultural dimension, and these rankings include the United States as well as the top ten trading partners of North America.[17] You can find rankings for other countries included in the GLOBE study in the online resources.

Individualism and Collectivism

Most intercultural communication scholars identify individualism and collectivism as the most influential cultural dimension. This dimension deals with the level of independence and interdependence that people in a society possess and encourage. **Individualism** refers to a mind-set that prioritizes independence more highly than interdependence, emphasizing individual goals over group goals, and valuing choice more than obligation. By contrast, **collectivism** refers to a mind-set that prioritizes interdependence more highly than independence, emphasizing group goals over individual goals, and valuing obligation more than choice.

Individualists view themselves as distinct and separate from their family members, friends, and colleagues. They pursue their own dreams and goals, even when it means spending less time with family members and friends. They enter friendships and relationships primarily based on common interests. They also leave relationships when they are no longer mutually satisfying, beneficial, or convenient. Decision making tends to be based on an individual's needs.[18]

On the other hand, collectivists view themselves as interdependent—forming an identity inseparable from that of their family members, friends, and other groups. They tend to follow the perceived dreams and goals of the group as a matter of duty and obligation, even when it means sacrificing their own hopes and ambitions. They form permanent and lifetime relationships. They also tend to stay in contact with and work through extended networks built on family relationships, schoolmates, and hometowns. Decisions are made by groups.[19] Figure 4.2 displays country rankings for individualism and

TABLE 4.4

Communication Practices in High-Individualist and High-Collectivist Cultures

High Individualism	High Collectivism
• Discuss individual rewards and goals • Emphasize opportunities and choices • Spend less time in group decision making • Socialize infrequently with colleagues outside of work • Network in loosely tied and temporary social networks • Communicate directly to efficiently deal with work tasks and outcomes	• Discuss group rewards and goals • Emphasize duties and obligations • Spend more time in group decision making • Socialize frequently with colleagues outside of work • Network in tightly knit and permanent social networks • Communicate indirectly to preserve harmony in work relationships

collectivism in society. Of the countries we are considering here, China has the highest ranking for collectivism and the Netherlands has the lowest. Japan, which many people think of as highly collectivist, falls in the middle of this group. Table 4.4 shows communication practices normally associated with high individualism and high collectivism.

Traditionally, North American and Western countries have been far more individualist than Asian, Latin American, and other countries. However, some countries have increasingly become individualist, such as Japan. Generally, as countries increase the standard of living, they develop more individualist tendencies.

A major distinction in individualism and collectivism can be made between norms and values in *society* versus norms and values in *organizations*. All companies tend to promote both individualist and collectivist values. For example, encouraging self-initiative and individual accountability are individualist values. Encouraging teamwork and team incentives are collectivist values. In practice, many companies in individualist countries have attempted to adopt more team-oriented strategies in recent decades. Thus, highly individualist countries such as the United States exhibit many collectivist characteristics within organizations. Figure 4.3 displays country rankings for individualism and collectivism within companies. In many cases, these rankings differ from norms and values in society at large.

As you read through this section on cultural dimensions and view the continuums with rankings for each country, note that cultures are more than a spot on a scale. For example, Figure 4.4 shows how the United States, which is considered to have one of the most individualist cultures, and China, which is considered among the most collectivist cultures, overlap to some extent on this dimension (the triangular area enclosed by the intersection of the red and blue curves). In other words, some Chinese individuals behave in more individualist ways than some American individuals. However, by and large, most Chinese are more collectivist than most Americans. Furthermore, norms within a culture typically evolve to reflect what *most* people value. Even within cultures, there is great variety. Research in the United States has shown that individualism and collectivism vary significantly by region, with the Mountain West region the most individualist and the Deep South the most collectivist.[20] By constantly reminding yourself that variety exists within cultures, you are less likely to typecast people (outgroup homogeneity effect).

Egalitarianism and Hierarchy

All cultures develop norms for how power is distributed. In **egalitarian** cultures, people tend to distribute and share power evenly, minimize status differences, and minimize special privileges and opportunities for people just because they have higher authority. In **hierarchical** cultures, people expect power differences, follow leaders without questioning them, and feel comfortable with leaders receiving special privileges and opportunities. Power tends to be concentrated at the top.

FIGURE 4.3

Individualism and Collectivism within Companies

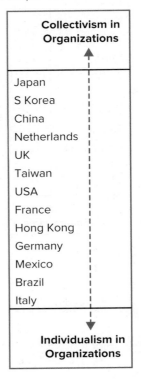

Collectivism in Organizations

Japan
S Korea
China
Netherlands
UK
Taiwan
USA
France
Hong Kong
Germany
Mexico
Brazil
Italy

Individualism in Organizations

FIGURE 4.4

Variety in Individualist and Collectivist Norms in the United States, Japan, and China

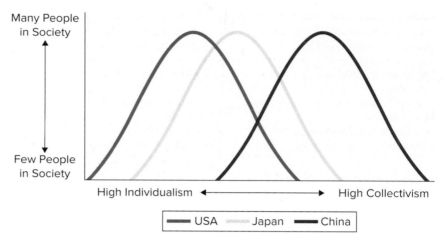

FIGURE 4.5

Hierarchy and Egalitarianism across Cultures

In egalitarian organizations, leaders avoid command-and-control approaches and lead with participatory and open management styles. Competence is highly valued in positions of authority. People of all ranks are encouraged to voice their opinions. Status symbols for leaders are discouraged. Salary ranges between the top and the bottom of the organization are quite narrow. By contrast, in hierarchical organizations, leaders expect employees to fall in line with their policies and decisions by virtue of their authority. Employees are discouraged from openly challenging leaders. Status symbols are common. Salary differences between the top and the bottom of the organization are extreme.[21] Figure 4.5 displays country rankings for hierarchy and egalitarianism. Table 4.5 presents communication practices normally associated with hierarchy and egalitarianism.

Performance Orientation

Performance orientation (PO) is "the extent to which a community encourages and rewards innovation, high standards, and performance improvement."[22] Of all cultural dimensions, societies cherish this one the most, especially in business. Yet many cultures are still developing a performance orientation.[23] To some degree, the distinctions between high-PO and low-PO cultures are captured in the phrase *living to work versus working to live*.

TABLE 4.5

Communication Practices in Egalitarian and Hierarchical Cultures

Egalitarianism	Hierarchy
• Decision making is more decentralized. • Protocol based on status is less important and is reserved for unusually formal business situations. • Subordinates speak more openly with leaders even during disagreements. • Subordinates do not take responsibility for the mistakes of leaders. • Leaders are approached directly.	• Decision making is more centralized. • Protocol (use of titles, seating arrangements) based on status is extremely important. • Subordinates defer to leaders during disagreements. • Subordinates take blame for and save face for leaders at all times. • Leaders are approached through intermediaries.

TABLE 4.6

Communication in High and Low Performance Orientation Societies

High Performance Orientation	Low Performance Orientation
• Emphasize results more than relationships	• Emphasize relationships more than results
• Prioritize measurable goals and objectives in meetings and communications	• Discuss goals and objectives casually without mechanisms for measuring them
• View feedback as essential to improvement	• View feedback as judgmental and uncomfortable
• Explicitly talk about financial incentives	• De-emphasize financial incentives; consider this motivation inappropriate
• Value statements of individual accountability	• Value expressions of loyalty and sympathy
• Expect urgency in communications and emphasize deadlines	• Show a relaxed view of time and view overemphasis on deadlines as pushy

The cultures of Far Eastern Asia, Western Europe, and North America are particularly high in performance orientation. For example, professionals in higher-PO cultures often perceive members of lower-PO cultures as not prioritizing results, accountability, and deadlines. By contrast, members of lower-PO cultures often perceive members of higher-PO cultures as impatient and even obsessed with short-term results.

Some cultures that are midrange-PO cultures such as China and India are rapidly developing performance orientations in work culture. Each of these countries has implemented major economic reforms in recent decades and is achieving stunning economic growth. These countries increasingly have companies and workforces that adopt norms and policies promoting innovation, improvement, and accountability systems. Figure 4.6 displays country rankings for performance orientation. Table 4.6 presents communication practices normally associated with high and low performance orientation.

Future Orientation

Future orientation (FO) involves the degree to which cultures are willing to sacrifice current wants to achieve future needs. Cultures with low FO (or present-oriented cultures) tend to enjoy being in the moment and spontaneity. They are less anxious about the future and often avoid the planning and sacrifices necessary to reach future goals. By contrast, cultures with high FO are imaginative about the future and have the discipline to carefully plan for and sacrifice current needs and wants to reach future goals.[24]

In future-oriented societies, many organizations create long-term strategies and business plans. Furthermore, they use these strategies and plans to guide their short-term business activities. By contrast, in present-oriented societies, organizations are less likely to develop clear long-term strategies and business plans. Moreover, they rarely focus short-term activities on long-term plans, even when they exist. Future orientation within organizations is a strong predictor of financial performance. High-FO cultures plan extensively for crises and unforeseen contingencies, whereas low-FO cultures take events as they occur.[25] Figure 4.7 displays country rankings for future orientation. Table 4.7 presents communication practices normally associated with high and low future orientation.

Assertiveness

The level of directness in speech varies greatly across cultures, and this can lead to miscommunication, misinterpretation of motivations, and hard feelings. The cultural dimension of **assertiveness** deals with the level of confrontation and directness that is considered appropriate and productive.[26] Typically, North Americans and Western

FIGURE 4.6

Performance Orientation across Cultures

High Performance Orientation

Hong Kong
S Korea
Netherlands
USA
France
Germany
China
Taiwan
Japan
UK
Brazil
Mexico
Italy

Low Performance Orientation

FIGURE 4.7

Time Orientation across Cultures

High Future Orientation

Netherlands
Germany
UK
Japan
USA
Brazil
S Korea
Hong Kong
Mexico
France
China
Taiwan
Italy

Low Future Orientation

TABLE 4.7

Communication Practices in High and Low Future Orientation Cultures

High Future Orientation	Low Future Orientation
• Emphasize control and planning for the future • Focus more on intrinsic motivation • Frequently discuss long-term strategies as part of business communications • Use flexible and adaptive language • Often mention long-term rewards and incentives • Appreciate visionary approaches to business problems	• Emphasize controlling current business problems • Focus more on extrinsic motivation • Rarely discuss long-term strategies as part of communications • Use inflexible and firm language • Often mention short-term rewards and incentives • Prioritize proven and routine approaches to problems

FIGURE 4.8

Assertiveness across Cultures

Europeans are the most assertive in business situations, whereas Asians tend to be less assertive. The mentality of "say it how it is," "cut to the chase," and "don't sugarcoat it" is emblematic of high assertiveness.

Members of highly assertive cultures often view members of less assertive cultures as timid, unenthusiastic, uncommitted, and even dishonest because they withhold or temper their comments. On the other hand, members of less assertive cultures often view members of highly assertive cultures as rude, tactless, inconsiderate, and even uncivilized.[27]

In particular, businesspeople notice differences in levels of assertiveness when a yes or no answer is expected. In less assertive cultures, the answer is sometimes vague; people are expected to read between the lines. As Guy McLeod, former president of Airbus China, stated, "In Europe or the States, 'yes' means 'yes,' so we can work together toward a common goal. Here, 'yes' doesn't always mean 'yes,' and 'no' doesn't always mean 'no.' . . . One piece of advice I give people about China: Everything is difficult, but everything is possible."[28] Figure 4.8 displays country rankings for assertiveness. Table 4.8 presents communication practices normally associated with high and low assertiveness.

Humane Orientation

Humane orientation (HO) is "the degree to which an organization or society encourages and rewards individuals for being fair, altruistic, friendly, generous, caring, and kind."[29]

TABLE 4.8

Communication Practices in High- and Low-Assertiveness Cultures

High-Assertiveness Cultures	Low-Assertiveness Cultures
• Emphasize direct and unambiguous language • Uncomfortable with silence and speak up quickly to fill the silence • Prioritize resolving issues over showing respect to others • Typically express more emotion • Use tough, even dominant, language • Stress equity and use competitive language • Value unrestrained expression of thoughts and feelings	• Emphasize indirect and subtle language • View silence as communicative and respectful • Prioritize showing respect over resolving issues • Typically express less emotion • Use tender and pleasant language • Stress equality and use cooperative language • Value measured and disciplined expression of thoughts and feelings

TABLE 4.9

Communication Styles in High and Low Humane Orientation Cultures

High Humane Orientation	Low Humane Orientation
• Express greetings, welcome, concern, and appreciation in most interactions • Consider taking time to talk about feelings as critical • Volunteer to help others • Smile and display other nonverbal signs of welcome frequently	• Express greetings and welcome in formal interactions • Consider taking time to talk about feelings as inefficient • Help others when asked • Smile and display other nonverbal signs of welcome infrequently

FIGURE 4.9

Humane Orientation across Cultures

In high-HO cultures, people demonstrate that others belong and are welcome. Concern extends to all people—friends and strangers—and nature. People provide social support to each other and are urged to be sensitive to all forms of unfairness, unkindness, and discrimination. Companies and shareholders emphasize social responsibility, and leaders are expected to be generous and compassionate.

In low-HO cultures, the values of pleasure, comfort, and self-enjoyment take precedence over displays of generosity and kindness. People extend material, financial, and social support to a close circle of friends and family. Society members are expected to solve personal problems on their own. Companies and shareholders focus primarily on financial profits, and leaders are not expected to be generous or compassionate.[30] Figure 4.9 displays country rankings for humane orientation. Table 4.9 presents communication practices normally associated with high and low humane orientation.

Uncertainty Avoidance

Uncertainty avoidance (UA) refers to how cultures socialize members to feel in uncertain, novel, surprising, or extraordinary situations. In high-UA cultures, people feel uncomfortable with uncertainty and seek orderliness, consistency, structure, and formalized procedures. People in high-UA cultures often stress orderliness and consistency, even if it means sacrificing experimentation and innovation. They prefer that expectations are clear and spelled out precisely in the form of instructions and rules. People in high-UA cultures prefer tasks with sure outcomes and minimal risk. They also show more resistance to change and less tolerance for breaking rules.[31]

In low-UA cultures, people feel comfortable with uncertainty. In fact, they may even thrive, since they prefer tasks that involve uncertain outcomes, calculated risks, and problem solving and experimentation. They often view rules and procedures as hindering creativity and innovation. Members of low-UA cultures develop trust more quickly with people from other groups and tend to be more informal in their interactions. They also show less resistance to change, less desire to establish rules to dictate behavior, and more tolerance for breaking rules.[32] Figure 4.10 displays country rankings for uncertainty avoidance. Table 4.10 presents communication practices normally associated with high and low uncertainty avoidance.

Gender Egalitarianism

Gender egalitarianism deals with the division of roles between men and women in society. In high gender-egalitarianism cultures, men and women are encouraged to occupy the same professional roles and leadership positions. Women are included equally in decision making. In low gender-egalitarianism cultures, men and women are expected to occupy different roles in society. Typically, women have less influence in professional

FIGURE 4.10

Uncertainty Avoidance across Cultures

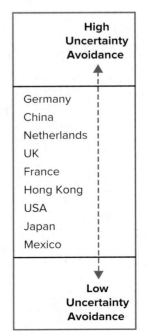

TABLE 4.10

Communication Styles in High and Low Uncertainty Avoidance Cultures

High Uncertainty Avoidance	Low Uncertainty Avoidance
• Document agreements in legal contracts • Expect orderly communication: keep meticulous records, document conclusions drawn in meetings • Refer to formalized policies, procedures, and rules as basis for decision making • Verify with written communication • Prefer formality in the majority of interpersonal business interactions	• Rely on the word of others they trust rather than contractual arrangements • Expect casual communication: less concerned with documentation and maintenance of meeting records • Feel unbound by formalized policies, procedures, and rules when discussing work decisions with others • Verify with oral communication • Expect informality in most interpersonal business interactions

decision making. However, in societies where gender roles are highly distinct, women often have powerful roles in family decision making.[33]

In Table 4.11, you will find communication practices normally associated with high and low gender-egalitarianism cultures.

Business Values around the World

To this point, we have discussed *norms,* or what cultures actually do. The GLOBE group also surveyed business professionals about *values,* or what they prefer for workplace culture. Refer to Table 4.12 to see which dimensions each culture prioritizes as their ideal work arrangements. Business cultures around the world show many convergences in terms of values—as a result of globalization and increased development. Business cultures, in particular, have converged more rapidly than other parts of society.

In the opening case, Eric wonders why Jae keeps calling him "Mr. Exum." He even thinks Jae is "formal and stuffy." Yet Jae's use of titles is more likely a sign of respect from a culture that is more *hierarchical* and in which *formal protocol* (titles, expensive clothes and vehicles) project status and garner respect. Eric also likely misinterprets Jae's motives for the agenda he has outlined. The day's activities, which include a lot of socializing and getting to know people in Jae's company, are consistent with a *collectivist* orientation. When he wonders why Jae isn't more accommodating to him, Eric is falling back on projected cognitive similarity, the tendency to assume others have the same norms and values as your own cultural group. In this case, he thinks Jae should act from Eric's own *individualist* orientation by giving him more time and privacy during the day.

TABLE 4.11

Communication Practices in High and Low Gender-Egalitarianism Cultures

High Gender Egalitarianism	Low Gender Egalitarianism
• Provide equal professional opportunities to men and women • Expect men and women to have the same communication and management styles • Avoid protocol that draws attention to gender	• Provide more professional leadership opportunities to men • Expect men and women to communicate in distinct masculine and feminine ways • Prefer protocol that draws attention to gender

TABLE 4.12

Preferred Priorities for Work Cultures around the World

Brazil	China	France
1. Performance orientation	1. Performance orientation	1. Performance orientation
2. Future orientation	2. Assertiveness	2. Humane orientation
3. Organizational collectivism	3. Humane orientation	3. Collectivism
4. Humane orientation	4. Uncertainty avoidance	4. Future orientation
5. Collectivism	5. Collectivism	5. Organizational collectivism
6. Uncertainty avoidance	6. Future orientation	6. Uncertainty avoidance
7. Assertiveness	7. Organizational collectivism	7. Assertiveness
8. Hierarchy	8. Hierarchy	8. Hierarchy

Germany	Hong Kong	Italy
1. Performance orientation	1. Performance orientation	1. Performance orientation
2. Humane orientation	2. Future orientation	2. Future orientation
3. Collectivism	3. Humane orientation	3. Collectivism
4. Organizational collectivism	4. Collectivism	4. Humane orientation
5. Future orientation	5. Assertiveness	5. Organizational collectivism
6. Uncertainty avoidance	6. Uncertainty avoidance	6. Uncertainty avoidance
7. Assertiveness	7. Organizational collectivism	7. Assertiveness
8. Hierarchy	8. Hierarchy	8. Hierarchy

Japan	Mexico	Netherlands
1. Assertiveness	1. Performance orientation	1. Performance orientation
2. Humane orientation	2. Collectivism	2. Humane orientation
3. Collectivism	3. Future orientation	3. Collectivism
4. Future orientation	4. Uncertainty avoidance	4. Future orientation
5. Performance orientation	5. Humane orientation	5. Organizational collectivism
6. Uncertainty avoidance	6. Organizational collectivism	6. Uncertainty avoidance
7. Organizational collectivism	7. Assertiveness	7. Assertiveness
8. Hierarchy	8. Hierarchy	8. Hierarchy

South Korea	United Kingdom	United States
1. Future orientation	1. Performance orientation	1. Performance orientation
2. Humane orientation	2. Collectivism	2. Collectivism
3. Collectivism	3. Humane orientation	3. Humane orientation
4. Performance orientation	4. Future orientation	4. Future orientation
5. Uncertainty avoidance	5. Organizational collectivism	5. Assertiveness
6. Organizational collectivism	6. Uncertainty avoidance	6. Organizational collectivism
7. Assertiveness	7. Assertiveness	7. Uncertainty avoidance
8. Hierarchy	8. Hierarchy	8. Hierarchy

Source: Based on a GLOBE study of work values among business managers in 62 countries.
Notes: Performance orientation is the most valued dimension in nearly all work cultures (in green shade).
Hierarchy is the least valued dimension in all work cultures (in red shade).
Humane orientation is highly valued among most cultures (in light blue shade).

Technology Tips

TRANSLATION APPS

Many translator apps are available. They are becoming more accurate, convenient, and accessible. For example, Google Translate and Bing Translator are two free translator apps that can be used online, integrated into messaging and other apps, and downloaded to your mobile devices for offline use.

These apps do much more than translate text from web-pages or digital files. They allow you to use your camera to recognize text (e.g., on road signs or physical objects such as books or magazines) or use audio recording to translate speech.

While these apps don't replace human translators and often miss the nuance of language use, they can help in many basic ways. They can provide help with real-time communication (e.g., checking meaning in a messaging conversation), provide help with needed phrases while traveling (e.g., "Where can I find a taxi?"), or even help you order in a foreign restaurant from a menu in another language.

Your challenge: Try out Google Translate and Bing Translator on some text of interest in another language. How well do these translators work? Which features work best? What situations do they work best in? What advice would you give someone about how to use these translators when going on an international business trip?

Dennizn/Alamy Stock Photo

You will notice that nearly all cultures value performance orientation. Note also that all cultures place the lowest priority on hierarchy. In other words, business professionals across the world nearly universally want to focus on performance in an egalitarian, participatory work environment. Furthermore, nearly all cultures value a humane orientation, thus demonstrating that results-focused communication remains critical, but members of most cultures will increasingly expect this strong performance orientation to be framed in a caring manner. As you conduct business across cultures, stay aware of these trends.

Building and Maintaining Cross-Cultural Work Relationships

Thus far, we have focused on aspects of cultural intelligence primarily related to understanding other cultures. In this section, we focus on the process of building relationships and co-creating success with members of other cultures. This process may involve communicating and working in entirely new ways for you and those of other cultures.

Establish Trust and Show Empathy

As in any other business relationships, trust is critical in cross-cultural work relationships. And as in other relationships, you can establish your credibility through competence, caring, and character. These aspects of credibility take more time to demonstrate and convey when working across cultures. People from other cultures may interpret behavior differently, so consider how each aspect of credibility is earned in other cultures. Similarly, allow members of other cultures to show their credibility and learn to interpret how they display competence, caring, and character in their cultures.

Business managers often start relationships from a position of needing to earn the trust of others. This is further complicated when working across cultures, where the beliefs that *most people can be trusted* may be less prominent than in North America (see Figure 4.11). The Netherlands, China, and Germany are considered to be high-trust cultures, meaning that their citizens are more conditioned to trust. The USA, Japan, India, and South Korea are generally considered moderately high-trust societies. In contrast, Spain, Mexico, and Brazil are considered to be low-trust cultures.[34]

One way of establishing trust is to show empathy. Developing empathy is more than showing you care. It also involves understanding members of other cultures as individuals and in terms of business goals and competencies. As you read on, you will notice that trust and credibility across cultures are built on many levels, chief of which is a vision of shared business potential.

Adopt a Learner Mind-Set

Developing strong cross-cultural relationships requires a learner mind-set. With the learner mind-set, you expect that members of other cultures possess unique types of knowledge and unique approaches to problem solving that will be helpful for shared business interests. You expect that they will be full partners in the decision-making process.

The opposite of the learner mind-set when working with other cultures is the judger mind-set. In cross-cultural working relationships, the judger mind-set is often referred to as **ethnocentrism**. It is the belief that your own culture is superior—that it provides better approaches for solving work problems or dealing with work relationships and contains a better knowledge base to conceptualize work. In all interpersonal relationships, the judger mind-set is damaging. In cross-cultural relationships, it is particularly damaging because most people have a great deal of self-respect and self-esteem tied to their cultural identities.[35]

Build a Co-culture of Cooperation and Innovation

When working across cultures, people generally adopt a unique set of communication and collaboration practices. These practices combine aspects of each culture. Over time, these practices, norms, and values form a **co-culture** that combines elements of each culture. One of the best signs that your cross-cultural working relationships are going well is when you have become comfortable enough with one another to form a co-culture. Doing so requires a mind-set that you are creating something new—a belief that you will adopt the best practices of the other culture and vice versa.

Business managers high in cultural intelligence recognize that developing effective co-cultures requires creating something new. This is one reason that seasoned executives select people for international assignments who can handle uncertainty. As Ekkehard Rathgeber, former president of Direct Group Asia, explained, "My belief is: If you pick the wrong person, no matter how much training you give, it won't work. You need to find a person who is very determined and can handle the ambiguity you find every day in China. . . . You must be very open to new things, excited by new things—not someone who wants to preserve his own culture and identity."[36]

Learning the Etiquette of Another Culture

Following the rules of etiquette in other cultures is one way of gaining favorable first impressions and showing respect. This is especially the case as you get to know potential partners or clients. On exploratory trips, you will participate in meetings and social engagements—banquets and meals, refreshments during meetings, and plenty of small talk. These are opportunities for members of each culture to get to know one another in a nonthreatening, casual environment.

FIGURE 4.11

Perceptions of Trust across Cultures

Note: % of adults who agree that *most people can be trusted.*

High-Trust Societies

Netherlands
China
Germany
USA
Japan
India
S Korea
Spain
Mexico
Brazil

Low-Trust Societies

IDEAS IN ACTION

LEARNING ANOTHER LANGUAGE

Mark Zuckerberg of Facebook

Did you know Mark Zuckerberg, CEO and founder of Facebook, speaks Chinese? He started learning it nearly ten years ago. Zuckerberg travels often to China to meet politicians, business professionals, and even students, and he's used his language skills to make speeches in Chinese to a variety of audiences.

Zuckerberg has strong business reasons for cultivating relationships in China. For now, Facebook is banned in China (it has been since 2009), and he clearly hopes it can enter the Chinese market at some point. His earnest efforts to learn more about the Chinese and their culture through its language have opened many opportunities for him to meet important Chinese officials and executives. While he may not have helped Facebook gain access to the Chinese market quite yet, Zuckerberg serves in a variety of influential roles in China, including as a board member for Tsinghua University (one of China's most prestigious universities).

Zuckerberg explained why he's invested so much time learning Chinese: "There are three reasons I decided to learn Chinese. The first, my wife is Chinese. Her grandmother can only speak Chinese. When I told her in Chinese I was going to marry Priscilla, she was very shocked. Then I want to study Chinese culture. The third: Chinese is hard and I like a challenge!"

Catwalker/Shutterstock

Like Zuckerberg, you can benefit from learning another language for a variety of reasons. It gives you many insights into the way people of other cultures think. It helps you appreciate the richness of other cultures. It fosters tremendous goodwill with others. And you may find yourself in situations where your language ability allows smoother communication than relying solely on English.

Sources: Leibowitz, G. (2017, February 2016). Mark Zuckerberg is learning Chinese. Here's why you should, too. *Inc.com.* Retrieved from https://www.inc.com/glenn-leibowitz/mark-zuckerberg-is-learning-chinese-heres-why-you-should-too.html; Snyder, B. (2014, October 23). Why Facebook's Mark Zuckerberg spent years learning Mandarin Chinese. *NBC News* online. Retrieved from https://www.nbcnews.com/tech/social-media/why-facebooks-mark-zuckerberg-spent-years-learning-mandarin-chinese-n232266; Moore, M. (2014, October 24). How good really is Mark Zuckerberg's Mandarin? *The Telegraph* online. Telegraph Media Group Limited. Retrieved from http://www.telegraph.co.uk/technology/mark-zuckerberg/11182575/How-good-really-is-Mark-Zuckerbergs-Mandarin.html.

LO4.3 Name and describe key categories of business etiquette in the intercultural communication process.

 **connect**

Visit http://connect.mheducation.com for an exercise on this topic.

You have many sources for learning about the appropriate customs and etiquette of other cultures. In Table 4.13, you will find examples from Mexico, Indonesia, Nigeria, and Turkey (often called the *MINT* countries because of their expected strategic importance as important emerging markets during the 21st century).[37] This table includes the types of customs and etiquette you should become aware of before traveling to another country for business, including appropriate versus taboo topics of conversation, conversation style, punctuality and meetings, dining, touching and proximity, business dress, and gift giving. Of course there is wide variation within each country. The countries in this table, like the United States, are multicultural. For example, Nigeria is home to roughly 250 ethnic groups and over 500 languages! As far as religion, roughly half of the population identifies with Christianity and roughly half identifies with Islam. Learn some broad tendencies in these cultures but stay aware of the immense diversity within each culture.

TABLE 4.13

Etiquette and Customs in the MINT Countries

	Mexico	Indonesia	Nigeria	Turkey
Meeting and Greeting	Shaking hands is common. Men often give a slight bow when greeting women. Embraces are common among acquaintances.	Shaking hands with a slight nod is common. A frequent greeting is "Selamat" (means *peace*). Some people may greet by placing their hand over their heart or bowing slightly.	Hearty welcomes are expected, with warm smiles, handshakes, and even a hand on the shoulder. Greeting should be in the order of seniority.	Shaking hands is appropriate. Focus should be on the most senior members first.
Appropriate Topics of Conversation	Small talk is important. Talking about family, health, and your enjoyment of Mexican music and food is appropriate.	Silence during conversations is appropriate. Talking about family, food, travel, and local communities is appropriate.	Talking about sports (especially soccer), food, and weather is appropriate.	Talking about politics is often appropriate, although it's important to speak diplomatically.
Private or Taboo Topics of Conversation	Comparing how things are done in the U.S. versus in Mexico; negative aspects of Catholicism; drug trafficking in Mexico.	Government or military corruption; politics; negative aspects of Islam.	Politics, ethnicity.	Negative aspects of Turkish politics; Armenia; Kurdish separatism.
Punctuality and Meetings	Loose with time: arriving 30 minutes after a meeting time may not be considered late. Agendas are viewed flexibly.	Foreigners are expected to be on time, although Indonesians are typically fairly loose with time when working with one another. Social events rarely start on time.	First meetings are typically formal and polite.	Punctuality is very important. Politeness and respect are important in meetings. Social events start on time. Avoid meetings during Ramadan or the Turkish summer.
Dining	Dining is important to build relationships and often occurs in your counterparts' homes. Social events rarely begin on time. Dinners generally include many dishes and last a long time. Alcohol is common at meals. Toasts are offered with the phrase "Salud," which means *health*.	Usually the guest of honor or the most senior person starts a meal. Some beverages and foods, such as alcohol and pork, are avoided because of the Muslim heritage. Both hands should be kept above the table while eating.	When dining in homes, guests often remove their shoes. Honored guests are often served first. The right hand should be used to pass and eat food.	Alcohol is less common largely due to the Muslim influence. Food should be handled only with the right hand.

TABLE 4.13

(Continued)

	Mexico	Indonesia	Nigeria	Turkey
Touching, Proximity, and Body Language	Typically stand close to one another and hold handshakes for longer. Gesture heavily and nod out of respect. Expect direct eye contact.	People touch often once they know each other. Men and women typically do not touch unless the woman initiates a handshake. Avoid extended eye contact. Sit with good posture and avoid crossing legs. Beckon with the entire hand. Avoid using the left hand (it is considered unclean).	Avoid using the left hand only. Eye contact is less direct. Lowering heads to more senior people is appropriate. Heavy use of gestures.	Typically stand close to another. Direct eye contact is expected. Avoid putting hands on hips or in pockets. A single nod means yes. Smiling in public at strangers feels strange. Shaking head means "I don't understand," not necessarily "no."
Business Dress	The quality of your clothes is an indicator of your status. Conservative, formal business attire is generally expected.	Skirts and blouses for women and suits for men are appropriate. Modesty is important.	Formal, conservative suits are appropriate.	Formal, conservative dress. Men generally wear ties and women generally wear suits or dresses.
Titles	Most people are referred to by professional titles such as Doctor, Accountant, or Engineer.	Common titles include Doctor, Professor, and Engineer. Indonesians often use kinship terms such as mother or father for those older than them.	Many titles are used, including Architect and Engineer.	Professional titles such as Doctor, Professor, Lawyer, and even Engineer are common.
Gift Giving	Gift giving is not always necessary. Items with corporate logos are appreciated. Flowers are appropriate when visiting homes.	Gifts are fairly rare. When gifts are given, they are after business is concluded.	When invited to homes, snacks such as nuts or chocolates are appropriate. Use your right hand to present gifts to others. Generally, men do not give gifts to women who are not relatives.	When invited to homes, modest gifts of flowers, candy, or chocolates are appropriate. Business gifts with corporate logos are appropriate but not common.

Generation, Gender, and Other Group Identities

Like culture on a global level, generational groups, gender, and other group identities can impact workplace communication. Often, members of these groups have been *socialized* in certain ways—they grew up with similar societal expectations and interacted with others as children and adults in ways that shaped what they came to view as acceptable and appropriate. The way members of these groups have been socialized often creates shared values, shared identities, and similar communication patterns in the workplace.

Working across Generations

Over the past decade, at least five generations have worked together in the workplace (see Figure 4.12). Professionals work across generations more so now for several reasons. Many workers are retiring later. More importantly, changes in technology and workplace cultures are dramatically affecting how often professionals of different generations interact. Technology allows easier access to colleagues and customers of all ages. Similarly, workplace cultures are moving to more flat, team-based structures that reduce the layers within organizations that, in the past, often separated colleagues by age.

Working with colleagues, clients, and customers of all ages presents many opportunities and challenges. Some of the challenges of working across generations involve distinct differences in working styles.[38] Other challenges are related to power and resources. Older professionals often hold positions with more power and clout, which some researchers suggest is the primary cause of conflict across generations. These challenges may be exacerbated when younger professionals hold leadership positions over older professionals. Many experts note that differences across generations are often a matter of life stages. For example, younger professionals are naturally eager to learn more and gain rapid advancement in their careers, whereas older professionals may feel more established and secure in their careers.[39] Yet other challenges are based on misperceptions and stereotyping. Savvy professionals with high CQ learn to see the best in the experiences and insights of professionals of all generations.

LO4.4 Identify how generational, gender, and other aspects of diversity affect workplace communication.

McGraw Hill **connect**

Visit http://connect. mheducation.com for an exercise on this topic.

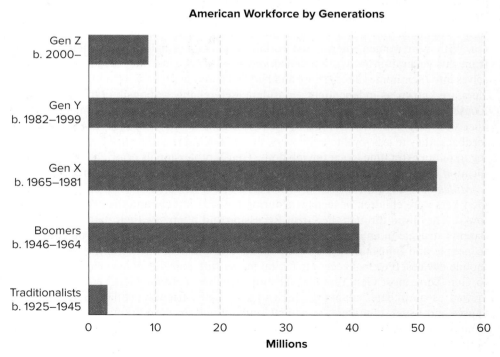

American Workforce by Generations

FIGURE 4.12

Five Generations in the American Workforce

Source: Fry, R. (2018, April 11). Millennials are the largest generation in the U.S. labor force. Pew Research Center. Retrieved from http://www.pewresearch.org/fact-tank/2018/04/11/millennials-largest-generation-us-labor-force/.

JGI/Jamie Grill/Blend Images/Getty Images

The *Silent Generation* or **Traditionalists** were born between 1925 and 1945. Traditionalists grew up during the Depression and World War II. Radio and telephones were emerging communication technologies during this time. Strong parental authority was the norm in most families. Traditionalists tend to be financially conservative, disciplined, patient, and respectful of authority. They believe in logic, hold a sense of right and wrong, and feel less comfortable with ambiguity. In the workplace, they are typically viewed as hardworking, loyal, and dedicated. They hold respect for titles and feel comfortable with command-and-control approaches to leadership and management.[40]

Baby Boomers or **Boomers** were born between 1946 and 1964. Boomers grew up during a prosperous World War II era. They also experienced major political and social changes, including the protest movements to the Vietnam War, the Civil Rights movement, the sexual revolution, Watergate, and the King and Kennedy assassinations. Most families were nuclear families with mothers staying at home. Families often gathered around the TV to watch shows together. Boomers are often considered optimistic, free spirited, and experimental. In the workplace, they hold a strong work ethic—in fact, the term *workaholic* was created for this generation. They hold strong loyalty to employers, and they prefer a professional work environment. Many Boomers have retired or are currently near retirement. Yet, they still comprise roughly 25 percent of the American workforce.[41]

Gen X refers to those who were born between 1965 and 1981. Gen Xers grew up during rapid globalization with growing and intense worldwide competition. Corporate downsizing was common. They also saw the end of the Cold War. They were the first generation to use desktop computers and home video games as children or teenagers. They experienced the rapid proliferation of entertainment options, including MTV and movie channels, on cable TV. The home environment shifted significantly during this era. With more women entering the workforce and more single-parent families, children from this generation were often called *latchkey kids* because they frequently let themselves into their homes after school and had less parental supervision and attention. Gen Xers are known as independent, confident, self-reliant, responsibility driven, results focused, and less formal. In the workplace, they work hard but attempt to maintain a balance with personal lives. Compared with prior generations, they seek more continuous feedback, they're less loyal to employers, they're not impressed by titles, and they're willing to put in extra time to get the job done. Gen X professionals prioritize open communication. Gen X professionals comprise roughly 33 percent of the workforce.[42]

Millennials, Digital Natives, or **Gen Y**ers were born between 1982 and 1999. Most Gen Yers were children or teenagers during the 9/11 attacks and the conflicts that followed. They lived through the Great Recession and often saw their parents or friends' parents struggle in an unpredictable economic environment. They grew up connected to people and information via social media and other online communication. With mobile devices, they had access to digital media with amazing convenience. Compared to Gen Xers, most Gen Yers had far more involved parents. Gen Yers are generally viewed as optimistic, adaptable, inclusive, sociable, friendly, collaborative, loyal to causes and issues, confident, impatient, and entitled. In the workplace, Gen Y professionals seek to strike a balance between work and lifestyle, want flexibility in work hours, enjoy working in teams, want to make an impact, seek continuous feedback and instant results, are less loyal to employers, prioritize a friendly and casual workplace, and enjoy multitasking. Gen Y comprise roughly 35 percent of the workforce.[43]

As you navigate your early professional life, understanding how other professionals view Gen Y professionals will help you play to your strengths and overcome possible misperceptions. It's important to be aware of common perceptions professionals hold toward various generations. Most older professionals regard Gen Y professionals as tech savvy, adaptable, enthusiastic, and entrepreneurial. They also see Gen Y professionals as strong brand ambassadors. Yet, most professionals also regard Gen Y professionals as entitled and inexperienced. These perceptions are common over time—every generation entering the workforce faces these stereotypes. Less than half of professionals view Gen Y employees as hardworking, strong in communication skills, and effective in decision making.[44] One common misperception is that Millennials don't want to talk face-to-face. In fact, Millennials prefer face-to-face communication as much as members of other generations.[45] Your credibility will grow as you disprove some of these common stereotypes and misperceptions.

Post-Millennials or **Gen Z**ers were born in 2000 or after. They amplify many of the traits associated with Gen Yers. For example, they are growing up even more connected, even more reliant on mobile devices, more focused on visual media, and even more accustomed to collaborative platforms.[46] Some Gen Z individuals have already entered the workforce. They are the smallest portion of the American workforce at roughly 6 percent. However, within five to ten years, they'll likely comprise up to 15 percent of the workforce. Members of each generation, particularly those entering the workforce, face stereotypes developed by members of other generations. Gen Y professionals have already formed stereotypes of Gen Z professionals. On the positive side, many Gen Y professionals consider Gen Z employees open-minded (41 percent) and creative (38 percent). On the negative side, many Gen Y professionals consider Gen Z employees lazy (45 percent), self-centered (37 percent), and easily distracted (35 percent).[47]

While work styles may vary across generations, keep in mind that media accounts of generational differences are often hyped or exaggerated.[48] As you work with colleagues, clients, and customers of all ages, consider the following tips:

Focus on individuals and their professional goals. This tip spans nearly all communication—people want to be recognized and respected for who they are on an individual level. While national, generational, gender, and other identities matter to most people, no one wants to be defined or stereotyped by these identities. Learning about others' individual goals and interests is the best way to understand them.

Recognize the similarities across generations. Members of various generations have far more similarities than differences in the workplace. For example, members of each generation are fairly aligned in what they consider the most important aspects of workplace culture. Members of each generation rank fairness, being ethical, and being straightforward as the most important aspects of workplace culture.[49] They also expect virtually the same traits of their leaders: credible, good listeners, forward-looking, and supportive. The Center for Creative Leadership has found that members of each generation hold quite similar life values, with strong importance attached to family, love, integrity, achievement, and happiness.[50] It's also worth noting that many childhood experiences occur in cycles and affect people of various generations in quite similar ways. For example, the two most financially conservative generations are the Traditionalists and the Gen Yers. Not surprisingly, the Traditionalists grew up during the Great Depression and the Gen Yers grew up during the Great Recession.[51]

Pay attention to preferred approaches to communicating. Members of various generations grew up with slightly different communication patterns that they carry throughout their lives. Communication technologies are often used quite differently by each generational group. Not surprisingly, Boomers and Gen Xers are most comfortable with phone calls, and Gen Yers are most comfortable with texting. Gen Xers are particularly comfortable on PCs and laptops, whereas Gen Yers are more comfortable on tablets and other mobile devices. (We discuss technology in more detail in Chapters 7 and 8.)

Beyond technology, however, members of various generations may differ in a variety of ways: word choice, turn-taking in meetings, choice of humor, and many other ways. Pay attention to these differences and enjoy fitting in!

Observe appropriate formality and attire. Professionals of various generations often hold distinct views of formality, etiquette, and attire. While some of these differences may seem more about style and less about substance, noticing, appreciating, and even adopting some of these practices can show respect and a touch of class in the eyes of others.

Gender and Communication Patterns

While some communication patterns of men and women in the workplace have converged over the past decades, differences still exist. Overall, women tend to be more relationship oriented, collaborative, and interconnected in thinking, whereas men tend to be more independent, competitive, and linear in thinking. These differences are somewhat similar to some of the cultural dimensions you read about at the beginning of the chapter. For example, a relational, group-oriented focus tends to describe a collectivist approach to work, and an independent, competitive focus tends to describe an individualist approach to work. In Figure 4.13, you'll notice several differences about the relationship between gender and collectivism that hold in nearly all societies. First, differences in national cultures are typically far greater than those of gender within societies. Second, women tend to be more relationship-oriented in individualist and collectivist societies. Third, there is significant overlap between men and women within societies. This suggests women and men may have general tendencies, but you can easily find many exceptions on an individual level.

One of the foremost experts on gendered communication in the workplace, Dr. Deborah Tannen, has spent the past half century exploring the ways women and men speak in the workplace. She has also studied how boys and girls grow up, and she has shown that the way men and women speak is often rooted in how they socialized and played as children. She has shown that the relational approach of women influences a variety of speech patterns in the workplace.[52] In this section, we explore speech patterns most often associated with women (see Table 4.14 for an overview). Historically, these speech patterns were not considered the dominant speech patterns in the workplace. Increasingly, these speech patterns are recognized and recommended as important ways to help professionals, teams, and organizations succeed.

Asking questions and listening are key leadership abilities. The frequency and purposes of questioning tend to differ slightly between women and men. Women

Visit http://connect.
mheducation.com for an
exercise on this topic.

FIGURE 4.13

Gender in Individualist
and Collectivist
Societies

Source: Chart created by author
based on dozens of research
studies that demonstrate women
tend to exhibit more collectivist,
relational attitudes and behaviors
in collectivist and individualist
societies.

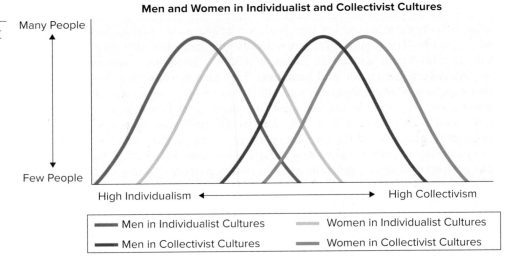

TABLE 4.14

Speech Patterns More Common among Women Than Men

	Pattern More Common among Women Than Men	Benefits	Risks
Asking Questions	Asking lots of questions	Opening up conversations; giving others a chance to speak; generating knowledge; gaining answers	Speaker appears to know less than others
Apologizing	Apologizing often	Expressing sympathy for others; smoothing over awkward situations; admitting mistakes and taking responsibility for them	Speaker appears to unnecessarily take responsibility or appears to lack authority
Sharing Credit	Using "we" rather than "I" when talking about accomplishments	Avoiding self-promotion and recognizing the contributions of others; maintaining a team orientation	Speaker doesn't get enough credit for individual accomplishments
Giving Feedback	Mentioning weaknesses only after citing strengths	Buffering criticism, maintaining high morale, and showing appreciation	Person receiving feedback doesn't recognize the importance of improving
Avoiding Verbal Opposition	Avoiding directly challenging others' ideas; hedging when stating one's own views	Allowing others to state their ideas freely; adopting flexible views of one another's ideas	Others conclude that speaker has weak ideas and lacks confidence
Being Indirect to Subordinates	Speaking indirectly rather than bluntly when talking to subordinates	Placing everyone on the same level and not coming across as commanding, domineering, or bossy	Subordinates conclude that manager lacks assertiveness and clear thinking
Complimenting	Showing genuine appreciation for the actions of others	Maintaining an enjoyable working relationship and showing others they're valued	Being known first and foremost as "nice" at the expense of being considered results driven

Sources: The table is primarily adapted from Tannen, D. (1995, September/October). The power of talk: Who gets heard and why. *Harvard Business Review*, 138–148. Tannen's work primarily focused on risks or unintended consequences of the various speech patterns. In the subsequent decades, many of these speech patterns have become much more in favor. In fact, many of these patterns are often recommended as the preferred approaches to teamwork, collaboration, and other forms of workplace communication. This adapted table also includes information from other sources, including the following: Tannen, D. (2007). *You just don't understand: Women and men in conversation*. New York: William Morrow Paperbacks; Annis, B., & Gray, J. (2013). *Work with me: The 8 blind spots between men and women in business*. New York: St. Martin's Press; Sandberg, S. (2013). *Lean in: Women, work, and the will to lead*. New York: Knopf.

tend to *ask questions* more than men do. In fact, in research about brainstorming meetings of about one hour in length, North American women ask about 19 questions compared with 15 questions for North American men. In similar meetings, East Asian women tend to ask about 11 questions compared with about 6 questions for East Asian men.[53] Whereas men are more likely to ask questions primarily to seek information, women are more likely to also ask questions to build consensus, to show concern, to offer feedback, or to ask for support. Because men view questions primarily as information seeking, they often miss the relational purposes women use for some questions. In the workplace, about 72 percent of men say they think women ask too many questions, and about 80 percent of women prefer to ask questions even when they know the answer.[54]

Women also apologize more than men do for several reasons. Women are more likely to view apologies as expressions of sympathy, whereas men are more likely to view apologies as expressions of responsibility.[55] With a relational focus, women generally have lower thresholds for rudeness, so they're more likely to offer an apology as a matter of politeness or to ease an awkward situation.[56] Women are also more likely to

mediaphotos/Getty Images

admit mistakes. Increasingly, employees respect leaders who can admit mistakes. A recent survey of 3,500 business professionals in 13 countries found that admitting mistakes was the third most important leadership ability—just slightly behind leading by example and communicating in an open, transparent way.[57] Still, apologies can be misinterpreted depending on how much others see them as statements of responsibility versus statements of politeness.

A variety of other speech patterns are more common among women. Women are more likely to *share credit* rather than state their individual contributions, *give feedback* by stating strengths first and then suggesting improvements, *avoid verbal opposition*, and *offer compliments*. Generally, women are more likely to be *indirect* to subordinates and *speak less* in meetings so they avoid sounding bossy. In fact, women who are more assertive and speak up more often are often judged more negatively (by men and women), whereas men are judged more positively for these same actions.[58] Recently, Sheryl Sandberg, COO of Facebook, has been a public advocate for overcoming this type of bias. She explained:

> The data show that success and likeability are positively correlated for men and negatively correlated for women. Which means that as women get more successful, they are liked less—both by men and by other women. That's because we want people to conform to our stereotypes. And when they don't, we don't like them as much. We expect men to have leadership qualities, to be assertive and competent, to speak out. We expect women to have communal qualities, to be givers and sharers, to pursue the common good. The problem is, we want to promote and hire people who are both competent and liked. And that's just much easier for men.[59]

As you work with others, you'll often notice people use these various speech patterns in different ways. Consider the following tips:

Notice when professionals use these speech patterns for task-based versus relationship-based reasons. While gender often plays a role in these speech patterns, many other factors are at play and you can easily think of some exceptions. Regardless, by observing the purposes behind asking questions, apologizing, indirectly offering feedback, and these other speech patterns, you can better understand the intentions of others.

Purposefully and consciously adopt your own style. Most professionals adopt these speech patterns without any thought. Take note of how you use these speech patterns. Be willing to experiment with alternative ways of speaking in the workplace. Find the mix of speech patterns that fits your personality, helps you work well with others, and helps you succeed.

Do your part to overcome biases. Women continue to be underrepresented in leadership positions. The reasons for this are complex and hard to pinpoint. Bias is likely a factor in many cases. For example, research shows that women continue to be judged less positively than men when they're assertive and direct.[60]

Displaying Cultural Intelligence with Other Groups and Appreciating Other Forms of Diversity

Professionals hold identities in many groups and generally adopt some of the shared values and norms of these groups.[61] Regional differences may impact communication. Phrases such as *Southern hospitality* or a *New York minute* often reflect distinct approaches to working with others and getting things done. Similarly, professionals who grew up in rural, suburban, and urban areas often gain lifelong attitudes and behaviors related to sense of community, pace of life, and communication patterns. Ethnicity likewise affects many professionals' values, attitudes, and identities in the workplace. Occupational groups often hold distinct ways of approaching work. For example, engineers and marketers are often socialized into distinct ways of discussing, approaching, and solving problems. Even companies have distinct cultures, which are influenced by many factors, including industry and size. For example, a small tech start-up in Silicon Valley likely has a markedly different culture than that of a large, established bank in New York City. The longer people work in companies, the more they adopt the ways of doing things in those organizations. Your ability to identify the norms and values associated with various groups will help you throughout your career as you work with others.

Gen Yers and Gen Zers are among the most sensitive to issues of diversity. You will improve your workplace and improve your communication skills as you consciously recognize and learn more about forms of diversity that have gained more attention in just the past few years. Increasingly, professionals recognize the the unique opportunities of working with people of neurodiverse backgrounds. **Neurodiversity** refers to people with conditions such as being on the autism spectrum or having attention-deficit/hyperactivity disorder (ADHD).[62] Much more attention has likewise recently focused on professionals and customers with physical challenges and disabilities, including visual impairment, hearing loss, and limited mobility, to name a few. Also, you should learn more about those who are affected by mental illness. Each year, roughly 20 percent of Americans experience mental illness. In fact, depression is the leading cause of disability in the workplace.[63]

Chapter Takeaway for *Global Communication and Diversity*

LO4.1 Describe characteristics of cultural intelligence, its importance for global business leaders, and approaches to developing it.

Principles of High Cultural Intelligence	
• Respect, recognize, and appreciate cultural differences. • Possess curiosity about and interest in other cultures. • Avoid inappropriate stereotypes. • Adjust conceptions of time and show patience. • Manage language differences to achieve shared meaning.	• Understand cultural dimensions. • Establish trust and show empathy across cultures. • Approach cross-cultural work relationships with a learner mind-set. • Build a co-culture of cooperation and innovation.

LO4.2 Explain the major cultural dimensions and related communication practices.

Cultural Dimensions
Individualism refers to a mind-set that prioritizes independence more highly than interdependence, emphasizes individual goals over group goals, and values choice more than obligation. **Collectivism** refers to a mind-set that prioritizes interdependence more highly than independence, emphasizes group goals over individual goals, and values obligation more than choice. **Egalitarianism** refers to cultures that distribute and share power evenly, minimize status differences, and minimize special privileges and opportunities for people just because they have higher authority. **Hierarchy** refers to cultures that expect power differences, follow leaders without questioning them, and feel comfortable with leaders receiving special privileges and opportunities. **Performance orientation** refers to cultures that encourage and reward innovation and set high standards of performance. **Future orientation** involves the degree to which cultures are willing to sacrifice current wants to achieve future needs. **Assertiveness** deals with the level of confrontation and directness that is considered appropriate and productive within a culture. **Humane orientation** refers to cultures that encourage and reward individuals for being fair, friendly, generous, and kind. **Uncertainty avoidance** refers to how cultures socialize members to feel in uncertain, novel, surprising, or extraordinary situations. **Gender egalitarianism** deals with the division of roles between men and women in society.

See *rankings of countries along these cultural dimensions* in Figures 4.2 through 4.10. See *related communication practices* in Tables 4.4 through 4.12. See a *comprehensive set of rankings* for 62 cultures in the online resources.

LO4.3 Name and describe key categories of business etiquette in the intercultural communication process.

Etiquette and Customs	
• Appropriate topics of conversation • Private or taboo topics • Punctuality and meetings • Dining • Touching and proximity	• Conversation style • Business dress • Titles • Gift giving

See *examples of etiquette and customs across the MINT countries* in Table 4.13.

LO4.4 Identify how generational, gender, and other aspects of diversity affect workplace communication.

Generations
Traditionalists were born between 1925 and 1945. **Boomers** were born between 1946 and 1964. **Gen X** individuals were born between 1965 and 1981. **Gen Y** individuals were born between 1982 and 1999. **Gen Z** individuals were born in 2000 or after.

Speech Patterns More Common among Women	
• Asking questions • Apologizing • Sharing credit • Giving feedback	• Avoiding verbal opposition • Being indirect to subordinates • Complimenting

See Table 4.14 for description of *benefits and risks of these speech patterns*.

Key Terms

assertiveness, 117

Boomers, 128

co-culture, 123

collectivism, 114

cultural dimensions, 114

cultural intelligence (CQ), 109

culture, 109

diversity, 109

egalitarian, 115

ethnocentrism, 123

future orientation (FO), 117

Gen X, 128

Gen Y, 128

Gen Z, 129

gender egalitarianism, 119

hierarchical, 115

humane orientation (HO), 118

individualism, 114

neurodiversity, 133

outgroup homogeneity effect, 112

performance orientation (PO), 116

projected cognitive similarity, 111

Traditionalists, 128

uncertainty avoidance (UA), 119

Discussion Exercises

4.1 Chapter Review Questions (LO4.1, LO4.2, LO4.3, LO4.4)

A. As you choose a culture or cultures to learn about, which do you think would be most helpful for your career? Why?

B. Explain what cultural intelligence is. How is it similar to and different from emotional intelligence?

C. What does it mean to embrace diversity in the context of conducting business across cultures?

D. How can you learn about another culture? Map out a plan for learning about a culture of interest.

E. How can stereotypes be productive and counterproductive? How does popular culture impact stereotypes of cultures?

F. What strategies can you use to overcome language barriers?

G. Describe each of the cultural dimensions and related communication practices.

H. Explain what is meant by a co-culture. Explain how a co-culture of communication practices might take form in a business setting.

I. Think of a culture of interest to you. Describe several things you could learn from that culture to enrich your life, deepen your business expertise, and improve your communication skills.

J. Describe what you think are the defining events in each of the generations. Explain how you think these events had long-lasting impacts on members of each of these generations.

K. Choose three of the speech patterns from the section about gender. Explain how these speech patterns may differ between individuals who view them primarily as task based versus those who view them primarily as relationship based?

4.2   Ideas in Action Discussion Questions (LO4.1, LO4.2, LO4.3)

Read the Ideas in Action section in this chapter. Based on Mark Zuckerberg's comments and your own experiences, respond to the following questions:

A. What are the reasons Zuckberg provides for learning Chinese? How do these apply to your reasons for studying another language?

B. What are additional reasons for studying a new language? Specifically, how can learning a new language help you in business and work?

C. If you had the chance to speak with Zuckerberg before a trip to China for business, what five questions would you ask him?

4.3   Leadership Lessons Learned through International Experiences (LO4.1)

Robert W. Selander, former president and CEO of MasterCard, was asked, "What are the most important leadership lessons you have learned?" He responded by describing some of his international experiences. He explained how English ability isn't necessarily reflective of managerial competence:

> I was out visiting a branch [in Brazil]. . . . [Since] he was struggling with his English, the coin sort of dropped that this guy really knows what he's talking about. He's having a hard time getting it out. . . . I realized this was probably the best branch manager I'd seen, but it would have been very easy for me to think he wasn't, because he couldn't communicate as well as some of the others who were fluent in English.[64]

Based on Selander's comments and your own experiences, respond to the following questions:

A. In what ways might you misjudge the competence of others based on language skills?

B. What are several strategies to overcoming language barriers?

C. How can you improve your ability to be a good listener for those with limited English abilities?

Evaluation Exercises

4.4   Evaluate Your Cross-Cultural Stereotypes (LO4.1)

Think about a culture of interest to you. Do the following:

A. Describe five preconceptions or stereotypes you have about the culture.

B. Conduct some research and find out how correct you are. Use books or articles written by experts on the culture. Or find a friend from that country or someone with a lot of experience working there and ask about the accuracy of your preconceptions and stereotypes.

C. Report your findings. For each preconception, describe causes and accuracy. Explain what this might mean about the way one develops impressions, holds preconceptions, and thinks in stereotypes of other cultures.

4.5   Evaluate Your Speech Patterns (LO4.4)

Based on the speech patterns described in Table 4.14, do the following for three of these speech patterns:

A. Explain how you use this speech pattern compared to others you know.

B. Evaluate the degree to which you hold task-based versus relationship-based purposes when you use this speech pattern.

C. Describe how others could potentially misinterpret your approach to this speech pattern.

Application Exercises

4.6   Analyze, Explain, and Make a Presentation about Your Own Business Culture (LO4.2)

Review the GLOBE rankings for the eight cultural dimensions for your culture. Also, go to a website that describes business etiquette in your country (e.g., http://www.ediplomat.com/np/cultural_etiquette/cultural_etiquette.htm, www.commisceo-global.com/resources/country-guides/). Assume you are going to train a group of business professionals from another country about doing business in your country. Also, assume the business professionals have read about the GLOBE rankings and learned about etiquette in your country. Create a presentation that includes the following:

A. Explain the five key norms and values that drive business culture in your country. Give at least one example of related communication behavior for each of the five key norms and values.

B. Describe the accuracy of the GLOBE rankings and information about business etiquette.

C. Explain three cases that involve exceptions to the rule. For example, if you say that performance orientation is one of the key norms and values, you could explain a few cases where views toward performance are more relaxed.

D. Provide three final tips for working effectively with members of your own culture that you won't find in books.

4.7   Analyze the Cultural Dimensions of a Country (LO4.2)

Choose a country of interest to you. (The GLOBE study rankings for 62 countries are provided in the online resources that accompany this book.) Analyze the country in terms of the following cultural dimensions:

· Individualism and collectivism.

· Egalitarianism and hierarchy.

· Performance orientation.

· Future orientation.

· Assertiveness.

· Humane orientation.

· Uncertainty avoidance.

· Gender egalitarianism.

In conclusion, describe five communication practices you think may be key when working with members from this country.

4.8 Analyze the Etiquette of a Business Culture (LO4.3)

Choose a country of interest to you. Go to the eDiplomat website, the Commisceo Global website (e.g., http://www.ediplomat.com/np/cultural_etiquette/cultural_etiquette.htm, www.commisceo-global.com/resources/country-guides/), and/or another website with cross-cultural comparisons of business etiquette. Read all the information about this country's business culture and then do the following:

A. Write about the five most intriguing aspects of the culture.

B. Write about the five aspects of etiquette you would observe when interacting with members of this culture.

C. Choose three relevant cultural dimensions (underlying sets of norms and values) and explain how they impact business etiquette in this country.

D. Write five questions about business etiquette you would like to ask a person from the country you chose.

4.9 Read News Stories Written by and for Members of Another Culture (LO4.1, LO4.2)

Read three online newspaper articles from a country of interest. You should be able to find an online English-language newspaper for your chosen country fairly easily. Go to these websites:

- www.world-newspapers.com
- www.onlinenewspapers.com
- www.refdesk.com/paper.html

After reading the three newspaper articles, write the following for each article:

A. *Article information:* article name, source (magazine name), date/edition, pages, web address if available.

B. *Summary:* a short summary of the article.

C. *Cultural lessons:* one paragraph that describes one or two aspects of culture that are illustrated by the article.

D. *Implications for business communication:* Explain how these aspects of the culture would impact conducting business with members of this culture.

4.10 Read a Magazine Article about Global Business (LO4.1, LO4.2)

Read a magazine article about global business that includes issues about cross-cultural differences. Consider the following online sources for an article:

- https://www.bloomberg.com/europe
- https://www.bloomberg.com/asia
- https://www.bloomberg.com/middleeast
- https://www.bloomberg.com/africa
- www.time.com/business
- https://www.cnbc.com/world/
- https://www.cnn.com/business

After reading an article about global business, write the following for each:

A. *Article information:* article name, source (magazine name), date/edition, pages, web address if available.

B. *Summary:* a short summary of the article.

C. *Cultural lessons:* one paragraph that describes one or two aspects of culture that are illustrated by the article.

D. *Implications for business communication:* Explain how these aspects of the culture would impact conducting business with members of this culture.

4.11 Interview a Professional with International Experience (LO4.1, LO4.2, LO4.3)

Interview someone you know who has worked extensively with members of other cultures. Spend an hour or two asking this person about his/her experiences. Report what this person had to say about five of the following ten areas:

- Etiquette.
- Preferred communication channels.
- Working in teams.
- Conducting meetings.
- Approaches to resolving differences of opinion.
- Negotiation style.
- Cultural values and norms.
- Adjusting to living in another country.
- Approaching conflicts or disagreements.
- Persuasion.

4.12 Interview an International Student (LO4.1, LO4.2)

Interview an international student at your university. Report about the interview in five of the following ten areas:

- Business in the student's country.
- Popular entertainment in the country.
- Changes occurring in the culture.
- Challenges in adapting to the food.
- Challenges in adapting to housing.
- Challenges in adapting to transportation.
- Experiences making friendships with Americans.
- Experiences working in teams with American students.
- Experiences working with American professors.
- Observations about American culture.

Conclude your report with three recommendations you have for people doing business with members of that culture.

4.13 Interview Professionals from Several Generations (LO4.4)

Interview at least two professionals from at least two generations. Ask them about their views of similarities and differences between professionals of various generations. Consider asking questions such as the following:

- What do you see as some of the differences in how people of various age groups use technology? (You might consider being specific about various types of communicating and computing, such as texting, calling, voice mail, email messages, word processing, and so on.)
- What are some differences in word choice across the generations?
- How do members of various generations approach meetings differently?
- How do members of various generations view etiquette and formality differently?
- What do you think members of the various generations can learn from each other?
- What do you see as the main similarities across generations?

Write a short report of your findings. Conclude your report with three recommendations for working effectively across generations.

Language Mechanics Check

4.14 Review the comma rules C1 through C10 in Appendix A. Then rewrite each sentence to add commas where needed.

A. China where most of our manufacturing is located offers advantages such as quality price and speed.

B. We manufacture in a location where we get superior quality and price.

C. To get the best quality we often need to locate our factories in Western Europe.

D. Between July 2020 and July 2024 we get tax breaks at our Poland factory.

E. We need to remit tax payments for this quarter between July 1 2020 and July 15 2020.

F. Often we relocate factories to gain tax advantages.

G. To gain tax advantages we often relocate factories.

H. Vietnam not China is the new destination for low-cost manufacturing.

I. Vietnam offers a low-cost highly educated workforce.

J. We also are considering opening factories in Malaysia Indonesia and the Philippines.

Endnotes

1. Earley, P. C., & Mosakowski, E. (2004, November). Cultural intelligence. *Harvard Business Review, 139*–146; Livermore, D. (2011, April 9). CQ: The test of your potential for cross-cultural success. *Forbes.* Retrieved from www.forbes.com/2010/01/06/cq-cultural-intelligence-leadership-managing-globalization.html.

2. Javidan, M., Steers, R. M., & Hitt, M. A. (2007). Putting it all together: So what is a global mindset and why is it important? In M. Javidan, R. M. Steers, and M. A. Hitts (Eds.), *The global mindset.* Oxford: Elsevier; Chaney, L. H., & Martin, J. S. (2011). *Intercultural business communication.* Upper Saddle River, NJ: Prentice Hall; Earley, P. C., & Mosakowski, E. (2004, November). Cultural intelligence. *Harvard Business Review, 139*–146.

3. Wheelan, S. A. (1999). *Creating effective teams: A guide for members and leaders.* Thousand Oaks, CA: Sage; Ribbink, K. (2002, November). Seven ways to better communicate in today's diverse workplace. *Harvard Management Communication Letter,* 3–5.

4. Cardon, P. W., & Marshall, B. (2010). International opportunities for business students. *National Business Education Yearbook, 48,* 223–235.

5. Bryant, A. (2010, July 31). Get a diploma, but then get a passport. *The New York Times.* Retrieved from www.nytimes.com/2010/08/01/business/01corner.html.

6. Cardon, P. W., Marshall, B. A., Patel, N., Goreva, N., & Fontenot, R. J. (2019). A comparison of study abroad and globalization attitudes among information systems, computer science, and business students: Recommendations for IS curriculum design. *Issues in Information System, 10*(1), 28–39.

7. Varner, I., & Beamer, L. (2005). *Intercultural communication in the global workplace* (3rd ed.). Boston: McGraw-Hill.

8. Briam, C. (2010). Outsourced: Using a comedy film to teach intercultural communication. *Business Communication Quarterly, 73*(4), 383–398; Cardon, P. W. (2010). Using films to learn about the nature of cross-cultural stereotypes in intercultural business communication courses. *Business Communication Quarterly, 73*(2), 150–165.

9. Verluyten, S. P. (2007). *Cultures: From observation to understanding.* Leuven, Belgium: ACCO; Verluyten, S. P. (2008, October 15). *The use of video excerpts in intercultural training.* Paper presented at the 73rd Annual Convention of the Association for Business Communication.

10. Varner, I., & Beamer, L. (2005). *Intercultural communication in the global workplace* (3rd ed.). Boston: McGraw-Hill; Neuliep, J. W. (2009).

Intercultural communication: A contextual approach. Thousand Oaks, CA: Sage; Cardon, P. W. (2010). Using films to learn about the nature of cross-cultural stereotypes in intercultural business communication courses. *Business Communication Quarterly, 73*(2), 150–165.

11. Berg, C. R. (2002). *Latino images in film: Stereotypes, subversion, resistance.* Austin: University of Texas; Wingfield, M., & Karaman, B. (1995). Arab stereotypes and American educators. *Social Studies and the Young Learner, 7*(4), 7–10; Mastro, D. E. (2003). A social identity approach to understanding the impact of television messages. *Communication Monographs, 70*(2), 98–113.

12. Wike, R., Poushter, J., & Zianulbhai, H. (2016, June 28). America's international image. *Pew Research Center Global Attitudes & Trends.* Retrieved from http://www.pewglobal.org/2016/06/28/americas-international-image/.

13. Fernandez, J. A., & Underwood, L. (2006). *China CEO: Voices of experience from 20 international business leaders.* Singapore: Wiley, 65.

14. Levine, R. V., & Norenzayan, A. (1999). The pace of life in 31 countries. *Journal of Cross-Cultural Psychology, 2,* 178–205.

15. Ribbink, K. (2002, November 1). *Seven ways to better communicate in today's diverse workplace.* Boston: Harvard Business Press.

16. House, R. J., Hanges, P. J., Javidan, M., Dorfman, P. W., & Gupta, V. (Eds). (2004). *Culture, leadership, and organizations: The GLOBE study of 62 societies.* Thousand Oaks, CA: Sage.

17. The scores in these rankings have been converted to a scale from 0 to 100 from the 7-point Likert scales provided in the GLOBE study. These conversions are similar in approach to how Geert Hofstede classified cultures to allow easier comprehension for readers.

18. Gelfand, M. J., Bhawuk, D. P. S., Nishii, L. H., & Bechtold, D. J. (2004). Individualism and collectivism. In R. J. House, P. J. Hanges, M. Javidan, P. W. Dorfman, and V. Gupta (Eds.), *Culture, leadership, and organizations: The GLOBE study of 62 societies* (pp. 437–512). Thousand Oaks, CA: Sage; Hofstede, G. (2001). *Culture's consequences: Comparing values, behaviors, institutions, and organizations across nations* (2nd ed.). Thousand Oaks, CA: Sage; Neuliep, J. W. (2009). *Intercultural communication: A contextual approach.* Thousand Oaks, CA: Sage.

19. Gelfand, M. J., Bhawuk, D. P. S., Nishii, L. H., & Bechtold, D. J. (2004). Individualism and collectivism. In R. J. House, P. J. Hanges, M. Javidan, P. W. Dorfman, and V. Gupta (Eds.), *Culture, leadership, and organizations: The GLOBE study of 62 societies* (pp. 437–512).

Thousand Oaks, CA: Sage; Hofstede, G. (2001). *Culture's consequences: Comparing values, behaviors, institutions, and organizations across nations* (2nd ed.). Thousand Oaks, CA: Sage; Neuliep, J. W. (2009). *Intercultural communication: A contextual approach.* Thousand Oaks, CA: Sage.

20. Vandello, J. A., & Cohen, D. (1999). Patterns of individualism and collectivism across the United States. *Journal of Personality and Social Psychology, 77*(2), 279–292.

21. Hofstede, G. (2001). *Culture's consequences: Comparing values, behaviors, institutions, and organizations across nations* (2nd ed.). Thousand Oaks, CA: Sage.

22. Javidan, M. (2004). Performance orientation. In R. J. House, P. J. Hanges, M. Javidan, P. W. Dorfman, and V. Gupta (Eds.), *Culture, leadership, and organizations: The GLOBE study of 62 societies* (p. 239). Thousand Oaks, CA: Sage.

23. Javidan, M. (2004). Performance orientation. In R. J. House, P. J. Hanges, M. Javidan, P. W. Dorfman, and V. Gupta (Eds.), *Culture, leadership, and organizations: The GLOBE study of 62 societies* (pp. 239–281). Thousand Oaks, CA: Sage.

24. Ashikanasy, N., Gupta, V., Mayfield, M. S., & Trevor-Roberts, E. (2004). Future orientation. In R. J. House, P. J. Hanges, M. Javidan, P. W. Dorfman, and V. Gupta (Eds.), *Culture, leadership, and organizations: The GLOBE study of 62 societies* (pp. 282–342). Thousand Oaks, CA: Sage.

25. Ashikanasy, N., Gupta, V., Mayfield, M. S., & Trevor-Roberts, E. (2004). Future orientation. In R. J. House, P. J. Hanges, M. Javidan, P. W. Dorfman, and V. Gupta (Eds.), *Culture, leadership, and organizations: The GLOBE study of 62 societies* (pp. 282–342). Thousand Oaks, CA: Sage.

26. den Hartog, D. N. (2004). Assertiveness. In R. J. House, P. J. Hanges, M. Javidan, P. W. Dorfman, and V. Gupta (Eds.), *Culture, leadership, and organizations: The GLOBE study of 62 societies* (p. 395). Thousand Oaks, CA: Sage.

27. den Hartog, D. N. (2004). Assertiveness. In R. J. House, P. J. Hanges, M. Javidan, P. W. Dorfman, and V. Gupta (Eds.), *Culture, leadership, and organizations: The GLOBE study of 62 societies* (pp. 395–436). Thousand Oaks, CA: Sage.

28. Fernandez, J. A., & Underwood, L. (2006). *China CEO: Voices of experience from 20 international business leaders* (p. 275). Singapore: Wiley.

29. Kabasakal, H., & Bodurm, M. (2004). Humane orientation in societies, organizations, and leader attributes. In R. J. House, P. J. Hanges, M. Javidan, P. W. Dorfman, and V. Gupta (Eds.), *Culture, leadership, and organizations: The GLOBE study of 62 societies* (p. 569). Thousand Oaks, CA: Sage.

30. Kabasakal, H., & Bodurm, M. (2004). Humane orientation in societies, organizations, and leader attributes. In R. J. House, P. J. Hanges, M. Javidan, P. W. Dorfman, and V. Gupta (Eds.), *Culture, leadership, and organizations: The GLOBE study of 62 societies* (pp. 564–601). Thousand Oaks, CA: Sage.

31. De Luque, M. S., & Javidan, M. (2004). Uncertainty avoidance. In R. J. House, P. J. Hanges, M. Javidan, P. W. Dorfman, and V. Gupta (Eds.), *Culture, leadership, and organizations: The GLOBE study of 62 societies* (pp. 602–653). Thousand Oaks, CA: Sage; Hofstede, G. (2001). *Culture's consequences: Comparing values, behaviors, institutions, and organizations across nations* (2nd ed.). Thousand Oaks, CA: Sage.

32. De Luque, M. S., & Javidan, M. (2004). Uncertainty avoidance. In R. J. House, P. J. Hanges, M. Javidan, P. W. Dorfman, and V. Gupta

(Eds.), *Culture, leadership, and organizations: The GLOBE study of 62 societies* (pp. 602–653). Thousand Oaks, CA: Sage.

33. Emrich, C. G., Denmark, F. L., & den Hartog, D. N. (2004). Cross-cultural differences in gender egalitarianism. In R. J. House, P. J. Hanges, M. Javidan, P. W. Dorfman, and V. Gupta (Eds.), *Culture, leadership, and organizations: The GLOBE study of 62 societies* (pp. 343–394). Thousand Oaks, CA: Sage.

34. Ortiz-Ospina, E., & Roser, M. (2014). Trust. *Our World in Data.* Retrieved from https://ourworldindata.org/trust.

35. Neuliep, J. W. (2009). *Intercultural communication: A contextual approach.* Thousand Oaks, CA: Sage.

36. Fernandez, J. A., & Underwood, L. (2006). *China CEO: Voices of experience from 20 international business leaders* (p. 265). Singapore: Wiley.

37. Information from this table comes from sources such as the following: eDiplomat. (2018). Cultural etiquette around the world. Retrieved from http://www.ediplomat.com/np/cultural_etiquette/cultural_etiquette.htm; Commisceo Global. (2018). Country guides to culture, customs and etiquette: Learn about different cultures. Retrieved from https://www.commisceo-global.com/resources/country-guides; Cultural Atlas. (2018). *Countries.* Retrieved from https://culturalatlas.sbs.com.au/countries; Morrison, T., & Conaway, W. A. (2006). *Kiss, bow, or shake hands.* (2nd ed.) Avon, MA: Adams Media.

38. Moore, S., Grunberg, L., & Krause, A. J. (2015). generational differences in workplace expectations: A comparison of production and professional workers. *Current Psychology, 34*, 346–362.

39. Levenson, A., & Deal, J. J. (2015). *Generational conflict at work: Separating fact from fiction.* Alexandria, VA: SHRM Foundation; Deal, J. J. (2007). *Retiring the generation gap: How employees young & old can find common ground.* San Francisco, CA: Jossey-Bass.

40. Tolbize, A. (2008). *Generational differences in the workplace.* Minneapolis: Research and Training Center on Community Living, University of Minnesota; Twenge, J. M., Campbell, S. M., Hoffman, B. J., & Lance, C. E. (2010). Generational differences in work values: Leisure and extrinsic values increasing, social and intrinsic values decreasing. *Journal of Management, 36*(5), 1117–1142; *EY.* (2013). Survey shows younger managers rise in the ranks. *EY.* Retrieved from http://www.ey.com/Publication/vwLUAssets/EY-Survey_shows_younger_managers_rising_in_the_ranks/$FILE/Executive-Summary-Generations-Research.pdf; Schullery, N. M. (2013). Workplace engagement and generational differences in values. *Business Communication Quarterly, 76*(2), 252–265; Nicholas, A. J., & Regina, S. (2009). Generational perceptions: Works and consumers. *Journal of Business and Economics Research, 7*(10), 47–52.

41. Tolbize, A. (2008). *Generational differences in the workplace.* Minneapolis: Research and Training Center on Community Living, University of Minnesota; Twenge, J. M., Campbell, S. M., Hoffman, B. J., & Lance, C. E. (2010). Generational differences in work values: Leisure and extrinsic values increasing, social and intrinsic values decreasing. *Journal of Management, 36*(5), 1117–1142; *EY.* (2013). Survey shows younger managers rise in the ranks. *EY.* Retrieved from http://www.ey.com/Publication/vwLUAssets/EY-Survey_shows_younger_managers_rising_in_the_ranks/$FILE/Executive-Summary-Generations-Research.pdf; Schullery, N. M. (2013). Workplace engagement and generational differences in values. *Business Communication Quarterly, 76*(2), 252–265; Nicholas, A. J., & Regina, S. (2009). Generational perceptions: Works and consumers. *Journal of Business and Economics Research, 7*(10), 47–52.

42. Tolbize, A. (2008). *Generational differences in the workplace.* Minneapolis: Research and Training Center on Community Living, University of Minnesota; Twenge, J. M., Campbell, S. M., Hoffman, B. J., & Lance, C. E. (2010). Generational differences in work values: Leisure and extrinsic values increasing, social and intrinsic values decreasing. *Journal of Management, 36*(5), 1117–1142; *EY.* (2013). Survey shows younger managers rise in the ranks. *EY.* Retrieved from http://www.ey.com/Publication/vwLUAssets/EY-Survey_shows_younger_managers_rising_in_the_ranks/$FILE/Executive-Summary-Generations-Research.pdf; Schullery, N. M. (2013). Workplace engagement and generational differences in values. *Business Communication Quarterly, 76*(2), 252–265; Nicholas, A. J., & Regina, S. (2009). Generational perceptions: Works and consumers. *Journal of Business and Economics Research, 7*(10), 47–52.

43. Tolbize, A. (2008). *Generational differences in the workplace.* Minneapolis: Research and Training Center on Community Living, University of Minnesota; Twenge, J. M., Campbell, S. M., Hoffman, B. J., & Lance, C. E. (2010). Generational differences in work values: Leisure and extrinsic values increasing, social and intrinsic values decreasing. *Journal of Management, 36*(5), 1117–1142; *EY.* (2013). Survey shows younger managers rise in the ranks. *EY.* Retrieved from http://www.ey.com/Publication/vwLUAssets/EY-Survey_shows_younger_managers_rising_in_the_ranks/$FILE/Executive-Summary-Generations-Research.pdf; Schullery, N. M. (2013). Workplace engagement and generational differences in values. *Business Communication Quarterly, 76*(2), 252–265; Nicholas, A. J., & Regina, S. (2009). Generational perceptions: Works and consumers. *Journal of Business and Economics Research, 7*(10), 47–52.

44. Randstad & Future Workplace. (2017). *Gen Z and Millennials collide at work.* Retrieved from https://experts.randstadusa.com/hubfs/Randstad_GenZ_Millennials_Collide_Report.pdf; *EY.* (2013). Survey shows younger managers rise in the ranks. *EY.* Retrieved from http://www.ey.com/Publication/vwLUAssets/EY-Survey_shows_younger_managers_rising_in_the_ranks/$FILE/Executive-Summary-Generations-Research.pdf.

45. Finn, D., & Donovan, A. (2013). "PwC's NextGen: A global generational study. *PwC.* Retrieved from http://www.pwc.com/gx/en/hr-management-services/publications/assets/pwc-nextgen.pdf.

46. Randstad & Future Workplace. (2017). *Gen Z and Millennials collide at work.* Retrieved from https://experts.randstadusa.com/hubfs/Randstad_GenZ_Millennials_Collide_Report.pdf; Knoll Workplace Research. (2014). What comes after Y? Generation Z: Arriving in the office soon. Knoll website. Retrieved from https://www.knoll.com/media/938/1006/What-Comes-After-Y.pdf.

47. Schawbel, D. (2014). Gen Y and Gen Z global workplace expectations study. *Millennial branding.* Retrieved from http://millennialbranding.com/2014/geny-genz-global-workplace-expectations-study/.

48. Winning the generation game (2013, September 28). *The Economist.* Retrieved from http://www.economist.com/news/business/21586831-businesses-are-worrying-about-how-manage-different-age-groups-widely-different; Hastings, R. R. (2012, October 18). Generational differences exist, but beware of stereotypes. SHRM. Retrieved from https://www.shrm.org/hrdisciplines/diversity/articles/pages/generational-differences-stereotypes.aspx.

49. Tolbize, A. (2008). *Generational differences in the workplace.* Minneapolis: Research and Training Center on Community Living, University of Minnesota.

50. 10 principles for working across generations. (n.d.). Center for Creative Leadership. Retrieved from http://insights.ccl.org/multimedia/podcast/10-principles-for-working-across-generations/.

51. Griswold, A. (2014, January 30). Millennials are the most financially conservative generation since the Great Depression. *Business Insider.* Retrieved from http://www.businessinsider.com/millennials-financially-conservative-generation-2014-1.

52. Tannen, D. (1995, September/October). The power of talk: Who gets heard and why. *Harvard Business Review,* 138–148; Tannen, D. (2007). *You just don't understand: Women and men in conversation.* New York: William Morrow Paperbacks.

53. Aritz, J., Walker, R., Cardon, P. W., & Zhang, L. (2017). Discourse of leadership: The power of questions in organizational decision making. *International Journal of Business Communication, 54*(2), 161–181.

54. Annis, B., & Gray, J. (2013). *Work with me: The 8 blind spots between men and women in business.* New York: St. Martin's Press; Sandberg, S. (2013). *Lean in: Women, work, and the will to lead.* New York: Knopf.

55. Crosley, S. (2015, June 23). Why women apologize and should stop. *The New York Times.* Retrieved from www.nytimes.com/2015/06/23/opinion/when-an-apology-is-anything-but.html?_r=2.

56. Ketchum. (2014, May). *Ketchum Leadership Communication Monitor.* Retrieved from https://www.ketchum.com/sites/default/files/2014_klcm_report.pdf.

57. Ignatius, A. (2013, April). Now is our time. *Harvard Business Review,* 84–88; Sandberg, S. (2013). *Lean in: Women, work, and the will to lead.* New York: Knopf; Sandberg, S., & Grant, A. (2015, January 12). Speaking while female. *The New York Times.* Retrieved from http://www.nytimes.com/2015/01/11/opinion/sunday/speaking-while-female.html; Tannen, D. (1995, September/October). The power of talk: Who gets heard and why. *Harvard Business Review,* 138–148.

58. Ignatius, A. (2013, April). Now is our time. *Harvard Business Review,* 87.

59. Sandberg, S. (2013). *Lean in: Women, work, and the will to lead.* New York: Knopf.

60. Jameson, D. (2007). Reconceptualizing cultural identity and its role in intercultural business communication. *Journal of Business Communication, 44*(3), 199–235.

61. Bryant, A. (2010, June 26). The X factor when hiring? Call it "presence." *The New York Times.* Retrieved from www.nytimes.com/2010/06/27/business/27corner.html.

62. Austin, R. D., & Pisano, G. P. (2017, May/June). Neurodiversity as a competitive advantage. *Harvard Business Review,* 96–103.

63. Gurchiek, K. (2017, October 26). SHRM chapters advocate for workers with disabilities. Society for Human Resource Management website. Retrieved from www.shrm.org/resourcesandtools/hr-topics/behavioral-competencies/global-and-cultural-effectiveness/pages/shrm-chapters-advocate-for-workers-with-disabilities.aspx.

64. Robert W. Selander as cited in Bryant, A. (2010, June 26). The X factor when hiring? Call it "presence." *The New York Times.* Retrieved from www.nytimes.com/2010/06/27/business/27corner.html.

Design elements: Set of universal icons for mobile app & web: ©Vitalex/Shutterstock; Learning Objective, Why Does This Matter?, Technology Tips, and Ideas in Action icons: ©McGraw-Hill

Principles for Business Messages

PART

THREE

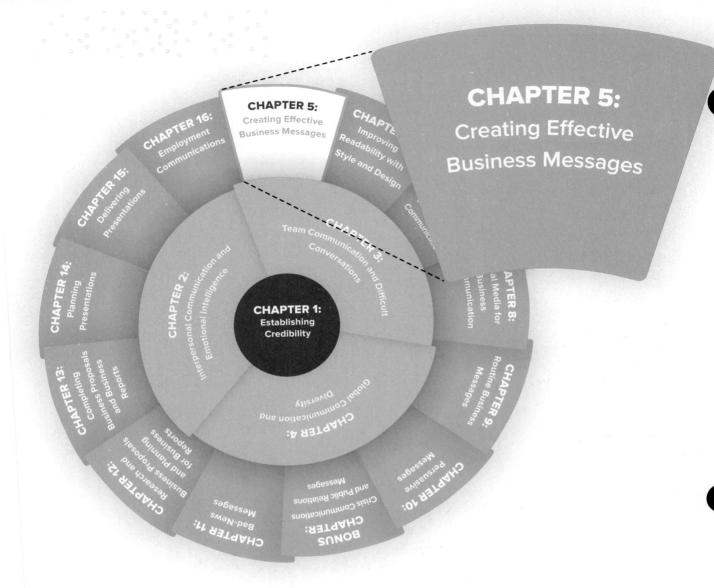

CHAPTER 5:
Creating Effective Business Messages

 ESTABLISHING CREDIBILITY

 **PRINCIPLES OF INTERPERSONAL COMMUNICATION**

 PRINCIPLES FOR & TYPES OF BUSINESS MESSAGES

 LEARNING OBJECTIVES

After studying this chapter, you should be able to do the following:

LO5.1 Explain the goals of effective business messages and the process for creating them.

LO5.2 Identify the needs of your audience in the AIM planning process.

LO5.3 Gather the right information and refine business ideas in the AIM planning process.

LO5.4 Develop your primary message and key points in the AIM planning process.

LO5.5 Explain and apply positive and other-oriented tone in business messages.

WHY DOES THIS MATTER?

You will have countless opportunities over your career to communicate important messages. Every situation will be unique and involve an array of business problems and recipients. In all your communications, however, this principle will remain constant: Effective messages emerge from a consistent planning process and a positive and other-oriented tone.

This chapter first explains the process of developing business messages. Then, we focus on the most critical stage—planning—followed by a discussion of tone. Although the chapter is concerned particularly with writing, the principles transfer effectively to any type of communication.

Throughout, we will provide examples from the chapter case about a challenging communication task. Not all communication tasks demand such rigorous planning and preparation. In fact, the majority will be fairly routine, meaning they will require less time and encounter little resistance from your readers. However, even routine messages require a strategic focus on planning and tone. As you apply these principles to your communications, you will find that you are far more effective and influential.

> **Hear Pete Cardon explain why this matters.**
>
> **bit.ly/cardon5**

CHAPTER CASE — JUSTIFYING A PAID PARENTAL LEAVE POLICY AT EASTMOND NETWORKING

WHO'S INVOLVED

Latisha Jackson

Summer Intern

- Working as a summer intern in the human resource department
- Assigned to research options for a new parental leave program

Jeff Brody

HR Director

- Has held current position for five years
- Trying to develop initiatives that improve employee well-being and morale amid steep budget cuts

Lisa Johnson

Finance Manager

- Has held current position for three years
- Specializes in developing budgets and financial forecasts

THE SITUATION

Jeff recently asked Latisha to spend around ten hours per week to develop a proposal for paid parental leave benefits as an effort to improve employee morale and retention. However, because the company is facing major budget constraints, executives are skeptical of resource-intensive initiatives. Jeff wants Latisha to focus her attention on the financial implications of paid parental leave first. He wants her to present her preliminary findings within one month.

Latisha was excited about the opportunity to keep working on paid parental leave options, even on this limited basis. She was also slightly nervous—one month was a short time to analyze how paid parental leave policies would affect the financial well-being of the company, and she wanted to prove she was up to the task. Each week, she gathered information. She talked to HR directors at several local businesses of roughly the same size that had introduced new parental leave policies.

One of the trickiest parts of the project was estimating the financial impacts. Latisha had taken a few classes in finance but had no real experience. So, she met with the finance manager, Lisa Johnson, and showed her the information she had collected. Lisa agreed to spend some time estimating the potential return on investment from various paid parental leave options. After Lisa provided an estimate, Latisha was ready to draft her initial findings and recommendations for Jeff.

TASK

1 How can Latisha address Jeff's and other key decision makers' needs and concerns? (See the section "The AIM Planning Process for Effective Business Messages.")

2 How should Latisha organize the information she has found? (See the section "The AIM Planning Process for Effective Business Messages.")

3 How should Latisha organize her message? (See the section "The AIM Planning Process for Effective Business Messages.")

4 How can Latisha strike the right tone? (See the section "Setting the Tone of the Message.")

The Process for Creating Business Messages

LO5.1 Explain the goals of effective business messages and the process for creating them.

Writing effective business messages involves a process—one that involves examining, developing, and refining business ideas in a way that provides business value to your audience. The very process that we explain in this section drives excellence in business thinking. Furthermore, it drives collaboration and productivity in your work relationships.

The process of developing business messages is fairly straightforward: *plan*, *write*, and *review*. You've likely been trained and coached in a similar process many times during your education. Nearly all business professionals have been trained in this process. Yet few business professionals excel at it and, consequently, few business professionals produce excellent written communication. Making this process a habit requires discipline and scheduling.

Notice Figure 5.1, which depicts the stages and goals for creating effective messages. We will focus on each of the three stages (planning, writing, and reviewing) in this chapter and the following one. It's worth noting that these stages are not necessarily linear and often overlap one another. Business writers frequently move back and forth between the stages.

Expert writers, however, more carefully and consciously break these stages apart. For example, they are more likely to analyze the needs of the audience, identify and collect the right information to tackle a problem, and identify the primary message and key points before starting a formal draft of a business message. On the other hand, poor and average writers are more likely to begin drafting or writing right away. They often address planning issues—audience analysis, information gathering, and message development—as they go. Consequently, they tend to write in a less organized, perhaps even haphazard, manner. They generally produce less strategic and influential messages.

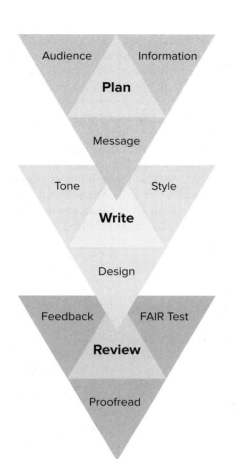

PLAN: Get the content right.

- Understand your *audience*.
- Gather the right *information*.
- Develop your *message*.

WRITE: Get the delivery right.

- Set the right *tone*.
- Apply a clear and concise *style*.
- Focus on navigational *design*.

REVIEW: Double-check everything.

- Get *feedback*.
- Ensure your message is *fair*.
- Make sure to *proofread*.

FIGURE 5.1

The Stages and Goals of Effective Message Creation

Developing expertise in this process makes you more effective, plus it makes you more efficient. In Figure 5.2, you'll see a chart that contrasts the time that poor, average, and expert business writers commit to planning, writing, and reviewing. Not surprisingly, poor writers spend less overall time than average and expert writers. They are aimless and sloppy. They generally spend little or no time planning and usually do not review their messages before sending them.[1]

The contrast between average business writers and expert business writers is most intriguing. Expert business writers not only produce more effective written

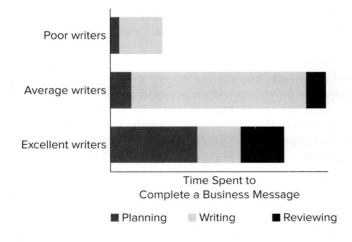

Time Spent to
Complete a Business Message

■ Planning　▨ Writing　■ Reviewing

FIGURE 5.2

Time Spent by Poor, Average, and Expert Writers Developing a Complete Business Message

Source: Time estimates based on author's observation of thousands of business students and consistent with decades of research about expertise as described in Pressley, M., & McCormick, C. B. (1995). *Advanced educational psychology for educators, researchers, and policymakers.* New York: HarperCollins.

communications, but they also do so more quickly than average writers. Their secret is to devote a much higher percentage of their time to the planning and reviewing stages. In particular, they spend far more time planning than average or poor writers. They take the time to understand the business issues well, piece together great ideas, make sure the ideas meet the needs of their audiences, and structure their messages for greatest clarity and impact. Once they start drafting, the content is essentially in place.

As you craft business messages, maintain a listener-centered approach (as opposed to a message-centered approach as described in Chapter 3). In the listener-centered approach to writing business messages, you seek as much input as reasonably possible from colleagues, clients, and customers. You ask them about their opinions, preferences, and areas of expertise. You find out what those to whom you are writing really want and expect. You adopt a learning, other-oriented approach to writing.

The AIM Planning Process for Effective Business Messages

LO5.2 Identify the needs of your audience in the AIM planning process.

The most important stage of creating effective business messages is planning. Throughout the remainder of the book, we will refer to the three-component AIM planning process for developing influential messages. It focuses on three areas: (1) **A**udience analysis; (2) **I**nformation gathering; and (3) **M**essage development. In short, the planning process should include analyzing the needs of your audience, gathering the right information to meet those needs, and then developing your message. The AIM planning process unleashes your best thinking and allows you to deliver influential messages.

Audience Analysis

Effective business communicators possess an uncanny ability to step into the shoes of their audience members. They think about their audience's needs, priorities, and values. They envision how their readers will respond when getting the message—in thought, feeling, and action. They also consider how the message will affect their working relationships. Effective business communicators regularly take the following actions to tailor their messages to others: identify reader benefits and constraints, consider reader values and priorities, estimate personal credibility, anticipate reactions, and consider secondary audiences.

Identifying Reader Benefits and Constraints   For many messages, this is the single most important planning step. Simply put, your readers respond when you provide them with something that they value. When you communicate no apparent benefits, your readers are unlikely to engage.

Similarly, think about the constraints your audience faces. Your readers will often see value in your messages but may not be able to respond as you hope because they don't have enough time, resources, or authority to make certain decisions.

In Latisha's case, she can point out to Jeff many potential benefits of paid parental leave (PPL). Presumably, Jeff cares about the employees and would like them to have more time with their families. Jeff would also like to save money for the company. And, like most employees, Jeff would likely want to be associated with any successful work initiative. In this regard, Latisha's challenge is choosing which reader benefits appeal most to Jeff in this situation.

Latisha should keep in mind that no matter how much Jeff views PPL as beneficial, he likely faces a number of constraints. He would certainly need to get agreement for a project of this size from other members of the leadership team. So, he would

Visit http://connect.
mheducation.com for an
exercise on this topic.

need to persuade others and risk his own credibility. In addition, since the company faces a financial crisis, any initiative may be viewed with higher-than-usual scrutiny and even skepticism. Latisha should anticipate these constraints and develop her message accordingly.

Considering Reader Values and Priorities   Being an effective business communicator requires that you learn about other people—what they value, prioritize, and prefer. **Values** refer to enduring beliefs and ideals that individuals hold. Because values are at the core of belief systems, appeals to an individual's values can have strong influence. Generally, people hold workplace values—beliefs and ideals about the appropriate way to approach business problems, resolve issues, and choose goals. **Priorities** involve ranking or assigning importance to things, such as projects, goals, and tasks. Priorities tend to shift more often than values.

Latisha has not known Jeff for long, but she can attempt to understand some of his values and priorities. She believes that he is fundamentally invested in the PPL initiative because of his strong commitment to employees. He seems to value detailed analysis and careful decision making. Based on his comments, he seems to prioritize efficiency and cost-cutting. This may be due to the current financial situation or it may be due to deeper, long-held values. He also refers frequently to the "company president," which suggests a respect for the chain of command. Jeff's frequent mention of the company president may mean that Jeff is under a great deal of pressure to perform according to the president's expectations.

Estimating Your Credibility   As discussed in Chapter 1, your readers will inevitably judge your recommendations, requests, and other messages based on their view of your credibility. If your credibility is low, consider how to strengthen your message in ways that overcome your lack of credibility.

Many entry-level professionals face this situation; they have relatively low professional credibility because they are viewed as the newcomers. Establishing a professional reputation takes time. It takes less time, however, if you stay aware of your strengths, weaknesses, and goals. Most important, your reputation depends on adding value in the workplace. Yet, overcoming a reputation as a newcomer isn't easy. Changing your reputation will likely take at least six months. To break out of a reputation as an inexperienced newcomer, consider the following options:[2]

- Set up a time to talk with your boss. Explain your growth in various areas and ask for his/her ideas about improving your professional reputation.
- Ask your boss if you can take on any higher-responsibility projects.
- Make sure you fit in with the corporate culture in terms of professional dress and communication style.
- Attend a lot of meetings to get to know as many colleagues as possible. Participate appropriately.
- Create a professional blog about a niche area.

As a newcomer, Latisha recognizes that Jeff has many reasons to doubt her credibility. She is an undergraduate business student without a degree or significant business experience. She has worked for Jeff for only a short time, so he can't make a good judgment about her ability to get things done. But he obviously saw promise in her or he wouldn't have hired her to develop a work initiative that was so important to him. Latisha felt that her credibility would be enhanced by including a trusted, competent voice in her memo. As a result, she sought the opinion of Lisa Johnson. By highlighting Lisa's estimate and opinions, Latisha elevates her own credibility. Lisa is competent in her area (finance) and reliable (she has a track record at Eastmond). Jeff will likely give more credence to Latisha's message because it references Lisa's cash flow estimate.

> **Audience Analysis Components**
>
> - Identify reader benefits and constraints.
> - Consider reader values and priorities.
> - Estimate your credibility.
> - Anticipate reactions.
> - Consider secondary audiences.

Anticipating Reactions   In the planning stage, envision how others will respond to your message. Imagine how your readers will think, feel, and act as they read it. Always think about what you want to achieve in terms of workplace relationships. Most business activities cannot be separated from the web of working relationships involved. Sometimes your positions or ideas may displease others. In these instances, consider how you can articulate your views most constructively.

Latisha believes that Jeff will respond sensibly to a clearly articulated, logical justification for a generous PPL policy. Based on the strength of the cash flow estimates, Latisha thinks he will respond favorably. Even if he disagrees, she assumes he will respect her hard work and reward her with challenging assignments.

Keeping Secondary Audiences in Mind   In most situations, you should anticipate that individuals other than your primary recipient will view your messages. In some cases, you will distribute your message to additional individuals whom it will affect. For example, you might copy team members on a correspondence between you and a client so that they are aware of project progress. In other cases, your primary recipient will forward your message or otherwise share the information with others. You should consider which secondary audiences will view your messages and, if necessary, modify them accordingly.

Latisha recognizes that her proposal for developing a PPL policy would impact everyone in the organization and would require significant resources. If Jeff finds merit in the proposal, he will undoubtedly share the message with a variety of individuals involved in the decision-making process.

Information Gathering

LO5.3 Gather the right information and refine business ideas in the AIM planning process.

Developing great business ideas involves sorting out the business issues and objectives, collecting as many relevant facts as possible, and making sound judgments about what the facts mean and imply. You are making sense out of often complex and confusing pieces of business information.

Excellent business thinkers possess a number of characteristics. First, they clearly and precisely identify and articulate key questions and problems. Second, they gather information from a variety of sources. Third, they make well-reasoned conclusions and solutions. Fourth, they remain open to alternatives to approaching and reasoning about the business problem—that is, they are mentally flexible. They can hold opposing views, avoid either/or thinking, avoid one-way linear thinking, and are open to nonconventional solutions. Finally, they are skilled at communicating with others to figure out and solve complex problems.[3]

Business professionals use many methods of bringing out their best thinking. Some write notes, some draw diagrams, some brainstorm with colleagues, some write ideas in outline form, and some just examine the ideas in their minds. Generally, for complex problems, such as the opening case, writing down ideas in some form is an important part of developing sound ideas from the information gathered. In this section, we focus on three broad areas: (1) identifying the business problem(s); (2) analyzing the business problem(s); and (3) clarifying objectives.

> **Information Gathering Components**
>
> * Identify the business problems.
> * Analyze the business problems.
> * Clarify objectives.

Visit http://connect.mheducation.com for an exercise on this topic.

Identifying the Business Problem(s)   To remain competitive and profitable, businesses constantly need to identify and overcome problems. One of the best reputations you can gain as a business professional is that of a problem solver. The first step in problem solving is identifying business problems. This involves understanding an organization's business objectives and related challenges. It involves asking many questions from a lot of angles. Once you're asking the right questions, you can gather the right information.

In Latisha's case, she has been given a charge: Find out how PPL would affect Eastmond. This is a classic business problem. Latisha can break down the problem by asking a variety of questions: How does PPL affect employee engagement and satisfactions? How do other businesses measure costs and return on investment for PPL initiatives? How do PPL initiatives impact productivity, retention, and recruiting? What are the ethical and legal considerations related to PPL?

Analyzing the Business Problem(s)   After gathering information to your questions, you can focus on analysis. Analyzing the business problem typically involves uncovering relevant facts, making conclusions, and taking positions. **Facts** are statements that can be relied on with a fair amount of certainty (most things are not absolutely certain in the business world) and can be observed objectively. **Conclusions** are statements that are reasoned or deduced based on facts. **Positions** are stances that you take based on a set of conclusions. In the workplace, you will often make recommendations, which are a type of position.

Latisha analyzed the business problem by collecting a variety of facts and making five or six broad conclusions about PPL based on those facts (see Figure 5.3). For example, she concluded that PPL increases retention based on findings from several studies, listed with bullet points. This form of outlining facts and conclusions can be particularly helpful once Latisha begins writing.

Latisha also relied on insiders for information. She asked Lisa Johnson, the company's finance manager, to estimate the financial impact PPL would have on Eastmond's cash flow (see details in Latisha's completed message at the end of the "Setting the Tone of the Message" section). In many cases, you conduct data gathering and analysis within your networks of colleagues and other business partners.

Clarifying Objectives   As you're gathering information and analyzing it, also clearly identify your goals. You are essentially asking yourself, "Now that I understand the problem, what exactly do I want to accomplish?" Knowing how committed you are to various work outcomes will help you decide how hard to push certain positions. It will also help you balance your preferred work outcomes with your work relationships.

Latisha has carefully thought about her attitudes toward creating a PPL policy for Eastmond. She is certain she wants the chance to work on the initiative. She is passionate about this issue and wants to gain experience combining her interests in management, equity, and family well-being. Latisha has thought about whether her self-interests are too strong. But, she feels confident that this initiative is good for the company: It will benefit the employees and it will save the company money. She is committed to taking a strong position.

Message Development

Once you have analyzed the needs of your audience and gathered the right information, you develop your basic message. This includes identifying and framing the primary message and setting up the logic with supporting points and a call to action (see the Ideas in Action box later in the chapter, featuring Jason Fried, that emphasizes how much developing clear and compelling messages can impact your career opportunities). The questions you will address include the following:

1. *Framing the primary message.*
   a. What is the primary message?
   b. What simple, vivid statement (15 words or fewer) captures the essence of your message?
2. *Setting up the logic of your message.*
   a. What are your supporting points?
   b. What do you want to explicitly ask your readers to do (call to action)?
   c. How will you order the logic of your message?

LO5.4 Develop your primary message and key points in the AIM planning process.

Visit http://connect.mheducation.com for an exercise on this topic.

FIGURE 5.3

Partial Analysis of Facts and Conclusions during Information Gathering

---

Analysis of Paid Parental Leave Policies

Most American companies offer no or limited paid parental leave (PPL), and Americans want much better PPL policies.

- Access to paid paternity leave is rare. Three states require equal access for mothers and fathers: California, New Jersey, and Rhode Island (U.S. Department of Labor, 2017).
- Access to paid paternity leave is rare. Three states require equal access for mothers and fathers: California, New Jersey, and Rhode Island (U.S. Department of Labor, 2017).
- 70 percent of fathers take fewer than ten days of leave after the birth or adoption of a child. (U.S. Department of Labor, 2017)
- The median length of leave is 11 weeks for mothers and just 1 week for fathers. Two-thirds of fathers say they want more time off (Schulte, Durana, Stout, & Moyer, 2017).
- In 2016, just 17 percent of employers offered paid parental leave (Onley, 2017).
- A 2017 estimate suggested 38 percent of U.S. organizations provide PPL. Of those that offer it, 58 percent offer the same amount to all new parents; 25 percent give more to birth mothers; and 15 percent differentiate between primary and secondary caregivers (WorldatWork, 2017).
- At organizations that provide PPL, women take 41 days compared to 22 days for men (Onley, 2017).
- At organizations that provide PPL, 80 percent offer full pay. The average paid parental leave is 4.1 weeks and the median length is 3 weeks (WorldatWork, 2017).

Progressive PPL policies cover offer generous options with many caregiver scenarios.

- Many PPL policies now cover any new parent and include options for birth, adoption, surrogacy, foster children, and any form of legal guardianship (Jackson, 2018).
- EY covers fertility treatments, surrogacy, and adoption (Onley, 2017).
- The most progressive and legally safe plans provide equal PPL for moms and dads for caregiving and bonding. JPMorgan Chase and Estee Lauder have been sued for discriminatory policies against dads (Jackson, 2018; Nowak, 2018; Rau & Williams, 2017). Women who carry children can receive additional time to recover from childbirth. Moms and dads must be treated equally for bonding leave (Nowak, 2018).
- Many PPL policies have flexible return-to-work policies (Jackson, 2018).
- "Primary caregiver" models are old-fashioned and reinforce gender stereotypes and gender roles (Rau & Williams, 2017). Primary versus secondary caregiver leave policies are difficult to administer (Nowak, 2018).
- Some companies have PPL for grandparents. For example, Cisco gives three days of PPL to grandparents (Miller, 2017).
- You don't need to provide benefits when hiring employees. You can require them to work a minimum amount of time first (Nowak, 2018).
- The most generous PPL plans tend to be offered by tech companies. Leading tech companies offer 12 to 26 weeks of PPL: Netflix, 52 weeks; Adobe, 26 weeks; Spotify, 26 weeks; Dell, 26 weeks; Etsy, 26 weeks; eBay: 24 weeks; Amazon, 20 weeks; Twitter, 20 weeks; Facebook, 4 months; Reddit, 4 months; Cisco, 13 weeks; Microsoft, 12 weeks. Other notable organizations include the following: Gates Foundation, 52 weeks; Change.org, 18 weeks; EY, 16 weeks, Johnson & Johnson, 8 weeks; Walmart: 6 weeks (Jackson, 2018; Miller, 2017; Onley, 2017).

PPL policies attract employees in the recruiting process.

- PPL policies attract the most well-qualified employees (Rau & Williams, 2017).
- PPL policies are particularly valued by women and Millennials. About 78 percent of Millennial parents are part of two-career couples (Rau & Williams, 2017).
- Well-educated professionals can be selective about employers because unemployment is just 2.5 percent for people over 25 with a college degree (Zhao, 2018).
- Most early-career professionals can easily find comparative information about PPL benefits. For example, the website FairyGodBoss has created a crowdsourced maternity leave resource center (Zhao, 2018).

FIGURE 5.3

(*Continued*)

Employers and their employees benefit in many ways from PPL policies.

- The OECD estimates that paid parental leaves of 15 weeks in the United States would increase productivity 1.1 percent (Schulte, Durana, Stout, & Moyer, 2017).
- Paid family medical leave (PFML) companies tend to be prepared for extended employee absences (EY, 2017).
- 71 percent of employees in companies with paid family leave for birth or adoption of a child are satisfied compared to 50 percent at companies without (EY, 2017).
- Creating better parental leave at the Gates Foundation has increased employee engagement (Zhao, 2018).
- When Google increased paid parental leave from 12 weeks to 18 weeks, attrition among mothers fell 50 percent. At Accenture, leave was extended from 8 weeks to 16 weeks and attrition among mothers dropped by 40 percent. At Aetna, an expansion of maternity leave led to a 14 percent increase in the percentage of women who returned to the workforce (Schulte, Durana, Stout, & Moyer, 2017).
- Organizations with family-supportive policies are 60 percent more likely to achieve above-average financial performance compared to organizations without these policies. That rises to 93 percent for organizations with paternity leave policies (Gray, 2002).
- Employers with PFML benefits overwhelmingly (over 90 percent) reported positive or neutral effects for improved morale, lower turnover, and higher profitability and productivity (EY, 2017).

PPL policies lead to more equitable outcomes for women and their families.

- 71 percent of Americans believe mothers and fathers should have equal bonding time with children (Schulte, Durana, Stout, & Moyer, 2017).
- Millennials expect both parents to be equally involved in parenting (Rau & Williams, 2017).
- Women are more likely to return to work when men take parental leave (Rau & Williams, 2017).
- Attrition of new mothers has dropped 50 percent at companies that have expanded parental leave policies (Rau & Williams, 2017).
- Paid family leave closes the gender pay gap, reduces family dependence on family assistance, and increases the rate at which women return to work (Schulte, Durana, Stout, & Moyer, 2017).
- Fathers who take parental leave share children duties more equally with mothers (U.S. Department of Labor, 2017).
- More time off for fathers is associated with higher gender equality, more involved parenting, less family stress, and better development of children (Schulte, Durana, Stout, & Moyer, 2017).
- Fathers who take longer paternity leaves tend to engage with and bond more with children. This leads to better developmental outcomes (U.S. Department of Labor, 2017).

References

Brody, J. (2020, January 15). *Key indicators of HR performance at Eastmond*; EY. (2017, March). *Viewpoints on paid family and medical leave*. London: Ernst & Young; Gray, H. (2002, May). *Family-friendly working: What a performance! An analysis of the relationship between the availability of family-friendly policies and establishment performance*. London: Centre for Economic Performance. Retrieved from http://eprints.lse.ac.uk/20082/1/Family-Friendly_Working_What_a_Performance%21_An_Analysis_of_the_Relationship_Between_the_Availability_of_Family-Friendly_Policies_and_Establishment_Performance.pdf; Jackson, A. E. (2018, September 6). 15 companies with the best parental leave policies. *Glassdoor*. Retrieved from https://www.glassdoor.com/blog/best-parental-leave-policies/; Miller, S. (2017, November 27). Companies add new twists to parental leave: Baby-bonding time for grandparents is among the new offerings. *Society for Human Resource Management* website. Retrieved from www.shrm.org/resourcesandtools/hr-topics/benefits/pages/parental-leave-twists.aspx; Nowak, J. (2018, August 10). Drafting a parental leave policy that won't get you sued. *Society for Human Resource Management* website. Retrieved from https://www.shrm.org/resourcesandtools/hr-topics/benefits/pages/tips-for-drafting-parental-leave-policies.aspx; Onley, D. (2017, February 22). Is paid family leave becoming a new standard for employers. *Society for Human Resource Management* website. Retrieved from www.shrm.org/hr-today/news/hr-magazine/0317/pages/is-paid-family-leave-becoming-a-new-standard-for-employers.aspx; Rau, H., & Williams, J. C. (2017, July 28). A winning parental leave policy can be surprisingly simple. *Harvard Business Review*. Retrieved from hbr.org/2017/07/a-winning-parental-leave-policy-can-be-surprisingly-simple; Schulte, B., Durana, A., Stout, B., & Moyer, J. (2017, June 16). Paid family leave: How much time is enough? *New America Better Life Lab*. Retrieved from https://www.newamerica.org/better-life-lab/reports/paid-family-leave-how-much-time-enough/#economic-impact; U.S. Department of Labor. (2013). Paternity leave: Why parental leave for fathers is so important for working families. Washington, D.C.: U.S. Department of Labor. Retrieved from https://www.dol.gov/asp/policy-development/PaternityBrief.pdf; WorldatWork. (2017, May). Survey of paid parental leave in the United States. New York: Mercer. Retrieved from https://www.worldatwork.org/docs/research-and-surveys/survey-report-survey-of-paid-parental-leave-in-the-us.pdf; Zhao, Jingcong. (2018, May 10). Why paid parental leave policies are becoming way more generous. *PayScale* website. Retrieved from https://www.payscale.com/compensation-today/2018/05/paid-parental-leave-benefit.

Framing the Primary Message Framing involves showcasing a message from an overarching theme. It focuses a reader or listener on a certain key idea or argument and highlights the premises and support for this key idea or argument. As one management communication expert said, "No communication skill . . . is more critical to the manager than the ability to frame an issue effectively."[4] Your job in framing the message is to help your reader see the issue from a strategic perspective. Just as a frame draws out particular aspects of a painting, the frame you apply to your message can create a unique prism through which your audience will read.

Message Development Components

- Frame the primary message.
- Set up the structure and logic of the message.

Strategic communicators consider alternative frames before they settle on the one that will be most compelling. Ideally, it should be a vivid statement with rational and emotional appeal. One standard you'll encounter frequently in this book is whether a reader would remember the frame later. Regarding your frame, ask questions such as the following: Will readers remember my primary message two hours from now? What about in two days or two weeks? Will this frame make readers more likely to support my call to action?[5]

The art of creating effective frames involves capturing your primary message in a short, memorable statement of 15 words or fewer. Eduardo Castro-Wright, former president and CEO of Wal-Mart Stores USA, discussed this strategy in the context of organizational communication: "We have a very clear view of what we do for consumers around the world. And we can describe our complete strategy in 10 words. And that makes it very easy to get everybody energized and aligned."[6]

As Latisha was thinking about how to justify a new PPL policy, she came up with three options for framing the message:

- Frame A—Providing PPL is the right thing to do. We are responsible for our employees and their families.
- Frame B—Providing PPL shows we are an employee-friendly company and will increase our profitability.
- Frame C—Providing PPL shows we're a progressive company that focuses on the changing needs of society.

She thinks each frame is powerful. She personally relates to Frame A with her passion for family well-being. However, she thinks this case is weakest in the current financial situation and with Jeff's apparent budgetary limitations. She believes that Frame B is strong. The company needs to cut costs, and Jeff has explicitly noted the company president's interest in improving morale. She also believes that Frame C is true but thinks it will not persuade Jeff or other decision makers.

Ultimately, Latisha selects Frame B for several reasons. With Jeff's preference for brief, to-the-point, results-oriented, and well-reasoned positions, she believes this frame is best suited for this communication approach. Also, she believes the concept of profitability emphasizes the return on investment for this project more so than any other frame. She wants to emphasize that a PPL policy is an asset—not a liability of any sort.

Setting Up the Message Framework   Most business arguments employ a **direct** or **deductive** approach. In other words, they begin by stating the primary message, which is typically a position or recommendation. Then they lay out the supporting reasons. Most business messages conclude with a call to action. The call to action in many cases is a more detailed and elaborate version of the initial position or recommendation.

Figure 5.4 illustrates the framework of most deductive business arguments. Generally, a reader could get the gist of your message—the primary message, rationale, and call to action—simply by reading the opening paragraph, the first sentence of each supporting paragraph, and the final paragraph. In fact, many of your readers, who are generally busy, will do exactly that. They will skim the communication to understand the main ideas and implications. If they see merit in your ideas, they will go back and read the entire message more carefully.

In upcoming chapters, we will focus on many types of messages for common business situations. The framework for these various messages may differ slightly from the one illustrated in Figure 5.4. For some messages, such as when delivering bad news (see Chapter 10), you may adopt a more **indirect** or **inductive** approach, in which you will provide supporting reasons first followed by the primary message. In all messages, however, the importance of framing and arranging supporting ideas to accentuate the main idea remains the same.

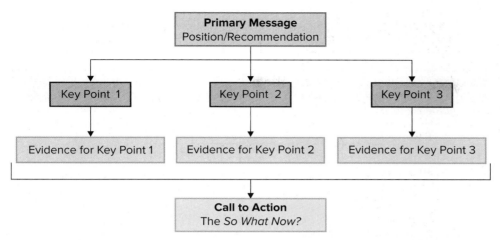

FIGURE 5.4

Typical Deductive
Framework for a
Business Argument
and Related Paragraph
Structure

One option for setting up the structure and appearance of various documents is to use templates. For ideas on enhancing the structure and appearance of various types of business messages, see the Technology Tips feature later in the chapter.

When you are setting up the logic of your message, you may find that sketching out or diagramming it is helpful. Latisha's logic for Frame B involves the claim that a generous PPL policy will show Eastmond is employee friendly and will increase profitability. It will do so by increasing employee engagement and satisfaction, reducing employee turnover, and attracting top talent. By diagramming her logic, she tightens her thinking about the problem and transfers her ideas more effectively into written form (Figure 5.5).

As you set up the structure of the message, carefully test its logic. Business decisions are consequential. Seasoned businesspeople expect solid business logic to support important decisions, and they dismiss ideas that are based on flimsy reasoning. If you ensure that your messages are built on strong reasoning, you will be far more influential because your company will benefit and you will gain credibility.[7] To build well-reasoned business positions, avoid the following types of logical inconsistencies: unsupported generalizations, faulty cause/effect claims, weak analogies, either/or logic, slanting the facts, and exaggeration.

FIGURE 5.5

Message Structure for Latisha's Justification of a PPL Policy

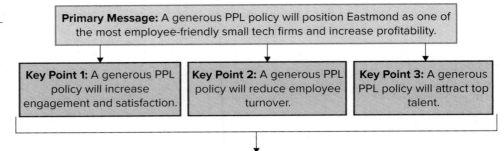

Primary Message: A generous PPL policy will position Eastmond as one of the most employee-friendly small tech firms and increase profitability.

Key Point 1: A generous PPL policy will increase engagement and satisfaction.

Key Point 2: A generous PPL policy will reduce employee turnover.

Key Point 3: A generous PPL policy will attract top talent.

Since a generous PPL policy will position Eastmond as one of the most employee-friendly small tech firms and increase profitability, we should do the following:

1. Develop the PPL policy (June 15 to July 31, 2020).
2. Promote the new PPL policy (August 1 to September 30, 2020).
3. Hire new employees (October 1, 2020, to March 31, 2021).
4. Evaluate the success of the PPL policy (April 1 to May 31, 2021)

Avoiding Unsupported Generalizations   This issue boils down to providing supporting facts for your claims. As you look at the examples in Table 5.1, notice that the less effective example is a blanket claim without support. The more effective example provides a variety of supporting facts.

Avoiding Faulty Cause/Effect Claims   As you analyze business issues, you are often trying to identify causes and effects. For example, when proposing new initiatives, you will generally claim that your actions will *cause* a certain result. The ability to precisely predict effects is always tricky, so choose your language and reasoning carefully. If readers are troubled by one of your cause/effect claims, they will become increasingly picky about your reasoning throughout the message (see Table 5.2).

Avoiding Weak Analogies   As you make sense of business issues, you will often try to identify analogies with other organizations, people, or things. Strong analogies serve to bolster your arguments. However, weak analogies may lead to inaccurate conclusions and recommendations. Be sure that the analogies you make are based on close and relevant similarities (see Table 5.3).

Avoiding Either/Or Logic   One of the main characteristics of critical thinking is to remain flexible and open to alternative explanations and options. In business, you will always want to stay aware of alternative ways of solving the same problem. Furthermore, most of your readers will respond better to you when they view you as

TABLE 5.1

Avoiding Unsupported Generalizations

Less Effective	More Effective
Eastmond has a turnover problem.	Eastmond faces an employee turnover problem. Employee turnover is at 23 percent compared to rates of between 10 to 15 percent at similar tech firms in our area.
Without any supporting facts, this broad generalization will be viewed skeptically by many readers.	This statement provides statistics to support the conclusion. The comparative data shows this is a problem.

TABLE 5.2

Avoiding Faulty Cause/Effect Claims

Less Effective	More Effective
Lisa Johnson's calculations show that Eastmond will definitely save at least $900,000 over the next five years by introducing PPL.	Lisa Johnson projected the financial impacts of a 20-week PPL policy. Considering increased productivity gains due to higher employee engagement, savings from reduced turnover, and higher employee costs to cover for employees on PPL, we anticipate saving about $900,000 over the next five years (see Lisa's attached estimate for assumptions and other details).
This statement assumes that a PPL policy will result in a definite result: at least $900,000 in savings. The certainty of this claim would raise skepticism among many readers, especially without data.	This statement provides facts, assumptions, and calculations to make a confident estimate. The statements are carefully crafted to avoid stating absolute outcomes. As a result, the statement will be perceived much more credibly.
Last year five promising early-career professionals turned down job offers. If we had PPL, they would have joined Eastmond.	Last year five promising early-career professionals turned down job offers. Two of them told us they were disappointed there wasn't any PPL. This leads us to believe we are losing some early-career professionals because we don't offer PPL.
This statement states a cause that is nearly impossible to demonstrate convincingly, especially without additional information.	This statement does not attribute the lack of PPL as the single cause of turned-down job offers. It provides more specific details about the lack of PPL as a concern for two of the individuals. The language is measured and objective.

flexible and open to other ideas (including their own). In the less effective example in Table 5.4, the claim is that a PPL policy is the only way to increase employee morale—that is, *either we provide a PPL policy and improve employee morale, or we don't provide a PPL policy and continue to have low morale.* In the more effective claim, providing a PPL policy is still identified as a way of increasing employee morale. However, this claim does not eliminate other options for improving employee morale.

TABLE 5.3

Avoiding Weak Analogies

Less Effective	More Effective
Organizations such as Netflix and the Gates Foundation have given a full year of PPL and dramatically increased employee retention. Therefore, we should adopt a 52-week PPL model to ensure we increase retention.	We found that the most generous PPL policies among small tech firms range from roughly 8 to 24 weeks. Therefore, in her estimate, Lisa assumed that Eastmond will gain the most employee retention benefits by offering 20-week PPL to new parents.
This statement is a weaker analogy because it compares a smaller organization, Eastmond, with large organizations that can take a different approach in terms of personnel, resources, and program options. Readers in smaller organizations would consider this a weak analogy.	This statement is a stronger analogy because it refers to similar-sized organizations with similar resources and constraints. Readers are far more likely to consider this a credible analogy.

TABLE 5.4

Avoiding Either/Or Logic

Less Effective	More Effective
Without providing PPL, employees will continue to suffer from low morale.	One way to reduce turnover is offering more employee-friendly benefits such as PPL.
This logic is either/or: without a PPL, employees will have low morale; with PPL, they will have high morale.	This statement does not imply that a PPL policy is the only option for reducing turnover. Readers will perceive this statement as confident but grounded and measured.

Avoiding Slanting the Facts　Slanting means presenting only those facts that are favorable to your position. To maintain your credibility, avoid slanting in all cases. While slanting may provide short-term benefits, many executives and managers have lost a lifetime of credibility when their gross misrepresentation was exposed. At a minimum, when readers notice that you have slanted the facts, they will be skeptical of the logic and reasoning of your entire message (see Table 5.5).

Avoiding Exaggeration　As with slanting, exaggeration impacts readers' perceptions of your overall credibility as well as the credibility of the message. Be careful not to make exaggerated claims, as illustrated in Table 5.6.

TABLE 5.5

Avoiding Slanting the Facts

Less Effective	More Effective
Employee turnover at Eastmond is at 23 percent compared to as low as 10 percent at similar tech firms in our area.	Employee turnover at Eastmond is at 23 percent compared to rates of between 10 to 15 percent at similar tech firms in our area.
This statement leaves out the top of the range to imply the separation between Eastmond and competing firms is even more dramatic than often is the case.	This statement provides the top of the range and thus provides complete information.

TABLE 5.6

Avoiding Exaggeration

Less Effective	More Effective
Providing PPL to our new parents would completely change our work environment for the better, allowing us to reach levels of performance previously unimagined.	Providing PPL options could significantly improve employee satisfaction, an issue that our company president is particularly interested in.
Many readers would view this statement with skepticism since the language seems exaggerated and unbelievable. This would lead some readers to call into question the credibility of the writer and the entire message.	This statement projects confidence but does not contain exaggerated, unrealistic, or overly ambitious language.

IDEAS IN ACTION

ARTICULATE YOUR IDEAS IN WRITING

Jason Fried of Basecamp

Jason Fried, CEO of the software company Basecamp, embraces the use of traditional and social media to build an effective professional persona that aligns with the reputation of his organization. As a TED Talks speaker and a prolific writer and contributor on platforms such as Twitter (twitter.com/jasonfried), Medium (medium.com/@jasonfried), LinkedIn (www.linkedin.com/in/37signals), Inc. (www.inc.com/author/jason-fried), and BigThink (bigthink.com/experts/jasonfried), he brings attention to issues such as productivity, project management, collaboration, workplace satisfaction, diversity, and business strategy. He is known for building a great workplace where all employees are encouraged not to work more than 40 hours per week.

Nicholas Hunt/Getty Images

Jason frequently talks about the importance of excellent writing skills. Here is his approach to hiring:

> Our top hiring criteria—in addition to having the skills to do the job—is, are you a great writer? You have to be a great writer to work here, in every single position, because the majority of our communication is written, primarily because a lot of us work remotely but also because writing is quieter. And we like long-form writing where people really think through an idea and present it. This is one of the reasons I don't like chat services. When companies start thinking one line at a time and everyone's rushed and you have to get your conversation in before it scrolls off the screen, I think it's a terrible, frantic way to work, and people are burning out because of it.

Jason explains that the company evaluates job candidates' cover letters, résumés, and email correspondence to determine whether they are strong writers. He views clear writing as a demonstration of clear thinking. So, remember to consistently improve your writing skills and, like Jason, find ways to build your professional reputation through traditional and social channels.

Sources: Orin, A. (2016, December 28). I'm Jason Fried, CEO of Basecamp, and this is how I work. *LifeHacker*. Retrieved from https://lifehacker.com/im-jason-fried-ceo-of-basecamp-and-this-is-how-i-work-1790556608; Bryant, A. (2017, September 1). Jason Fried of Basecamp on the importance of writing skills. *The New York Times*. Retrieved from https://www.nytimes.com/2017/09/01/jobs/corner-office-jason-fried-basecamp.html.

Setting the Tone of the Message

How many times have you heard phrases such as these? "It's not what he said, but how he said it," or "She said one thing but meant another." People often build resistance not to the content of a message but to the way it is delivered. One of your primary goals as a communicator is to express your messages in ways that respect and inspire others. Readers judge a message partially by its **tone**—the overall evaluation the reader perceives the writer to have toward the reader and the message content. Readers will judge your message based on how positive and concerned they think you are.

LO5.5 Explain and apply positive and other-oriented tone in business messages.

Business communicators generally aim to project positivity and concern for others in all business messages. By following the suggestions in this section, you will more effectively project messages with these tones. Many of the examples provided focus on the sentence level (primarily due to space constraints). However, tone is generally perceived across an entire message. Applying these principles across an entire message will dramatically alter the overall tone of the message.

Positivity

A positive attitude in the workplace improves work performance, allows more creativity, provides more motivation to excel, facilitates more helpfulness between co-workers, and gains more influence on clients and customers.[8] Bottom line, your ability to remain positive and exude optimism in your communications can strongly influence others. You can adopt a number of techniques to make your messages more positive.

Display a Can-Do, Confident Attitude   Focus on actions you can accomplish, and demonstrate a realistic optimism, as illustrated in Table 5.7. At the same time, be careful not to exaggerate or set unrealistic expectations.

Focus on the Positive Rather Than Negative Traits of Products and Services   Emphasize what products and services are rather than what they are not (see Table 5.8).

Use Diplomatic, Constructive Terms Related to Your Relationships and Interactions   Find ways to avoid terms that unnecessarily focus on differences and may imply opposing or even adversarial relationships or positions (see Table 5.9).

Principles for Setting the Right Tone

- Demonstrate positivity.
- Show concern for others.

Visit http://connect.mheducation.com for an exercise on this topic.

TABLE 5.7

Displaying a Can-Do, Confident Attitude

Less Effective	More Effective
Let me know if you want me to keep working on the implementation plan.	I look forward to putting together a detailed implementation plan.
This statement is weak—it expresses little enthusiasm or passion for pursuing this project.	This statement is strong. It expresses an enthusiasm for putting together a successful plan.
Based on the information I have access to, and if everything goes according to Lisa's analysis, I think that a PPL policy might increase profitability at Eastmond.	Using conservative assumptions, Lisa Johnson projected the financial impacts of a 20-week PPL policy. Considering increased productivity gains due to higher employee engagement, savings from reduced turnover, and higher employee costs to cover employees on PPL, we anticipate saving about $900,000 over the next five years.
This statement is qualified with too many weak words—based on . . . , if, think, might. Collectively, these words display a lack of confidence in the program.	This statement expresses confidence that the program will be profitable based on well-developed estimates. It does not seem exaggerated.

TABLE 5.8

Focusing on Positive Traits

Less Effective	More Effective
A PPL policy is not just a perk for the few new parents in the organization.	A PPL policy shows that Eastmond is an employee-friendly organization.
Without any additional elaboration, this sentence does not provide any positive information about a PPL policy.	This sentence effectively frames the positive impacts of a PPL policy. It is a strategic statement.
A PPL policy does require significant expenses.	A PPL policy would be an asset to our company, bringing in a strong return on investment.
Without any follow-up sentences, this statement falls short of what it could accomplish with positive phrasing.	This positive statement effectively frames the PPL policy as an asset.

TABLE 5.9

Using Diplomatic, Constructive Terms

Less Effective	More Effective
I would like to present my argument for why we should immediately implement a PPL policy.	Thank you for the opportunity to share my analysis of how a paid parental leave (PPL) policy can impact Eastmond Networking.
The term *argument* unnecessarily implies contention and difference of opinion.	This statement prefaces the goal of the communication with a compliment, which is a show of solidarity.
Your characterization of the PPL policy as a perk is inaccurate since the program would actually save the company money.	The PPL policy would feel like a perk to employees, which could boost morale. Yet, unlike most perks, it would actually save us money.
The phrase *your characterization* immediately creates a me-versus-you tone.	By stating the perception of the PPL policy being a perk in neutral terms, the statement would not be perceived as confrontational or divisive.

Concern for Others

In every facet of business communication, focusing on others is important. It is a basic component of your credibility (caring). In content and form, your message should show that you have the interests of your audience in mind. Therefore, avoid any sense of self-centeredness. Also aim for a tone that is inviting—that implies your interest in your readers' opinions, feelings, needs, and wants. The following guidelines will help you demonstrate concern for others (also referred to as *other-oriented language* in some parts of the book).

TABLE 5.10

Using You-Voice, We-Voice, Impersonal Voice, and I-Voice Appropriately

	Appropriate Situations	**Examples**
You-Voice	*Use when focus is solely on the reader.* It is particularly well suited to describing how products and services benefit customers, clients, and colleagues. *Avoid* when pointing out the mistakes of others or when the statement may be presumptuous.	**Effective:** You will receive regular updates about how to use PPL and related services to meet your family needs. **Effective:** You may be interested in Lisa's cash flow analysis. She found that a 20-week PPL policy would save about $900,000 over five years.
We-Voice	*Use when focus is on shared efforts, interests, and problems.* It is particularly well suited to messages within a company (i.e., work team).	**Effective:** Were we to offer PPL, we could actively promote this benefit to potential hires. **Effective:** We could further discuss the estimates for how a PPL policy could impact Eastmond.
Impersonal Voice	*Use when rational and neutral analysis is expected.* It is well suited for explaining business ideas, plans, and reports.	**Effective:** A PPL policy can increase employee engagement and satisfaction, reduce turnover, and attract top talent. **Effective:** Creating and implementing a PPL policy will require several steps.
I-Voice	*Use with nonthreatening verbs (i.e., think, feel) when there is bad news, difference of opinion, or even blame involved.* It is well suited for situations that could result in personal disappointments. Used most often in oral communication.	**Effective:** I think right now is not the right time to focus on creating a PPL policy. **Effective:** I think your ideas about a PPL policy make a lot of sense, but the company is not in a position to make the initial investments to get it started.

Avoid Relying Too Heavily on the I-Voice   The subject of a sentence almost always becomes the focus or emphasis. Generally, place the focus on your reader (you-voice), your shared interests with the reader (we-voice), or simply the business issue at hand (impersonal voice). Table 5.10 provides guidelines for selecting appropriate subjects for sentences.

Typically, readers sense tone over an entire message. The guidelines for choosing appropriate subjects for your sentences influence tone—for good or bad—over the entirety of a paragraph or message. Notice in Table 5.11 how the repeated use of the I-voice amplifies the self-centered tone, whereas the repeated use of we-voice and you-voice amplifies a tone that reflects other-orientation.

Respect the Time and Autonomy of Your Readers   The business world can be a hectic, deadline-filled environment. In many situations you will want fast responses. If you show consideration for others' time as well as for their sense of autonomy, you will often achieve your intended results more effectively than if your words sound bossy and demanding (see Table 5.12). Keep in mind that statements you can say with a nonpushy tone may be decoded as pushy when in written form.

Give Credit to Others   *What comes around goes around* is a maxim that holds true in many situations in the business world. Show your genuine appreciation and sincere

TABLE 5.11

Ineffective Use of I-Voice

Less Effective	More Effective
I would like to know as soon as possible when you could meet. I want to go over the estimates with you to show you how strong the case is for pursuing this option. Also, I have developed a timeline for writing the implementation plan that I want to show you right away.	Please let me know when there is a convenient time to meet. We could further discuss the estimates for how a PPL policy program could impact Eastmond. Also, if you think we should pursue this initiative, we could discuss the timeline for developing an implementation plan.
The repeated use of I-voice may be perceived as self-centered, inconsiderate, or pushy.	The repeated use of we-voice will likely be perceived as team-oriented and flexible.
I've set up the PPL program with extensive pregnancy information, health care options for newborns, and advice to bond with your new child. I'm especially proud of the wealth of information that I compiled for you about bonding with a new child. In my experience, the longer a parent can be with a new child, the better. I've made sure that you can take a full 20 weeks to bond with your child.	The PPL program provides you with extensive pregnancy information, health care options for your new child, and advice to bond with your child. You have a full 20 weeks of paid leave time to bond with your child.
The repeated use of I-voice may come off as self-absorbed or insincere.	The repeated use of you-voice frames everything in terms of reader benefits.

TABLE 5.12

Showing Respect for Time and Autonomy

Less Effective	More Effective
Call me as soon as you get out of your meeting.	Please give me a call when it's convenient.
This abrupt and demanding sentence would sound bossy to some people.	Using the courteous term *please* and focusing on the message recipient's convenience (rather than your own) shows respect.
We need to meet before Monday to go over the proposal. Have your administrative assistant set up a time for us and get back to me as soon as you know a time.	I think discussing the proposal with you before Monday would give us a chance to include your ideas in the proposal before we submit it on Wednesday. I'm available anytime before noon on Thursday or Friday. Is there a time that works for you? We could meet at your office, talk by phone, or meet online.
These sentences will be interpreted as overly demanding to some readers. In written form, these statements can easily be misinterpreted.	These statements focus on achieving results together by a deadline while still respecting the time of the message recipient.

TABLE 5.13

Giving Credit to Others

Less Effective	More Effective
The PPL policy could result in a significant return on investment for Eastmond.	Lisa also helped me understand how a PPL policy could result in a significant return on investment for Eastmond.
This statement implies that the writer is responsible for this analysis.	This statement implies that Lisa was instrumental in the analysis.
I gave Lisa information about PPL policies so she could plug in the numbers and see what it meant for Eastmond. As I anticipated, the estimate showed that Eastmond would save about $900,000 over six years.	Lisa Johnson estimates a 20-week PPL policy would save about $900,000 over the next five years.
These statements give credit to Lisa yet imply that the *real* analysis was conducted by the writer.	This sentence gives full credit to Lisa for her time-consuming, thorough, and insightful work.

recognition for the efforts of others (see Table 5.13), and it will pay off in many ways, including through improved camaraderie and willingness of others to give you ample and deserved credit in other situations. In short, make sure not to take credit for the work of others.

Sending the Right Meta Messages

A related notion to tone is that of meta messages. Whereas tone relates to the overall attitudes or feelings that writers convey toward a message and its recipients, **meta messages** are the overall but often underlying messages people take away from a communication or group of communications. Meta messages are encoded and decoded as a combination of content, tone, and other signals.

In your written and oral communications, think about the lasting meta messages you send. Over the course of many communications—conversations, email exchanges, content on user profiles, comments on social networking websites, discussions during meetings—you send meta messages that become the basis for your reputation. These meta messages form others' impressions of your credibility: your competence, caring, and character. Some positive meta messages that business professionals might hope to send include "I'm skilled in my area" (competence), "I want you to succeed on this project" (caring), and "I will follow our corporate code of conduct" (character).

Mixed signals occur when the content of a message conflicts with the tone, nonverbal communication, or other signals. Sending mixed signals is not only confusing, but it also frequently results in negative meta messages. Even if a business message is well reasoned and justified, if readers perceive a selfish or manipulative tone, they may decode meta messages such as "I'm not being straight with you" or "I'm opportunistic." In a job interview, an applicant may say the right things but because of unprofessional dress send meta messages such as "I'm not serious about this job" or "I don't understand the culture of this company."

Notice Latisha's final memo in Figure 5.6. It is well analyzed, positive, and other-oriented. She intends the memo to appeal logically and emotionally to Jeff and others who read it. Ideally, it will send meta messages such as "I can be trusted with important

FIGURE 5.6

Latisha's Message to Justify a PPL Policy

Refer to Figure 5.5 to see how the planned message structure matches the final document.

To:	Jeff Brody, HR Director
Cc:	Lisa Johnson, Finance Manager
From:	Latisha Jackson, HR Intern
Date:	June 5, 2020
Subject:	Paid Parental Leave (PPL) at Eastmond
Attached:	Lisa Johnson's 5-Year Financial Impact Study of PPL

Thank you for the opportunity to share my analysis of how a paid parental leave (PPL) policy can impact Eastmond Networking.

> Primary message as a topic sentence in the opening of the document.

With a generous PPL policy (20 weeks of PPL), Eastmond can become known as one of the most employee-friendly small tech firms while generating immediate returns on investment. Specifically, a PPL policy can increase employee engagement and satisfaction, reduce turnover, and attract top talent.

> Introduction of the key supporting conclusion.

Increasing Employee Engagement and Satisfaction due to PPL

Eastmond has relatively low employee engagement and satisfaction compared to competing tech firms. Only 31 percent of employees are highly engaged, just 56 percent of employees say they are proud of the company, and only 59 percent of our employees think we offer competitive benefits. Current and former employees give us mediocre Glassdoor ratings for compensation and benefits: a 3.4 on a scale of 5 compared to an average score of 4.1 at competing tech firms (Brody, 2020).

> **Key Point 1.** Each key point has a heading and a topic sentence.

Eastmond can develop an employee-friendly reputation by offering benefits such as a generous PPL policy. Several recent studies show that PPL policies increase engagement and satisfaction (Zhao, 2018). An EY study showed that in companies with PPL policies, 71 percent of employees were satisfied compared to employee satisfaction of 50 percent in companies without PPL options (EY, 2017).

Reducing Turnover due to PPL

Eastmond faces an employee turnover problem. Employee turnover is at 23 percent compared to rates of between 10 to 15 percent at similar tech firms in our area. This is an enduring problem. Eastmond has faced turnover between 21 and 27 percent for each of the past five years (Brody, 2020).

> **Key Point 2.**

One way to reduce turnover is offering more employee-friendly benefits such as PPL. Attrition following the introduction or expansion of these benefits leads to much less attrition, with an average of 50 percent less attrition among women (Rau & Williams, 2017). When Google increased PPL from 12 weeks to 18 weeks, attrition among mothers fell 50 percent. When Accenture extended PPL from 8 weeks to 16 weeks, attrition among mothers dropped by 40 percent (Schulte, Durana, Stout, & Moyer, 2017).

> Problem–solution pattern is followed in each section.

Attracting Top Talent due to PPL

Eastmond has consistently struggled to attract top talent, particularly among early-career professionals under 35 years old. One way to attract more qualified, early-career professionals is with generous benefits such as PPL, which are particularly valued by women and Millennials. Because about 78 percent

> **Key Point 3.**

FIGURE 5.6

(Continued)

of Millennial parents are part of two-career couples, many of these early-career professionals may not consider Eastmond unless we offer PPL (Rau & Williams, 2017). Further, since unemployment is just 2.5 percent for people over 25 years old with a college degree, job seekers can be selective in their choice of employers (Zhao, 2018).

Financial Impacts of a PPL Policy ← **Estimates based on key points.**

Using conservative assumptions, Lisa Johnson projected the financial impacts of a 20-week PPL policy. Considering increased productivity gains due to higher employee engagement, savings from reduced turnover, and higher employee costs to cover employees on PPL, we anticipate saving about $900,000 over the next five years. This estimate does not factor in the benefits of attracting top talent to our company.

Table of Financial Estimates (in thousands of dollars)

	Year 1	Year 2	Year 3	Year 4	Year 5	Total
Productivity gains	$ -	$ 193	$ 196	$ 200	$ 204	$ 793
Savings from reduced turnover	$ 252	$ 532	$ 543	$ 553	$ 565	$ 2,445
Additional employee costs	$(438)	$(451)	$(465)	$(479)	$(493)	$(2,325)
Overall financial impact	$(186)	$ 273	$ 274	$ 275	$ 276	$ 913

Assumptions:
(1) Productivity gains are based on a 0.5 percent productivity gain across our 350 employees starting in Year 2;
(2) Savings from reduced turnover assumes a drop from 23 percent to 15 percent with average hiring costs of $19,000 per employee;
(3) Additional employee costs assume the addition of six employees to ensure we can consistently cover employees who take PPL. See attached PPL Financial Impact Study for full details about these estimates.

Recommendations for Implementing a PPL Policy ← **Call to Action.**

Creating and implementing a PPL policy will require several steps. The benefits team recommends the following timeline of activities:

1. *Develop the PPL policy* (June 15 to July 31, 2020). We currently recommend 20 weeks of PPL. The benefits team will need to continue evaluating PPL policies at progressive organizations to finalize details about the amount of PPL offered, return-to-work options, coverage scenarios, and eligibility requirements.
2. *Promote the new PPL policy* (August 1 to September 30, 2020). We will develop a communication plan that promotes our new policy internally to our employees and externally to the media, prospective employees, and other partners.
3. *Hire new employees* (October 1, 2020, to March 31, 2021). We anticipate hiring six new employees to ensure we can cover for employees taking PPL. The financial estimate report contains additional details about this necessary investment.
4. *Evaluate the success of the PPL policy* (April 1 to May 31, 2021). Soon after implementing the PPL policy, we recommend the benefits team collects data about the perceptions of our stakeholders toward the policy and the experiences of those who have used it. This evaluation will inform whether we should make any modifications to the policy.

projects" or "A PPL policy makes financial sense for this company, and I'm the right person to continue working on it."

In addition to reviewing the final memo for its tone and meta messages, take a few moments to notice its logic and structure. It clearly distinguishes between facts, conclusions, and positions. Immediately following the final memo, you'll find the Technology Tips feature about AI tone analyzers. These emerging tools will increasingly help professionals improve the tone of business messages.

Technology Tips

AI TONE ANALYZERS

Many tone analyzers based on artificial intelligence (AI) technologies can evaluate the tone of various messages. Nearly all customer service chat bots rely on these types of tools to gauge how customers are feeling. Some companies use these tools to understand the sentiment of employees in emails and other messages placed on digital platforms.

You can use these analyzers to get a sense of the tone you project. For example, you can try out IBM's Watson tone analyzer (https://natural-language-understanding-demo.ng. bluemix.net/; https://www.ibm.com/watson/services/tone-analyzer/; https://tone-analyzer-demo.ng.bluemix.net/). It evaluates mood and sentiment based on how you use words and phrases. Specifically, it evaluates tones in terms of anger, fear, joy, sadness, analytical, confident, and tentative. It also evaluates overall sentiment (positive versus negative).

Your challenge: Try out the Watson tone analyzer or another similar tool on several recent emails you've written (although you should avoid any content that you think is private or confidential). What did you learn? How much do you trust this tool? What do you think it got right and wrong? What are the implications of companies using these tools to evaluate employee sentiments?

Chapter Takeaway for *Creating Effective Business Messages*

LO5.1 Explain the goals of effective business messages and the process for creating them.

The Stages and Goals of Effective Message Creation

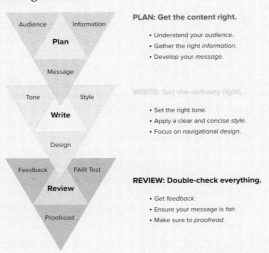

PLAN: Get the content right.

- Understand your *audience*.
- Gather the right *information*.
- Develop your *message*.

WRITE: Get the delivery right.

- Set the right *tone*.
- Apply a clear and concise *style*.
- Focus on navigational *design*.

REVIEW: Double-check everything.

- Get *feedback*.
- Ensure your message is *fair*.
- Make sure to *proofread*.

LO5.2 Identify the needs of your audience in the AIM planning process.

Audience Analysis		
• Identify reader benefits and constraints. • Consider reader values and priorities.	• Estimate your credibility. • Anticipate reactions.	• Consider secondary audiences.

LO5.3 Gather the right information and refine business ideas in the AIM planning process.

Information Gathering		
• Identify the business problems.	• Analyze the business problems.	• Clarify objectives.

See an *example of information gathering* in Figure 5.3.

LO5.4 Develop your primary message and key points in the AIM planning process.

Message Development	Testing Logic	
• Frame the main point. • Set up the structure/logic of the message.	**Avoid** the following: • Unsupported generalizations • Faulty cause/effect claims • Weak analogies	• Either/or logic • Slanting of facts • Exaggeration

See an *example of a deductive framework* in Figure 5.4.
See *typical paragraph structure* in a deductive business message in Figure 5.5.

LO5.5 Explain and apply positive and other-oriented tone in business messages.

Setting the Right Tone	
Demonstrate positivity.	**Show concern for others.**
• Display a can-do, confident attitude. • Focus on positive rather than negative traits. • Use diplomatic, constructive terms.	• Avoid relying too heavily on I-voice. • Respect the time and autonomy of your readers. • Give credit to others.

Key Terms

conclusions, 149
deductive, 152
direct, 152
facts, 149

indirect, 152
inductive, 152
meta messages, 162
positions, 149

priorities, 147
tone, 157
values, 147

Discussion Exercises

5.1 Chapter Review Questions (LO5.1, LO5.2, LO5.3, LO5.4, LO5.5)

A. Describe each of the three components in the AIM planning process for business messages: audience analysis, idea development, and message structuring.

B. Explain the general nature of excellence in business thinking and how it applies to the idea development stage of planning messages.

C. Discuss basic considerations in the audience analysis stage of planning messages.

D. Describe the nature of framing for business messages.

E. Explain common types of logical inconsistencies in business messages.

F. Discuss the importance of achieving positive and other-oriented tone in business messages.

5.2 Ideas in Action Discussion Questions (LO5.1, LO5.2, LO5.3, LO5.4, LO5.5)

Read the comments and advice of Jason Fried in the Ideas in Action feature. Respond to the following questions:

A. What does Fried say about assessing writing in the hiring process? Why does he think writing skills are so important?

B. What does he say distinguishes long-form writing from other forms of writing in the workplace? What are the benefits of long-form writing?

C. He suggests many people are burning out. What do you think he's referring to as the cause? What do you think he suggests are the solutions?

5.3 Worst Words to Use at Work? Displaying Confidence with Words (LO5.5)

In a *Forbes* magazine article called "Worst Words to Say at Work," business consultant and psychotherapist Linda Durre listed nine words or phrases that show someone is not confident.[9] These phrases, according to Durre, cause others to perceive you as undependable and untrustworthy. To read the article, go to www.forbes. com/2010/04/26/words-work-communication-forbes-woman-leadership-career.html. Then respond to each of the following, which are excerpted from her article, with four to five sentences about whether you agree or disagree with her point of view:

A. *Try* is a weasel word. "Well, I'll try," some people say. It's a cop-out. They're just giving you lip service when they probably have no real intention of doing what you ask.

B. *Whatever*—This word is a trusted favorite of people who want to dismiss you, diminish what you say, or get rid of you quickly. . . . It's an insult and a verbal slap in the face. It's a way to respond to a person without actually responding.

C. *Maybe* and *I don't know*—People will sometimes avoid making a decision and hide behind these words. Sometimes during a confrontation people will claim not to know something or offer the noncommittal response "maybe," just to avoid being put on the spot.

D. *I'll get back to you*—When people need to buy time or avoid revealing a project's status, they will say, "I'll get back to you," and they usually never do.

E. *If*—Projects depend on everyone doing his or her part. People who use *if* are usually playing the blame game and betting against themselves. They like to set conditions rather than assuming a successful outcome.

F. *Yes, but* . . . —This is another excuse. You might give your team members suggestions or solutions and they come back to you with "Yes, but . . ." as a response. They don't really want answers, help, or solutions.

G. *I guess* . . . —This is usually said in a weak, soft-spoken, shoulder-shrugging manner. It's another attempt to shirk responsibility—a phrase is muttered only when people half agree with you, but want to leave enough leeway to say, "Well, I didn't really know. . . . I was only guessing."

H. *We'll see* . . . —How many times did we hear our parents say this? We knew they were buying time, avoiding a fight or confrontation, or really saying no.

Evaluation Exercises

5.4 Evaluating Latisha's Proposal for a New PPL Policy (LO5.2, LO5.3, LO5.4, LO5.5)

Based on the completed message from Latisha in Figure 5.6, answer the following questions:

A. How effectively is this message framed? Would you suggest any changes?

B. How effective is the business logic? Would you suggest any changes?

C. How effective is the tone? Would you suggest any changes?

5.5 Evaluating a Business Message (LO5.2, LO5.3, LO5.4, LO5.5)

Choose a business message to evaluate. You could find a recent letter you have received from a business, go to a website and choose a message for customers or stockholders, or use a message specified by your instructor. Select a message that contains at least three or four paragraphs. Evaluate the message in the following ways:

A. How effectively are facts and conclusions written?

B. How effectively is the message targeted to its audience? Do you have any suggestions for how it could have been better adapted for the audience?

C. Does it have any logical inconsistencies? Explain.

D. Does the message portray a tone of positivity? Other-orientation? Describe your viewpoint with examples.

5.6 Self-Assessment of Approach to Writing (LO5.2, LO5.3, LO5.4, LO5.5)

Evaluate yourself with regard to each of the practices listed in the table below. Circle the appropriate number for each.

Before sending important written messages, I . . .	1 (Rarely/Never)	2 (Sometimes)	3 (Usually)	4 (Always)
Make sure I gather all the facts.	1	2	3	4
Think carefully about what the facts mean.	1	2	3	4
Take time to think about what my audience wants and needs.	1	2	3	4
Spend time envisioning how my audience will respond.	1	2	3	4
Think about how the gist of my message could be captured in one short statement.	1	2	3	4
Map out the main supporting ideas for my primary message.	1	2	3	4
Check the message for logical consistency.	1	2	3	4
Make certain the tone is positive (as appropriate).	1	2	3	4
Ensure that the tone is other-oriented.	1	2	3	4
Reread the message to make sure everything is correct.	1	2	3	4

Add up your score and consider the following advice:

35–40: You are a strategic writer. You nearly always think carefully about the strength of your message and its intended influence on your audience. Keep up the great work.

30–34: You are a careful writer. You have many good habits in writing preparation. Identify the areas where you need to improve. By preparing slightly more in these areas, you will become a powerful, strategic writer in the workplace.

25–29: You are a somewhat careful writer. Sometimes and in some ways you are careful about your writing. You occasionally ask the right questions about getting your message right for your audience. You are inconsistent, however. Focus on preparing carefully for all important messages.

Under 25: You are a casual writer. You rarely take enough time to think carefully about your written messages. Even if you are a gifted and savvy writer, at some point your lack of preparation will harm your work achievements. Make a habit of spending more time in the preparation stage asking questions about how to construct your message to appropriately influence your audience.

Once you've completed the short assessment, write about three areas of writing preparation in which you intend to improve. Describe specific steps you will take to improve and benchmarks for checking your progress.

Application Exercises

5.7 Avoiding Logical Errors (LO5.4)

For each of the following sentences, identify what you consider to be logical inconsistencies. Explain whether these inconsistencies relate to unsupported generalizations, faulty cause/effect claims, either/or logic, slanting the facts, or exaggeration. Then revise the sentences to eliminate the logical inconsistencies.

A. Jim's Old Fashioned Burgers provides the best management training program in the industry.

B. The training consists of five stages: manager-in-training, second assistant manager, first assistant manager, restaurant manager, and regional director. The training places you on the fast track to success; advancing from one stage to the next takes from as few as three months up to just two years.

C. Many trainees eventually become upper-level executives, showing that hands-on training is better than getting a business degree.

D. Eventually, approximately 10 percent of trainees become regional directors. Employees from this elite group are those who show perseverance and determination to reach their professional goals.

E. Because just 5 percent of Jim's employees are selected for the training program, your acceptance in the program shows that you have great leadership potential.

F. We encourage you to apply for the training program so that you avoid staying in the same position without making career progress.

G. Restaurant managers make approximately $35,000 to $40,000 per year. The annual salary has grown at approximately 5 percent per year during the past three years, far outpacing income growth for restaurant managers at McDonald's or Burger King. So reaching the restaurant manager stage places you in a better economic position than you would be in at competing restaurants.

5.8 Displaying a Can-Do, Confident Tone (LO5.5)

For each of the following items, rewrite the sentences to achieve a better can-do, confident tone.

A. Even though I do not have any supervisory experience, I think I have excellent leadership skills.

B. I have excellent leadership skills and will certainly increase profitability as I am promoted through the ranks of the training program.

C. I might be a good candidate for the training program since I work so hard.

D. We feel that next year's annual profits could increase if the economy picks up and if we are able to fill all of our management positions.

E. We believe that improving customer service is one way of driving increased revenues.

5.9 Focusing on Positive Traits (LO5.5)

For each of the following items, rewrite the sentences to achieve a more positive tone.

A. All employees who show commitment and strong leadership skills are eligible for the management training program, even if they lack any higher education.

B. None of the training requires you to go through a traditional, businesslike educational program.

C. You will begin as a manager-in-training and will do far more than flip burgers.

D. Those employees who do not show exceptional leadership skills at the manager-in-training stage do not advance to the next stage of training.

E. We are seeking individuals who do not settle for average customer service.

F. You will lose your opportunity to be considered for the program unless we receive your application by July 1.

G. Employees who have not done poorly on their performance reviews are eligible to apply for the program.

5.10 Using Diplomatic, Constructive Terms (LO5.5)

For each of the following items, rewrite the sentences to achieve a more positive, constructive tone.

A. You probably won't be accepted into the management training program because you haven't worked here long enough to show any commitment.

B. Your contention that you have enough supervisory experience to make you qualified is questionable.

C. I think you must reconsider your views on the management training program if you expect it to succeed. You're just not in

touch with reality if you expect to get quality managers without paying them higher salaries sooner in the program.

5.11 Using Appropriate Voice (LO5.5)

For each of the following items, rewrite the sentences in you-voice, we-voice, or I-voice to achieve a more effective tone.

A. I'm happy to offer you a spot in the manager-in-training program.

B. I'm positive that this opportunity will help your career.

C. You must turn in the application before July 1.

D. I will lead the first orientation session for the program, and then I'll turn over the remainder of the afternoon meetings to my colleague.

E. I've come up with some ideas for the training program, and I'd like to meet as soon as possible to get some discussion going. I want us to focus on a conversation about the salaries and benefits that would motivate more employees to apply for the program.

5.12 Respecting the Time and Autonomy of Others (LO5.5)

Rewrite each of the following items twice. Rewrite the first time assuming that you are writing to a peer. Rewrite the second time assuming that you are writing to a subordinate.

A. Get back to me before Friday afternoon about your availability for an interview.

B. I think we should review the manager-in-training applicants. Please come to my office on Tuesday at 9:30 a.m.

C. I have chosen the five applicants who are most strongly suited for the training program. Could you send me an email confirming that you agree with my selections?

D. I'm swamped with other projects, and we need to make the selections for the training program. Please take care of it yourself before this Friday at noon. You can count on me agreeing with your selections.

Case for Problems 5.13 through 5.15: Learning about Stress Management Programs for Eastmond Networking

When Jeff arrived back at the office, he spent 15 minutes reading Latisha's proposal to work on a PPL program. He found the work impressive and insightful. If only more of his employees had the same drive, initiative, and analytical skills as Latisha, thought Jeff, Eastmond would be far more successful. If Latisha kept up this level of analysis in her work, Jeff would definitely find a way to employ her full-time at Eastmond. Her thorough and thoughtful approach to this business problem showed she could excel in many of the entry-level management positions at the company.[10]

Jeff approached Latisha and explained that now he wanted to consider how to help employees avoid stress. Latisha spent the next week learning about corporate stress management programs. She learned the following:

- Health care costs of people suffering chronic, extreme stress are 46 percent higher than for those who are not.
- According to the American Medical Association, stress is as bad for your heart as smoking and high cholesterol.
- Forty percent of job turnover is due to stress.
- Stress reduction programs can have major impacts. In one company, 42 percent of 5,900 employees suffered moderate to severe stress. In fact, 80 percent of doctor visits for these

employees were related to stress. After a stress reduction program, employee physician services dropped from $7.4 million annually to $5.3 million annually.

• Employees with various health risks directly increase health care costs to employers. For example, compared to employees with low health risks, employees with the following conditions significantly increase costs to the employer: depression (70.2 percent higher cost); stress (46.3 percent); glucose (34.8 percent); weight (21.4 percent); tobacco (19.7 percent); blood pressure (11.7 percent); exercise (10.4 percent).

• According to the Department of Health and Human Services, employees suffer the following risk factors: stress, 44 percent; overweight, 38 percent; use alcohol excessively, 31 percent; high cholesterol, 30 percent; have cardiovascular disease, 25 percent; don't exercise, 24 percent; smoke, 21 percent; don't wear seat belts, 20 percent; are asthmatic, 12 percent; are diabetic, 6 percent.

• One study showed the annual per-employee absenteeism costs for the following conditions as follows: stress, $136; weight issues, $70; tobacco use, $44; glucose problems, $29.

• The Canadian Institute of Stress showed the following results for corporate stress management programs: work stress: 32 percent improvement; work satisfaction: 38 percent improvement; absenteeism: 18 percent reduction; disability days: 52 percent reduction; grievances: 32 percent reduction; productivity: 7 percent improvement; quality measures: 13 percent improvement; work engagement: 62 percent improvement.

• Stress management programs are most effective when offered in conjunction with broad wellness programs.

• Setting up stress management programs is challenging. Other disease management programs are more easily defined in terms of who has conditions and how to treat them (i.e., diabetes, heart disease).

• Most employees do not enroll in stress management programs unless there are incentives.

• Stress management can be achieved through workplace policies that alleviate work and personal stress. Some companies have tried flextime, allowing work at home, child care initiatives, sick child care, and other incentives to help employees reduce stress and be more productive.

• Stress management can also involve training through workshops and professional coaching.

• Lisa estimates that hiring a full-time professional coach for the workplace would cost approximately $60,000 per year (salary plus benefits and other related costs). The coach would run workshops, distribute educational materials, and also offer one-to-one coaching in stress relief. The coach would be qualified to work on other wellness areas such as weight loss, exercise, and dietary improvements. Assuming that Eastmond offered $150 reductions on health care premiums per year, Lisa estimates the company could achieve 90 percent participation (about 175 employees) in a basic stress management program. She thinks it's reasonable to assume that Eastmond could save about $500 per enrolled employee between health care and absenteeism costs.

5.13 Idea Development by Organizing Facts into Conclusions and Recommendations (LO5.2)

Assume you are Latisha and you will write a proposal to Jeff asking that Eastmond develop a stress management program. You can use any of the facts she has discovered and even search for some online (there's lots of information about stress management), but your task is to make sense of the facts you've gathered. Organize them into groups that support three or four major conclusions (in a format similar to Figure 5.4). Then write three or four recommendations you would make based on your conclusions.

5.14 Writing a Proposal in Support of Developing a Stress Management Program (LO5.2, LO5.3, LO5.4, LO5.5)

Assume the role of Latisha. Write a proposal to develop a stress management program. Use well-justified logic to support your conclusions and recommendations.

5.15 Writing a Proposal to Broaden the Focus of a Stress Management Program (LO5.2, LO5.3, LO5.4, LO5.5)

Assume the role of Latisha. You have concluded that although a stress management program would be beneficial, focusing on stress management without a comprehensive wellness program is shortsighted and less cost-effective. Use well-justified logic to support your conclusions and recommendations.

Language Mechanics Check

5.16 Review the semicolon and colon rules in Appendix A. Then rewrite each sentence to add semicolons and colons where needed (you may need to replace other forms of punctuation in some instances).

A. IBM's two most important business units are Global Technology Services and Global Business Services.

B. IBM primarily focuses on B2B business, on the other hand, Microsoft primarily focuses on B2C business.

C. IBM has U.S. offices in Armonk, New York, New York City, New York and Santa Clara, California.

D. Even though IBM is a well-recognized brand, most people don't know much about its products or services for many reasons, including that it focuses mostly on B2B products and services, that its products and services are highly technical, and that it doesn't explain its well-known products, such as Watson, to the public.

E. IBM's two most important business units are the following Global Technology Services and Global Business Services.

F. IBM was forced to lay off roughly 15 percent of its North American employees, however, that does not indicate a decline in revenues.

G. IBM's top executive team includes the following individuals; Virginia M. Rometty, chair, president, and CEO, Michelle H. Browdy, Senior VP of Legal and Regulatory Affairs, Ray Day, chief communications officer, and Mark Foster, Senior VP of IBM Services and Global Business Services.

H. IBM faces several major challenges; it's so large that it's difficult to lead and manage, it faces stiff challenges from cloud providers, and it's not well equipped to deal with growing demand for rented software and computer systems.

I. The top vendors for enterprise social networking platforms are IBM, Jive, Microsoft, Cisco, and Salesforce.

J. I originally wanted to apply for a job at IBM: however, I ended up deciding to apply at Cisco.

Endnotes

1. These time estimates are based on observing thousands of business students and are consistent with decades of research about expertise as described in Pressley, M., & McCormick, C. B. (1995). *Advanced educational psychology for educators, researchers, and policymakers.* New York: HarperCollins.

2. Garone, E. (2008, October 8). How to escape a reputation as a novice. *The Wall Street Journal.*

3. Martin, R. (2007, June). How successful leaders think. *Harvard Business Review,* 72–83; Paul, R., & Elder, L. (2008). *The miniature guide to critical thinking concepts and tools.* Dillon Park, CA: Foundation for Critical Thinking Press; Carrithers, D., & Bean, J. C. (2008). Using a client memo to assess critical thinking of finance majors. *Business Communication Quarterly, 71*(1), 10–26.

4. Raffoni, M. (2002). Framing for leadership. *Harvard Management Communication Letter, 5*(12), 3–4.

5. Sussman, L. (1999). How to frame a message: The art of persuasion and negotiation. *Business Horizons, 42*(4), 2–6.

6. Bryant, A. (2009, May 23). In a word, he wants simplicity. *The New York Times.* Retrieved from www.nytimes.com/2009/05/24/business/24corner.html.

7. Thomas, J. (2004). *Guide to managerial persuasion and influence.* Upper Saddle River, NJ: Pearson Education.

8. Judge, T. A., & Ilies, R. (2004). Is positiveness in organizations always desirable?" *Academy of Management Executive, 18*(4), 151–155.

9. Durre, L. (2010, August 5). Worst words to say at work. *Forbes.* Retrieved from www.forbes.com/2010/04/26/words-work-communication-forbes-woman-leadership-career.html.

10. This case problem uses information from several additional resources, including the following: American Institute for Preventive Medicine. (2009). *A worksite wellness white paper.* Farmington Hills, MI: Author. Retrieved from www.healthylife.com/template.asp?pageID=75; Calarco, C., & Cryer, B. (2009). *Return on investment paper.* Boulder Creek, CA: HeartMath; HealthAdvocate. (2010). *Setting up a stress management program: A checklist for success.* Plymouth Meeting, PA: Author.

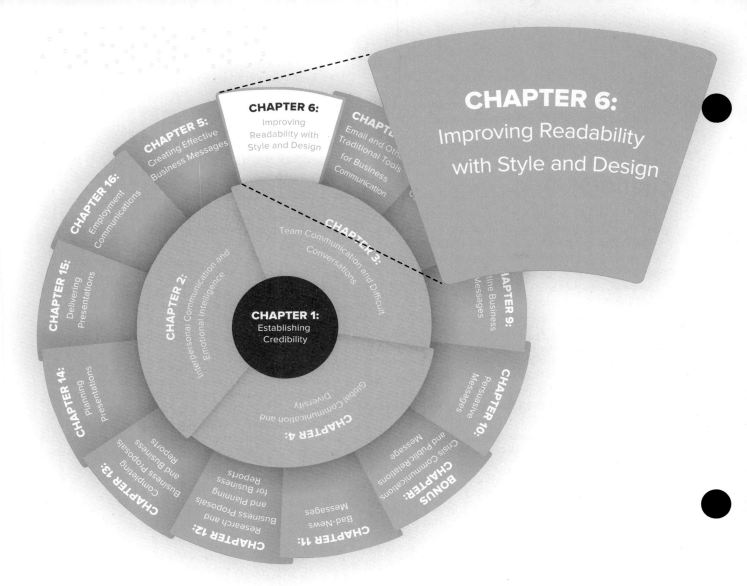

CHAPTER 6:
Improving Readability with Style and Design

CHAPTER 5:
Creating Effective Business Messages

CHAPTER 16:
Employment Communications

CHAPTER 15:
Delivering Presentations

CHAPTER 2:
Interpersonal Communication and Emotional Intelligence

CHAPTER 1:
Establishing Credibility

CHAPTER 3:
Team Communication and Difficult Conversations

CHAPTER 14:
Planning Presentations

CHAPTER 13:
Completing Business Proposals and Business Reports

CHAPTER 12:
Research and Business Proposals and Planning for Business Reports

CHAPTER 11:
Bad-News Messages

CHAPTER 4:
Global Communication and Diversity

BONUS CHAPTER:
Crisis Communications and Public Relations Message

CHAPTER 10:
Persuasive Messages

CHAPTER 9:
Routine Business Messages

  **ESTABLISHING CREDIBILITY**

 PRINCIPLES OF INTERPERSONAL COMMUNICATION

 PRINCIPLES FOR & TYPES OF BUSINESS MESSAGES

LEARNING OBJECTIVES

After studying this chapter, you should be able to do the following:

LO6.1 Describe and apply the following principles of writing style that improve ease of reading: completeness, conciseness, and natural processing.

LO6.2 Explain and use navigational design to improve ease of reading.

LO6.3 Describe and apply the components of the reviewing stage, including a FAIR test, proofreading, and feedback.

? WHY DOES THIS MATTER?

In Chapter 5, we focused on getting your message right with the AIM planning process. Then we introduced the importance of tone as you begin formally drafting your message. In this chapter, we focus on style and design—the next considerations as you draft your message. At this point, *your entire focus should be making your message easy to read*.

In short, your audience members—whether executives, managers, other professionals, or clients and customers—are typically preoccupied with many projects and overwhelmed with messages and information. When you make your messages easy to read, your audience is more likely to read them carefully and understand them as you intended.[1]

Many of the principles in this chapter focus on simplifying your words and sentences. This should not be confused with oversimplifying and minimizing your message. Your messages should contain the best of ideas with strong support. If your message is difficult to read, however, your ideas may not even be considered.

In this chapter, we discuss four broad goals. The first three goals relate to writing style and include being complete, concise, and natural. The final goal is to design your document for rapid navigation. Throughout the chapter, you will find less effective and more effective examples of each of these style and design elements. These examples come directly from the chapter case. Make sure to skim Stephanie's original difficult-to-read draft (see Figure 6.1) so you understand the context for the chapter examples. By the end of the chapter, you will see the revisions that result in the final version of the brochure (see Figure 6.3).

> **Hear Pete Cardon explain why this matters.**
>
> **bit.ly/cardon6**

CHAPTER CASE · PROMOTING VOLUNTEERISM AT PEAK HARVEST FOOD BANK

WHO'S INVOLVED

Stephanie Jorgenson

President of the Peak Harvest Food Bank

- Started the food bank 20 years ago
- Exploring ways to increase donations and involve members of the community

THE SITUATION

Over the past 20 years, Peak Harvest Food Bank has served the needs of tens of thousands of low-income members of the community. Stephanie Jorgenson started the food bank to ensure low-income families had enough food. She has expanded the food bank's mission over the years. For example, it now offers

(Stephanie Jorgenson character): Ariel Skelley/Blend Images LLC nutritional guidance to many adults, particularly seniors, who have diseases such as diabetes and high blood pressure. The food bank also now provides clothing and books.

To accomplish the food bank's mission, Stephanie relies heavily on donations and volunteerism. In the past few years, she started a social ambassador program. These ambassadors post information on their social media accounts that generate awareness about hunger and nutrition and call for donations and volunteerism at the food bank.

The social ambassador program has been successful, but the turnover is high. Most ambassadors post actively for a few months and then discontinue posting. Stephanie is seeking to find more social ambassadors—particularly those who will stay active longer and who are younger members of the community.

Stephanie drafted a message (see Figure 6.1) to post to the website, send to an email list of prior volunteers, and place in her social channels. She asked several of her colleagues for input on the content. They all told her the same thing: "This is hard to read."

TASK

1

How can Stephanie improve the writing style of the message so that potential social ambassadors will easily read it? (See the "Improving Ease of Reading with Completeness," "Improving Ease of Reading with Conciseness," and "Improving Ease of Reading with Natural Style" sections.)

2

How can Stephanie improve the navigational design of the message so that potential social ambassadors can find important pieces of information rapidly? (See the "Improving Ease of Reading with Navigational Design" section.)

Improving Ease of Reading with Completeness

LO6.1 Describe and apply the following principles of writing style that improve ease of reading: completeness, conciseness, and natural processing.

Visit http://connect.mheducation.com for an exercise on this topic.

Most of your messages in the workplace have a clear goal: to update your team members, to promote a service to a client, to give an assignment, and so on. Your goal of completeness means that your message provides all the information necessary to meet that purpose. Your colleagues, clients, and other contacts expect complete information so they can act on your message immediately. Otherwise, they will need to contact you to get additional information or, worse yet, ignore your message altogether. You can achieve completeness with three basic strategies: (1) providing all relevant information, (2) being accurate, and (3) being specific.

Provide All Relevant Information

One challenge is to judge which information is relevant for your message. After all, providing too much information can distract your readers and weigh down your document. On the other hand, not providing enough information can leave your reader wondering how to respond. The key to providing *all but only* relevant information is to plan, write, and review your message strategically. Repeatedly asking yourself what information is necessary for the purpose of your message will help you accomplish this.

A survey of corporate recruiters from 2,092 companies showed which elements of writing style are most important. Accuracy was the most sought-after characteristic of writing style (95 percent), followed by clarity (75 percent), language mechanics (59 percent), conciseness (41 percent), precision (37 percent), and visual appeal (11 percent).[2]

FIGURE 6.1

Stephanie's Original, Difficult-to-Read Message to Potential Social Ambassadors

The Peak Harvest Food Bank Needs More Volunteers

Do you want to change the world? With very little time commitment, you can catapult the life opportunities of kids and their families in our community. In the past few years, we've used a new way of getting the word out about what we do—social ambassadors. Social ambassadors help get the word out about the food bank to raise awareness about our community's needs, help people get assistance, increase donations, and promote volunteerism. Last year our top social ambassadors made a huge impact. Across the board, every metric has skyrocketed. Donations increased so much that we could serve many more families. On top of that, volunteer hours increased and we were able to receive far more clothing donations. There are so many valuable skills and lessons that social ambassadors gain, from using social media for good causes to marketing to excellent teamwork to simply giving back to the community.

Unfortunately, about 20 percent or one in five people in our community is food insecure. Experts examine food insecurity in many ways, but their definitions generally coalesce around the idea that people not only don't have enough money for food but it's also not healthy food they eat. This creates worry, embarrassment, hunger, and poor health. Those who are food insecure are generally in low-income households (under $300000), but that's not always the case. Surprise medical bills, extended family caretaking responsibilities, and sudden loss of employment are common reasons other households are affected. We worry the most about children. In all the research about food security, kids in food insecure households are much more likely on a path to poor school performance, much more likely in a condition of stress, and much more likely on the road to many lifelong challenges. More than ever, we've started to serve the senior citizen community, with nearly 15 percent of our clients who are retired without enough income for regular, nutritious meals and who often face extra challenges with diseases such as diabetes and high blood pressure and who need dietary guidance as a result.

A lot of people wonder exactly what we do. That's a fair question. In an effort to support people in need, we provide food in a well-balanced and nutritious manner. We have an on-site food pantry and a food pantry truck to provide delivery. We also serve hot meals on-site for breakfast, lunch, and dinner. The food bank bestows our clients with bountiful and sustainable food. In 2019, we served 2,152 households, 5,327 children were served, another 986 senior citizens were served, and altogether we served 23,887 meals! Our food bank is also a dietary guidance organization. Generally, impoverished families simply don't have the wherewithal to procure healthy foods. We have done research that shows 83 percent of the people we serve usually purchase inexpensive unhealthy foods. As a result, many of our clients need more education about proper dietary needs. We also provide clothing assistance and give away books. *We have helped thousands of members of the community get back on their feet. The charity watchdog group Charity Navigotor has given us a perfect rating for the past five years because of our ability to serve our community with the resources we receive.*

Social ambassadors are needed to help with promoting the food bank and raising donations. They use social media to share information about food insecurity in our community. Most of our social ambassadors are also volunteers at the food bank for at least one shift (three hours) per month so they have their own personal experiences working with clients.

To help you succeed, we provide you with many resources so you can complete your role effectively. Needless to say, you receive training about how to influence your followers on Facebook, Instagram, LinkedIn, Twitter, and other social sites. Social ambassadors are given weekly tips, suggestions, and examples about how to increase impact each and every week. They are also given content to post and suggestions for how to personalize it. By being in attendance at the monthly social ambassador meeting, there is a lot that can be learned about running a nonprofit. To apply to serve as a social ambassador, email Stephanie Jorgenson at sjorgenson@phfb.org.

TABLE 6.1

Being Accurate

Less Effective	More Effective
Those who are food insecure are generally in low-income (under $<u>300000</u> per year) households, but that's not always the case.	Those who are food insecure are generally in low-income (under $<u>30,000</u> per year) households, but that's not always the case.
A typo (300,000) implies an income level that is ten times too high. It's an obvious mistake that will detract from the credibility of the message.	The revised version contains the corrected figure.
The average social ambassador increased donations by $2,312—that's enough to help a food-insecure family of four eat nutritious meals for nearly <u>four weeks</u>!	The average social ambassador increased donations by $2,312—that's enough to help a food-insecure family of four eat nutritious meals for nearly <u>four months</u>!
Incorrect word (*weeks* rather than *months*) leads to one of the figures dramatically underestimating the impact.	The revised version contains the corrected phrase to show the true impact.

In Stephanie's case, her basic purpose is to attract passionate, qualified individuals to volunteer as social ambassadors. She wants to accomplish several objectives: explain the need for a food bank, describe what her food bank does, and persuade people to volunteer as social ambassadors. As long as she keeps these objectives in mind, she can ensure that the brochure contains only relevant information.

Be Accurate

Accuracy is a basic objective of all business communications because your colleagues, customers, and clients base important decisions on your communications. In short, accurate information is true, correct, and exact. You should aim for accuracy in facts, figures, statistics, and word choice. Inaccuracies may result from miscalculations, misinformation, poor word choice, or simply typos (see Table 6.1 for examples). Accuracy, like specificity, strongly impacts your readers' perceptions of your credibility. Just one inaccurate statement can lead readers to dismiss your entire message and lower their trust in your future communications as well.

Be Specific

Your readers expect you to be precise and avoid vagueness in nearly all business situations. The more specific you are, the more likely your readers are to have their questions answered. If you are not specific, your readers may become impatient and begin scanning and skimming for the information they want. If they can't find that information, they are unlikely to respond to your message as you intend.

Being specific also affects the judgments your readers make about your credibility. Specific statements lead your readers to believe that you know what you're talking about (competence), that you are not hiding anything (character), and that you want your readers to be informed (caring). Being vague, on the other hand, detracts from your credibility. See Table 6.2 for examples of less specific and more specific writing.

TABLE 6.2

Being Specific

Less Effective	More Effective
<u>With very little time commitment</u>, you can dramatically improve the lives of kids and their families in our community.	In just <u>one to two hours per week</u>, you can dramatically improve the lives of kids and their families in our community.
The phrase *very little time commitment* is not specific.	The phrase *one to two hours per week* is specific and avoids ambiguity.
Across the board, <u>every metric has skyrocketed</u>. Donations <u>increased so much</u> that we could serve many more families. On top of that, volunteer hours <u>increased</u> and we were able to receive <u>far more</u> clothing donations.	Since we started the social ambassadors program in 2018, cash donations have <u>increased 32 percent</u>; food donations, <u>18 percent</u>; book donations, <u>42 percent</u>; clothing donations, <u>55 percent</u>; and volunteer hours, <u>155 percent</u>.
All these terms are vague.	By stating specific figures for increases in donations, the impacts are not open to interpretation.

Improving Ease of Reading with Conciseness

When you write concisely, your message is far easier to read. Conciseness does not imply removing relevant information. Rather, it implies omitting needless words so that readers can rapidly process your main ideas. In response to the question "[Do you have] any thoughts on how language is used in the business world?" Clarence Otis Jr., former CEO of Darden Restaurants, responded this way:

> I think writing in the business world is more functional than elegant. I felt that way making the transition from law to business. Lawyers write much better. They spend a lot more time on it. In the business world, it's less about how well you say it and more about how efficiently you say it.[3]

Otis's primary point is that your language should be efficient. You should say as much as you can in as few words as possible. His distinction between functionality and elegance means that your primary focus is not impressing with words, but rather impressing with ideas. In this section, we describe strategies for writing concisely, including controlling paragraph length, using shorter sentences, avoiding redundancy, avoiding empty phrases, and avoiding wordy phrases.

Control Paragraph Length

Before they even begin to read, readers form impressions about ease of reading by looking at paragraph length. When they see long paragraphs, they often enter skim mode—searching for certain words and ideas rather than reading. Long paragraphs can signal disorganization and even disrespect for the reader's time.

Typically, paragraphs should contain 40 to 80 words. For routine messages, paragraphs as short as 20 to 30 words are common and appropriate. As the level of information and analysis grows deeper, some paragraphs will be longer. Rarely should paragraphs exceed 150 words. In a matter of seconds, you can easily check how many words are in your paragraphs with nearly all word processing software.

Improving Ease of Reading with Writing Style

Completeness
- Provide all relevant information.
- Be accurate.
- Be specific.

Conciseness
- Control paragraph length.
- Use short sentences.
- Avoid redundancy.
- Avoid empty phrases.
- Avoid wordy prepositional phrases.

Natural Style
- Use action verbs when possible.
- Use active voice.
- Use short and familiar words and phrases.
- Use parallel language.
- Avoid buzzwords and figures of speech.
- Avoid *it is/there are.*

TABLE 6.3

Controlling Paragraph Length

Less Effective	More Effective
A lot of people wonder exactly what we do. That's a fair question. In an effort to support people in need, we provide food in a well-balanced and nutritious manner. We have an on-site food pantry and a food pantry truck to provide delivery. We also serve hot meals on-site for breakfast, lunch, and dinner. The food bank bestows our clients with bountiful and sustainable food. In 2019, we served 2,152 households, 5,327 children were served, another 986 senior citizens were served, and altogether we served 23,887 meals! Our food bank is also a dietary guidance organization. Generally, impoverished families simply don't have the wherewithal to procure healthy foods. We have done research that shows 83 percent of the people we serve usually purchase inexpensive and unhealthy foods. As a result, many of our clients need more education about proper dietary needs. We also provide clothing assistance and give away books. We have helped thousands of members of the community get back on their feet. The charity watchdog group Charity Navigator has given us a perfect rating for the past five years because of our ability to serve our community with the resources we receive.	We provide well-balanced, nutritious foods to anyone in need. We have an on-site food pantry and a food pantry truck to provide delivery. We also serve hot meals on-site for breakfast, lunch, and dinner. We ensure all clients receive dairy products, fresh produce, meats, and breads.

Impact	2019
Households served	2,152
Children served	5,327
Seniors served	986
Meals served	23,887

We also provide dietary guidance. Many low-income families can't consistently afford healthy foods. Our research shows that 83 percent of our clients usually purchase inexpensive and unhealthy foods. As a result, many of our clients need more education about proper dietary needs. We also provide clothing assistance and give away books.

We have helped thousands of members of the community get back on their feet. *The charity watchdog group Charity Navigator has given us a perfect rating for the past five years* because of excellent use of donations to support our clients.

This paragraph contains 195 words. It also contains excessive numerical figures.	This paragraph contains the same information but has been edited for conciseness and divided into three paragraphs (46, 51, and 41 words) and a table for numerical information.

Mc Graw Hill connect

Visit http://connect. mheducation.com for an exercise on this topic.

One primary cause of overly lengthy paragraphs is placing more than one main idea or topic in the paragraph. Your readers can process the information in your message far more easily if you create unified paragraphs in which each paragraph focuses on one idea or topic. Paragraphs with more than one idea often confuse readers. Even worse, readers may miss some ideas altogether. The process of unifying helps you control paragraph length and even tighten your business reasoning (see Table 6.3).

Use Short Sentences in Most Cases

Like relatively short paragraphs, short sentences allow your readers to comprehend your ideas more easily. Consider Figure 6.2, which depicts the data from a study conducted by the American Press Institute.[4] Readers were tested on their overall comprehension based on the length of sentences. When sentences had 10 words or fewer, readers had nearly 100 percent comprehension. Once sentence lengths reached around 20 words, comprehension dropped to about 80 percent. Thereafter, comprehension dropped rapidly. Sentence lengths of 28 words resulted in just 30 percent comprehension.

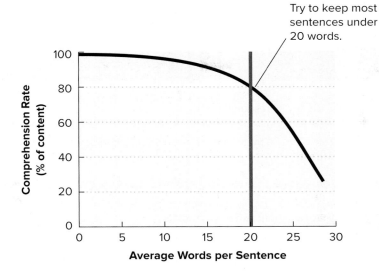

Try to keep most sentences under 20 words.

FIGURE 6.2

Comprehension Rate and Sentence Length

Source: Figure adapted from Wylie, A. (2009, January 14). How to make your copy more readable: Make sentences shorter. *Comprehension.* Retrieved from http://comprehension. prsa.org/?p=217.

As a rule of thumb, then, for routine messages, aim for average sentence length of 15 or fewer words. For more analytical and complex business messages, you may have an average sentence length of 20 or fewer words. Of course, you will often deal with complex ideas and need to go above 20 words in some of your sentences. Use your judgment to minimize sentence length (see Table 6.4).

Avoid Redundancy

One way to reduce word count and make your messages easier to read is to avoid redundancies, which are words or phrases that repeat the same meaning. For example, consider the phrase *past history*; history can only be past, so there's no need to

TABLE 6.4

Using Short Sentences

Less Effective	More Effective
Experts examine food insecurity in many ways, and their definitions generally coalesce around the idea that people not only consistently don't have enough money for food but it's also not healthy food they eat.	Generally, food insecurity means people don't have enough money to consistently eat enough healthy food.
This sentence contains 34 words.	This sentence contains the same ideas in just 15 words.
More than ever, we've started to serve the senior citizen community, with nearly 15 percent of our clients who are retired without enough income for regular, nutritious meals and who often face extra challenges with diseases such as diabetes and high blood pressure and who need dietary guidance as a result.	Increasingly, seniors need support as well. Nearly 15 percent of our clients are retired without enough income for regular, nutritious meals. Many of these seniors require nutritional guidance as they face extra challenges with diseases such as diabetes and high blood pressure.
This sentence contains 51 words.	The less effective sentence has been split into three sentences with 7, 15, and 21 words, respectively.

TABLE 6.5

Avoiding Redundancy

Less Effective	More Effective
<u>To help you succeed,</u> we provide you with many resources <u>so you can complete your role effectively.</u>	To help you <u>succeed</u>, we provide you with many resources.
This sentence has 17 words. *To help you succeed* and *so you can complete your role effectively* are redundant phrases.	This sentence has 10 words. It removes redundancy.
You will receive <u>weekly tips, suggestions,</u> and examples about how to increase your impact <u>each and every week</u>.	You will receive <u>weekly tips</u> and examples about how to increase your impact.
This sentence has 18 words. *Weekly* and *each and every week* are redundant. *Tips* and *suggestions* are redundant.	This sentence has 13 words. It removes redundancies.

use both words. By eliminating redundancies, you can reduce overall word count (see Table 6.5).

Avoid Empty Phrases

Many phrases simply fill space without adding additional meaning. Many of these phrases are common in conversations but are not needed for written messages (see Table 6.6).

Avoid Wordy Prepositional Phrases

Eliminating extra words allows you to get your ideas across as efficiently as possible. You will often find that you can reduce word count by 30 to 40 percent simply by converting many of your prepositional phrases into single-word verbs. Like other elements of style we have discussed already, prepositional phrases are not bad in themselves. In many cases, they are perfectly appropriate. Rather, their overuse leads to wordiness and less clarity (see Table 6.7).

TABLE 6.6

Avoiding Empty Phrases

Less Effective	More Effective
<u>Needless to say,</u> you receive training about how to influence your followers on Facebook, Instagram, LinkedIn, Twitter, and other social sites.	You receive training about how to influence your followers on Facebook, Instagram, LinkedIn, Twitter, and other social sites.
This sentence contains 21 words.	This revision contains 18 words.
<u>With all due respect,</u> we recommend you avoid posting unapproved content.	We recommend you avoid posting unapproved content.
This sentence contains 11 words.	This revision contains 7 words.

TABLE 6.7

Avoiding Wordy Prepositional Phrases

Less Effective	More Effective
In an effort to support people in need, we provide food in a well-balanced and nutritious manner.	We provide well-balanced, nutritious foods to anyone in need.
This sentence contains 18 words.	This revision of the less effective sentence contains 10 words.
In all the research about food security, kids in food insecure households are much more likely on a path to poor school performance, much more likely in a condition of stress, and much more likely on the road to many lifelong challenges.	Research shows that kids who face food insecurity experience more stress, perform more poorly at school, and face many lifelong challenges.
This sentence contains 42 words.	This revision of the less effective sentence contains 21 words.

Improving Ease of Reading with Natural Style

The closer you match your writing style to the way your readers think and talk, the easier it is for them to process the information you present. Ease of processing means your readers need less mental effort to understand your message, which is especially important for readers who are busy and preoccupied with other work challenges.

Several broad principles support the strategies in this section. First, people can generally process information more quickly when writers use action verbs. Second, people tend to think in a doer-action-object pattern, so using this pattern in your writing enhances comprehension. Furthermore, when the subject or doer is missing from the sentence, readers may become confused. Third, people generally process simple, short words more quickly than long, complex ones.

Visit http://connect.
mheducation.com for an
exercise on this topic.

Use Action Verbs When Possible

As a business writer, you want to project a positive, can-do, action-oriented tone whenever possible. Indeed, fostering action is the basic purpose of most workplace communication. Using action verbs focuses on the goal of coordinating action in the workplace and livens up your writing. Also, it usually reduces word count.

Typically, then, you can focus on two types of revisions to achieve more effective action verbs. First, find nouns that you can convert to action verbs. For example, *have a meeting* becomes *meet* or *have a discussion* becomes *discuss*. Second, find forms of the verb *to be* (e.g., be verbs such as *is, are, am*) and convert them to action verbs (see Table 6.8). For example, *The food bank is a great place for new skill development* becomes *The food bank gives you many opportunities to develop new skills.*

Use Active Voice

One way to immediately improve your writing is to use active rather than passive voice in most sentences. Active voice and passive voice contain the following grammatical patterns:

Active voice: Doer as Subject + Verb + Object
Passive voice: Object as Subject + Be Verb + Verb + Doer (Optional)

TABLE 6.8

Using Action Verbs

Less Effective	More Effective
Most of our social ambassadors <u>are volunteers</u> at the food bank.	Most of our social ambassadors <u>volunteer</u> at the food bank.
This sentence contains 11 words.	This revision contains 10 words.
Our food bank <u>is</u> also a dietary guidance organization.	We also <u>provide</u> dietary guidance.
This sentence contains 9 words.	This revision contains 5 words.

Consider the following examples:

Active voice: The food bank provides training for all social ambassadors.

Passive voice: Training is provided to all social ambassadors.

In active voice, this sentence immediately identifies the doer (the food bank). It then uses a strong verb (provides) and proceeds to the object (training). In passive voice, this sentence begins with the object of the action (training), proceeds to a weak verb (is), then employs a strong verb (provided), and leaves out the doer, thus lacking the clarity of active voice.

Using active voice in writing includes many benefits. The doer-action-object allows for faster processing because most people's natural thinking occurs in this way. It also emphasizes the business orientation of action. Perhaps most important, it specifies the doer. Because business activities depend on accountability and coordination, knowing the identity of the doer of an action is usually important. Furthermore, writing in the active voice usually results in fewer words (see Table 6.9).

TABLE 6.9

Using Active Voice Appropriately

Less Effective (Passive Voice)	More Effective (Active Voice)
Social ambassadors <u>are provided</u> with content to post and <u>are also given</u> suggestions about how to make it personalized.	We give you content to post and suggest how to personalize it.
This passive sentence de-emphasizes who provides the content and lacks an action-oriented tone. At 19 words, it is unnecessarily wordy.	The active verb construction in this sentence helps achieve a more engaging, action-oriented tone. At 12 words, it is easier to process.
<u>By being in attendance</u> at the monthly social ambassador meeting, there is a lot that <u>can be learned</u> about running a nonprofit.	You can join the food bank's monthly social ambassador meeting and learn about running a nonprofit.
This sentence contains two sets of passive verbs. It de-emphasizes who will run the meeting and who will learn about nonprofits. It lacks an action-oriented tone. At 22 words, it is wordy.	This sentences clearly identifies a benefit to *you* (social ambassadors). It is clear the food bank runs the meeting. At 16 words, it is easier to read.

TABLE 6.10

Using Passive Voice Appropriately

Less Effective (Active Voice)	More Effective (Passive Voice)
<u>Since you did not provide enough information in your application</u>, <u>we cannot provide a decision</u> about you being a social ambassador.	<u>Since some application information wasn't completed</u>, a <u>decision</u> about you being a social ambassador <u>hasn't been made.</u>
This active verb construction emphasizes the applicant's mistakes. It also emphasizes the controlling nature of the food bank in the decision.	This passive verb construction provides the bad news without assigning blame or directly pointing out failure.
<u>You need to complete the application forms carefully</u> for us to seriously consider your application.	<u>Application forms that are completed carefully</u> allow us to better determine the merit of your application.
This active verb construction might be perceived as bossy (sounds like an order) or demeaning (implies the reader is not smart enough to understand basic procedures).	This passive verb construction emphasizes the importance of carefully completing the forms without directly implying the reader is likely to make elementary mistakes.

While active voice is the preferred writing style for most business writing, passive voice is sometimes better when attempting to avoid blaming others or sounding bossy. Some research reports also use passive voice to emphasize neutrality (see Table 6.10).

Use Short and Familiar Words and Phrases

Whenever possible, choose short, conversational, and familiar words. Using longer, less common words to "sound smart" rarely pays off. They slow processing and distract from your message. They may even inadvertently send the signal that you are out of touch, quirky, or even arrogant (see Table 6.11).

TABLE 6.11

Using Short, Familiar Words and Phrases

Less Effective	More Effective
Generally, <u>impoverished</u> families simply don't have the <u>wherewithal</u> to <u>procure</u> <u>wholesome</u> foods.	Generally, <u>low-income</u> families can't always <u>afford</u> <u>healthy</u> foods.
Impoverished, wherewithal, procure, and *wholesome* are all words that are less familiar to many readers and take longer to process than words such as *low-income, afford,* and *healthy.*	This sentence contains short, familiar words that allow for ease of reading.
The food bank <u>bestows</u> our clients with <u>bountiful</u> and <u>sustainable</u> food.	We ensure all clients receive dairy products, fresh produce, meats, and breads.
This sentence contains infrequently used or exaggerated words *(bestows, bountiful, sustainable).* These terms sound overblown and will confuse many readers.	This sentence contains shorter, more familiar terms and concrete items that capture the intended meaning.

TABLE 6.12

Using Parallel Language

Less Effective	More Effective
Social ambassadors are <u>generous</u> and <u>know how to influence others on social media sites</u>.	Social ambassadors are <u>generous with their time</u> and <u>savvy with social media</u>.
The two characteristics of customers are not parallel. They are in the following pattern: adjective and verb–object.	The two characteristics of customers are parallel. They are both adjectives.
	OR
	Social ambassadors <u>give their time freely</u> and <u>influence their followers on social media sites</u>.
	The two characteristics of social ambassadors are parallel. They both follow verb–object patterns.
We will work directly with you to <u>influence social media followers, select appropriate content, and personalized posts</u>.	We will work directly with you to <u>influence social media followers, select appropriate content, and personalize your posts</u>.
The three items in the list are not parallel. They are in the following pattern: verb–object, verb–object, noun.	The three items in the list are parallel. They are each in a verb–object pattern.
	OR
	We will work directly with you to achieve the following: <u>appropriate content selection, personalized posts, and widespread influence</u>.
	The three items in the list are parallel. They are each in adjective–noun patterns.

Use Parallel Language

Using parallel language means that you apply a consistent grammatical pattern across a sentence or paragraph. Parallelism is most important when you use series or lists. For example, when you describe a product with three characteristics, use the same grammatical pattern for each—that is, for example, choose adjectives or nouns or verbs for all of them. When you use consistent grammatical patterns for items in lists and series, readers can process the information far more naturally and quickly (see Table 6.12).

Avoid Buzzwords and Figures of Speech

To keep your writing natural and engaging, make sure you don't distract your readers with overused or out-of-place words or phrases. Buzzwords, which are workplace terms that become trite because of overuse, can stir negative feelings among some readers. In Table 6.13, you can see one list of annoying buzzwords cited in a recent survey of executives.[5] (Dozens of such lists exist because business professionals become so agitated by these overused words.)

Figures of speech, such as idioms and metaphors, which contain nonliteral meanings, are generally out of place or inappropriate in business writing. Because they are nonliteral, they lack the precise meanings needed in business. Also, some idioms and metaphors have become so clichéd that they have lost almost all meaning (see Table 6.14).

TABLE 6.13

The Most Annoying Buzzwords

Leverage	At the end of the day
Reach out	Synergy
It is what it is	Solution
Viral	Think outside the box
Game changer	On the same page
Disconnect	Customer-centric
Value-add	Do more with less
Circle back	Downsizing
Cutting edge	Overworked

Source: What's the buzz? Survey reveals most overused workplace terms. Online article. Retrieved July 2014.

Avoid *It Is/There Are*

Readers naturally want to know precisely *who* or *what* the subject of a sentence is, particularly in business writing, where specificity is so important. Most sentences that begin with *it is* or *there are* fail to provide a specific subject and generally contain more words than necessary. A message can be particularly awkward when many of the sentences begin with *it is* or *there are*. By rewording *it is/there are* statements, you generally liven up your writing.

One way of recognizing when to reword *it is* statements is to ask the question *what does* **it** *refer to?* If you don't know the answer, your readers won't either. Consider the

TABLE 6.14

Avoiding Buzzwords and Figures of Speech

Less Effective	More Effective
Do you want to change the world? With very little time commitment, you can catapult the life opportunities of kids and their families in our community.	Do you want to help the most vulnerable members of our community? In just one or two hours per week, you can dramatically improve the lives of kids and their families in our community.
Change the world and *catapult* are figures of speech that sound unbelievable to most readers.	This sentence is more believable. It avoids exaggerated figures of speech but remains extremely positive and future-oriented.
We organize an annual retreat that is a total blast for our social ambassadors and that provides synergistic, win–win solutions and proactive approaches to managing their social media influence.	We organize a fun-filled annual retreat for social ambassadors where they can share and discuss problems, solutions, and opportunities to increase their social media influence.
These sentences contain various figures of speech that readers may not receive well. A *total blast* is slang. Not only can slang be misunderstood, but it can also serve as a generation marker. Slang goes out of style and can make you look out of date. Other slang will highlight how young you are. The combination of buzzwords (*synergistic, win–win, proactive*) in the second portion of the sentence will annoy some readers.	This sentence, without the excessive slang and buzzwords, is easy to read. Readers can rapidly process this sentence and relate to its tone.

TABLE 6.15

Avoiding *It Is* and *There Are*

Less Effective	More Effective
<u>There are</u> many ways you can help out as a social ambassador.	As a social ambassador, you can help in many ways.
This sentence contains 12 words.	This sentence contains 10 words.
<u>It is</u> wonderful to see kids not worrying about where their next meal comes from.	Seeing kids not worrying about their next meal is wonderful.
This sentence contains 15 words.	This sentence contains 10 words.
<u>It is</u> great to be in a nonprofit where <u>there are</u> so many extremely loyal volunteers.	In nonprofits, so many volunteers are extremely loyal.
This sentence contains 16 words.	This sentence contains 8 words.

second sentence in Table 6.15: *It is wonderful to see kids not worrying about where their next meal comes from.* What does *it* refer to? Recognizing what *it* is requires you to think for a few seconds. By rewording the sentence, you can provide a more descriptive, concise, and natural statement: *Seeing kids not worrying about their next meal is wonderful.* After considering the examples in Table 6.15, read the Technology Tips in the "Reviewing Your Message" section for ways that you can use your word processing program to further improve your writing.

Improving Ease of Reading with Navigational Design

LO6.2 Explain and use navigational design to improve ease of reading.

Your primary goal for document design is making your message easy to navigate. Ask yourself these questions: How can I get my readers to see my main ideas and messages quickly? How can I make sure my readers can find the information they are most interested in? Several features will help you improve navigational design, including headings, highlighting, lists, white space, and simplicity. Later in the book, we will focus on additional ways of enhancing the appearance of your document with charts, figures, and graphics.

Use Headings

In information-rich and complex messages, headings can help your readers identify key ideas and navigate the document to areas of interest. As you create headings and subheadings, be consistent in font style and formatting throughout your document. One way to be consistent with your headings is to apply formatting features available in most word processing programs. For example, in Microsoft Word, you can assign heading levels for major heads and subheads (Heading 1, Heading 2, and so on). You have many options for the formatting styles you apply, and the software ensures that the formatting remains consistent throughout the document.

As you develop your headings, make sure you concisely and accurately convey the contents of a section. For example, notice the heading "Who Needs Our Help?" in the more effective example in Table 6.16. In contrast, the heading "How Do We Determine Who Needs Help the Most and Then Target Those High-Need Individuals?" is likely too long for most documents. On the other hand, a subheading such as "Community Needs" may not give readers accurate information about the contents of the section.

> **Improving Ease of Reading with Navigational Design**
> - Headings
> - Highlighting
> - Lists
> - White space
> - Simplicity

TABLE 6.16

Using Headings

Less Effective	More Effective

Less Effective

Unfortunately, about 20 percent or one in five people in our community is food insecure. Experts examine food insecurity in many ways, but their definitions generally coalesce around the idea that people not only don't have enough money for food but it's also not healthy food they eat. This creates worry, embarrassment, hunger, and poor health. Those who are food insecure are generally in low-income (under $300000) households, but that's not always the case. Surprise medical bills, extended family caretaking responsibilities, and sudden loss of employment are common reasons other households are affected. We worry the most about children. In all the research about food security, kids in food insecure households are much more likely on a path to poor school performance, much more likely in a condition of stress, and much more likely on the road to many lifelong challenges. More than ever, we've started to serve the senior citizen community, with nearly 15 percent of our clients who are retired without enough income for regular, nutritious meals and who often face extra challenges with diseases such as diabetes and high blood pressure and who need dietary guidance as a result.

A lot of people wonder exactly what we do. That's a fair question. In an effort to support people in need, we provide food in a well-balanced and nutritious manner. We have an on-site food pantry and a food pantry truck to provide delivery. We also serve hot meals on-site for breakfast, lunch, and dinner. The food bank bestows our clients with bountiful and sustainable food. In 2019, we served 2,152 households, 5,327 children were served, another 986 senior citizens were served, and altogether we served 23,887 meals! Our food bank is also a dietary guidance organization. Generally, impoverished families simply don't have the wherewithal to procure healthy foods. We have done research that shows 83 percent of the people we serve usually purchase inexpensive and unhealthy foods. As a result, many of our clients need more education about proper dietary needs. We also provide clothing assistance and give away books. We have helped thousands of members of the community get back on their feet. The charity watchdog group Charity Navigator has given us a perfect rating for the past five years because of our ability to serve our community with the resources we receive.

These two paragraphs contain 384 words with far too many numbers. Many readers would have a hard time locating the key information.

More Effective

Who Needs Our Help?

About one in five people in our community is food insecure. Generally, this means they don't have enough money to consistently eat enough healthy food. This creates worry, embarrassment, hunger, and poor health.

Those who are food insecure are generally in low-income (under $30,000 per year) households, but that's not always the case. Surprise medical bills, extended family caretaking responsibilities, and sudden loss of employment are common reasons other households are affected.

We worry the most about children. Research shows that kids who face food insecurity experience more stress, perform more poorly at school, and face many lifelong challenges. Increasingly, seniors need support as well. Nearly 15 percent of our clients are retired without enough income for regular, nutritious meals. Many of these seniors require nutritional guidance as they face extra challenges with diseases such as diabetes and high blood pressure.

What Does Peak Harvest Food Bank Do?

We provide well-balanced, nutritious foods to anyone in need. We have an on-site food pantry and a food pantry truck to provide delivery. We also serve hot meals on-site for breakfast, lunch, and dinner. We ensure all clients receive dairy products, fresh produce, meats, and breads.

Impact	2019
Households served	2,152
Children served	5,327
Seniors served	986
Meals served	23,887

We also provide dietary guidance. Many low-income families can't consistently afford healthy foods. Our research shows that 83 percent of our clients usually purchase inexpensive and unhealthy foods. As a result, many of our clients need more education about proper dietary needs. We also provide clothing assistance and give away books.

We have supported thousands of members of the community get back on their feet. The charity watchdog group *Charity Navigator has given us a perfect rating for the past five years* because of excellent use of donations to support our clients.

Visually, these paragraphs are far more appealing and inviting. The headings immediately orient the reader to the content. Key figures are placed in the table for better emphasis.

TABLE 6.17

Applying Formatting to Key Words and Phrases

Less Effective	More Effective
We have helped thousands of members of the community get back on their feet. The charity watchdog group Charity Navigator has given us a perfect rating for the past five years because of excellent use of donations to support our clients.	We have helped thousands of members of the community get back on their feet. The charity watchdog group *Charity Navigator has given us a perfect rating for the past five years* because of excellent use of donations to support our clients.
By italicizing everything, nothing is highlighted.	By italicizing one short phrase, you emphasize it.
We provide **<u>free training</u>** for all new social ambassadors.	We provide **free training** for all new social ambassadors.
Applying two formatting features (bold and underlining) may appear overbearing.	Applying one formatting feature (bold) is sufficient to highlight the phrase.

Readers skimming the document to learn who is served by the food bank might miss this section on the first pass. You can find more information about headings in Chapters 12 and 13 about reports.

Highlight Key Words and Phrases

When you want to highlight ideas or phrases, consider using **bold**, *italics*, or <u>underlining</u> to draw and keep your readers' attention. Typically, you will apply this type of formatting sparingly; if you use too much special formatting, your main ideas will not stand out. In general, apply only one type of formatting to a highlighted word or words (i.e., only bold or italics, not bold *and* italics) (see Table 6.17).

Use Bulleted and Numbered Lists

You will often use lists in business writing. When you set these items apart with bullets or numbers, your readers notice and remember the items more easily (see Table 6.18).

TABLE 6.18

Using Bulleted and Numbered Lists

Less Effective	More Effective
To help you succeed, we provide you with many resources. You receive training about how to influence your followers on Facebook, Instagram, LinkedIn, Twitter, and other social sites. You receive weekly tips and examples about how to increase your impact. You receive content to post and suggestions for how to personalize it. You can join the food bank's monthly social ambassador meeting and learn about running a nonprofit.	To help you succeed, we provide you with many resources. • You receive training about how to influence your followers on Facebook, Instagram, LinkedIn, Twitter, and other social sites. • You receive weekly tips and examples about how to increase your impact. • You receive content to post and suggestions for how to personalize it. • You can join the food bank's monthly social ambassador meeting and learn about running a nonprofit.
Without bullets, this paragraph contains a lot of items that are difficult for the reader to remember. Furthermore, it takes longer for the reader to visualize the components of the brochure.	With bullets, this paragraph allows the reader to rapidly process the information and visualize the components of the brochure. Furthermore, the use of enumeration and bullets more clearly distinguishes the overarching goals and components of the brochure.

Use White Space Generously

Your readers will form an immediate impression about your document based on how much white space (areas without text) it has. Documents with too much text and not enough white look daunting or cluttered. On the other hand, documents with too much white space may look insufficient. Many students are trained in the university setting to double-space documents. In the workplace, double-spaced documents are rare, however.

Keep It Simple

Visual appeal is not the first consideration for most written business communications. Rather, the goal is to get your message across in an easy-to-read manner. As you design your document, focus first on easy navigation for your reader. Avoid formatting features that distract from the main message. See Figure 6.3 for effective use of navigational features and white space.

FIGURE 6.3

Stephanie's Final, Easier-to-Read Brochure (compare to original version in Figure 6.1)

Statistical Comparison of Original and Final Versions of Brochure		
	Original Version	**Revised Version**
Paragraphs (#)	8	21
Longest Paragraph	216 words	95 words
Average Paragraph Length	143 words	55 words
Average Sentence Length	23 words	15 words

Become a Social Ambassador for Peak Harvest Food Bank

In just one or two hours per week, you can dramatically improve the lives of kids and their families in our community. Social ambassadors for the food bank get the word out about our community's needs, help people get assistance, increase donations, and promote volunteerism.

Last year our top social ambassadors made a huge impact. The average social ambassador increased donations by $2,312—that's enough to help a food-insecure family of four eat nutritious meals for nearly four months! Since we started the social ambassadors program in 2018, cash donations have increased 32 percent; food donations, 18 percent; book donations, 42 percent; clothing donations, 55 percent; and volunteer hours, 159 percent.

Social ambassadors also gain valuable skills and lessons, such as using social media for good causes, marketing, working in teams, and giving back to the community. *Local employers tell us they highly value the skills the social ambassadors develop.*

Who Needs Our Help?

About one in five people in our community is food insecure. Generally, this means they don't have enough money to consistently eat enough healthy food. This creates worry, embarrassment, hunger, and poor health.

Those who are food insecure are generally in low-income (under $30,000 per year) households, but that's not always the case. Surprise medical bills, extended family caretaking responsibilities, and sudden loss of employment are common reasons other households are affected.

We worry the most about children. Research shows that kids who face food insecurity experience more stress, perform more poorly at school, and face many lifelong challenges. Increasingly, seniors need support as well. Nearly 15 percent of our clients are retired without enough income for regular, nutritious meals. Many of these seniors require nutritional guidance as they face extra challenges with diseases such as diabetes and high blood pressure.

Lisa Poole/AP Photo

FIGURE 6.3

(Continued)

What Does Peak Harvest Food Bank Do?

We provide well-balanced, nutritious foods to anyone in need. We have an on-site food pantry and a food pantry truck to provide delivery. We also serve hot meals on-site for breakfast, lunch, and dinner. We ensure all clients receive dairy products, fresh produce, meats, and breads.

Impact	2019
Households served	2,152
Children served	5,327
Seniors served	986
Meals served	23,887

We also provide dietary guidance. Many low-income families can't consistently afford healthy foods. Our research shows that 83 percent of our clients usually purchase inexpensive and unhealthy foods. As a result, many of our clients need more education about proper dietary needs. We also provide clothing assistance and give away books.

We have helped thousands of members of the community get back on their feet. The charity watchdog group *Charity Navigator has given us a perfect rating for the past five years* because of excellent use of donations to support our clients.

Steve Debenport/ E+/Getty Images

What Do Social Ambassadors Do?

Social ambassadors promote the food bank and raise donations. They use social media to share information about food insecurity in our community. Most of our social ambassadors also volunteer at the food bank for at least one shift (three hours) per month so they have their own personal experiences working with clients.

What Can Social Ambassadors Expect and Receive from the Food Bank?

To help you succeed, we provide you with many resources.

- You receive training about how to influence your followers on Facebook, Instagram, LinkedIn, Twitter, and other social sites.
- You receive weekly tips and examples about how to increase your impact.
- You receive content to post and suggestions for how to personalize it.
- You can join the food bank's monthly social ambassador meeting and learn about running a nonprofit.

To apply to serve as a social ambassador, fill out the online form or email Stephanie Jorgenson at sjorgenson@phfb.org.

Reviewing Your Message

LO6.3 Describe and apply the components of the reviewing stage, including a FAIR test, proofreading, and feedback.

You will recall from Chapter 5 that expert business writers use their time differently than do average business writers (see Figure 5.2 in Chapter 5). They devote more time to planning and reviewing and proportionately less time to drafting. They spend most of their time—before and after drafting—carefully thinking about how the message will influence and affect others.

Many business professionals get anxious to send their messages as soon as they finish drafting them. It is human nature to want to move on to the next task. Resist the urge to move on without carefully reviewing your messages. During the reviewing stage, you will improve your message, making it far more successful. You will also minimize the possibility of embarrassing and damaging mistakes.

The reviewing process includes three interrelated components: conducting the FAIR test, proofreading, and getting feedback (not generally needed for routine messages). These reviewing components ensure that you show fairness, get the message right, avoid errors, and get perspectives from trusted colleagues. For short, routine messages (one

Technology Tips

USING SPELLING AND GRAMMAR CHECKS

Most word processing software programs contain spelling and grammar checks to help you avoid misspellings and grammatical mistakes. Many of these programs, such as Microsoft Word, also have tools to evaluate writing style and ease of reading. Typically, these tools are not set by default. You will need to manually select them. (In Microsoft Word, you can access these additional tools by changing settings in the *Proofing* area of *Word Options*.)

When you run spelling and grammar checks, you can review your document sentence by sentence for passive voice, noun clusters, and other elements. Once you finish the check, you will see a final calculation of readability statistics. Keep in mind that the software is not perfect. Generally, however, it will help you improve your writing style.

Your challenge: Use Microsoft Word to calculate the readability statistics of a recent assignment you turned in. What do the statistics tell you? What can you change based on these statistics?

Become a Social Ambassador for Peak Harvest Food Bank

In just one or two hours per week, you can dramatically improve the lives of kids and their families in our community. Social ambassadors for the food bank get the word out about our community's needs, help people get assistance, increase donations, and promote volunteerism.

Last year our top social ambassadors made a huge impact. The average social ambassador increased donations by $2,312 – that's enough to help a food-insecure family of four eat nutritious meals for nearly four months! Since we started the social ambassadors program in 2018, cash donations have increased 32 percent; food donations, 18 percent; book donations, 42 percent; clothing dontations, 55 percent; and volunteer hours, 159 percent. |

Social ambassadors also gain valuable skills and lesson~~s~~ marketing, working in teams, and giving back to the c~~o~~ the skills are social ambassadors develop.

Who Needs Our Help?

About one in five people in our community is food ins~~e~~ enough money to consistently eat enough healthy foo~~d~~ and poor health.

Those who are food insecure are generally in low-inco~~me~~ that's not always the case. Surprise medical bills, exte~~nded~~ sudden loss of employment are common reasons othe~~r~~

We worry the most about children. Research shows th~~at~~ stress, perform more poorly at school, and face many support as well. Nearly 15 percent of our clients are re~~ceiving~~ nutritious meals. Many of these seniors require nutritional guidance as they face extra challenges with diseases such as diabetes and high blood pressure.

Readability Statistics	?	X
Counts		
Words		612
Characters		3,303
Paragraphs		31
Sentences		41
Averages		
Sentences per Paragraph		2.0
Words per Sentence		14.3
Characters per Word		5.2
Readability		
Flesch Reading Ease		49.3
Flesch-Kincaid Grade Level		9.6
Passive Sentences		0.0%

OK

What Does Peak Harvest Food Bank Do?

We provide well-balanced, nutritious foods to anyone in need. We have an on-site food pantry and a food pantry truck to provide delivery. We also serve hot meals on-site for breakfast, lunch, and dinner. We ensure all clients receive dairy products, fresh produce, meats, and breads.

Impact	2019
Households served	2,152
Children served	5,327
Seniors served	986
Meals served	23,887

We also provide dietary guidance. Many low-income families can't consistently afford healthy foods. Our research shows that 83 percent of our clients usually purchase inexpensive and unhealthy foods. As a result, many of our clients need more education about proper dietary needs. We also provide clothing assistance and give away books.

Readability Statistics box: Microsoft Word Readability Statistics

to four paragraphs), expert business writers can often check for fairness and proofread in just a few minutes. For long, important messages, such as business proposals or business plans, the reviewing stage may take weeks or months.

Conduct a FAIR Test

In Chapter 1, we introduced the FAIR test as a way of ensuring ethical business communication. Of course, you will consider such issues during the planning and writing stages. Also, during the review process you can also take the time to think about the degree to which your entire message conforms to standards for facts, access, impacts, and respect. For important messages—particularly those that involve complicated business issues—apply the FAIR test:

- *Facts:* Are you confident in your facts? Are your assumptions clear? Have you avoided slanting the facts or made other logical errors?
- *Access:* Have you granted enough access to message recipients about decision making and information? Have you granted enough access to the message recipients to provide input? Are you open about your motives, or do you have a hidden agenda?
- *Impacts:* Have you thought about how the message will impact various stakeholders? Have you evaluated impacts on others from ethical, corporate, and legal perspectives?
- *Respect:* Have you demonstrated respect for the inherent worth of others: their aspirations, thoughts, feelings, and well-being? Have you shown that you value others?

Proofread

Proofreading involves rereading your entire document to make sure it is influential and accurate. You might consider rereading each sentence several times, each time with a different focus. On your first pass, place yourself in the position of your audience members. Imagine how they will respond. On your second pass, check for problems with writing style and language mechanics.

Get Feedback

As one business writing expert stated, one of the best ways to ensure that your communication is effective and fair is to get feedback from others:

> Ask some people whose judgment you respect to give it a test read and get their reaction. Do they think it's too energetic or hyperbolic for the audience and the occasion? Or is it too frosty? Similarly, do they think the writing is too distant or too familiar? What are the offending words or phrases? How can they be changed to do the job at hand? Using test readers is hardly rocket science, but those willing to go through this trouble invariably produce more effective writing.[6]

This advice reveals an important point: Your trusted colleagues are giving your message a trial run—trying to simulate how the intended message recipient will respond. As they review your message, they can provide insights about making it better. Before they begin to read, ask them to consider whether you have framed the idea correctly, whether the business logic holds up, whether the message has the intended effects, whether the tone is appropriate, and so on. Effective business communicators make a habit of getting this advance feedback for important messages.

IDEAS IN ACTION

WRITE LIKE WARREN BUFFETT

Warren Buffett, one of the world's most successful investors and CEO of Berkshire Hathaway, has personally written annual letters to his shareholders for well over 50 years. Investors and analysts look forward to these letters each year because of Buffett's wit, charm, and style.

Drew Angerer/Getty Images

One reason his letters are so effective is his ability to take complex information and state it simply and elegantly. One set of indexes created by Legal Writing Pro gives him perfect scores for using plain English, writing in short paragraphs, avoiding passive voice, and maintaining sentence variety. His 2016 letter has an average sentence length of 13.5 words.

Importantly, people feel like Buffett is speaking directly to them and giving them valuable tips. In fact, many people who are not shareholders read the letters because they think he gives such good advice. One indicator of his focus on the readers is his use of the you-view. For example, in his most recent letter, he used the words *you* or *your* 71 times. In his 2016 letter, he used *you* or *your* more than 100 times!

Sources: Gallo, C. (2018, February 25). Warren Buffett loves this ancient tool of persuasion to enliven his annual letters. *Forbes*. Retrieved from www.forbes.com/sites/carminegallo/2018/02/25/warren-buffett-loves-this-ancient-tool-of-persuasion-to-enliven-his-annual-letters/; Guberman, R. (2018, February 27). Five ways to write like Warren Buffett. *Legal Writing Pro*. Retrieved from www.legalwritingpro.com/blog/five-ways-write-like-warren-buffett/; Sullivan, J. (2017, March 2). How to write like Warren Buffett—or not. *Forbes*. Retrieved from www.forbes.com/sites/jaysullivan/2017/03/02/how-to-write-like-warren-buffett-or-not/.

Chapter Takeaway for *Improving Readability with Style and Design*

LO6.1 Describe and apply the following principles of writing style that improve ease of reading: completeness, conciseness, and natural processing.

Improving Ease of Reading with Writing Style		
Completeness	**Conciseness**	**Natural Style**
• Provide all relevant information. • Be accurate. • Be specific.	• Control paragraph length. • Use short sentences. • Avoid redundancy. • Avoid empty phrases. • Avoid wordy prepositional phrases.	• Use action verbs when possible. • Use active voice. • Use short and familiar words and phrases. • Use parallel language. • Avoid buzzwords and figures of speech. • Avoid *it is/there are*.

See *examples of writing style improvements* in Tables 6.1 through 6.15.

LO6.2 Explain and use navigational design to improve ease of reading.

Improving Ease of Reading with Navigational Design		
• Headings • Highlighting	• Lists • White space	• Simplicity

See *examples of navigational design* in Tables 6.16 through 6.18.

LO6.3 Describe and apply the components of the reviewing stage, including a FAIR test, proofreading, and feedback.

FAIR test: Evaluate your message in terms of facts, access, impacts, and respect.
Proofreading: Ask trusted colleagues to review your message for effectiveness and accuracy.
Feedback: For important messages, ask trusted colleagues to give input about effectiveness and fairness.

Discussion Exercises

6.1 Chapter Review Questions (LO6.1, LO6.2, LO6.3)

Answer the following questions:

A. How does complete writing improve ease of reading?

B. How does concise writing improve ease of reading?

C. How does natural writing improve ease of reading?

D. How does document design improve ease of reading?

E. Do you think that complete and concise writing are competing goals? Explain.

6.2 Ideas in Action Discussion Questions (LO6.1)

Answer the following questions based on the Ideas in Action box that features Warren Buffett as well as your own experiences:

A. What elements of tone make Buffett's messages so appealing?

B. What elements of style make Buffett's messages so appealing?

C. Which aspects of style are most important to you? Why?

D. Find one of Buffett's recent annual letters. What are your observations about the tone, paragraph length, sentence length, and use of active verbs?

Evaluation Exercises

6.3 Analyzing a Corporate Message (LO6.1, LO6.2)

In July 2015, Stephen Elop announced major changes at Microsoft. Read the message at http://news.microsoft.com/2014/07/17/stephen-elops-email-to-employees/.

Analyze this message for ease of reading in the following ways:

A. Identify and revise five sentences that are not complete.

B. Identify and revise five sentences that are not concise.

C. Identify and revise five sentences that are not natural.

D. Explain three strategies for designing the document for faster navigation.

E. Revise the document. Attempt to cut the length in half. Use headings and other design features to improve navigation.

6.4 Identifying Areas for Personal Improvement (LO6.1, LO6.2)

Identify three writing principles from this chapter that you most need to work on. For each principle, write a paragraph about why you want to improve in this area and how you will go about doing it. Choose from the following writing principles: be specific; be accurate; control paragraph length; use short sentences in most cases; avoid redundancy; avoid empty phrases; avoid wordy phrases; use action verbs when possible; use active voice; use short and familiar words and phrases; use parallel language; avoid buzzwords and figures of speech; avoid *it is* and *there are*; use headings; apply formatting to key words and phrases; use bulleted and numbered lists; use white space generously.

Application Exercises

Case for Exercises 6.5 through 6.18: Promoting the Supply Chain Management Club

Your roommate is the president of the Supply Chain Management Club. She wants you to help her revise a flyer that she has drafted to attract more members. Here is her draft.

Joining a Student Club

Have you thought about joining a student club? If so, we are organizing an information session to orient you to our club.

The purpose of the Supply Chain Management Club (SCMC) that we have here on campus is to support Supply Chain and Operations Management (SCOM) majors as well as other interested majors if they choose to gain a broader and balanced understanding of the opportunities, career paths, trends, and current burning issues in global supply chain management. Each and every semester, SCMC has facility tours, discussion panels, faculty interactions, and résumé workshops in order for our members to gain a glimpse into the real world of global supply chain management and the nature of this constantly evolving and developing business field.

There are many, many reasons for being an SCMC member. It goes without saying that many of you want financial aid, and SCMC has received boatloads of generous donations to offer scholarships for qualifying SCMC students. All SCMC club members learn to market themselves more effectively by joining the club. There is an SCMC Placement Coordinator specifically directed to search for every possible job that you could apply for, and these jobs are placed on the SCMC website where you can view them anytime and anywhere. These jobs are in a plethora of industries, like Business Services, Consumer Products and Services, Food and Beverage, Health, Industrial, Public Sector, and Technology and Communications. Also, through SCMC and by also gaining a membership in ISM, certification opportunities will be at your fingertips. The sky's the limit in this club. SCMC board members are currently looking for new opportunities and are researching the potential of funding future group workshops and certification programs that we haven't had access to in the past.

The most popular part of the club that students like the most are the abundant events that are scheduled. Plant tours and speeches by supply chain professionals are constantly being scheduled for SCMC club members to attend. These events create a big impact on your future career by giving you the opportunities to gain exposure to real-world professionals. One of the great opportunities you have as a member in the club is the opportunity to be in touch with the SCMC alumni group, which gives you a networking chance with people already working in supply chain management.

There are many opportunities to learn special skills since there are special-interest groups within the club. For example, there is a special-interest group devoted to learning about various software tools for global supply chain management. In the software group, you can learn statistical software programs such as POM for Windows, Excel Solver, ProcessModel, and SPSS as well as learning mapping software such as MapPoint. Skills acquired in these special-interest groups can be placed on your résumé in conjunction with other skills developed in your studies from the SCOM major. It can't be stated enough how much these extra skills can enhance your qualifications to be a supply chain manager.

The Supply Chain Management Club (SCMC) is designed to help club members understand the critical and essential organizational function of global supply chain and operations management that creates and distributes products and services; measures their quality and instigates the processes whereby quality improvement occurs; and simultaneously creates nimble, streamlined, and efficient business processes and supply chains. This critical business function is responsible for short-term survival and long-term profitability and growth of the organization in all types of businesses, such as large or small, manufacturing or service, or even for-profit or nonprofit. In today's globally interconnected economy, prowess in global supply chain and operations management is the benchmark of the great manufacturers, retailers, and major companies, such as Dell, Walmart, Southwest Airlines, Toyota, and Bank of America. Supply chain management is the fundamental competency that determines success in today's business world, and by joining the SCMC club, you literally have success in your hands since so many major businesses will need your services.

The Supply Chain Management Club (SCMC) is extremely practical with many career options in global manufacturing firms in production, purchasing, quality control, distribution and supply chain management; in service firms as general operations management and logistics/supply chain management; and in consulting firms as business process and quality improvement consultants. In fact, even if you are pursuing other professions as primary careers, SCOM skills and competencies make one a better accountant, better at financial analysis, better as marketing manager, or even better at managing human resources or managing information technology for a company.

The club is affiliated with the Institute for Supply Chain Management (ISM), which was founded in the year 1915 and is the biggest supply chain management association in the world and is recognized by supply chain professionals far and wide as the repository of best practices in the field. The ISM website can be visited at the following website: www.ism.ws/.

A pizza party will be held in the business building on January 29 to introduce you to the club. This meeting will provide a lot of information about reasons for joining the club.

All of our regular meetings are at the Marriott next to the business school. A speech is *always given by an important industry professional. Dinner is served at just $10.*

Rewrite each of the following sentences from her draft to be complete, concise, and natural. The sentences are organized by principles from the chapter; however, note that many sentences contain additional style issues for you to correct. Make reasonable embellishments as necessary.

6.5 Be Specific (LO6.1)

A. Have you thought about joining a student club? If so, we are organizing an information session to orient you to our club.

B. A pizza party will be held in the business building on January 29 to introduce you to the club.

C. This meeting will provide a lot of information about reasons for joining the club.

D. All of our regular meetings are at the Marriott next to the business school.

6.6 Be Accurate (LO6.1)

A. Supply chain management is the fundamental competency that determines success in today's business world, and by joining the SCMC club, you literally have success in your hands since so many major businesses will need your services.

B. All SCMC club members learn to market themselves more effectively by joining the club.

6.7 Use Short Sentences in Most Cases (LO6.1)

Cut these sentences by more than 50 percent. Use more than one sentence if necessary.

A. The purpose of the Supply Chain Management Club (SCMC) that we have here on campus is to support Supply Chain and Operations Management (SCOM) majors as well as other interested majors if they choose to gain a broader and balanced understanding of the opportunities, career paths, trends, and current burning issues in global supply chain management.

B. The Supply Chain Management Club (SCMC) is designed to help club members understand the critical and essential organizational function of global supply chain and operations management that creates and distributes products and services; measures their quality and instigates the processes whereby quality improvement occurs; and simultaneously creates nimble, streamlined, and efficient business processes and supply chains.

C. This critical business function is responsible for short-term survival and long-term profitability and growth of the organization in all types of businesses, such as large or small, manufacturing or service, or even for-profit or nonprofit.

6.8 Avoid Redundancy (LO6.1)

Remove redundancies and shorten these sentences.

A. Each and every semester, SCMC has facility tours, discussion panels, faculty interactions, and résumé workshops in order for our members to gain a glimpse into the real world of global supply chain management and the nature of this constantly evolving and developing business field.

B. There is an SCMC Placement Coordinator specifically directed to search for every possible job that you could apply for, and these jobs are placed on the SCMC website where you can view them anytime and anywhere.

C. The most popular part of the club that students like the most are the abundant events that are scheduled.

6.9 Avoid Empty Phrases (LO6.1)

Remove empty phrases and shorten these sentences.

A. It goes without saying that many of you want financial aid.

B. It can't be stated enough how much these extra skills can enhance your qualifications to be a supply chain manager.

6.10 Avoid Wordy Prepositional Phrases (LO6.1)

Rewrite these sentences to reduce wordy prepositional phrases.

A. Skills acquired in these special-interest groups can be placed on your résumé in conjunction with other skills developed in your studies from the SCOM major.

B. One of the great opportunities you have as a member in the club is the opportunity to be in touch with the SCMC alumni group, which gives you a networking chance with people already working in supply chain management.

6.11 Use Action Verbs When Possible (LO6.1)

Rewrite these sentences to include action verbs.

A. The Supply Chain Management Club (SCMC) is extremely practical with many career options.

B. These events create a big impact on your future career by giving you the opportunities to gain exposure to real-world professionals.

6.12 Use Active Voice (LO6.1)

Rewrite these sentences to use active voice instead of passive.

A. Plant tours and speeches by supply chain professionals are constantly being scheduled for SCMC club members to attend.

B. A speech is always given by an important industry professional.

6.13 Use Short and Familiar Words and Phrases (LO6.1)

Replace uncommon words with familiar words and phrases.

A. These jobs are in a plethora of industries.

B. In today's globally interconnected economy, prowess in global supply chain and operations management is the benchmark of the great manufacturers, retailers, and major companies, such as Dell, Walmart, Southwest Airlines, Toyota, and Bank of America.

6.14 Use Parallel Language (LO6.1)

Rewrite these sentences so the language is parallel.

A. SCOM skills and competencies make one a better accountant, better at financial analysis, better as marketing manager, or even better at managing human resources or managing information technology for a company.

B. In the software group, you can learn statistical software programs such as POM for Windows, Excel Solver, ProcessModel, and SPSS as well as learning mapping software such as MapPoint.

6.15 Avoid Buzzwords and Figures of Speech (LO6.1)

Rewrite these sentences to eliminate buzzwords and figures of speech.

A. Also, through SCMC and by also gaining a membership in ISM, certification opportunities will be at your fingertips.

B. The sky's the limit in this club.

C. SCMC has received boatloads of generous donations to offer scholarships for qualifying SCMC students.

6.16 Avoid *It Is* and *There Is/Are* (LO6.1)

Rewrite these sentences to improve clarity.

A. There are many opportunities to learn special skills since there are special-interest groups within the club.

B. There is a special-interest group devoted to learning about various software tools for global supply chain management.

6.17 Setting Up Effective Navigational Design (LO6.2)

A. If you were going to use headings in this document, how would you group sections? What headings would you use?

B. Which parts of the document would you consider converting to bulleted or numbered lists?

C. What other strategies would you consider for making the document easy to navigate?

6.18 Revising the Supply Chain Management Club Flyer (LO6.1, LO6.2)

Revise the entire student club flyer. Create an effective flyer to help promote the Supply Chain Management Club. Make sure the document is as easy to read as possible while retaining all relevant information.

Use the following table with statistics about the cereal industry[7] for Problems 6.19 through 6.30. In some cases, you will need to carefully review the information in the table to get the correct answers.

Comparisons between Kellogg Company and General Mills

	Kellogg Company (K)	General Mills (GM)
Top-Selling Cereal	Special K	Cheerios
Market Share in Cereal Industry	34 percent	31 percent
Number of Employees	30,900	33,000
Headquarters	Battle Creek, Michigan	Minneapolis, Minnesota
CEO Annual Salary	$11.5 million	$11.1 million
Main Products	Ready-to-eat cereals, cookies, toaster pastries, cereal bars, frozen waffles, and meat alternatives	Ready-to-eat cereals, yogurt, ready-to-serve soup, dry dinners, frozen vegetables, dough products, baking mixes, frozen pizza, snacks
Newly Introduced Products	Special K crackers, fruit crisps, and chocolate pretzel bars. New Special K flavors such as cinnamon pecan, fruit and nut clusters, and blueberry	Chocolate Cheerios, Yoplait Delights yogurt parfaits, Wanchai Ferry frozen foods, Betty Crocker gluten-free dessert mixes, new Häagen-Dazs ice cream flavors
North American Revenues	67.7 percent of total revenues	81.6 percent of total revenues
Worldwide Revenues	$12.5 billion	$14.8 billion
Worldwide Advertising Expenses	$1.1 billion	$908 million
Net Sales Percentage to Walmart	44 percent	30 percent
Negative Media Attention	Product recalls due to potential salmonella contamination	Ammonia leaks at its manufacturing facilities
Least Nutritious Children's Cereals (NPI is a nutritional ranking for cereals ranging from 34 [worst] to 72 [best] and issued by the Rudd Center.)	Corn Pops (NPI: 35.8); Froot Loops (NPI: 38.0); Apple Jacks (NPI: 40.0)	Reese's Puffs (34.0); Golden Grahams (36.0); Lucky Charms (36.0); Cinnamon Toast Crunch (36.6); Trix (38.0); Count Chocula (38.0)
Yogurt Sales	N/A	General Mills yogurt brands include Yoplait, Trix, Yoplait Kids, Go-GURT, Fiber One, YoPlus, and Whips! Approximately $1.5 billion in yogurt sales

Other statistics about the breakfast cereal industry:

- Approximately two-thirds of all cereals are sold with a deal (discounts, coupons).
- The total cereal market in the United States is approximately $9 billion.
- Gross profit margins in the breakfast cereal industry average between 40 percent and 45 percent.
- The global cereal market is approximately $28.7 billion.
- The ten cereals most marketed on TV to children are the following (company and percentage of sugar content displayed in parentheses): 1. Cinnamon Toast Crunch (GM; 33 percent); 2. Honey Nut Cheerios (GM; 32 percent); 3. Lucky Charms (GM; 41 percent); 4. Cocoa Puffs (GM; 44 percent); 5. Trix (GM; 38 percent); 6. Frosted Flakes (K; 37 percent); 7. Fruity and Cocoa Pebbles (Post; 37 percent); 8. Reese's Puffs (GM; 41 percent); 9. Corn Pops (K; 41 percent); 10. Froot Loops (K; 41 percent).

6.19 Being Accurate (LO6.1)

Use the preceding table to proofread the following items and correct them as needed.

A. Please address correspondence to the following address: General Mills, PO Box 1493, Minneapolis, MI.

B. The annually salary for General Mills' CEO is higher than that of Kellogg Company's CEO by approximately $400 thousand.

C. With nearly half of their net sales to Walmart, General Mills and Kellogg Company are extremely dependent on a single retailer.

D. General Mills has six children's cereals with NPI rankings below 40, whereas Kellogg's has just three.

F. General Mills spends approximately 8.1 percent of its total revenues on advertising, whereas Kellogg Company spends roughly 8.8 percent of its total revenues on advertising.

F. Kellogg's children's cereals are the least nutritious cereals in the industry.

G. Since only about one in four boxes of cereal is sold without deals of some kind, cereal producers must constantly market new and exciting discounts and coupons.

H. General Mills reached $1.5 million in yogurt sales last year.

I. One of Kellogg Company's worst negative publicity resulted from ammonia leaks at some its manufacturing facilities.

J. The United States cereal market accounts for approximately 35.1 percent of the world market.

6.20 Being Specific (LO6.1)

Use information from the preceding table to revise the following sentences and make them more specific.

A. General Mills markets through television to children far more than other cereal makers.

B. Gross profit margins in the breakfast cereal industry are quite high.

C. Kellogg Company and General Mills have each experienced negative media attention recently.

D. General Mills is more dependent on the North American market than Kellogg Company.

E. While General Mills and Kellogg Company have similar product mixes, they each market several products not offered by the other.

F. Kellogg Company and General Mills are the top two cereal makers.

G. Kellogg Company and General Mills have each introduced new flavors for their products in recent years.

H. General Mills offers the least nutritious children's cereal on the market.

I. Kellogg's cereals include three children's cereals with NPI scores at 40 or below: Corn Pops, Froot Loops, and Apple Jacks.

6.21 Using Short Sentences in Most Cases (LO6.1)

Revise each of the following items to make the sentences shorter and more readable.

A. General Mills is a dominant player in the American yogurt industry with $1.5 billion in sales, and it sells yogurts under a variety of brands, including Yoplait, Trix, Yoplait Kids, Go-GURT, Fiber One, Whips!, and YoPlus.

B. The two cereal giants, Kellogg Company and General Mills, do not remain complacent with their existing products lines but

rather routinely develop and market new products—after all, Kellogg Company has recently introduced new products such as Special K crackers, fruit crisps, and chocolate pretzel bars, and General Mills has recently added new products such as Chocolate Cheerios, Yoplait Delights yogurt parfaits, Wanchai Ferry frozen foods, and Betty Crocker gluten-free dessert mixes.

C. The total cereal market in the United States is $9 billion, which is just a small and decreasing portion—31.4 percent—of the worldwide market, which is seeing robust growth in the BRIC countries of Brazil, Russia, India, and China.

6.22 Avoid Redundancy (LO6.1)

Revise each of the following sentences to eliminate redundancy.

A. Discount coupons for select Kellogg's cereals contain rebates of between 10 and 20 percent that can save you money.

B. Kellogg Company definitely needs to view crisis communications for the salmonella outbreak as absolutely necessary.

C. Please make advance reservations for the bloggers conference hosted at General Mills to see how you can connect and cooperate together with other corporate bloggers.

6.23 Avoid Empty Phrases (LO6.1)

Revise each of the following items to eliminate empty phrases.

A. Needless to say, General Mills is by all accounts among the worst offenders of marketing less healthy cereals to children.

B. In my personal opinion, Kellogg's children's cereals are in a very real sense superior to General Mills in terms of nutritional value.

C. The point I am trying to make is that parents, for all intents and purposes, are usually unaware of how unhealthy most children's cereals are.

6.24 Avoid Wordy Prepositional Phrases (LO6.1)

Revise each of the following items to eliminate wordy prepositional phrases.

A. In view of the recent rankings about nutritional values for cereals, I think we should focus for the next product development cycle on a reduction in sugar content and an increase in fiber content.

N. For companies in the food industry, a heavy proportion of sales to Walmart provides advantages in terms of higher revenues and a boost in name recognition but disadvantages in terms of lower margins on sales and reduction in customer perceptions of quality.

C. In light of the product recalls in recent times, Kellogg Company is in no position to tout a reputation for food safety.

6.25 Use Action Verbs When Possible (LO6.1)

Improve each of the following sentences by using action verbs.

A. Kellogg Company has new product developments and marketing efforts as part of its rebranding strategy that demonstrates a healthy-food focus.

B. General Mills is a company with strong yogurt brand, and it is in a position of leverage in this regard to achieve higher visibility for healthy foods.

C. The CEO of Kellogg will provide an announcement about new corporate strategy, give his explanation for how the company will reach its goals, and do a presentation about the current financial situation.

6.26 Use Active Voice (LO6.1)

Revise each of the following sentences to switch them from passive to active voice.

A. The NPI rankings were widely publicized in media outlets and were a cause for concern among many cereal executives.

B. The new Special K flavors—cinnamon pecan, fruit and nut clusters, and blueberry—were introduced last year, and Kellogg reports that they have been a huge success.

C. Market strategies to promote healthier cereals were the focus of discussions among industry insiders.

D. Your inaction in confronting the potential salmonella contamination lost us millions of dollars in revenues.

E. Quick crisis communications were the key to General Mills quickly eliminating negative press about the ammonia leaks.

6.27 Use Short and Familiar Words and Phrases (LO6.1)

Revise the following sentences to eliminate unnecessarily long and/or unfamiliar words and phrases.

A. General Mills has abated the public's denouncements of its high-sugar children's cereals by curtailing sugar content by 8 percent on average.

B. The preeminent cereal brands for the dominant duo of cereal makers, Kellogg Company and General Mills, are Special K and Cheerios, respectively.

C. By incentivizing discount programs with multi-purchase point allocations and associated rewards, cereal makers could develop enhanced affinity to brands.

6.28 Use Parallel Language (LO6.1)

Revise the following sentences for parallelism.

A. Kellogg Company and General Mills produce ready-to-eat cereals and also are selling cereal bars.

B. At the bloggers conference hosted by General Mills, the sessions will include the following: (a) reaching a business audience, (b) best practices in tagging, and (c) how to partner with companies.

C. Special K is Kellogg's leading cereal and is continuing to match sales targets.

D. Wanchai Ferry frozen foods are named after the famous tourist spot in Hong Kong, which is known for excitement, attracting boisterous crowds, and creates an exotic atmosphere.

E. Make sure to sign up for RSS feeds from the General Mills Investor Relations page to stay updated with stock prices and for gaining the latest news about the company.

6.29 Avoid Buzzwords and Figures of Speech (LO6.1)

Revise the following sentences to eliminate buzzwords and clichéd figures of speech.

A. The latest hot news for the industry is that Kellogg's and General Mills will develop synergistic working relationships with international partners to get a piece of the pie in the BRIC countries.

B. General Mills's latest strategy is nothing more than a swing for the fence.

C. Just as an FYI, I want everyone to come ready to our next meeting to think outside of the box.

6.30 Avoid *It Is/There Are* (LO6.1)

Revise the following sentences to eliminate the phrases *it is* and *there are*.

A. It is gratifying that General Mills has reduced sugar content in its children's cereals so that there are fewer children who face obesity.

B. There are several new product lines for Kellogg Company that it hopes will show that there is still plenty of innovation and creativity at the company.

C. It is critical for Kellogg Company to tell the public that there is a risk of salmonella contamination in some of its products and that there will be full rebates for products purchased with peanuts as ingredients.

Case for Problems 6.31 and 6.32: Creating a Database of Prospects

Kip recently hired Tia for a marketing internship. Kip arranged to meet her next Tuesday and explain the major project that she would complete during her internship. The project involves creating a database of meeting planners (people who organize large conventions and off-site meetings). Unfortunately, Kip had to leave on a sudden business trip and would miss the meeting. He wanted to make sure Tia could start working on the project right away. So, he emailed her from the airport to give her the information she needed. His email message, however, was rushed and somewhat confusing.

SUBJECT: Work Schedule

Hi Tia, I was just asked to make a quick business trip to a trade show that will have me gone from the office for the next four days during next week. We had scheduled to meet on Tuesday, at which time I was going to walk you through the process of developing a full, complete, and comprehensive database of meeting planners at state and federal agencies nearby. Since I will be unable to attend our meeting and give you direction, I thought I would give you some ideas so you can get started. I'm currently waiting for a flight at the airport, so I apologize for any typos.

As you know, one of your responsibilities this summer will be to help us develop a database of prospects. What we are looking for, in particular, are meeting planners at state and federal agencies located within 500 miles. We feel that this could be an opportunity if we choose to start developing our capacity to hold green meetings and to include green meetings as part of our core strategic initiatives moving forward. One reason for this is that we think government agencies are more likely to seek out green meetings, and another reason is that, in our past experience, government agencies that hold meetings here are more likely to give us repeat business, thus allowing us to gain more reliable and loyal business.

In order to allow us to act swiftly if we start to market green meetings to government agencies, we want you to create a database that includes information of designated meeting planners in these state and federal agencies located within 500 miles of us that will allow us to send out periodic marketing messages via email, mail, and phone. On top of this contact information, we would like to gather information such as how often they hold meetings, for how many people, etc.

We also want to find out the extent to which they have prioritized green (or eco-friendly) meetings in the past. Some of the information is already assembled and organized in our current database that contains all federal and state agencies (this file is located on the intranet). For some of these state and federal governmental agencies, we have some information in the database already that states who the meeting planners are and whether we've met with them in the past; however, this information is mostly incomplete (probably less than 5 to 10 percent complete). We want you to contact all of the agencies to find out as much information as you can. For each meeting planner you talk to, you should ask them what their key criteria are in making their venue selection. Also, please include a field with a rating for how promising the lead is that contains your estimation (or whoever is updating the database) of how likely you think this particular client could be.

As far as the process for making contact with meeting planners, we've generally found that it's best to phone first so that you get in direct contact with a meeting planner and get more accurate and reliable information. You should make a call to find out which person is in charge of meetings. Once you get the contact information for this person (or office), try calling them directly. If your call is not returned within three business days, then make one more direct call. If they do not return the call, then use email to try to arrange information. Of course, it goes without saying, make sure that you are polite as possible so that these meeting planners will want to do business with us in the future.

In the event that you have questions, please give me a call on my mobile phone.

Thanks, Tia, for working on this. Kip

Sent from iPad. Please excuse brevity and typos.

6.31 Identify and Rewrite Nonconcise Sentences (LO6.1)

For each of the following issues, identify three sentences from the email message that are problematic and rewrite to make them more concise: (a) unnecessarily long sentences, (b) redundancy, (c) empty phrases, and (d) wordy prepositional phrases.

6.32 Rewrite the Email Message (LO6.1)

Ensure that the message is more concise. In addition to making sentence-level changes, also ensure that paragraph length is appropriate and eliminate unneeded information. As you rewrite the message, focus on making the message as clear as possible.

Language Mechanics Check

6.36 Review the dashes and hyphens rules in Appendix A. Then, rewrite each sentence to add dashes and hyphens where needed.

A. My supervisor is well known for her expertise in predictive analytics.

B. Training that is the key to keeping skills up to date.

C. One well known approach to maintaining up to date skills is to enroll in two analytics courses per year.

D. Her consulting role with demanding clients is high stress.

E. She has had a high stress consulting role for a long time.

F. She applies a statistics based approach to developing solutions.

G. Her long time philosophy has been to break even on new initiatives.

H. Let's take an easy does it approach to implementing this changes.

I. Her calm and collected temperament helps her in high pressure situations.

J. I would definitely describe her as solutions oriented.

Endnotes

1. Toogood, G. N. (1996). *The articulate executive: Learn to look, act, and sound like a leader.* New York: McGraw-Hill.

2. The National Commission on Writing for America's Families, Schools, and Colleges. (2004). *Writing: A ticket to work—or a ticket out: A survey of business leaders.* New York: CollegeBoard.

3. Clarence Otis Jr. as cited in Bryant, A. (2009, June 6). Ensemble acting, in business. *Corner Office* (blog), *The New York Times*, www.nytimes.com/2009/06/07/business/07corner.html.

4. Figure adapted from Wylie, A. (2009, January 14). How to make your copy more readable: Make sentences shorter. *Comprehension.* Retrieved from http://comprehension.prsa.org/?p=217.

5. Accountemps. What's the buzz? Survey reveals most overused workplace terms. Retrieved March 3, 2012, from http://accountemps. rhi.mediaroom.com/Buzzwords.

6. Bierck, R. (2001). Find the right tone for your business writing. *Harvard Management Communication Letter, 4*(9), 10-11.

7. Cereal nutrition facts are based on 2009 figures from the Rudd Center: www.cerealfacts.org/media/Marketing_Rankings/Brand_Nutrition.pdf.

Design elements: Set of universal icons for mobile app & web: ©Vitalex/Shutterstock; Learning Objective, Why Does This Matter?, Technology Tips, and Ideas in Action icons: ©McGraw-Hill

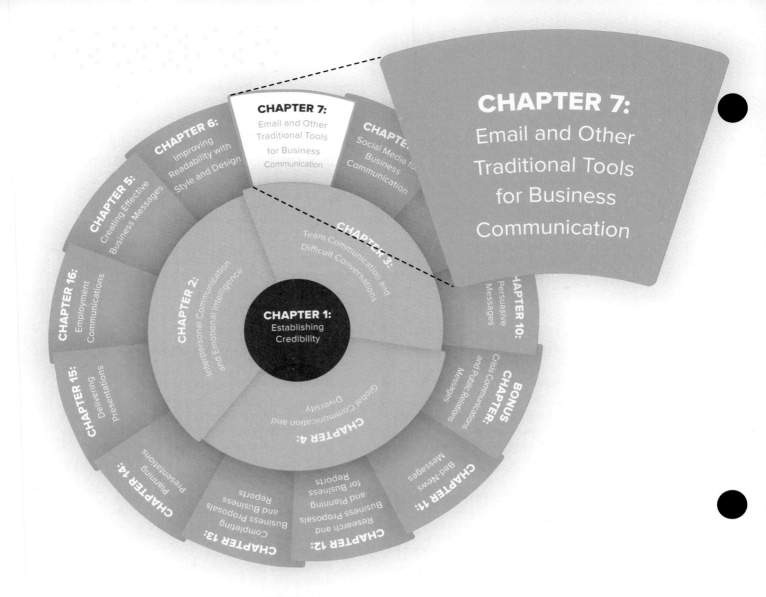

CHAPTER 7:
Email and Other Traditional Tools for Business Communication

ESTABLISHING CREDIBILITY

PRINCIPLES OF INTERPERSONAL COMMUNICATION

PRINCIPLES FOR & TYPES OF BUSINESS MESSAGES

LEARNING OBJECTIVES

After studying this chapter, you should be able to do the following:

LO7.1 Explain the trade-offs associated with richness, control, and constraints when choosing a communication channel.

LO7.2 Apply principles for writing effective emails.

LO7.3 Explain how to handle emotion effectively in online communications.

LO7.4 Describe strategies for effective instant messaging in the workplace.

LO7.5 Describe strategies for managing digital message overload.

LO7.6 Explain principles for effective phone conversations and videoconferences.

For nearly 25 years, email has been the primary written business communication tool. Even with so many emerging communication tools, *email remains the channel of choice for most professionals.*

Writing emails will likely consume much of your time early in your career. One study showed that professionals spend about 4.1 hours per day on email-related tasks.[1] The average business professional receives 76 emails per day and sends 33 emails per day.[2]

In this chapter, we first focus on principles for adopting the right communication channel. Then, we focus on the most common form of written business communication: emails. We also discuss other important communication channels such as texts, phone calls, and group voice and video calls.

> **Hear Pete Cardon explain why this matters.**
>
> **bit.ly/cardon7**

CHAPTER CASE — COMMUNICATING WITH EMAILS, TEXTS, AND CALLS AT BETTER HORIZONS CREDIT UNION

WHO'S INVOLVED

Haniz Zogby

Marketing Specialist

Jaclyn Peha

Technology Intern

Haniz Uses Emails with Clients to Establish Terms

Haniz is helping Better Horizons Credit Union run an annual financial literacy fair. One of her responsibilities is to develop sponsorship agreements with local businesses. One of her clients, Diane Sanchez, called Haniz this morning and discussed making some changes to the sponsorship agreement. Diane negotiated a 10 percent reduction in the sponsorship fee. She also wanted clarification about issues such as logo displays and booth size. Haniz wants to immediately update the agreement and send an email to Diane with a summary of changes.

SITUATION 1

Haniz and Jaclyn Handle a Delicate Situation by Email

Haniz and Jaclyn recently met about making changes to the website. Haniz thought the conversation went well and they reached some agreements about how to proceed. Jaclyn, on the other hand, thought she wasn't given a fair chance to express some of her ideas. She wrote a late-night email to Haniz with her complaints. Now Haniz wants to resolve an uncomfortable situation with Jaclyn and also make progress on improving the website.

SITUATION 2

(Haniz Zogby character): Ingram Publishing; (Jaclyn Peha character): Onoky/SuperStock

Jaclyn Works with Colleagues and Customers via Texting and Calls
Jaclyn is supporting several colleagues and clients with tech support. She uses texts and calls to help coordinate and arrange meetings.

TASK

1
How can Haniz use email effectively with clients?

2
How can Haniz handle an emotionally charged email?

3
How can Jaclyn use texts and calls to collaborate with her colleagues?

Strategically Selecting Channels for Communication

LO7.1 Explain the trade-offs associated with richness, control, and constraints when choosing a communication channel.

Mc Graw Hill connect

Visit http://connect. mheducation.com for an exercise on this topic.

You have so many useful communication tools and technologies for getting in touch with your colleagues, your customers, and other contacts. Having so many options, however, also presents dilemmas about selecting an appropriate **communication channel**—the medium through which a message is transmitted. Examples of communication channels include emails, phone conversations, and face-to-face dialogue. Each communication channel has strengths and drawbacks, the topic we explore in this section.

Strategically selecting a communication channel means that you choose the one that is best able to meet your work objectives. Sometimes a quick phone call or text message is the most efficient way to figure out a meeting time. Other times you will need a face-to-face meeting to clarify misunderstandings about projects. In many of your working relationships, you'll use many communication channels—email, social media, calls, face-to-face conversations—on a daily or weekly basis. Strategically choosing a communication channel involves three basic considerations related to their limitations: richness, control, and constraints.

Richness involves two considerations: the level of immediacy and the number of cues available. **Immediacy** relates to how quickly someone is able to respond and give feedback. In high-immediacy communication, people have immediate access to a variety of **cues**, including social cues (turn-taking), verbal cues (tone of voice), and nonverbal cues (gestures, facial expressions). Generally, face-to-face communication is considered the richest, since each person involved can get immediate verbal and nonverbal feedback. Richer communication typically leads to more trust-building, rapport, and commitment. It is generally the most efficient way to accomplish communication objectives quickly and is less likely to lead to misunderstandings.[3]

Control refers to the degree to which communications can be planned and recorded, thus allowing strategic message development. **Planning** implies that the communication can be tightly drafted, edited and revised, rehearsed, and otherwise strategically developed before delivery. **Permanence** refers to the extent to which the message can be stored, retrieved, and distributed to others. Control may be your primary concern for many important communications.

Constraints refer to the practical limitations of coordination and resources. **Coordination** deals with the effort and timing needed to allow all relevant people to participate in a communication. **Resources** include the financial, space, time, and other investments necessary to employ particular channels of communication. A meeting of ten corporate employees who fly in from different cities is a high-constraint communication that requires extensive coordination and resources.

At the most basic level, communication channels can be divided between the spoken and the written. Spoken messages in the workplace are generally high in richness but low in control. In other words, when people speak to one another face-to-face, they get immediate verbal and nonverbal feedback and respond accordingly. This leads to rapid understanding and bonding. However, they cannot prepare a set message (low planning) or keep a permanent record that can be reviewed and distributed to others (low permanence).

In terms of constraints, spoken communication can range from low to high depending on a number of factors. For example, speaking to a colleague in the next office might require little scheduling (coordination) and few additional monetary and time resources. However, if colleagues are dispersed in various offices separated by time zones, scheduling could be challenging, and the company and the employees might invest a great deal of money and time on travel and related expenses to facilitate rich face-to-face conversation.

By contrast, written messages in the workplace are generally low in richness since they typically do not allow immediate feedback and lack a variety of social, verbal, and nonverbal cues. Yet, they present a number of benefits. Individuals can carefully craft messages at their own pace and on their schedule (high in planning and low in coordination). Moreover, many business professionals consider writing to be conducive to deep thinking on business matters. Furthermore, writing creates a permanent record. Because written records are text-based, it is far easier to search and retrieve relevant information. Generally, the constraints (resources and coordination) of writing are quite low.

Broadly speaking, the benefits of spoken versus written messages reflect an important point: Choosing between communication channels is generally a matter of trade-offs. There is no such thing as a perfect communication channel. Written business communication complements the weaknesses of spoken business communication and vice versa.

The distinctions between spoken and written business messages mirror the relative benefits and weaknesses of synchronous and asynchronous communications. **Synchronous communication** occurs in real time; the individuals involved give immediate responses to one another and engage in turn-taking. **Asynchronous communication** does not occur in real time. Individuals involved in such communication can pay attention to and respond to communications at a time of their choosing. Most successful working relationships depend on both synchronous and asynchronous communication. Scholars Arvind Malhotra, Ann Majchrzak, and Benson Rosen have studied hundreds of virtual teams over nearly a decade and concluded the following about successful communication between teams:[4]

> Most successful virtual team leaders establish a synchronous as well as an asynchronous collaboration rhythm. . . . Successful virtual teams use the time between meetings to asynchronously (through use of electronic discussion threads and annotation of documents in the repository) generate and evaluate ideas. By working asynchronously virtual team members can pick and choose when they can make their contributions. This allows team members with diverse backgrounds to have a different rhythm and pace of generating their own ideas and digesting others' ideas. Leaders also use asynchronous discussion threads to identify areas of disagreements because the discussion threads give members with different language capabilities time to share their thoughts in their non-native languages in ways that they find difficult in synchronous (fast-paced audio-conference) sessions.[5]

Table 7.1 summarizes the features of several communication channels in terms of richness, control, and constraints. Of course, the evolving nature of communication technologies impacts the richness, control, and constraints. For example, many messaging platforms now allow video chat, which make them richer than in the past.

TABLE 7.1

Richness, Control, and Constraints of Various Communication Channels

Red indicates a major limitation. Green indicates a major strength.

Communication Channel	Richness Immediacy + Cues	Control Planning + Permanence	Constraints Coordination + Resources	When to Use
Written messages	✗ Low	✔ High	✔ Low	Ideal for asynchronous communication, matters that require documentation, and messages that need to be crafted with a lot of thought and precision.
Spoken communication	✔ High	✗ Low	✔ Low to ✗ High	Ideal for matters that require rapport-building, discussion, brainstorming, clarification, and immediate feedback. Preferred for sensitive and emotion-packed situations.
Asynchronous Communication Channels				
Email	✗ Low	✔ High	✔ Low	For one-to-one or one-to-many business messages. Email is the dominant communication tool for private, written business messages.
Messaging (including texting)*	✗ Low to ✔ High	Medium	✔ Low	For short, one-to-one, one-to-many, and many-to-many messages. Ideal for quick announcements and scheduling. Not well suited for important or complex business messages.
Social media	✗ Low to ✔ High	Medium to ✔ High	✔ Low to Medium	For team and networked communication. Facilitates a one-stop work space containing project and meeting information, shared files, and communication platforms (see Chapter 8).
Synchronous or Real-Time Communication Channels				
Phone conversations	Medium to ✔ High	✗ Low to Medium	✔ Low to Medium	For one-to-one conversations between parties in different locations. A fairly rich communication channel to quickly discuss and clarify workplace issues.
Conference calls	Medium to ✔ High	✗ Low to Medium	Medium to ✗ High	For team conversations. Typically less rich than one-to-one phone conversations because many participants do not provide cues continuously during the conversation.
Web conferences/ webinars	Medium to ✔ High	Medium to ✔ High	Medium to ✗ High	For team meetings/sales presentations. A richer form of interacting than conference calls but typically requires more coordination due to technology requirements.
Videoconferences	✔ High	✗ Low to Medium	Medium to ✗ High	For team meetings. A richer form of interacting than conference calls but typically requires more expensive equipment and careful scheduling and planning.

Note: Table is modified and adapted from Pearn Kandola's *The Psychology of Effective Business Communications in Geographically Dispersed Teams.*

*As a communication channel, messaging (including texting) isn't simple to classify. You can see in this table that messaging may be considered asynchronous. In the workplace, many professionals are not able to respond immediately because they are in meetings or events that make it difficult to respond immediately. Yet, in many situations, professionals use messaging in a synchronous manner. See the section later in the chapter about instant messaging.

As ambiguity and sensitivity in your communications increase, you will generally seek richer forms of communication, such as face-to-face conversations, meetings, phone calls, and online conferences. For less ambiguous, highly detailed, and highly analytical messages, you will likely turn to higher-control channels. Thus, communicating with letters, emails, blogs, podcasts, and other asynchronous communication channels may be particularly helpful.

Many work factors affect the communication channels you choose. In some cases, companies develop protocols for communicating. The stage of a project may be important, for instance. Generally, projects begin with face-to-face meetings because rich communication is particularly important to develop trust, establish work roles, and brainstorm in the early stages of a project. Later in the project, more control and fewer constraints may allow business professionals to work on their own schedules with less face-to-face meeting time. As a result, more of the communication may become mediated by communication technologies (i.e., email, messaging, discussion forums, phone calls, online conferences).

Furthermore, some types of communication are considered more formal and appropriate for certain types of business activities. Typically, written communication is considered more formal. Proposals, agreements, contracts, and similar documents are written because that implies that the content is in certain and unambiguous terms. In the remainder of this chapter, we'll explore a variety of essential business communication tools, including emails, instant messaging, phone calls, and group voice and video calls.

Creating Effective Emails

Email communication is the primary form of written business communication. Most business professionals spend between 20 and 50 percent of their time reading and writing email (see Figure 7.1).[6] Most analysts expect email to be the primary tool for at least the next five years in most companies. Many forward-thinking companies also encourage employees to use internal digital platforms for communication (discussed in Chapter 8); however, even in companies that adopt these platforms, employees will continue to use private electronic messages within these platforms, which function nearly identically to emails. Furthermore, many of your colleagues, clients, and other contacts will likely prefer to use email systems for many years to come.

Writing effective emails involves applying the principles of writing style that we discussed in Chapters 5 and 6. It also involves adapting to the unique characteristics of email. In this section, we explain basic principles for using emails effectively, including the basic components that ensure ease of reading. Then, we focus on managing emotion and maintaining civility in electronic communications.

Use Email for the Right Purposes

Email is easy and convenient. Before quickly sending out an email, however, consider whether it is the best communication channel for your work purposes.

Because emails are not rich—meaning lacking in virtually all verbal and nonverbal cues associated with face-to-face communication and lacking immediate feedback—they are best suited for routine, task-oriented, fact-based, and nonsensitive messages. Emails may be used to praise others but should rarely be used to criticize others.[7]

Email communication has few constraints (low cost, little coordination) and high control (the writer can think them out carefully, and they provide a permanent record). Yet because it is not a rich form of communication, it is rarely appropriate for sensitive or emotional communication tasks. It is also less efficient than real-time conversations for making joint decisions.

LO7.2 Apply principles for writing effective emails.

Visit http://connect. mheducation.com for an exercise on this topic.

Principles of Effective Emails

- Use for the right purposes.
- Ensure ease of reading.
- Show respect for time.
- Protect privacy and confidentiality.
- Respond promptly.
- Maintain professionalism and appropriate formality.
- Manage emotion effectively.
- Avoid distractions.

FIGURE 7.1

Time Devoted to Email by Business Professionals

Source: Based on survey of 1,004 marketing, R&D, and IT managers in the following industries: Finance, Banking, and Insurance; Health Care and Social Assistance; Manufacturing; and Retail and Wholesale Trade. Findings of this survey first presented at the following academic conference: Cardon, P. W. (2016, April 23). *The role of leadership communication and emotional capital in driving internal social media use.* Presentation at the Association for Business Communication Southeast/Midwest Regional Conference. St. Louis, MO.

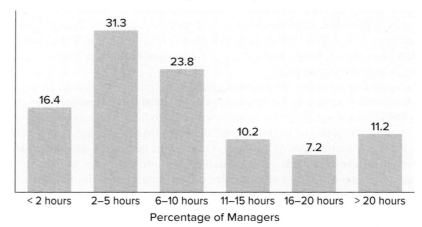

Time Spent Reading and Writing Email per Week

- < 2 hours: 16.4
- 2–5 hours: 31.3
- 6–10 hours: 23.8
- 11–15 hours: 10.2
- 16–20 hours: 7.2
- > 20 hours: 11.2

Percentage of Managers

Ensure Ease of Reading

In all written communication, ensuring ease of reading is critical. It is even more critical in emails and other digital messages. Simply put, your readers are unlikely to read your message unless you make it easy for them. Compare the ease of reading in the less effective and more effective examples of emails in Figures 7.2 and 7.3. Think about how quickly a reader can process the information. Also, use the following tips to ensure ease of reading in your emails.

FIGURE 7.2

Less Effective Email

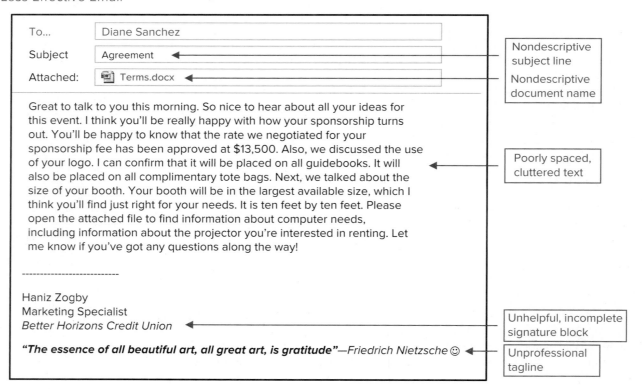

To... Diane Sanchez

Subject: Agreement ← Nondescriptive subject line

Attached: Terms.docx ← Nondescriptive document name

Great to talk to you this morning. So nice to hear about all your ideas for this event. I think you'll be really happy with how your sponsorship turns out. You'll be happy to know that the rate we negotiated for your sponsorship fee has been approved at $13,500. Also, we discussed the use of your logo. I can confirm that it will be placed on all guidebooks. It will also be placed on all complimentary tote bags. Next, we talked about the size of your booth. Your booth will be in the largest available size, which I think you'll find just right for your needs. It is ten feet by ten feet. Please open the attached file to find information about computer needs, including information about the projector you're interested in renting. Let me know if you've got any questions along the way! ← Poorly spaced, cluttered text

----

Haniz Zogby
Marketing Specialist
Better Horizons Credit Union ← Unhelpful, incomplete signature block

"The essence of all beautiful art, all great art, is gratitude"—*Friedrich Nietzsche* ☺ ← Unprofessional tagline

FIGURE 7.3

More Effective Email

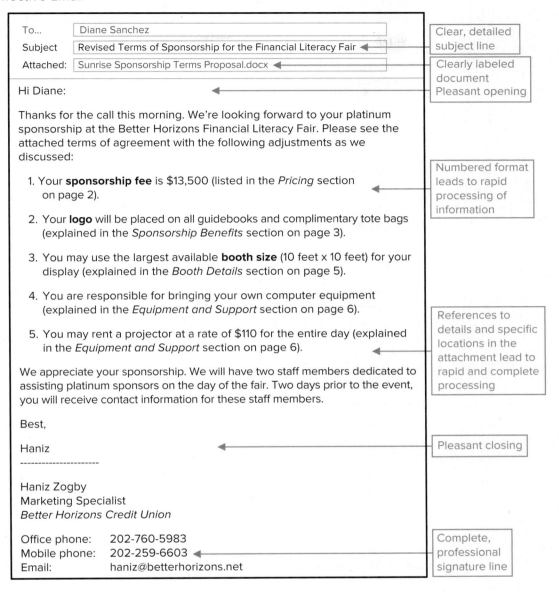

Provide a Short, Descriptive Subject Line Message recipients make immediate judgments about the importance of a message based on the subject line. If it is not clear and compelling, recipients may not open the message right away. Furthermore, when business professionals search for prior email messages, they often scan the subject lines in their in-boxes. Without a descriptive subject line, they may miss the message. Good subject lines are generally 5 to 10 words long. By contrast, poor subjects are either too short (1 or 2 words) and thus nondescriptive or too long (12 words or longer) and thus difficult to process. Fundamentally, subject lines frame your entire message; they serve the same role that headlines do in newspapers and magazines.

Components of Effective Emails

- Subject line
- Greeting*
- Message
- Closing*
- Signature block*
- Attachments*

*optional

Keep Your Message Brief Yet Complete   Get to the point within three or four sentences, and keep your paragraphs about half the size of those in business documents—ideally 30 to 50 words long. Consider placing the most critical information at the beginning so readers gather the most relevant information immediately. This is an important strategy because most people are so inundated with messages that they often pay more attention to the beginning, skimming or skipping latter portions. This is especially important as business professionals increasingly use mobile devices.

Clearly Identify Expected Actions   Most emails are intended to spur action. Effective emails contain specific and clear requests so that recipients know exactly how to respond. In many cases, you can place these directions in the subject line for greatest clarity.

Provide a Descriptive Signature Block   Signature blocks should provide clear contact information. This allows recipients to easily contact you through richer communication channels if needed. It also enhances your professional image.

Use Attachments Wisely   Attachments allow business professionals to share files that do not display effectively in an email window. Messages that are more than several paragraphs long are typically appropriate as attachments. Also, pictures and other graphics, spreadsheets, databases, and many other types of files are nearly always more appropriate as attachments. However, be careful about sending attachments that are too large, since they may fill others' email boxes. Also, consider whether these documents are more appropriate as shared files on a company intranet or another location (such as Google Drive or Dropbox).

Show Respect for Others' Time

Because email communication is so convenient, some people overuse and even abuse it. With business professionals sending and receiving hundreds of emails each week, they often experience information overload and email fatigue. Every time you write an email, you might want to envision your colleagues and clients who are receiving them. Imagine their time pressures and the line of emails awaiting their response. Assume they will likely have low tolerance for poorly written, sloppy, unclear emails.

In the business world, where time pressures can be overwhelming, you can engender goodwill by writing emails that are professional, relevant, easy to read, and other-oriented. To show your respect for others when sending email, consider the following advice.

Select Message Recipients Carefully   Before sending an email, think about the workload you are creating for your colleagues or other message recipients. Not only do they commit time to reading your email, but they also often interrupt another work task to do so. If you are requesting information or action, your colleagues are further committed in terms of time. So, make sure the email is necessary and relevant for each of your message recipients.

Provide Timelines and Options   If you use email to coordinate tasks with deadlines, provide detailed information about time frames and your availability. If you are setting up appointments, make sure you have provided several options. By clearly providing timelines and schedules, you minimize the number of emails needed to coordinate your efforts, thus saving time. By providing options, you show respect for your colleagues' schedules.

Be Careful about Using the Priority Flag   You will routinely make requests of others that are time-sensitive. If you too often set the priority flag on such emails, your colleagues may become annoyed, perceiving you as pushy. In fact, some business professionals are more likely to ignore emails when the priority flag is set. If you need something urgently, mention it politely in the subject line or use a rich communication channel such as a phone call to gain buy-in.

Let Others Know When You Will Take Longer Than Anticipated to Respond or Take Action   If you can't respond to a request made in an email, reply immediately and explain how soon you can respond in full. You might use phrases such as "I will respond to your email by next Tuesday," or "I can take care of this by the end of next week." When you make your commitment, make sure to place the task on your calendar so you follow through.

Avoid Contributing to Confusing and Repetitive Email Chains   Email chains are groups of emails that are sent back and forth among a group of people. As the number of messages and people involved in an email chain increases, confusion can build. Consider the following complaint of a business professional:

> One of my biggest pet peeves has to do with forwards. My company will often send out a corporate email to the all-hands list, then a program manager will forward that email to the same all-hands list "in case you didn't get this," then the department head will forward the same email back to the same all-hands list "in case you didn't get this." Often another layer or two of management feels compelled to forward the same email down to their organizational levels for the same reason. I'm not exaggerating when I say that I often have to delete the same email five or six times! Please, if you're in the habit of forwarding announcements for "FYI" reasons, pay attention to which lists you're forwarding to and which people are already on those lists.[8]

Three features contribute to email chains: *forward*, *copy*, and *reply to all*. The forward feature allows you to send any message you receive to others with the click of the mouse. As always, make sure that those you are forwarding the message to *need* to see the email. Also, consider whether the original sender would consider it appropriate for you to forward the email to others; after all, he or she did not place those people on the original email. Similarly, many business professionals consider use of the *blind carbon copy* feature a breach of privacy. Furthermore, the ease of forwarding and copying can create other problems. Once you send an email, you have no control over whether others will forward it, and to whom, which leads to a good standard articulated by Tony DiRomualdo, strategy and IT researcher: "Don't say anything you would not want the entire planet to read at some point."[9]

Many business professionals use the *copy* feature liberally to let everyone in a department or work unit in on the conversation. Of course, one of your goals is transparency, allowing others in your relevant work group to know how decisions are being made. But copying too many people can lead to information overload. Furthermore, copying too many people on an email can dilute responsibility. When five or six people receive an email about accomplishing a specific task, uncertainty may arise about exactly who is supposed to do what. The more people you copy, the less likely you will get a response. Also, some people perceive copying a direct supervisor or boss on emails between peers as a subtle power play.[10]

The *reply to all* feature can contribute to confusing email chains in many of the same ways as the *forward* and *copy* features. In an email conversation of more than four or five people, various message recipients can lose track of the sequence of messages or miss some messages altogether. Reply email chains become especially confusing when some colleagues are using just the *reply* feature whereas others are using the *reply to all* feature. One advantage of team messaging platforms is that they remove some of the inefficiencies and confusion of email chains by placing messages and shared content in a central location rather than in various, separate email boxes.

Protect Privacy and Confidentiality

Be careful about not spreading—purposely or inadvertently—sensitive or confidential information. Because emails are so convenient to send, even the rare mistake in an address line can result in damaging professional consequences. Consider, for example, that eight out of ten marketing and advertising executives say they have made mistakes via email, such as sending job offers to the wrong people or revealing confidential salary information to the entire company.[11] Double-checking that you have placed the correct people in the address line before you hit the send button is a worthwhile habit that requires just a few extra moments.

Respond Promptly

Most business professionals expect fast responses to emails. Of course, what seems like a quick response to one person seems like a delayed response to another. One recent study of business professionals found that most business professionals expect an email response within one to four hours.[12] Younger professionals are more likely to expect a response immediately. If you choose not to check your email more than four to five times a day (a strategy recommended later in the chapter), let others know how soon to expect replies.

Maintain Professionalism and Appropriate Formality

Email communication is typically considered fairly formal. Many business professionals are particularly sensitive to "sloppy" email. Unfortunately, because so many more people can potentially see an email than would ever see a hard copy of a message, having high standards is even more important. In the past few years, a preference has emerged for less formal, stuffy writing. Still, you'll want to achieve a balance between formality and the friendliness associated with casual writing. Generally, you are better off erring on the side of too much formality as opposed to too much casualness. Consider the following recommendations.

Avoid Indications That You View Email as Casual Communication Certain casual ways of writing and formatting appear unprofessional—for example, using all lowercase letters or nonstandard spelling (i.e., *hey barbara, how r u*), using excessive formatting (i.e., flashy background colors, unusual fonts), providing extraneous information in the signature line (i.e., favorite quotations), and typing in all caps for full phrases and sentences (IMPLIES ANGER). Humor and sarcasm, too, can be misinterpreted in digital communications, even among close colleagues. Furthermore, even when considered funny, it can draw attention away from your central message.

Casual forms of communication in email can be appropriate for close colleagues with whom you work often. For example, some professionals enjoy emoticons and emoji in emails. These can make emails fun and light. Notice, for example, two nearly identical emails in Figures 7.4 and 7.5. The first email is much too casual because it is sent to a client. The second email is more appropriate since it is written to a close colleague. However, stay aware of how your message recipients will react. Some research has shown people who use smiley emojis in emails are considered less competent.[13]

FIGURE 7.4

Less Effective Email with a Casual Tone to a Client

To	Diane Sanchez
Subject	Happy Birthday to an Amazing Partner

Diane, we appreciate working with you. You're such a pleasure to work with. Hope it's a special day!!! 🌕 🎇 🎁 Haniz

| To | Jaclyn Peha |
| Subject | Happy Birthday! |

Jaclyn, thanks so much for all you do at Better Horizons. Hope you enjoy an amazing birthday! 🎂 🎉 🎁 🐣 Haniz

FIGURE 7.5

More Effective Email with a Casual Tone to a Close Colleague

Apply the Same Standards of Spelling, Punctuation, and Formatting You Would for Other Written Documents   Carefully review your message for typos, spelling, punctuation, or grammatical problems before sending it. For important messages, consider first composing with word processing software. This will help you apply a higher level of seriousness. In addition, you'll be able to use spell-check and grammar-check features that are more reliable than those within email systems. Finally, you can ensure that you do not inadvertently send the message without making sure it is polished and complete.

Use Greetings and Names   Although not technically required, consider using short greetings and the names of your message recipients. As one of Dale Carnegie's most famous pieces of networking advice goes, "A person's name is to that person the sweetest most important sound in any language."[14] This advice applies to most communication situations, including emails. People leave out names in emails for several reasons. Some professionals view the use of greetings and names as excessively formal, resembling letters. Other professionals view emails as the equivalent of memos. In fact, the layout of most emails—with a recipient line, sender line, and subject line—resembles memos. Traditionally, the format for memos calls for omitting a personal greeting and name.

In a study about morale within organizations, a communication researcher was given access to the emails in two organizations. One was a low-morale organization and one was a high-morale organization. She found that the presence or absence of greetings and names at the beginning of emails was a strong indicator of company climate (see Figure 7.6).[15] In the low-morale organization, just 20 percent of the emails contained greetings, and just 36 percent contained names. By contrast, in the high-morale organization, 58 percent contained greetings, and 78 percent contained names. The same trend was shown in closings. In the low-morale organization, just 23 percent of the emails contained a polite closing and a name compared to 73 percent in the high-morale organization.

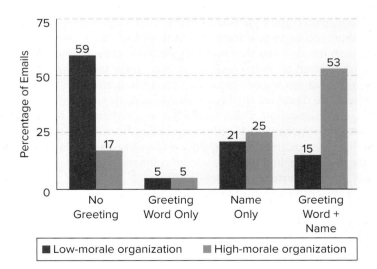

FIGURE 7.6

Use of Email Greetings and Names in a Low-Morale and a High-Morale Organization

Source: Data from Waldvogel, J. (2007). Greetings and closings in workplace email. *Journal of Computer-Mediated Communication, 12*(2), 456–477.

The conventions of using greetings and names are sometimes dropped as an email chain emerges and functions much like a conversation. Typically, professionals with blue and hub MVSs (see Chapter 2) (those with the strongest people-orientation) show a stronger preference for greetings and names. If you're having an ongoing email exchange with a blue or a hub and you notice that he or she is using a formal greeting in each email, consider reciprocating. On the other hand, if you're a blue or a hub and like to see greetings and names in every email but your colleagues are not doing so, avoid getting hung up on it. Assume that they view emails much like memos or that they view excessive use of greetings and names in back-and-forth email chains as repetitive and unnecessary.

Manage Emotion and Maintain Civility

LO7.3 Explain how to handle emotion effectively in online communications.

Visit http://connect. mheducation.com for an exercise on this topic.

Many managers cite the lack of emotion in emails as positive. They see email as a channel that allows the exchange of messages in minimal form—objective, task-based, and straightforward. As one manager explained, "With email I find myself answering without all the kindness necessary to keep people happy with their job."[16]

Yet, avoiding emotion entirely, even for task-based messages, is nearly impossible. Business professionals often want to invoke some emotion—perhaps enthusiasm or a sense of urgency. Even when senders intend to convey a relatively nonemotional message, recipients may experience an emotional reaction.

In the absence of face-to-face communications, emails tend to elicit either the neutrality effect or the negativity effect. The **neutrality effect** means that recipients are more likely to perceive messages with an intended positive emotion as neutral. That is, the sender may wish to express enthusiasm about an event, but the receiver decodes the information without "hearing" the enthusiasm. The **negativity effect** means that recipients are more likely to perceive messages that are intended as neutral as negative. The effects of emotional inaccuracy due to the neutrality and negativity effects can lead to conflict escalation, confusion, and anxiety.[17] Expert business communicators remain aware of these tendencies.

Two characteristics of asynchronous electronic communications can lead to feelings of anger and frustration more so than in face-to-face communications. First, people often feel comfortable writing things they would not say in person.[18] This level of directness is often perceived as rudeness by others.

The second aspect of asynchronous electronic communications that can lead to anger and frustration is **cyber silence**, which is nonresponse to emails and other communications. During the nonresponse stage, message senders often misattribute explanations for the silence. They sometimes wonder if message recipients are purposely avoiding or even ignoring them. As the length of time between messages increases, they often experience more frustration and anger.[19]

As a message sender, grant the benefit of the doubt to your recipients when responses take longer than you expected. Instead of getting frustrated, consider giving them a phone call. Keep in mind that they may have different expectations about a reasonable time frame to respond to your email. If they routinely take longer than you expect, politely mention that you would appreciate quicker responses.

In Chapter 2, we discussed the importance of civility. Civility is likewise important in electronic communication. **Cyber incivility** is the violation of respect and consideration in an online environment based on workplace norms. Research has shown that "fast-paced, high-tech interactions may add to incivility, as people believe that they do not have time to be 'nice' and that impersonal contacts [such as electronic communications] do not require courteous interaction."[20]

Shockingly, recent research shows that 91 percent of employees reported experiencing either active or passive cyber incivility from supervisors in the workplace.[21] **Active incivility** involves direct forms of disrespect (i.e., being condescending, demeaning, saying something hurtful). **Passive incivility** involves indirect forms of disrespect (i.e., using emails for time-sensitive messages, not acknowledging receipt of emails,

Active and Passive Incivility through Emails of Supervisors
(Percentage of Employees Who Stated Their Current Supervisor Had Engaged in Email Incivility)

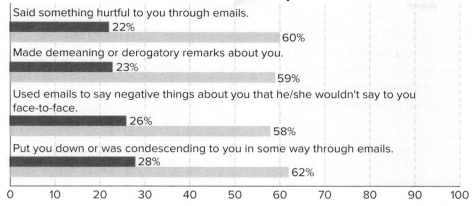

Active Email Incivility

Said something hurtful to you through emails. — 22% / 60%

Made demeaning or derogatory remarks about you. — 23% / 59%

Used emails to say negative things about you that he/she wouldn't say to you face-to-face. — 26% / 58%

Put you down or was condescending to you in some way through emails. — 28% / 62%

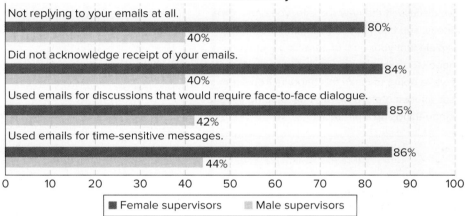

Passive Email Incivility

Not replying to your emails at all. — 80% / 40%

Did not acknowledge receipt of your emails. — 84% / 40%

Used emails for discussions that would require face-to-face dialogue. — 85% / 42%

Used emails for time-sensitive messages. — 86% / 44%

■ Female supervisors   ▨ Male supervisors

FIGURE 7.7

Active and Passive Incivility from Supervisors

Source: Based on information from Lim, V. K., & Teo, T. S. H. (2009). Mind your e-manners: Impact of cyber incivility on employees' work attitude and behavior. *Information & Management, 46,* 419–425.

not replying to emails). Cyber incivility has been shown to lead to lower job satisfaction and organizational commitment. Active incivility was the most damaging. In Figure 7.7, you can see a summary of this research. One interesting finding was that male and female supervisors engaged in different types of incivility. Male supervisors were far more likely to engage in active incivility, whereas female supervisors were far more likely to engage in passive incivility.

Inevitably, you will be the target of what you consider uncivil electronic communications. In nearly all situations, your goal should be to avoid escalation. You can take several steps to constructively address uncivil emails: reinterpretation, relaxation, and defusing. **Reinterpretation** involves adjusting your initial perceptions by making more objective, more fact-based, and less personal judgments and evaluations. When people are distressed, they often make extreme, subjective, and overly personal judgments. By reinterpreting the event, you allow yourself to take the communication less personally. This is easier said than done. Many people engage in relaxation techniques to help constructively reinterpret the event. **Relaxation** involves releasing and overcoming anger and frustration so that you can make a more rational and less emotional response. People use a variety of methods to alleviate the physiological impact of anger, including counting to ten, taking time-outs, engaging in deep breathing, and looking for the humor in the situation.[22]

FIGURE 7.8

Less Effective Response to an Angry Email

To:	Jaclyn Peha
Subject:	Re: Issues

We need to talk about this email when I get back in a week after the holiday. I thought we had a productive conversation but you obviously were not candid or professional. Also, please empty your voice mail. I tried reaching you several times only to get your full voice mail box.

From: Jaclyn Peha [jaclyn@betterhorizons.net]
Sent: Saturday, July 1 9:54 p.m.
To: Haniz Zogby [haniz@betterhorizons.net]

Subject: Issues

Haniz, the other day when we discussed the new website, you didn't give me a chance to explain my ideas, and I don't think you made the conversation fair. I tried to explain that your goal of attracting younger customers is good, but we need to create a more interactive website that's plugged into social media if we're going to make this happen. You seem to just want the easiest, quickest solution. Before we start developing the site any more, let's meet and change things up a bit. Jaclyn

Impersonal. Leaves out greeting and name.

Confrontational. Immediately creates a *me-versus-you* approach with the phrase "We need to talk about this email."

Defensive/attacking. Focuses on defending rather than understanding Jaclyn's point of view.

Accusatory. Jaclyn lays blame on Haniz in every regard. The repeated use of *you-voice* increases the accusatory tone.

In the opening case, Jaclyn expressed frustration with a conversation she had with Haniz. Jaclyn, perhaps unwisely, fired off an angry email (see the bottom message in Figure 7.8), and Haniz responded (the top message in Figure 7.8). Regardless of whether Jaclyn was correct about Haniz's approach to developing the website, email is rarely an effective communication channel to air complaints or to discuss emotionally charged issues. Figure 7.9 presents a more effective response from Haniz to this exchange.

Defusing involves avoiding escalation and removing tension to focus on work objectives. You can take several steps to defuse the situation when you receive an uncivil email. First, focus on task-related facts and issues in your reply. Second, focus on shared objectives and agreements. Third, express interest in arranging a time to meet in person. If this is not possible, attempt a richer channel of communication such as a phone call or an online video meeting. Defusing the situation with an immediate email is only part of the process in restoring or perhaps even strengthening a working relationship. A follow-up meeting is nearly always essential to renew cooperation on shared work efforts.

You often will need to respond to electronic messages that you feel are unfair or inappropriate. Notice how Haniz escalates the problem in the less effective response by writing in an impersonal, defensive, and confrontational manner. By contrast, notice how she defuses the situation in the more effective response by avoiding defensiveness, focusing on shared interests, and arranging for a time to meet face-to-face. Your ability to defuse uncivil electronic communications during your career will pay off in many ways: It will help your colleagues and teams stay on task and perform better; it will help you develop a reputation for constructively

FIGURE 7.9

More Effective Response to Defuse an Angry Email

To:	Jaclyn Peha
Subject:	Meeting to Improve the Website

Hello Jaclyn,

I'm sorry to hear that you did not think our conversation was fair. I'm glad you're thinking about how we can use the website to better attract younger customers.

When we're both back in the office, let's set up a time to discuss plans for the website. Would you be willing to come up with your three major ideas for making the website more interactive and connected to our social media platforms?

When we meet, I'd like to get a sense for the resources we would need to commit to your ideas. We need to make sure more ambitious plans make business sense.

Would you like to include anyone else in our meeting? Do you think the entire marketing team should participate in this discussion?

Enjoy your holiday weekend!

Haniz

Cordial and personal. Uses Jaclyn's name and extends warm wishes.

Validating. Compliments Jaclyn on her desire to improve the website.

Inviting. Asks for Jaclyn's input in terms of ideas and people who should be included in a decision-making process.

Nondefensive. Haniz makes it clear that making "business sense" is an important part of the discussion. Yet, she does so without sounding defensive or intimidating (she is in the position of a superior).

resolving differences; and it will lead to more satisfying work experiences. The ability to defuse such situations requires high emotional intelligence, especially in self-awareness and self-management.

Instant Messaging in the Workplace

Instant messaging (IM) or texting are among the most popular features on mobile phones. American adults IM on their phones more frequently than they access the Internet, send or receive email, or participate in video chats.[23] Instant messaging is ideal for short and simple business messages that contain announcements, questions, confirmations of plans, quick tips, support, and congratulations. Most business professionals consider IM a less formal communication channel than email.

Instant messaging is a relatively new and undeveloped form of communication in the workplace, and attitudes toward it vary significantly. Many professionals consider IM impersonal, uninteresting, rude, intrusive, or inadequate. On the other hand, many professionals associate IM in the workplace with exactly the opposite qualities: warm and personal, nice, less intrusive than calls, fun, inviting, and helpful. As you message with colleagues and other contacts, consider the following tips.

LO7.4 Describe strategies for effective instant messaging in the workplace.

Evaluate the Meta Message of Instant Messaging

In Chapter 5, you read about *meta messages*, the overall but often underlying messages that others decode from your communications. Because professionals hold so many attitudes toward instant messaging, think about how they'd interpret your use of IM. One colleague might decode your instant message as saying, "You're not important enough for a phone call." Another colleague might decode the *same* instant message as saying, "I want to keep you in the loop, so I'm messaging you."

Use IM for Simple and Brief Conversations, Not for Important Decisions

IMs are best used for short, uncomplicated messages and conversations. If there's any level of complexity or ambiguity, you're better off speaking to others directly or sending an email where you have more space for detailed information. Generally, if the exchange requires more than three or four instant messages, you should probably use an email or make a call.

FIGURE 7.10

Instant Messages to Show Support

FIGURE 7.11

Mismatched Messaging Styles

Make Sure Your Tone Is Positive, Supportive, and Appropriately Fun

You should reserve most messaging for straightforward, positive messages. IM can be a particularly effective way to send quick notes of support, congratulations, and appreciation to close colleagues (see Figure 7.10). Messaging is also a chance to use a light and fun tone when you're sure that's a style that message recipients will appreciate. One risk of IM is that with a focus on conciseness, IM messages may come across as commanding, abrupt, or unfeeling. Similarly, an excessively casual tone may diminish the perceived importance of your message. In nearly all cases, avoid using IM for bad or unpleasant news.

Don't Ask Questions You Can Get Answers to Yourself

Many tools such as instant messaging allow professionals to get questions answered quickly by their colleagues. Be careful about overusing this approach to getting information, especially when you can get the information yourself without much effort. When professionals ask questions and offload their own work via instant messages or emails too often, they get reputations as *takers* rather than *givers*.

Be Careful about Abbreviated Language, Emoticons, Acronyms, and Emoji

Abbreviated language, acronyms, emoticons, and emoji are some of the fun features of instant messaging. Until you know the IM style of others in the workplace, you should err on the side of complete sentences and standard language conventions. In Figure 7.11 , you will notice how Jaclyn uses a short message to tell Haniz the location of a business meal. Jaclyn uses complete sentences and standard language conventions, while Haniz uses abbreviated language and acronyms. Haniz should consider adopting more standard language conventions to match Jaclyn's style. On the other hand, Jaclyn should notice that Haniz enjoys using some abbreviated language. Jaclyn might consider using some nonstandard language conventions when instant messaging with Haniz.

Avoid Sarcasm and Jokes in Most Cases

While most people use IM playfully and with humor in their personal lives, trying to use sarcasm and jokes in the workplace is often misunderstood or misinterpreted. Even colleagues who know one another well often misinterpret attempts at humor and sarcasm in instant messages.

Avoid Rescheduling Meeting Times or Places

Instant messaging is often a convenient way of confirming meeting plans, especially those that involve offsite locations. It's also a convenient way of saying you're running a few minutes late. While slightly changing meeting plans via IM is handy in rare cases, avoid doing so unless absolutely necessary. Many professionals have gained reputations as not being reliable because they frequently adjust meeting times and locations at the last minute via IM. In situations where you must change plans, consider placing a call as a show of courtesy and as a way of efficiently and clearly adjusting plans.

Consider Turning Off Sound Alerts for Incoming Messages/Emails

This can be especially distracting when you work in shared workspaces. It's also a matter of productivity (as we'll discuss in the next section).

Identify Yourself

Other than for people you text or IM often, you can't be certain whether you're part of your message recipients' address lists. Simply stating your name ("Hi. This is Jaclyn . . .") will help avoid confusion in many cases.

Clearly End the IM Exchange

Some IM exchanges become awkward as they drag on. Send signals that the exchange is complete ("Thanks for the update. Talk to you tomorrow.").

Avoid Personal IM during Work Hours

Increasingly, professionals bring their home lives into the workplace. This isn't surprising given the convenience of so many communication tools. Most workplaces have some policies about avoiding personal communications (including IM), although these policies are generally loosely enforced. You'll notice that exercising discipline and avoiding personal digital messages will help you gain the respect of your colleagues and establish your professionalism.

Avoid Sending Instant Messages after Work Hours

Many new communication tools lead to professionals blurring the line between personal time and work time. IM, compared to emails and other communication tools, may be considered even more intrusive when sent after hours because of the expectation of immediate responses.

Establish Rules with Your Colleagues for Instant Messaging in Meetings

Instant messaging is increasingly common during meetings in *some* organizations. Texting can be used to prompt team members about topics to cover, give quick updates as needed to team leaders, ask for information from colleagues or clients outside of the meeting, and assist teammates in a variety of ways (see Figure 7.12). Some organizations' cultures encourage this, whereas others strictly discourage it. So, pay attention to the culture of texting at your company. Of course, even where texting is encouraged in meetings, it can also be abused (see Figure 7.13). In any case, discuss with your teammates what you consider appropriate in meetings. Similarly, use the messaging app or platform that is recommended and supported by your organization.

FIGURE 7.12

A Potentially Effective Instant Message in a Meeting

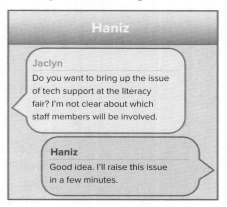

FIGURE 7.13

An Ineffective Instant Message in a Meeting

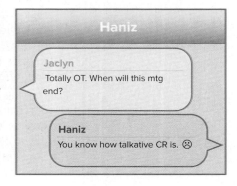

Managing Your Digital Communication Efficiently

LO7.5 Describe strategies for managing digital message overload.

Constantly checking incoming messages—emails, texts, IMs, and other digital messages—or simply hearing message alerts distracts business professionals from concentrating on the tasks at hand. As you are bombarded with incoming messages, your productivity decreases for two reasons: You are distracted from your immediate tasks, and you try to multitask.

Rawpixel.com/Shutterstock

Interruptions from digital messages, or *e-interruptions*, are extremely costly to your performance. One recent study found that the average worker several hours per day due to interruptions. Many of these distractions are email and other incoming messages. On average, professionals check their email or texts every six minutes, which amounts to 80 e-interruptions in an eight-hour day![24] Distractions affect your performance for much longer than the few moments you take to acknowledge and respond to incoming messages. A Microsoft study found that it takes 15 minutes on average to refocus after an interruption. Furthermore, these disruptions have been shown to reduce attention spans, increase stress, and even reduce creativity. The cost to companies is enormous. Intel estimates that large companies lose about $1 billion per year because of email overload.[25]

Many business professionals erroneously assume they can respond immediately to all incoming messages *and* focus sufficiently on work tasks. This is simply not the case. A University of Michigan study found that productivity drops by up to 40 percent when people try to do two or more things at once. A variety of research about the brain shows that it is not hardwired to multitask effectively.[26]

In most business positions, however, you need to respond to others as soon as possible. This places you in a delicate balancing act; how can you stay responsive to others yet focus enough to achieve peak performance in your work tasks? Consider the following guidelines:[27]

- *Check digital messages just four to five times each day at designated times.* Unless your job calls for it (or your boss demands it!), try not to check your messages more than every 45 minutes. Consider taking some interruption-free periods during the day exclusively devoted to email so you can concentrate on communicating with others. For example, you might schedule 30 minutes to an hour at 8 a.m., 11 a.m., 1 p.m., and 4 p.m. each day to communicate via email and other online tools.

- *Wean yourself off checking your mobile devices constantly.* Most professionals get anxious if they don't check their phones every 15 minutes or even more frequently. A variety of anxieties, such as FOMO (fear of missing out) and FOBO (fear of being offline), drastically cut many professionals' productivity. Consciously extending the periods between when you glance or check your devices can dramatically improve your effectiveness.

- *Develop strategies to manage your inbox.* Experiment with various ways of staying current with your email. Common strategies include LIFO (last in, first out), reverse chronological, and inbox zero. *LIFO* is most common and involves top-down reading of your email list. This helps you deal with your most current emails. Some of the older email messages sometimes involve issues that have been worked out already. The risk is you may read and respond to a more current message

ⓘ Technology Tips

SCHEDULING EMAILS

For decades, marketers have scheduled emails to reach consumers at the right time. Similarly, savvy professionals increasingly schedule professional emails to arrive at the most appropriate time.

To respect others' time and create a healthy work environment, you should generally avoid off-hours emails (i.e., weekends, late evenings). Let's say you write an email to you colleague at 11 p.m., well past the end of work. You don't want to disturb your colleague while she's off work, so you set the email to send the next morning at 8 a.m. when she'll be back in the office.

To exert the most influence, you should choose the most favorable times to email important messages. Research shows that professionals are most likely to positively respond to emails early in the week and before noon.[28] Let's say you write several emails on Friday afternoon. You can set the emails to send on Monday morning at 9 a.m. when your colleagues are more likely to open your emails and respond favorably to your requests.

Most email programs require a few extra steps to delay the message. For example, in Gmail you need to download a Chrome extension. In Outlook, you need to go into the Options tab to set the delivery options.

Source: Google INC

Your challenge: In your favorite email program, send several delayed messages to yourself. How easy was it to send delayed messages? What strategies should you use to schedule your email messages more effectively?

without the context needed from prior messages. The *reverse chronological* solves this problem by ensuring you see the original messages first. It also rewards people in the order they sent messages to you. Yet, you may also expend time reading and responding to issues that have already been addressed or solved. *Inbox zero* is a strategy of immediately taking action on every email and keeping your inbox empty by the end of each session. You can use a variety of email tools such as filters and rules to efficiently read and respond to your most important email.

- *Turn off message alerts*. Over the course of a day, these alerts can distract you and reduce your focus.

- *Use rich channels such as face-to-face and phone conversations to accomplish a task completely*. Back-and-forth email chains and other sets of asynchronous digital messages may repeatedly draw attention away from tasks at hand. As appropriate, use rich, synchronous communication to take care of the matter immediately so that distractions do not compound themselves.

- *Reply immediately only to urgent messages*. When you reply immediately to nonurgent messages, you set a precedent. Others form an expectation that you can be interrupted at any time for any matter.

- *Avoid unnecessarily lengthening an email chain*. You can shorten email chains by placing statements such as "no reply necessary" in the subject line. You can also shorten email chains by not sending messages such as "got it" or "thanks." At the same time, make sure you don't abruptly end an email chain when others would appreciate a reply. For example, some business professionals appreciate short notes of gratitude and confirmation.

- *Use automatic messages to help people know when you're unavailable*. Set up automatic messages to let people know when you are out of the office for more than one day.

Building Connections with Phone Conversations

LO7.6 Explain principles for effective phone conversations and videoconferences.

Michaeljung/123RF

Compared to less rich channels such as email, phone calls generally allow business professionals to connect more deeply, resolve problems more quickly, make important decisions better, and manage conflict more effectively.[29] In the past decade, mobile phones have transformed business communication. Most business professionals carry at least one phone at all times for calls, texting, Internet use, scheduling, and much more. In many ways, mobile phones increasingly serve as a communication center for many managers and executives.

Ironically, the increased use of mobile phones in people's personal lives has actually led to a downward trend in calls. In fact, making calls is just the fifth most used function of smartphone users on their phones.[30] However, business professionals continue to use landline and mobile calls extensively (see Figure 7.14).[31] For most business professionals, less calling translates into lost opportunities. Refining the art and skills of phone calls can help you become a more dynamic and savvy communicator. Keep in mind the following guidelines for one-to-one calls in the workplace.

Schedule and Plan for Your Phone Calls

Like other forms of business communication, think ahead about your key discussion topics and points. Many phone conversations are much like meetings, so consider sending an invitation with an agenda to your conversation partner (see Figure 7.15 for an example). For less formal conversations, at least plan your purpose and major points to cover. Out of respect for your conversation partners' time, let them know roughly how long the call will take.

Ensure Quality Audio

Especially for important calls, you should test your audio quality before the call. Although mobile phones provide reliable audio quality in most locations, they're still less predictable than landline connections. You might consider using landline calls whenever possible to enhance audio quality.

FIGURE 7.14

Time Devoted to Calling among Business Professionals

Source: Based on survey of 1,004 marketing, R&D, and IT managers in the following industries: Finance, Banking, and Insurance; Health Care and Social Assistance; Manufacturing; and Retail and Wholesale Trade. Findings of this survey first presented in the following academic conference: Cardon, P. W. (2016, April 23). *The role of leadership communication and emotional capital in driving internal social media use.* Presentation at the Association for Business Communication Southeast/Midwest Regional Conference. St. Louis, MO.

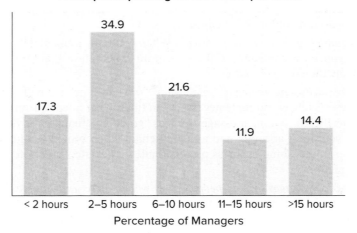

Time Spent Speaking on the Phone per Week

< 2 hours	2–5 hours	6–10 hours	11–15 hours	>15 hours
17.3	34.9	21.6	11.9	14.4

Percentage of Managers

FIGURE 7.15

Sample Meeting
Request and Agenda
for a Phone Call

Open with a Warm Greeting and Use Your Caller's Name

You've read this advice several times in this book, and you'll hear it several more times: Calling others by name personalizes and elevates your communications with them.

After Brief Small Talk, Direct the Conversation to the Issues at Hand

Most callers appreciate a few light comments to start a conversation, but be careful not to let this initial small talk drag on. Most effective business calls get to the issues at hand within one to two minutes.

Speak with a Pleasant, Enthusiastic Voice

Although others cannot see you, your nonverbal behaviors are often reflected in your voice. Consider sitting up straight or standing up, breathing deeply, intonating clearly, gesturing, and even smiling as you would if you were in person. These nonverbal actions will often carry through in a pleasant, professional voice and help you avoid a monotone. From time to time, consider listening to your recorded voice to pick up on ways in which you can speak more professionally and energetically.

Share Conversation Time Equally

Phone calls are a great opportunity to deepen relationships and get work done when each person shares conversation time equally. Make sure you're not dominating a conversation by taking up more than your fair share of speaking time. Similarly, if your conversation partner is taking too much of the time, politely interject now and then to balance the speaking time.

Apply the Rules of Active Listening and Avoid Multitasking

Enter a phone call eager to learn about the ideas of your conversation partner and ready to express your views as well. Amazingly, roughly six in ten professionals admit to multitasking during phone calls.[32] Make sure the call is your entire focus. Also, make sure

FIGURE 7.16

Sample Follow-up
Message with Action
Items

Reply   Reply All   Forward

Follow-up to Our Phone Call about the Website

Peha, Jaclyn

To: Haniz Zogby

Cc: Raj Naykodi

Hello Haniz,

Thanks for the opportunity to talk about ideas for the new website. I've attached a document with detailed notes. I believe we agreed to finish the final proposal for new features on the website by August 5. We agreed to the following roles:

- **Haniz:** marketing strategy, integration of social media into website, budgeting, project timeline
- **Jaclyn and Raj:** analysis of competitors' websites, mock-ups of new features intended to attract new members (with a focus on younger members), analytics options

Let me know if my notes and these roles match your recollections of our conversation.

Best,
Jaclyn

---

you don't sound rushed—this often sends a signal that you're more interested in other people or matters.

Take Notes on Important Points and Summarize Next Steps at the End of the Call

As you're speaking, take some notes so you can recall the most important points of agreement. At the end of the call, take a few minutes to wrap up and summarize next steps.

Close with Appreciation

In nearly all calls, you should find a way to express appreciation to your conversation partner. Simple phrases such as "thanks for taking the time to . . ." or "it has been great to get your ideas about . . ." can end the call on a warm note and pave the way for easier follow-up.

Follow Up on Agreements

Many professionals often don't follow through on commitments they make to each other on calls. This happens most often when neither person documents the content and agreements of their conversation. Consider sending a message within a few hours of your call while the conversation is still fresh in your minds (see Figure 7.16 as an example). This dramatically improves the likelihood that you will accomplish your shared objectives.

Participating in and Leading Group Voice and Video Calls

Increasingly, you'll participate in video conferences, web conferences, and conference calls to meet with groups of colleagues and other professional contacts. Most business professionals spend at least five hours each week on video and web conferences.[33] Sometimes you'll have video and other times you may only have audio. You'll sometimes use high-end videoconferencing platforms and other times use web conferencing tools such as Zoom, Google Hangouts, or Skype. Many of the tips that we discussed for one-to-one calls apply, as do the guidelines for effective virtual meetings discussed in Chapter 3. In addition, consider the following tips.

Practice Using the Technology before the Group Call

There are many options for group voice and video calls. Even if you often participate in or even lead these calls, you may not be up to date with various platforms or new tools. If you're leading the call, send out information about the technology to participants so they can be prepared. When the first five to ten minutes of group calls are consumed by participants trying to figure out the technology, the meetings rarely turn out productive or engaging.

Blend Images/Alamy Stock Photo

Use Your Webcam Effectively

The power of group video calls is the ability to have rich conversations full of nonverbal cues. You lose this advantage unless you carefully position your webcam so you are speaking directly to your listeners. Make sure that you've got good lighting and a clean background. Also, maintain direct eye contact with your webcam as much as possible so that other meeting participants can see your interest level and understand your nonverbal cues.

Use Interactive Tools Wisely

Most videoconference platforms have many options to make meetings interactive, including screen sharing, polling, online chat, and other features. These tools are excellent when used with purpose. Be careful, however, not to use the tools simply for the sake of being interactive.

Start the Call with Purpose and Take Charge

Many professionals make a judgment within the first few minutes about the importance of the call. Unless you get people interested and engaged quickly, many participants will tune out and start multitasking.

Follow the Guidelines of Effective Virtual Meetings

The tried-and-true practices of using an agenda, getting each participant involved, and following up with minutes and action items are essential.

💡 IDEAS IN ACTION

TAKING CONTROL OF YOUR EMAIL

Conversations with Current Business Professionals

Arianna Huffington is among the most successful business women in the world and is most well known for co-founding the *Huffington Post*. In recent years, she has started another company called Thrive Global, which focuses on helping people avoid stress and burnout. Huffington is keenly aware of the impact of media and technology on professional and personal lives. She promotes threes daily rules of email to focus on a higher quality life: (1) no emails for half an hour before bed, (2) no emails immediately after waking up, and (3) no emails while she is with her children.

Jason Smith/Everett Collection/Alamy Stock Photo

Huffington also promotes a no-email rule on vacations. In fact, she uses a tool that deletes incoming email while she's on vacation and notifies the sender to re-send an email when she's back in the office. Regarding how this strategy impacted a recent vacation, she explained, "It felt so different to be able to be fully present—for meals, for conversation, for taking walks, for all the felicitous things that can happen only when we don't have our heads down in a screen. And the recharging I got wasn't immediately burned off by a mountain of email facing me the morning I got back to the office."

Huffington often points to research that shows people who limit digital use during portions of the day and who take vacations from media are more successful in their careers and their relationships. So, make sure to figure out the rules for email and other digital messages that help you strike the right balance between professionalism and personal fulfillment.

Sources: Huffington, A. (2017, August 23). How to keep email from ruining your vacation. *Harvard Business Review.* Retrieved from hbr.org/2017/08/how-to-keep-email-from-ruining-your-vacation; Clarkson, N. (2015, March 13). What habits do Jack Dorsey, Mark Zuckerberg and other successful people have in common? *Virgin Entrepreneur.* Retrieved from www.virgin.com/entrepreneur/what-habits-do-jack-dorsey-mark-zuckerberg-and-other-successful-people-have-in-common.

LO7.1 Explain the trade-offs associated with richness, control, and constraints when choosing a communication channel.

See *summaries of trade-offs* of communication channels in Table 7.1.

LO7.2 Apply principles for writing effective emails.

Principles of Effective Emails		Components of Effective Emails	
• Use for the right purposes. • Ensure ease of reading. • Show respect for time. • Protect privacy confidentiality.	• Respond promptly. • Maintain professionalism and appropriate formality. • Manage emotion effectively. • Avoid distractions.	• Subject line • Greeting* • Message *optional	• Closing* • Signature block* • Attachments*

See *examples of ineffective and effective emails* in Figures 7.2 and 7.3.

LO7.3 Explain how to handle emotion effectively in online communications.

Responding to Uncivil Communications		
• Reinterpret	• Relax	• Defuse

See *examples of ineffective and effective responses to uncivil emails* in Figures 7.8 and 7.9.

LO7.4 Describe strategies for effective instant messaging in the workplace.

Guidelines for Texting in the Workplace	
• Evaluate the meta message of an instant message or text. • Use IMs or texts for simple and brief messages, not for conversations. • Make sure your tone is positive, supportive, and appropriately fun. • Don't ask questions you can get answers to yourself. • Be careful about abbreviated language, emoticons, acronyms, and emoji.	• Avoid sarcasm and jokes in most cases. • Avoid rescheduling meeting times or places. • Consider turning off sound alerts for incoming IMs/emails. • Identify yourself. • Clearly end the instant messaging exchange. • Avoid personal IMs during work hours. • Avoid sending IMs after work hours. • Establish rules with your colleagues for instant messaging in meetings.

See *examples of instant messaging* in Figures 7.10 through 7.13.

LO7.5 Describe strategies for managing digital message overload.

Principles for Managing Emails to Avoid Distractions	
• Check digital messages just two to four times each day at designated times. • Turn off message alerts. • Use rich channels such as face-to-face and phone conversations to accomplish a task completely.	• Reply immediately only to urgent messages. • Avoid unnecessarily lengthening an email chain. • Use automatic messages to help people know when you're unavailable.

LO7.6 Explain principles for effective phone conversations and videoconferences.

Guidelines for Phone Calls and Videoconferences	
• Schedule and plan for your phone calls. • Ensure quality audio. Open with a warm greeting and use your caller's name. After a brief chat, direct the conversation to the issues at hand. • Speak with a pleasant, enthusiastic voice. Share conversation time equally. • Apply the rules of active listening and avoid multitasking.	• Take notes on important points and summarize next steps at the end of the call. • Close with appreciation. • Follow up on agreements. • Practice using the technology before the group call. • Use your webcam effectively. • Use interactive tools wisely. • Start the call with purpose and take charge. • Follow the guidelines of effective virtual meetings (see Chapter 3).

See an *example of a meeting request and agenda for a phone call* in Figure 7.15 and an *example of a follow-up email after a call* in Figure 7.16.

Key Terms

active incivility, 214

asynchronous communication, 205

communication channel, 204

constraints, 204

control, 204

coordination, 204

cues, 204

cyber incivility, 214

cyber silence, 214

defusing, 216

immediacy, 204

negativity effect, 214

neutrality effect, 214

passive incivility, 214

permanence, 204

planning, 204

reinterpretation, 215

relaxation, 215

resources, 204

richness, 204

synchronous communication, 205

Discussion Exercises

7.1 Chapter Review Questions (LO7.1, LO7.2, LO7.3, LO7.4, LO7.5, LO7.6)

A. Compare and contrast spoken versus written communication in terms of richness, control, and constraints.

B. Describe three communication channels not listed in Table 7.1 and their strengths and weaknesses in terms of richness, control, and constraints.

C. What strategies can you use to ensure ease of reading in your emails and other digital communications?

D. What strategies can you use to show respect for the time of others?

E. Explain the neutrality effect and negativity effect in digital communications. What do they imply for how you write digital messages?

F. What strategies can you use to avoid email overload and, as a result, increase your productivity?

G. Explain the following components of constructively responding to uncivil digital messages: reinterpretation, relaxation, and defusing.

H. What strategies do you think are most important for effective texting in the workplace?

I. What are some strategies you can use to make better phone calls in the workplace?

7.2 Questions about Ideas in Action Feature (LO7.1, LO7.2, LO7.3)

Read the Ideas in Action featuring Arianna Huffington. Answer the following questions:

A. What principles does Huffington use for email? How might you apply these principles to your life?

B. Do you think it's practical to avoid email on vacations? Do you agree with Huffington's approach of deleting incoming email during vacations?

C. Huffington suggests people who limit digital use are more successful in their careers. In what ways do you agree and disagree with this view?

D. What are the five rules of digital communication you want to live by?

7.3 Information Overload Due to Digital Messages (LO7.5)

Go to the Information Overload Research Group's website (iorgforum.org). Read a research article, blog entry, or other content about a topic of interest. In three to five paragraphs, explain the following: (a) main points in the article, (b) your views of the main points, and (c) three strategies you will adopt to avoid information overload in the workplace.

7.4 Internet Communication Taking Over (LO7.1, LO7.4, LO7.5, LO7.6)

As researchers Simon Wright and Juraj Zdinak stated, "Internet communication is slowly taking over traditional phone-based voice communication and face-to-face communication. Restrictions to local or regional communities no longer apply: The Internet has enabled easy global communication."[34] Think about your future career and answer the following questions:

A. Is the prospect of communicating primarily via the Internet liberating? Explain.

B. Do you view the possibility of less face-to-face communication as disappointing? Explain.

C. What personal characteristics and skills are particularly well suited to success for predominantly Internet-based communication?

Evaluation Exercises

7.5 Evaluating Email Messages (LO7.2)

Compare the less effective and more effective emails in Figures 7.2 and 7.3 in the following ways:

A. Analyze the writing for each email based on tone, style, or design.

B. Evaluate them based on three of the principles for effective emails from this chapter.

C. Make two recommendations for improving the more effective email.

7.6 Description of Past Work or School-Related Emails (LO7.2)

Think of recent emails you have received related to work and school. Describe three effective email practices and three ineffective email practices you have observed. Describe each of these practices in detail (a paragraph each) and provide specific examples from emails you have received. You don't need to reveal who sent the emails.

7.7 Self-Assessment for Email Practices (LO7.2)

Evaluate your typical practices with regard to email for school or work by circling the appropriate number for each of the following items.

	1 (Disagree)	2 (Somewhat Disagree)	3 (Somewhat Agree)	4 (Agree)
I almost always reread my email message in its entirety before sending it.	1	2	3	4
I write emails in a professional and sufficiently formal manner.	1	2	3	4
I think carefully about what to write in the subject line.	1	2	3	4
I use a spell-checker for important email messages.	1	2	3	4
I envision how the recipient of my email message will respond when she/he receives it.	1	2	3	4
I think about the preferred communication channel of my message recipient before writing an email.	1	2	3	4
I read emails from others carefully and in their entirety before responding.	1	2	3	4
Before sending a reply email, I make one last check to see that I have responded to everything requested.	1	2	3	4
I regularly schedule uninterrupted time to focus on reading and responding to emails.	1	2	3	4
I set up an automatic email response or in other ways let others know when I will not be responsive to emails for an extended period (e.g., during vacation time).	1	2	3	4

Add up your score and consider the following advice:

35–40: You are a *strategic* communicator by email. You carefully plan your emails and make sure that you send a professional communication. Notice the items you did not place a 4 next to and focus on improving in these areas.

30–34: You are a *careful* communicator by email. You generally plan your emails well. However, you sometimes send them without enough thought or without reviewing them sufficiently. Focus on spending slightly more time in the planning stage.

25–29: You are an *above average* communicator by email. Sometimes you plan your emails well. Make sure to spend more time before sending an email. Always make sure your content is completely professional before sending it.

Under 25: You *need to improve* your approach to writing emails. You are too casual. Consider altering your orientation so that you view email as an important, formal business communication tool in which slight mistakes can damage your career.

Write three goals you have for becoming a more effective communicator by email. Go through the items in the survey one by one to help you think of areas where you most need to improve.

7.8 Assessment of Prior Email or Other Electronic Communication (LO7.2, LO7.3)

Think of an important email or other electronic communication you have sent in which others misunderstood your emotions and/or intent. How did the other person respond? Did you think the response was fair? Why did this person misunderstand? Did the lack of richness of the communication channel have an impact? How could you have written or approached your message differently to avoid misunderstandings?

7.9 Responding to Cyber Incivility (LO7.3)

Respond to the following questions:

A. What types of cyber incivility have you observed or heard about?

B. Based on your own experiences or those of your friends or colleagues, describe a situation in which someone was the target of cyber incivility. Describe the cyber incivility. How well did the target respond? How well did the target reinterpret, relax, and/or defuse the situation?

C. Compare the less effective and more effective responses to an angry email depicted in Figures 7.8 and 7.9. Explain three specific ways in which the more effective response defuses the situation. Also, suggest two improvements you would make to the more effective response in Figure 7.9.

7.10 Responding to Digital Messages and Managing Your Time (LO7.5)

Answer the following questions about appropriately responding to digital messages:

A. What do you think is an appropriate response time to the following types of digital messages: texts, microblog messages (such as tweets), and emails?

B. Have others ever found your response time surprisingly fast? Have others ever found your response time to be slow enough to be considered impolite or uncivil? How can you influence the expectations of others regarding how quickly you respond to their digital messages?

C. Explain cyber silence. Provide three examples that you have observed.

D. What is the best way to respond to cyber silence when you need a response from someone else?

E. What three strategies do you or will you use in the upcoming five years to avoid e-interruptions in the workplace?

Application Exercises

7.11 Choose the Right Communication Channel (LO7.1)

Assume the role of Jaclyn (from the chapter case prior to writing an angry email). She has just had a conversation with Haniz about developing a new website. Jaclyn feels that Haniz dominated the conversation and didn't allow her to express her ideas. She thinks the plan to develop the website is incomplete because it doesn't involve the integration of social media. She wants to approach Haniz and discuss the web development plan in more detail. However, she doesn't know how to start the conversation. She is just an intern. Haniz technically isn't Jaclyn's boss, but she is the lead person on the web development project. What would be the best communication channel for this discussion under each of the following circumstances? You may select more than one communication channel or even a combination of communication channels. Defend each answer with a discussion of richness, control, and constraints.

A. Haniz is in her office with the door open.

B. Haniz is in her office with the door closed, and she is not taking calls.

C. Haniz is out of town for two weeks.

D. Jaclyn is out of town for two weeks.

E. Jaclyn is nervous and uncomfortable about approaching Haniz.

F. Jaclyn thinks Haniz doesn't want to complicate the project by focusing on social media.

G. Haniz has a green MVS (see Chapter 2 for a description of MVSs) and Jaclyn has a blue MVS.

H. Jaclyn has a red MVS and Haniz has a hub MVS.

Language Mechanics Check

Review the quotation marks, italics, and parentheses rules in Appendix A. Then, rewrite each sentence to add quotation marks, italics, and parentheses where needed.

A. The term big data gets misused and overused at marketing conferences.

B. Geraldine gave the speech Making Big Data Work for You.

C. A Wall Street Journal reporter interviewed her after the speech.

D. She has received the Marketer of the Year Award twice 2015, 2019.

E. I think her key catchphrase was big data is a big mess without planning.

F. Big data refers to the exponential growth in data volume, data velocity, and data variety.

G. Geraldine cited a study called Managing Big Data in the Journal of Marketing Science.

H. She sent us the slide deck an attachment in a May 15 email with all the findings from her study.

I. After finishing her presentation, she told our employees, I'm happy to help your marketing team make a plan to use big data in your business.

J. She told us that we could find a lot of useful information in the Harvard Business Review and MIT Sloan Management Review.

Endnotes

1. Dewey, C. (2016, October 3). How many hours of your life have you wasted on work email? Try our depressing calculator. *Washington Post*. Retrieved from https://www.washingtonpost.com/news/the-intersect/wp/2016/10/03/how-many-hours-of-your-life-have-you-wasted-on-work-email-try-our-depressing-calculator/.

2. Radicati Group. (2015). Email statistics report, 2015–2019. *Radicati* website. Retrieved from http://www.radicati.com/wp/wp-content/uploads/2015/02/Email-Statistics-Report-2015-2019-Executive-Summary.pdf.

3. Kandola, P. (2006). *The psychology of effective business communications in geographically dispersed teams*. San Jose, CA: Cisco; Maruping, L. M., & Agarwal, R. (2004). Managing team interpersonal processes through technology: A task-technology fit perspective. *Journal of Applied Psychology, 89*(6), 975–990.

4. Malhotra, A., Majchrzak, A., & Rosen, B. (2007). Leading virtual teams. *Academy of Management Perspectives, 21*, 64.

5. Malhotra, A., Majchrzak, A., & Rosen, B. (2007). Leading virtual teams. *Academy of Management Perspectives, 21*, 60–70.

6. Based on survey of 1,004 marketing, R&D, and IT managers in the following industries: Finance, Banking, and Insurance; Health Care and Social Assistance; Manufacturing; and Retail and Wholesale Trade. Findings of this survey first presented at the following academic conference: Cardon, P. W. (2016, April 23). *The role of leadership communication and emotional capital in driving internal social media use.* Presentation at the Association for Business Communication Southeast/Midwest Regional Conference. St. Louis, MO.

7. Murray, A. (2010, July 15). Should I use email? *The Wall Street Journal* website. Retrieved from http://guides.wsj.com/management/managing-your-people/should-i-use-email/.

8. Hyatt, M. (2010, July 15). *Email etiquette 101.* Retrieved from http://michaelhyatt.com/2007/07/email-etiquette-101.html.

9. Morgan, N. (2002, August). Don't push that send button! *Harvard Management Communication Letter, 4.*

10. Bixler, S., & Dugan, L. S. (2001). *How to project confidence, competence, and credibility at work: 5 steps to professional presence.* Avon, MA: Adams Media.

11. Wright, G. (2010, June 28). Twitter with care: Web 2.0 usage offers few second chances. *Society for Human Resource Management.* Retrieved from www.shrm.org/hrdisciplines/technology/Articles/Pages/TwitterCarefully.aspx.

12. Plummer, M. (2019, January 22). How to spend way less time on email every day. *Harvard Business Review.* Retrieved from hbr.org/2019/01/how-to-spend-way-less-time-on-email-every-day.

13. Blackman, A. (2018, March 11). The smartest ways to use email at work. *The Wall Street Journal.* Retrieved from www.wsj.com/articles/the-smartest-ways-to-use-email-at-work-1520820300.

14. Carnegie, D. (1981). *How to win friends and influence people.* New York: Simon & Schuster, 83.

15. Waldvogel, J. (2007). Greetings and closings in workplace email. *Journal of Computer-Mediated Communication, 12*(2), 456–477.

16. Byron, K. (2008). Carry too heavy a load? The communication and miscommunication of emotion by email. *Academy of Management Review, 88*(2), 313.

17. Byron, K. (2008). Carry too heavy a load? The communication and miscommunication of emotion by email. *Academy of Management Review, 88*(2), 309–327.

18. Alonzo, M., & Aiken, M. (2004). Flaming in electronic communication. *Decision Support Systems, 36*, 205.

19. Johnson, N. A., Cooper, R., B., & Chin, W. W. (2009). Anger and flaming in computer-mediated negotiation among strangers. *Decision Support Systems, 46*(3), 660–672.

20. Based on information from Lim, V. K., & Teo, T. S. H. (2009). Mind your e-manners: Impact of cyber incivility on employees' work attitude and behavior. *Information & Management, 46*, 419–425.

21. Lim, V. K., & Teo, T. S. H. (2009). Mind your e-manners: Impact of cyber incivility on employees' work attitude and behavior. *Information & Management, 46*, 419–425.

22. Johnson, N. A., Cooper, R. B., & Chin, W. W. (2009). Anger and flaming in computer-mediated negotiation among strangers. *Decision Support Systems, 46*(3), 660–672.

23. Pew Research Internet Project. (2014, January). Mobile technology fact sheet *Pew Research Internet Project.* Retrieved from www.pewinternet.org/fact-sheets/mobile-technology-fact-sheet/.

24. Macdonell, R. (2018, August 17). The truth about digital distraction in the workplace. *HR Daily Advisor.* Retrieved from https://hrdailyadvisor.blr.com/2018/08/07/truth-digital-distraction-workplace/.

25. Robinson, J. (2010, March). Email is making you stupid. *Entrepreneur,* 61–63.

26. Robinson, J. (2010, March). Email is making you stupid. *Entrepreneur,* 61–63.

27. Robinson, J. (2010, March). Email is making you stupid. *Entrepreneur,* 61–63; McGhee, S. (2010, July 15). 4 ways to take control of your email inbox. *Microsoft At Work.* Retrieved from www.microsoft.com/atwork/productivity/email.aspx; Cavoulacos, A. (2016). 4 strategies for keeping your inbox empty: Which one is right for you? *The Muse.* Retrieved from www.themuse.com/advice/4-strategies-for-keeping-your-inbox-empty-which-one-is-right-for-you; Rosen, L., & Samuel, A. (2015, June). Conquering digital distraction. *Harvard Business Review,* 110–113.

28. Blackman, A. (2018, March 11). The smartest ways to use email at work. *The Wall Street Journal.* Retrieved from www.wsj.com/articles/the-smartest-ways-to-use-email-at-work-1520820300.

29. Tjan, A. K. (2011, November 1). Don't send that email. Pick up the phone! *Harvard Business Review.* Retrieved from http://blogs.hbr.org/2011/11/dont-send-that-email-pick-up-t/.

30. Kluger, J. (2011, March 18). We never talk any more: The problem with text messaging. *CNN.* Retrieved from www.cnn.com/2012/08/31/tech/mobile/problem-text-messaging-oms/; Paul, P. (2011, March 8). Don't call me, I won't call you. *The New York Times.* Retrieved from www.nytimes.com/2011/03/20/fashion/20Cultural.html; O^2, Making calls has become fifth most frequent use for a smartphone for newly-networked generation of users. *The Blue.* Retrieved from http://news.o2.co.uk/?press-release=Making-calls-has-become-fifth-most-frequent-use-for-a-Smartphone-for-newly-networked-generation-of-users.

31. Cardon, P. W. (2016, April 23). *The role of leadership communication and emotional capital in driving internal social media use.* Presentation at the Association for Business Communication Southeast/Midwest Regional Conference. St. Louis, MO.

32. Young, K. (2014, January 14). The high cost of multitasking. *The Fuze.* Retrieved from http://blog.fuze.com/the-high-cost-of-multitasking-infographic/.

33. Based on Cardon, P. W. (2016, April 23). *The role of leadership communication and emotional capital in driving internal social media use.* Presentation at the Association for Business Communication Southeast/Midwest Regional Conference. St. Louis, MO.

34. Wright, S., & Zdinak, J. (2008). *New communication behaviors in a Web 2.0 world changes, challenges, and opportunities in the era of the Information Revolution.* Paris: Alcatel-Lucent, 6.

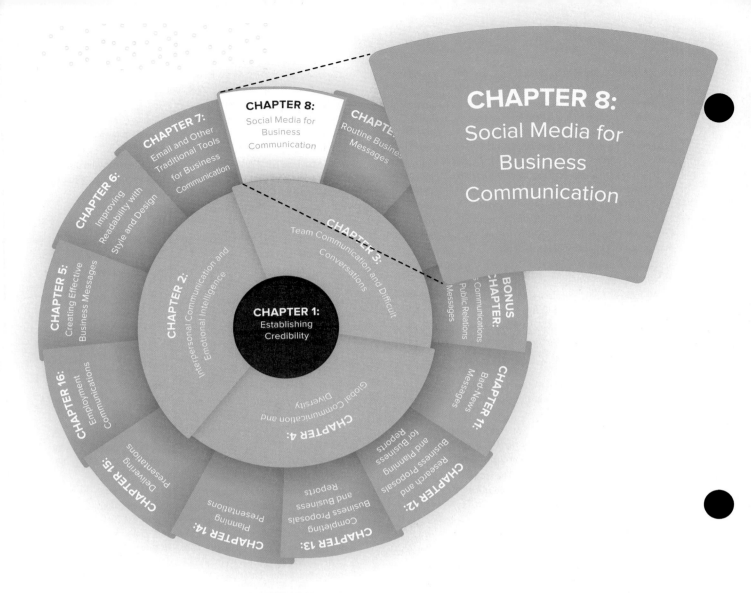

CHAPTER 8:
Social Media for Business Communication

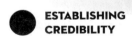 ESTABLISHING CREDIBILITY

 PRINCIPLES OF INTERPERSONAL COMMUNICATION

 PRINCIPLES FOR & TYPES OF BUSINESS MESSAGES

 LEARNING OBJECTIVES

After studying this chapter, you should be able to do the following:

LO8.1 Explain characteristics of the emerging Social Age.

LO8.2 Use blogs, forums, and other social tools for effective communication within organizations.

LO8.3 Create blogs and other social posts for effective external communications.

LO8.4 Build a credible online reputation.

LO8.5 Describe the ethical use of social media for work.

With all the social media tools available to collaborate and communicate with others, you're entering the workplace at an exciting time! These social tools include shared files and work spaces, blogs, microblogs (such as Twitter), and other collaboration tools. Compared to email and other nonsocial technologies, these social tools can dramatically improve productivity. The average knowledge worker in the United States spends about 28 hours per week reading and sending emails, searching for information, and collaborating internally. By transitioning to social tools, the average knowledge worker can save roughly six to eight hours per week and produce better work.[1]

Even for professionals familiar with using social media in their personal lives, using social tools for work isn't always natural or simple. It takes some hard work to figure out how to use these tools well and establish your professional voice. While these social tools can help you gain professional opportunities more quickly than ever, these same tools can magnify and broadcast mistakes as well. So, it's worth carefully thinking about how to use these tools well in your career. This chapter provides a variety of strategies for you to use social tools to connect and collaborate with colleagues, customers, and other contacts.

> **Hear Pete Cardon explain why this matters.**
>
> **bit.ly/cardon8**

CHAPTER CASE COMMUNICATING WITH SOCIAL MEDIA AT AICASUS TOURS

WHO'S INVOLVED

Andrea Garcia

Nancy Jeffreys

Barbara Brookshire

Director of Marketing   **Director of Market Research**   **Director of Marketing Operations**

Jeff Anderton

Kip Yamada

Market Research Associate   **Group Tours Associate**

The Marketing Team Uses a Collaboration Platform to Complete Its Work
The marketing team has recently started using enterprise social software, which functions in many ways like Facebook but is customized for use within an organization. Team members are using online discussions, status updates, shared files,

SITUATION 1

and other tools to follow up with one another related to action items agreed on in meetings, discuss ongoing projects and campaigns, and update one another about their accomplishments.

SITUATION 2

The Marketing Team Discusses Policies for Giving Discounts

Nancy and Kip recently disagreed about how to handle authorization for discounts and refunds. Kip thought generous discounts would lead to repeat business. Nancy was concerned these discounts would result in lost profits. She also thought a clear authorization policy should exist. Nancy and Kip agreed to open up a forum to marketing team members to see what their views are on this issue.

SITUATION 3

The Marketing Team Uses Blogs for External Communications

The marketing team has started using blog posts on its website and social media platforms to give customers, prospects, and other stakeholders an inside view of the company. It hopes to better promote the organization to its stakeholders.

TASK

1

How will the marketing team use social tools to work together more efficiently?

2

How can the marketing team discuss the issue of authorization for refunds on a discussion forum?

3

How can the marketing team use blogs to improve the Aicasus Tours brand?

Communicating in the Workplace in the Social Age

LO8.1 Explain characteristics of the emerging Social Age.

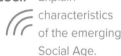

Visit http://connect. mheducation.com for an exercise on this topic.

Many online communication tools used in business—social networking, blogs, messaging, discussion forums, and others—are driving profound changes in how people connect and collaborate in the workplace. These changes are so profound that workplace culture is moving into a new era: from the Information Age to the Social Age (see Figure 8.1). The **Social Age** is an era in which people engage in networked communication, collaborate across boundaries, and solve problems communally.[2] However, even though the communication technologies that have paved the way for the Social Age are changing rapidly (in months and years), workplace culture is relatively slow to change (in years and decades). So, as you read this section, keep in mind that cultural norms and values more significantly influence the impact of social media in the workplace than do the capabilities of social media.

The evolution of the Internet during the past 20 years from Web 1.0 to Web 2.0 platforms is the primary driver of the Social Age. In the original Internet, referred to as **Web 1.0**, most web pages were read-only and static. As the Internet evolved, referred to as **Web 2.0**, what emerged was the read-write web, where users interact extensively with web pages—authoring content, expressing opinions, and customizing and editing web content among other things. Web 2.0 communication tools, often referred to as **social media**, include social networks, blogs, wikis, gaming, podcasts, and information tagging. In simple terms, Web 1.0 communication tools are primarily passive and static. By contrast, Web 2.0 communication tools are interactive, customizable, and *social*.[3] **User 1.0** refers to an individual who primarily uses and prefers Web 1.0 tools, whereas **User 2.0** refers to an individual who primarily uses and prefers Web 2.0 tools (see Table 8.1).[4] The emerging Social Age involves adopting many workplace norms and values from users of Web 2.0 tools.

FIGURE 8.1

The Evolving Workplace

Industrial Age	Information Age	Social Age
Command-and-control (Little communication between teams and units)	Mass two-way communication (Extensive communication between teams and units)	Networked communication (Extensive communication between individuals with shared interests)
Respect for position	Respect for expertise and position	Respect for expertise and contributions to the network
Holding authority is power	Holding knowledge is power	Sharing knowledge is power
Efficiency, competitiveness, and authority are key values	Autonomy, innovation, and achievement are key values	Transparency, honesty, and camaraderie are key values

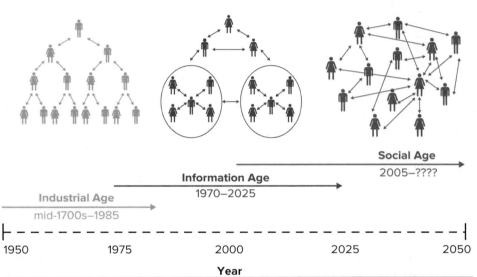

Increasingly, companies are adopting social networking platforms that contain Web 2.0 communication tools (also called *enterprise social software* and *Enterprise 2.0*) in the workplace. These platforms contain many of the features available on social networking websites: user profiles, status updates or microblogs, blogs, co-authoring tools or wikis, shared files, and group messaging or chat boxes. They often include a variety of other communication and collaboration tools as well, including online audio and video calls, shared work spaces, calendars, and private messaging (or email) systems. Thus, most companies—especially medium- to large-sized businesses—are increasingly moving toward corporate intranets that contain both Web 1.0 and Web 2.0 tools.

TABLE 8.1

Comparisons between User 1.0 and User 2.0

User 1.0	User 2.0
Passively reads and searches for content.	Actively creates and shares content online.
Depends on content creator; does not express own opinion.	Can express opinions and even change the content presented.
Gets the web as is.	Customizes web pages and content.
Email is the main communication tool.	Peer-to-peer programs are the main communication tools.
The computer is the main access point.	Connects from mobile devices.
Connected online for time-limited sessions.	Connected online all the time.

TABLE 8.2

Benefits and Challenges of Social Media in the Workplace

Benefits of Social Media	Challenges and Risks of Social Media
To companies: • Team communication and collaboration • Succession planning • Recruitment and on-boarding • Idea sharing/knowledge management • Skills development and training • Interfacing with customers, suppliers, and partners • Decreased time to market for new products and services • More innovative, creative, effective, and profitable approaches to work problems • Less time and fewer resources needed for business travel	*To companies:* • Lack of adoption and penetration • Lack of permanence • Confusion over which communication channels to use • Distraction from work, too much socializing • Lack of control of information provided externally and internally • Lack of systems for rewarding networked and team communication and collaboration
To business professionals: • Build professional networks internally and externally • Access business expertise and knowledge more rapidly • Enhance camaraderie with peers	*To business professionals:* • Lack of boundaries between professional and private lives • Lower productivity due to multitasking • Excessive opportunism and self-promotion • Mistakes and incompetence broadcast to larger audiences

Major Components of Social Networking Platforms

• User profiles
• Status updates/microblogs
• Blogs
• Co-authoring tools and wikis
• Group messaging/chat boxes
• Private messaging
• Discussion forums
• RSS feeds
• Social bookmarking
• Rating and tagging
• Video sharing
• Podcasts
• Mashups

The emerging work culture associated with the Social Age presents many benefits to companies and business professionals in the context of team and networked communication (see Table 8.2).[5] When social media are used for professional purposes, teams can communicate more efficiently; companies can interface more responsively with customers, clients, and suppliers; customers and other interested individuals can be directly involved in the development of products and services; and anyone with shared professional interests can communicate easily, not needing to travel to see one another.

Social media also present many challenges and risks. The primary challenges are cultural. Some of them are age-based: Older employees are more accustomed to the communication tools they have used for years and decades. Typically, the Web 1.0 tools reinforce many older employees' work values, such as privacy and autonomy. The use of social media creates a free flow of information that, in many cases, runs counter to traditional business approaches to decision making, lines of authority, team formation, performance incentives, and so on.

One basic challenge of using social media internally is getting employees to participate. In most companies, participation on enterprise social platforms with related collaboration tools is fairly low. The case of Wikipedia is instructive. Although millions of Internet users consider Wikipedia to be a reliable source of information, only a small fraction of users are also Wikipedia authors and contributors. Wikipedia is consistently among the ten most visited websites. Yet, less than 1 percent of users ever contribute to its entries.[6]

Social media use also presents a variety of risks. For companies, social media can lead to lower productivity when employees use them for social and entertainment purposes, release confidential and proprietary information, post inappropriate comments that lead to reputation loss for companies, and go around lines of authority. On an individual level, social media can lead to major credibility loss (discussed further in "Managing Your Online Reputation").

Using Social Media Tools for Communication within Organizations

Using social tools for everyday communication has dramatic impacts in the workplace. Various research suggests that productivity can grow by between 10 and 25 percent.[7] In this section, we briefly touch on several of the social software tools you can expect to use in the workplace: dashboards, user profiles, blogs and status updates, and discussion forums (usually simply called *forums*). We focus on these tools for a few reasons. They are among the most widely used and most effective social tools, and they involve significant written communication.

Organize Your Dashboard to Control Your Communication and Information Flow

Nearly all social software systems contain a *dashboard*, your front page when you log in, which operates as your communication and information hub. Your dashboard gives you many opportunities to learn and connect with others. By setting up your dashboard strategically, you can learn more about the people in your organization and develop business expertise each day. You can also allow others to learn more about you and enhance your credibility within your organization.

In most cases, you can customize the dashboard to display the features that most interest you. For most teams, displaying status updates and other project notifications should be most prominent. You can also display your mail, your schedule, the communities you belong to, people you follow in the organization, and even use plug-ins for external social readers to learn more about your industry and your field (the "Guidelines for Using Social Media in the Workplace" section contains information about using social readers).

Create a Complete and Professional Profile

In your profile, you provide information about yourself, such as your position, contact information, professional interests, and current projects. You can usually provide a picture and list personal interests outside of work. Profiles are an excellent way of finding people within an organization with needed expertise or shared professional interests. Profiles as part of enterprise social software systems appear much like those in Facebook and LinkedIn.

In your profiles, make sure you provide complete information. This is a chance for colleagues and clients who do not know you well to learn about your professional background, abilities, and interests. Colleagues in your organization who do not know you well may be more likely to contact you for projects and other opportunities based on what they learn from your profile. Notice in Figure 8.2 how Kip edits his profile by providing a professional picture, information about his role, and contact information.

Use Blogs and Status Updates for Team Communication

Blogs are posts that are arranged chronologically, similar to a journal format. Traditionally, most blogs have included entries by just one or a few individuals, although many provide the option for reader comments. Increasingly, teams and other professional groups write blogs. In the workplace, they allow business professionals to share their ideas and experiences. By focusing on specific topics and areas of expertise, bloggers can attract and connect with other employees with similar professional interests.[8] A variety of blog types have emerged in the workplace, including individual expert blogs, company executive blogs, company team blogs, company update blogs, company crisis blogs, and internal company blogs.[9]

LO8.2 Use blogs, forums, and other social tools for effective communication within organizations.

Visit http://connect. mheducation.com for an exercise on this topic.

Edit your profile

Full name

Kip Yamada

Profile photo

Display name (optional)

Kip

This could be your first name, or a nickname — however you'd like
people to refer to you in Slack.

What I do

Group Tours

Let people know what you do at Aicasus Tours.

Phone number

213-740-0633

Enter a phone number.

Time Zone

(UTC-08:00) Pacific Time (US and Canada ▼

Your current time zone. Used to send summary and notification
emails, for times in your activity feeds, and for reminders.

Skype

grouptours-kip

This will be displayed on your profile.

Blog posts are excellent opportunities for leaders, managers, and supervisors to keep employees aware of announcements and updates. By using the comment features on these blogs, employees can ask questions and share their opinions. This helps create a more interactive, transparent decision-making process within organizations, business units, and teams. Notice in Figure 8.3 how Andrea makes a short announcement via a blog post. Kip has a question and Andrea quickly responds. This process helps Andrea get input from her colleagues to make better decisions. It also gives all employees the sense that their concerns and opinions matter.

Status updates (also known as **microblogs**) are short comments that typically contain just a few sentences. The most popular public social networking platform for microblogs is Twitter. As part of enterprise social networking platforms, status updates are tools for broadcasting quick announcements and urgent information. Members of a network can also use them to ask questions that need immediate responses. They are particularly useful in teams so team members can coordinate their efforts effectively. Notice in Figure 8.4 how the marketing team uses updates throughout the day to ensure they work well together.

Organizations are increasingly using team blogs and project blogs (many-to-many communication). **Team blogs** are typically organized around formal work teams, and **project blogs** are organized around particular projects that generally involve temporary teams. Team and project blogs are excellent ways to place all of the team's communications in a single place, such as updates, progress reports, problem-solving discussions, project timelines and goals, announcements, and a variety of other coordination tasks. These team and project blogs are also excellent for sharing success stories to build and shape organizational and team culture.

FIGURE 8.3

Blog Used for Internal Announcements

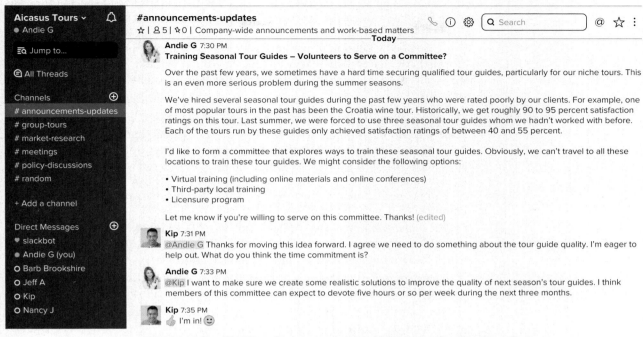

Slack; Photos: Andres Rodriguez/123RF; John A Rizzo/Pixtal/SuperStock; Andres Rodriguez/123RF; John A Rizzo/Pixtal/SuperStock

FIGURE 8.4

Status Updates for Team Coordination

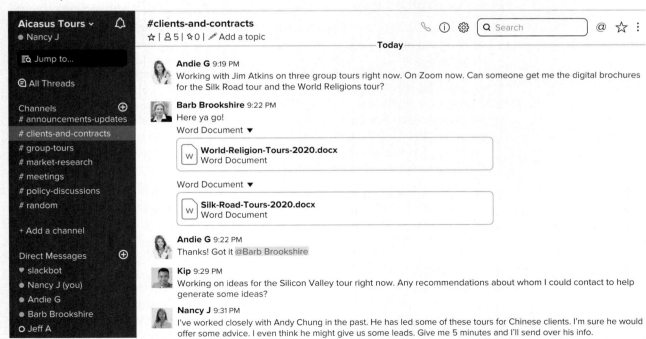

Slack; photos: Andres Rodriguez/123RF; Corbis/VCG/Getty Images; Andres Rodriguez/123RF; John A Rizzo/Pixtal/SuperStock; Photodisc/Getty Images

Use Shared Files to Collaborate

Smart teams rely on shared files on a central platform to co-edit and coordinate their work. In the past few decades, the most common approach to sharing files was sending files back and forth via email. This approach has several limitations, including the challenges of maintaining version control, co-editing at the same time, and relying on a single location for all important files. Most enterprise social networking platforms have shared files platforms that operate much like Google Docs. As you share files with team members and other colleagues to collaborate, consider the following tips:

* *Discuss with your team members and colleagues what the protocol should be for sharing and co-editing files.* As discussed in Chapter 3 about teams, you should always be explicit about your preferences and expectations. Some colleagues prefer simultaneously co-editing, whereas others prefer a single author who relies on the comments on others. Your team has a variety of decisions to make, including how to name documents, how to track and manage edits, and how to respond to comments.
* *Organize your files by project.* Unless you organize your files by project (or topic), shared files can become difficult to track and find. Discuss with your team members which folders and naming conventions you intend to use.
* *Manage permissions.* Often, you'll keep sensitive, even confidential, information in shared files. Make sure you manage permissions and allow only the right people access to this information.
* *Add comments constructively and carefully read your colleagues' comments.* You and your teams will make one another's work much stronger by carefully making comments. You should avoid generic comments and provide enough detail to help your colleagues. For example, simply writing "Great job!" isn't particularly helpful. Notice in Figure 8.5 how a variety of teammates provide comments to Jeff's report draft. They compliment Jeff *and* provide concrete suggestions to make his report even more valuable and useful.

Solve Problems with Discussion Forums

All enterprise social networking platforms contain discussion forums. These forums allow team members and colleagues to continue holding conversations between meetings. As a result, important team conversations stay more current and fresh in each team member's memory. Some business professionals prefer forums over face-to-face meetings because forums allow them to make thoughtful, carefully prepared, and well-documented comments. Typically, introverts express themselves more easily in forums. So, using face-to-face meetings together with forums creates a work environment that brings out the contributions and best ideas of *all* team members. However, forums are not always successful. Generally, you should help your teams avoid the following actions that hinder productive team communication:

* *Avoid leading posts.* Just as leading questions hinder listening in face-to-face communication, leading posts harm online discussions. Figure 8.6 displays an abbreviated discussion forum that is not effective. Take a few minutes to read it. One of the first things you'll notice is the leading subject line, which is nothing more than Kip's strong opinion. This immediately places the forum on the wrong trajectory.
* *Avoid ignoring competing points of view*s. Many ineffective forums are the result of professionals sharing their own views but not acknowledging the views of others. You'll notice a variety of posts in the ineffective forum (Figure 8.6) where Kip and Nancy state their views but don't directly acknowledge one another's points. Professionals, even in forums, often "talk over" one another. This doesn't help

FIGURE 8.5

Appropriate Reactions to Shared Files

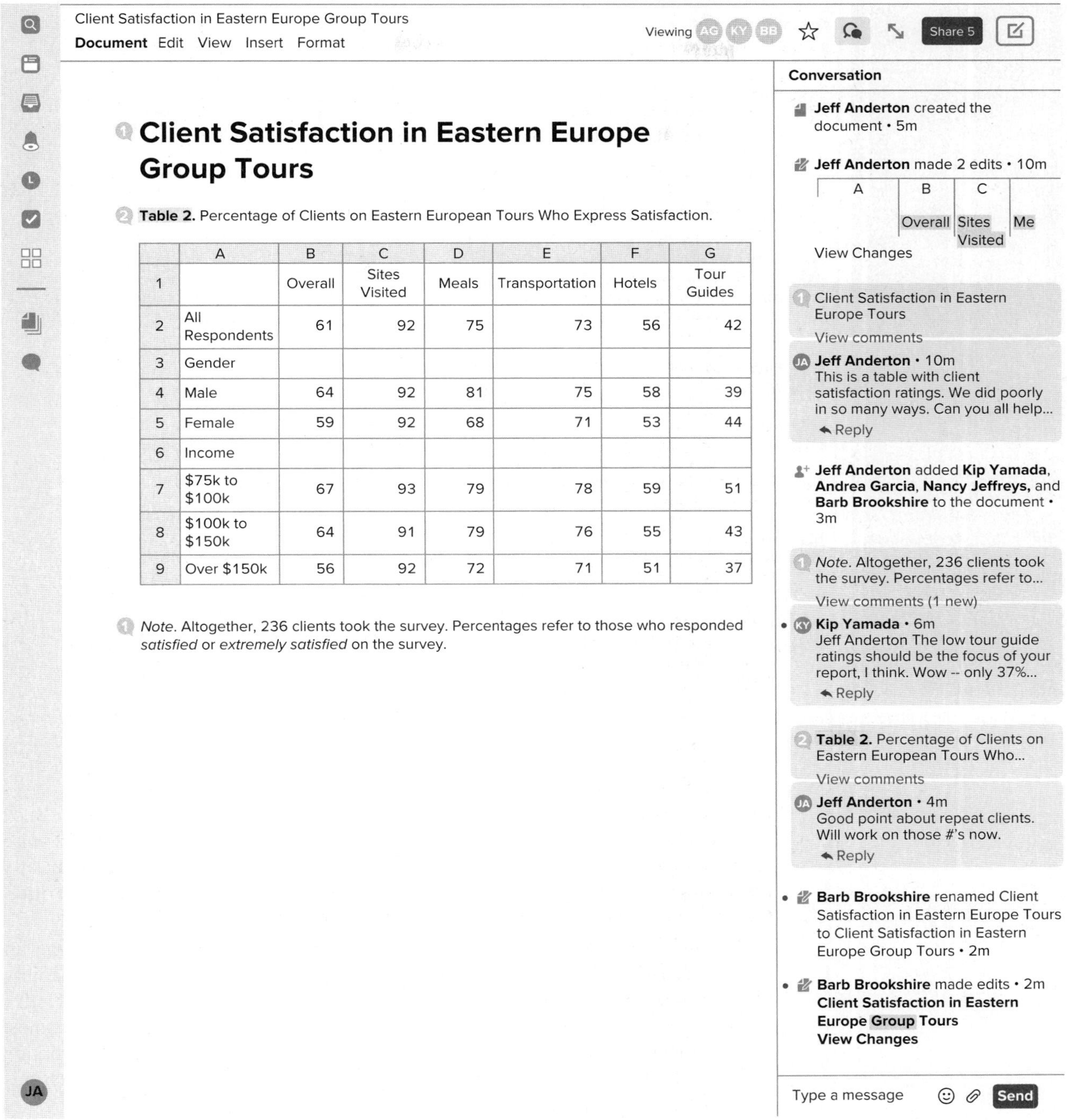

Client Satisfaction in Eastern Europe Group Tours
Document Edit View Insert Format

Viewing (AG) (KY) (BB) ☆ 💬 ↘ | Share 5 | ☑

Client Satisfaction in Eastern Europe Group Tours

Table 2. Percentage of Clients on Eastern European Tours Who Express Satisfaction.

	A	B	C	D	E	F	G
1		Overall	Sites Visited	Meals	Transportation	Hotels	Tour Guides
2	All Respondents	61	92	75	73	56	42
3	Gender						
4	Male	64	92	81	75	58	39
5	Female	59	92	68	71	53	44
6	Income						
7	$75k to $100k	67	93	79	78	59	51
8	$100k to $150k	64	91	79	76	55	43
9	Over $150k	56	92	72	71	51	37

Note. Altogether, 236 clients took the survey. Percentages refer to those who responded *satisfied* or *extremely satisfied* on the survey.

Conversation

Jeff Anderton created the document • 5m

Jeff Anderton made 2 edits • 10m

A	B	C	
	Overall	Sites Visited	Me

View Changes

Client Satisfaction in Eastern Europe Tours
View comments

Jeff Anderton • 10m
This is a table with client satisfaction ratings. We did poorly in so many ways. Can you all help...
↩ Reply

Jeff Anderton added **Kip Yamada**, **Andrea Garcia**, **Nancy Jeffreys**, and **Barb Brookshire** to the document • 3m

Note. Altogether, 236 clients took the survey. Percentages refer to...
View comments (1 new)

Kip Yamada • 6m
Jeff Anderton The low tour guide ratings should be the focus of your report, I think. Wow -- only 37%...
↩ Reply

Table 2. Percentage of Clients on Eastern European Tours Who...
View comments

Jeff Anderton • 4m
Good point about repeat clients. Will work on those #'s now.
↩ Reply

Barb Brookshire renamed Client Satisfaction in Eastern Europe Tours to Client Satisfaction in Eastern Europe Group Tours • 2m

Barb Brookshire made edits • 2m
Client Satisfaction in Eastern Europe Group Tours
View Changes

Type a message ☺ 🔗 | Send |

Kip or Nancy influence others. It also discourages teammates from participating in the forum.

- *Avoid strong, rigid language.* Rarely are forums the right outlet to persuade others from the outset. Rather, the goal of forums is to explore one another's ideas and build solutions together. Strong and rigid language signals that people are not open to the ideas of the team. This language can come in the form of *either/or options*

FIGURE 8.6

An Ineffective Example of a Forum Conversation

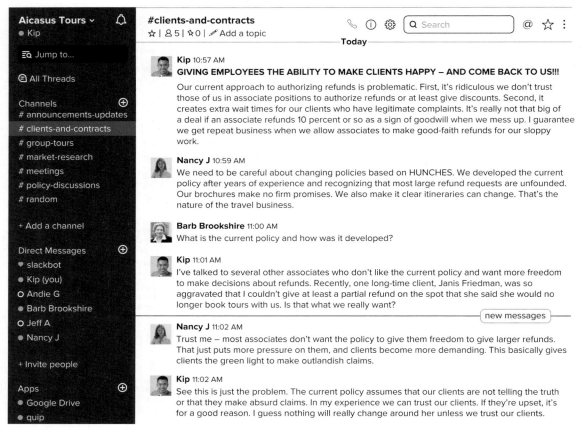

Slack; photos: John A Rizzo/Pixtal/SuperStock; Photodisc/Getty Images; Corbis/VCG/Getty Images; John A Rizzo/Pixtal/SuperStock; Photodisc/Getty Images; John A Rizzo/Pixtal/SuperStock

(i.e., "the only way to . . ."), *finality*—implying the issue is not open to debate (i.e., "we already decided to . . ."), *exaggeration* (i.e., "the best way to . . ."), and otherwise *judgmental terms* (i.e., "ridiculous"). As a rule of thumb, if you sense that you or others are trying to "win the argument," you should stop and reflect whether the direction of the discussion is helpful for your team and its goals.

- *Avoid complaining.* Complaining can drag down any conversation, including an online discussion. The major problem with complaining is dwelling on the inability to avoid negative outcomes. You'll notice that Kip's comments in the ineffective forum often contain this sense of exasperation and certainty of poor outcomes. Many professional forums contain rants. These rants on enterprise social networking platforms remain as permanent records and sometimes serve as the first impressions colleagues have of one another.

- *Avoid blaming.* Blaming is similar to complaining in that it often places responsibility entirely on others. It is more serious, however, because it often serves as an attack on others. In the ineffective forum, Kip and Nancy indirectly blame one another throughout the forum. Kip blames Nancy for not understanding the needs of front-desk employees and guests. Nancy blames Kip for forming his conclusions based on hunches rather than careful research.

- *Avoid off-topic points.* The major value of forums is holding targeted, specific conversations. When professionals start discussing unrelated issues, the forum loses its value for several reasons: (a) the discussion is unlikely to produce results for the original purpose, (b) some participants discontinue participating, and (c) the discussion loses its appeal as a reference in later conversations.

- *Avoid excessively short or lengthy posts.* Typically, posts that are too short show that participants aren't engaging the forum sufficiently. On the other hand, excessively lengthy posts often go unread. They also may signal that the writer is disinterested in a back-and-forth discussion with teammates.
- *Avoid sarcasm.* Sarcasm is usually misinterpreted on forums. One reason sarcasm doesn't work on forums is that it generally applies to a context at a shared moment. Since forums often run over days and weeks, this shared context at a point in time is missing.

You can use a variety of strategies to make forums effective ways for your teams to produce better work. Consider the following strategies:

- *Read your peers' comments completely and carefully.* You'll save time by making sure you read every comment carefully. By doing so, you provide better comments and show that you care about your teammates. In fact, you'll often realize your influence grows as others see your efforts to learn from them.
- *State the purpose of the forum clearly.* The subject line for the forum should clearly lay out the question or purpose of the forum. In the effective forum in Figure 8.7, you can see that the forum subject is posed as a clear, specific question. It is also posted in the correct channel (#policy-discussions), which signals this is an open conversations. Also, make sure the first few posts clearly describe why the issue is important and provide some background. This motivates other team members to participate.
- *Use flexible, open, and inviting language.* You can express your views with confidence while also signaling that you want to hear from others. Using phrases such as *I think*, *I suggest*, or *perhaps we should* allows you to voice your opinions while staying open to others.
- *Build on the ideas of others and pose questions.* The best forums result from team members referencing and connecting each other's ideas. Posing questions will often help draw out the ideas of teammates.
- *Show appreciation for your teammates and their ideas.* You don't have to agree with everything your colleagues suggest to show appreciation. Find ways to see merit in their ideas. Use their names to show your interest in them individually. Assume that they are acting in the interest of the team and the organization.
- *Participate often.* Forums work well when all team members visit the forum regularly. One major threat to productive discussions is inconsistency. First comers sometimes state their views and then never return to the forum. Latecomers may disrupt the process by not entering the discussion until after other team members have developed a consensus. If these latecomers go against the hard-earned consensus of the team, they cost the whole team time and morale. Consistent participation by each team member makes the process smooth and productive.
- *Meet in real time for touchy points.* Forums are excellent for fairly routine conversations. If the online discussion gets contentious or raises sensitive issues, schedule a time for the team to discuss the issues in real time. You'll accomplish much more in a real-time conversation and reduce the likelihood of misunderstandings.
- *Summarize and, as appropriate, identify next steps.* The purpose of most forums is to help a team discuss an issue and arrive at solutions. By the end of the forum, summarize the discussion and identify actions your team will take.
- *Talk with your team about ways to make forums help your decision making and coordination.* Much like we discussed in Chapter 3 about team communication, your team should evaluate its performance. As part of this process, your team should periodically discuss how well forums work and how you can improve them.

FIGURE 8.7

An Effective Example of a Forum Conversation

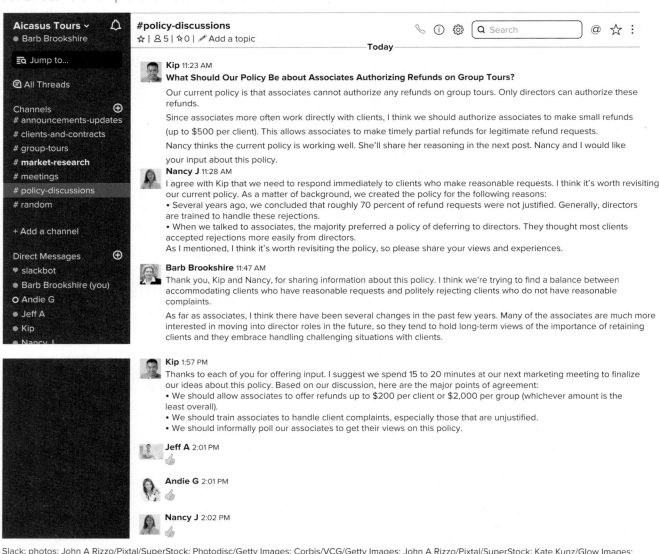

Slack; photos: John A Rizzo/Pixtal/SuperStock; Photodisc/Getty Images; Corbis/VCG/Getty Images; John A Rizzo/Pixtal/SuperStock; Kate Kunz/Glow Images; Andres Rodriguez/123RF; Photodisc/Getty Images

Other Social Media Tools

Many other communication tools exist on social networking platforms. Furthermore, Enterprise 2.0 platforms are constantly evolving and adding communication tools. You would be wise to experiment with all the communication tools available on these platforms so you can identify and use the channels best suited for your audiences.

Writing Blogs for External Audiences

Increasingly, stakeholders expect an insider view of organizations. One effective way of *telling the story* of your organization is through blog posts. Usually, these posts originate on a corporate website. Then, these posts are generally linked to a variety of public social networking platforms, such as Facebook, LinkedIn, Instagram, and Pinterest. Also, many professionals now write blogs about their professional interests. These blogs are a powerful way of personal branding. In this section, we'll discuss these two forms of writing blogs for external audiences.

Write Posts for Your Organization

The primary goal of blogs for organizations is effective public relations (PR). Traditionally, PR was viewed as media relations, and the primary vehicles for PR messages were press releases. Over the past several decades, during the Information Age, the scope of PR broadened and it became a key component of the marketing mix. PR has been defined as "the management function that establishes and maintains mutually beneficial relationships between an organization and the various publics on whom its success depends."[10] In other words, PR is fundamentally about *building relationships* with employees, customers, communities, the media, and other stakeholders.

A primary goal of building these relationships is to improve corporate reputation or credibility. Elliot Schreiber, one of the foremost authorities on public relations, defined **corporate reputation** on the Institute for Public Relations website:

> From the perspective of the organization, reputation is an intangible asset that allows the company to better manage the expectations and needs of its various stakeholders, creating differentiation and barriers vis-à-vis its competitors. From the perspective of stakeholders, reputation is the intellectual, emotional and behavioral response as to whether or not the communications and actions of an organization resonate with their needs and interests.[11]

This definition reveals several key aspects of reputation. First, it is an asset; it has value. Studies suggest that reputation directly contributes to between 3 and 7.5 percent of annual revenues. For some companies, reputation can increase revenue even more. Second, having a positive reputation is not enough. A company's reputation must differentiate it from its competitors. Third, a primary goal of public relations is managing the expectations of stakeholders. And most important, through public relations, a company develops a reputation that delivers value to stakeholders based on their own needs and interests.[12]

Idea Development for Public Relations Messages   Because a primary goal of PR is to create distinctive brand value for a company, any individual message should be considered a piece in this larger effort. So, the first step is to clarify your company's brand and, through discussion, gain a shared sense of the brand message. Without this agreement among colleagues, a company may produce nonunified, perhaps even confusing, messages.

Many PR messages center on drawing positive attention to products and services, especially those that are newly launched, recently improved, or recently awarded or otherwise recognized. Developing your ideas for PR messages involves understanding these products and services completely and accurately. Furthermore, it involves identifying which products and services the company intends to highlight. Thus, it requires discussions of the company's strategy for promoting various products and services. Once you have done all this, you are ready to act much like a news reporter. You gather accurate and reliable information that tells a compelling story of what the company has done.

Message Structure for Public Relations Messages   In the press-release style, which still accounts for most written PR messages, the main components include a headline, dateline, the story, a boilerplate, and contact information. The *headline* immediately captures the attention of stakeholders. Next, the *dateline* allows readers to identify when the story occurred. Then, the *PR story*—whether it's announcing a product

LO8.3 Create blogs and other social posts for effective external communications.

Visit http://connect. mheducation.com for an exercise on this topic.

Components of Press-Release Style Blog Posts

- Headline
- Dateline
- PR story
- Boilerplate
- Contact information
- Call to action

FIGURE 8.8

A Press-Release Style
Blog Post

Aicasus Tours Adds Silicon Valley Tour to the World Revolutions Series

Published on February 11

 Kip Yamada | ✓ Following
Group Tours Associate at Aicasus Tours
12 articles, 37 likes, 7 comments, 19 reposts

 0 0 0

Aicasus just added to its acclaimed lineup of World Revolutions tours. The newest tour explores—in hands-on fashion—the companies and personalities that are changing our world right before our eyes. Like all tours in this series, clients see how history is informing our future.

The Silicon Valley tour includes site visits to Google, Apple, Tesla, Facebook, and several startups. Unlike most Silicon Valley tours, Aicasus gives access to executives, managers, and engineers at each site. Each tour also includes attendance at a major product launch event.

All the buzz in recent years is artificial intelligence. Aicasus gives tour participants the ultimate AI experience! Participants interact with AI-powered robots and even create their own chat bot (no technical experience necessary). They also compete in a variety of games against AI-powered machines.

The tour concludes with a day of reflection in the Redwood Forest. Tour participants enjoy several meditation exercises and a one-of-a kind hike that exposes the majesty of our planet.

Tour participants gain rich perspectives about the future and see where science fiction may become reality. They also rub shoulders with some of the most interesting innovators on the planet. The wine tasting and gourmet meals also add a unique flavor to the tour!

Aicasus Tours creates novel and surprising travel experiences for the sophisticated traveler. You can contact Kip Yamada directly by email or Twitter to learn more about group tours.

launch, an act of charity, an event, or some other type of notable corporate activity—is written in third person in what is often referred to as *inverted pyramid style*.

The *story* should answer the basic questions of *who*, *what*, *when*, *where*, and *why* quickly within the first paragraph. The story then provides supporting details—the second tier of the inverted pyramid. At the end of the PR story, a *boilerplate* or *positioning statement* briefly explains background about the company: the nature of its business, its products and services, its customers, and its *unique selling position*, meaning what distinguishes it from competitors. Typically, minor PR announcements are just 100 to 300 words, and major announcements are generally 500 to 800 words.[13] You can see an example of this type of blog post in Figure 8.8.

FIGURE 8.9

An Op-Ed Style Blog Post

Why Every Traveler Should Try Homestay

Published on February 11

Kip Yamada | ✓ Following
Group Tours Associate at Aicasus Tours
12 articles, 72 likes, 21 comments, 24 reposts

0   0   0

It's not also convenient. In fact, sometimes it's tiring, challenging, and even frustrating. But, staying in the home of another family in another country can be among the most enriching, eye-opening, and even life-changing travel experiences.

At Aicasus tours, we provide homestay experiences to about 2,500 travelers each year. We match travelers with the right host families for anywhere between three days and one month. The most common destinations are in China, India, and Germany. We place people in big cities, small towns, and even on farms!

People often ask why they should do it. The reasons differations generally all relate to building deep connections and bridge *You simply can't understand another culture until you've liv family's home.* Pierre Jackson, a 33-year-old business exec countries on regular tours. Then, we placed him with a fami describes the experience:

Nothing prepared me for this experience. I had traveled the world. But, until I stayed with the Chen family in a modest Beijing neighborhood, I never understood what it meant to be part of another family. And, I never really understood Chinese culture until I stayed with the Chens.

—Pierre Jackson

Every serious traveler should enjoy a homestay experience. All the simple things—eating and preparing meals together, stumbling through conversations when you don't know the language too well, helping with family chores, attending neighborhood get-togethers, and a million little things—help you feel part of our world family.

So, take that leap with a new kind of travel experience: spend just a few days or even a month with a homestay family.

Aicasus Tours creates novel and surprising travel experiences for the sophisticated traveler. You can contact Kip Yamada directly by email or Twitter to learn more about group tours.

Photos: John A Rizzo/Pixtal/SuperStock; Leila/ZUMA Press Inc/Alamy Stock Photo

Another common approach to PR messages is the op-ed style. Traditionally, a corporate leader would write an opinion piece in first person about a challenge or issue shared by the company and the public. As with press releases, the scope of the op-ed approach for PR has grown. Just a decade ago, op-eds were written for newspapers and other periodicals on an irregular basis. Now, however, the op-ed style is common on corporate blogs, where business leaders can regularly share their opinions and experiences. You can see an example of this type of op-ed in Figure 8.9.

Write Posts for a Professional Blog

Increasingly, business professionals have opportunities to build personal brands with social media tools. One of the best ways of establishing thought leadership is to create blog posts that focus on areas of expertise or interests. Many professionals create their own blogs (many free platforms exist such as WordPress and Medium). Other professionals post their entries on well-known social networking platforms such as LinkedIn. While you can distinguish yourself on these external platforms, you can also write blog posts on enterprise social networking platforms that help give you a reputation of expertise within your organization.

Typically, you can employ several strategies on your own professional blogs. First, develop a theme that readers easily recognize and that captures your areas of expertise or interests. Second, make sure your blog posts maintain a professional, fun, and helpful tone. Third, make sure your content is accurate. You can quickly gain a reputation as an expert with strong posts yet gain a reputation as a novice if there are obvious mistakes in your content. Most blog writers enhance their credibility by providing hyperlinks to their source or reference material. This helps readers make judgments about the quality of your posts. Also, make sure your content is interesting and front-loaded. You've got only 5 to 15 seconds to draw your readers in, so make sure you capture their interest immediately. Finally, stay responsive to your readers' comments. You can often learn what your readers are looking for by sifting through comments. Because so many styles exist for professional blogs, you should read the blogs of popular business and management bloggers to figure out some options that might work for you. You can see one example of a professional blog in Figure 8.10. Jeff Anderton, a market research associate at Aicasus, has his own blog about digital marketing and customer loyalty. This blog can serve as a way for Jeff to continue to develop professional knowledge and develop a personal brand that will provide professional opportunities.

Guidelines for Using Social Media in the Workplace

Many communication tools fall under the social media platform. Generally, you can apply the following advice to any of them.

Be an Active Contributor and Join Communities

If your company or professional group has committed to using social networking platforms, make sure you contribute regularly and respond to the comments and work of others. As an example, for individual blogs, those employees who gain the largest followings (and thus a reputation for thought leadership) regularly make blog entries and other posts two to three times per week.

Online communities are excellent places to network and participate with professionals in your organization and those with shared professional interests outside your organization. Your company's digital platform will likely offer many ways to join online communities. Some communities are built around committees, task forces, and teams with specific charges or tasks. Other communities are built around shared professional interests, such as finance or project management. These communities are often called *communities of practice* and allow you to share and learn from other professionals in your area. Yet other communities are focused on personal interests and hobbies. Generally, actively participating in these communities will open up many professional and learning opportunities.

Read, Listen, and Learn

Social media offer an ideal means of continuously learning about your company, your industry, and your discipline. In Chapter 3, we focused on the importance of having a

Principles for Professional Social Media Use

- Be an active contributor.
- Read, listen, and learn.
- Focus on content.
- Make your content accessible.
- Make your messages authentic and friendly.
- Be responsive and help others.
- Respect boundaries.
- Participate in communities.

FIGURE 8.10

An Example of a Personal Professional Blog

The Digital Strategies and Customer Loyalty Blog

Home   **About**   **Past Blog Posts**

How Much Service and Content Should You Give Away for Free?

August 1, 2020
Posted by Jeff Anderton

About Jeff

"I'm a market research associate at Aicasus Tours. I write about digital marketing and customer loyalty. All views are my own."

Many software and consulting companies rely on a business model of giving away content and services. To make money, of course, these companies need paying customers. This business model is called *freemium* (combines the words *free* and *premium*). A well-known freemium company is LinkedIn. Most customers pay nothing for free profiles with a small proportion of customers paying for premium services.

In the recent *Harvard Business Review* article "Making 'Freemium' Work," Vineet Kumar provides an overview of the freemium business model. He presents the cases of LinkedIn, NYTimes.com, Spotify, and Dropbox. Kumar explains that freemium companies must figure out how to offer some features for free to attract new users, yet retain other features that are reserved for premium users. So, how do you do that? Kumar gives some hints but not any specific answers.

Over the past few weeks, I've read articles by many of the experts on freemium business models. They generally recommend the following strategies to find the "sweet spot" between offering too much or too little free content:

1. *Use the RIGHT MODEL.* Freemium expert Lincoln Murphy has examined this business model for nearly a decade and identified seven distinct freemium business models. Some companies even use more than one business model for various products and services. To know which model to use, freemium companies should know answers to the following questions: (a) Will the content or services remain free forever? (b) Will users or organizations purchase the content or services? (c) Is the primary purpose to get customers to upgrade or to get them to purchase other products or services (a cross-sell strategy)? (d) Is the base product intended to create an ecosystem? Without answering these questions carefully, companies may choose the wrong model and get the free/premium mix wrong.

2. *Keep track of the RIGHT METRICS.* One company that's mastered the mix between free and premium content is Breaking Into Wall Street, an educational service about landing a finance position. Its founder and president, Brian DeChesare, recently sat down for an interview with *Forbes* and mentioned all freemium companies must measure the following: (a) What is the cost of content creation? (b) How long will free content attract new customers? (c) What are the costs of updating free content? (d) What is the expected ROI on free content?

3. *Hire the RIGHT PEOPLE to oversee the process.* Among the most successful creators of a freemium company was David Sacks, founder and CEO of Yammer. He recently guest authored the article "When Freemium Beats Premium" for the *WSJ*. Sacks says that "a lot of effort, experimentation, and fine-tuning" are needed to succeed with freemium. So, yes, it's important to capture the right metrics. You need people who understand data. But, it's also important to hire people who embrace uncertainty and use a trial-and-error process to figure out what to give away for free and what to reserve for paid customers.

Photo: Kate Kunz/Glow Images

listening-centered approach to communication. Used wisely, social media give you many ways to read, listen, and learn.

With the wealth of online information, you can take steps on a weekly basis to learn more about your areas of expertise, your industry, and other topics of interest. Using social reading platforms (such as LinkedIn, Feedly, or Flipboard), you can weed out less relevant information and efficiently access information to develop your knowledge and skills. Ideally, you will set apart at least several hours per week to read and learn with a social reader. To make the best use of these platforms, consider the following strategies:

- *Identify the 20 to 50 sources of information that are most helpful to you.* This is the most time-consuming part of setting up a social reader. You'll likely need to experiment over time to identify the best mix of information for you. Consider following professionals you admire (inside and outside your company), companies of interest (including competitors), and news sources related to your professional interests and expertise (set up as RSS feeds to important periodicals and thought leaders).

- *Use hashtag and other topical searches to track important information to you.* In addition to following sources of information, wisely using automated searches allows you to get relevant information for your professional interests. You can use a variety of platforms to automate this process. Notice in Figure 8.11 how Kip uses TweetDeck to create a news feed based on various automated searches (with hashtags such as #hotelmarketing and #eventprofs). With several weeks or months of experimentation, you can generally set up search-based news feeds that help you find the best of your company's digital platform and the Internet with little effort on your part.

- *Take time to read important articles and posts.* Most online readers are skimmers. Skimming is important to quickly extract key ideas. You will learn more deeply and notice you are more informed than many of your peers by setting aside at least a few hours per week for dedicated, comprehensive reading of key articles and posts in your area. Commit to taking enough time to process this information well.

- *Recognize and praise the contributions of others.* Make sure to like and compliment the well-developed content of others. Many of your colleagues and other contacts will greatly appreciate your well-crafted, specific praise. They'll also likely return that appreciation when you post your own content.

Focus on Content

Blogs, wikis, forums, and even news feeds are collaborative tools. In other words, they are intended to help you work more effectively with your team members, other colleagues, and clients. The primary goal is not to entertain; it is to provide value to others and increase your professional, not social, credibility (as discussed in "Managing Your Online Reputation").[14] The content of your posts should focus on your work projects, meetings, shared goals, experiences, and expertise and knowledge.

Of course, social media are called *social* for a reason. They provide professionals with rich and exciting communication tools. Including social content is good to a point. In high-performing teams, 60 to 70 percent of all comments are directly related to work, about 15 to 20 percent of comments are supportive, and about 10 to 15 percent are primarily social. This is also the case for business communication via social media. As a good rule of thumb to achieve your professional goals, roughly 70 percent of your social media content should be directly related to work, roughly 20 percent should be supportive, and roughly 10 percent should be social.

FIGURE 8.11

A Customized News Feed on TweetDeck

Twitter

Make Your Content Accessible

Contributing to blogs and wikis increases your organization's knowledge. However, if other people can't find and use your contributions, you have not accomplished your purpose. By naming, labeling, indexing, and tagging (applying keywords to your blogs and other posts) well, you help others find your information (see the Technology Tips about tagging in the "Managing Your Online Reputation" section). Also consider using links to your files to help others open them immediately.

Make Your Messages Authentic and Friendly

Authenticity is key to effective social media messages. Social media readers expect sincerity and the raw truth. Your messages should not come off as spin and should not contradict who you really are. Be clear about your intentions. Your messages should also have a friendly tone. However, authenticity and friendliness do not mean sloppy writing or rudeness. When engaging in collaborative writing, keep a friendly tone even when you disagree with others. Avoid any urges to delete the comments of others or engage in edit wars.[15]

Be Responsive and Help Others

One expectation of social networks is that you are a good member of the community. As a good member, you respond positively to the requests of others and help when possible. As you gain a reputation for responding and helping others, you can expect that other community members will respond and help you.

Respect Boundaries and Avoid Oversharing

The many communication tools available in the emerging Social Age allow people to communicate with nearly anyone at nearly anytime from nearly any location about nearly anything. In other words, the division between professional and private lives is becoming increasingly blurred. Stay observant about where your colleagues draw lines to preserve their lives away from work.

Similarly, notice the frequency with which your colleagues and other contacts appreciate new posts and other social media content. Some employees gain a reputation for oversharing in overall content. They may also overshare when they post so much more than their colleagues that they appear domineering or self-centered.

Managing Your Online Reputation

LO8.4 Build a  credible online reputation.

Mc Graw Hill connect

Visit http://connect. mheducation.com for an exercise on this topic.

Although nearly all business professionals are aware of social networking and the importance of strong online reputations, most are still learning to manage their online presences strategically. And although younger people are often expert at developing an online social persona, they are less skilled at developing an online professional presence.[16] As you read this section, think about the opportunities and risks for you as you develop your online reputation.

First, think carefully about developing a **personal brand** in a professional sense—a unique set of professional skills and attributes that others associate with you.[17] In the final chapter of this book, when we turn to job applications, we discuss the notion of promoting your personal brand in more detail. Here, we introduce the idea of building your personal brand and using it as an asset in your career progression. Increasingly, you will express your personal brand through social media tools. One major goal, then, for your online activities is to build a reputation that showcases your credibility and personal brand.

Whether or not you have intentionally created an online presence, potential and current employers, colleagues, and clients will judge your credibility based on online information about you. Thus, you need to take as much control as you can of your online reputation. As portrayed in Table 8.3, one helpful approach is to consider the meta messages, or overall and underlying messages that others decode from your online communications. These meta messages become one basis for your online reputation.

For example, consider two students, Jenny and Regina, who create blogs about their study-abroad experiences in Spain. Jenny's blog describes her observations of her homestay family, the people in the community, and her efforts to learn Spanish. She frequently talks about the generosity they extend to her. She posts pictures of cultural and historical sites as well as many of the people she meets. Her blog sends a meta message, "I'm grateful to the people in Spain for providing me with such a rich learning experience." This meta message feeds into a reputation for open-mindedness, flexibility, curiosity, and appreciation of others.

Technology Tips

GOOGLE YOURSELF

Most people have casually Googled themselves. Adopting a strategy to periodically Google yourself will help you manage your online reputation. Consider doing the following:

- *Use several combinations of search terms to see what potential employers or others are likely to use.* In addition to your name, consider adding your hometown, city of residence, university, and/or employer.

- *Search through several pages of results.* Most people give up after three to five pages of search results.

- *Sign up for Google alerts.* You can set alerts on Google and other search engines whenever your name is mentioned on the Internet.

- *Search in private or incognito mode.* This will ensure you see the results the way a random person would see them. (Otherwise, the search results are influenced by aspects of your personal information collected through cookies and search history.)

- *Use advanced search tools.* For example, you might limit search results to the past one or two years.

- *Check on other search engines as well,* including Yahoo and Bing.

Robin Beckham/BEEPstock/Alamy Stock Photo

Your challenge: Conduct a search of yourself on several search engines. What is the most visible information? What surprised you? How would you characterize your online reputation? Ideally, what would you like to see in the top ten results when people search your name?

Regina, on the other hand, mostly posts pictures of herself at pubs. She describes the many friends she has made who are also American study-abroad students. Her longest entry explains how glad she was to go to the Hard Rock Café and get a hamburger "just like back at home." To many readers, the meta message Regina sends is, "I'm having a great time with my American friends in Spain." This meta message may feed into a reputation for complacency and closed-mindedness.

Take a few minutes to think about Table 8.3. You will notice a variety of positive meta messages and related reputations. You can see that these meta messages and reputations are grouped into four areas: personal and private, professional and private, personal and public, and professional and public. In each domain of your online communications, you should think about the meta messages you would like to send so that you build a credible reputation. Also, because many of your online communications are accessible to personal friends as well as professional contacts, you need to consider whether you are prioritizing your professional or your social reputation.

Social media tools make developing a personal brand easier than ever. You can broadcast your expertise and business interests to an ever-growing network of business professionals. However, social media tools also make it easier than ever to damage your personal brand and online reputation. When you make inaccurate or unprofessional posts, your incompetency, unprofessionalism, and other mistakes are broadcast to a much larger network. In fact, one mistake can undermine your reputation.[18]

Some business professionals damage their reputations because their social media use sends meta messages that they are self-promoters and careerists. Other employees view

TABLE 8.3

Developing a Credible Online Reputation

	Positive Meta Messages	Sought-After Reputations
Personal and Private (for family and friends) *Example:* a family blog	*I'm a good listener* (competence) *I can take care of you* (competence) *I hope the best for you* (caring) *You can always count on me* (caring) *You can trust me* (character) *I'm a fun person* (character)	Communicative, interpersonal skills Dependable, reliable, capable Considerate, caring, concerned Loyal, committed Honest, trustworthy Fun-loving, exciting
Professional and Private (for work colleagues) *Example:* a corporate blog	*I will get the job done* (competence) *I am a good team member* (competence) *I want you to succeed* (caring) *I want to work with you* (caring) *I will do what I say* (character) *I abide by the rules* (character)	Competent, skilled, dependable Bring out the best in others Supportive, caring Team-oriented, collaborative Sincere, genuine, integrity Moral, ethical, fair
Personal and Public (for society) *Example:* social networking website such as Facebook	*I have certain abilities* (competence) *I have certain interests* (competence) *I want to share my experiences and ideas* (caring) *I want to learn about you* (caring) *I have certain social values and priorities* (character) *I live my life according to certain beliefs* (character)	Talented, skilled, capable Determined, focused, driven Open, networked, independent Inquisitive, curious, considerate Activist, cause-driven, passionate Moral, understanding
Professional and Public (for professional peers) *Example:* professional social networking website such as LinkedIn	*I am an expert* (competent) *I want to lead a professional discussion* (competent) *I want to share my ideas with you* (caring) *I want to understand your experiences* (caring) *I am committed to my industry* (character) *I think my profession should maintain high standards* (character)	Thought leader, forward-thinking Initiative, leadership, open-minded Generous, giving, collaborative Learning, inquisitive, curious Professional, passionate, committed Ethical, disciplined, consistent

their online communications as opportunistic and self-centered, believing the self-promoters place their personal career interests ahead of the organization's interests.[19] Generally, the reputation as a self-promoter comes from excessively drawing attention to one's own professional skills and interests. As you adopt other-oriented, listening-centered approaches to social media use, you can highlight your own professional skills and interests without reaching what others consider excessive self-promotion.

Compare several common types of ineffective and effective posts by Kip (in Figures 8.12, 8.13, 8.14, and 8.15). As far as establishing a professional reputation, two of the most common types of ineffective posts involve political posts and complaining about work. Notice in Figure 8.12 that Kip makes a strongly worded political comment. Even those who agree with him will be surprised by this statement in a professional context. Notice in Figure 8.13 that Kip publicly complains about his work. Not only can this type of statement lead to demotions or job loss in a current position, they can leave a lasting impact on job prospects at future employers.

By contrast, notice the more effective posts in Figures 8.14 and 8.15. These are two of the most common types of effective posts: promoting you employer and sharing positive, motivational, and relevant content. Generally, you should always think

FIGURE 8.12

Less Effective Post
because of Political
Orientation

John A Rizzo/Pixtal/SuperStock;
HERIKA MARTINEZ/AFP/Getty
Images; LinkedIn

about the meta messages you may send with your posts. What type of reputation are you building?

Social media use is particularly well suited for networked communication. As we have discussed, working in networks is an increasingly important skill and integral to success in the emerging Social Age. As part of large professional networks, seek a reputation as a giver, not a taker. Similarly, always honor your commitments. In networked communication, word gets around quickly about which members are considered givers, which honor commitments, and which do not.

FIGURE 8.13

Less Effective Post due
to Complaining

John A Rizzo/Pixtal/SuperStock;
LinkedIn

FIGURE 8.14

More Effective Post due to Promotion of Business

John A Rizzo/Pixtal/SuperStock; Dpa picture alliance/Alamy Stock Photo; LinkedIn

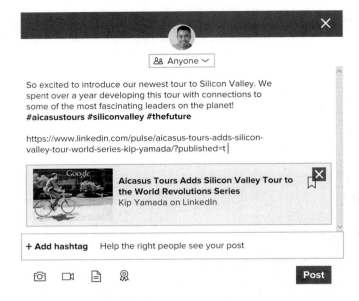

FIGURE 8.15

More Effective Post due to Promotion of Business

John A Rizzo/Pixtal/SuperStock; Matt Anderson Photography/ Moment Open/Getty images; LinkedIn

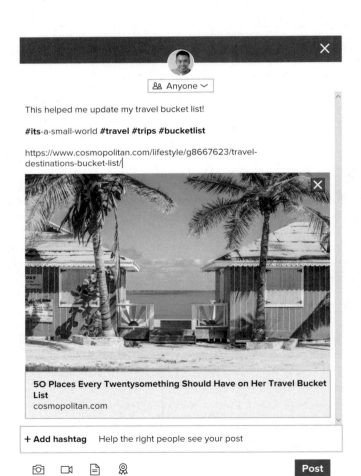

Using Social Media Ethically

The use of social media—even private use—complicates your relationship with your employer. Consider the following cases:[20]

> An employee who works in research and development updates his Facebook status, bemoaning the fact that he has to cancel his weekend golf plans due to yet another project delay. Other Facebook users connect this with a highly anticipated product launch, and the company's stock price declines.

> A salesperson posts a derogatory comment on Twitter about a prospective client's headquarters city as he lands there the day before a critical presentation. Someone forwards the tweet to the CEO, who cancels the meeting.

> An employee is terminated for cause. A few weeks later, she asks a former colleague to recommend her on LinkedIn. The former colleague writes a glowing recommendation. The terminated employee later uses this recommendation as evidence in a discrimination suit, claiming she was terminated unfairly.

LO8.5 Describe the ethical use of social media for work.

As these various examples illustrate, much more than your online reputation is at stake with social media use; the reputation and performance of your company is at stake as well. The line between what you believe is private use of social media and your role as an employee can be murky because your private actions can damage your employer and hurt your career.

In short, constantly try to understand evolving norms for social media use in a professional context. For your own protection and that of your company, become familiar with your company's acceptable-use policies for social networking websites. Coca-Cola recently compiled a set of social media guidelines for its employees (see the guidelines at this link: www.coca-colacompany.com/stories/online-social-media-principles). The guidelines include statements such as the following: "You are responsible for your actions. We encourage you to get online and have fun, but use sound judgment and common sense." "You are an important ambassador for our Company's brands, and you're encouraged to promote them as long as you *make sure you disclose that you are affiliated with the Company.*" "When you see posts or commentary on topics that require subject matter expertise, such as ingredients, obesity, the Company's environmental impacts, or the Company's financial performance, avoid the temptation to respond to these directly."[21] In addition to understanding your organization's external social media policies, seek advice about using social media tools within the organization.

IDEAS IN ACTION

BUILDING YOUR PERSONAL BRAND THROUGH SOCIAL MEDIA

Conversations with Current Business Professionals

Sir Richard Branson is the charismatic and energetic founder of the Virgin Group, a group of companies in travel and leisure, music and entertainment, financial services, and even aerospace, among other industries. Aside from his immense business success, Branson is known for his philanthropy, humanitarianism, and commitment to his employees. Interestingly, he started his career as a journalist. This natural tendency to develop content for wide audiences has served him well on social media. He is among the most widely followed executives on social media. For example, he has roughly 13 million followers on Twitter who enjoy the career advice and motivational quotes he dispenses.

Sir Richard Branson Uses Social Media Extensively to Promote His Businesses and Many Social Causes.

Alex Wong/Getty Images

Branson adopts many strategies to build his own professional brand and draw positive attention to the Virgin Group. Whether it's career advice, social causes, or exciting developments (i.e., travel to space!), he focuses on content that is helpful and inspirational. He often interacts with people who post on his social media sites. He uses a conversational, friendly tone and makes it fun! Importantly, he drives traffic to the Virgin website.

As you think about your own professional persona, check out how Branson uses his social channels. Also, check out how other professionals in your target profession are using social media to build their own professional reputations. That will help you develop your own unique style.

Sources: Branson, R. (2017, October 20). Richard Branson on how social media changed the way he does business: Even in social media's early days, it spread like wildfire. *Thrive Global*. Retrieved from thriveglobal.com/stories/richard-branson-on-how-social-media-changed-the-way-he-does-business/; Mitchell, D. (2016, June 6). 4 ways Richard Branson does social media better than you. *Entrepreneur*. Retrieved from www.entrepreneur.com/article/275472.

Chapter Takeaway for *Social Media for Business Communication*

LO8.1 Explain characteristics of the emerging Social Age.

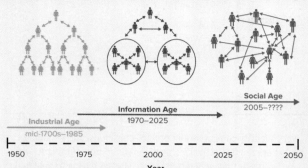

Characteristics of the Social Age
• Networked communication.   • Respect for expertise and contributions to the network.   • Knowledge sharing.   • Transparency, honesty, and camaraderie.

LO8.2 Use blogs, forums, and other social tools for effective communication within organizations.

Principles for Using Forums
• Read your peers' comments completely and carefully.   • State the purpose of the forum clearly.   • Use flexible, open, and inviting language.   • Build on the ideas of others and pose questions.   • Show appreciation for your teammates and their ideas.   • Participate often.   • Meet in real time for touchy points.   • Summarize and, as appropriate, identify next steps.   • Talk with your team about ways to make forums help your decision making and coordination.

Principles for Using Internal Communication Tools in the Social Age
• Organize your dashboard to control your communication and information flow.   • Create a complete and professional profile.   • Use blogs and status updates for team communication.   • Use shared files to collaborate.   • Solve problems with discussion forums.

General Principles for Using Social Media
• Be an active contributor and join communities.   • Read, listen, and learn.   • Focus on content.   • Make your content accessible.   • Make your messages authentic and friendly.   • Be responsive and help others.   • Respect boundaries and avoid oversharing.

See *examples of a profile* in Figure 8.2, a *blog used for announcements* in Figure 8.3, *status updates for team coordination* in Figure 8.4, and *appropriate reactions to shared files* in Figure 8.5.
See an *ineffective example of a forum* in Figure 8.6 and an *effective example of a forum* in Figure 8.7.

LO8.3 Create blogs and other social posts for effective external communications.

See a *press-release style corporate blog post* in Figure 8.8, an *op-ed style blog post* in Figure 8.9, and an *example of a professional blog post* in Figure 8.10.

LO8.4 Build a credible online reputation.

See Table 8.3 for *types of positive meta messages you seek to establish your online reputation.*
See *examples of ineffective and effective social posts* in Figures 8.12 through 8.15.

LO8.5 Describe the ethical use of social media for work.

Key Terms

blogs, 237

corporate reputation, 245

microblogs, 238

personal brand, 252

project blogs, 238

Social Age, 234

social media, 234

team blogs, 238

User 1.0, 234

User 2.0, 234

Web 1.0, 234

Web 2.0, 234

Discussion Exercises

8.1 Chapter Review Questions (LO8.1, LO8.2, LO8.3, LO8.4, LO8.5)

A. What are some characteristics of the Social Age?

B. What are some strategies for organizing a dashboard to help you work more efficiently with your teams?

C. What do you think are some of the most important pieces of information for a professional profile on an enterprise social networking platform?

D. When do you think you should use blogs and status updates in teams? How should you decide which to use?

E. What do you think are the primary challenges to running an effective forum?

F. Which strategies do you consider most important when leading a forum? Explain.

G. What elements of tone are most important for social media messages?

H. What strategies can you use to build a credible online reputation?

I. How can you use social media ethically from the perspective of your employer?

8.2 Ideas in Action Discussion Questions (LO8.1, LO8.2, LO8.5)

A. What influence do you think Sir Richard Branson's background in journalism had on his current social media behavior? What can you learn from journalists as you think about your social media presence?

B. Based on the Ideas in Action feature as well as your review of Branson's social media activity, how would you categorize the content of his posts? Which posts are most effective and why?

C. Based on the Ideas in Action feature as well as your review of Branson's social media activity, how would you categorize the tone of his posts? What type of tone would you like to adopt in your posts?

8.3 Social Media, Online Expression, and Collaboration (LO8.1, LO8.2, LO8.4)

Vineet Nayar, former CEO of HCL Technologies, commented about the use of new communication channels. He specifically mentioned the use of social networking and the growing importance of Web 2.0 tools:

> As my kids became teenagers, I started looking at Facebook a little more closely. It was a significant amount of collaboration. There was open understanding. They didn't have a problem sharing their status. Nothing seemed to be secret, and they were living their lives very openly, and friends were commenting on each other and it was working. Here is my generation, which is very security-conscious and privacy-conscious, and I thought, what are the differences? This is the generation coming to work for us. It's not my generation. So we started having people make their presentations and record them for our internal website. We open that for review to a 360-degree workshop, which means your subordinates will review it. Your managers will read it. Your peers will read it, and everybody will comment on it. I will be, or your manager will be, one of the many who read it. So, every presentation was reviewed by 300, 400 people. What happened? There were two very interesting lessons that I learned. One, because your subordinates are going to see the plan, you cannot lie. You have to be honest. Two, because your peers are going to see it, you are going to put your best work into it. Third, you didn't learn from me. You learned by reviewing somebody else's presentation. You learned from the comments somebody else gave you. For the 8,000 people who participated, there was a massive collaborative learning that took place.[22]

Based on Nayar's comments and your own experiences, answer the following questions:

A. What are the potential personal and group benefits from using Web 2.0 communication channels?

B. What are some of the differing attitudes between generations about online expression? What impact might these differences have on workplace communication?

C. In what ways do online communications lead to more honesty and higher-quality work?

D. In what ways might online communications lead to less honesty and lower-quality work?

8.4 Challenges to Adopting Social Media for Professional Use (LO8.1, LO8.2, LO8.5)

Andrew McAfee, one of the premier experts on Enterprise 2.0 systems, commented about the challenges of adopting such systems and the shift in orientation needed by management to unleash a culture of User 2.0.

> I thought these technologies [such as Facebook, Wikipedia, Flickr, and YouTube] were essentially so cool that when you dropped them in an organization, people flocked to them. That was the assumption I carried around in my research. I very quickly had that overturned. This is not an overnight phenomenon at all. And while there are pockets of energy, getting mass adoption remains a pretty serious challenge for a lot of organizations.
>
> If you're a middle manager who essentially views your job as one of gatekeeping or refereeing information flows, you should be pretty frightened by these technologies, because they're going to greatly reduce your ability to do that. If you're someone who

sees your job as managing people and fundamentally getting the human elements right that will lead your part of the organization to succeed, these technologies are not at all harmful to you. One of the things that we've learned is that there's no technology—even these great new social technologies—that's a substitute for face time. If you have another view of yourself, which is that you're someone who's responsible for output, these tools should be your best friend. Because all the evidence we have suggests that Enterprise 2.0 helps you turn out more and better products and actually is not a vehicle for time wasting or for chipping away at what you're supposed to be doing throughout the day.[23]

Based on McAfee's comments, contents of the chapter, and your own experiences, respond to the following questions:

A. What are the major obstacles to adopting Web 2.0 communication tools in the workplace?

B. McAfee distinguishes between information gatekeepers and managers of people. Explain what you think he means by this distinction and its relevance to the adoption of social software.

C. When are Web 2.0 communication tools more efficient than Web 1.0 communication tools such as email?

D. When are Web 1.0 communication tools such as email better choices than Web 2.0 communication tools?

E. Place yourself in the position of a middle or upper manager. Describe two ways in which the use of social media tools by your subordinates would benefit you and two ways in which they would threaten you.

8.5 Setting Boundaries (LO8.4, LO8.5)

In a survey of corporate employees, 76 percent thought it was OK to friend another employee who was a peer. Only 35 percent thought it was OK to friend a supervisor, and only 30 percent thought it was OK to friend a supervisee.[24] Answer the following related questions:

A. Do you think it is appropriate to friend a supervisor or supervisee on Facebook or another social networking website? What problems could arise by doing so? What work benefits might you achieve? What social boundaries should exist between supervisors and supervisees?

B. Do you think the boundaries between private life and work life are blurred by communication technologies such as social networking? What standards or principles do you want to use to keep parts of your private life separate from your colleagues?

C. Have you ever talked to your colleagues or classmates about your communication preferences? For example, have you discussed preferences for certain communication channels or expected response times? Describe your experiences.

8.6 Ethical Use of Social Media (LO8.5)

Reread the three examples of personal social media use that hurt employers (see the beginning of the "Using Social Media Ethically" section). For each item, do the following:

A. Explain why the social media use was unethical.

B. Describe a similar behavior you have observed.

C. Recommend how employees can avoid such problems.

8.7 Corporate Social Media Guidelines (LO8.5)

Read Coca-Cola's social media guidelines at the following link: http://www.coca-colacompany.com/stories/online-social-media-principles. Respond to the following items:

A. Generally, what is the difference between speaking "on behalf of the Company" and speaking "about" the company?

B. The policy states that employees are responsible for following the Code of Business Conduct in all public settings. Do you think your online activities on public social networking websites constitute a public setting? Explain.

C. The policy tells employees they should be "conscientious when mixing your business and personal lives." Give five examples of posts that many people might consider private or personal *and* that could damage a company's image.

D. The policy encourages employees to post items that "inspire moments of optimism and happiness." Give five options for employees to make these types of posts. What value do these types of posts provide to Coca-Cola? How might posting as a Coca-Cola employee create opportunities for employees?

E. What types of online conversations about the company are appropriate? Inappropriate?

Evaluation Exercises

8.8 Choosing the Right Type of Digital Message (LO8.1, LO8.2)

For each of the following communication tasks, identify which communication channel you think would work best: email, blogs, or wikis. Write several sentences explaining why you would choose that communication channel. Assume you are a manager sending these messages to your subordinates:

A. Giving updates about an ongoing project.

B. Providing feedback on individual performance.

C. Sending a note of appreciation to one of your subordinates for excellent work.

D. Providing meeting minutes.

E. Setting up a working document about ground rules for participation in meetings.

F. Extending birthday wishes.

G. Sharing ideas with a few but not all of your subordinates.

H. Announcing a meeting for the whole team.

I. Announcing a meeting with two of the team members.

J. Working on a joint marketing proposal.

8.9 Evaluation of a Professional Blog (LO8.3, LO8.4)

Choose a professional blog of interest to you. Read a minimum of ten posts. Then, in one to two pages, respond to the following questions:

A. What is the name and web address of the blog?

B. What is the target audience for this blog?

C. How does the content meet the needs of readers?

D. Why would the target audience choose this blog over other similar blogs?

E. How does the blog author(s) establish credibility?

F. What type of online reputation does the blog author(s) create?

G. What design features make the blog effective?

H. What three aspects of this blog will you apply most to your blog?

8.10 Evaluation of the Tweets of Business Leaders (LO8.3, LO8.4, LO8.5).

View the recent tweets of two or three business leaders (you might consider looking for accounts of business leaders you're interested in, or you could find lists of business leaders' accounts such as the following: https://cultbizztech.com/10-ceos-follow-twitter/). Then, write a short report about your observations of these business leaders' tweets. Include the following in your short report:

A. Comparisons between the tweets of your chosen business leaders in terms of the following: (1) style and content of tweets, (2) frequency of tweets, and (3) goals of tweets.

B. Three tips for business leaders when they create tweets.

8.11 Evaluating Your Online Reputation (LO8.4)

A. Currently, what type of online reputation do you have in a professional sense?

B. In four or five sentences, explain the personal brand you would like to develop over the next five years.

C. Explain three strategies you will employ to develop your personal brand in your online communications. Devote at least one paragraph to each strategy.

8.12 Sending the Right Meta Messages with Your Online Communications (LO8.4)

Using Table 8.3 as a guide, do the following for each domain of your online reputation: personal and private, professional and private, personal and public, and professional and public:

A. What are the online communication channels you will use for each domain?

B. Will you use the same channels for more than one domain? If you share any of the communication channels for more than one domain, how will you prioritize which audiences to choose content for?

C. What are the primary meta messages you want to send? Choose two meta messages for each domain and explain how you intend to send these meta messages.

Application Exercises

8.13 Digital Sabbatical (LO8.1, LO8.5)

For 24 hours, avoid using your mobile device or a computer for any communication or accessing online information. (You might consider notifying your friends and family that you will be unavailable during this period.) Write a one- to two-page account of your experience. Consider including discussion about the following:

A. How you felt going without communication (anxiety, relief, stress, peace, etc.).

B. How you felt going without access to digital information (empowered, helpless, out of the loop, etc.).

C. How you think going without digital communications impacts your quality of life, productivity, and/or routines.

D. Based on your experience, give two or three recommendations for how professionals should go about handling digital communication and information.

8.14 Social News Reader (LO8.2, LO8.4)

Using a social reading platform (such as LinkedIn, Flipboard, or Feedly), set up a feed of articles and posts that match your professional interests. At a minimum, take the following actions:

A. Follow at least five feeds in your business discipline (e.g., marketing, finance).

B. Follow at least five feeds from an industry of interest.

C. Follow at least five feeds from organizations of interest.

D. Follow at least five feeds of professionals you admire.

Experiment with your social reader for at least one week. Then, report the following:

A. What are the professional interests that you cater to with your social reader?

B. What platform did you use? How easy was it to set up feeds for information of interest?

C. What content is most useful and interesting?

D. What adjustments have you made to make your social reader more useful?

E. What strategies will you use in the future to use social readers for professional purposes?

8.15 Twitter News Feed (LO8.2, LO8.4)

Using TweetDeck or another similar platform, set up a news feed based on searches. Use a minimum of ten hashtags for your searches. Experiment with your search-based news feed for at least one week. Then, report the following:

A. What are the professional interests that you cater to with your search-based news feed?

B. What platform did you use? How easy was it to set up feeds for information of interest?

C. What content is most useful and interesting?

D. What adjustments have you made to make your searches more effective at providing interesting content?

E. What strategies will you use in the future to use search-based news feeds for professional purposes?

8.16 LinkedIn Profile (LO8.4)

Based on your LinkedIn profile, respond to the following items:

A. What is your LinkedIn profile address?

B. What are the main traits that stand out about you on your LinkedIn page?

C. What are the main abilities that stand out about you on your LinkedIn page?

D. Which parts of your LinkedIn profile best promote who you are as a professional?

E. Which parts of your LinkedIn profile least promote who you are as a professional?

F. What are three changes you intend to make to improve your LinkedIn profile?

G. What three groups would you like to join and participate in?

H. Which three organizations should you follow? Why?

I. Which three professionals should you follow? Why?

8.17 Professional Blog (LO8.3, LO8.4)

Write a blog about a business issue or topic of interest to you and that provides content that is valuable to others. You should develop the blog with a specific audience in mind and provide original,

insightful entries. Also, you should develop your blog with your own career interests and desired online reputation in mind. You will write five entries. Each entry should be roughly 700 to 1,000 words. The five entries should combine to meet the needs of your target audience and develop your personal brand. For each blog post, consider applying the following formula: (a) one or two takeaway messages; (b) a catchy title and opening; (c) a winning tone for blogs—helpful, personalized, positive, informative, fun, and interesting; (d) hyperlinks to interesting articles, videos, etc.; (e) images if you'd like (not required); and (f) concise writing with fairly short paragraphs.

Language Mechanics Check

8.22 Review the numbers, dates, and currency rules in Appendix A. Then, rewrite each sentence to correct the numbers, dates, and currency where needed.

A. We should focus on these 2 markets for now.

B. We should focus on seven of the fifteen geographic regions.

C. 15 regions will have new supervisors as of June 20th, 2020.

D. Each purchase above 500 dollars must be approved by June 31st, 2019 to get reimbursed.

E. Employees can contribute up to 7.5% of their salaries to the retirement plan.

F. Nearly 1/3 of our employees contribute the maximum amount to retirement plans.

G. Employees may have up to 4 2MB websites.

H. Employees make an average of 23 dollars per hour.

I. Our revenue for the year topped $2,500,000,000.

J. We gave employee recognition awards to nearly 2/3 (65.3%) of our employees last quarter.

Endnotes

1. Chui, M., Manyika, J., Bughin, J., Dobbs, R., Roxburgh, C., Sarrazin, H., Sands, G., & Westergren, M. (2012, July). *The social economy: Unlocking value and productivity through social technologies.* McKinsey Global Institute.

2. Azua, M. (2010). *The social factor: Innovate, ignite, and win through mass collaboration and social networking.* Upper Saddle River, NJ: IBM Press.

3. Chui, M., Miller, A., & Roberts, R. P. (2010). Six ways to make Web 2.0 work. *McKinsey Quarterly.*

4. Wright, S., & Zdinak, J. (2008). *New communication behaviors in a Web 2.0 world—Changes, challenges and opportunities in the era of the Information Revolution.* Paris: Alcatel-Lucent, 10.

5. Wright, S., & Zdinak, J. (2008). *New communication behaviors in a Web 2.0 World—Changes, challenges and opportunities in the era of the Information Revolution.* Paris: Alcatel-Lucent; Kaplan, A. M., & Haenlein, M. (2010). Users of the world, unite! The challenges and opportunities of social media. *Business Horizons, 53*(1), 59–68; AON Consulting. (2009, March). *Web 2.0 and employee communications: Summary of survey findings.* Chicago: AON Consulting; Bughin, J., Chui, M., & Miller, A. (2009). How companies are benefiting from Web 2.0. *McKinsey Quarterly, 17*(9); McAfee, A. (2009). *Enterprise 2.0: New collaborative tools for your organization's toughest challenges.* Boston: Harvard Business Press.

6. McAfee, A. (2009). *Enterprise 2.0: New collaborative tools for your organization's toughest challenges.* Boston: Harvard Business Press.

7. Chui, M., Manyika, J., Bughin, J., Dobbs, R., Roxburgh, C., Sarrazin, H., Sands, G., & Westergren, M. (2012, July). *The social economy: Unlocking value and productivity through social technologies.* McKinsey Global Institute.

8. Wright, S., & Zdinak, J. (2008). *New communication behaviors in a Web 2.0 World—Changes, challenges and opportunities in the era of the Information Revolution.* Paris: Alcatel-Lucent.

9. Beal, A., & Straus, J. (2008). *Radically transparent: Monitoring and managing reputations online.* Indianapolis, IN: Wiley Publishing.

10. Schreiber, E. S. (2011, January 14). Reputation. *Institute for Public Relations.* Retrieved from www.instituteforpr.org/topics/reputation/.

11. Schreiber, E. S. (2011, January 14). Reputation. *Institute for Public Relations.* Retrieved from www.instituteforpr.org/topics/reputation/.

12. Deutsche, P. (2011). *Elements of a PR plan.* San Francisco: e-agency.

13. Nations, D. (2010, November 20). The business wiki. Retrieved from http://webtrends.about.com/od/wiki/a/business-wiki.htm.

14. Goetz Boue, *Don't Say Web 2.0, Say Intranet 2.0* (London: Concentra, 2009); Dutta, S. (2010, November). Managing yourself: What's your personal social media strategy. *Harvard Business Review.* Retrieved from hbr.org/2010/11/managing-yourself-whats-your-personal-social-media-strategy; Beal, A., & Straus, J. (2008). *Radically transparent: Monitoring and managing reputations online.* Indianapolis, IN: Wiley Publishing.

15. Dutta, S. (2010, November). Managing yourself: What's your personal social media strategy. *Harvard Business Review.* Retrieved from hbr.org/2010/11/managing-yourself-whats-your-personal-social-media-strategy.

16. Hyatt, J. (2010, August 16). Building your brand and keeping your job. *Fortune,* 74.

17. Adapted from Dutta, S. (2010, November). Managing yourself: What's your personal social media strategy. *Harvard Business Review,* 129. Retrieved from hbr.org/2010/11/managing-yourself-whats-your-personal-social-media-strategy.

18. Hyatt, J. (2010, August 16). Building your brand and keeping your job. *Fortune,* 74.

19. Arnold, J. T. (2009, December 1). Twittering and Facebooking while they work. *HR Magazine, 54*(12).

20. Arnold, J. T. (2009, December 1). Twittering and Facebooking while they work. *HR Magazine, 54*(12).

21. Coca-Cola. (n.d.). *Social media principles.* Retrieved from http://www.coca-colacompany.com/stories/online-social-media-principles.

22. Bryant, A. (2010). He's not Bill Gates, or Fred Astaire. *The New York Times.*

23. Roger P. Roberts, R. P. (2010). An interview with MIT's Andrew McAfee. *McKinsey Quarterly, 1.*

24. Edelman Trust Barometer 2007 as presented in Beal, A., & Straus, J. (2008). *Radically transparent: Monitoring and managing reputations online.* Indianapolis, IN: Wiley Publishing.

Types of Business Messages

PART FOUR

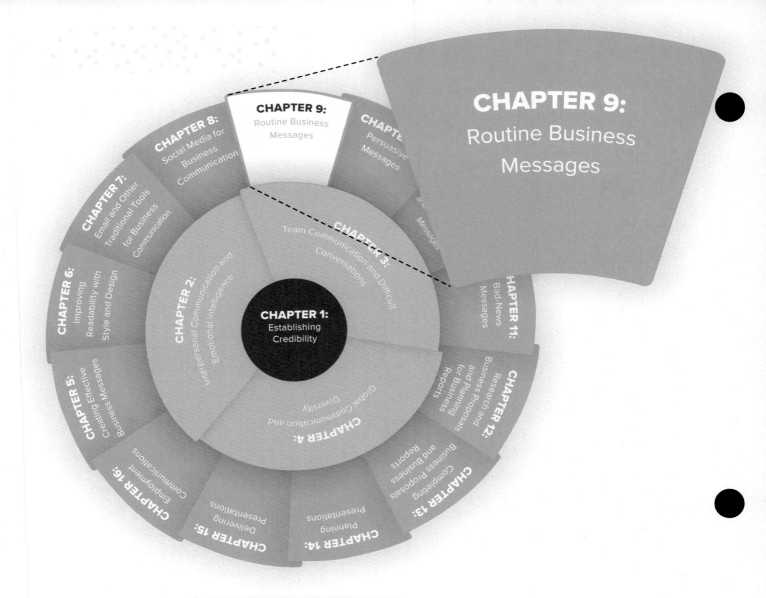

CHAPTER 9:
Routine Business
Messages

CHAPTER 9:
Routine Business
Messages

ESTABLISHING CREDIBILITY

PRINCIPLES OF INTERPERSONAL COMMUNICATION

PRINCIPLES FOR & TYPES OF BUSINESS MESSAGES

LEARNING OBJECTIVES

After studying this chapter, you should be able to do the following:

LO9.1 Describe how delivering routine messages impacts credibility.

LO9.2 Describe the process for developing routine business messages.

LO9.3 Construct task-oriented routine messages, including requests, expectations, directions,

responses to inquiries, announcements, and claims.

LO9.4 Construct relationship-oriented routine messages, including appreciation, congratulations, apologies, and expressions of sympathy.

The vast majority of business messages are routine. In routine messages, you are dealing with straightforward information that does not require in-depth analysis, so you generally expect your readers to react positively, and you do not anticipate resistance.

Most routine messages are simple. Yet, routine messages should not be treated as unimportant or inconsequential. They are the glue that holds together most coordinated business actions. In this chapter, we discuss common types of routine messages. Many of them primarily focus on work tasks, such as making requests, setting expectations, providing directions, making inquiries, providing announcements, and making claims. Other routine messages focus on maintaining and improving workplace relationships, such as showing appreciation, giving congratulations, offering apologies, and expressing sympathy. The final two types of messages, apologies and expressions of sympathy, are unlike other messages in this chapter in that they occur far less frequently. However, like other messages in this chapter, they are fairly straightforward and require you to compose them fairly quickly.

The day-in-and-day-out routine messages you send may be among the most important for establishing your credibility in the workplace, especially early in your business career. Your approach to routine business messages strongly influences how others evaluate your responsiveness, reliability, attention to detail, commitment, and professionalism.

Read the chapter case about a typical morning at work for Bryan Atkins, an account executive at an advertising firm. Throughout the chapter, you'll see the routine messages Bryan completes before 11 a.m. While Bryan can answer most routine messages with emails of less than one paragraph, we focus on those examples that require slightly more effort. As a result, the examples are generally three to five paragraphs long.

> **Hear Pete Cardon explain why this matters.**
> **bit.ly/cardon9**

LO9.1 Describe how delivering routine messages impacts credibility.

CHAPTER CASE ROUTINE EMAILS AT SMITH & SMITH ADVERTISING

Bryan Atkins

WHO'S INVOLVED

Account Executive at Smith & Smith Advertising
- Works extensively with clients to ensure they are satisfied with various advertising campaigns
- Leads and coordinates work with the creative teams working on these campaigns

Bryan Requests Software Licenses for Several Marketing Analysts
Bryan and several marketing analysts had spent the past few weeks discussing the purchase of statistical software. The software would help the analysts better target customers with online ads and predict online campaign performance. Bryan

SITUATION 1 (8 A.M.)

michaeljung/123RF

needs approval from one of the partners, Andrea Johansen, to purchase the software licenses. He thought this was a straightforward request but knew Andrea expected him to provide a rationale for and details about the software purchases.

SITUATION 2 (9 A.M.)

Bryan Responds to Messages in His Inbox from Employees and Prospects

After the meeting, Bryan sat down at his computer to find 37 new messages from colleagues, clients, and prospects. Bryan thought all of the messages were important enough that he needed to respond to them within two to three hours. Several were most urgent:

- A member of the creative team, Barry Evermore, said he and his partner, John Anderson, had just finished an account and were waiting for new assignments.
- A new member of the creative team, John Anderson (Barry Evermore's partner), was scheduled to take a company trip, but he was unfamiliar with travel procedures at Smith & Smith. He was asking Bryan how to set up his trip.
- A potential client emailed Bryan about services offered by Smith & Smith.

SITUATION 3 (9:30 A.M.)

Bryan Makes an Announcement

Bryan works on a committee of account executives and IT specialists to create policies for the firm. The committee just created new bring your own device (BYOD) policies. He will finish drafting a memo to let all employees know about the new policies.

SITUATION 4 (9:40 A.M.)

Bryan Takes Care of Overcharges from a Vendor

This morning, Bryan noticed that a hotel had overcharged Smith & Smith by not applying a negotiated rate to several hotel stays for members of his creative team. He wanted to resolve the matter immediately.

SITUATION 5 (10:05 A.M.)

Bryan Shows Appreciation to His Creative Team

During the morning, Bryan took a call from a recent client, Ana Galleraga, director of the local zoo. "Hey, Bryan," she said. "Just wanted to let you know what a great success we're having with the ad campaign you developed. Since we started putting up billboard ads and running the radio spots last month, we've increased participation in all of our community educational programs. We're also getting lots of comments about how beautiful the billboards are. Please let everyone over there know what a great job they've done. And, we'd like to figure out how to use the campaign concept in our online marketing." Of course, Bryan told her that the agency could help her out in that regard.

SITUATION 6 (10:30 A.M.)

Bryan Issues a Brief Apology

Over the weekend, Bryan worried about insensitive comments he made in last Friday's leadership team meeting. Bryan had accused his colleagues of caring more about one of their clients than about their own employees. This particular client frequently made unreasonable requests, but Bryan and other members of the executive management team never pushed back because the client accounted for nearly one-quarter of Smith & Smith's total revenues. Bryan will apologize quickly at the beginning of the team's 10:30 meeting.

SITUATION 7 (11:30 A.M.)

Bryan Expresses Sympathy to a Longtime Client

Bryan wanted to write a sympathy card to his close client Felipe Bravo. Over the weekend, Felipe's wife, Rosa, passed away after a long battle with cancer. Bryan and Felipe have worked together for nearly a decade, and Bryan wanted to express his genuine sympathy to Felipe.

TASK

1
How will Bryan write a routine request for the purchase of new software? (See the "Making Requests" section.)

2
- How can Bryan best set expectations for Barry and John's upcoming work schedule? (See "Setting Expectations.")
- How can Bryan most efficiently help John make travel plans? (See "Providing Directions.")
- How can Bryan respond in a way that best answers the potential client's questions and maximizes the likelihood that he will become a client? (See "Responding to Inquiries.")

3
How should Bryan announce the firm's new BYOD policy so that his colleagues will get all the key information rapidly? (See the "Creating Announcements" section.)

4
How should Bryan make sure the excessive charges are refunded or credited? (See "Making Claims.")

5
How should Bryan go about congratulating his creative team on its excellent work? (See "Showing Appreciation.")

6
How can Bryan make amends for his inappropriate comments? (See the "Making Apologies" section.)

7
How should Bryan express condolences to his client? (See "Expressing Sympathy.")

Developing Routine Messages

Since you will send and receive so many routine messages in any given business day, one of your primary goals is efficiency: You need to produce credible messages quickly. Excellent business communicators can develop routine written messages—even those that require several paragraphs—in a matter of minutes. The examples in this chapter should generally take 5 to 15 minutes to complete.

Typically, routine messages require less time to complete than other types of business messages. Also, compared to other types of business messages, routine messages require proportionately less time for planning and reviewing. *Developing routine messages quickly, however, does not mean abandoning the writing process of planning, drafting, and reviewing.*

For most routine messages, you can accomplish the AIM planning process fairly quickly (see Figure 9.1). Because you generally are working with straightforward matters and your audience is likely to respond positively, you don't need much time for *audience analysis* or *information gathering*. Still, make sure to identify and gather relevant, accurate, and up-to-date information. Ask yourself questions such as the following: *How would my audience want to receive this information? How much detail do my audience members expect?*

The most important planning step is *message development*. Since routine messages are so common and your readers are likely overloaded with so many other messages and tasks, your primary challenge is to make sure your readers pay attention. Therefore, your message should be direct and front-loaded. The primary message should have ten words or fewer, and you should typically place it in the subject line of your email to immediately capture attention. Furthermore, the primary message should appear in the first sentence or two of the message and again in the closing if your message is several paragraphs long.

In the body of the routine message, you should provide short paragraphs with related details. To make sure your message receiver will comply, include all needed information. Not only are readers less likely to comply when you don't provide enough information, but you also lose credibility. Once you establish a reputation for providing

LO9.2 Describe the process for developing routine business messages.

McGraw Hill connect

Visit **http://connect. mheducation.com** for an exercise on this topic.

Components of Routine Messages

- State the *primary message* (ten words or fewer).
- Provide *details* in paragraphs of 20 to 80 words.
- *Restate* the request or key message in more specific terms.
- State *goodwill*.

FIGURE 9.1

The Writing
Process for Routine
Messages

PLAN: Get the content right.

- Identify the exact needs of your *audience*.
- Gather relevant, accurate, and up-to-date *information*.
- Create a front-loaded, direct, complete, and detail-oriented *message*.

WRITE: Get the delivery right.

- Aim for a helpful, professional, reader-centered *tone*. Show respect for your readers' time.
- Apply a concise, easy-to-read, action-oriented *style*.
- Use subject lines and formatting to create a simple navigational *design*.

REVIEW: Double-check everything.

- Get *feedback* when writing on behalf of a team or unit.
- Ensure your message is *FAIR*.
- Make sure to *proofread*.

incomplete, overly general messages, your readers are less likely to pay close attention to your future messages.

As you *write* the message, aim for a helpful, professional, and reader-centered tone. Focus on making the message easy to read. Readers expect to understand your primary message in under 10 to 15 seconds, so use short sentences and paragraphs. Design your message so readers can find information in just moments. Use bullets, numbering, special formatting, and external links to relevant information to highlight key ideas.

Your proofreading in the *reviewing* stage should take a minute or two. Since business professionals send so many routine messages each day and their content can be repetitive, they often do not take time to reread them. Avoid this impulse to hit "send" without rereading your messages. By rereading, you will make sure the content is complete and without errors. Even minor typos can distract your readers from complying with your messages.

Since routine messages are straightforward and rarely sensitive, you generally do not need to ask for feedback from trusted colleagues. However, when you speak on behalf of your team, you might check with other team members to ensure they agree about the content. The most important aspect of the FAIR test is checking for accuracy—that is, making certain your information is accurate and reliable.

LO9.3 Construct task-oriented routine messages, including requests, expectations, directions, responses to inquiries, announcements, and claims.

Making Requests

You will make thousands of requests of others during your career, and others will make thousands of requests of you. Requests are the essence of people coordinating work efforts, buying and selling products and services, and maintaining work relationships.

Routine requests involve cases where you expect little or no resistance from message recipients. Like all routine messages, routine requests should contain clear and specific subject lines, often stating the entire *request*. As you reread the message before sending it, one question you'll ask yourself is whether the message recipient will understand exactly what to do.

For most requests, you will use a portion of the message to provide the *rationale* for the request. Since you expect a favorable response, you typically do not need to be particularly persuasive. However, justifying the request shows your professionalism and attention to detail. It also helps a company maintain transparency by keeping written records of why certain decisions were made.

One primary goal for routine requests is to retain *goodwill* with the recipient. No one wants to feel bossed around, so make sure you achieve a positive, other-oriented tone. Also, when working with superiors, be careful about setting deadlines. Even in today's flatter organizations, being bossy to the boss can be counterproductive. Finally, when making requests, showing respect for the recipient's time goes a long way in maintaining goodwill.

In Bryan's request memo to Andrea for new software (see Figures 9.2 and 9.3), the request is routine because Andrea will likely approve his request. The primary goal is to convey the information in an easy-to-read, complete format. In the more effective message (see Figure 9.3), Bryan justifies the request with sufficient rationale and detail. He is direct but not bossy or domineering, which is important since he is writing to his boss.

Mc Graw Hill **connect**

Visit http://connect. mheducation.com for an exercise on this topic.

> **Components of Requests**
> ___
> - Make request.
> - Provide rationale.
> - Call to action.*
> - State goodwill.
>
> *Optional—appropriate at the end of lengthy messages

FIGURE 9.2

Less Effective Routine Request

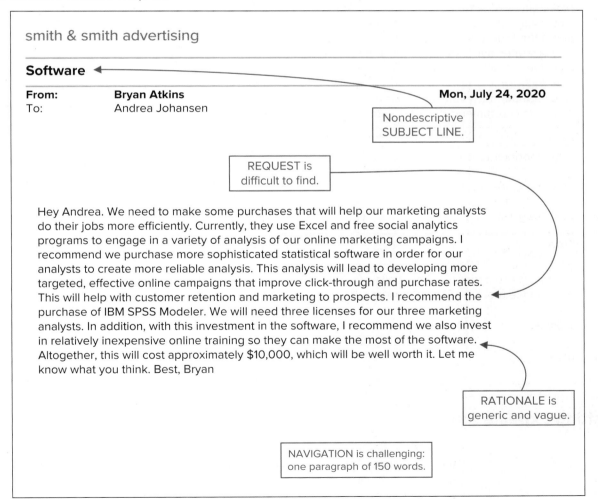

smith & smith advertising

Software ← *Nondescriptive SUBJECT LINE.*

From: **Bryan Atkins**   **Mon, July 24, 2020**
To: Andrea Johansen

REQUEST is difficult to find.

Hey Andrea. We need to make some purchases that will help our marketing analysts do their jobs more efficiently. Currently, they use Excel and free social analytics programs to engage in a variety of analysis of our online marketing campaigns. I recommend we purchase more sophisticated statistical software in order for our analysts to create more reliable analysis. This analysis will lead to developing more targeted, effective online campaigns that improve click-through and purchase rates. This will help with customer retention and marketing to prospects. I recommend the purchase of IBM SPSS Modeler. We will need three licenses for our three marketing analysts. In addition, with this investment in the software, I recommend we also invest in relatively inexpensive online training so they can make the most of the software. Altogether, this will cost approximately $10,000, which will be well worth it. Let me know what you think. Best, Bryan

RATIONALE is generic and vague.

NAVIGATION is challenging: one paragraph of 150 words.

FIGURE 9.3

More Effective Routine Request

---

smith & smith advertising

SUBJECT LINE short (9 words) but effective.

Purchase of IBM SPSS Modeler for Our Marketing Analysts

From: **Bryan Atkins**   **Mon, July 24, 2020**

To: Andrea Johansen

REQUEST stated clearly and upfront.

Dear Andrea:

Can you provide a purchase authorization for statistical software for our three marketing analysts?

During the past month, our marketing analysts (Moku Singh, Elissa Morales, and Josh Liebowitz) and I have explored ways to improve the prediction and tracking of online ad campaigns. Over the past few years, the analyst team members have relied primarily on spreadsheets and other basic statistical software. With more complex data than ever, they now need more sophisticated tools.

RATIONALE is specific and clear.

Moku and Josh attended several workshops this past month about using various statistical software packages. They also talked to marketing analysts at other firms about the tools they use. One of their contacts showed them how she improved click-through rates and purchases on several online ad campaigns by more than 40 percent by using predictive modeling and other techniques.

After comparing several software packages and learning about training options, Moku and Josh recommend purchasing the following items:

Item	Number	Cost	Note
SPSS Modeler License	3	$9,399	Negotiated discounted rate of $3,133 per license
SPSS Modeler Online Training	3	$2,250	2-day online training at $750 per student
Estimated Tax	1	$816	Based on 7.5% sales tax
Total		**$12,465**	

Andrea, we're eager to make these purchases and allow the analyst team to begin using these tools. Please let me know if you can authorize these purchases.

Thanks,

NAVIGATION is easy: Paragraphs are 14, 60, 59, 58, and 27 words long.

Bryan

Setting Expectations

Working with others involves setting expectations, especially when you are in management and supervisory roles. Many young business professionals—especially first-time managers—are not comfortable with telling others what to do. They are nervous about overstepping their authority and disrupting a friendly feeling with subordinates. Yet, setting expectations is directly tied to your credibility and ability to foster interpersonal trust in the workplace. Dennis S. Reina and Michelle L. Reina have examined the nature of trust in hundreds of companies over the past few decades and say this about setting clear expectations:

> A lack of clarity regarding expectations causes misperceptions and misconstrued intentions. When people's expectations are not met, they may feel a range of emotions. They may feel disappointed, discounted, taken advantage of, angry, or hurt. The result may be distrust and feelings of betrayal. . . . When people don't find out what is expected of them until they run into a wall, go down the wrong road, or fail to get a promotion or pay raise, it's too late. In these kinds of situations, people may experience a range of emotions from disappointment to betrayal.[1]

So, although setting expectations is often a routine matter, failure to do it can lead to lasting professional disappointments and breakdowns in working relationships.

Three components are central in setting expectations for those you manage: describing responsibilities, providing deadlines, and discussing coordination. Describing *responsibilities* means designating tasks and work outcomes to certain employees, providing *deadlines* means setting out the timeline by which the work should be accomplished satisfactorily, and discussing *coordination* involves providing guidelines for how employees should communicate and cooperate with one another. From time to time, you should also describe your own role and responsibilities to supervisees. When you do so, they see they are accountable to you and you are also accountable to them. This means you may need to occasionally own up to your own mistakes and accept responsibility when everything has not gone as expected.

Notice the differences between the less effective and more effective expectation-setting messages in Figures 9.4 and 9.5, in which Bryan makes a new assignment and sets out the deadlines for Barry and John, two of his supervisees. The less effective example violates the basic requirements of routine messages because it does not provide the key message clearly at the beginning. It is also difficult to read. In the more effective message, Barry and John can grasp the key messages within seconds. They can process all of the information rapidly and understand the responsibilities, deadlines, and coordination associated with these new accounts.

Components of Expectations

- Explain overall expectation.
- Describe responsibilities.
- Provide deadlines.
- Discuss coordination.
- State goodwill.

FIGURE 9.4

Less Effective Example of Setting Expectations

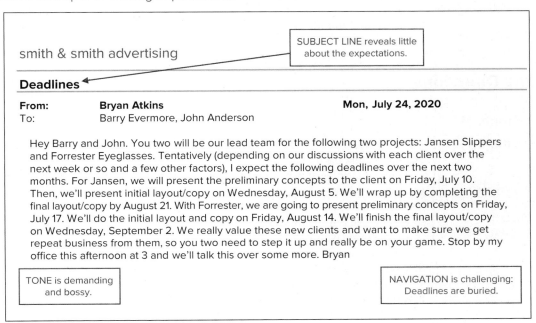

FIGURE 9.5

More Effective
Example of Setting
Expectations

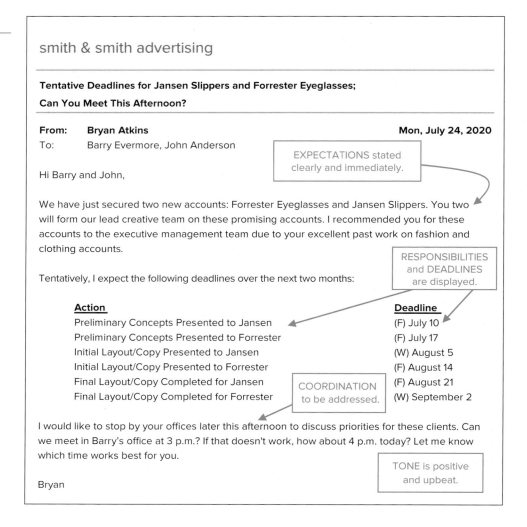

Increasingly, workplaces uses project management software with task items to help set expectations. The same principles apply as you use this software: describing responsibilities, providing deadlines, and discussing coordination. Even in workplaces with this software, not all your colleagues will consistently use it. Be prepared to use other channels (e.g., in-person conversations, emails) to politely reinforce your expectations.

Providing Directions

Components of Directions

- State goal.
- Give step-by-step directions.
- State goodwill.

Another common type of routine message provides directions for others. Messages that provide directions share many similarities with those that set expectations. The primary distinction is that directions typically include specific—often step-by-step—guidelines for accomplishing particular tasks.

Since describing step-by-step procedures is so specific, insufficient detail can frustrate your readers. For routine matters, you are generally safe reviewing your own work and making sure it is complete. For more technical and complicated procedures, make sure you have several people test the procedures to find where you can better clarify the steps involved.

In messages with procedures and directions, make the steps stand out clearly by enumerating each one. This helps your reader keep track of progress completing the tasks. Steps that are written in narrative form within a paragraph are typically difficult to follow.

Notice the differences between the less effective and more effective messages in Figures 9.6 and 9.7, where Bryan gives directions to John on how to make company

FIGURE 9.6

Less Effective
Directions

smith & smith advertising | SUBJECT LINE is not descriptive.

Travel

From:	**Bryan Atkins**	**Mon, July 24, 2020**
To:	John Anderson	

TONE is careless and sloppy. Use of passive voice makes message impersonal.

The process is fairly simple. Once there is a determination that the trip is necessary (I've determined that already), a T/A is required. The form should be filled out and signed by your direct supervisor. Then, the form should be taken to HR. It will then be sent directly to our travel agency and you will be contacted about setting up your trip. After the trip, any receipts need to be turned in to HR and reimbursement generally takes about 10 days. Hope this helps.

FIGURE 9.7

More Effective Directions

smith & smith advertising | DIRECTIONS are specific and clear.

Procedures for Setting Up Travel

From:	**Bryan Atkins**	**Mon, July 24, 2020**
To:	John Anderson	

John,

For complete details, go to the *Travel* section of the **Human Resources intranet portal**. You will immediately find all policies and forms that you need.

Here are the basic steps pasted directly from the HR intranet portal with several *comments from me inserted in italics.*

1. Complete a "Travel Authorization" (T/A) form with approval signature from your immediate supervisor.

   (I'm the supervisor. You can get the latest T/A form off the HR intranet portal at the following link: T/A Form *.)*

2. Submit the T/A to Human Resources (HR). HR will forward it directly to our designated travel agency.

   (Our current designated travel agency is Dawson Travel.)

3. An agent from the travel agency will contact you directly and develop your trip itinerary with you. The travel agency will bill Smith & Smith directly for your airfare, accommodations, and car rentals.

   (You should do this right away. You may be able to choose an airline that you have frequent flier miles with if you can book far enough in advance. If you book within two weeks of the travel, you are required to use discount airlines.)

4. After completing your trip, turn in receipts for incidental expenses to HR. You will be reimbursed for these expenses and receive a daily stipend to cover meals.

   (Make sure to review the company policies so you know which incidental expenses are covered and how much your daily stipend will be.)

This should get you started. For questions about filling out the T/A, you'll get more help from HR. As soon as you get the T/A form filled in, just let me know and I'll sign it right away.

Bryan

TONE is professional and helpful.

travel arrangements. The less effective example in Figure 9.6 has an unhelpful and careless tone, written almost entirely in passive voice. The message is abrupt and insufficiently detailed. Many readers will decode a meta message of "I don't have time for you." In the more effective example in Figure 9.7, Bryan provides clear directions by pasting the human resources policies into the message and inserting his own comments as additional guidelines and tips. He also tells John where to go for more information. In reality, Bryan could have simply emailed "check the HR intranet portal." Yet, this more effective message, written in just three to four minutes, is a strong sign of Bryan's willingness to help John. Many readers will decode a meta message of "I want to help you out as much as possible."

Responding to Inquiries

Components of Inquiry Responses

- Provide responses.
- State goodwill.

The very nature of working with others involves asking and responding to questions. One of the most important strategies for responding to inquiries is to set off each question so your readers can quickly identify responses to particular questions. You generally can do this using bullets or numbered lists and/or special formatting (i.e., bold or italics). When choosing between bullets or numbered lists, consider whether the order of the items is important. If the order is important, use numbered lists. Otherwise, use bullets. Also, consider telling your readers where to get additional and more specific information by providing links to FAQ web pages or other relevant web pages.

Notice the difference between Bryan's less effective and more effective responses to an inquiry from a prospect in Figures 9.8 and 9.9. In the less effective response in Figure 9.8, Bryan mixes responses in a single paragraph. (The original inquiry is located at the bottom of Figure 9.8; it is a poorly written inquiry with all the questions embedded in one paragraph.) In the more effective response in Figure 9.9, Bryan gives each question its own section and highlights each in bold. By structuring the email this way, he helps the reader easily navigate the various answers. He also uses links to web pages with further information and attempts to schedule a face-to-face meeting where he can answer questions in a richer medium.

Creating Announcements

Components of Announcements

- Gain attention.
- Give announcement.
- Provide details.
- Call to action.*
- State goodwill.

*For some announcements

Business executives and managers routinely make announcements. Announcements are updates to policies and procedures, notices of events, and other correspondences that apply to a group of employees and/or customers. Announcements are one form of one-to-many communications.

Since announcements are generally broadcast to a large number of receivers (often as emails or corporate intranet posts), many employees and customers gloss over them. To prevent employees and customers from ignoring announcements, the subject line must be specific and must create interest. Furthermore, announcements, especially for events, should be designed to let readers gather all relevant information in 10 to 15 seconds. Thus, formatting is especially important.

In the less effective announcement from Bryan about new computing policies (see Figure 9.10), he provides most of the necessary information about the new policies but buries most of it in long paragraphs. He leaves out some important information, such as dates. Missing dates are among the most common mistakes on announcements. While most announcements of this type (for new policies) are tempered in tone, they should still carry some enthusiasm when the announcements include good news. This announcement has quite positive news for most employees. Bryan's more effective announcement (see Figure 9.11) contains complete information in concise form. The formatting allows employees to grasp all essential information in about 15 seconds. It also contains more positive, inviting language. One reason that the more effective announcement is better than the less effective announcement is the grouping and arrangement of information.

FIGURE 9.8

Less Effective Response to an Inquiry

To... Joel Yang [joel.yang@doityourselfsports.com]

Subject: RE: Questions about Advertising

Arial 10 B I U

Hello Joel:

Thanks for getting in touch with us here at Smith & Smith. Answers to all of your questions can be found on our website (Smith & Smith website). Generally, you'll find that our rates are extremely competitive with other agencies. More important, we have a great record of return on investment and help you track this figure. Also, our agency has been at the forefront of all forms of online advertising and marketing for the past fifteen years. We have been instrumental in helping small companies rapidly grow their revenues and expand. See the following web page about our online advertising with examples of our work: Smith & Smith online advertising and social media. We can meet at a time and place convenient for you. This week I'm available from 2 to 4 on Tuesday, 9 to 11:30 on Wednesday, and in the morning or afternoon on Thursday. Please let me know a time that is best for you.

Bryan

Nonunified Response: A single paragraph contains answers to all of the questions.

From: Joel Yang [joel.yang@doityourselfsports.com]
Sent: Mon, July 24, 2020 at 8:34 AM
To: Bryan Atkins [bryanatkins@smith+smith.com]
Subject: Questions about Advertising

Hi Bryan, I contacted Andrea Johansen about developing some ads. She recommended that I contact you directly. Basically, I'm interested in pricing for various advertising options. You've probably seen our used sports equipment stores around town. We've decided to change our business model and devote half of our retail space to new sports equipment. Anyway, we want to get the word out. We've always developed in-house advertising which I think has been amateurish. Of course, we don't have a big budget. So, we want quality advertising but we're concerned about pricing. How do your rates compare to other advertising agencies? Do you have any specialists in online advertising? What about with social media? When could we meet and talk about what you might provide us? Thanks a lot. Joel

By taking an extra five to ten minutes to organize the information carefully, Bryan ensures that employees have a far better understanding of the new policies.

Components of Claims

- Make claim.
- Provide rationale.
- Call to action.
- State goodwill.

Making Claims

Claims are requests for other companies to compensate for or correct the wrongs of mistakes they have made. As with other requests, you should immediately state what the *claim* is and what you expect the company to do for you. You also will provide a

FIGURE 9.9

More Effective Response to an Inquiry

To... Joel Yang [joel.yang@doityourselfsports.com]

Subject: Responses to Your Questions; Setting Up a Time to Meet

---

Arial   10   **B** *I* U̲   ☰ ☰ ☲ ☲ ᵃᵇʸ ▾ **A** ▾ ⊗

Hello Joel:

Thanks for getting in touch with us here at Smith & Smith. I suggest that we meet in person so we can learn more about your marketing and advertising needs. After we talk for 15 to 30 minutes, I could give you a good idea of what your options are and whether our agency is a good fit for you.

Our website (**Smith & Smith website**) has answers to each of your questions. I've responded briefly below with links to our website for more information:

How do your rates compare to other advertising agencies?

Our rates are extremely competitive with other agencies. More important, we have a great record of return on investment and help you track this figure. We also specialize in building brands, which is particularly important in your case since you are adjusting your business model to include new sports equipment. See the following web page with ten case studies of our clients and the returns they received on their advertising: **Smith & Smith case studies**.

Do you have any specialists in online advertising? What about in social media?

Yes. Our agency has been at the forefront of all forms of online advertising and marketing for the past 15 years. We have been instrumental in helping small companies rapidly grow their revenues and expand. See the following web page about our online advertising with examples of our work: **Smith & Smith online advertising and social media**.

When could we meet and talk about what you might provide us?

At a time and place convenient for you. I would be more than happy to visit your office. I am available during the following times this week:

Tuesday:	2 p.m.–4 p.m.
Wednesday:	9 a.m.–11:30 a.m.
Thursday:	9 a.m.–11:30 a.m., 2 p.m.–4 p.m.

Please let me know a time that is best for you. You can call directly anytime.

Bryan

Bryan Atkins
Account Executive
Smith & Smith Advertising
803-777-1848

> SPECIFIC responses
> to all questions.

> NAVIGATION is easy with
> questions as headings.

FIGURE 9.10

Less Effective Announcement

MEMORANDUM

TO:	Smith & Smith Advertising Employees
FROM:	Bryan Atkins
DATE:	Mon, July 24, 2020
SUBJECT	New Policies

> INFORMATION is incomplete (missing key dates) and difficult to read. The TONE lacks enough enthusiasm.

On behalf of the Committee for Technology, I'm sharing several new policies that impact employees at S&S. We deliberated carefully about these new policies to meet our stated objectives of making computing more accessible and convenient for employees while also safeguarding information systems security for our advertising firm. These policies will go into effect in the next week. All these policies relate to using your own devices for work.

The first set of BYOD policies makes mobile computing easier for employees. Employees who use their own mobile phones for work can receive reimbursement for up to $75 per month for voice and data plans (previously this was capped at $30 per month). We felt that this amount more accurately reflected the costs many employees incur for voice and data on behalf of the firm. Also, several policies directly address the major expenses of owning your own computers that you use for work. S&S will reimburse employees for up to $1,200 per year for desktop computers, laptops, tablets, or other mobile computer devices used primarily for work purposes. The great news is that any unused money will roll over for use in the following year. Finally, S&S must use a new ticketing system through the HelpDesk for all requests.

There will also be new security measures. We've learned that many of our S&S resources and information are vulnerable to attacks. These new policies will be minimally inconvenient for employees yet make substantial improvements to our security. All devices—including mobile phones—are now required to have a log-in. Also, employees will need to update their log-in passwords to the S&S intranet every six months. Your supervisors will continue updating you about the new policies, and you can read all BYOD and computing policies on the intranet.

---

rationale for your claim in the body of the message and close with a call to *action*—a specific request.

As you write claims, keep in mind that your goal is to have your claim honored. Focus on facts first and emotions second, if at all. Lay out a logical, reasonable, and professional explanation for your claim. Emotional claims are far more likely to be rejected. Also, remember that you will often work with the same people again and again. So, be polite and focus on the long-term working relationship.

In Bryan's less effective claim to the Prestigio Hotel about a billing error (see Figure 9.12), phrases such as "you have not honored" and "you overcharged" unnecessarily and perhaps unfairly question Jeff's intent. The message focuses first on frustration and second on the merits of the claim. Abrupt phrases such as "please take care of this matter immediately" can easily be misinterpreted as rude. Notice how the more effective claim (see Figure 9.13) balances directness with politeness. Bryan justifies the claim with an objective description of the overbilling and provides an attachment with the agreement. He politely asks for an adjustment to the account while also complimenting Jeff on the excellent service the hotel provides.

FIGURE 9.11

More Effective Announcement

MEMORANDUM

TO:	Smith & Smith Advertising Employees
FROM:	Bryan Atkins
DATE:	Mon, July 24, 2020
SUBJECT	New Bring Your Own Device (BYOD) Policies

> **INFORMATION** is complete and easy to process. Most readers will recognize all essential information within 15 seconds. **RATIONALE** is clear and concise. **TONE** is positive and helpful

Beginning on July 1, 2020, several new BYOD policies will go into effect to provide employees with more mobile and home computing options and ensure better security for Smith & Smith.

These new policies were developed by a committee comprised of IT managers and account executives. The policies were approved by the executive team on June 19, 2020.

New Policies to Support Mobile and Home Computing

- *Reimbursement for voice/data plans:* Employees who use their own mobile phones for work can receive reimbursement for up to $75 per month for voice and data plans (previously this was capped at $30 per month).

- *Reimbursement for mobile and home computers:* S&S will reimburse employees for up to $1,200 per year for desktop computers, laptops, tablets, or other mobile computer devices used primarily for work purposes. Any unused money will roll over for use in the following year.

- *IT Support:* S&S employees must use a new ticketing system through the HelpDesk for all requests. IT support will now be available Monday through Saturday, 8 a.m. to 7 p.m.

New Security Policies

- *Log-in on all devices:* All devices—including mobile phones—are now required to have a log-in.

- *S&S intranet password updates:* Employees will need to update their log-in passwords to the S&S intranet every six months. Passwords must contain at least eight characters and must include at least one letter, one number, and one special character.

Your supervisors will continue updating you about the new policies. Also, *you can read all BYOD and computing policies in the "Computing" section located on your S&S dashboard.*

Showing Appreciation

Components of Appreciation Messages
• Give thanks.
• Provide rationale.
• State goodwill.

Employees at all levels of an organization desire to feel appreciated. Sadly, polls show that employees express thanks to one another less now than ever since polling on this issue began. Just 10 percent of employees say supervisors thank them daily. More than half (55 percent) of employees say they are thanked never, seldom, or only occasionally.[2]

A sincere expression of thanks also helps achieve business goals and strengthens work relationships. Joseph Ungoco of a popular public relations agency in New York is a staunch believer that thank-you notes help his agency maintain effective working relationships and strongly impact repeat business. He sends handwritten thank-you notes within 48 hours to partners and clients.[3]

FIGURE 9.12

Less Effective Claim

To... Jeff Anderton [jeffanderton@theprestigiohotel.com]

Subject: Please Correct Billing Mistakes on Hotel Stays Immediately

Hello Jeff:

I'm quite frustrated that we made an annual agreement with you at a rate of $124 per night for our employees that you have not honored. Within the past two months, two of our employees have stayed at the Prestigio for a total of 15 nights at a rate of $169. By my calculations, you overcharged us by $675. In addition, there should be a minor adjustment for taxes that we paid on a higher rate.

Please take care of this matter immediately by refunding us the overpaid amount. Thanks a lot.

Bryan

TONE is accusatory and demanding.

FIGURE 9.13

More Effective Claim

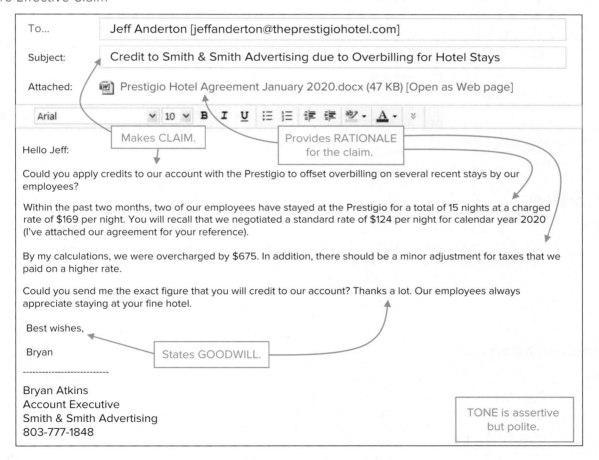

To... Jeff Anderton [jeffanderton@theprestigiohotel.com]

Subject: Credit to Smith & Smith Advertising due to Overbilling for Hotel Stays

Attached: Prestigio Hotel Agreement January 2020.docx (47 KB) [Open as Web page]

Makes CLAIM.

Provides RATIONALE for the claim.

Hello Jeff:

Could you apply credits to our account with the Prestigio to offset overbilling on several recent stays by our employees?

Within the past two months, two of our employees have stayed at the Prestigio for a total of 15 nights at a charged rate of $169 per night. You will recall that we negotiated a standard rate of $124 per night for calendar year 2020 (I've attached our agreement for your reference).

By my calculations, we were overcharged by $675. In addition, there should be a minor adjustment for taxes that we paid on a higher rate.

Could you send me the exact figure that you will credit to our account? Thanks a lot. Our employees always appreciate staying at your fine hotel.

Best wishes,

Bryan

States GOODWILL.

Bryan Atkins
Account Executive
Smith & Smith Advertising
803-777-1848

TONE is assertive but polite.

FIGURE 9.14

Less Effective
Appreciation Message

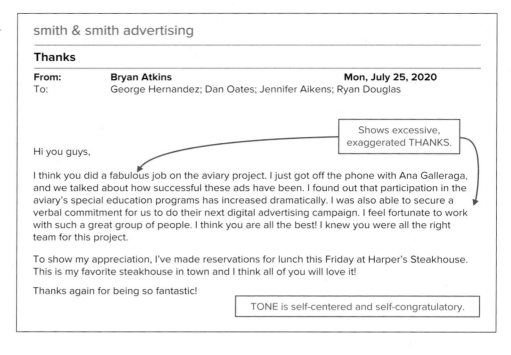

smith & smith advertising

Thanks

| From: | Bryan Atkins | Mon, July 25, 2020 |
| To: | George Hernandez; Dan Oates; Jennifer Aikens; Ryan Douglas | |

Hi you guys,

I think you did a fabulous job on the aviary project. I just got off the phone with Ana Galleraga, and we talked about how successful these ads have been. I found out that participation in the aviary's special education programs has increased dramatically. I was also able to secure a verbal commitment for us to do their next digital advertising campaign. I feel fortunate to work with such a great group of people. I think you are all the best! I knew you were all the right team for this project.

> Shows excessive, exaggerated THANKS.

To show my appreciation, I've made reservations for lunch this Friday at Harper's Steakhouse. This is my favorite steakhouse in town and I think all of you will love it!

Thanks again for being so fantastic!

> TONE is self-centered and self-congratulatory.

LO9.4 Construct relationship-oriented routine messages, including appreciation, congratulations, apologies, and expressions of sympathy.

 **connect**

Visit http://connect.
mheducation.com for an exercise on this topic.

Appreciation messages vary significantly in terms of formality. Thank-you notes for customers and clients or for special occasions demand more formality. Thank-you messages for colleagues and others you see each day should be less formal and should not feel over the top. In any case, several components are standard for appreciation messages. They should begin with an expression of *thanks*, provide a quick *rationale* for the thanks, and end with a statement of *goodwill*.

Appreciation messages should be genuine, simple, warm, and personal. To show your sincerity, focus exclusively on the recipient. Appreciation messages should not appear self-serving in any way; state any reference to yourself carefully to avoid drawing attention away from those you are thanking.

In the workplace, showing your appreciation will help build connections. Be careful, however, about excessive or exaggerated displays of gratitude. First, readers may view them as insincere. Second, they may cross boundaries of what is considered professional.

Notice the differences between Bryan's less effective and more effective appreciation messages to his team in Figures 9.14 and 9.15. In the less effective example, the exaggerated and excessive phrases of gratitude (i.e., "a fabulous job," "feel fortunate," "you are all the best!") appear unprofessional or insincere. Also, the message contains far too much focus on Bryan and implies he now deserves thanks for his own actions (securing a new deal, providing lunch). In the more effective example, Bryan focuses entirely on the group. He shows enthusiasm within professional boundaries.

Congratulations and Celebrations

Quite similar to expressions of appreciation are congratulation and celebration messages. While appreciation messages should be expressed constantly among colleagues, congratulations are typically reserved for major professional milestones: securing a major deal, getting an important new client, reaching a work anniversary (i.e., ten years of service), gaining a promotion, and even reaching retirement. For close colleagues and clients, professionals should also celebrate many nonprofessional milestones: marriages, births, graduations, home purchases, and other major life events.

FIGURE 9.15

More Effective Appreciation Message

Typically, you should express deep and positive emotion in congratulation messages. It's appropriate to project a tone of joy and happiness. Also, you should consider validating others for their milestone. For someone who has been promoted, you could express how well deserved the promotion is. For someone who has just purchased a home, you could express what a good decision it is. Finally, since milestones generally represent the beginning of a new journey, you should consider expressing confidence in their future. For someone who has secured a major deal, you might suggest it's the beginning of securing other deals. For someone who has just married, you could express your confidence in a long and happy union. Many professionals differ as far as the level of formality for these messages, but they generally ensure these messages are emotional, validating, and forward looking. Notice in Figure 9.16 how Bryan offers a congratulation message to a colleague who has taken a new and better position in a competing firm.

> **Components of Congratulation and Celebration Messages**
>
> - Display happiness, joy, and other positive sentiments.
> - Validate their accomplishment or milestone.
> - Express confidence in their future.

Making Apologies

Even with the best of intentions, colleagues sometimes let one another down. Differences in communication style, personality clashes, and careless comments are sometimes factors in personal offenses. Business professionals who are high in emotional intelligence notice how their actions impact others. When they intentionally or unintentionally do harm, they seek to improve the workplace relationships right away. In some cases, making apologies is the appropriate response.

FIGURE 9.16

A Congratulations Message

---

smith & smith advertising

Congratulations on Your New Role

| From: | Bryan Atkins | Mon, July 25, 2020 |
| To: | Sandy Cartier | |

> Displays EMOTION throughout the message.

Dear Sandy:

Congratulations on receiving a director role at DGS. This offer doesn't surprise me in the least. You have succeeded in every campaign you've led here. Your leadership skills and strategic vision are exactly what are needed for a director role. I'm so happy for you.

> Expresses VALIDATION for the milestone.

I expect you'll make an immediate impact at DGS. Keep up the great work!

Of course we'll miss you tremendously here at Smith & Smith. Thank you for all the work you've done here. Mostly, thank you for your constant encouragement and friendship.

> Shows CONFIDENCE in Sandy's future success.

Best wishes in your new adventure!

Bryan

> TONE is positive, joyful (yet appropriately bittersweet), and forward-looking.

However, all apologies are not necessarily good apologies. As stated by management communication specialist Holly Weeks, "Offering the right apology, particularly in the corporate world, is not as simple as saying, 'I'm sorry.' Done right, an apology can enhance both reputations and relationships. Done wrong, an apology can compound the original mistake, sometimes to disastrous consequences."[4]

Effective apologies achieve several important results. First, they help repair working relationships so that you can refocus on solving problems together. Second, they can rebuild your reputation. When you've made offenses or mistakes that harm others, your credibility is weakened. Your reputation for competence, caring, and/or character may be questioned.[5]

Typically, an apology includes the following elements: *acknowledgment* of a mistake or an offense, an expression of *regret* for the harm caused, acceptance of *responsibility*, and a *commitment* that the offense will not be repeated. Effective apologies should be timely and sincere.

Apologies are ineffective when they are vague and clichéd. For the apology to be effective, others must sense that the apologizer is sincere, genuine, and acting without an agenda. Effective apologies must focus on others, not you. During an apology, if the recipient decodes any behavior as defensive, it casts doubt on the apologizer's sincerity.[6]

Components of Apologies

- Make acknowledgment.
- Express regret.
- Take responsibility.
- Offer commitment.
- State goodwill.

Before apologizing, consider the business implications. If you are dealing with customers and clients, an apology may imply legal responsibility. For serious matters, you might seek the company's legal counsel. Internally, an apology may become a permanent record in a performance review or other files (in rare situations). So, you might consider the potential costs of an apology to your company and your career. Generally, however, apologies for routine mistakes and offenses pose little risk to either your company or your career. They are likely to restore and perhaps even enhance your company's and your personal credibility.

Notice Bryan's oral apology in Figure 9.17 for unfair statements he made at a meeting. The apology contains the basic elements: acknowledgment, regret, responsibility, and commitment. It is short, simple, sincere, and forward-looking. Colleagues who have known Bryan for years will likely accept the apology quickly and redirect their efforts to working together effectively.

Technology Tips

USING APPS TO CREATE A ROUTINE OF APPRECIATION AND CELEBRATION

For most professionals, the busyness of the workplace gets in the way of appropriately expressing gratitude, celebrating others, and taking time for relaxation and recharging. You can use a variety of apps to make a routine for these activities. Consider the following:

- *Set recurring dates on your online calendar for special occasions.* For example, make sure your calendar has birthdays of all your close contacts. Many professionals make sure they receive a notification at least three days before birthdays so they have time to plan for these occasions, even if it's as small as a birthday card.

- *Experiment with recognition apps* that remind you and give you tools to show gratitude to others. Apps such as iAppreciate, Sparcet, and Kudos help you show recognition to your colleagues and others. Make sure you express your thanks in person as well.

- *Try out apps that track your happiness, gratitude, stress, and other emotions.* Many apps help you recognize your emotional states throughout the day. For example, Worry Watch tracks your stress and anxiety, iMood Journal assesses your happiness, and Headspace recommends various forms of meditation based on your moods. Dozens of similar apps exist.

Your challenge: Select two apps with reminders and suggestions to help you recognize and thank others and monitor your own moods. Try them out for one week. How were these apps helpful? What didn't you like about the apps? What features would help you better develop routines for recognizing and celebrating others and taking better care of yourself?

Expressing Sympathy

When your colleagues and other close professional contacts encounter personal losses—such as the sickness or even the passing away of loved ones—it is appropriate for you to extend your sincere sympathies. Although you may have maintained strictly

FIGURE 9.17

An Apology

"Good morning, everyone. I want to take just a few moments to apologize. Last Friday in our executive management meeting, I made several unfair comments."

"I complained that several of you care more about our clients than you do about our employees. I also said that you ask our employees to work excessive hours on weekends and evenings because you are never willing to say 'no' to our clients, even when they make unreasonable demands."

ACKNOWLEDGMENT of mistake.

"These statements were inaccurate and unfair. I have known each of you for many years, and I am certain that all of you care deeply about our employees."

Statement of REGRET.

"Over the weekend, I thought about my comments a lot. I am frustrated that we—myself included—give in to unreasonable demands from a few of our clients. I think we end up putting too much stress on our employees as a result. I am sorry that I misdirected my frustration with the demands of our clients at all of you."

Statement of RESPONSIBILITY.

"At some point, I hope we can discuss how to negotiate with our clients when we view their demands as unreasonable. For my part, I will avoid any blaming. I would certainly like to hear your experiences, perspectives, and suggestions."

COMMITMENT to avoid such behavior in the future and approach frustrations constructively.

IDEAS IN ACTION

SHOWING GRATITUDE

Indra Nooyi, former CEO of PepsiCo

Routine notes of appreciation are always welcome, but some people find ways to extend gratitude in unique ways. Shortly after becoming CEO of PepsiCo in 2006, Indra Nooyi returned to her mom's home in India for a short visit. Person after person visited her mother's home. They didn't say anything to Nooyi. Rather, they'd walked up to her mother and thanked her for raising such a wonderful daughter!

This experience inspired her to pass gratitude on in a similar way. Each year, Nooyi sent more than 400 thank-you letters to the parents of her employees. She feels parents deserve much of the credit for the performance of their children. She would write, "Thank you for the gift of your child to our company." These thank-you notes made her employees and their parents feel proud and appreciated.

Monica Schipper/Getty Images

The power of thank-you messages is profound. You may not necessarily send notes to parents, but you can find many distinct and creative ways to spread gratitude with your colleagues and other contacts.

Source: Ward, M. (2017, February 1). Why PepsiCo CEO Indra Nooyi writes letters to her employees' parents. *CNBC.* Retrieved from www.cnbc.com/2017/02/01/why-pepsico-ceo-indra-nooyi-writes-letters-to-her-employees-parents.html.

Components of Sympathy Messages

- Express sympathy.
- Offer support.
- State goodwill.

professional relations with others, expressing condolences, concern, and support can help them cope with personal grief and pain.

The foremost requirement of any expression of sympathy is that it be sincere. These difficult moments are challenging and awkward. You may feel uncertain about what to say, which words to use. Your genuine concern will compensate for any deficiencies in the words you use. Typically, keep your expressions of sympathy brief. For deaths, state your support and concern to the person who has experienced the loss. Make the note personal by mentioning the deceased person by name and your positive impressions and memories. When possible, handwrite your expression of sympathy on a nice card (see Figure 9.18 for an example of a sympathy message).

FIGURE 9.18

An Expression of Sympathy

Flowers on card: Burke/Triolo Productions/Getty Images; postage stamp: Mark Steinmetz/ McGraw-Hill Education

Chapter Takeaway for *Routine Business Messages*

LO9.1 Describe how delivering routine messages impacts credibility.

Delivering effective routine messages improves your **reputation for personal credibility.**

It shows **competence** when you know how to manage and resolve routine business tasks.	It shows **caring** when you are responsive to others and show respect for their time.	It shows **character** when you live up to your promises and your company's commitments.

LO9.2 Describe the process for developing routine business messages.

Components of Routine Messages	
• State primary message (ten words or fewer). • Provide details in paragraphs of 20 to 80 words.	• Restate request or key message in more specific terms. • State goodwill.

LO9.3 Construct task-oriented routine messages, including requests, expectations, directions, responses to inquiries, announcements, and claims.

Construct routine business requests.

Components of Requests	
• Make request. • Provide rationale.	• Call to action (for some). • State goodwill.

See *examples of business requests* in Figures 9.2 and 9.3.

Compose routine sets of expectations.

Components of Expectations		
• Explain overall expectation. • Describe responsibilities.	• Provide deadlines. • Discuss coordination.	• State goodwill.

See *examples of expectation-setting messages* in Figures 9.4 and 9.5.

Construct routine sets of directions.

Components of Directions		
• State goal.	• Give step-by-step directions.	• State goodwill.

See *examples of directions* in Figures 9.6 and 9.7.

Compose routine responses to inquiries.

Components of Inquiry Responses	
• Provide responses.	• State goodwill.

See *examples of responses to inquiries* in Figures 9.8 and 9.9.

Construct routine announcements.

Components of Announcements		
• Gain attention. • Give announcement.	• Provide details. • Call to action (for some).	• State goodwill.

See *examples of announcements* in Figures 9.10 and 9.11.

Compose routine claims.

Components of Claims	
• Make claim. • Provide rationale.	• Call to action. • State goodwill.

See *examples of claims* in Figures 9.12 and 9.13.

LO9.4 Construct relationship-oriented routine messages, including appreciation, congratulations, apologies, and expressions of sympathy.

Components of Appreciation Messages		
• Give thanks.	• Provide rationale.	• State goodwill.

See *examples of appreciation messages* in Figures 9.14 and 9.15.

Compose apologies.

Components of Congratulations and Celebration Messages		
• Display happiness, joy, and other positive sentiments.	• Validate their accomplishment or milestone.	• Express confidence in their future.

See an *example of a congratulations message* in Figure 9.16.

Compose apologies.

Components of Apologies		
• Make acknowledgment. • Express regret.	• Take responsibility. • Offer commitment.	• State goodwill.

See an *example of an apology* in Figure 9.17.

Construct routine expressions of sympathy.

Components of Sympathy Messages		
• Express sympathy.	• Offer support.	• State goodwill.

See an *example of a sympathy message* in Figure 9.18.

Discussion Exercises

9.1 Chapter Review Questions (LO9.1, LO9.2)

A. Describe the AIM planning process for routine messages.

B. Explain the importance of reviewing for routine messages. What considerations should you make? What are your primary goals?

C. Identify the preferable message structures for various types of routine messages.

9.2 Ideas in Action Discussion Questions (LO9.4)

A. What's your reaction to Indra Nooyi's mother's friends congratulating her mother rather than her? How did this inspire Nooyi?

B. What was unique about Nooyi's thank-you messages? What are several unique traditions you could create to thank colleagues?

C. What is your view of physical thank-you notes? What are the advantages and disadvantages compared to digital thank-you notes?

Evaluation Exercises

9.3 Evaluating Routine Requests (LO9.3)

A. Compare Bryan's less effective and more effective requests for a new server in Figures 9.2 and 9.3. Identify three ways in which Bryan improved the message.

B. How do you think the more effective message will impact work outcomes?

C. How do you think the more effective message will impact workplace relationships?

D. What two changes could you make to improve the more effective example?

9.4 Evaluating Routine Expectations Messages (LO9.3)

A. Compare Bryan's less effective and more effective messages regarding his expectations for Barry and John in their new assignment (see Figures 9.4 and 9.5). Identify three ways in which Bryan improved the message.

B. How do you think the more effective message will impact work outcomes?

C. How do you think the more effective message will impact workplace relationships?

D. What two changes could you make to improve the more effective example?

9.5 Evaluating Routine Directions Messages (LO9.3)

A. Compare Bryan's less effective and more effective messages giving directions for how to arrange company travel (see Figures 9.6 and 9.7). Identify the ways in which he improved the message.

B. How do you think the more effective message will impact work outcomes?

C. How do you think the more effective message will impact workplace relationships?

D. What two changes could you make to improve the more effective example?

9.6 Evaluating Routine Inquiries (LO9.3)

A. Compare Bryan's less effective and more effective responses to an inquiry from a client (see Figures 9.8 and 9.9). Identify three ways that he improved the message.

B. How do you think the more effective message will impact work outcomes?

C. How do you think the more effective message will impact workplace relationships?

D. What two changes could you make to improve the more effective example?

9.7 Evaluating Routine Announcements (LO9.3)

A. Compare Bryan's less effective and more effective announcements about the firm's new computing policies (see Figures 9.10 and 9.11). Identify three ways that he improved the message.

B. How do you think the more effective message will impact work outcomes?

C. How do you think the more effective message will impact workplace relationships?

D. What two changes could you make to improve the more effective example?

9.8 Evaluating Routine Claims (LO9.3)

A. Compare Bryan's less effective and more effective claims to the Prestigio Hotel about its rate (see Figures 9.12 and 9.13). Identify three ways that he improved the message.

B. How do you think the more effective message will impact work outcomes?

C. How do you think the more effective message will impact workplace relationships?

D. What two changes could you make to improve the more effective example?

9.9 Evaluating Routine Appreciation Messages (LO9.4)

A. Compare Bryan's less effective and more effective messages of appreciation to his staff (see Figures 9.14 and 9.15). Identify three ways that he improved the message.

B. How do you think the more effective message will impact work outcomes?

C. How do you think the more effective message will impact workplace relationships?

D. What two changes could you make to improve the more effective example?

9.10 Evaluating Routine Congratulations Messages (LO9.4)

A. Examine Bryan's congratulations message in Figure 9.16.

B. How do you think this message will impact work outcomes?

C. How do you think this message will impact workplace relationships?

D. What two changes could you make to improve the message?

9.10 Evaluating Routine Apologies (LO9.4)

A. Examine Bryan's apology in Figure 9.17. How do you think this apology will impact work outcomes?

B. How do you think this apology will impact workplace relationships?

C. What two changes could you make to improve the apology?

9.11 Evaluating Sympathy Messages (LO9.4)

A. Examine Bryan's sympathy message in Figure 9.18. How do you think this sympathy message will impact work outcomes?

B. How do you think this sympathy message will impact workplace relationships?

C. What two changes could you make to improve the sympathy message?

9.12 Evaluating Your Approach to Writing (LO9.1, LO9.2)

Evaluate yourself with regard to each of the writing practices listed in the table below. Circle the appropriate number for each.

	1 – Rarely/Never	2 – Sometimes	3 – Usually	4 – Always
Before I write routine messages, I make sure I've gathered all of the relevant information.	1	2	3	4
Before I write routine messages, I spend a significant amount of time analyzing and piecing together the information.	1	2	3	4
Before I write routine messages, I learn as much as I reasonably can about the needs of the message receiver(s).	1	2	3	4
As I write routine messages, I think about how the message receiver(s) will feel while reading the message.	1	2	3	4
As I write routine messages, I think about how the message receiver(s) will respond.	1	2	3	4
As I write routine messages, I think about how quickly and easily the message receiver(s) will be able to read the message.	1	2	3	4
Before sending a routine message, I place myself in the position of the message receiver(s) and reread the message imagining how the message will be interpreted.	1	2	3	4
Before sending a routine message, I carefully double-check the entire message to make sure it is appropriate and accurate.	1	2	3	4
Before sending a routine message, I frequently ask people I trust to read the message or ask them how they would handle the communication.	1	2	3	4
Before sending a routine message, I use a spell-checker.	1	2	3	4

Add up your score and consider the following advice:

35–40: You are a *strategic, other-oriented* writer. You think about how to send a well-thought-out message that meets the needs of others. Continue with such awareness of the impact of your written messages.

30–34: You are a *careful, considerate* writer. You spend time thinking about the content of your message and the needs of your message receiver(s). Consider taking more time in the planning process to think your message through even more carefully, and pay close attention to the needs and potential responses to your written messages by message receivers.

25–29: You are an *inconsistent but self-aware* writer. Sometimes you are careful about developing your message

and considerate of the needs and reactions of others. Other times you are not. Always engage in excellent analysis when you craft your message and think carefully about your message receiver(s).

Under 25: You *need to improve* your approach to writing. You likely send most messages without spending enough time to think through the problems and impacts on others. Often this approach is harmless. Sometimes, however, you will not be influential in the way you want. Change your orientation to writing to spend most of your time preparing and reviewing.

After going through the self-assessment exercises, identify three specific goals you have for improving your approach to writing. Write four or five sentences about each goal.

Application Exercises

9.13 Request for a Letter of Recommendation (LO9.1, LO9.2, LO9.3)

Find a specific job, internship, or graduate study listing that you would be interested in pursuing. Make sure it requires a letter of recommendation. Your task is to request a letter of recommendation from one of your instructors. Assume that you will write an email making the request.

Answer the questions listed below to help you plan your request. Then write the request.

A. Why would your instructor want to write a letter of recommendation for you? What would increase your instructor's willingness and delight in writing a letter for you?

B. What tone will you try to project in your email?

C. What information about you would your instructor need to write an effective letter of recommendation?

D. How can you make it easier for your instructor to write a letter of recommendation?

E. How can you show courtesy to your instructor since she/he is using her/his own time to do a favor for you?

F. How will you order your message? What will be the subject line?

G. Write the email request for a letter of recommendation.

9.14 Writing a Memo with Group Goals and Expectations (LO9.3)

Think about a group project you've worked on in school or at work. Ideally, you will choose a currently active group project. Assume the role of group leader (you can make up facts as necessary). Write a document that includes the following:

- Group member names.
- Group goals and ultimate outcomes.
- Group member roles.
- Timeline for completing various activities and coordinating with one another.

9.15 Writing Procedures for Getting into Graduate School (LO9.3)

Go to the website of a graduate school you are interested in or to the graduate school website for your current university. Rewrite the

directions for applying to a graduate program of interest to you. Make them clearer and simpler to read.

9.16 Responding to Inquiries (LO9.3)

Assume you are an advisor for students in your program or major. A prospective student sends you the following message: "Hi, I'm interested in your major. Can you give me some information about it? What is the placement rate of your students in the workplace upon graduation? How much money do they usually get? What are the professors like? Do I have to have a minimum GPA to get in the program? Any information would be helpful. Thanks, Jack." Respond to this message with sufficient detail. Remember your goal is to make a favorable impression on this prospective student.

9.17 Making Announcements (LO9.3)

Place yourself in the position of an advisor in your program. The upcoming semester will begin soon. Send an announcement to all current students with items they should be aware of for the upcoming semester. Include deadlines and make sure students will pay attention to the announcement.

9.18 Changing the Vacation Policy at APECT Consulting (LO9.3)

Ruth Weinstein had worked at APECT Consulting for the past 18 years. Shortly after becoming president several years ago, she recognized that turnover was quite high. The average consultant at the firm left after 5 to 6 years of employment. In exit interviews, departing consultants consistently talked about "being burned out" or "needing an extended break." Most of these departing employees still had months of unused paid vacation leave, which consistently prompted Ruth to ask, "Why didn't you use your vacation time?" Consultants often said they felt a pressure to avoid vacation, especially if they were early-career professionals trying to prove themselves. Some consultants said they thought they'd lose certain client accounts if they took time off.

After several years of concerns about employees overworking, Ruth decided to learn more about how vacation time might affect the business. She started examining research about vacation time. She read a 2013 study jointly conducted by the Society for Human Resource Management and the U.S. Travel Association.[7] The study showed that human resources (HR) professionals overwhelmingly thought vacation affected job performance (94%), morale (92%), wellness (92%), a positive culture (90%), productivity (90%), and retention (88%). Strong majorities of human resources professionals also thought vacation time impacted creativity (70%), employee engagement (68%), staying with the organization longer (60%), and taking fewer sick days (58%).

The current policy allows APECT employees to take paid time off (PTO) based on years of employment: 5 vacation days for employees with fewer than 3 years of employment; 10 vacation days for employees with between 3 and 5 years of employment; 15 days for employees with between 5 and 10 years of employment; and 20 days for employees with more than 10 years of employment.

As Ruth talked to her human resources team, she was told how the current roll-over policy did not provide an incentive to take vacation days during any given year. Since employees could simply roll over their vacation days at the year's end, they could accumulate large numbers of vacation days. The human resources team told Ruth that the average consultant had accumulated 23 days of PTO. Furthermore, when consultants left the firm, they received cash payouts for unused PTO. With an average payout at approximately $330 per accumulated PTO day, most consultants did not feel motivated to use all their vacation time.

After talking to the human resources team for roughly three months, examining vacation plan policies at competing firms, and informally talking to about a dozen consultants at the firm, Ruth and the HR team developed a new vacation policy. Beginning on January 1, 2020, employees with fewer than 10 years of employment at the firm will receive 15 days of vacation per year, and employees with more than 10 years of employment will receive 20 days of vacation per year. The amount of roll-over and cash payouts will be dramatically reduced. Employees can only roll over a maximum of 5 days per year and cannot accumulate more than 25 total days of vacation. Employees will no longer gain cash pay-outs from unused PTO days after January 1, 2020. On January 1, 2020, the firm will give employees cash pay-outs for all accumulated PTO vacation days. Ruth drafted the following announcement to employees:

SUBJECT: Mandatory Vacation Policy Effective January 1

As I hold exit interviews with departing consultants, I've been troubled by how many of our employees have failed to take all of their vacation time. Our average consultant has 33 days of accumulated PTO. While I understand many of the pressures many of you feel to stay working and keep commitments to our clients, this amount of unused vacation time is unacceptable. Research convincingly shows that employees who use more vacation time are happier and more productive at work.

I have been reviewing this matter with the HR team for months. I have come to the firm conclusion that our firm needs a change in policy that incentivizes you employees to take time off so that you are more productive when you're here in the workplace.

Beginning on January 1, 2020, employees with fewer than 10 years of employment at the firm will receive 15 days of vacation per year, and employees with more than 10 years of employment will receive 20 days of vacation per year. The amount of roll-over and cash payouts will be dramatically reduced. Employees can only roll over a maximum of 5 days per year and cannot accumulate more than 30 total days of vacation. Employees will no longer gain cash pay-outs from unused PTO days after January 1, 2020. On January 1, 2020, the firm will give employees cash pay-outs for all accumulated PTO vacation days.

I will hold town hall meetings on November 2 and November 11 to tell you about the changes in more detail and explain how they help you out.

Best, Ruth

Your task: Rewrite the message to improve its tone and more adequately announce the changes. Make sure to briefly mention the rationale for the changes and explain the impacts on employees.

9.19 Building a Culture of Safety: Providing Directions at Fordham Springs Manufacturing (LO9.3)

About three months ago, an assembly worker at Fordham Spring Manufacturing (FSM) narrowly avoided a fatal assembly-line accident. While the company had avoided an accident with an injury for nearly 950 days, the company's president, Jackie Bentworth, was extremely concerned. The narrowly avoided accident was one of at least three such incidents in the past year. As a result, she formed the Safety Guidelines Committee to develop new procedures to improve the safety culture. Jackie assigned Roy Bang, an engineer, to lead this seven-person committee.

The committee developed a 65-page, comprehensive guidebook called the Fordham Spring Manufacturing Safety Guidelines. Roy placed the guidelines on the company's intranet where all employees could see them. He also broke the guidelines into separate webpages so that employees could easily find sought-after information quickly. He also planned to lead employee town hall meetings about the new safety guidelines on June 3, June 8, and June 10. He hoped all managers would attend these town hall meetings.

Roy wanted to share the new responsibilities and guidelines with employees throughout the organization. He decided to personally contact each of the managers to provide an overview of their responsibilities. First, he decided to contact mid-level managers because they played a major role in promoting safety among supervisors and assembly-line employees. FSM currently had eight mid-level managers. Each of these managers oversaw production of one of FSM's core products. The current managers included Steve Easton, Jeffrey Thompson, Deshawn Miles, Angie Zambroni, Brad Wilhemson, Parker Jones, Sandra Argesion, and Daniel King. Roy drafted the following message to send to the mid-level managers:

SUBJECT: New Procedures

Hi everyone,

Congratulations! We have now gone nearly 950 days without any major accidents or injuries! A new set of safety guidelines will be of assistance in continuing this excellent record of safety and concern for the well-being of all employees. After all, we have had at least three close calls that could have been devastating accidents for employees and the company. So, we can never be complacent.

During the past nine months, our Safety Guidelines Committee has undertaken the responsibility to develop definitions of various duties and responsibilities of managers at various levels of the organization. The duties and guidelines were developed after extensive review of industry standards and ten meetings were undertaken in the pursuit of the development of clear-cut, concrete, and unambiguous roles and responsibilities for employees at every level or the organization, from the shop floor to the C-suite.

Since you are a mid-level manager, I wanted to take this opportunity to share with you the pertinent responsibilities and guidelines that apply to you. All mid-level managers are expected to adhere to the following responsibilities: all mid-level managers should understand, implement, and monitor safety guidelines (the new guidelines are attached to this message); all mid-level managers are in charge of the quarterly evaluation of supervisors' adherence to relevant safety guidelines; all mid-level managers are responsible for making sure that all employees conduct Work Activity Safety Planning before the beginning of all new projects; all mid-level managers are responsible for the provision of safety training and certification of all supervisors and assembly workers; all mid-level managers have the responsibility of the placement of safety performance expectations in the job position descriptions of all supervisors and all assembly workers; all mid-level managers are responsible for the conducting of weekly inspections of all assembly line areas with the accompaniment of relevant supervisors; responsibility of the coaching and mentoring of supervisors and assembly line workers in new safety procedures; responsible for participation in accident review procedures in order to communicate "lessons learned" to all relevant supervisors and assembly-line workers.

If by chance there is a serious injury in your assigned work area, please be advised that the committee has identified the followed procedures: ensuring immediate medical treatment for the injured employee; securing the accident area; contacting of the Director of Personnel as soon as the employee is under appropriate medical treatment and the accident area is secured; creation of an official accident report with all information completed as directed to the Director of Personnel within 24 hours.

Thank you for all you do for the safety of your designated employees. You truly make a difference.

Best wishes, Roy Bang

Your task: Rewrite this message to mid-level managers. Rewrite with a focus on the following goals: (1) make the responsibilities and directions more clear, (2) improve the writing style to make the message easier to read, (3) make the message more personable, and (4) briefly provide the background and rationale for the new safety responsibilities and guidelines.

9.20 Making Claims (LO9.3)

Think about a product or service you have purchased in the past that did not work properly. Write a claim to the company about it. Explain why your claim is justified and suggest action. Focus on achieving an assertive but friendly tone.

9.21 Expressing Appreciation (LO9.4)

Assume that you just received and accepted an offer for a job you've wanted. You believe one of your references may have been instrumental in helping you get the job. Write a note of appreciation.

9.22 Making Apologies (LO9.4)

Assume you lost your temper when discussing a group project with one of your classmates. You left the meeting early because you were frustrated that your classmate insisted on doing everything his way. You still feel that he is dominating the project, but your behavior was inappropriate. Write an apology to your classmate in a way that repairs some of the damage between the two of you and allows the group to work more effectively together.

9.23 Expressing Sympathy (LO9.4)

Assume your boss's mother has just passed away. Write a note that you could include in a card.

Language Mechanics Check

9.24 Review the grammar rules in Appendix A. Then, rewrite each sentence to correct grammatical mistakes where needed.

A. Each customer should provide their complete purchase information for all refund requests.

B. Either Jake or Jen will give you their laptop when it's your turn to present.

C. Jen gave her presentation about giving back to your communities at the board meeting.

D. I serve our clients in the Western region, she serves our clients in the Southeastern region.

E. Jim's organization and the Chinese delegation is creating a Sino-American think tank.

F. The training manual for managers are online.

G. She thinks that we should keep a 6-week supply of inventory, he thinks we should keep a 2-week supply of inventory.

H. Getting 90 percentile, the GMAT score should help him get into a top MBA program.

I. The benefits at this company is one of the key attractions for new employees.

J. Jen's company provides their employees with many benefits.

Endnotes

1. Reina, D. S., & Reina, M. L. (2006). *Trust and betrayal in the workplace.* San Francisco: Berrett-Koehler Publishers, 19–20.

2. Krotz, J. L. (2010, July 7). The power of saying thank you. *Microsoft Business.* Retrieved from www.microsoft.com/business/en-us/resources/marketing/customer-service-acquisition/the-power-of-saying-thank-you.aspx#Thepowerofsayingthankyou.

3. Krotz, J. L. (2010, July 7). The power of saying thank you. *Microsoft Business.* Retrieved from www.microsoft.com/business/en-us/resources/marketing/customer-service-acquisition/the-power-of-saying-thank-you.aspx#Thepowerofsayingthankyou.

4. Weeks, H. (2003, April). The art of the apology. *Harvard Management Update, 8*(4), 10–11.

5. Kellerman, B. (2006, April). When should a leader apologize—and when not? *Harvard Business Review,* 72–81; Weeks, H. (2003, April). The art of the apology. *Harvard Management Update, 8*(4), 10–11.

6. Kellerman, B. (2006, April). When should a leader apologize—and when not? *Harvard Business Review,* 72–81; Weeks, H. (2003, April). The art of the apology. *Harvard Management Update, 8*(4), 72–81.

7. Society for Human Resource Management. (2013, November 12). Vacation time is time well spent, HR professionals say in new SHRM survey. Retrieved from https://www.shrm.org/about-shrm/press-room/press-releases/pages/vacationbenefits.aspx.

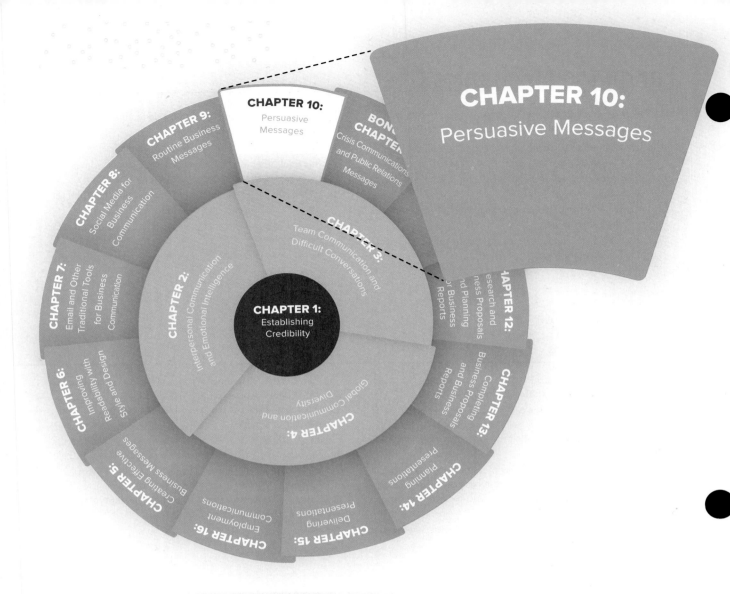

CHAPTER 10:
Persuasive Messages

  **ESTABLISHING CREDIBILITY**

 PRINCIPLES OF INTERPERSONAL COMMUNICATION

PRINCIPLES FOR & TYPES OF BUSINESS MESSAGES

 LEARNING OBJECTIVES

After studying this chapter, you should be able to do the following:

LO10.1 Describe the relationship between credibility and persuasion.

LO10.2 Explain the AIM planning process for persuasive messages and the basic components of most persuasive messages.

LO10.3 Explain how the tone and style of persuasive messages impact their influence.

LO10.4 Create compelling internal persuasive messages.

LO10.5 Explain how to influence professionals with various decision-making styles.

LO10.6 Compose influential external persuasive messages.

LO10.7 Construct effective mass sales messages.

LO10.8 Evaluate persuasive messages for effectiveness and fairness.

? WHY DOES THIS MATTER?

In many business situations, you hope to persuade others. In internal business communications, you may want your boss, peers, or colleagues to consider or adopt your ideas when their perspectives differ from yours. In external business communications, you will want to persuade your clients, customers, and prospects to use your products and services. Persuasion involves influencing others to see the merits of your ideas and act on your requests, even when they initially resist. In this chapter, we explore strategies for persuading others through writing.

In some ways, all business messages contain an element of persuasion—that is, you are hoping to influence the way others think, feel, or behave. Many of the concepts in this chapter will enhance your ability to make any kind of request. However, the approaches in this chapter are most applicable to situations in which your audience will initially resist your requests.

Throughout this chapter, you will see examples of persuasive messages at Better Horizons Credit Union. The chapter case provides the background.

> **Hear Pete Cardon explain why this matters.**
>
> **bit.ly/cardon10**

CHAPTER CASE — SHIFTING COURSE AT BETTER HORIZONS CREDIT UNION

Haniz Zogby

Christine Russo

WHO'S INVOLVED

Marketing Specialist

- Started working at Better Horizons nearly five years ago. She has worked 20 to 30 hours per week while attending college with a major in finance and a minor in event management.
- Started as a teller. Within a few years, she was promoted to positions of teller supervisor, loan officer, and marketing specialist.
- Currently working on marketing initiatives under the direction of Christine Russo.

President and CEO

- Has worked at Better Horizons for approximately ten years.
- Currently interested in increasing the number of young members. With declining numbers of young members, she is concerned that the credit union does not have good long-term prospects.

Haniz and Christine Want to Attract New Members by Focusing on Financial Planning

Christine recognized that people under the age of 25 were not joining the credit union. Christine asked Haniz and several marketing team members to develop a plan to attract more college students. After several months of work, Haniz and the team have a plan, but they know the executive team is deeply skeptical of plans to draw younger members. These plans have failed often in the past.

SITUATION 1

SITUATION 2

Christine and Haniz Promote a Mentorship Program to Attract and Retain New Hires

Christine recognizes that Better Horizons needs to hire younger, early-career professionals for several reasons. She thinks hiring early-career professionals will help with the strategy to attract younger members. She recently asked several of her employees to develop a mentoring program, which would help attract and retain new hires. She wants to persuade employees to volunteer as mentors for this program. Also, she wants Haniz to use the mentorship program as part of a pitch about career opportunities to soon-to-be college graduates.

SITUATION 3

Haniz Is in Charge of Recruiting Participants for a Local Charity Event

Christine asked Haniz to be in charge of recruiting credit union members to join this year's Hope Walkathon to support research on breast cancer. Better Horizons has assembled a walkathon team for this prominent community event each year for nearly a decade. Haniz is writing an email to send to all credit union members. The message will be modified slightly to appear as an announcement on the credit union website as well.

SITUATION 4

Haniz Needs to Create a Flyer Explaining the Benefits of Credit Union Membership Compared to Banks

Haniz is working on a flyer describing the benefits of membership at Better Horizons Credit Union. The flyer will be part of a packet of materials that is distributed to community members who participate in free financial planning and income tax assistance seminars offered by Better Horizons. Haniz is using the message to highlight the benefits of Better Horizons compared to local banks.

SITUATION 5

Haniz Is Helping Develop a Sales Message for Auto Loans

Haniz and several other employees are working on sales messages for auto loans. In recent months, Better Horizon's senior management decided the credit union should become a "player" in the auto loans market. Few Better Horizons members take advantage of car loans, most assuming that dealer financing is cheaper and easier to get.

TASK

1 How will Haniz write a message to Christine and the executive team that motivates them to invest in a new campaign? (See the section "Creating Internal Persuasive Messages.")

2 How will Christine solicit volunteers for the mentorship program? (See "Creating Internal Persuasive Messages.") How will Haniz pitch career opportunities at Better Horizons to soon-to-be college graduates? (See the section "Composing Mass Sales Messages.")

3 How will Haniz persuade credit union members to join the Hope Walkathon? (See the section "Constructing External Persuasive Messages.")

4 How will Haniz develop a general-purpose flyer that shows the broad benefits of choosing Better Horizons Credit Union over banks? (See "Constructing External Persuasive Messages.")

5 How will Haniz develop sales messages for an auto loan campaign? (See "Composing Mass Sales Messages.")

The Importance of Credibility in an Era of Mistrust and Skepticism

While credibility is critical to all business communications, its importance is heightened for persuasive messages. By definition, persuasion implies that you are communicating with someone who does not think or feel the same way as you do. So, your goal is to help your audience members identify with and find merit in your positions. If they question your credibility, they are unlikely to carefully consider your ideas, requests, or recommendations.

Persuasion is becoming more difficult as we live in a time of increasing mistrust. In Chapter 1, we discussed the declining levels of trust for nearly all professional groups, particularly business-related occupations. Michael Maslansky, one of the leading corporate communications experts, has labeled this the post-trust era (PTE):

> Just a few years ago, salespeople, corporate leaders, marketing departments, and communicators like me had it pretty easy. We looked at communication as a relatively linear process. . . . But trust disappeared, things changed. . . . In a word, trust is out, skepticism is in.[1]

Over the past decade, Michael Maslansky and his colleagues have examined how language is used to persuade and motivate others. By interviewing hundreds of thousands of employees and customers in some 30 countries, they have found that the language of trust is more important than ever. Furthermore, they have noticed emerging trends in how language impacts trust. Strategies for persuasion that once worked are less effective in the PTE. Other strategies continue to work well. In this chapter, we sort through some of these basic principles of persuasive writing and identify those strategies that are most effective in the PTE.

LO10.1 Describe the relationship between credibility and persuasion.

In the post-trust era, persuasion is more challenging.
Gajus/Shutterstock

Applying the AIM Planning Process to Persuasive Messages

Persuasion involves extensive planning: analyzing your *audience* to understand their needs, values, and how they are influenced; gathering the right *information* as you wrestle with the complicated business issues at hand; and developing a *message* that most effectively reduces resistance and gains buy-in. Many effective business communicators spend weeks and months learning about their target audiences, gathering information, and piecing together persuasive messages.

Understand Your Audience

To convince others to modify their own ideas and accept yours, you need to show that you care about them and that your ideas fit into their interests. This is the approach communication specialist Liz Simpson recommends:

> To succeed at the persuasion game, you have to be absolutely committed to understanding the other side's position as well as your own. Without that willingness to try on the other side's arguments, you simply cannot be persuasive. From that understanding will come the insights you need to move the other side over to your camp.[2]

This is true not only for ideas but also for products and services. Your best argument is always one that meets the needs and wants of your audience.

Understanding the needs and values of others is *not* simple. It requires a strong listening orientation. You will need to ask lots of questions to get beyond a surface understanding about the hopes, expectations, and hidden assumptions of your target audience. Once you know your target audience's needs and values, you are in a strong position to explain how your product, service, or idea benefits them.

LO10.2 Explain the AIM planning process for persuasive messages and the basic components of most persuasive messages.

Visit http://connect. mheducation.com for an exercise on this topic.

As you consider the needs of others in the workplace, you should always keep in mind the deep and underlying hopes of others. Your colleagues will generally want to help when they share the same purposes and values. Similarly, your colleagues nearly always want to feel appreciated and needed. For colleagues and customers, you can consider a variety of psychological principles of influence. Also, you should consider whether you are making a logical appeal or an emotional one in your persuasive messages.

Persuade through Shared Purpose and Shared Values In today's networked and more open work environment, professionals increasingly work in teams and communities (within organizations) tied together by a shared purpose and shared values. As a result, many professionals are highly motivated by appeals to support their organizations, their teams, and their colleagues because colleagues genuinely want to help.

When you make appeals to shared purpose and shared values, your credibility is typically the most important factor in gaining your colleagues' support. You can influence others best when they believe you are sincerely acting on behalf of the organization and them (caring), you are candid about the reasons behind your requests (character), and others are confident that your ideas will really make a positive difference (competence). While these types of appeals are often effective, use them sparingly. When overused, appeals to purpose and values may be interpreted as self-serving or insincere. You'll notice a persuasive message later in the chapter (Figure 10.5) that is primarily based on an appeal to shared purpose.

Show People They Are Sincerely Needed and Appreciated You can influence colleagues and partners far more easily when they know you appreciate them for their hard work, their abilities, and their good intentions. By complimenting them and expressing appreciation to them, they often will want to return that goodwill to you (discussed further in a few paragraphs in relation to the principle of *reciprocity*). Similarly, most of your colleagues want to feel needed. They want to feel that they are essential to getting work done. Your ability to persuade colleagues is often closely tied to how needed and appreciated you make them feel. Of course, your colleagues must trust your sincerity when you show them they are needed and appreciated.

Understand Methods of Influence Dr. Robert Cialdini, a marketing psychologist, has spent his career studying how people are influenced in business and marketing environments. He has examined research in this area for four decades, plus he spent three years taking undercover jobs in car dealerships, telemarketing firms, fundraising organizations, and other buyer–seller environments to learn the most influential ways of getting people to say yes. Based on his work, he has identified six principles of persuasion (aside from the price and quality of products and services). These principles include reciprocation, consistency, social proof, liking, authority, and scarcity.[3] Haniz's message to recruit credit union members for the Hope Walkathon offers an interesting example for applying these various principles (see Figure 10.9 for her completed message).

Reciprocation is a principle of influence based on returning favors. As defined by Cialdini, "We should try to repay, in kind, what another person has provided us."[4] Cialdini cited an interesting study in which a professor sent Christmas cards to a random sample of strangers to see what would happen. Many of the card recipients reciprocated, sending cards to the professor without attempting to find out who he was. The study showed that even card receivers who did not know the card sender and who might not interact with the card sender in the future felt compelled to return the favor of sending a card. People tend to feel obligated to pay back others when they've received something of value.[5]

Haniz uses the principle of reciprocation in her message in several ways. For example, she focuses on a lengthy reciprocal relationship that the credit union has with the local breast cancer center, and the walkathon serves as the mechanism that draws the two organizations together. The credit union helps the center by generating walkathon donations, and the center helps the credit union and the larger community through more effective breast cancer treatment and education. Furthermore, the message implies a reciprocal relationship between the credit union and its members by offering various free items, such as a T-shirt, a water bottle, and a cancer guide, to members who are willing to participate in the walkathon.

Consistency is based on the idea that once people make an explicit commitment, they tend to follow through or honor that commitment. In other words, they want to stay consistent with their original commitment. Cialdini cited several studies to make this point. In one, psychologists found that horse racing fans become more confident that their horses would win after placing a bet. Once they made a final commitment, they were further convinced of the correctness of their choice.[6]

Haniz appeals to commitment and consistency in several ways. Foremost, she appeals to the credit union's long commitment to the fight against breast cancer. Some credit union members will want to continue to honor this long-standing collective commitment and will appreciate that their credit union is doing so. She also provides links in the message for people to immediately act on their interest in the walkathon. A link to register right now serves as an immediate commitment to participate.

Social proof is a principle of influence whereby people determine what is right, correct, or desirable by seeing what others do. Haniz employs several appeals to social proof in her letter. She describes the level of participation and contribution among members in last year's walkathon, implying that the popularity and financial impact of this event make it a good cause. Also, the walkathon itself is a type of social proof; the gathering of thousands of people wearing team T-shirts and marching in unison for a cause is powerful imagery.[7]

Liking is a principle of influence whereby people are more likely to be persuaded by people they like.[8] Haniz appeals directly to this principle by describing Betty Williams, who is a breast cancer survivor, the benefactor of the breast center, a credit union member, and a participant in the walkathon. Betty Williams is presumably a person most people in the community know and like, a woman many of the credit union members may know from running into her at the credit union or other community events, and a woman who is passionate about an important cause (a reason for liking). Haniz emphasizes in the message that walkathon participants will join this likable and respected community member at the walkathon.

Authority is a principle of influence whereby people follow authority figures. The number of celebrity endorsements in advertising is evidence of how authority can impact persuasion.[9] Although Haniz does not appeal to a national celebrity, she does appeal to a prominent local community member—again Betty Williams. With Betty's level of influence and personal experience combating cancer, she is likely seen as an authority. Furthermore, Haniz also appeals to members to support the Betty Williams Breast Center, a group of expert professionals who collectively are authorities on breast cancer.

Scarcity is a principle of influence whereby people think there is limited availability of something they want or need, so they must act quickly.[10] Haniz employs this principle in terms of time. She explains that the walkathon occurs only once each year (limited time period to participate) and that participants must sign up by a given deadline (limited time period to sign up).

You will apply these principles most often in external persuasive messages, and you should always apply them fairly. Cialdini describes them as "weapons of influence."[11] The very term *weapons* implies that they are powerful and can do harm. In the "Apply the FAIR Test" section near the end of the chapter, we further discuss the appropriate use of these principles.

Persuade through Emotion and Reason   Most people justify their business decisions based on the soundness of ideas, not feelings. Savvy business communicators, however, understand the importance of injecting emotion into their persuasive messages. While they appreciate the place of reason in business and consumer decisions, they understand that resistance to ideas, products, and services is often emotional. Conversely, they are aware that their target audiences often possess strong emotional attachment to competing ideas, products, and services. Thus, effective communicators find ways to appeal to the core emotional benefits of products, services, and ideas.[12]

Even in internal persuasive messages, emotional appeals are critical, as indicated by Craig Conway, former president and CEO of PeopleSoft:

> Good communicators have an enormous advantage over poor communicators because so much of running a company is inspirational. . . . You just have to be able to persuade people that they are a part of something bigger. If you have a creative vision and you can communicate it in a compelling way to get people excited, you will recruit better people as a result. Then, it is easy to convince the world that you have a more dynamic company.[13]

Part of understanding your audience is identifying the needs and values that resonate emotionally for them.

Typically, internal persuasive messages focus mostly on logical appeals. External persuasive messages, with the exception of those that emphasize price, generally include strong emotional appeals. As you develop persuasive messages, think about how to get the right mix of logical and emotional appeals. Generally, you will supply both but emphasize one or the other. Keep in mind that even when you choose to make strong emotional appeals in written messages, you should generally avoid the tone of mass advertising, where exaggeration, sarcasm, and over-the-top appeals are acceptable and even effective. Later in the chapter, you will notice several messages created by Haniz and Christine—two based more strongly on logical appeals (Figures 10.7 and 10.10) and two on emotional appeals (Figures 10.9 and 10.11).

Gather the Right Information

Gathering the right information and developing your ideas for persuasive messages is critical. Since your audience is resistant to the message, one of your key tasks is to establish credibility. Developing strong ideas in the interest of your audience helps you demonstrate your voice of competence. It involves gaining a deep understanding of the benefits and drawbacks of your ideas, products, and services. In addition, it involves gaining a thorough understanding of competing ideas, products, and services.

Thus, before attempting to persuade others, expert business communicators seek to understand products, services, and ideas in great depth so that they can speak from an authoritative and *competent* perspective. To address the issue of attracting younger credit union members, Christine and Haniz spend months learning about the strategies that other credit unions use. When Haniz works on a message that promotes her credit union over local banks, she carefully analyzes and compares the major products and services offered by her credit union and those of competing banks. When Haniz works on a message to persuade credit union members to join the Hope Walkathon, she learns all she can about participation in this event and how it helps in the fight against breast cancer.

Set Up the Message

Most business writing is **direct** and **explicit**. It is direct in that you begin with a main idea or argument and then provide the supporting reasons. It is explicit in that nothing is implied; statements contain full and unambiguous meaning. When you write directly and explicitly, you help your readers understand your message and you show respect for their time.

Components of Persuasive Messages

- Gain attention.
- Raise a need.
- Deliver a solution.
- Provide a rationale.
- Validate the views, preferences, and concerns of others.
- Give counterpoints (optional).
- Call to action.

TABLE 10.1

Effective Attention-Getters

Type of Attention-Getter	Example
Rhetorical question	Did you know that average credit union members save $400 per year compared to bank customers?
Intriguing statistic	In the past five years, we've lost over 200 members—over 10 percent of our membership.
Compelling and unusual fact(s)	You've probably heard car dealers boast about their near-zero percent interest rates—but there's a catch! By financing with car dealers, you give up your opportunity to receive manufacturer rebates and your power to negotiate on price.
Challenge	Please join our team in this year's Hope Walkathon in the fight against breast cancer.
Testimonial	"I never knew I could have so much negotiating power with a preapproved loan. By getting my car loan through Better Horizons, I negotiated a great deal with the car dealer. This is the way to buy cars!"

Compared to other business messages, persuasive messages are sometimes more **indirect** and **implicit**. They are sometimes indirect in that they provide the rationale for a request before making the specific request. They are sometimes implicit in that the request or some of the rationale for the request may be implied. In other words, sometimes the reader needs to read between the lines to grasp the entire meaning. Implicit statements politely ask people to do or think differently. Also, explicitly stating some types of benefits is considered poor form—for example, matters of financial or career gain in internal persuasive requests.[14]

Attention   The first task of most persuasive messages is to gain the attention of your readers. You can do this in a variety of ways, including asking a rhetorical question, providing a compelling or interesting fact, revealing a compelling statistic, issuing a challenge, or posting a testimonial.[15] For internal persuasive messages, the primary means of gaining attention is demonstrating a business need—a gap between what is and what could be.[16] You generally have more flexibility in external persuasive messages as you choose your attention-getters. See Table 10.1 for examples of attention-getters Haniz might use for some of her communication tasks.

Need, Solution, and Rationale   In the body of your message, your first task is to tie your product, service, or idea to the *needs* of your readers. The best way to reduce the resistance your reader may have is to show that your message meets your readers' needs. Once you've stated the need, you may describe your *solution,* which is a recommended product, service, or idea. Many readers will remain skeptical unless you provide convincing support. So, you will need to provide a strong *rationale,* meaning solid reasons why your product, service, or idea really benefits them. After all, you are more than likely attempting to influence skeptics.[17]

As you structure your message, consider how *direct* you should be. If your audience members are strongly and emotionally resistant to your solution, consider a more indirect approach so they warm up to your ideas before you suggest a solution. To make your message less direct, provide the rationale before the solution.

Validation   At some point in the body of the message, you should validate your readers by showing appreciation for their views, preferences, and concerns. **Validation** implies that you recognize and appreciate others' needs, wants, ideas, and preferences as legitimate and reasonable, "especially when they are different than your own." By validating your readers, you show respect for them and demonstrate a balanced perspective.[18]

Counterpoints   Traditionally, communicators overcame objections by providing counterpoints to any of the audience members' objections. In other words, they showed how their own ideas, products, or services were superior to the competing ideas, products, or services the audience favored.

Overcoming objections with counterpoints, however, is risky in the post-trust era. This approach may unnecessarily carry a *me-versus-you* tone and delegitimize the readers' concerns. Michael Maslansky, in his research about emerging trends in sales messages in the PTE, states that validation is "using words to let people know that their concerns are valid," and that it is the "polar opposite of overcoming objections."[19] He says the "new sales mantra [is to] agree with objections."[20] This perhaps ironic approach shows respect and balance because you validate the potential customer's feelings and ideas. When you validate your readers, they are more likely to accept the merits of your persuasive message.

Thus, consider carefully whether to include counterpoints to your readers' objections. When you know people well and believe that you will not create a *me-versus-you* adversarial stance, tactfully state how your ideas, products, and services outperform those of your readers.

Skilled business communicators understand that building support for their ideas takes time. Especially for persuasion within companies, you will generally use a mix of communication channels. Rarely will your ideas be accepted and enacted with one written message. However, one written message can make a powerful statement and open avenues of communication that lead to acceptance and adoption of your ideas.

Action   You conclude persuasive messages with a call to action, which asks your readers to take a specific step toward the purchase of a product or service or acceptance of an idea. However, a call to action should not be a hard sell; pressuring others is increasingly ineffective in the PTE.[21] In external persuasive messages, the call to action is typically a specific and explicit step. In internal persuasive messages, the call to action is sometimes explicit and sometimes implicit. It is more likely to be implicit for controversial change ideas and when corresponding with superiors who have ultimate decision-making authority.

Getting the Tone and Style Right for Persuasive Messages

LO10.3   Explain how the tone and style of persuasive messages impact their influence.

Visit http://connect.mheducation.com for an exercise on this topic.

The tone for persuasive messages should be confident and positive, yet at the same time avoid exaggeration or hype. This is tricky! You will no doubt need to make some trade-offs. The more confident and positive you make your message, the more you risk being perceived as pushy or exaggerated. As you reduce confidence and positivity, you risk your product, service, or idea being perceived as weak or unexciting. One benefit of asking colleagues to read your persuasive message before you send it is they can help you decide if you have achieved the right level of confidence and positivity without sacrificing believability.

The writing style of your message should be action-oriented and lively. But again, you risk being perceived as unbelievable or overly enthusiastic if you overdo the language. However, you risk being perceived as dull or unexceptional if you don't use engaging, lively language. Proofreading by yourself and with the help of colleagues will help you get the right writing style to set your message apart.

Apply the Personal Touch

Recently, a number of competing developers delivered presentations to a property owner, each hoping to persuade him to sell them 4,000 acres of much-sought-after property. The presentations were nearly identical, so the property owner was unsure how to choose the best developer. A few days later, the property owner received a handwritten thank-you note from one candidate. The property owner immediately awarded the deal to that developer because he had taken the time to write a message of appreciation.[22]

Often, your competitors are nearly identical to you. Your colleagues and customers will be more easily persuaded when you show interest in them personally, speak to them in personal terms, understand their specific needs, and demonstrate that you are seeking benefits for them. Personalizing your messages is not easy, though, as Michael Maslansky points out:

> For all of us, selling ideas or products or ourselves begins with a need to talk about something that we have and the audience should need, want, or agree with. The problem is that too often, we focus on the first part—what we want to sell, and too little on the second—why they want to buy . . . and yet, our audience demands increasingly that messages, products, and services speak directly to them.[23]

Creating messages that *speak directly* to customers and colleagues requires that you use language that helps your customers and colleagues feel the product, service, or idea is just for them.[24]

One of the primary strategies you can use to personalize persuasive messages is your selection of voice—either you-voice, we-voice, I-voice, or impersonal voice (as introduced in Chapter 2). Table 10.2 offers guidance on choosing the appropriate

---

Guidelines for Tone for Persuasive Messages

- Apply the personal touch.
- Use action-oriented, lively language.
- Write with confidence.
- Offer choice.
- Show positivity.

TABLE 10.2

Voice in Persuasive Messages

Voice	Appropriate Cases	Cautions	Examples
You-voice	Use in external persuasive messages to emphasize reader benefits.	Presumptuousness— assuming you know what is good for someone else	When you take out an auto loan, you get a variety of resources to help you in your car shopping, including a free copy of a *Kelley Blue Book*, access to free Carfax reports, Mechanical Breakdown Insurance (MBI), and Guaranteed Auto Protection (GAP). In this example, you-voice helps show direct benefits to the customers. Overuse across an entire message, however, may come across as presumptuous, overbearing, or exaggerated.
We-voice	Use in internal persuasive messages to emphasize shared work goals.	Presumptuousness— assuming you share common beliefs, ideas, or understanding with your colleagues	At Better Horizons, we've instilled a personal touch into every aspect of our business. We've reinforced this culture with face-to-face services. Our tellers welcome members by name. When members come into the credit union, they know we care about them as people, not just as customers. The warm, friendly, genuine, and personal approach we take to serving our members is why I'm so proud to work here. In this passage, we-voice instills a sense of shared values, priorities, and goals. We-voice can instill a strong sense of teamwork. When audience members have different perspectives, however, they may resent that you are stating agreement where it does not exist.
I-voice	Use in all persuasive messages sparingly.	Overuse implies self-centeredness	After examining the results of other credit unions, I am convinced that these tools can build emotional connections and loyalty with our members. In this example, I-voice is used to show a personal opinion and shows respect for audience members who are not yet fully persuaded. Frequent use of I-voice across an entire message, however, may come across as emphasizing your interests rather than those of the audience.
Impersonal voice	Use in persuasive messages to emphasize objectivity and neutrality.	Overuse may depersonalize the message	The basic difference between credit unions and banks is that credit union members own and control their credit unions whereas bank account holders have no stake or control in their financial institutions. In this example, impersonal voice helps show objectivity. An entire persuasive message in impersonal voice, however, may fail to connect on a personal level with the audience.

voice. Generally, you-voice is more effective in external persuasive messages to customers and clients because it emphasizes the benefits they receive from your products and services. From the customer's perspective, the you-voice shows them that they are the center of attention.

Writing in the you-voice to customers is more than just a stylistic choice. It forces you to consciously consider the readers' needs and wants. It forces you to personalize the message for them. By contrast, the we-voice in external messages can focus too much attention on your company and de-emphasize benefits to the customer. Notice the difference in overall tone in the two messages in Figures 10.4 and 10.5. In the less effective example, the you-voice is hardly used at all compared to the dominating we-voice. In the more effective example, the you-voice takes center stage over the we-voice. The extensive use of you-voice in the more effective message sends a strong meta message: *This message is about you.*

Another method of personalizing a message is to make your statements tangible. By definition, *tangible* means something can be touched; it is material or substantial. In a business communications context, making the statement **tangible** implies that the readers can discern something in terms that are meaningful to them. This allows the reader to sense the impact on a personal level.[25] You often can achieve a tangible feel by combining you-voice with specificity. Consider the examples in Table 10.3, from messages that Haniz is working on for the credit union.

As you reread your message, keep in mind the following advice from sales specialist Ralph Allora: "Read the letter aloud. If it doesn't sound like you're having a conversation with the client over the phone, then you're not using the right tone."[26] This in part is a test of whether you have personalized your message enough.

TABLE 10.3

Making Tangible Statements

Less Effective	More Effective
Credit unions save members about $8 billion a year thanks to better interest rates and reduced fees.	On average, credit union members save $400 each year compared to bank customers thanks to lower loan rates and fees.
The benefit is not tangible. Customers are not sure what the benefit would be for them personally.	This benefit is tangible; the customers know how much they will save on an individual level.
In recent years, many credit unions have lost membership because younger individuals are not attracted to them.	In the past five years, we've lost over 200 members—over 10 percent of our membership. And we simply aren't attracting younger members.
This statement focuses on a general trend for credit unions but does not indicate an impact on a particular credit union.	This statement invokes a sense of what is happening right here at our credit union. Identifying the amount (as well as a percentage) helps the reader discern the impact.
We provide lower rates on car loans. Our car loan rates are between 1.5 and 1.75 percentage points lower than at any of the banks in town.	**You pay lower rates on car loans.** You can get car loan rates at Better Horizons that are 1.5–1.75 percentage points lower than at any other bank in town. Consider the savings: • On a 4-year $15,000 new car loan: You save about $680. • On a 4-year $5,000 used car loan: You save about $200.
This statement doesn't help the customers understand how much in dollars they would save on a car loan at Better Horizons.	This statement allows customers to easily think about how much savings they would receive by getting a car loan with Better Horizons.

TABLE 10.4

Using Action-Oriented and Lively Language

Less Effective	More Effective
The Betty Williams Breast Center has a nationally accredited program for treatment of breast cancer.	The Betty Williams Breast Center runs a nationally accredited program for treatment of breast cancer.
The weak verb *has* implies little action on the part of the Betty Williams Breast Center.	The action verb *runs* implies a full-fledged and active effort on the part of the Betty Williams Breast Center.
Better Horizons has always been known for its personal approach to our members. Our transactions have always occurred through face-to-face services. Our tellers are friendly to all members.	At Better Horizons, we've instilled a personal touch into every aspect of our business. We've reinforced this culture with face-to-face services. Our tellers welcome members by name. When members come into the credit union, they know we care about them as people, not just as customers.
Uses unexciting, weak verbs: *has been known, have occurred, are* (notice how passive verbs detract from a sense of action and engagement). The central theme of personalized service does not come through. For example, consider the contrast between *our tellers are friendly* versus *our tellers welcome members by name*.	Uses a positive, diverse set of action verbs: *instilled, reinforced, welcome, care*. Uses adjectives and nouns to further emphasize a central theme of personalized service: *personal touch, face-to-face services, name*.

Use Action-Oriented and Lively Language

In persuasive messages, you have somewhat more license to write creatively. Focus on using action-oriented and lively words to achieve a sense of excitement, optimism, or other positive emotions. Use strong nouns and verbs to add to the excitement of the message. Some sales messages sound dull because of overuse of and reliance on words such as *provide* and *offer*.[27] Across the entire message or thought, the action-oriented and lively language should emphasize a central theme. See Table 10.4 for examples from documents Haniz is working on for two of her projects.

Write with Confidence

As you display more confidence in your idea, your product, or your service, you can more effectively influence your audience. Effective persuaders provide compelling and simple reasons for action. They should show confidence in these ideas, as illustrated in Table 10.5, again with examples from two of Haniz's projects. Emotionally, the writer's confidence allows the audience to gain confidence in the message. In internal persuasive messages, expressing confidence in key players, who can make the change occur, is crucial. These key players include upper-level executives who will actively endorse and authorize resources as well as those managers and employees who will put the ideas into motion.[28]

Offer Choice

Michael Maslansky and his research team have examined the reactions of tens of thousands of customers and clients to many types of written messages. In this section, we illustrate a few findings from the financial industry. For example, in Figure 10.1, you see four statements that were sent to respondents. In the hypothetical scenario that was presented to them, a company is attempting to do a good thing—give its employees an opportunity to put money in a retirement account.

TABLE 10.5

Writing with Confidence

Less Effective	More Effective
If the executive team is interested, we could share more information about how we arrived at our conclusions.	We are eager to meet with the executive team and present our findings and recommendations in more detail. Could we set a time within the next two weeks to share with the team?
This statement is unassertive and, by extension, not confident. It does not show conviction in her message.	These statements imply confidence in the writer's message and confidence that a meeting will further her goals. These statements maintain a respectful tone.
Please think about how Better Horizons can help you in your banking.	We encourage you to stop by Better Horizons and make direct comparisons with your current bank. You'll find that banking with Better Horizons saves you money, provides convenience when you travel, and offers services to meet nearly any banking need.
This nonspecific request sounds weak and not confident. It gives the reader an excuse to easily dismiss the message.	This request lays down a challenge to make direct comparisons, confidently implying that Better Horizons can outperform competitors. It then directly states specific benefits to the potential member.

The four statements state essentially the same thing but are phrased differently. Each is written fairly well and appeals to some individuals. The statement that appeals to the most people (40 percent) emphasizes choice rather than intent. It uses the you-voice rather than the we-voice, which is preferable for many messages written to consumers (this is most similar to a consumer situation). It contains three short sentences with 7, 2, and 29 words. The emphasis on choice (other-orientation),

FIGURE 10.1

Most Effective Statements to Persuade Skeptical Employees *(Creating Salary Deduction for 401[k] Scenario)*

Source: Maslansky, M., S. West, & G.DeMoss, (2010). *The language of trust: Selling ideas in a world of skeptics.* Van Kampen Investor Services, Inc.

Note: The survey involved a hypothetical situation where employers would automatically deduct 7 percent of an employee's salary and place it into a 401(k). This process would help employees save money for the future. The employees would have the option to opt-out.

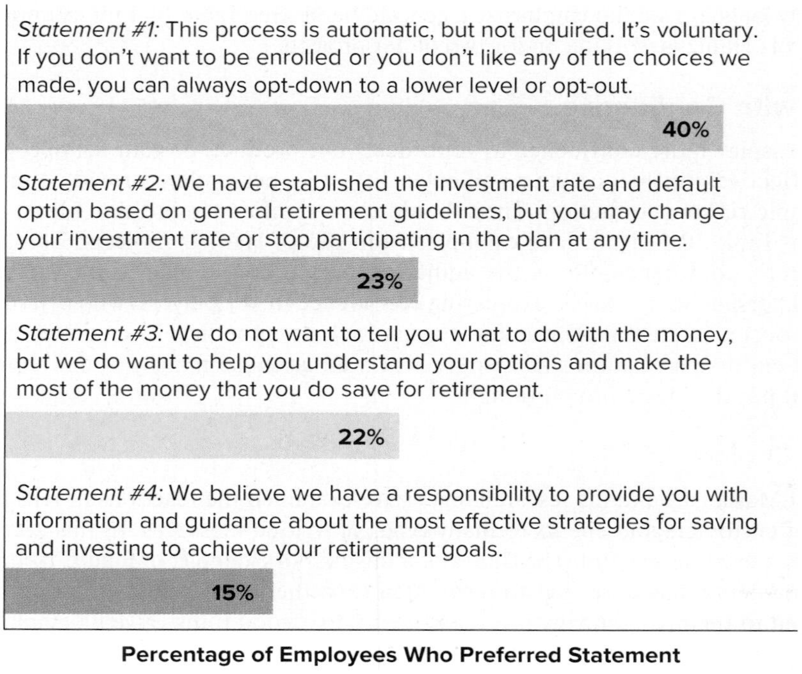

Statement #1: This process is automatic, but not required. It's voluntary. If you don't want to be enrolled or you don't like any of the choices we made, you can always opt-down to a lower level or opt-out.
40%

Statement #2: We have established the investment rate and default option based on general retirement guidelines, but you may change your investment rate or stop participating in the plan at any time.
23%

Statement #3: We do not want to tell you what to do with the money, but we do want to help you understand your options and make the most of the money that you do save for retirement.
22%

Statement #4: We believe we have a responsibility to provide you with information and guidance about the most effective strategies for saving and investing to achieve your retirement goals.
15%

Percentage of Employees Who Preferred Statement

TABLE 10.6

Emphasizing Choice

Less Effective	More Effective
You owe it to the women in your lives to make a difference.	You can help make a difference for women here in our community.
This appeal focuses on obligation and pressure. Most readers will not respond positively.	This appeal focuses on volunteerism and contribution to the community without telling the readers what to do.
The walkathon will be held on Saturday, October 6 at 9:00 a.m. at Central Park. Do your part to improve the lives of women in our community!	The walkathon will be held on Saturday, October 6 at 9:00 a.m. at Central Park. Please join Betty and the rest of the Better Horizons team for a day of fun, excitement, and hope!
This request is a guilt trip; it emphasizes the readers' duty.	This request recognizes the readers' choice to participate in a fun and exciting approach to a good cause.

use of you-voice (other-orientation), and simple language combine to make this the most influential statement. By contrast, the other options each contain one long sentence (30, 36, and 27 words).

In the PTE, customers and clients consider choice an indicator of credibility. They view simple language (not implying lack of sophisticated knowledge) as a display of transparency and respect. In contrast, they view overly complex language as potentially deceptive.[29] Similarly, effective persuasive messages avoid statements that may be perceived as pressure tactics. Hard sells are increasingly ineffective in a PTE, especially in written format.[30] Compare Haniz's less effective and more effective persuasive statements in Table 10.6, all of which you will see again in her messages located later in the chapter.

In persuasive messages, always be careful about being perceived as presumptuous—unfairly assuming that you know or even share the thoughts, feelings, and intentions of others. Many people are easily offended when you presume to know or even dictate how they will think, feel, or react to your messages.[31]

Show Positivity

Positivity in persuasive messages helps your audience focus on the benefits rather than the drawbacks of what you are trying to promote. Maslansky and his team's research helps demonstrate that subtle changes to more positive wording are generally more persuasive. For example, they asked consumers to identify which of three pairs of phrases were more persuasive in promotional material about investment options.

In the first pair of statements, 90 percent of consumers thought the statement *making sure you have enough money as long as you live* was more effective than the statement *managing longevity risk*. Overwhelmingly, the consumers thought the benefit (having long-term financial security) was more influential than the possible drawback (avoiding financial loss).

For the second pair of statements, 81 percent of consumers thought the statement *making sure you can afford to maintain your lifestyle* was more persuasive than the statement *managing inflation risk*. Similarly, the vast majority of consumers in the case thought that the benefit (maintaining your lifestyle) was more compelling than the drawback (possibly losing your current buying power).

TABLE 10.7

Statements to Avoid in the Post-Trust Era

Type	Examples That Don't Work
Trust me	"Trust me" or "We speak your language"
Unbelievable	"Your call is important to us" or "We care about our customers"
Too good to be true	"This is the right product for you" or "We give you guaranteed results"
Excuses	"What you need to understand is . . ." or "Our hands are tied"
Explanations	"This was taken out of context" or "I can explain"
Fear tactics	"Are you concerned about the security of your family?" or "Act now or you'll miss this opportunity"

Source: Maslansky, M., West, S., & DeMoss, G. (2010). *The language of trust: Selling ideas in a world of skeptics.* Van Kampen Investor Services, Inc.

For the third pair of statements, 63 percent of consumers thought the statement *making sure you can participate in the gains while reducing your downside risk* was more persuasive than *managing market risk*. In this case, consumers were more positively influenced by the statement about risk (a drawback) when it was preceded by a phrase about gains (the benefit).[32]

In addition to being positive, avoiding superlatives gives you the best chance of persuading your audience. Phrases such as *best product on the market*, *state-of-the-art technology*, or *best-in-class service* sound increasingly hollow. Maslansky's research with consumers shows that terms such as *comfortable retirement* rather than *dream retirement*; *protection* rather than *guarantee*; *financial security* rather than *financial freedom*; *effective* rather than *best of breed* are more persuasive.

Consumers perceive too-good-to-be-true statements as attempts to convince them of "the merits without making a rational argument. And they [too-good-to-be-true statements] fail because they suggest an inherent bias that ruins the integrity of the communicator."[33] Table 10.7 highlights the kinds of phrases that are increasingly ineffective with today's skeptical consumers. Table 10.8 contrasts messages from Haniz's projects that persuade with and without exaggeration.

TABLE 10.8

Avoiding Exaggeration and Superlatives

Less Effective	More Effective
You can trust us at Better Horizons to make your financial dreams come true.	As a nonprofit, member-controlled financial institution, Better Horizons can provide you with higher rates on savings accounts, better terms on loans, and lower fees.
This statement uses phrases that seem unbelievable *(you can trust us)* and exaggerated *(make your financial dreams come true)*. It is positive but not plausible.	This statement focuses on specific benefits and uses words that nearly all people view positively *(nonprofit, member-controlled, savings, better, lower fees)*. It is both positive and plausible.
Pay attention to these facts or risk losing money to banks.	Consider some of the following reasons to join Better Horizons and start saving today.
This statement focuses on fear and applies pressure. Most customers would consider the writer not credible.	This statement is inviting and nonthreatening. It uses pressure-free *(consider)* and positive *(join, start saving)* words.

Creating Internal Persuasive Messages

Internal and external persuasive messages contain many common elements: They gain *attention*, raise a *need*, deliver a *solution*, provide a *rationale*, show *appreciation* for differences of opinion, give *counterpoints*, and call readers to *action*. Nevertheless, internal and external persuasive messages differ in some ways (see Table 10.9). Internal messages more often focus on promoting ideas, whereas external messages more often focus on promoting products and services. Also, internal persuasive messages tend to be slightly more direct and explicit, and they tend to be based more so on logical appeals. In contrast, external persuasive messages tend to be slightly more indirect and implicit, and they often rely heavily on emotional appeals.

LO10.4 Create compelling internal persuasive messages.

Visit **http://connect.mheducation.com** for an exercise on this topic.

Influencing a Superior

You often rely on your supervisors and other superiors to work on interesting projects and follow through on ideas of interest. Christine asked Haniz to work on a plan to attract younger members to the credit union. When Haniz thought the report was ready, Christine said, "Haniz, send me an email with the report. I'll forward it to the executive team. Several members of that group are always naysayers, so we want to make sure you can present to them and field their questions." In the less effective message (see Figure 10.2), Haniz shows little confidence and specificity in the new ideas. The message generally contains short, dull, and nontangible comments.

In the more effective message (see Figure 10.3), Haniz begins with a tangible business problem. Then, she tactfully discusses her ideas and concludes with calls to action. The message contains conviction without sounding too pushy. This message will open avenues for constructive conversations when Haniz and Christine meet with the executive team.

TABLE 10.9

Components of Internal and External Persuasive Messages

	Internal Messages (Typically for Ideas)	**External Messages (Typically for Products and Services)**
Attention	Overview of a business problem	Catchy statement
Need	Description of a business problem	Description of unmet *needs* or *wants* of your customers
Solution	Description of *how* your idea or policy addresses the business problem	Description of *how* your product or service benefits customers
Rationale	Elaboration about *why* your idea or policy is the best option	Elaboration about *why* your product or service will benefit the customer
Appreciation	Appreciation for decision makers' perspectives and resistance to your ideas	Recognition of customers' resistance to your product or service
Counterpoints	Explanation of why your ideas are better than competing ideas (typically those of decision makers who comprise your target audience)	Explanation of why your product/service is better than competing products/services (typically those favored by the target audience)
Action	Recommendations for a course of action or further discussion about an idea or policy	Description of a specific step for the customer to take toward purchase of a product or service

FIGURE 10.2

Less Effective Internal Persuasive Message

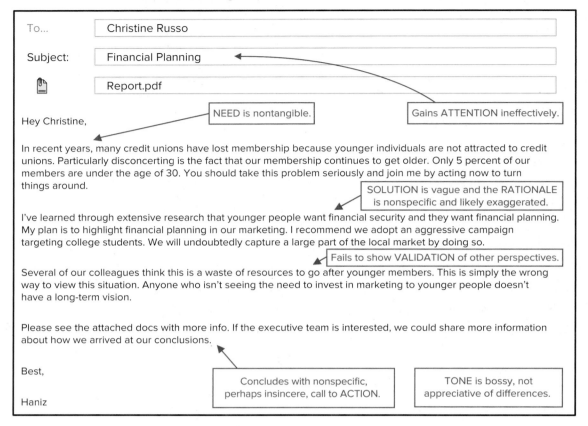

To...   Christine Russo

Subject: Financial Planning

Report.pdf

> Gains ATTENTION ineffectively.

Hey Christine,

> NEED is nontangible.

In recent years, many credit unions have lost membership because younger individuals are not attracted to credit unions. Particularly disconcerting is the fact that our membership continues to get older. Only 5 percent of our members are under the age of 30. You should take this problem seriously and join me by acting now to turn things around.

> SOLUTION is vague and the RATIONALE is nonspecific and likely exaggerated.

I've learned through extensive research that younger people want financial security and they want financial planning. My plan is to highlight financial planning in our marketing. I recommend we adopt an aggressive campaign targeting college students. We will undoubtedly capture a large part of the local market by doing so.

> Fails to show VALIDATION of other perspectives.

Several of our colleagues think this is a waste of resources to go after younger members. This is simply the wrong way to view this situation. Anyone who isn't seeing the need to invest in marketing to younger people doesn't have a long-term vision.

Please see the attached docs with more info. If the executive team is interested, we could share more information about how we arrived at our conclusions.

Best,

Haniz

> Concludes with nonspecific, perhaps insincere, call to ACTION.

> TONE is bossy, not appreciative of differences.

Influencing Employees

In Figures 10.4 and 10.5, you can see a less effective and a more effective example of Christine asking employees to volunteer as mentors to new employees. In the less effective example, Christine comes across as bossy and demanding. Leaders rarely capture the hearts and minds of their employees when they fail to offer choice, portray problems in excessively negative terms, and don't validate legitimate concerns. You'll notice that Christine makes all these mistakes in the less effective example. In the more effective example, Christine offers choice throughout the message, appeals to shared purpose throughout the message, offers a positive vision, and validates the employees' real concerns about time commitments. Although this is a relatively simple message, Christine is likely to inspire many employees to volunteer as mentors as long as employees view her as credible and sincere.

LO10.5 Explain how to influence professionals with various decision-making styles.

Taking Initiative, Showing Persistence, and Adapting to Various Decision-Making Styles

In practice, persuasion may a long time. It requires initiative and it requires persistence. It often takes many conversations and many written messages. It usually requires courage to start the conversation and determination to gain the commitment of others. Successful businessman and *Wall Street Journal* writer Andy Kessler suggests persuasion requires at least five touch points with decision makers. He suggests five meetings in the following pattern: the sniff, the story, the data, the ask, and the close.[34] Kessler's point is clear: You should view persuasion as a process with several stages.

FIGURE 10.3

More Effective Internal Persuasive Message

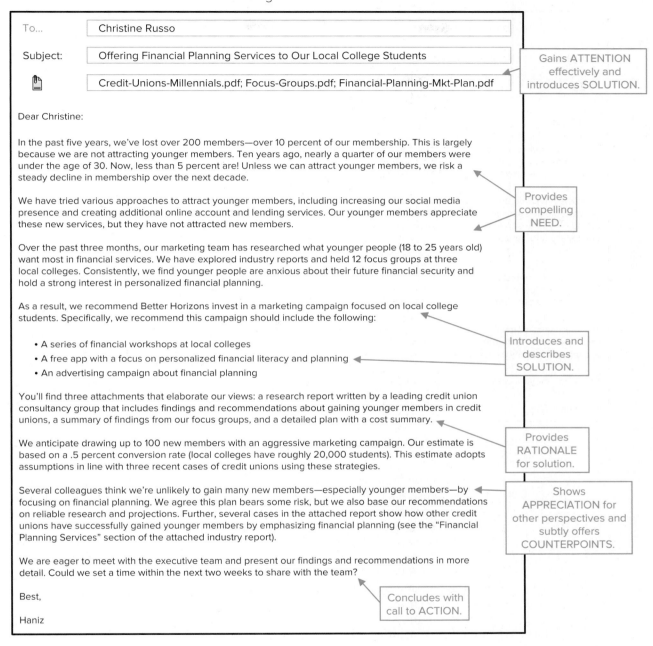

To...	Christine Russo
Subject:	Offering Financial Planning Services to Our Local College Students
📄	Credit-Unions-Millennials.pdf; Focus-Groups.pdf; Financial-Planning-Mkt-Plan.pdf

> Gains ATTENTION effectively and introduces SOLUTION.

Dear Christine:

In the past five years, we've lost over 200 members—over 10 percent of our membership. This is largely because we are not attracting younger members. Ten years ago, nearly a quarter of our members were under the age of 30. Now, less than 5 percent are! Unless we can attract younger members, we risk a steady decline in membership over the next decade.

We have tried various approaches to attract younger members, including increasing our social media presence and creating additional online account and lending services. Our younger members appreciate these new services, but they have not attracted new members.

> Provides compelling NEED.

Over the past three months, our marketing team has researched what younger people (18 to 25 years old) want most in financial services. We have explored industry reports and held 12 focus groups at three local colleges. Consistently, we find younger people are anxious about their future financial security and hold a strong interest in personalized financial planning.

As a result, we recommend Better Horizons invest in a marketing campaign focused on local college students. Specifically, we recommend this campaign should include the following:

- A series of financial workshops at local colleges
- A free app with a focus on personalized financial literacy and planning
- An advertising campaign about financial planning

> Introduces and describes SOLUTION.

You'll find three attachments that elaborate our views: a research report written by a leading credit union consultancy group that includes findings and recommendations about gaining younger members in credit unions, a summary of findings from our focus groups, and a detailed plan with a cost summary.

We anticipate drawing up to 100 new members with an aggressive marketing campaign. Our estimate is based on a .5 percent conversion rate (local colleges have roughly 20,000 students). This estimate adopts assumptions in line with three recent cases of credit unions using these strategies.

> Provides RATIONALE for solution.

Several colleagues think we're unlikely to gain many new members—especially younger members—by focusing on financial planning. We agree this plan bears some risk, but we also base our recommendations on reliable research and projections. Further, several cases in the attached report show how other credit unions have successfully gained younger members by emphasizing financial planning (see the "Financial Planning Services" section of the attached industry report).

> Shows APPRECIATION for other perspectives and subtly offers COUNTERPOINTS.

We are eager to meet with the executive team and present our findings and recommendations in more detail. Could we set a time within the next two weeks to share with the team?

Best,

> Concludes with call to ACTION.

Haniz

Effective persuaders also learn to recognize various decision-making styles. Gary Williams and Robert Miller studied the decision-making styles of 1,600 executives. They found most executives can be classified in the following ways based on their decision-making approaches: charismatics, thinkers, skeptics, followers, and controllers. Typically, executives have adopted these styles because they led to success in their early careers. Williams and Miller found that the content of half of all persuasion attempts are mismatched with the decision-making style of decision makers.[35]

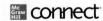

Visit http://connect. mheducation.com for an exercise on this topic.

FIGURE 10.4

Less Effective Message to Employees

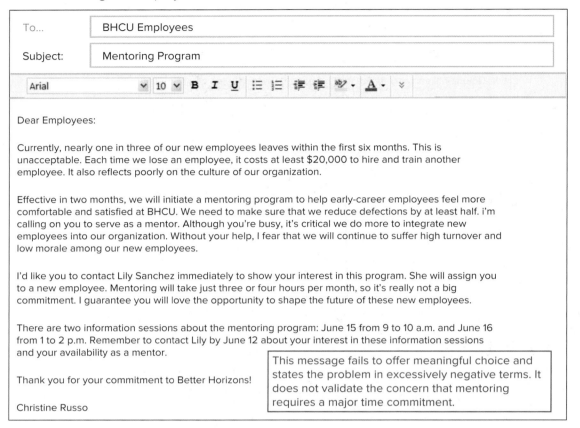

To... BHCU Employees

Subject: Mentoring Program

Arial   10   **B** *I* <u>U</u>

Dear Employees:

Currently, nearly one in three of our new employees leaves within the first six months. This is unacceptable. Each time we lose an employee, it costs at least $20,000 to hire and train another employee. It also reflects poorly on the culture of our organization.

Effective in two months, we will initiate a mentoring program to help early-career employees feel more comfortable and satisfied at BHCU. We need to make sure that we reduce defections by at least half. i'm calling on you to serve as a mentor. Although you're busy, it's critical we do more to integrate new employees into our organization. Without your help, I fear that we will continue to suffer high turnover and low morale among our new employees.

I'd like you to contact Lily Sanchez immediately to show your interest in this program. She will assign you to a new employee. Mentoring will take just three or four hours per month, so it's really not a big commitment. I guarantee you will love the opportunity to shape the future of these new employees.

There are two information sessions about the mentoring program: June 15 from 9 to 10 a.m. and June 16 from 1 to 2 p.m. Remember to contact Lily by June 12 about your interest in these information sessions and your availability as a mentor.

> This message fails to offer meaningful choice and states the problem in excessively negative terms. It does not validate the concern that mentoring requires a major time commitment.

Thank you for your commitment to Better Horizons!

Christine Russo

Haniz and Christine would like the executive team to approve a new campaign to younger prospects that focuses on financial planning. They can tailor their persuasion to the most important decision makers. You'll read about the decision-making types and how Haniz and Christine can adapt their approach.

Followers make decisions based on what has worked in the past. They are quite risk-averse and tend to follow how other successful executives have made similar decisions. To persuade followers, use references, testimonials, and successful precedents. They want to feel sure they're making a good decision. Followers comprise roughly 36 percent of executives.

If Haniz and Christine know a key decision maker is a follower, they should more prominently feature similar examples that have worked in the past. They might even arrange a conference call with someone at another credit union or bank who has implemented a similar strategy. Their goal should be to show the strategy is safe and proven.

Charismatics tend to get excited when they hear new ideas. They are enthusiastic and talkative. Yet, they've often made mistakes by making decisions based on their initial excitement. They ultimately make decisions based on simple but factual arguments that focus on results. Charismatics are less fearful of risk and most likely to act quickly. To persuade charismatics, avoid the instinct to join in their excitement. Stay measured in your arguments, lay out the benefits of your argument in straightforward terms, use visual aids, and provide clear next steps. Charismatics comprise roughly 25 percent of executives.

FIGURE 10.5

More Effective Message to Employees

To... BHCU Employees

Subject: Creating a Mentoring Program—We Need You!

> Gain ATTENTION with an appeal to shared purpose and a request for help.

[Arial | 10 | B I U | ≡ ≡ | 律 律 | ᵃᵇ⁄ ▾ | A ▾ | ⥌]

Dear Colleagues:

> Describes a SOLUTION briefly in the opening and in more detail later on.

Within the next one to two months, we will formally start the BHCU Mentoring Program. This is an exciting way to connect with new employees and help them in their careers. You have so much knowledge and experience to share with our new employees. Please consider taking a mentoring role to make this new program a success.

> Describes the NEED.

Currently, nearly one in three new employees leaves within the first six months. This is costly and disruptive. One major reason we're creating a mentoring program is to boost employee retention. Studies show that mentoring can increase retention by over 55 percent.

We also view a mentoring program as a key differentiator in attracting top talent. Research consistently shows that between 80 and 85 percent of early-career professionals seek mentoring programs. Yet, just 20 percent of employers offer mentoring. Among companies we complete against for local talent, none offer mentoring programs.

> Describes RATIONALE in terms of company needs and individual benefits.

While our primary goals of the mentorship program are attracting and retaining early-career professionals, we also view the program as an opportunity for our mentors. Mentoring is a rewarding way to meet and coach our early-career professionals. It lets you help shape the culture of our organization.

We envision a flexible and meaningful mentoring program. You would mentor one entry-level employee during his/her first year at Better Horizons. Your would spend three to four hours per month with your mentee. Ideally, you'd share an informal lunch or two with your mentee each month to talk about your areas of expertise and career development. Also, you'd involve your mentee in one of your projects so that he/she could get an up-close look at how you add value to challenging and complex problems.

I know mentoring can add to your busy schedule. We will help you succeed in this role and try to free up time by reducing some of your other responsibilities.

We will hold two information sessions about the mentoring program: June 15 from 9 to 10 a.m. and June 16 from 1 to 2 p.m. You can learn more about the nature of mentoring and available resources at these information sessions. You'll also have the opportunity to ask any questions. Please RSVP for one of these sessions to Lily Sanchez by June 12.

If you already know you'd like to serve as a mentor, please fill out this mentor volunteer form. Once you fill out the form, you'll work directly with Lily to pair you up with the right mentee.

Sincerely,

Christine

Christine Russo

> Includes calls to ACTION that are based on the principle of consistency.

If Haniz and Christine know a key decision maker is a charismatic, they should share the benefits of their idea in a measured, visually appealing way. They should be clear about the benefits, costs, *and* risks of the idea. Their goal should be to show the strategy is ambitious but well calculated.

Skeptics are suspicious of every data point, especially those that run counter to their own views. They are argumentative, even combative. To persuade a skeptic, no issue is more important than credibility. They must trust you to even consider your viewpoints. If you don't have time to establish credibility, you might consider aligning

The decision-making styles of others should influence your persuasion strategy.
Convisum/123RF

yourself with someone the decision maker trusts. Skeptics comprise roughly 19 percent of executives.

If Haniz and Christine know a key decision maker is a skeptic, they should carefully prepare for a back-and-forth conversation. Yet, they should realize that ultimately they must garner trust. They might discuss the strategy with several of the skeptic's close colleagues. If these close colleagues agree with the strategy, they can be enlisted to offer their views to the skeptic. The goal should be to show the strategy is vetted by someone who is trusted.

Thinkers are impressed by data-driven arguments. They make decisions slowly because they expect to see all possible data and carefully conduct cost–benefit analyses. They pride themselves on acting objectively and dispassionately. To persuade thinkers, make sure to have as much data ready as possible, provide all perspectives, and give them time to carefully evaluate the facts. Thinkers comprise roughly 11 percent of executives.

If Haniz and Christine know a key decision maker is a thinker, they should gather as much information as possible. They should recognize the thinker needs enough time to carefully evaluate all the information and form their own views. So, they should send all of this information well in advance of a meeting. They should be prepared to do more research based on the thinker's questions. Their goal should be to show the strategy has undergone objective, multisourced, time-intensive analysis.

Controllers dread uncertainty. They want all the facts in a structured manner, but they want to form their own conclusions. They resent feeling pushed or persuaded by others. To persuade controllers, give them as much information as possible. You might even periodically provide additional data to keep their attention on the issue. Yet, you should allow them to make up their own minds and ideally feel like they are the ones who came up with the solution. Controllers comprise roughly 9 percent of executives.

If Haniz and Christine know a key decision maker is a controller, they should prepare for a longer time until the decision is made. They might give the controller pieces of information periodically to keep the controller aware of the issue. Yet, they should avoid pushing the controller too hard. Their goal should be to allow the controller to own the issue so he/she can claim it as his/her own.

Constructing External Persuasive Messages

LO10.6 Compose influential external persuasive messages.

Haniz writes two external persuasive messages. The first is a flyer for community members who are participating in free financial planning and tax assistance workshops sponsored and led by Better Horizons. The second is an email encouraging Better Horizons members to join the Hope Walkathon. The first message uses more logical appeals. It deals with reasons Better Horizons is a better option than local banks. The second message uses more emotional appeals. It focuses on pride in team and community, a sense of contribution to an important cause, and an exciting and hope-filled activity. It contains many facts but relies most heavily on garnering feelings of dedication and enthusiasm.

FIGURE 10.6

Less Effective External Persuasive Message Based on Logical Appeals

| This message does not highlight key ideas. | **BETTER HORIZONS CREDIT UNION**
Est. 1937 | This message is not personalized or tangible. |

8 Reasons to Join Better Horizons Credit Union

Credit unions save members about $8 billion a year thanks to better interest rates and reduced fees. So, you can trust us to make your financial dreams come true. Pay attention to these facts or risk losing money to banks:

1. We are a member-based organization. That means our members can have a voice. They can serve on committees and even be elected to the Board of Directors.
2. We provide lower rates on car loans. We offer car loan rates at between 1.5 and 1.75 percentage points lower than any of the banks in town.
3. We provide lower rates on unsecured loans. We offer unsecured loans at a full 2 percentage points lower than any bank.
4. We provide mortgages more conveniently and at lower costs to our members. For example, a 30-year mortgage is as low as 5.31 percent compared to rates of 5.35 to 5.42 percent at competitor banks in town. The average closing costs are $1,900 compared to between $2,800 and $3,000 at competitor banks.
5. We provide higher interest on checking and savings accounts. Currently, we offer between .3 and .5 percentage points more interest than any bank in town.
6. We charge less in fees. For example, overdraft fees at Better Horizons are $19 compared to $35 to $50 at other local banks.
7. We provide a free retirement and financial planning advisor. Better Horizons has always employed a full-time financial planning advisor to help members with any of their financial planning questions.
8. Credit unions are safer than banks. In the recent economic downturn, banks were five times more likely to fail than credit unions. Better Horizons has always been in excellent financial condition, even during economic downturns.

Please think about how Better Horizons can help you in your banking. Please stop by anytime and meet with Ms. Norah Stevens or another membership specialist to learn more. Or, fill out the online membership application. We look forward to seeing you!

2737 Better Horizons Loop, Pescaloosa, FL 91214 • Phone: 803-784-7300 • Email: info@bhcu.org • Web: www.bhcu.org

Notice the differences between the less effective and more effective examples in Figures 10.6 and 10.7. In the less effective message (Figure 10.6), most components of persuasive messages are present except for a show of appreciation and a call to action. However, it employs we-voice when the potential customer should be the entire focus of the message, and it does not provide tangible benefits.

By contrast, in the more effective flyer (Figure 10.7), Haniz wrote a message that employs you-voice and describes tangible benefits to focus the entire message on the customer. The formatting makes each benefit stand out. The tangible statements help the customer quickly identify with the worth of the benefits; for example, saving $680 on a car loan (more effective message) is a far clearer benefit than paying 1.5 to 1.75 percentage points less (as in the less effective message).

FIGURE 10.7

More Effective External Persuasive Message Based on Logical Appeals

---

BETTER HORIZONS CREDIT UNION
Est. 1937

When You Join Better Horizons Credit Union, You're Not a Customer—You're an Owner

Eight Reasons to Join Better Horizons Credit Union   Gains ATTENTION.

Did you know that average credit union members save $400 per year compared to bank customers? The basic difference between credit unions and banks is that credit union members own and control their credit unions whereas bank account holders have no stake or control in their financial institutions. As a nonprofit, member-controlled financial institution, Better Horizons can provide you with higher rates on savings accounts, better terms on loans, and lower fees. Consider some of the following reasons to join Better Horizons and start saving today:

1.   **You come first.** You are not just a customer; you are an owner and member. That means you have a voice in how the credit union is run. You can serve on committees and even be elected to the Board of Directors.

2.   **You pay lower rates on car loans.** You can get car loan rates that are between 1.5 and 1.75 percentage points lower than at any of the banks in town. Consider the savings: Provides a NEED and SOLUTION.
     - On a 4-year $15,000 new car loan: You save about $680.
     - On a 4-year $5,000 used car loan: You save about $200.

3.   **You pay lower rates on unsecured loans.** You can get unsecured loans for unforeseen expenses at much lower rates at credit unions than banks. On average, unsecured loans are a full 2 percentage points lower than any bank. Consider the savings:
     - On a 3-year $15,000 unsecured loan: You save about $640.   Provides RATIONALE.
     - On a 3-year $5,000 unsecured loan: You save about $215.

4.   **You can get mortgages more conveniently and at lower costs.**
     - You can get mortgages approved within one business day at Better Horizons.
     - On a 30-year mortgage, you can get a rate as low as 5.31 percent compared to rates of 5.35 to 5.42 percent at competitor banks in town. For a $200,000 mortgage, that amounts to a savings of between $1,800 and $4,900 over the course of the loan.
     - You can get closing costs that average $1,900 compared to between $2,800 and $3,000 at competitor banks.

5.   **You earn higher interest on your checking and savings accounts.** Currently, you earn between .3 and .5 percentage points more interest than at any bank in town. That can add up fast. For an account with an average of $5,000, that will bring you an extra $15 to $25 per year.

6.   **You pay less in fees.** If banking fees bother you, credit unions are the place for you. Overdraft fees, late payment fees on credit cards, and many other fees are lower at Better Horizons than at any local bank. For example, overdraft fees at Better Horizons are $19 compared to $35 to $50 at other local banks.

7.   **You will have a free retirement and financial planning advisor.** Better Horizons has always employed a full-time financial planning advisor who can help you with your financial planning questions.

8.   **Your savings are safest at credit unions.** In the recent economic downturn, banks were five times more likely to fail than credit unions. Better Horizons has always been in excellent financial condition, even during economic downturns.   Shows VALIDATION of other perspectives.

With all these benefits, why wouldn't everyone choose credit unions? That's a good question. Some people prefer banks because they often have branches and ATMs throughout the country, which is convenient for travel. Also, some people say that banks offer more services. And, many people don't know much about credit unions at all. We encourage you to stop by Better Horizons and make direct comparisons with your current bank. You'll find that banking with Better Horizons saves you money, provides convenience when you travel, and offers services to meet nearly any banking need.

Please stop by anytime and meet with Ms. Norah Stevens or another membership specialist to learn more. Or, fill out the online membership application. New members who complete an application before September 1 will receive $50 cash in their new checking account.   Concludes with call to ACTION.

2737 Better Horizons Loop, Pescaloosa, FL 91214 • Phone: 803-784-7300 • Email: info@bhcu.org • Web: www.bhcu.org

To...	Anderson, Jamal; Anderson, Jennifer; Baker, William; Belk, Crystal; Belk, Jonathan; Belk, Ralph; Belk, Sally; Bi, Hu; Cardwell, Stephanie; Carter, Branson; Carter, Elizabeth; Casey, Stephen; Casey, Rick; Cedar, Brian; Cedar, Rebeka
Subject:	Your Duty to the Women in Your Lives

Arial ⌄ 10 ⌄ **B** *I* <u>U</u> ≔ ≔ 帚 帚 ✎ · **A** · ⌄

Dear Credit Union Member:

> This message is not personalized, shames the readers, and employs excessive negative language.

Please join Better Horizons in our fight against breast cancer, one of the deadliest cancers for women. You owe it to the women in your lives to make a difference. Think about the following facts:

- About 182,460 women will develop breast cancer this year in our country.
- Breast cancer ranks second among cancer deaths in women.

Breast cancer affects all of us deeply—a mother, a wife, a daughter, a friend. If you really care, you'll join us in this fight.

All proceeds of the Hope Walkathon are for the Betty Williams Breast Center and are used for community education, research, and support for low-income patients and families. The Betty Williams Breast Center has a nationally accredited program for treatment of breast cancer. It helps do research in a national network of breast centers that are at the forefront of research for improving treatments. The breast center is active in educating our community about detecting breast cancer early. It spreads the word about breast self-exams and mammograms. The Betty Williams Breast Center began with an initial donation by Betty Williams, a breast cancer survivor and longtime Best Horizons member. Betty would certainly want to see you out there trying to help the victims of this horrible disease.

Registration is just $50 per person. If you are not able to participate in the walkathon, you are still welcome to register and make your donation to the Betty Williams Breast Center. Each Better Horizons participating member will receive a Hope Walkathon T-shirt, a Better Horizons water bottle, and a copy of *Lifestyle Choices to Help Avoid Cancer*. Best of all, you are part of the Better Horizons effort to stop breast cancer.

To join the Better Horizons Credit Union team, complete an online application or send your application by mail. Just complete the application by September 21 to secure your spot and Better Horizons T-shirt. Your T-shirt will be mailed to you so that you can wear it for the walkathon and represent Better Horizons with pride! The walkathon will be held on Saturday, October 6 at 9:00 a.m. at Central Park. Do your part to improve the lives of women in our community!

The more effective example also provides an influential appreciation statement (the less effective example provides no appreciation statement) that anticipates the thoughts of skeptical consumers. In italics, it asks, *With all these benefits, why wouldn't everyone choose credit unions?* This validates the thinking of customers who might otherwise dismiss all these benefits as too good to be true. The paragraph explains why some people prefer banks and encourages customers to make direct comparisons themselves. Finally, the message concludes with a call to action—a cash reward to new members who join before September 1. Most effective sales messages provide incentives to motivate purchase of products or services.

Now notice the differences between the less effective and more effective external persuasive messages in Figures 10.8 and 10.9, both of which use emotional appeals to rally people to sign up for the Hope Walkathon. In the less effective example (Figure 10.8), Haniz includes several statements that readers could perceive as guilt trips. It uses a series of extremely negative terms within the first few sentences (i.e., *deadliest, cancer deaths*) without providing hopeful words, an approach that could lead readers to think participating in the walkathon would make little difference. Furthermore, the message is not personalized. Rather than focusing on the local and credit union communities, it exclusively examines the problem in a national context.

In the more effective example (Figure 10.9), the message is far more personalized, upbeat, positive, and pressure-free. Instead of citing national statistics, it provides statistics about the local community and the credit union. It places more emphasis on Betty Williams, who is tied to the community and credit union. It describes the fun and excitement the reader will feel being part of a team. It does not avoid some of the

FIGURE 10.9

More Effective External
Persuasive Message
Based on Emotional
Appeal

To...	Anderson, Jamal
Subject:	Join the Better Horizons Team to Fight Breast Cancer; Register for the Hope Walkathon by September 21

Hello Jamal:

> This message is personalized, exciting, inspiring, and motivating. It lives up to the theme: hope.

Please join our team in this year's _Hope Walkathon_ in the fight against breast cancer. Last year, our team of 415 members raised $23,000 for the Betty Williams Breast Center, located right here in our town.

Breast cancer affects our community deeply—but there is hope! Many advances in prevention and treatment are made possible by the proceeds from the Hope Walkathon. You can help make a difference for women here in our community.

Consider the following facts:

- About 50 women per year in our county are diagnosed with breast cancer.
- Seven of our credit union members were diagnosed with breast cancer last year (that we know of).
- About 1 in 8 women in our community will be diagnosed with breast cancer during their lifetime.
- Breast cancer is the second deadliest cancer in women.
- _The five-year survival rate for breast cancer is 95 percent when it is detected early._

All proceeds of the walkathon go directly to the Betty Williams Breast Center and promote community education, research, and support for low-income patients and families. The Betty Williams Breast Center runs a nationally accredited program for treatment of breast cancer. It also contributes to a national network of breast centers that are at the forefront of research for improving treatments. The breast center is active in educating our community about detecting breast cancer early. It spreads the word about breast self-exams, mammograms, and other forms of prevention.

The Betty Williams Breast Center began with an initial donation by Betty Williams, a breast cancer survivor and longtime Best Horizons member. You can see her at the walkathon, where she will be participating for the 17th consecutive year!

Registration is just $50 per person. If you are not able to participate in the walkathon, you are still welcome to register and make your donation to the Betty Williams Breast Center. Each Better Horizons participating member will receive a Hope Walkathon T-shirt, a Better Horizons water bottle, and a copy of _Lifestyle Choices to Help Avoid Cancer_. Best of all, your money goes to a great cause.

To join the Better Horizons Credit Union team, complete an online application or send your application by mail. Please complete the application by September 21 to secure your spot and T-shirt. Your shirt will be mailed to you so that you can wear it for the walkathon.

The walkathon will be held on Saturday, October 6 at 9:00 a.m. at Central Park. Please join Betty and the rest of the Better Horizons team for a day of fun, excitement, and hope!

Thanks,

Haniz

negative terms (i.e., _deadliest_, _diagnosed_) associated with breast cancer; however, it uses far more positive and constructive words and phrases (i.e., _hope, prevention, treatment, survival, you can make a difference, 95 percent_) to create an overall hopeful and inspiring message. While both messages contain a call to action, the call to action in the more effective example includes a direct link to sign up online. The more effective example provides other links as well so readers can learn more about the walkathon and the Betty Williams Breast Center.

Composing Mass Sales Messages

LO10.7 Construct effective mass sales messages.

Even if you are not in a marketing position, you may participate in developing **mass sales messages**—messages sent to a large group of consumers and intended to market a particular product or service. Often in the form of mass emails, online ads, or sales letters, these messages generally have low success rates (ratio of number of purchases

ⓘ Technology Tips

ARTIFICIAL INTELLIGENCE (AI) TOOLS AND PERSUASION

Increasingly, AI systems are capable of developing arguments on complex and sophisticated topics. These systems can explore issues that do not have black-and-white answers. They can even listen to the arguments of humans and develop counterarguments.

One well-known system is IBM's Project Debater. It has debated many people, including debate champions, on diverse topics. IBM explains that Project Debater can "help people reason by providing compelling, evidence-based arguments and limiting the influence of emotion, bias, or ambiguity."

Your challenge: Watch IBM's Project Debater (based on AI technologies) compete in a debate against a debate champion (for example, you can watch a debate here: https://www.youtube.com/watch?v=m3u-1yttrVw). Think about the value of this type of tool for the workplace. Explain how using a tool like this could improve your argumentation and persuasive skills.

IBM/Splash News/SplashNews/Newscom

Sources: Gallo, C. (2019, January 13). IBM's AI machine makes a convincing case that it's mastering the human art of persuasion. *Forbes.* Retrieved from www.forbes.com/sites/carminegallo/2019/01/13/ibms-ai-machine-makes-a-convincing-case-that-its-mastering-the-human-art-of-persuasion/; IBM. (n.d.). Project Debater. *IBM AI research.* Retrieved from https://www.research.ibm.com/artificial-intelligence/project-debater/.

---

to number of message recipients). For example, a company sending out 7,000 sales letters may achieve only a 2 percent success rate (140 sales directly attributable to the mailings)—enough to make the effort profitable. Since mass emails and online ads are much less expensive than hard-copy sales letters (costs generally involve purchasing consumer email lists and online ads but no paper or postage), expected success rates may be much lower.

A secondary benefit of mass sales messages is that even when consumers do not respond with immediate purchases, these messages can raise a company's brand awareness. Consumers may keep the company in mind when making a purchase one, two, or more years in the future. On the other hand, many consumers resent mass sales messages. Excessive sales letters and spam emails may lower brand value in some cases.

While most of the principles from this chapter apply to sales messages, the structure of mass sales messages is adjusted to increase the success rate. Even modest improvements in the success rate—for example, from 2 percent to 3 percent—can make tens of thousands of dollars' difference in revenue. The most common model for mass sales messages is the AIDA approach: *a*ttention, *i*nterest, *d*esire, and *a*ction. This approach begins and ends like other persuasive messages; it must first gain *attention* and it should end with a specific call to *action*.

Typically, the attention-getter needs to be livelier and even more provocative than with internal persuasive messages. After gaining attention, the next step is to build interest and curiosity. Then, the sales message should focus on building *desire*. That is, you want potential customers thinking, "I want this product or service." You conclude with a specific call to action that the potential customer can take to begin the purchase process.

Structure of Mass Sales Messages

- Gain attention.
- Generate interest.
- Build desire.
- Call to action.

Most effective sales messages contain a **central sales theme**. Like other messages, sales messages are strongest when they contain a coherent, unified theme that consumers can recognize quickly. However, whereas your colleagues and clients who know you will grant you a window of 30 seconds or so to provide your main point, recipients of mass sales messages may give you only a few seconds. Thus, your sales message should stick to a single, recognizable theme that resonates within seconds.

One of the most common sales themes is price. Sales messages that focus on price tend to emphasize it immediately, generally in the attention-getter. Sales messages that emphasize other attributes typically de-emphasize price by making a brief mention of it near the end of the message. Some sales messages omit any references to price. This is a risky strategy for mass sales messages since most consumers expect at least some information about price right away.

Recent research suggests mass sales messages may be more effective by employing a more direct approach.[36] With so much messaging in social media and other digital channels, many people have shorter attention spans and block unwanted messages quickly. Further, Gen Yers and Gen Zers expect more direct messages. While the AIDA approach culminates in a specific call to action, you'll notice in the effective mass sales messages below that the central sales theme and ultimate call to action are clear in the subject lines and easy to understand within seconds. Make sure your audiences recognize your request within seconds.

In Figures 10.10 and 10.11, you can see two mass sales messages that Haniz and her colleagues created to promote the credit union's auto loans. In the first message

FIGURE 10.10

A Mass Sales Message with a Strong Logical Appeal

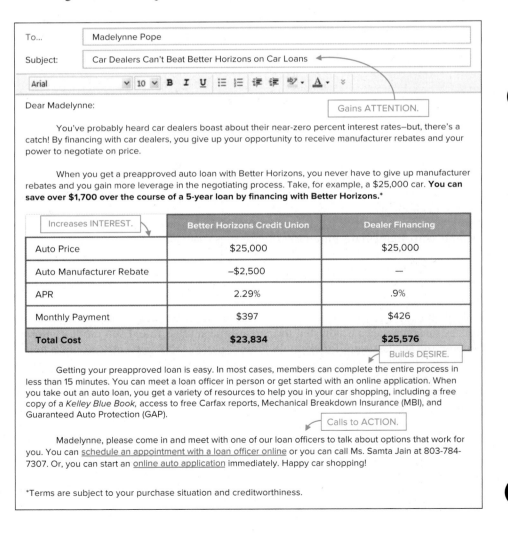

To...	Madelynne Pope
Subject:	Car Dealers Can't Beat Better Horizons on Car Loans

Dear Madelynne:

You've probably heard car dealers boast about their near-zero percent interest rates—but, there's a catch! By financing with car dealers, you give up your opportunity to receive manufacturer rebates and your power to negotiate on price.

When you get a preapproved auto loan with Better Horizons, you never have to give up manufacturer rebates and you gain more leverage in the negotiating process. Take, for example, a $25,000 car. **You can save over $1,700 over the course of a 5-year loan by financing with Better Horizons.***

	Better Horizons Credit Union	Dealer Financing
Auto Price	$25,000	$25,000
Auto Manufacturer Rebate	–$2,500	—
APR	2.29%	.9%
Monthly Payment	$397	$426
Total Cost	**$23,834**	**$25,576**

Getting your preapproved loan is easy. In most cases, members can complete the entire process in less than 15 minutes. You can meet a loan officer in person or get started with an online application. When you take out an auto loan, you get a variety of resources to help you in your car shopping, including a free copy of a *Kelley Blue Book,* access to free Carfax reports, Mechanical Breakdown Insurance (MBI), and Guaranteed Auto Protection (GAP).

Madelynne, please come in and meet with one of our loan officers to talk about options that work for you. You can schedule an appointment with a loan officer online or you can call Ms. Samta Jain at 803-784-7307. Or, you can start an online auto application immediately. Happy car shopping!

*Terms are subject to your purchase situation and creditworthiness.

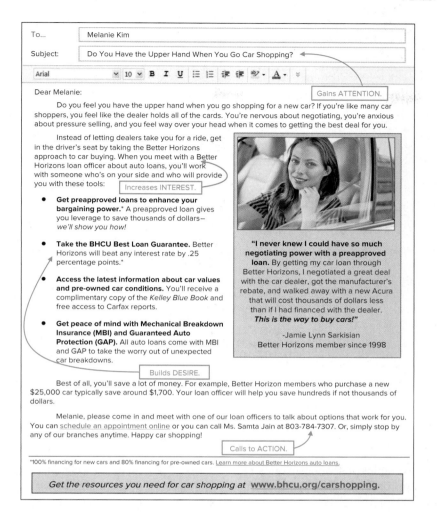

FIGURE 10.11

A Mass Sales Message with a Strong Emotional Appeal

Eric Audras/Getty Images

(Figure 10.10), the central selling theme is price: Better Horizons Credit Union's auto loans cost less than dealer financing. So, the attention-getter focuses on this theme in the subject line and opening paragraph. The first paragraph arouses interest by pointing out the perhaps underappreciated fact that accepting low-rate dealer financing generally involves sacrificing rebates and negotiating power. The prominent and well-designed table likewise increases interest with its easy-to-process comparison between getting an auto loan versus dealer financing. The final paragraphs build desire by showing the ease and perks of getting an auto loan and providing information about how to apply right away. This sales message primarily makes a logical appeal.

In the next sales message (Figure 10.11), Haniz and her colleagues highlight a different sales theme with a primarily emotional appeal. In this message, they focus on going car shopping with confidence and strength, directly addressing an anxiety many car shoppers have of getting taken advantage of when making a car purchase. The emotional appeal involves several influence strategies, including social proof (with the testimonial of a satisfied member who has saved money by taking out an auto loan) and reciprocation (with the warm offer to get help from a loan officer and an invitation to "work as a team" against the car dealers). You typically have much more freedom of creative expression in mass sales messages than you do with other types of persuasive messages. Haniz uses this creative license with metaphorical language tied to playing cards ("upper hand," "dealer holds the cards") and driving ("take you for a ride," "get in the driver's seat").

FIGURE 10.12

Less Effective Mass Email

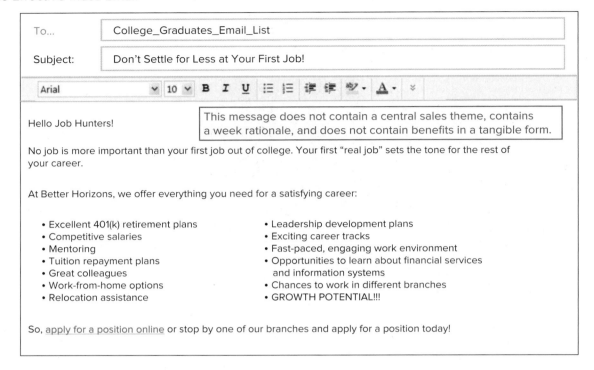

The examples you've observed so far focus on consumers. You can also apply the AIDA approach to other types of mass promotions. For example, Better Horizons seeks to attract the best college graduates to apply for open positions. It has access to an email list of current college students who have attended job fairs nearby. In Figures 10.12 and 10.13, you can see a less effective example and a more effective example of Haniz encouraging college students to apply for open positions. In the less effective example, you'll notice that Haniz tries a strategy of stating all the benefits of working at Better Horizons. This generic strategy fails because it ends up emphasizing nothing. In other words, it lacks a central sales theme. This message also fails to explain benefits in tangible terms. In the more effective example, Haniz focuses on a central sales theme (employer programs that create career advantages for early-career professionals). She focuses on just three programs, allowing her to provide specific and concrete statements of benefits to potential employees. Also, by formatting with italics, bold fonts, and other features, she ensures potential employees get the gist of the message rapidly.

Reviewing Persuasive Messages

LO10.8 Evaluate persuasive messages for effectiveness and fairness.

Always carefully review your persuasive messages, especially since nearly all of them are high-stakes communications. They can potentially provide you with more professional opportunities and enhanced credibility, or they can close off future opportunities and diminish your credibility. Likewise, because you are a representative of your organization, your persuasive messages may raise or decrease customer loyalty, revenues, and brand value.

FIGURE 10.13

More Effective Mass Email

Laflor/Getty Images

To...　Emily Smith

Subject:　Get Your Career on the Right Track at Better Horizons Credit Union

Arial　　10　**B** *I* <u>U</u>

Gains ATTENTION with a central sales theme: employer programs that help early-career professionals the most.

Dear Emily:

No job is more important than your first job out of college. Your first "real job" sets the tone for the rest of your career.

Builds INTEREST with evidence-based conclusions.

Finding an employer that invests in you will make a dramatic impact on your career opportunities. Check out how much difference various employer programs make for early-career professionals:

- *Employees who received early-career mentoring earn between $5,500 and $22,500 more per year compared to employees who did not receive mentoring.* <u>Read more...</u>

- *Employees who participate in leadership development programs are twice as likely to gain managerial or supervisory positions within their first two years after college.* <u>Read more...</u>

- *Employees with employer-based student loan repayment plans purchase homes three years sooner than employees without these repayment plans.* <u>Read more...</u>

At Better Horizons, we're committed to your career success. That's why all new employees have access to mentoring programs, leadership development programs, and student loan payback plans:

- **Better Horizons Mentoring Program**. All new employees are assigned a seasoned mentor who has worked in financial services or information services. Mentors generally take mentees out for lunch once or twice per month, spend several hours coaching mentees each month, involve mentees in important projects, and share ideas about career development.

- **Better Horizons Leadership Development Program**. All employees are eligible to participate in our various leadership programs catered to specialties in mortgages, investment services, and information technology.

  Increases DESIRE with a list of tangible benefits at Better Horizons.

- **Better Horizons Student Loan Repayment Program**. Once employees have been with us for six months, we reimburse them for student loans up to $300 per month.

So, please check out our <u>open positions for tellers, financial specialists, IT specialists, loan officers, and more</u>. Also, my team and I would enjoy meeting you in person at the upcoming <u>PCC Job Fair</u>.

Calls to ACTION with a link to open positions and an invitation to a job fair.

Best wishes,

Haniz

Haniz Zogby

The entire message sticks to a tight, unified CENTRAL SALES THEME.

Get Feedback and Reread

Persuasive messages are directed to others who *resist* your ideas, products, or services. Read your message carefully. Imagine yourself in your audience members' position and consider how they would respond. Make sure you ask trusted colleagues to read your messages. Ask them how they would respond and how they think you can better construct the message to get your intended results. You may be best served to seek out trusted colleagues who may be resistant in the same way as your audience. These colleagues may provide the most insight to you about crafting your message carefully.

Apply the FAIR Test

Persuasive messages can be intentionally designed to manipulate colleagues and customers. In a business communications context, **manipulation** involves attempting to influence others by some level of deception so you can achieve your own interests. You may face many strong temptations to manipulate others through persuasive messages—to elevate your career, get a commission on that extra sale, get that bonus for exceptional performance, or pad your ego for being right.

By applying the FAIR test, you can avoid sending persuasive messages that manipulate others. This is especially the case for sales messages because any misrepresentation of your product or service is unethical. Use Figure 10.14 as a guide as you discuss with your colleagues whether your persuasive messages are fair. And by considering the experience of a business professional (see the Ideas in Action), you can learn to be more thoughtful and skillful when crafting persuasive messages.

FIGURE 10.14

Are Your Persuasive Messages FAIR?

Facts (How *factual* is your persuasive message?)
- Have you presented *all* the facts correctly?
- Have you presented information that allows colleagues, customers, and consumers to make informed decisions that are in their best interests?
- Have you carefully considered various interpretations of your data? Have you assessed the quality of your information?

Access (How *accessible* or *transparent* are your motives, reasoning, and information?)
- Are your motives clear or will others perceive that you have a hidden agenda? Have you made yourself accessible to others so that they can learn more about your viewpoints?
- Have you fully disclosed information that colleagues, customers, or consumers should expect to receive?
- Are you hiding any information that casts your recommendations in a better light? Are you hiding real reasons for making certain claims or recommendations?
- Have you given stakeholders the opportunity to provide input in the decision-making process?

Impacts (How does your communication *impact* stakeholders?)
- Have you carefully considered how your ideas, products, and services will impact colleagues, customers, and consumers?
- Have you made recommendations to colleagues, customers, and consumers that are in their best interests?

Respect (How *respectful* is your communication?)
- If you were the customer or the colleague, would you feel that the tone of the message was appropriate?
- Does the message offend or pressure? Does it show that your colleagues' and customers' needs are important?
- Would a neutral observer consider your communication respectful?

IDEAS IN ACTION

PERSUADING BY UNDERSTANDING OTHERS ON A PERSONAL LEVEL

Stephen Curry of the Golden State Warriors

Stephen Curry is among the most popular professional basketball players in the world. He was signed with Nike until 2013. Then, he signed with Under Armour. His move away from Nike to Under Armour was in part due to the Nike pitch team's ineffective persuasion and the Under Armour pitch team's effective persuasion.

Nike's team pitched to Curry in August 2013. Nike's most powerful representative didn't come to the meeting, perhaps indicating Curry wasn't Nike's highest priority. Curry wanted to run a Nike-sponsored youth basketball camp because he had been inspired when he was younger at these camps. Nike failed to give him a camp. During the

Icon Sportswire/Getty Images

pitch meeting, team members mispronounced Curry's first name (repeatedly saying "Steph-on"). The PowerPoint slides they used had Kevin Durant's (another famous basketball player) name on them. Every signal in the meeting was that Curry was not a top-tier athlete.

Whereas Nike's pitch was sloppy and poorly planned, the Under Armour team spent years planning its pitch to Curry. Without a direct link to Curry, the Under Armour team recruited one of Curry's close teammates to act as an intermediary. Curry's teammate periodically gave him Under Armour shoes and gear and suggested meeting with the Under Armour team. Finally, Curry met with Under Armour's top representative. In every interaction, the Under Armour team treated Curry as a top-tier athlete for the brand. Now, Curry is signed through 2024 with Under Armour.

Sources: Strauss, E. S. (2016, March 23). You won't believe how Nike lost Steph to Under Armour. *ESPN*. Retrieved from http://www.espn.com/nba/story/_/id/15047018/how-nike-lost-stephen-curry-armour; Haden, J. (2016, March 28). The $14 billion man: Why Nike lost NBA superstar Stephen Curry to Under Armour. *Inc.com*. Retrieved from https://www.inc.com/jeff-haden/the-14-billion-man-why-nike-lost-nba-superstar-stephen-curry-to-under-armour.html.

Chapter Takeaway for *Persuasive Messages*

LO10.1 Describe the relationship between credibility and persuasion.
Delivering effective persuasive messages improves your **reputation for personal credibility**.

It shows **competence** when you know everything about your product, service, or idea.	It shows **caring** when you explain how your product, service, or idea benefits others.	It shows **character** when you provide completely reliable and honest information.

LO10.2 Explain the AIM planning process for persuasive messages and the basic components of most persuasive messages.

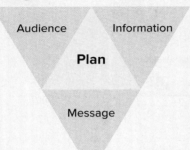

Audience Analysis: Identify the needs of your audience and learn how it is influenced.

Information Gathering: Gather extensive information about products, services, and ideas that you are writing about.

Message Development: Gain attention, tie needs to benefits, provide rationale, show appreciation, and call your audience to action.

Components of Persuasive Messages		
• Gain attention. • Raise a need. • Deliver a solution.	• Provide a rationale. • Validate the views, preferences, and concerns of others.	• Give counterpoints (optional). • Call to action.

Types of Attention-Getters		
• Rhetorical question • Intriguing statistic	• Compelling and unusual facts • Challenge	• Testimonial

See *examples of attention-getters* in Table 10.1.

LO10.3 Explain how the tone and style of persuasive messages impact their influence.

Guidelines for Tone and Style for Persuasive Messages
• Apply the personal touch. • Use action-oriented, lively language. • Write with confidence. • Offer choice. • Show positivity.

Tone   Style

Write

Design

See *examples of tone and style choices* in Tables 10.2 through 10.8.

LO10.4 Create compelling internal persuasive messages.

Components of Internal Persuasive Messages	
• Gain attention: overview of a business problem. • Raise a need: description of a business problem. • Deliver a solution: description of *how* your idea or policy addresses the business problem. • Provide a rationale: elaboration about *why* your idea or policy is the best option. • Validate: appreciation for decision makers' perspectives and resistance to your ideas.	• Give counterpoints (optional): explanation of why your ideas are better than competing ideas (typically those of decision makers who comprise your target audience). • Call to action: recommendations for a course of action or further discussion about an idea or policy.

See *examples of internal persuasive messages* in Figures 10.2 through 10.5.

LO10.5 Explain how to influence professionals with various decision-making styles.

• **Followers** make decisions based on what has worked in the past. They are quite risk-averse and tend to follow how other successful executives have made similar decisions. • **Charismatics** tend to get excited when they hear new ideas. They are enthusiastic and talkative. Yet, they've often made mistakes by making decisions based on their initial excitement. They ultimately make decisions based on simple but factual arguments that focus on results. • **Skeptics** are suspicious of every data point, especially those that run counter to their own views. They are argumentative, even combative.	• **Thinkers** are impressed by data-driven arguments. They make decisions slowly because they expect to see all possible data and carefully conduct cost–benefit analyses. They pride themselves on acting objectively and dispassionately. • **Controllers** dread uncertainty. They want all the facts in a structured manner, but they want to form their own conclusions. They resent feeling pushed or persuaded by others.

LO10.6 Compose influential external persuasive messages.

Components of External Persuasive Messages	
• Gain attention: catchy statement. • Raise a need: description of unmet *needs* or *wants* of your customers. • Deliver a solution: description of *how* your product or service benefits customers. • Provide a rationale: elaboration about *why* your product or service will benefit the customer. • Validate: recognition of customers' resistance to your product or service.	• Give counterpoints (optional): explanation of why your product/service is better than competing products/services (typically those favored by the target audience). • Call to action: description of a specific step for the customer to take toward purchase of a product or service.

See *examples of external persuasive messages* in Figures 10.6 through 10.9.

LO10.7 Construct effective mass sales messages.

Structure of Mass Sales Messages
• Gain attention. • Generate interest. • Build desire. • Call to action.

See *examples of mass sales messages* in Figures 10.10 through 10.13.

LO10.8 Evaluate persuasive messages for effectiveness and fairness.

Feedback: Have trusted colleagues check for accuracy, honesty, and influence.

FAIR Test: Make sure your claims are factual and nondeceptive.

Proofreading: Carefully reread the message several times. Envision the response of the audience.

Key Terms

Discussion Exercises

10.1 Chapter Review Questions (LO10.1, LO10.2, LO10.3)

A. Describe how credibility forms a basis for persuasion.

B. Explain how the tone and style of persuasive messages impact their persuasiveness. Specifically, address how personal touch, action-oriented language, confidence, choice, and positivity affect how message recipients respond.

C. Explain the AIM planning process for persuasive messages and the basic components of most persuasive messages.

10.2 Applying Key Terms (LO10.1, LO10.2, LO10.3)

Explain each key term above and provide a concrete example of how it impacts persuasive messages.

10.3 Ideas in Action Discussion Questions (LO10.1, LO10.2, LO10.3)

Read the Ideas in Action section about Stephen Curry. Respond to the following questions:

A. What were some of the mistakes Nike made in its pitch to Stephen Curry? What does this imply about principles of persuasion?

B. What did Under Armour do right in its pitch to Stephen Curry? What does this imply about principles of persuasion?

C. If you were a shoe or apparel company pitching to a rising athlete, which three principles of persuasion from this chapter do you think are most important? Why?

D. How is pitching to a high-profile athlete similar and different that persuading your colleagues in the workplace? Explain.

10.4 Should You Use Persuasion Sparingly? (LO10.1, LO10.3)

Some people suggest that all business communication is a form of persuasion—that is, you are attempting to motivate others to think and/or do as you suggest. Others suggest that you should use persuasion only in rare circumstances. For example, in the recent Dale Carnegie Training book called *The 5 Essential People Skills*, the authors write the following:

It has been said that persuasion is like a savings account: The less you use it, the more you've got. Learn how to use your powers of persuasion well and at the appropriate moments.

With time and practice, you'll be able to have positive influence on people's decisions in any number of areas.[37]

Write three or four paragraphs describing your perspectives on how often and when you should use persuasion in the workplace.

10.5 Character and Persuasion (LO10.1, LO10.8)

As Aristotle famously stated, "Character may almost be called the most effective means of persuasion." Do you think this is true in today's business world? Explain your viewpoints with three or four supporting points and examples.

Evaluation Exercises

10.6 Analyzing a Sales Message (LO10.7)

Find an interesting sales message that you have received recently in the mail or through email. If you can't find one readily, go to the website of a company that sells products or services that interest you. Find a sales message of sufficient length to analyze. Analyze it in the following ways:

A. Which psychological tools of influence (consistency, reciprocation, social proof, authority, liking, scarcity) does it use? Provide examples.

B. What emotional appeals are used? What about logical appeals? Would you consider this sales message to be catering more to emotion or logic? Explain.

C. Do you consider this sales message warm and inviting?

D. Do you consider this sales message plausible?

E. Do you consider this sales message respectful?

F. Do you trust the sales message?

G. What are two changes you think could be made to improve its effectiveness?

10.7 Analyzing the Better Horizons Promotional Message (LO10.6)

Analyze the Better Horizons flyer (Figure 10.9) in the following ways:

A. Which psychological tools of influence (consistency, reciprocation, social proof, authority, liking, scarcity) does it use? Provide examples.

B. What emotional appeals are used? What about logical appeals? Would you consider this message as catering more to emotion or logic? Explain.

C. Do you consider this message warm and inviting?

D. Do you consider this sales message plausible?

E. Do you consider this sales message respectful?

F. Do you trust this message?

G. What are two changes you think could be made to improve its effectiveness?

10.8 Persuasion Self-Assessment (LO10.1, LO10.2, LO10.3, LO10.8)

Evaluate yourself with regard to each of the persuasive practices listed in the table below. Circle the appropriate number for each.

	1 – Rarely/Never	2 – Sometimes	3 – Usually	4 – Always
I can persuade others to see merit in my ideas even when they initially disagree.	1	2	3	4
Before trying to persuade others, I think about what their needs are.	1	2	3	4
Before trying to persuade others, I think about the best ways to influence them.	1	2	3	4
I feel comfortable expressing my viewpoints even when I know others disagree.	1	2	3	4
I can persuade others without offending them.	1	2	3	4
Even when others disagree with me, I offer my perspective without putting down their opinions.	1	2	3	4
I can write strong persuasive messages.	1	2	3	4
When I persuade others, I try to open up avenues for future discussion.	1	2	3	4
I realize that most people are not persuaded immediately. I communicate with others realizing that the process will likely involve many steps.	1	2	3	4
I show respect for others with whom I disagree.	1	2	3	4

Total your score and consider the following advice:

35–40:   You are an *effective persuader*. You likely influence others as intended in most cases. Continue honing your persuasive skills and ensure that you always act with the interests of others in mind.

30–34:   You are a *conscientious persuader*. You are aware of the needs of others, you are confident of presenting your perspectives, and you feel that you can show respect to others who think differently. Continue working on developing your persuasive abilities.

25–29:   You are an *average persuader*. You are persuasive in many cases, but you will be far more effective if you consistently apply principles of effective persuasion. Identify those areas where you most need to improve and you will see rapid improvement.

Under 25:   You are a *less effective persuader*. Think carefully about the areas in which you can most improve. You can dramatically change your influence on others by mastering just a few principles of persuasion.

Based on the self-assessment, identify three areas in which to improve your approach to persuasion. Write three goals and elaborate on each with a supporting paragraph.

Application Exercises

Case for Exercises 10.9 through 10.11: Promoting New Services at Better Horizons Credit Union

Christine Russo works at Better Horizons and is developing several new services the credit union could offer. One idea is for credit union members to take a five-day cruise to the Bahamas. Two afternoons of the cruise will be devoted to financial planning workshops, including choices such as retirement planning, trusts and estates, insurance, charitable giving, taxes, and college savings. Also, a finance boot camp for teenagers will provide basic information about savings and checking accounts, loans, and budgeting.

In another initiative, Christine wants to set up a new rewards program for credit union members who use their Better Horizons debit or credit cards. Each purchase with the debit or credit card will contribute to their total reward points, which customers can redeem for brand-name merchandise, hotel accommodations, airline tickets, cruises, and other travel options (detailed in an online and paper merchandise and travel catalog). Members get one point for each dollar spent on their credit cards and one point for every two dollars spent on their debit cards. One advantage of the program is that points can be combined across accounts. So, family members or friends who are members of the credit union can transfer their points to one another's accounts and more quickly gain rewards. The program involves no fee, and members with the cards are automatically enrolled in the program.

10.9 Selling an Idea to the Better Horizons Board (LO10.4)

Assume the role of Christine and write a letter to the board describing your ideas for the financial planning cruise and the new rewards program.

10.10 Promoting the Financial Planning Cruise to Better Horizons Credit Union Members (LO10.6)

Write a sales message to Better Horizons members to promote the financial planning cruise. Feel free to add additional details (i.e., price and dates for the cruise).

10.11 Writing a Sales Letter for the New Better Horizons Special Rewards Card (LO10.6, LO10.7)

Write a sales message to Better Horizons members to promote the new rewards programs. Feel free to add additional details (i.e., types of rewards).

10.12 Creating a Message to Promote Joining a Student Club (LO10.5, LO10.6, LO10.7)

A. Select a student club of interest to you. You may already be a member or you may know little about the club. In any case, write a message to encourage other students to join. Describe benefits that membership brings and specific steps for joining the club or learning more about it.

B. In a separate message, describe the students you are targeting; reasons for resistance among these students, how your message appeals to this group, and the mix of communication channels you'll use to distribute the message. Address the message to the president of the club.

10.13 Writing a Sales Letter for Your Computer Store (LO10.7)

Assume you own a computer retail store located near your campus (give the store any name you want). You have sold fewer PCs in recent years due to the strong demand for Macs among university students. You will write a sales letter to reach all student housing units. Your goal is to encourage students to purchase PCs at your store. You can do online research to help you contrast PCs with Macs and identify pricing levels. In the sales letter, attempt to show students the advantages of PCs compared to Macs and get them to take specific steps to learn more about or even purchase a PC at your store.

10.14 Writing a Sales Letter for a Credit Union That Targets University Students (LO10.7)

Write a sales letter that targets university students and promotes joining a local credit union. In addition to using materials from this chapter, go online and find comparisons of benefits between credit unions and banks. It's easy to find plenty of information in just 20 to 30 minutes.

10.15 Writing a Sales Letter for a Bank That Targets University Students (LO10.7)

Write a sales letter that targets university students and promotes joining a local bank. Find information online about local credit unions and banks, select the financial institution that interests you the most, and then promote it with an effective sales letter.

10.16 Persuading University Students to Start a Retirement Account
(LO10.6, LO10.7)

Write a message that targets university students and persuades them to start a retirement account. You'll find lots of information online about the benefits of starting a retirement account early. Spend a few hours learning about options before writing your letter.

10.17 Developing a Promotional Message at the EdFirst Foundation
(LO10.6, LO10.7)

Angela Nguyen, director of donor relations, sighed. She glanced at the statistics for the last quarter. Donations to the EdFirst were down 6 percent. Even worse, donations were down nearly 23 percent from two years ago. The foundation received about 5 percent of its revenue from program participants, about 35 percent from federal and state grants, and roughly 60 percent from individual donations. The foundation would need to drop critical services if donations didn't pick up soon.

The EdFirst Foundation provided mentoring, after-school programs, and other resources for K–12 children from low-income families in inner cities. Any child in any of the ten cities EdFirst operated in qualified for the program. Children from families that fell below the federal poverty line received all services for free. Children from families above the poverty line received the services at highly discounted rates of between $25 and $75 per year. Approximately 92 percent of children participating in EdFirst programs came from families that fell under the federal poverty line.

The foundation employed some full-time center directors and part-time staff members. However, most of the work was done by volunteers. For example, all mentors were volunteers. The average mentor had served for nearly 7 years and volunteered an average of 2.3 hours per week to help struggling students. Volunteers also helped with after-school programs held in EdFirst facilities, developed educational materials, and recruited children to join the programs.

Recently, Angela commissioned several third parties to evaluate the performance of the foundation. In the first evaluation, an independent evaluator identified the following impacts for children participating in EdFirst programs:

- Reading levels improved by 1.4 grade levels after 6 months of active participation.
- Reading levels improved by 2.3 grade levels after 12 months of active participation.
- Math scores improved by 1.9 grade levels after 6 months of active participation.
- Math scores improved by 2.6 grade levels after 12 months of active participation.
- High school graduation rates in areas served by EdFirst stood at 43 percent. In these same areas, the high school graduation rate for individuals who had participated for at least one year between the ages of 12 and 18 years old was 72 percent. The high school graduation rate for individuals who had participated for at least three years between the ages of 12 and 18 years old was 96 percent.

In the second evaluation, a separate independent accreditor found the following about the foundation:

- 92 percent of all donations were used directly for the educational programs. In other comparable non-profit organizations, an average of 78 percent of all donations were used directly for educational programs.

- 89 percent of EdFirst volunteers had undergraduate degrees, and 38 percent had graduate degrees.
- 97 percent of parents of EdFirst program participants were "extremely satisfied" with EdFirst services.

While EdFirst aimed to keep expenses as low as possible, it incurred significant costs to rent and own various education centers, supply textbooks and other curricular materials, provide transportation to and from its centers for program participants and volunteers, and run various after-school activities.

Angela was extremely frustrated. With all the good news about the positive impacts on inner-city kids and operational efficiency, she realized the foundation would have to cut back services for some kids or even close some centers if donations didn't pick up. Based on her calculations, the average cost to support a child in the program for an entire year was just $236.

She decided that she would send a message to prior donors who had not donated in over a year. She would ask these prior donors to enroll in the "EdFirst Support a Kid" program. Enrolling in this program involved a $20 monthly donation.

Your Task: Assume you are in charge of sending a message to past donors. Write a message to past donors asking them to join the "EdFirst Support a Kid" program.

10.18 A Message Do-Over for a Persuasive Message to a Colleague
(LO10.4)

Samantha Parkinson works as a marketing intern for a start-up software company. She is working on an account for a new social networking platform for professionals. The platform, called *LinkedB2B*, allows professionals to connect in many ways similar to LinkedIn. However, it also sets up in-person networking events in several major cities and focuses on geographic proximity to connect professionals. The platform also emphasizes business-to-business (B2B) relationships rather than recruiting and consulting.

Currently, LinkedB2B charges a rate of $19 per month to all professionals on the network. It charges businesses $149 to have up to ten users on the network. So far, the network has nearly 9,000 members, most of which are in three major cities: Houston, Dallas, and Los Angeles. Typically, LinkedB2B hosts networking events three times per year in these cities. To attend the events, attendees must be LinkedB2B members. Generally, admission prices for the networking events are around $30.

Samantha believes the network should offer free accounts, like LinkedIn, so that LinkedB2B can grow its membership base. She thinks that members should pay for only premium services. Samantha decided to share her conclusions with her boss, Bianca Genova. Bianca originally created LinkedB2B and considers it her greatest professional achievement. Samantha sent the following message:

SUBJECT: Changing Our Pricing Model

Hey Bianca,

Unfortunately, our current pricing model simply doesn't bring in enough members for us to be lucrative. 9,000 members really is next to nothing in our business. To survive, we will need to get far more paying members. Ironically, we can get more paying members only by offering our membership for free. LinkedIn is the model we must follow in order to do this. It makes so much money because it gets professionals hooked to free memberships, then professionals see the added value of premium services and can't resist paying. If we changed to a free model up front, we could get hundreds of thousands or even millions of members. I estimate that within one year, we could get at least 500,000 members if we opened up LinkedB2B for free. If we could get just 10 percent of these members to purchase premium services, we would have roughly 50,000 paying members, which is a fivefold increase over where we are now. The way to make this happen involves focusing on the following cities: Houston, Dallas, Los Angeles, San Francisco, Portland, and Seattle. We will offer free memberships to all professionals. At the free membership level, professionals can display their profiles. Our pricing for premium services would remain the same at the individual and organization levels. At the premium level, members would be able to do the following: attend networking events at discounted rates (generally 30 to 50 percent less), send ten free messages per month to non-contacts, use the blogging platform, and organize groups. I know you want this platform to succeed, so let's plan on meeting this Friday and I can give a more specific plan for making this happen.

Samantha

Complete the following tasks:

A. Evaluate the effectiveness of Samantha's message.

B. Rewrite the message to improve it. Feel free to reasonably embellish the message as directed by your instructor.

10.19 A Message Do-Over for a Sales Message (LO10.7)

Bianca Genova is the VP of sales for a social networking platform called LinkedB2B (see Exercise 10.18 for more background). One of her goals is to increase attendance at in-person networking events for LinkedB2B members. She is currently using Los Angeles as a test market to explore new ways of attracting members to the events. The Los Angeles market now has approximately 2,500 members. On average, just 40 members attend in-person networking events. This is enough to cover costs of the events but does little to generate profits. Bianca believes that by increasing attendance at these events to between 150 and 200 people, the events will help her company in the following ways: they will make the events more profitable; they will make LinkedB2B membership more valuable; and they will increase LinkedB2B's brand value of growing business-to-business relationships. Bianca created a message to attract more members to these events.

SUBJECT: Come Network to Find New Business Partners!!!

Dear LinkedB2B Members of Southern California!

We are so happy to bring you more and better networking events to help you build your professional networks and build your careers. As a LinkedB2B member, you know how important it is to cultivate your networks and find the next great business partner. But, did you know how much difference it makes to not only meet people online but also in person? Our internal surveys show that members who attended LinkedB2B events in the last year say they found three new business partners at these events. Ninety-three percent of these members also say they gained new business insights. We're now going to take our networking events to the next level by making more opportunities for you to find business partners and more opportunities for you to get cutting-edge business knowledge to transform your organizations' performance. Beginning on May 3, we will begin holding networking events every two months that involve a speaker series. On May 3 the speaker will be Jeff Sedgewick, an expert in B2B social media. On July 7 the speaker will be Janna Chen, an expert in B2B ecosystems. Then, on September 4, we're fortunate to have world-renowned author and expert of deal-making and conflict resolution Madison Avery talk about how to get a deal done. Now, all events will include two complimentary drinks and light refreshments. Also, we're adding a new e-introduction feature that will allow you to see who is attending the event ahead of time. This same tool will help you follow up with people you meet at the event.

Sincerely,

Bianca

Complete the following tasks:

A. Evaluate the effectiveness of Bianca's message.

B. Rewrite the message to improve it. Feel free to reasonably embellish the message as directed by your instructor.

Language Mechanics Check

10.20 Review the "Commonly Misspelled and Confused Words" section in Appendix A. Then, rewrite each sentence to make any needed corrections.

A. We want your advise on the affects of this monetary policy.

B. She said the team lacked complimentary skills, which was one reason for such moral.

C. Your order is already, so please pick it up sooner then 6 p.m.

D. His key incite was that the new policy had no effects at all.

E. This initiative will insure that all employees will not loose their retirement options.

F. It's okay to accept credit cards.

G. The principal behind this guideline is that we trust our employees.

H. Since she's already accepted the offer, let's precede as if she's a current employee.

I. We provided complimentary items to all attendees accept for employees.

J. Please apprise her performance and then send her advice.

Endnotes

1. Maslansky, M., West, S., DeMoss, G., & Saylor, D. (2010). *The language of trust: Selling ideas in a world of skeptics.* New York: Prentice Hall, 6.

2. Simpson, L. (2003). Get around resistance and win over the other side. *Harvard Management Communication Letter, 3.*

3. Cialdini, R. B. (2007). *Influence: The psychology of persuasion.* New York: HarperCollins.

4. Cialdini, R. B. (2007). *Influence: The psychology of persuasion.* New York: HarperCollins, 17.

5. Cialdini, R. B. (2007). *Influence: The psychology of persuasion.* New York: HarperCollins.

6. Cialdini, R. B. (2007). *Influence: The psychology of persuasion.* New York: HarperCollins.

7. Cialdini, R. B. (2007). *Influence: The psychology of persuasion.* New York: HarperCollins.

8. Cialdini, R. B. (2007). *Influence: The psychology of persuasion.* New York: HarperCollins.

9. Cialdini, R. B. (2007). *Influence: The psychology of persuasion.* New York: HarperCollins.

10. Cialdini, R. B. (2007). *Influence: The psychology of persuasion.* New York: HarperCollins.

11. Cialdini, R. B. (2007). *Influence: The psychology of persuasion.* New York: HarperCollins.

12. Allora, R. (2009). *Winning sales letters—from prospect to close.* New York: McGraw-Hill.

13. Ashby, M. D., & Miles, S. A. (2002). *Leaders talk leadership: Top executives speak their minds.* New York: Oxford University Press, 160–161.

14. Mazzei, M. J., Shook, C. L., & Ketchen, D. J., Jr. (2009, November). Selling strategic issues: Crafting the content of the sales pitch. *Business Horizons, 52,* 539–543.

15. Ballaro, B. (2003). Six ways to grab your audience right from the start. *Harvard Management Communication Letter, 3–5.*

16. Mazzei, M. J., Shook, C. L., & Ketchen, D. J., Jr. (2009, November). Selling strategic issues: Crafting the content of the sales pitch. *Business Horizons, 52,* 539–543.

17. Sant, T. (2004). *Persuasive business proposals: Writing to win more customers, clients, and contracts* (2nd ed.). New York: AMACOM; Allora, R. (2009). *Winning sales letters—from prospect to close.* New York: McGraw-Hill.

18. Simpson, L. (2003). Get around resistance and win over the other side. *Harvard Management Communication Letter, 3.*

19. Maslansky, M., West, S., DeMoss, G., & Saylor, D. (2010). *The language of trust: Selling ideas in a world of skeptics.* New York: Prentice Hall, 35.

20. Maslansky, M., West, S., DeMoss, G., & Saylor, D. (2010). *The language of trust: Selling ideas in a world of skeptics.* New York: Prentice Hall, 35.

21. Allora, R. (2009). *Winning sales letters—from prospect to close.* New York: McGraw-Hill; Sant, T. (2004). *Persuasive business proposals: Writing to win more customers, clients, and contracts* (2nd ed.). New York: AMACOM.

22. Covey, S. M. R. (2006). *The speed of trust.* New York: Free Press.

23. Maslansky, M., West, S., DeMoss, G., & Saylor, D. (2010). *The language of trust: Selling ideas in a world of skeptics.* New York: Prentice Hall, 39.

24. Allora, R. (2009). *Winning sales letters—from prospect to close.* New York: McGraw-Hill.

25. Maslansky, M., West, S., DeMoss, G., & Saylor, D. (2010). *The language of trust: Selling ideas in a world of skeptics.* New York: Prentice Hall, 39.

26. Allora, R. (2009). *Winning sales letters—from prospect to close.* New York: McGraw-Hill.

27. Allora, R. (2009). *Winning sales letters—from prospect to close.* New York: McGraw-Hill.

28. Mazzei, M. J., Shook, C. L., & Ketchen, D. J., Jr. (2009, November). Selling strategic issues: Crafting the content of the sales pitch. *Business Horizons, 52,* 539–543.

29. Maslansky, M., West, S., DeMoss, G., & Saylor, D. (2010). *The language of trust: Selling ideas in a world of skeptics.* New York: Prentice Hall.

30. Maslansky, M., West, S., DeMoss, G., & Saylor, D. (2010). *The language of trust: Selling ideas in a world of skeptics.* New York: Prentice Hall.

31. Allora, R. (2009). *Winning sales letters—from prospect to close.* New York: McGraw-Hill.

32. Maslansky, M., West, S., DeMoss, G., & Saylor, D. (2010). *The language of trust: Selling ideas in a world of skeptics.* New York: Prentice Hall.

33. Maslansky, M., West, S., DeMoss, G., & Saylor, D. (2010). *The language of trust: Selling ideas in a world of skeptics.* New York: Prentice Hall, 232–242.

34. Kessler, A. (2018, November 18). Anything good takes exactly five meetings: From deals to dating, you should pitch yourself piece by piece, building the close. *The Wall Street Journal.* Retrieved from www.wsj.com/articles/anything-good-takes-exactly-five-meetings-1542578334.

35. Williams, G. A., & Miller, R. B. (2002, May). Change the way you persuade. *Harvard Business Review,* 65–73.

36. Austin, T. L., Clark, L. C., & Sigmar, L. S. (2018). Practical persuasive communication: The evolving attitudes of the iGeneration student. *e-Journal of Business Education & Scholarship of Teaching, 12*(3), 14–33.

37. Dale Carnegie Training. (2009). *The 5 essential people skills: How to assert yourself, listen to others, and resolve conflicts.* New York: Simon & Schuster, 137.

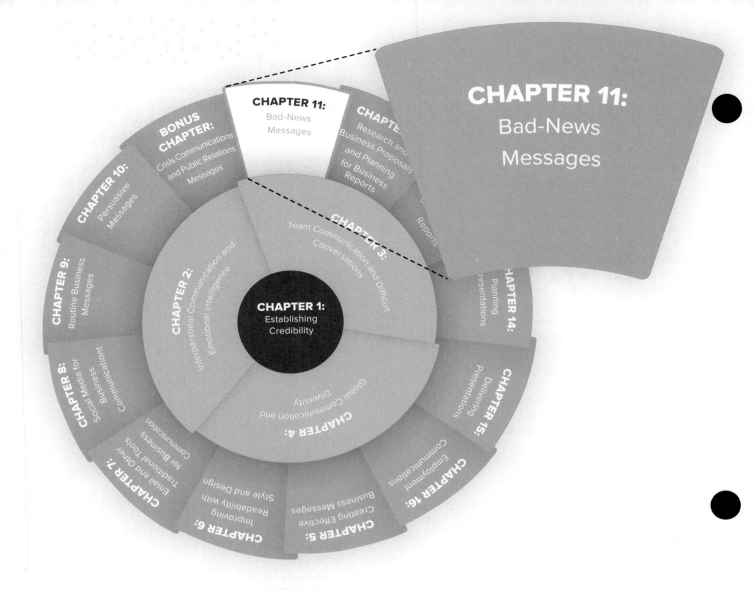

PRINCIPLES FOR & TYPES OF
BUSINESS MESSAGES

PRINCIPLES OF INTERPERSONAL
COMMUNICATION

ESTABLISHING
CREDIBILITY

LEARNING OBJECTIVES

After studying this chapter, you should be able to do the following:

LO11.1 Describe how delivering bad news impacts your credibility.

LO11.2 Explain considerations for deciding which channels to use when delivering bad-news messages.

LO11.3 Summarize principles for effectively delivering bad-news messages.

LO11.4 Compose effective bad-news messages in person and in writing for various audiences, including colleagues, external partners, and customers.

LO11.5 Deliver and receive negative performance reviews constructively.

LO11.6 Review bad-news messages for effectiveness and fairness.

WHY DOES THIS MATTER?

Business inevitably involves giving bad or disappointing news to people. Perhaps you need to turn down a proposal, reject the business of a supplier, deny the claim of a customer, give a negative performance review to a subordinate, reject the idea of a colleague, explain that you do not like a product or service, notify your boss of mistakes you've made, or even tell employees that they will be laid off. Not all communications in business are pleasant. Because business is competitive by nature, turning down others is common.

Delivering really bad news is extremely stressful to most business professionals. Management consultant Mark Blackham explained this uncomfortable predicament: "Bad news is bad news no matter how you spin it. It changes people's futures. This is one part of life that is not much fun, and you cannot make it better with words."[1]

In this chapter, we focus on several principles for delivering bad news in person and in writing. In the majority of workplace situations, you and your organization will continue to hold a working relationship with the recipients of bad news—whether they are colleagues, external partners, or customers. Therefore, your overarching goal is to create a path forward that is in the long-run interests of each person involved in the situation. Moreover, one of your goals is to help bad-news recipients maintain a positive image of your organization. Read the following short case, which will be the basis for five examples of delivering bad news shown throughout this chapter.

> **Hear Pete Cardon explain why this matters.**
>
> **bit.ly/cardon11**

CHAPTER CASE BAD NEWS AT MARBLE HOME MAKEOVERS

WHO'S INVOLVED

Juan Hernandez

Business Manager at Marble Home Makeovers (The business fabricates marble countertops, tiles, vanities, and bathtubs. It also installs and remodels home bathrooms and kitchens.)

- Oversees fast growth as the company transitions from a small, regional company to a large, nationwide supplier

Cindy Cooper

Loan Officer at Wilson Citizen Bank

- Has acted as a small-business loan specialist for the prior four years

Jake Adelman

Shift Supervisor at Marble Home Makeovers

- Promoted to shift supervisor two years ago largely due to his ability to improve employee morale

Cindy Cooper Informs Juan That Marble Home Makeovers's Credit Line Will Be Reduced Substantially

Cindy is in charge of small-business loans. Bank officials just decided that the bank was holding excessively risky credit lines with the majority of its small-business clients. Cindy was told to rein in dozens of these credit lines by reducing

SITUATION 1 (TUESDAY AFTERNOON)

them by 50 to 75 percent. She called and met with several of these clients over the past week, many of whom stated they did not know how to meet the bank's sudden demands.

Next, Cindy needed to contact Juan and inform him that the bank would be cutting the credit line from $100,000 to between $30,000 and $50,000. She knew this would be difficult news for Juan because Marble Home Makeovers faced some challenging cash constraints.

Juan Needs to Break the News to All Employees That Work Hours Will Be Reduced

Juan Hernandez sighed in frustration. He'd slept poorly last night because of anxiety. Today was going to be a long day. He had lots of bad news to pass around—to employees, suppliers, and customers. Juan had delivered bad news many times before, but it never got easy.

Juan gathered most of the employees for a 30-minute meeting. He broke the news that the company was temporarily suspending any overtime work and cutting back on shifts. Juan knew some of the workers lived from month to month and that these new changes would hurt them. When the meeting ended, Juan thought the employees still had some questions. Also, not all employees were at work today, so Juan needed to send out an email to clarify the news he had delivered in the meeting. He definitely wanted to get out more complete information right away.

Juan Needs to Turn Down the Request of a Supervisor

One of the supervisors, Jake Adelman, requested that two production workers get to retain all their shifts. Jake is sympathetic to these two workers' personal financial situations. Jake's well-intentioned request is not fair to other employees. Juan needs to tactfully turn down this request.

Juan Needs to Inform an Unhappy Customer That He Is Rejecting Her Claim

Juan needs to respond to an email complaint from a customer who complained that a marble countertop the company had installed in her home had a crack. She requested that Marble Home Makeovers replace the countertop or pay her $495 (the original price). The countertop had been manufactured and installed five years previously, well beyond the two-year warranty.

Juan Delivers Negative Feedback to an Employee

Juan conducts quarterly performance reviews for each of his shift supervisors. Today, he is meeting with Jake Adelman, who is one of the most popular employees in the company. Jake is outgoing, friendly, and inspiring to his workers. Juan has become close friends with Jake, and they regularly go out for lunch together.

One of Jake's primary responsibilities is to ensure that each outgoing shipment to construction wholesalers is complete and that all items are free of defects. In the past few months, however, several wholesalers have complained that Jake's shipments did not contain the correct items. In two cases, nearly every item in the shipments contained defects. Juan deemed Jake's quarterly performance as poor and knew he needed to confront Jake about these problems.

TASK

1 — How can Cindy inform Juan of changes to his credit line and also preserve business with Marble Home Makeovers? (See the section "Delivering Bad News to Clients.")

2 — How can Juan write a message to employees informing them that they will have reduced work hours without excessively reducing employee morale and commitment? (See the section "Delivering Bad-News Announcements.")

3 — How can Juan turn down a supervisor's request and still maintain goodwill? (See the section "Turning Down Requests and Ideas.")

4 — How can Juan reject this customer's claim but retain her loyalty? (See the section "Delivering Bad News to Customers.")

5 — How can Juan tell one of the most popular employees that he is not performing well? (See the section "Delivering and Receiving Negative Performance Reviews.")

Maintaining Credibility When Delivering Bad News

How you deliver bad news strongly impacts your credibility. Any perceived dishonesty or deception can damage your credibility.[2] Communication specialist Dave Zielinski described how failing to effectively deliver bad news during tough times can damage credibility over the long term:

> Employees, who have long memories, tend to remember how they were treated, not what marching orders they received, in times of corporate turmoil. When it comes to how they perceive the organization in the aftermath of such troubles, those who communicated openly, honestly and frequently will lay the foundation for future loyalty and overall organizational health.[3]

LO11.1 Describe how delivering bad news impacts your credibility.

Zielinski's point is clear: Honesty and openness are key. Although people do not like to get bad news, they expect the truth.

Research shows that honesty and openness can lead to more trust in the bad-news bearer. The consulting firm Siegel+Gale conducted research about delivering bad news. Based on responses from hundreds of customers of financial service companies, the consultants concluded the following:

> Many organizations struggle to communicate unfavorable news— from lower earnings and shrinking market share, to cuts in service and increases in prices. While many assume that communicating bad news to customers shakes relationships and breeds mistrust, Siegel+Gale's latest . . . survey reveals that delivering bad news the right way can actually strengthen customer relationships and lay the foundation for increased trust when conditions improve.[4]

Although one should never view the delivery of bad news opportunistically, those who deliver bad news appropriately enhance their credibility. It shows character on your part to tell people the truth, even when it's hard for all parties

Professionals often enhance their credibility by delivering bad news in an honest, caring, and timely fashion.
Michaeljung/123RF

337

involved. In particular, bearing responsibility for your own role in causing the bad news shows your commitment to transparency and honesty, further bolstering character. It shows caring when you do all you can to lessen the impact of bad news on others and exhibit forward thinking that considers their needs. It shows competence when you have a track record of success in tough situations and demonstrate a good plan for overcoming the challenges you face.

Applying the AIM Planning Process for Bad-News Messages

Planning is critical to delivering bad news in a way that best serves all parties involved and leaves the door open for productive cooperation in the future. Yet, since bad news should be delivered in a timely manner, planning must be tackled as soon as possible. Many times, bad-news recipients are hurt less by the bad news than by how long it took to receive it. Your challenge, then, is to start planning efficiently as soon as you discover the unpleasant news.

Understand How the Bad News Will Affect Your Audience

Delivering bad news often creates stress, anxiety, and other strong emotions. You may feel eager to relieve yourself of these feelings. More than with other types of messages, you may need to work hard to focus your message on serving others. You can make the situation better for the recipients by understanding the nature of the bad news and its impacts on them, delivering the news in a timely manner, and choosing the right mix of communication channels.

Deliver the Bad News in a Timely Manner The adage *no news is bad news* applies when colleagues, clients, or customers know you are in the process of making decisions that can impact them. In the absence of information, they often assume the worst. Sometimes, as people are wondering what the bad news may be, they may even pass on their speculations as part of the rumor mill. In these cases, you lose control of the message and can lose credibility if others think you have wrongfully withheld information. Never wait too long to deliver bad news.[5]

On the other hand, don't deliver bad news when you don't know the details because this can cause unnecessary anxiety. For example, announcing that there *might* be budget cuts or layoffs or pay cuts without any specifics could cause more alarm than is warranted. You will be the judge of this.[6]

Choose the Right Mix of Channels Generally, bad news is best delivered in person. This allows rich communication, where you can use verbal and nonverbal cues to show your concern and sensitivity. You get immediate feedback from those receiving bad news and can respond to their discomforts right away. In many unpleasant situations, you can immediately come up with options and solutions.

However, delivering bad news in writing also has advantages. By placing the bad news in writing, you can control the message more carefully and ensure that you state the bad news precisely and accurately. However, you do not have the ability to respond immediately if the message recipients misinterpret the bad news. Moreover, many people view bad news in written form as callous and impersonal. See Table 11.1 for a summary of advantages and disadvantages of delivering bad news in person and in writing.

As you consider which communication channels to use, analyze the nature of the bad news. In research from medical and social psychology literature, researchers have

Guidelines for Bad-News Messages

- Deliver the bad news in a timely manner.
- Choose the right mix of channels.
- Sympathize with the bad-news recipients and soften the blow.
- Provide a simple, clear rationale.
- Explain immediate impacts.
- Focus on solutions and long-term benefits.
- Show goodwill.

LO11.2 Explain considerations for deciding which channels to use when delivering bad-news messages.

TABLE 11.1

Advantages and Disadvantages of Bad News in Verbal and Written Forms

Verbal Delivery	Written Delivery
Advantages	*Advantages*
• Can use and observe nonverbal cues • Can more easily demonstrate intentions • Can more effectively clarify and explain the bad news • Can respond to concerns immediately	• Can craft message more carefully • Can document the message more easily • Can provide a message that serves as a reference (provide directions, suggestions, and options for future actions) • Can deliver message to more people more efficiently
Disadvantages	*Disadvantages*
• May hinder effective delivery, interpretation, and discussion of bad news due to strong emotions • Requires more time • Less able to document the bad news Less able to provide directions that bad-news recipients can reference later	• Unable to demonstrate concern through nonverbal cues • Unable to immediately respond to concerns • Unable to work out mutual solutions • Less able to control long-term impacts on working relationships

identified three aspects of the bad news that impact how you approach delivering it: severity, controllability, and likelihood. **Severity** is how serious or detrimental the bad news is. **Controllability** is the degree to which the bad-news message receiver can alter the outcome. **Likelihood** relates to the probability of the bad event occurring.[7]

As controllability decreases and likelihood and/or severity increase, richer channels of communication are most appropriate. For example, laying off someone should certainly be done in person. There is no controllability (the employee cannot undo being laid off), there is complete likelihood, and there is high severity (the employee will be unemployed and potentially without income and other benefits such as health insurance). When bad news becomes more controllable, less likely, and/or less severe, less rich channels are more often justified. In Table 11.2, you can see appropriate responses in terms of richness for various combinations of severity and controllability.

Of course, your preferred communication channel is not always available. For example, if you work in a virtual team, you may not have the option of delivering bad news in person. Or if you hold a high-level leadership position, you simply cannot take time to speak to each person affected by your decisions. Where possible and appropriate, choose richer communication channels.

Gather Information from a Variety of Sources

Gathering the facts from a variety of sources is critical for bad-news messages. Often, you are dealing with emotionally charged issues, situations that are open to multiple interpretations, and/or situations where the potential consequences are severe. If you gather as much information as you can from a variety of sources, you're more likely to make objective judgments and propose fair solutions. Make sure you are aware of your own emotions and how they impact your thinking. You might ask yourself whether your reaction to the situation involves any defensiveness, rashness, or favoritism.

Visit **http://connect. mheducation.com** for an exercise on this topic.

LO11.3 Summarize principles for effectively delivering bad-news messages.

TABLE 11.2

Types of Bad News and Richness of Communication Channels

Type of Bad News	Example	Written Only (Example: Email)	Verbal Not in Person (Example: Phone)	Verbal + Nonverbal Not in Person (Example: Video Call)	Verbal + Nonverbal in Person (Example: Meeting)	In Person + Written (Example: Meeting + Follow-up Memo)
Low Severity + High Controllability	Colleague's idea is rejected (Figure 11.6)	*	*	*	*	*
Low Severity + Low Controllability	Customer claim is rejected (Figure 11.8)	*	*	*	*	*
Medium Severity + High Controllability	Vendor chooses another supplier	*	✔	✔	✔	✔
Medium Severity + Low Controllability	Employees given fewer work hours (Figure 11.4)	✗	✗	✔	✔	✔
High Severity + High Controllability	Employee receives poor performance rating (Figure 11.10)	✗	✗	✗	✔	✔
High Severity + Low Controllability	Employee laid off	✗	✗	✗	✗	✔

* = depends on communication channel in use or preferred by bad-news recipient; ✗ = rarely acceptable; ✔ = preferred.

Components of *Indirect* Bad-News Messages

- Ease in with a buffer.
- **Provide a rationale.**
- **Deliver the bad news.**
- Explain impacts.
- Focus on the future (as appropriate).
- Show goodwill.

Mc Graw Hill connect

Visit http://connect. mheducation.com for an exercise on this topic.

Develop Your Message

One choice you'll make when delivering bad news is whether to make your message more or less direct. For most bad-news messages, you'll ease into the bad news and allow the affected person to prepare for the potential shock. In less direct messages, you'll describe the rationale for the bad news first, whereas in more direct messages, you'll give the bad news and then provide the rationale.

Generally, you will deliver less direct bad news when you work with customers, clients, and contacts you don't know very well. When working with colleagues, you can typically be more direct than you are with customers and clients. In particular, you should generally be most direct when delivering bad news to superiors, who have limited time and need the key pieces of information up front. Still, in most of your relationships with colleagues, some indirectness helps prepare your colleagues to accept the bad news or negative feedback constructively.

You also can make judgments based on the motivational values of others (as you learned about in Chapter 2). Professionals with assertive-directing motivational values (reds) prefer more directness in all situations, including those involving bad news. Professionals with analytic-autonomizing motivational values (greens) prefer less direct bad news that is characterized by the most attention to the rationale. Professionals with hub motivational value systems (roughly equal focus on assertiveness, analysis, and altruism) also prefer less direct bad news that is characterized by a focus on the future and a desire for harmony. Professionals with altruistic-nurturing motivational values (blues) prefer the least direct bad news with heavy attention paid to displays of concern and shows of goodwill.

BAD-NEWS MESSAGES **CHAPTER ELEVEN** 341

Sympathize with the Bad-News Recipient and Soften the Blow   When bad-news message recipients know you are concerned about them, they generally respond without antagonism and even appreciate your honesty. In person, most people make a judgment about your genuine concern for them based on many factors, including your past treatment of them and your nonverbal behavior. In writing, you are less able to use nonverbal behavior to show your sincere concern and appreciation.

For written messages, several techniques help the bad-news recipient prepare emotionally. First, using a neutral subject line often helps the reader recognize that the news will likely not be positive. However, since it is not direct (does not state the bad news), it allows the reader to momentarily adjust psychologically to accept the bad news.

Also, in some communications, you may use a one- or two-sentence buffer to start the bad-news message, which softens the blow. A **buffer** is a statement to establish common ground, show appreciation, state your sympathy, or otherwise express goodwill. Table 11.3 provides several examples, each of which is intended to draw connections between the message sender and message recipient and reduce the sudden emotional impact for the recipient.

When you show sympathy to your readers, you let them know you share their sorrow or trouble in some part. However, limit such expressions to one or two sentences, and make them sincere and professional. Avoid taking responsibility if you are not at fault. For example, the statement "We're sorry to hear about the crack in your countertop" does not imply responsibility, whereas the statement "We're sorry that the countertop we installed has malfunctioned" may.

When delivering bad news, you may choose to use a form of buffer referred to as a **teaser message**. These messages, often written, signal to recipients that an upcoming conversation or other communication may involve unpleasant news. The teaser message prepares recipients emotionally yet does not reveal specific information. Neutral statements such as "I have some feedback to give you this afternoon" or "I'll share with you what our clients thought of your ideas" help employees prepare for news that may be partially negative.

Deliver the Bad News   Throughout the delivery of bad news, find ways to express concern for recipients. By showing that you care, you may help them bear the news better and respond constructively. Generally, make the expression of concern brief, and stay attentive to the receiver's response. Be aware that excessive displays of concern may sound like a pity trip.

Get to the point fairly quickly—that is, express the bad news and explain the reasons for it clearly. Recipients of bad news generally expect an explanation for why a decision was made. Stick to the facts so recipients will not try to fill in the blanks and come to

> **Components of *Direct* Bad-News Messages**
>
> - Ease in with a buffer.
> - **Deliver the bad news.**
> - **Provide a rationale.**
> - Explain impacts.
> - Focus on the future (as appropriate).
> - Show goodwill.

TABLE 11.3

Buffers for Bad-News Messages

Type of Buffer	Example
Neutral statement	SUBJECT: Decision on Bid for Annual Contract with Marble Home Makeovers
Appreciation	Thank you for submitting your competitive bid to supply and deliver plastic resins for the upcoming year.
Sympathy	We're sorry to hear about the crack in your countertop.
Common ground	Reducing work hours creates unwanted financial challenges for our employees.
Compliment	Thank you for your excellent work, especially during this temporary period of cash flow challenges.

the wrong conclusions. If you skirt around the bad news, your audience often views your efforts as evasive, thus weakening your credibility.[8]

In written bad-news messages, the neutral subject line and short buffer can soften the blow and show sympathy. However, make the buffer statement short, and, again, get to the bad news fairly quickly. You don't want readers to feel you are purposely downplaying or hiding the bad news by burying it within the message. You also don't want readers to get their hopes up only to have them dashed later in the message. In these instances, bad-news recipients may even feel misled. If you find yourself writing an extremely indirect bad-news message, ask yourself whether you should instead meet in person or pick up the phone.

Provide a Clear Rationale and Specific Feedback   Recently, research about delivering bad news to customers in the financial industry has shown that when banks clearly explained the reasons for the bad-news decision, customers felt more trust toward the bank. In response to letters that offered little (i.e., "market conditions and maintaining profitability on your account") or no explanation, customers made comments such as the following: "This makes me feel like the bank wants to squeeze me for all they can. They're not interested in me as a loyal customer; I'm just a number to them." By contrast, customers who received full explanations in the letters were twice as likely to consider the organizations credible. They used statements such as the following: "They seemed honest and up front. They were forthcoming and direct with their information, which is always good." Furthermore, the researchers showed that clear, specific, and simple language built trust, whereas vague, general, and legal language created suspicion and anger.[9]

The most obvious and primary benefit of using simple and specific language is that recipients are more likely to interpret the information as honest and up front. An additional reason to use simple and specific language is that bad-news recipients struggle to process information in bad-news situations. Since many recipients may experience strong emotions and begin thinking ahead about what the bad news means for them, they are less capable of processing complex information.

Explain Immediate Impacts   Once you've explained the bad news and the reasons for it, discuss the immediate impacts on recipients. In most situations, avoid moving directly to a discussion of what the bad news means for the company. Your focus should now be on the bad-news recipients, who will naturally be wondering, "What does this mean for me right now?"

Resist the impulse to minimize the negative impact. By honestly describing the negative impacts, you address the foremost concern in the recipients' minds—themselves. If you skip this step, which many people prefer to do since it is not pleasant, you may lose the attention of the bad-news recipients for two reasons. First, they can't process other topics. They are fixated only on the potential impacts on themselves. Second, they may be annoyed if you move immediately to what you consider the silver lining, showing you are detached from their immediate needs.

Focus on Solutions and Long-Term Benefits   Most bad news is not permanent. In other words, it usually involves a temporary setback. So once you've described the immediate impacts on the recipients, move to a constructive, forward-looking approach. Where possible, describe realistic solutions, steps to overcoming the current problems, and/or the benefits that current sacrifices make possible. Ideally, you can describe solutions and benefits that the bad-news recipient can control.[10]

Recent research has shown that when managers take a solution-oriented approach to negative situations, employees receiving the bad news respond much more positively and productively. In fact, one study showed that when bad-news recipients are offered options to solve problems, they are 20 percent more effective at solving subsequent tasks and 19 percent less agitated.[11]

Focusing on solutions and long-term benefits should take a positive tone. However, be careful about the good news/bad news approach. The recipients of bad news may react negatively if they perceive that you are downplaying the impact of the bad news on them.[12]

Show Goodwill Keeping the door open to working together constructively in the future should be one of your top priorities in nearly all cases. You may be demoting an employee from a current position today but promoting that same employee two or three years down the road. You may be denying the claim of a customer today but hoping for that customer's repeat business far into the future, and you're definitely trying to ensure that customer tells others that you are credible. You may say no to a supplier today but expect good terms on contracts from that same supplier in the future. It's not even uncommon for companies to ask laid-off employees to return to the company. In the process of delivering bad news, try not to burn bridges.

Getting the Tone, Style, and Design Right

When you discuss bad news with others, use your tone and nonverbal behaviors to show your interest and concern. Notice the recipient's nonverbal behavior as you deliver the news. Your ability to manage emotions—yours and others'—during a bad-news discussion strongly influences your future working relationship. Research about providing feedback in performance reviews has shown that providing negative feedback with a positive tone actually makes employees feel more positive than when they receive positive feedback with a negative tone. In other words, the power of delivery often outweighs the content of your message in feedback situations.[13]

When you write your bad-news messages, carefully consider tone, style, and design. Aim for a *tone* of genuine concern in a professional manner. Also inject some positive direction to the message, but don't provide false hope or seem out of touch with the impacts on message recipients. Use a writing *style* that is simple, accurate, and jargon-free. Doing so helps people process information quickly and accurately. Since bad-news recipients may be experiencing strong emotions and allowing their thoughts to wander, they are less able to process information accurately. Therefore, use clear language that they will not misinterpret. Finally, maintain a simple *design*. If your message looks too slick, bad-news recipients may believe the message is designed more to impress than to meet their needs. Increasingly, artificial intelligence (AI) can help evaluate the tone of written and oral messages. See the Technology Tips feature for more details about these emerging tools.

Your tone is often as important as the message itself when delivering bad news.
Echo/Getty Images

Technology Tips

USING AI-BASED SOFTWARE TO GAUGE YOUR RAPPORT

Nonverbal communication and tone of voice are critical elements of bad-news and difficult conversations. Bad-news recipients often judge the bearers of bad news more so on nonverbal communication and tone than the message itself.

Bad-news conversations become especially tricky in online environments. Professionals increasingly work remotely from one another and rely on online feedback. In these situations, resist the urge to deliver significant bad news by email or messaging. Make sure you hold an online videoconference so others can clearly see your nonverbal and tonal displays of sincerity and concern.

One routine that many professionals are adopting is using AI-powered video recording to improve rapport-building communication. These tools evaluate your nonverbal communication, tone of voice, and even word choice to determine how well you're likely connecting with others. For example, jargon.ai (pictured here) is a tool that helps you evaluate these aspects of your communication.

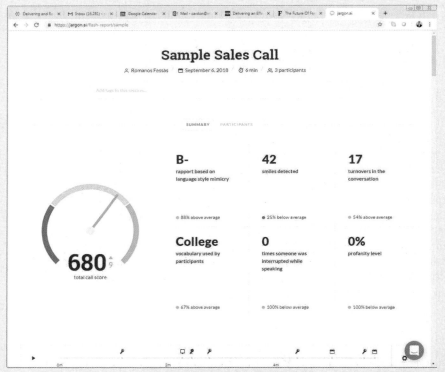

Once a meeting is recorded in jargon.ai, the system evaluates the entire team's and individual team member's communication. In this practice example, the team's overall communication was rated as a B–, meaning the team is above average but could improve its overall communication. The team was given a B– for rapport-building. The example shows that the system evaluates for the number of smiles, pauses, swear words, and interruptions. Finally, it also determines the complexity of the words used. In this case, team members used words that require a college-level education; by altering vocabulary, the level may drop to a high school level. Avoiding overly complex language can help many teams build consensus more rapidly, especially when the meeting involves team members who speak English as a second language.

ThinkLoot, Inc. (2019). Jargon.ai.

Your challenge: Try out an AI-powered video recording tool such as jargon.ai (there are many free tools emerging all the time). With a partner, practice using the software. Simulate a feedback situation and see how the software evaluates your nonverbal communication. In what ways can this software help you more effectively deliver bad news in in-person and online environments?

Delivering Bad News to Clients

In any business, you develop close working relationships with clients over time. You become aware of their needs and hopes. In many cases, you've had to struggle to gain their business and you're constantly working to keep them satisfied with your products and services. Providing bad news to these clients is stressful, since you do not want to let them down, and you know that your success depends on their business.

In the first situation from the chapter case, Cindy Cooper needs to inform Juan Hernandez that the bank will reduce the credit line to his business by between 50 and 75 percent within a few months. Since Marble Home Makeovers is currently in a poor cash position, this new policy is serious and could be viewed as medium severity. Because the bank has some flexibility in establishing the new credit line terms (reduction of between 50 and 75 percent within 60 to 90 days), Juan may be able to negotiate the best possible terms. Therefore, he does have some control. In Cindy's less effective approach (see Figure 11.1), she writes an email message, which is not as rich and personal as required based on the severity of this situation. In the more effective delivery (see Figure 11.2), Cindy calls Juan, meets with him, and follows principles for delivering bad news effectively.

Delivering Bad-News Announcements

One characteristic of high-performing organizations is that employees volunteer information with one another, even when it is bad news. In many organizations, however, employees are reluctant to share bad news. They do not want to disappoint others, and they do not want to be blamed. When many employees in an organization avoid sharing bad news, the result is the mum effect. The **mum effect** occurs when the chain of messages within an organization is filtered at each level to leave out or inaccurately state the bad news. The message that top executives often hear ends up being unrealistically rosy.

One tragic example of the mum effect is the 1986 space shuttle explosion. During the investigation, Nobel laureate Richard Feynman found that engineers had predicted the probability of a main engine failure at between 1 in 200 and 1 in 300. Top decision

LO11.4 Compose effective bad-news messages in person and in writing for various audiences, including colleagues, external partners, and customers.

Visit http://connect. mheducation.com for an exercise on this topic.

FIGURE 11.1

Less Effective Delivery of Bad News to a Client

To...	Juan Hernandez
Subject:	Lower Credit Line Effective in 60 Days

Arial   10   **B** *I* U ☰ ☰ ☰ ☰ ✎ ▾ **A** ▾ ⌄

Dear Mr. Hernandez:

Effective 60 days from now, the outstanding credit line for Marble Home Makeovers will be reduced to $30,000. Your current outstanding balance of $94,345 far exceeds this new limit. We will move to collect if you are unable to meet these new requirements.

As you know, recent economic situations have resulted in changes in regulation standards as well as banks taking a closer look at the risk they bear. Accordingly, it has been deemed important to adjust our outstanding loans so that we bear an acceptable level of risk. In exhaustively examining our small-business loans and credit lines, it was determined that our credit lines should be lowered to achieve a more acceptable risk level. Due to the fact that we have deemed your credit line excessively risky, this adjustment is necessary.

Please call if you have any questions about the new credit line limits. I will be happy to help in any way.

Cindy Cooper

> Given the long-term working relationship between Cindy and Juan, this written message is impersonal. Furthermore, the message contains unnecessarily complex language.

FIGURE 11.2

More Effective Delivery of Bad News to a Client

Cindy was tired of telling her small-business clients the disappointing news that their credit lines would soon be severely reduced. She sighed and called the next person on her list: "Juan, the bank is making some adjustments to small-business credit lines. I'd like to meet in person as soon as possible to explain what this means for your business." Juan replied, "I can stop by this afternoon since I'm in town today." Having worked with Juan for over five years, she knew meeting the bank's demands would be challenging for his business.

> Phone call with a somewhat urgent but neutral tone serves as a BUFFER and allows Juan to prepare emotionally.

[Later at the bank]

Cindy: Juan, thanks for stopping by on such short notice. The bank is making some major changes to the terms of our small-business credit lines, and I wanted to let you know about these changes right away. Because of so many recent bank failures around the country, we requested an audit to help us evaluate our situation. The audit results showed that we hold far too much debt, and we're implementing several policies to place the bank in a safer financial position. These policies will impact your business, so I wanted to explain the new terms and discuss how we can work together in meeting them.

> Provides RATIONALE for changes in credit line terms.

Juan: This sounds serious. What are the changes?

Cindy: For most small-business credit lines, including yours, we're reducing the credit line by between 50 and 75 percent. We expect to make the policy effective in 60 to 90 days, and the bank will move to collect on outstanding credit above the new limits. Today, I'd like to discuss ways to lower your outstanding credit so that you'll remain on good terms once the new policy goes into place.

> Delivers the BAD NEWS.

Juan: Well, Cindy, this comes as quite a surprise. This will put tremendous strain on our business. Exactly how much do we need to pay back and in what time frame?

Cindy: In your case, you're currently using nearly $94,000 of your $100,000 credit line. We will cut the credit line to between $30,000 and $50,000 in 60 to 90 days. Based on our conversation today, including your ideas for reducing your outstanding balance, I'll make a determination this afternoon. What are your projections for cash flow over the next three to six months? What can you do to improve your cash situation rapidly?

> Explains IMMEDIATE IMPACTS.

Juan: We are facing some challenging cash constraints, but the long-term position looks strong. We've expanded during the past two years from a regional market to a national one. Our revenue has grown by 400 percent in just one year, and we've increased the number of employees from 15 to 50 in a year and a half. With all this growth, we've moved into a new building and invested heavily in new equipment and facility improvements.

We currently have five bids on several large projects. I expect us to get at least two of these. If we receive any of the five bids, we could immediately pay back the credit line.

Cindy: What if you do not receive any of the bids?

> Adopts a listening orientation.

Juan: In that case, our only option would be to lay off employees or reduce work hours. We do currently hold some excess inventory. We could temporarily reduce work hours and thus lower payroll expenses by relying on this inventory . . .

> Focuses on the FUTURE and shows GOODWILL.

[After continued discussion, Cindy decides to cut the credit line to $50,000 in 90 days since Juan has agreed to temporarily reduce payroll expenses. The employees will not be happy about this change.]

Photos: Cindy: Mike Powell/Getty Images; Juan: Purestock/Getty Images makers at the National Aeronautics and Space Administration (NASA), however, had been informed by reports that had progressively gotten more positive through several layers of bureaucracy, and they had thus believed the probability of main engine failure was closer to 1 in 100,000. While the shuttle disaster is an extreme example, businesses repeatedly underperform and even fail on projects due to the mum effect.[14]

When most employees deliver bad news and negative feedback to one another in open, honest, caring, and rich environments, organizations tend to exhibit higher morale. On the other hand, when most employees do not share bad news or do so impersonally, organizations tend to exhibit lower morale. In practice, many companies have cultures of delivering bad news impersonally. McGraw Wentworth, a consulting firm, recently issued a report about delivering bad news and explained, "Using an impersonal e-mail format to deliver bad news is very poor business form. Your employees will feel your organization has no respect for them. They will not forget the callous way they received bad news and when the economy turns around, they may be the first people looking for new opportunities."[15]

In all management positions, you will need to give bad news to your boss, your peers, or those you supervise from time to time. Your ability to deliver bad-news messages constructively will foster a transparent and open work culture. As appropriate, internal bad-news messages should show appreciation for the efforts of employees and look to the future.

In Juan's case, he is delivering a bad-news announcement to the production workers that the company needs to reduce their hours for three months. He broke the news first in a rich environment—a meeting. Next, he is writing a follow-up to provide complete details and serve as a reference to employees. In the less effective example (see Figure 11.3),

FIGURE 11.3

Less Effective Bad-News Message to Employees

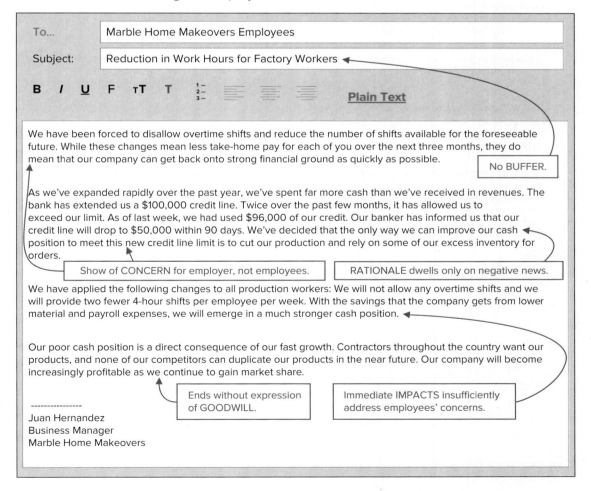

FIGURE 11.4

More Effective Bad-News Message to Employees

To... Marble Home Makeovers Employees

Subject: Temporary Change in Work Shifts over Next Three Months

B *I* <u>U</u> **F** ᴛT T ₁—₂—₃— ☰ ☰ ☰ **Plain Text**

Hello Marble Home Makeovers Team:

> Neutral subject line as BUFFER.

I want to further explain our *temporary* policy of eliminating overtime shifts and reducing the number of shifts available. While these changes mean less take-home pay for each of you over the next three months, I want to assure you that we are doing all we can to quickly get back to normal work hours.

> Shows CONCERN.

Why We Must Change Work Shifts

Your great work has contributed to our rapid expansion over the past year. Expansion has brought growing pains, and we've spent far more cash than we've received in revenues. Our bank has extended us a $100,000 credit line. Twice over the past few months, it has allowed us to exceed our limit. As of last week, we had used $96,000 of our credit line. Our banker has informed us that in 90 days, our credit line will be lowered to $50,000. To meet this new credit line limit, we need to make some temporary changes.

Working with our banker and our four shift supervisors, we've decided that the only way we can improve our cash position is to cut our production and rely on our excess inventory for orders. Production expenses, including payroll, account for nearly 75 percent of our expenses. So, temporarily lowering production is our only option for improving the cash position quickly.

> Provides RATIONALE.

What These Temporary Changes Mean for You

The changes in work shifts will be applied to all production workers. The following two changes apply for the next three months:

> Explains immediate IMPACTS.

- No overtime shifts
- Two fewer 4-hour shifts per employee per week

We estimate that these changes will cost each of you between $175 and $325 per month. We know many of you depend on your full wages, and this temporary change creates an unwanted burden. We are putting these changes into place as a last resort. We will do all we can to get your take-home pay back to normal as quickly as possible.

How We'll Keep You Updated

I will update you weekly about progress we are making to improve our cash position. Please feel free to drop by my office anytime if you have specific questions. I expect that we will emerge with a strong cash position within three months.

What the Future Holds at Marble Home Makeovers

> Discusses the FUTURE.

Our poor cash position is a direct consequence of our fast growth. Contractors throughout the country want our products, and none of our competitors can duplicate our products in the near future. As we continue to grow, we will need experienced employees to move into management and other exciting positions, creating many opportunities for each of you in the next few years. Thank you for helping us grow so quickly in the past year and helping us get over this temporary financial hurdle.

Juan

> Concludes with statement of GOODWILL.

Juan leaves out a buffer and focuses primarily on the needs of the company. This approach will anger many employees and reduce company loyalty. In the more effective example (see Figure 11.4), Juan focuses on the employees—their needs and concerns. He does not sugarcoat the news. He clearly describes the reasons for reducing work hours. He also clearly explains the likely negative impacts (specific ranges of loss in income). Many employees will likely respect him for his openness and honesty. Juan concludes the message with forward-looking and positive thoughts about opportunities for the employees. This is appropriate as long as Juan can deliver on these promises.

Turning Down Requests and Ideas

Your colleagues will often approach you with requests and ideas. Turning down colleagues is challenging because you want to preserve productive and comfortable working relationships. Most often, you should use richer communication channels if possible—that is, in person or by phone. Writing makes sense, however, when the bad news is not severe, when your audience prefers corresponding in written form, or when you're responding to a written request. When you break bad news in writing, you should generally follow up with a phone call or visit.

When turning down requests or ideas with close colleagues, one of the most common mistakes is to offer **token appreciation.** Token appreciation is an expression of thanks or gratitude for a request or idea while immediately dismissing the request or idea as implausible or even inappropriate. While token appreciation is often given with the intent of not hurting feelings, it is often perceived as insincere or manipulative. One of the most common forms of token appreciation is the *yes-but* statement. Statements such as "I like your idea, but . . ." or "You make a good point, however . . ." are often stated in a way that dismisses the requests or ideas of others without any intention of taking the ideas or requests seriously.

When turning down requests and ideas, appealing to values and principles is often appropriate. Yet, savvy communicators do so without coming across as morally superior. Bad-news recipients often become defensive when they feel their requests are denied *and* their requests are viewed as invalid or illegitimate.

Also, excellent communicators avoid turning down requests and ideas in a way that closes the conversation. While they may say "no" to the particular request or idea, they remain open to related solutions. They also take time to hear people out and strengthen the working relationship.

After Juan sent out the bad-news announcement to temporarily reduce work hours for production workers, one of the supervisors requested that Juan continue to allow full shifts for two of the workers. In the less effective response (see Figure 11.5; Jake's original message is in the bottom of this figure), Juan is dismissive of Jake's idea, which is amplified by *yes-but* statements. Unnecessarily using negative words such as *unfortunately* also accentuates the dead-end nature of this idea and request.

In the more effective response (see Figure 11.6), Juan shows genuine appreciation for Jake's request. Juan tactfully states that meeting the request is unlikely but remains open to other ways of helping the employees. He's clear that any solutions should be available to all employees without indicating Jake's original idea is potentially *unfair* by benefiting just a few of the employees. By seeking to meet with Jake in person, Juan shows his sincere interest in hearing Jake's ideas.

Delivering Bad News to Customers

In many positions, you will have direct contact with customers. You have probably already worked in jobs where you interacted extensively with customers and likely had to deliver bad news. You certainly have been an angry customer who has received bad news, so you can relate! Bad-news messages to customers contain the same essential components as other bad-news messages. However, when writing this kind of bad-news message, you want to emphasize the options available—solutions the customer has control over. In most bad-news situations, customers are interested only in solutions. They do not want long descriptions of why you can't meet their demands. Also, they do not want to be blamed for anything. Even when customers are at fault, use neutral language (avoid you-voice and use passive verbs) to point out mistakes.

Juan is in a situation with a customer who has made an unreasonable claim, so he is not going to replace the product or provide a refund. You will often encounter

FIGURE 11.5

Less Effective Example of Turning Down a Request

To...	Jake Adelman
Subject:	Re: Idea to Maintain Shifts for Several Workers

B *I* <u>U</u> F ᴛT T 1—2—3— ≡ ≡ ≡ **Plain Text**

Jake,

> This statement could appear to accuse Jake of being unethical.

Thanks for your idea, but it's not really appropriate or fair to continue rewarding just a few employees. We can't take our employees' personal financial situations into account when making wage decisions. We have to pay what we fairly can based on their contributions.

> Several *yes-but* statements appear dismissive of Jake's ideas.

Again, I'm glad you're sympathetic to your guys, but you need to learn that as a supervisor, you can't get so emotionally tied to your workers' personal lives. Unfortunately, we'll need to stick to our plan and apply it to everyone.

> This message is full of token appreciation.

Thanks a lot.

Juan

Dear Juan:

I've been thinking about ways to inspire our production workers right now. These shift reductions really come at bad time. I know two workers who took out car loans in the past month with the expectation they would continue to have a higher paycheck. I've talked to them. They're planning on looking for some second jobs to make up the difference. These are great guys. Let's find a way to help them out and make sure we hold on to them.

So, this is my idea. How about we continue offering these two workers all their regular shifts. I'm sure that will have minimal impact on our overall cash position, but it will definitely help out two of our loyal employees.

Jake

Jake Adelman
Shift Supervisor
Marble Home Makeovers

similar situations. In the less effective example (see Figure 11.7), Juan unnecessarily blames the customer. Because he uses you-voice ("since you did not purchase the countertop with a warranty, you will not receive a refund"), the tone is accusatory and even confrontational. Furthermore, the message is not helpful enough. It offers some hastily written, vague advice. The customer will likely decode this response as uncaring.

In the more effective message (see Figure 11.8), Juan provides both a buffer and an expression of sympathy in the first sentence. Although Juan denies the claim, he provides thorough, detailed options for helping this customer. Most customers would be delighted with this level of responsiveness. This message expresses goodwill. In every part of the letter, the attention to detail and expressed hope to get the countertop fixed show goodwill.

In jobs where you interact often with customers, you are unlikely to have enough time to write an original bad-news message like Juan's to each customer. However, you

FIGURE 11.6

More Effective Example of Turning Down a Request

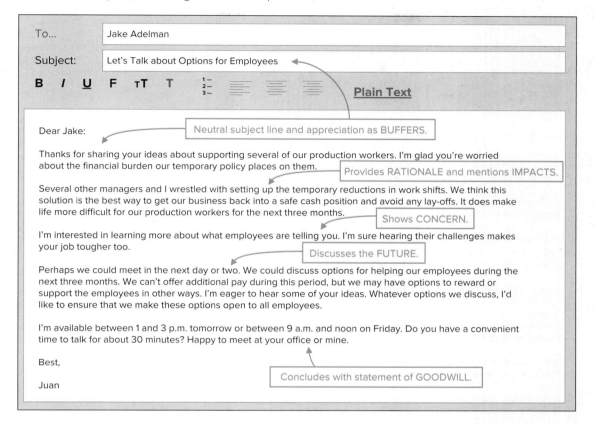

To... Jake Adelman

Subject: Let's Talk about Options for Employees

B *I* U F ᴛT T 1—2—3— **Plain Text**

Dear Jake:

> Neutral subject line and appreciation as BUFFERS.

Thanks for sharing your ideas about supporting several of our production workers. I'm glad you're worried about the financial burden our temporary policy places on them.

> Provides RATIONALE and mentions IMPACTS.

Several other managers and I wrestled with setting up the temporary reductions in work shifts. We think this solution is the best way to get our business back into a safe cash position and avoid any lay-offs. It does make life more difficult for our production workers for the next three months.

> Shows CONCERN.

I'm interested in learning more about what employees are telling you. I'm sure hearing their challenges makes your job tougher too.

> Discusses the FUTURE.

Perhaps we could meet in the next day or two. We could discuss options for helping our employees during the next three months. We can't offer additional pay during this period, but we may have options to reward or support the employees in other ways. I'm eager to hear some of your ideas. Whatever options we discuss, I'd like to ensure that we make these options open to all employees.

I'm available between 1 and 3 p.m. tomorrow or between 9 a.m. and noon on Friday. Do you have a convenient time to talk for about 30 minutes? Happy to meet at your office or mine.

Best,

> Concludes with statement of GOODWILL.

Juan

FIGURE 11.7

Less Effective Bad-News Message to a Customer

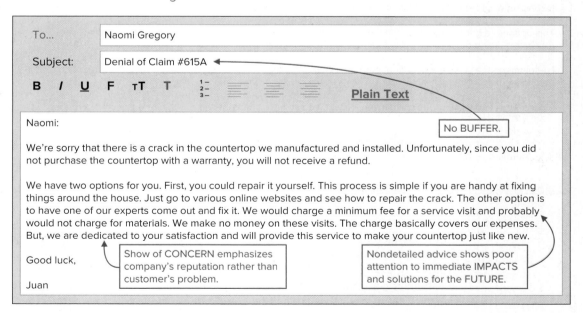

To... Naomi Gregory

Subject: Denial of Claim #615A

B *I* U F ᴛT T 1—2—3— **Plain Text**

Naomi:

> No BUFFER.

We're sorry that there is a crack in the countertop we manufactured and installed. Unfortunately, since you did not purchase the countertop with a warranty, you will not receive a refund.

We have two options for you. First, you could repair it yourself. This process is simple if you are handy at fixing things around the house. Just go to various online websites and see how to repair the crack. The other option is to have one of our experts come out and fix it. We would charge a minimum fee for a service visit and probably would not charge for materials. We make no money on these visits. The charge basically covers our expenses. But, we are dedicated to your satisfaction and will provide this service to make your countertop just like new.

Good luck,

> Show of CONCERN emphasizes company's reputation rather than customer's problem.

Juan

> Nondetailed advice shows poor attention to immediate IMPACTS and solutions for the FUTURE.

FIGURE 11.8

More Effective Bad-News Message to a Customer

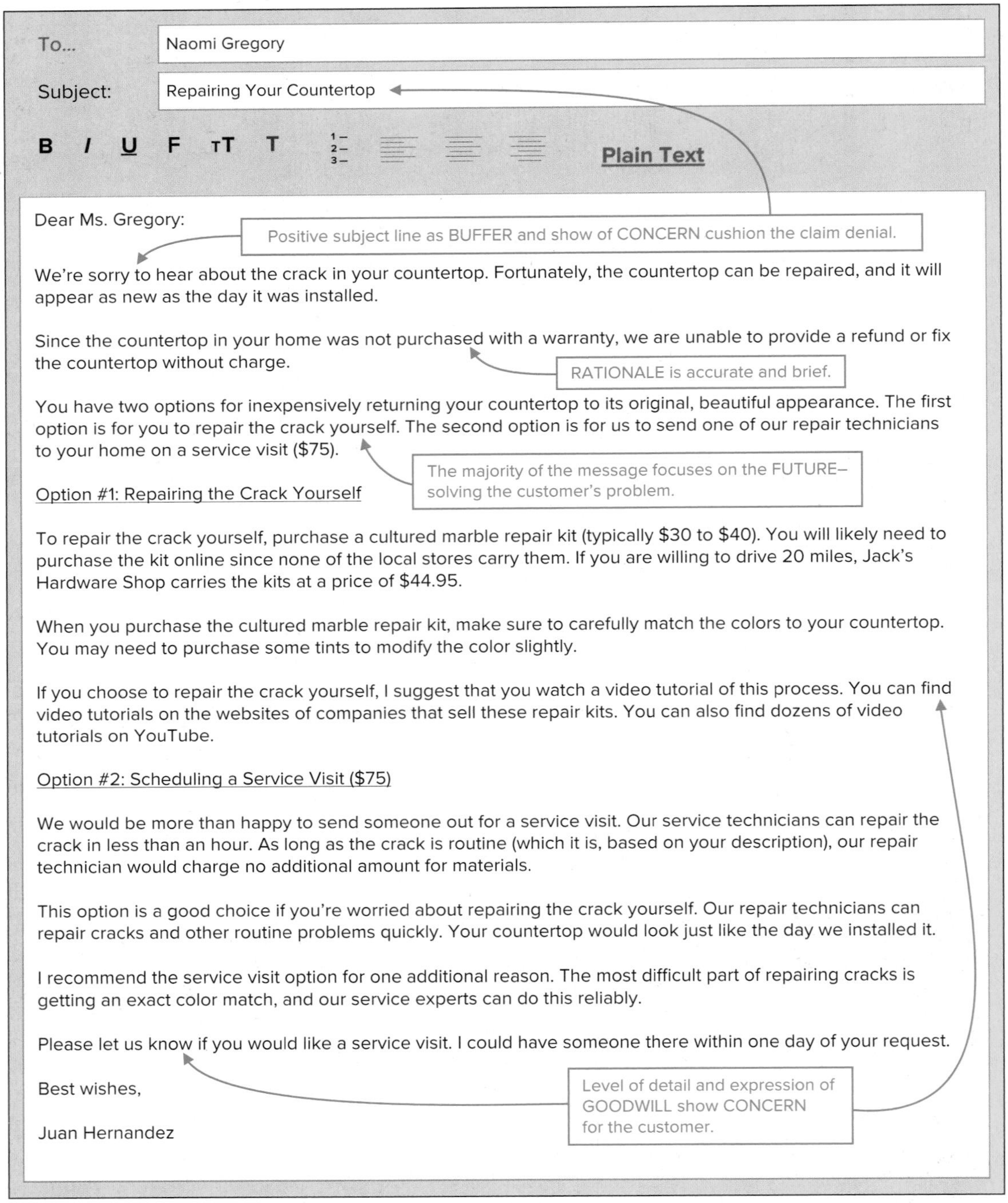

To...　Naomi Gregory

Subject:　Repairing Your Countertop ◀

B *I* <u>U</u> F ᴛT T ¹⁻²⁻³⁻ ☰ ☰ ☰　　**Plain Text**

Dear Ms. Gregory:

> Positive subject line as BUFFER and show of CONCERN cushion the claim denial.

We're sorry to hear about the crack in your countertop. Fortunately, the countertop can be repaired, and it will appear as new as the day it was installed.

Since the countertop in your home was not purchased with a warranty, we are unable to provide a refund or fix the countertop without charge.

> RATIONALE is accurate and brief.

You have two options for inexpensively returning your countertop to its original, beautiful appearance. The first option is for you to repair the crack yourself. The second option is for us to send one of our repair technicians to your home on a service visit ($75).

> The majority of the message focuses on the FUTURE— solving the customer's problem.

Option #1: Repairing the Crack Yourself

To repair the crack yourself, purchase a cultured marble repair kit (typically $30 to $40). You will likely need to purchase the kit online since none of the local stores carry them. If you are willing to drive 20 miles, Jack's Hardware Shop carries the kits at a price of $44.95.

When you purchase the cultured marble repair kit, make sure to carefully match the colors to your countertop. You may need to purchase some tints to modify the color slightly.

If you choose to repair the crack yourself, I suggest that you watch a video tutorial of this process. You can find video tutorials on the websites of companies that sell these repair kits. You can also find dozens of video tutorials on YouTube.

Option #2: Scheduling a Service Visit ($75)

We would be more than happy to send someone out for a service visit. Our service technicians can repair the crack in less than an hour. As long as the crack is routine (which it is, based on your description), our repair technician would charge no additional amount for materials.

This option is a good choice if you're worried about repairing the crack yourself. Our repair technicians can repair cracks and other routine problems quickly. Your countertop would look just like the day we installed it.

I recommend the service visit option for one additional reason. The most difficult part of repairing cracks is getting an exact color match, and our service experts can do this reliably.

Please let us know if you would like a service visit. I could have someone there within one day of your request.

Best wishes,

> Level of detail and expression of GOODWILL show CONCERN for the customer.

Juan Hernandez

probably face three or four broad types of complaints. By using templates with common explanations and solutions, you can quickly tailor a message to individual situations. For example, Juan could create a template that contained two options—one for customers who might fix the products themselves and the other for customers who might want a service visit. Then he could rapidly modify various details for the individual situation.

Delivering and Receiving Negative Performance Reviews

Nearly all professionals engage in regular performance appraisals; sometimes they are appraising others, and sometimes they are themselves being appraised. Face-to-face reviews are often among the most stressful experiences for employees and sometimes for managers. These situations are particularly stressful when the manager must deliver negative performance reviews.[16] In this section, we will first consider the appraisal from the manager's point of view and then turn to the employee who is being appraised.

Deliver Negative Feedback

In most performance appraisals, you are evaluating excellent or good performers. In these cases, you should focus on an overall positive message. When evaluating poor performers, however, you should be clear about the need for improvement. You can generally apply the principles we have discussed earlier in the chapter regarding delivering bad news. In addition, keep the following in mind:[17]

- *Adopt a team-centered orientation.* Even when you are evaluating a poor performer, maintain a mentality that you are working together as a team. Maintain a constructive, forward-looking tone.
- *Avoid sugarcoating the bad news.* Make sure the poor performer realizes she/he must improve (the next few sections will give tips for doing this tactfully and constructively).
- *Explain the impacts of the individual's poor performance on organizational performance.* One major goal of performance appraisals is to help poor performers understand how they are hurting organizational performance.
- *Link to consequences.* Another major goal of performance appraisals is to help employees understand how poor performance impacts their employment opportunities at the organization as well as their ability to meet their career goals.
- *Probe for reasons performance is not higher.* Ask employees to discuss their perspectives on their poor performance. Often, you will identify root causes of poor performance that will help the employee improve rapidly. You may even uncover issues that impact the organization more broadly.
- *Emphasize problem solving rather than blaming.* As much as possible, adopt a positive, forward-looking tone. You are seeking solutions that help the poor performer improve. This is good for the poor performer's career, work relationships, and morale.
- *Be firm.* Many managers want to shrink from delivering negative feedback, especially when poor performers are defensive. Remain firm that the employee must improve.

You will undoubtedly need to deliver negative performance reviews from time to time. Your overall approach to these conversations and your choice of words are important in determining how useful the reviews are. Thus, use statements that offer clear and targeted feedback, focus on actions and results rather than attitudes and intentions, and establish measurable and realistic expectations.

In the final situation from the opening case, Juan needs to give a negative performance evaluation to Jake, one of the shift supervisors. Juan does not want to harm his working relationship with Jake, and he's nervous about how Jake will react. In the next few pages, you'll find Juan's less effective and more effective approaches to talking to Jake. You'll also find abbreviated versions of the performance appraisal in Figures 11.9 and 11.10.

Give Clear and Targeted Feedback When providing feedback for poor performance, many managers want to soften the bad reviews so they employ the sandwich approach of good news–bad news–good news (compliment–negative feedback–niceties). However, the sandwich approach may inadvertently encourage poor

LO11.5 Deliver and receive negative performance reviews constructively.

Visit http://connect. mheducation.com for an exercise on this topic.

FIGURE 11.9

Less Effective Delivery of Bad News during a Performance Review

Juan: Jake, did you watch last night's game?
Jake: Yeah, that was awesome . . . [talk about sports for several minutes].

Juan: Well, let's get down to business. I'd like to thank you for how supportive you are of the employees. You really boost morale around here more so than anyone else . . . [continues talking about accomplishments and strengths for ten minutes].

Juan: One issue I want to raise for the review is that our customers have complained about several of your shipments. I think we should talk about how to avoid shipments that contain any items with defects.

Jake: I'll try to make sure that we don't have any mistakes on future orders. The other shift supervisors and I have talked about some ways of avoiding any future problems.

Juan: Jake, none of the other shift supervisors have had these problems—only you. I think this shows that you've been careless, and you're not really looking out for our customers.

Jake: Look, I'm sorry that there were some mistakes. But I'm not the one who packs the shipments. Those who are careless are the employees packing the shipments.

Juan: But, Jake, you're the one responsible for inspecting and approving the shipments, not the employees on your shift. Remember, every time our shipments have mistakes, it comes back on me. I have to take the fall for it with our owner. And I'm the one who has to hear the complaints from our customers.

Jake: OK, well, I'll make sure the employees on my shift are more careful.

Juan: We need to really focus on getting everything right from now on. I'm counting on you. Well, again, thank you for your efforts for the company and all your great work. See you later on for lunch.

> The sandwich approach to delivering bad news dilutes the message and gives Jake a false sense that his performance is acceptable. Feedback and expectations are vague.

Juan encodes: I value you as an employee.

Jake decodes: Juan values my positive impact here.

Juan encodes: You have performed poorly with shipments. I want you to improve.

Jake decodes: Juan is making a blanket judgment by calling me *careless*. He is overlooking all the good work I do.

Jake encodes: You need to hold everyone responsible.

Juan decodes: Jake is making excuses and blaming others.

Juan encodes: You are the supervisor; you are responsible.

Jake decodes: Juan wants me to spend my time micromanaging my employees. And, he just cares about making himself look good.

Jake encodes: OK, I'll watch out for problems.

Juan decodes: Good, Jake's gotten the message he needs to improve.

Juan encodes: Now that you know my position, let's go to lunch.

Jake decodes: Great. Juan is generally happy with me and my performance.

Photos: Juan: Purestock/Getty Images; Jake: David Sacks/Getty Images

performers. Instead, the review should emphasize the bad news so employees know how important it is for them to improve (see Table 11.4 for less effective and more effective examples of giving clear and targeted feedback).

Focus on Actions and Results, Not Attitudes and Intentions Provide feedback only on that which is observable. You can accurately observe actions and results; however, you can never know the thoughts and feelings of others with certainty. Furthermore, if you focus on attitudes and intentions, you are far more likely to be

FIGURE 11.10

More Effective Delivery of Bad News during a Performance Review

Juan: Jake, for today's performance review, I want to focus most of our attention on one issue: making sure all your shipments contain the correct items and that they are all defect-free. We have received four complaints about your shipments in the past month. In the most serious complaint, your shipment to Carnegie Homebuilders contained 14 sinks of the wrong size. Four of those sinks were cracked or chipped. What do you think are some of the reasons for the incorrect shipments and the defective items?

Jake: I rely on my crew to produce defect-free items and pack the shipments. As a result, I don't actually see every shipment that goes out. Since I don't micromanage, I believe that my approach shows trust in the employees. Even though we have made a few mistakes, overall I think the working climate results in higher overall productivity.

Juan: I appreciate your focus on the employees, and I do think morale is high in your production crew. Ultimately, you bear responsibility for their performance, so I would like to discuss how to avoid costly shipment mistakes. The problems with the shipment to Carnegie Homebuilders cost us approximately $5,000 due to material and labor costs. I'm also concerned that they'll be less likely to choose us in the future. What are some ways you can manage your crew to avoid shipment mistakes in the future?

[Jake and Juan discuss approaches to managing the crew and improving quality for 30 minutes.]

Juan: Jake, for this quarter, I've given you an overall performance rating of 2, which indicates poor performance. This means that in the short term you're unlikely to receive a promotion or bonus. However, I'm confident in your ability and that of your crew to get all shipments correct . . . [Jake and Juan continue discussing the rating].

Juan: In our next quarterly performance review, we'll discuss how well you've done with your shipments. The standard will be to receive no complaints from customers for incorrect orders or deficient products. Also, we'll discuss your progress on the goals you've outlined for managing your production crew. Thanks, Jake, for your ideas today, and I look forward to discussing your progress during the next few weeks and months.

> Jake realizes the severity of his poor performance. Juan's open, clear, specific, and problem-solving approach is not threatening and shows his commitment to supporting Jake's improvement efforts.

Juan encodes: I want to focus on your ability to get shipments correct.

Jake decodes: Juan is serious that I need to improve my shipments.

Jake encodes: My management style may cause some problems, but it also results in higher morale and productivity.

Juan decodes: Jake is not taking responsibility for the mistakes.

Juan encodes: Your management style has many benefits. It's still your responsibility to make sure shipments are correct. Incorrect shipments harm the company. Let's discuss ways to manage employees and avoid mistakes.

Jake decodes: Juan is looking out for the best interests of the organization.

Juan encodes: Your overall performance was poor for this quarter. I want you and your crew to succeed.

Jake decodes: I need to avoid any mistakes on shipments if I'm going to get promoted. Jake will support me if I show positive results.

Juan encodes: This is exactly how we will evaluate your performance.

Jake decodes: I know what Juan wants me to do.

Photos: Juan: © Purestock/Getty Images RF; Jake: © David Sacks/Digital Vision/Getty Images RF

TABLE 11.4

Giving Clear and Targeted Feedback

Less Effective	More Effective
Juan: Jake, as usual, I'd like to thank you for how supportive you are of the employees. You really boost morale around here more than anyone else. . . . One thing I want to raise for the review is that on several of your shipments, our customers have complained. I think we should talk about how to avoid shipments that contain any items with defects. . . . Well, again, thank you for your efforts for the company and all your great work. See you later on for lunch.	***Juan:*** Jake, for today's performance review, I want to focus on one issue: making sure all your shipments contain the correct items and that they are all defect-free . . . [spends most of time discussing how to improve in this area].
This sandwich approach to bad news (compliment–bad news–niceties) combined with Juan's roundabout language dilute the primary message that Jake needs to improve his performance. Juan may inadvertently send the signal that Jake's performance is not poor or that his mistakes are relatively insignificant.	This approach is clear and targeted. Jake will recognize the importance of improving in this area.

perceived as judgmental and provoke defensiveness (see the less effective and more effective examples in Table 11.5).

Establish Measurable and Realistic Expectations   Negative performance reviews without measurable and realistic goals may demoralize employees. Employees who receive negative reviews generally want a clear path to regaining positive ratings; they want to be on good terms with their supervisors, and they usually take pride in doing well. Make sure to discuss how they can improve performance in specific ways. You might even set up a development plan that includes action steps, timelines, specific goals, training, and resources needed. By setting clear expectations for improvement, you lay the groundwork for accountability later on (see Table 11.6 for less effective and more effective examples).

TABLE 11.5

Focusing on Actions and Results, Not Attitudes and Intentions

Less Effective	More Effective
Juan: Jake, we've gotten a number of complaints from wholesalers that your shipments are not correct. I think this shows that you've been careless, and you're not really looking out for our customers. None of the other shift supervisors have had these problems—only you.	***Juan:*** Jake, we have received four complaints about your shipments in the past month. In the most serious complaint, your shipment to Carnegie Homebuilders contained 14 sinks of the wrong size. The invoice you placed in the shipment did show the correct order, however. In addition, four of the sinks you shipped were cracked or chipped.
This critique focuses exclusively on characteristics of Jake—carelessness and inattentiveness.	This critique focuses on Jake's actions and the results of those actions. These comments are less likely to provoke defensiveness or a counterproductive response from Jake.

TABLE 11.6

Establishing Measurable Expectations

Less Effective	More Effective
Juan: Jake, we need to really focus on getting everything right from now on. I know you and your crew will do great and turn things around for our next performance review.	*Juan:* Jake, in our next quarterly performance review, we'll discuss how well you've done with your shipments. The standard will be to receive no complaints from customers for incorrect orders or for deficient products. Also, we'll discuss your progress on the goals you've outlined for managing your production crew. Thanks, Jake, for your ideas today, and I look forward to discussing your progress during the next few weeks and months.
This closing statement is vague. Jake does not know the standard by which Juan will evaluate him for the next performance review.	This closing statement is specific and measurable. Jake knows the standards by which Juan will evaluate him for the next performance review.

Increasingly, companies provide options for all or part of performance reviews to be conducted online. Typically, these online reviews allow you to give more frequent feedback to your employees.

Receive Negative Feedback

In nearly all business positions, from entry-level to executive, you will have many opportunities to get feedback about your performance and potential. Seeking and receiving feedback, even when it's negative, will help you develop the skills you need to make an impact in the workplace and move into new positions. To accept negative feedback and respond to it well requires high emotional intelligence, since you may feel many emotions, including fear, anxiety, and perhaps even anger. To avoid counterproductive responses to negative emotions, learn to recognize and name these emotions. Then develop a reframing statement to respond more effectively. See Table 11.7 for ideas about reframing statements.[18]

TABLE 11.7

Reframing Your Thoughts to Initiate Feedback Conversations

Possible Negative Emotion	Counterproductive Response	Reframing Statement
Anger (*I'm mad at my boss because she doesn't pay attention to my work.*)	Acting out (complaining, showing irritability)	It's my responsibility to get feedback and guidance from my boss.
Anxiety (*I don't know what to expect.*)	Avoiding (*I'm too busy to get feedback.*)	Getting feedback can provide me with opportunities.
Defensiveness (*My boss doesn't know what he's talking about.*)	Not supporting the boss (*I'm not going to make him look good.*)	Being defensive prevents me from knowing what he thinks.
Fear of Reprisal (*I don't want to do this.*)	Denial (*I'm doing fine so I don't need feedback.*)	Getting an honest assessment of my work will help me.
Fear of Personal Rejection (*I'm worried she doesn't like me.*)	Withdrawal (being quieter than usual, feeling demotivated)	My performance on the job isn't related to whether she likes me.

IDEAS IN ACTION

GIVING FEEDBACK THAT ALLOWS INCREMENTAL IMPROVEMENTS

Karen May of Google

Google is renowned for its performance-driven but fun and friendly culture. Karen May, vice president of people development at Google since 2011, is one of the primary architects of that culture. She oversees learning and development for Google's roughly 100,000 employees. Over her career, she has personally coached hundreds of executives. Among the capabilities she focuses on most with executives are listening and empathy.

Christoph Dernbach/dpa picture alliance/Alamy Stock Photo

To give helpful feedback to others and serve well as a coach, she gives several important tips. Once you've identified a performance problem in others, you should be prepared to provide specific guidance in the feedback conversation. You should also get your information from several people so you have a well-rounded view of the performance problem. You should also approach the conversation with realistic goals. Most people can't make major changes immediately, so she suggests helping people make incremental improvements.

May experiments with ways to facilitate honest feedback among colleagues. For example, she puts managers in fast-paced exercises together to increase openness. At the end of these exercises, she places them facing one another and sitting knee-to-knee in chairs. She gives them three minutes to provide as much feedback as possible. This exercise that she calls "speed-back" breaks down some of the normal inhibitions and allows managers to learn about the strengths and weaknesses of their leadership styles.

Finally, May emphasizes the importance of getting enough sleep. She says you bring your best self to work and make everyone else around you better as a result. Perhaps the most telling aspect of her philosophy toward giving good feedback is how she describes herself: "I'm a thought partner through tough challenges."

Sources: Bryant, A. (2012, December 29). Conquering your fears of giving feedback. *The New York Times*. Retrieved from https://www.nytimes.com/2012/12/30/business/karen-may-of-google-on-conquering-fears-of-giving-feedback.html; Meet Karen May of Google: #EWlive14 featured speaker. *Emerging Women*. Retrieved from https://blog.emergingwomen.com/2014/08/karen-may-featured-ewlive14-speaker; May, K. (2016, September 2). Getting more sleep, and sticking with it. *Huffington Post*. Retrieved from https://www.huffpost.com/entry/getting-more-sleep_n_8078278.

Reviewing Bad-News Messages

LO11.6 Review bad-news messages for effectiveness and fairness.

The reviewing stage of bad-news messages is extremely important. Bad news involves unpleasant impacts on others, so you should carefully consider whether you are handling the situation appropriately. Also, since recipients can easily take bad news the wrong way and feel disappointed or angry, make sure to review your written and oral messages carefully so you can deliver the news respectfully.

Get Feedback and Reread

When writing bad-news messages, always reread them several times. Place yourself in the position of the recipients so you can try to imagine how they may feel and react. An extra 10 to 30 minutes of proofreading can lead to constructive work together in the future and avoid time lost resolving an unnecessarily escalated difference. Also, if the message does not need to be delivered immediately, consider writing it, waiting a few hours or days, and then rereading it. Often, you will find that your strong emotions,

FIGURE 11.11

Are Your Bad-News Messages FAIR?

Facts (How *factual* is your communication?)
- Have I gathered all the relevant facts? Have I examined various accounts of the same events?
- Is my perspective of the facts influenced by defensiveness, favoritism, or some other bias?
- Is the rationale for this bad news based on sound facts and conclusions?

Access (How *accessible* or *transparent* are your motives, reasoning, and information?)
- Are my motives clear, or will others perceive that I have a hidden agenda?
- Is it clear how the decision was made?
- Am I giving enough information to bad-news recipients for them to respond well?
- Am I hiding any information that casts me in a better light or concealing the real reasons for the bad news?

Impacts (How does your communication *impact* stakeholders?)
- Have I considered all the ways in which this message will impact others in the near term and long term?
- What have I done to lessen the negative impacts on recipients?
- Am I doing what I can to provide opportunities—as appropriate—to the bad-news recipients?

Respect (How *respectful* is your communication?)
- Would recipients consider my communication respectful?
- Have I stated the message in a way that recognizes the inherent worth of others?

such as anxiety and nervousness, affected the tone of the original message. When you deliver a bad-news message in person, you have less control. Yet, you can still prepare your intended message (mentally or in note form) and review it as you would a written bad-news message.

In some situations, consider asking trusted colleagues to review your message and give feedback. They may be able to give you a neutral and objective view of the situation. Generally, it is appropriate to talk to colleagues about bad-news messages that you plan to deliver to groups of customers or employees. However, it is not appropriate to ask others to read messages that include confidential matters. For example, negative feedback for an individual employee should typically be private.

Apply the FAIR Test

For all bad news, spend time reflecting on each component of the FAIR test before delivering the message. Since bad-news messages impact others in undesirable ways, take the time to make sure you have been as fair as possible. Read through some of the questions you might ask yourself in Figure 11.11.

Chapter Takeaway for *Bad-News Messages*

LO11.1 Describe how delivering bad news impacts your credibility.

Delivering effective bad-news messages improves your **reputation for personal credibility.**

It shows **competence** when you generate a forward-looking plan to overcome challenges.	It shows **caring** when you lessen the negative impacts on others and focus on their needs.	It shows **character** when you are completely transparent and honest.

LO11.2 Explain considerations for deciding which channels to use when delivering bad-news messages.

Guidelines for Choosing the Right Communication Channel for Bad-News Messages		
• **Advantages of oral communication:** can use and observe nonverbal cues; can more easily demonstrate intentions; can more effectively clarify and explain the bad news; can respond to concerns immediately.	• **Advantages of written communication:** can craft message more carefully; can document the message more easily; can provide a message that serves as a reference (provide directions, suggestions, and options for future actions); can deliver message to more people more efficiently.	• When a bad-news message is more severe, more likely, and/or less controllable, **choose richer communication channels when possible.**

LO11.3 Summarize principles for effectively delivering bad-news messages.

Audience   Information

Plan

Message

Audience Analysis: Understand how the bad news will impact others and think carefully about how best to convey it.

Information Gathering: Get your facts straight and understand competing versions of events before delivering the bad news.

Message Development: Deliver the bad news in a productive manner. Ease into the bad news but avoid sugarcoating it.

Guidelines for Bad-News Messages		
• Deliver the bad news in a timely manner. • Choose the right mix of channels.	• Sympathize with the bad-news recipients and soften the blow. • Provide a simple, clear rationale.	• Explain immediate impacts. • Focus on solutions and long-term benefits. • Show goodwill.

LO11.4 Compose effective bad-news messages in person and in writing for various audiences, including colleagues, external partners, and customers.

Components of *Indirect* Bad-News Messages	
Show CONCERN.	
• Ease in with a buffer. • **Provide a rationale.** • **Deliver the bad news.**	• Explain impacts. • Focus on the future (as appropriate). • Show goodwill.

Components of *Direct* Bad-News Messages	
Show CONCERN.	
• Ease in with a buffer. • **Deliver the bad news.** • **Provide a rationale.**	• Explain impacts. • Focus on the future (as appropriate). • Show goodwill.

See *examples of bad-news messages* in Figures 11.1 through 11.8.

LO11.5 Deliver and receive negative performance reviews constructively.

Principles for Delivering Negative Performance Reviews	
• Adopt a team-centered orientation. • Avoid sugarcoating the bad news. • Explain the impacts of the individual's poor performance on organizational performance.	• Link to consequences. • Probe for reasons performance is not higher. • Emphasize problem solving rather than blaming. • Be firm.

Style for Delivering Negative Performance Reviews
• Give clear and targeted feedback. • Focus on actions and results, not attitudes and intentions. • Establish measurable and realistic expectations.

See *examples of delivering negative performance reviews* in Figures 11.9 and 11.10.

LO11.6 Review bad-news messages for effectiveness and fairness.

Feedback: Ask several trusted colleagues who can empathize with the bad-news recipients to review your message.

FAIR Test: Pay particular attention to the *Impacts* of the bad news on others and how to express it with *respect*.

Proofreading: Reread your message several times slowly, imagining how your message recipients will feel and respond.

Key Terms

Discussion Exercises

11.1 Chapter Review Questions (LO11.1, LO11.2, LO11.3, LO11.6)

A. Describe reasons for hesitancy in delivering bad news and the impact of the mum effect.

B. Explain how delivering bad-news messages impacts credibility.

C. Describe the criteria for evaluating bad-news messages in terms of controllability, likelihood, and severity.

D. Explain considerations for deciding which channels to use when delivering bad-news messages.

E. Summarize principles for effectively delivering bad-news messages.

11.2 Key Terms (LO11.1, LO11.2, LO11.3, LO11.6)

Explain each key term and how it would impact a specific business communication situation.

11.3 Ideas in Action Questions (LO11.1, LO11.2, LO11.3, LO11.6)

Read the Ideas in Action feature of Google's Karen May. Respond to the following questions:

A. Karen May suggests you shouldn't hold a feedback conversation unless you have some guidance or solutions. In what ways do you agree and disagree?

B. Why do you think May suggests getting information from several people before holding a feedback conversation?

C. May holds fast-paced exercises to get people to open up with candid feedback. Under what circumstances do you think this would work well?

D. How does positioning yourself as a "thought partner" help you give effective feedback?

Evaluation Exercises

11.4 Analyzing a Bad-News Message from Microsoft Executive Vice President Stephen Elop to Employees (LO11.3, LO11.6)

In 2014, Stephen Elop of Microsoft announced layoffs of 12,500 employees. Read his email to employees: https://news.microsoft.com/2014/07/17/stephen-elops-email-to-employees/. Then, answer the following questions:

A. Is the bad news delivered immediately? Do you think it is delivered too directly? Too indirectly? Explain.

B. Is there a buffer? Is there an attempt to soften the blow? Explain.

C. How effective is the opening paragraph?

D. How effectively does the message explain immediate impacts?

E. Is the tone appropriate?

F. Conduct a FAIR test of the message.

G. Overall, what three changes would you suggest to make the bad-news message more effective?

11.5 Analyzing a Bad-News Message Delivered to You (LO11.3, LO11.6)

Describe a bad-news message you received in the workplace or at school. Evaluate the message in the following ways:

A. Was the bad news delivered in a timely manner? Do you think it was delivered too directly? Too indirectly? Explain.

B. Was there a buffer? Was there an attempt to soften the blow? Explain.

C. Were you told of or did you discuss immediate impacts?

D. Was the tone appropriate?

E. Was the delivery of bad news to you FAIR?

F. Overall, what three changes would have made the delivery of the bad news more effective?

11.6 Assess Your Ability to Deliver Bad News (LO11.1, LO11.2, LO11.3, LO11.6)

Evaluate yourself with regard to each of the practices listed in the table below. Circle the appropriate number for each.

	1 – Rarely/Never	2 – Sometimes	3 – Usually	4 – Always
When I need to pass on bad news, I avoid it as long as possible.	1	2	3	4
I have a hard time breaking bad news.	1	2	3	4
When I break bad news, I understate how bad it really is.	1	2	3	4
When I pass on bad news, I use texts, emails, or other non-face-to-face messages to avoid conflict or uncomfortable situations.	1	2	3	4
When I share unpleasant news, I say as little as possible and expect others to read between the lines.	1	2	3	4

Add up your score and consider the following advice:

16–20:　You are *conflict avoidant.* You usually avoid delivering bad news because you feel uncomfortable doing so. When you break bad news, you understate it. You generally have good intentions, but sometimes you make matters worse by not confronting uncomfortable situations. Try thinking about the benefits to you and the bad-news recipients when delivering bad news right away.

12–15:　You are *somewhat conflict avoidant.* You often avoid unpleasant conversations and communications. Sometimes, you prefer to leave issues unresolved rather than risk the uncomfortable interactions to address these issues.

10–11:　You *sometimes confront bad news in a timely manner.* In many situations, you confront uncomfortable situations right away, yet you shy away from doing so in other cases.

Under 10:　You *usually confront bad news in a timely manner.* You confront bad news and difficult situations immediately and with sensitivity.

Write three goals you have for constructively delivering bad news in the workplace.

11.7 Assess Your Prior Experiences Delivering Bad News (LO11.1, LO11.2, LO11.3)

Briefly describe your own experiences delivering bad news in the following ways:

A. Delivering it too late and negatively affecting the bad-news recipient more than you intended.

B. Delivering it right away and creating the best possible outcomes for all involved.

C. Delivering it using a communication channel that wasn't appropriate.

D. Delivering it using a communication channel that was appropriate.

E. Not telling the whole truth.

Based on these experiences, write three principles for delivering bad news that you will live by in the workplace. Elaborate on each with one paragraph.

11.8 Assess Token Appreciation (LO11.4)

Over the course of one week, keep a journal about token appreciation. Focus on situations where people may hold differences of opinion. Think about various ways in which people use *yes-but* statements. As you write, feel free to use pseudonyms or non-identifying information. Each day, describe the following:

A. Give an example of token appreciation you heard someone else say. Why do you think it was token appreciation? How might this person have addressed this situation more honestly and constructively?

B. Give an example of token appreciation that you engaged in. What were your intentions? Could you have approached this situation more honestly and constructively? How?

At the end of the journal, describe what you learned by assessing token appreciation over the course of a week. List three principles that you think would help people avoid token appreciation and more meaningfully manage differences of opinion.

Application Exercises

Case for Problems 11.9 through 11.11: Bad News at Jensen Chemicals and Hardware Depot

Juan Hernandez for many years had worked with Jensen Chemicals to supply plastic resins. However, Juan had recently accepted a bid from another supplier. Juan sent the following message to Nick Jensen:

Hi Nick:

Thank you for submitting your competitive bid to supply and deliver plastic resins for the upcoming year.

We reviewed the bids with three chief criteria in mind: price, delivery schedule, and inventory management.

We have accepted Hunter Chemical's bid to supply and deliver plastic resins for the upcoming year. Hunter Chemicals offered us slightly better pricing. Also, we were impressed with Hunter Chemical's ability to deliver product on shorter notice and link their online order system directly to our online inventory system.

Nick, we have always appreciated the dependable service your company has provided. We will continue purchasing lumber supplies from you, and I will notify you next year when we are ready to accept bids again for chemical supplies.

Best wishes, Juan

Nick Jensen shook his head in frustration as he read Juan Hernandez's email notifying him that his company had lost the bid to supply chemicals to Marble Home Makeovers for the upcoming year. He'd had a hunch that his uncle's store, Jensen Chemicals and Hardware Depot, would not get the bid. However, it was still disappointing, and he was worried that unless the store changed its business model, it would be out of business within five years. The store had lost nearly 30 percent of its business in supplying chemicals in the past two years. It simply couldn't compete with larger regional companies.

Nick knew he needed to talk to his uncle, Mike Jensen, the owner. Mike owned five businesses but no longer got involved much in managing them. He spent about half of his time on vacations. Nick thought he should email Uncle Mike and tell him what he considered ominous signs for his company. He might recommend that they sell this portion of the business to a larger chemical manufacturer and supplier, and get out of chemicals altogether. They would probably take a loss to do so, but selling now could also help them cut their losses. Nick knew his uncle loved having a stake in chemicals. He was also embarrassed that while Mike had entrusted him with a management position, the chemical portion of the business was performing so poorly. The good news, however, was that business-to-business hardware sales were in great shape.

Nick dreaded several other pieces of bad news he needed to deliver right away. Over a decade ago, during their most profitable years, management at Jensen Chemicals and Hardware Depot had implemented many benefits. One program allowed employees to be reimbursed for their tuition for up to two classes per semester if they received grades of a B or higher. Currently, 20 employees consistently took advantage of the program. Nick needed to inform all employees that the program would be discontinued immediately, as it cost the company too much. Employees currently enrolled could be reimbursed for courses during the present semester. Employees who had fewer than four courses left to receive an undergraduate degree would continue receiving reimbursement until they graduated. This included just three employees.

Finally, Nick needed to inform customers that the Jensen Chemicals and Hardware Depot Elite Customers program would be discontinued after the current rewards cycle. Under the program, customers who spent more than $1,000 in a calendar year automatically qualified for a 10 percent discount on all purchases in the following year. The program had been quite popular, and Nick knew that many customers would be upset. However, he had done the math and felt it was a money loser for the company. To soften the disappointment to customers, in letters to all previous Elite Customers, he was including a 20 percent discount coupon on any single purchase. In addition, customers could still reach Elite Customer status for this year and qualify for discounts next year.

11.9 Writing a Bad-News Message about Jensen Chemicals and Hardware Depot (LO11.4)

Assume the role of Nick and write an email to your uncle explaining why you think the company needs to get out of chemicals. You think the chemicals division could be sold for around half a million dollars. You currently have about $740,000 in debt related to the chemicals division. You would need to lay off ten employees, all of whom have been loyal to the company for many years. However, you think it's necessary because the chemical division lost nearly $200,000 last year, and you expect things to get worse.

11.10 Writing a Bad-News Message about Elimination of Tuition-Reimbursement Program (LO11.4)

Assume the role of Nick and write a bad-news announcement to all employees explaining the elimination of the tuition-reimbursement program. Explain that the company has lost money in three of the four prior years and that you need to take actions to make the company profitable again.

11.11 Writing a Bad-News Message about Elimination of Elite Customer Program (LO11.4)

Assume the role of Nick and write a bad-news announcement to all former Elite Customers explaining the elimination of the program.

11.12 Rewriting a Corporate Bad-News Message (LO11.4)

In 2014, Stephen Elop of Microsoft announced layoffs of 12,500 employees. Read his email to employees—https://news.microsoft.com/2014/07/17/stephen-elops-email-to-employees/—and then rewrite it to make it more effective.

11.13 Message Do-Over for a Bad-News Message to a Colleague (LO11.4)

Recently, Samantha Parkinson, a marketing intern, sent a message to Bianca Genova, her boss, about changing the pricing model for a social networking platform (see Exercise 10.18 for background). Bianca was upset when she read Samantha's message. She thought Samantha's ideas were poorly developed. She also thought the message was disrespectful and unappreciative. She sent the message below:

SUBJECT: Re: Changing Our Pricing Model

Samantha,

LinkedB2B is not LinkedIn. Period.

We are a premier social networking service for professionals. We focus on B2B networking. Our competitive advantage is that we are not LinkedIn. We are far more valuable to our members than LinkedIn. THAT IS WHY WE CHARGE FOR ALL MEMBERS. As soon as we reduce our service to a free service, we lose our advantage. Furthermore, we send the message that anyone can join. Quite frankly, we only want professionals who are serious about networking to join. As soon as we open the service up to anyone willing to create a username and a password, then our loyal members will recognize that most of the members are no longer as valuable as contacts.

Please avoid spending any time developing your own ideas. We've set up a variety of activities for you to work on—identifying prospects to contact directly about our service, developing content to help in B2B relationship-building, and contacting professionals who have failed to renew their memberships. This is all we want you to do. You've done a fine job at this so far, and we want you to DEVOTE ALL OF YOUR ENERGIES TO YOUR JOB DESCRIPTION.

Best,

Bianca

Complete the following tasks:

A. Evaluate the effectiveness of Bianca's message.

B. Rewrite the message to improve it. Feel free to reasonably embellish the message as directed by your instructor.

11.14 Message Do-Over for a Bad-News Message to a Professional Contact (LO11.4)

Bianca Genova has worked hard to make networking events for LinkedB2B more attractive to members (see Exercises 10.18, 10.19, and 11.13 for background). She developed a speaker series as one strategy to attract members to attend the events. Several months ago, she invited a prominent author and speaker, Madison Avery, to an event on September 4. On August 21, Madison sent the following note:

SUBJECT: Speaking Cancellation

Dear Bianca,

I regret to inform you that I cannot speak at your September 4 networking event. I will return the $2,000 advance that you sent me.

In the past month, I have suffered some health issues. I anticipated recovering more quickly. My doctor has advised that I avoid all travel for several months to avoid some of these problems. On top of that, my father-in-law died two weeks ago. As a result, I've spent most of my time attempting to help my husband deal with this tragic time. I appreciate your understanding.

Madison

At this time, 179 professionals have signed up for the event. Bianca needs to write a message to all professionals who have RSVP'd and paid for the event. She will explain that she will find a fill-in speaker on the same topic and she will offer refunds to any person who no longer wants to attend the event.

Complete the following tasks:

A. Evaluate how well Madison delivers bad news.

B. Rewrite Madison's note to more effectively deliver bad news.

C. Assume the role of Samantha and write a message to members that delivers the bad news and also helps promote the networking event even in the absence of Madison as a speaker.

Language Mechanics Check

11.16 **Review all rules in Appendix A about punctuation, number usage, and grammar. Then, rewrite each sentence to make all needed corrections.**

A. If you go to just about any companies website you'll find many references to corporate social responsibility, or CSR for short.

B. In fact many companies have dedicate entire sections on they're websites to CSR. They even publish CSR reports under names such as Giving Back, Sharing the Wealth, and Citizenship Report.

C. The reality however, is corporate giving to charity are far less than it was twenty years ago.

D. In 1986 the average company donated 2.1% of it's profits to charity.

E. Now the average company donates around .8% of it's profits to charity.

F. Some of the most profitable and most well known companies in the technology sector gives less than .5% of its profits.

G. Some companies are extremely generous yet do not give much to local, communities.

H. For example Google gives roughly 8% of its profits to charity.

I. Yet almost none of this money goes to communities in cities near their corporate headquarters.

J. Unless companies can increase charitable giving to these local communities their efforts to promote their CSR activities will come across as insincere.

Endnotes

1. InTouch. (2008). Comment on breaking bad news. *New Zealand Management, 55*(9), 16.

2. Young Entrepreneur Council. (2018, January 11). Sharing tough company news? 18 strategies for minimizing stress among employees. *Forbes.* Retrieved from www.forbes.com/sites/theyec/2018/01/11/sharing-tough-company-news-18-strategies-for-minimizing-stress-among-employees/; McGraw Wentworth. (2009). Tips on delivering bad news. *The ViewsLetter, 12*(2), 1-4.

3. Zielinski, D. (2001, February 1). Crisis presenting: How to deliver bad news. *Presentations.*

4. Siegel+Gale. (2009). *Turning bad news into good vibes.* New York: Author, 1.

5. Barbosa, B. (2017, October 28). This is the best way to deliver bad news, according to science. *Fortune.* Retrieved from www.inc.com/brenda-barbosa/this-is-best-way-to-deliver-bad-news-according-to-science.html; Young Entrepreneur Council. (2018, January 11). Sharing tough company news? 18 strategies for minimizing stress among employees. *Forbes.* Retrieved from www.forbes.com/sites/theyec/2018/01/11/sharing-tough-company-news-18-strategies-for-minimizing-stress-among-employees/.

6. Young Entrepreneur Council. (2018, January 11). Sharing tough company news? 18 strategies for minimizing stress among employees. *Forbes.* Retrieved from www.forbes.com/sites/theyec/2018/01/11/sharing-tough-company-news-18-strategies-for-minimizing-stress-among-employees/; McGraw Wentworth. (2009). Tips on delivering bad News. *The ViewsLetter, 12*(2), 1-4.

7. Sweeny, K., & Shepperd, J. A. (2007). Being the best bearer of bad tidings. *Review of General Psychology, 11*(3), 235-257.

8. Dixon, L. (2010, April 13). Good practices for delivering bad news. Retrieved July 20, 2010, from http://webatsimon.com/good-practices-for-delivering-bad-news/.

9. Siegel+Gale. (2009). *Turning bad news into good vibes.* New York: Author, 4.

10. Maslansky, M. (2010). *The language of trust.* New York: Prentice Hall.

11. Gielan, M. (2016, March 21). You can deliver bad news to your team without crushing them. *Harvard Business Review.* Retrieved from hbr.org/2016/03/you-can-deliver-bad-news-to-your-team-without-crushing-them.

12. McGraw Wentworth. (2009). Tips on delivering bad news. *The ViewsLetter, 12*(2), 1-4; Law, S. (2006, August 18). How to soften the blow when you have to give bad news. *Denver Business Journal.*

13. Goleman, D., Boyatzis, R., & McKee, A. (2001, December). Realizing the power of emotional intelligence: Primal leadership. *Harvard Business Review,* 42-51.

14. Park, C., Im, G., & Keil, M. (2008). Overcoming the mum effect in IT project reporting: Impacts of fault responsibility and time urgency. *Journal of the Association for Information Systems, 9*(7), Article 17; Tesser, A., & Rosen, S. (1975). The reluctance to transmit bad news. *Advances in Experimental Social Psychology, 8,* 193-232.

15.   McGraw Wentworth. (2009). Tips on delivering bad news. *The ViewsLetter, 12*(2), 1-4.

16.   Knight, R. (2011, November 3). Delivering an effective performance review. *Harvard Business Review*. Retrieved from https://hbr.org/2011/11/delivering-an-effective-perfor.

17.   Knight, R. (2011, November 3). Delivering an effective performance review. *Harvard Business Review*. Retrieved from https://hbr.org/2011/11/delivering-an-effective-perfor; Jordan, K. (2009). *Performance appraisal: The basics.* Boston: Harvard Business Press; Miller, B. C. (2006). *Keeping employees accountable for results.* New York: American Management Association.

18.   Adapted from table in Jackman, J. M., & Strober, M. H. (2003, April). Fear of feedback. *Harvard Business Review,* 101-107.

Reports and Presentations

PART

FIVE

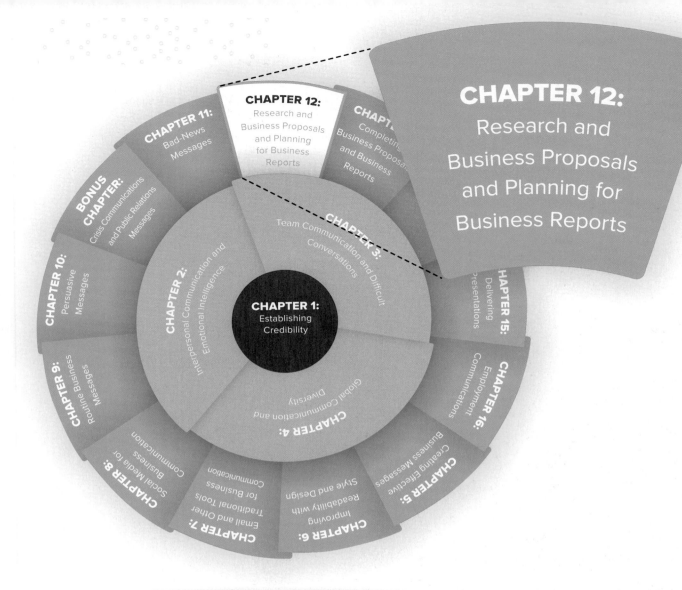

CHAPTER 12:
Research and Business Proposals and Planning for Business Reports

CHAPTER 12:
Research and Business Proposals and Planning for Business Reports

 ESTABLISHING CREDIBILITY

 PRINCIPLES OF INTERPERSONAL COMMUNICATION

 PRINCIPLES FOR & TYPES OF BUSINESS MESSAGES

 LEARNING OBJECTIVES

After studying this chapter, you should be able to do the following:

LO12.1 Explain how planning and conducting business research for reports impacts your credibility.

LO12.2 Create research objectives that are specific and achievable.

LO12.3 Explain principles of effective design for survey questions and choices.

LO12.4 Develop charts and tables to concisely display data and accentuate key messages.

LO12.5 Evaluate the usefulness of data sources for business research.

LO12.6 Conduct secondary research to address a business problem.

LO12.7 Evaluate research data, charts, and tables for fairness and effectiveness.

In your career, you'll be responsible for reading and preparing an amazing variety of business reports. Common types include business plans, project reports, status or progress reports, financial plans, marketing plans, strategic plans, and technical reports. Reports can range from a single page to thousands of pages. One characteristic is common to all types: the purpose is to provide sound information, analysis, and advice to decision makers.

Compared to most daily business correspondence, reports are considered more reliable, authoritative, thorough, and final. As decision-making tools, they are typically commissioned by and written for middle-level or upper-level managers or external stakeholders (i.e., loan officers, stockholders). Because of their role in decision making, most reports take much more time to create than daily business correspondence. Furthermore, many reports are written collaboratively since they contain complex information that requires the talents and resources of many professionals.

Many reports rely on business research. A person who can conduct business research will have many opportunities for success and advancement. Research is the process of searching for knowledge. In business, you may want to know how consumers think and feel, understand employees' attitudes about a new policy, forecast sales based on past performance and carefully selected assumptions, use internal data to identify consumer behavioral patterns, or examine data to address a variety of business problems.

Conducting and reporting research can enhance your credibility in a variety of ways. You demonstrate an often-rare competency in the workplace when you can zero in on core business problems and collect and analyze data that relates to these problems. You show caring by involving key decision makers in the process and conducting research that meets their needs. Also, your character is significantly enhanced when decision makers recognize that they can count on you to deliver results in an objective and unbiased fashion.

In this chapter, we consider several approaches to planning and conducting research for reports. Overall, the purpose is to gather and analyze data that will drive excellent decision making and high organizational performance. First, we focus on setting research objectives, a process that ensures you identify the most relevant data for your business goals. Then, we examine the processes of primary and secondary research to ensure that you will gather reliable data. We also discuss how to effectively present numerical and other information in charts, graphs, and tables so that your complex data is easy to understand and supports your key messages. Read the following case, which serves as the basis for examples provided in Chapters 12 and 13.

Hear Pete Cardon explain why this matters.
bit.ly/cardon12

LO12.1 Explain how planning and conducting business research for reports impacts your credibility.

CHAPTER CASE   CONDUCTING MARKET RESEARCH AT AICASUS TOURS

Jeff Anderton

Andrea Garcia

WHO'S INVOLVED

Market research associate

- Has worked at Aicasus Tours for three months
- Roles include conducting research about new markets and tracking customer satisfaction
- Graduated a year ago with a marketing major and statistics minor

Director of marketing

- Has worked as director of marketing for one year
- Started at Aicasus Tours nearly nine years ago in a position similar to Jeff's market research associate position
- Expects thorough data and analysis before making decisions

Andrea recently asked Jeff to work on two market research projects. She expects him to complete them in roughly three months.

Aicasus Tours owns several hotels and resorts around the world, including the Prestigio Hotel. For the first project, Andrea wants Jeff to analyze guest satisfaction at the Prestigio Hotel compared with its three chief competitors: the Grand Swan, Great Falls, and Wyatt. She wants Jeff to use an online hotel rating system to conduct the analysis. Andrea also wants to know if satisfaction ratings have improved in relation to two recent initiatives: increasing the guest-to-staff ratio and increasing the amount of customer service training. Jeff determines that he can best gather the data with primary research, through a survey he will develop.

For the second project, Andrea wants Jeff to gather information about the use of virtual reality (VR) technologies for group tours. Andrea thinks VR headsets can help bring tour experiences to life and help clients engage with history, wildlife, music, and other aspects of tours in new ways. Yet, she's uncertain whether clients really want these experiences and whether it's worth the investment. Jeff is excited to tackle this interesting project.

THE SITUATION

(Jeff Anderton character): Kate Kunz/Glow Images; (Andrea Garcia character): Andres Rodriguez/123RF

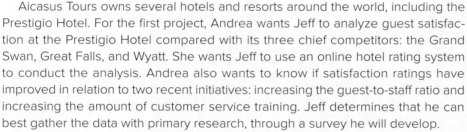

TASK

1 Gather and analyze guest satisfaction ratings for the Prestigio and its competitors.

2 Gather information about the use of VR technologies for group tours.

Analyzing Your Audience for Business Reports

The planning stage for many types of business reports—especially those based on research—often takes months, even years. Like other communications, you can apply the AIM planning process to develop your message based on good ideas that meet the needs of decision makers.

The first step in developing research-based business reports is identifying what decision makers want to accomplish. In many cases, they will commission the reports and have clear goals in mind. In other cases, they do not have clear goals. In all cases, you should spend time with your target audience of decision makers to carefully consider their primary business goals, research objectives, and expectations.[1]

During the research and report writing process, consider updating decision makers and involving them in the process. This increases the likelihood that you will develop a report that is useful to them.

Gathering Information through Primary Research

With a clear understanding of what decision makers want from reports, you are ready to begin research. For important business decisions, gathering data can take weeks, months, and even years. Since many reports are intended to aid high-stakes decision making, getting the right information, analyzing it correctly, and making related recommendations needs to be done carefully and completely.

Business research can be broadly categorized as primary and secondary. **Primary research** refers to the analysis of data that you, people from your organization, or others under your direction (i.e., consultants) have collected. **Secondary research** refers to the analysis of data collected by others with no direction from you or members of your organization.

Primary research is generally most reliable and useful for your business reports because you can focus it to meet your specific research objectives and get feedback directly related to your organization and its needs. However, conducting primary research is often time-consuming, intrusive, and expensive. In some cases, primary research might suffer from a bias toward preexisting opinions and beliefs. For example, a marketing director who is convinced that a new product will be successful when it hits the market may misinterpret consumer research to fit his/her preexisting opinions. Common types of primary research include analysis of internal data, survey research, focus groups, interviews, and case studies.

In this chapter, we focus on one of the most common types of primary research: surveys. Survey research is increasingly common because of the ease with which online surveys can be administered (see Technology Tips). Generally, survey research involves administering written questionnaires. Most survey questions are **closed questions**, which restrict respondents to certain answers (rating scales, multiple choice, etc.). Some survey questions are **open-ended questions**, allowing respondents to answer in any way they choose. Closed questions can be more easily quantified and analyzed. However, open-ended questions allow you to understand an issue in more depth.

Develop Research Objectives

Once you have identified what your audience of decision makers needs, you will carefully define your research problems. Defining research problems involves stating your research objectives in specific, targeted, and achievable statements. Notice in Table 12.1 how Jeff develops research objectives for two of his research projects.

LO12.2 Create research objectives that are specific and achievable.

Create Surveys

With online survey technology readily available and easy to use, you will likely have many opportunities to use it in the workplace. Surveys are particularly useful because

TABLE 12.1

Creating Research Objectives

Less Effective	More Effective
Determine how satisfied our conference guests are.	Determine guest satisfaction among conference attendees for key conference amenities and services.
This objective is not specific enough. The statement does not lead to a focused approach to research.	This objective is specific. The statement leads to a focused approach to research.
Understand VR technologies.	Identify use cases of and market demand for VR technologies in group tourism
This objective is not specific. It is too broad and lacks context.	This objective is specific. It focuses on a context that is relevant to Aicasus Tours.

LO12.3 Explain principles of effective design for survey questions and choices.

Mc Graw Hill connect

Visit http://connect.mheducation.com for an exercise on this topic.

Principles for Survey Questions

- Simple to answer
- Non-leading
- Exhaustive and unambiguous
- Single idea

you can quickly get the responses of dozens if not hundreds of colleagues, current or potential customers, or members of other groups of interest. Online surveys are a nice tool because you can automatically dump all the data you collect into a spreadsheet. Of course, online surveys are not always convenient or possible, so you will sometimes use traditional paper-and-pencil questionnaires.

Ideally, you will have opportunities to learn about effective survey design, data collection, and analysis in some of your university courses. If you don't have this opportunity, many excellent books can help you develop your survey research skills. However, to develop your survey skills, you will need more than how-to knowledge. You also need to practice several times; there's no substitute for conducting several surveys and using the data to solve business problems in the workplace.

Generally, surveys should be short. Rarely can you get accurate data from surveys that take longer than five minutes to complete. Most consumer research questionnaires contain fewer than five or six questions. If the survey takes too long, respondents may become impatient and provide less-than-accurate responses or skip questions. The exception is when you pay respondents to take a survey. The obvious drawback is the high cost.

Another key to getting reliable data is designing the survey questions effectively. Survey questions should be (1) simple to answer, (2) non-leading, (3) exhaustive and unambiguous, and (4) limited to a single idea.

Survey Questions Should Be Simple to Answer As you design most surveys, envision respondents who are eager to complete the items quickly and who will spend minimal time thinking about any given item. Survey questions should contain short questions and short response options. Thus, respondents should be able to read the entire question in 10 to 20 seconds and select a response that matches their true opinions and feelings within just a few seconds. In Table 12.2, you will notice how Jeff is developing survey questions for his research about guest satisfaction.

Survey Questions Should Be Non-Leading Be sure the questions in your survey are **non-leading**. A leading question is one that suggests an answer. Often, the leading question is designed to gain a preferred response from the survey designer's perspective. Sometimes, leading questions are phrased to imply how a respondent should answer. For example, the following leading question would likely lead many respondents to provide insincere answers: *As a citizen in the country with the most per capita carbon emissions in the world, how interested are you in learning about green*

TABLE 12.2

Creating Simple Survey Questions

Less Effective	More Effective
On a scale from 1, not satisfied, to 4, extremely satisfied, how satisfied were you in the following areas related to your conference experience (if you have no opinion or did not use the following services, simply mark N/A)?	**How satisfied were you with the following aspects of your conference experience?**

Less Effective

	1	2	3	4	N/A
Conference Meals	○	○	○	○	○
Internet Pricing	○	○	○	○	○
Internet Speed in Rooms	○	○	○	○	○

More Effective

	1– Not Satisfied	2– Somewhat Satisfied	3– Satisfied	4– Extremely Satisfied	N/A– Not Applicable
Conference Meals	○	○	○	○	○
Internet Pricing	○	○	○	○	○
Internet Speed in Rooms	○	○	○	○	○

Less Effective	More Effective
The question is 39 words long. Many respondents will be confused about how to answer the questions without labels for the numerical values.	The question contains just 12 words. Formatting and labels allow respondents to quickly and precisely process the information.

Less Effective	More Effective
Rank-order each of the following guest services and amenities in providing value to you during your conference stay. (Rank-order each item. Place a 1 next to your favorite item, a 2 next to your second-favorite item, and so on. Do not place a number next to an amenity or service that you did not use during your stay.) _____ Spa _____ Fitness center _____ Outdoor swimming pool _____ Prestigio golf course _____ Prestigio comedy club _____ One of the Prestigio restaurants	Which of the following GUEST SERVICES AND AMENITIES did you use during your conference stay? **Check ALL that apply.** ☐ Spa　　　　　☐ Prestigio golf course ☐ Fitness center　　☐ Prestigio comedy club ☐ Outdoor swimming pool　☐ One of the Prestigio restaurants
This question is complicated to answer. Many respondents will not spend time to carefully rank each item. Other responses may be inaccurate or unreliable.	This question is easy to answer. Respondents are given just one choice and can make this judgment within a few seconds.

meeting options? Leading questions often do not allow respondents to provide their genuine thoughts or impressions. So, leading questions in surveys can produce unreliable and unusable information (see Table 12.3).

Survey Choices Should Be Exhaustive and Unambiguous Survey choices should be complete. Being **exhaustive** means that all possibilities are available, and being **unambiguous** means that only one choice is appropriate (see Table 12.4).

Survey Questions Should Contain One Idea Survey questions that contain more than one idea are difficult for respondents to answer (see Table 12.5). Furthermore, they are impossible to correctly analyze. Notice Jeff's completed survey in Figure 12.1.

TABLE 12.3

Creating Non-Leading Survey Questions

Less Effective	More Effective
To show my support for the green meeting movement, I would recommend the Prestigio as a good site for a business conference. 1. Strongly disagree 2. Disagree 3. Neutral 4. Agree 5. Strongly agree	I would recommend the Prestigio as a good site for a business conference. 1. Strongly disagree 2. Disagree 3. Neutral 4. Agree 5. Strongly agree
This survey question is leading. It suggests to respondents a correct or right answer. It would not provide reliable or useful results.	This survey question is non-leading. It does not suggest or manipulate a response. It would likely provide useful data.

TABLE 12.4

Creating Exhaustive and Unambiguous Survey Choices

Less Effective	More Effective
Age: A. Under 30 B. 31 to 40 C. 41 to 50 D. 50 to 64	Age: A. 30 and under B. 31 to 40 C. 41 to 50 D. 51 to 65 E. Over 65
These choices are neither exhaustive nor unambiguous. They are not exhaustive because respondents who are 65 and over would not have a choice to select. They are not unambiguous because two of the choices overlap (C and D); in other words, a person who is 50 could select either option.	These choices are both exhaustive and unambiguous. Any respondent of any age would find just one correct response.

TABLE 12.5

Creating Survey Questions with a Single Idea

Less Effective	More Effective
How much do you know about green meetings and possible savings on these meetings? A. Nothing at all B. A little C. Some D. A lot	How much do you know about green meeting options for your business? A. Nothing at all B. A little C. Some D. A lot
This question contains two ideas: (1) what the respondent knows about green meetings and (2) what the respondent knows about possible savings on green meetings. This is confusing to the respondent and impossible for the researcher to interpret.	This question contains one idea. As a result, the question is easy for the respondent to answer and easy for the researcher to analyze.

FIGURE 12.1

Example of Simple, Easy-to-Complete Online Survey

Feedback on Your Conference Stay at *The Prestigio*   Exit This Survey

Thanks for your participation in this survey. When you complete this survey by clicking the "Done" button, you will be given a printable coupon worth $10 at any Target store.

1. Gender:

○ Male

○ Female

2. Age:

○ Under 30   ○ 51 to 65

○ 31 to 40   ○ Over 65

○ 41 to 50

3. Income Level:

○ Under $30,000   ○ $50,000–$74,999

○ $30,000–$39,999   ○ $75,000–$100,000

○ $40,000–$49,999   ○ Over $100,000

4. How many days of Internet service did you purchase during your conference visit?

○ 0   ○ 2

○ 1   ○ 3

5. How satisfied were you with the following aspects of your conference experience?

	1– Not Satisfied	2– Somewhat Satisfied	3– Satisfied	4– Extremely Satisfied	N/A– Not Applicable
Conference Meals	○	○	○	○	○
Internet Pricing	○	○	○	○	○
Internet Speed in Rooms	○	○	○	○	○
Business Center	○	○	○	○	○
Staff & Service	○	○	○	○	○
Meeting Rooms	○	○	○	○	○

6. Please respond to the following statements based on your experiences during your recent conference at the Prestigio.

	1– Strongly Disagree	2– Disagree	3– Neutral	4– Agree	5– Strongly Agree
Overall, I was satisfied with the conference experience.	○	○	○	○	○
I would like to attend another business conference held at the Prestigio.	○	○	○	○	○
I would recommend the Prestigio as a good site for a business conference.	○	○	○	○	○

Which of the following GUEST SERVICES AND AMENITIES did you use during your conference stay? Check ALL that apply.

☐ Spa   ☐ Outdoor swimming pool   ☐ Prestigio comedy club

☐ Fitness center   ☐ Prestigio golf course   ☐ One of the Prestigio restaurants

Done

Analyze Your Data

Once you've conducted your surveys, your next step is to analyze the data. This job may feel exhilarating. Or it may feel overwhelming and even daunting. Even small sets of data from relatively few survey questions can be analyzed and configured in nearly limitless ways. As you develop your primary research skills, consider the following advice:

1. *Learn as much as you can about forecasting and other forms of statistical and quantitative analysis.* Unless you apply good principles of analysis, you can easily get flawed results. Furthermore, unless you are careful you can, without any intention of doing so, allow your preconceived ideas and biases to affect how you interpret the data.

2. *Learn as much as you can about spreadsheet, database, and statistical software.* You likely will have a course in spreadsheet software (i.e., Excel). Make the most of this training and continue experimenting with the software to feel comfortable analyzing data. Also, develop a basic understanding of databases. All companies store tremendous amounts of information in databases. If you understand basic database design, you will know what types of information you can extract to answer your research questions. Finally, statistical software (i.e., SPSS, SAS, SYSTAT) can help you conduct analyses far more rapidly and efficiently than can spreadsheet software.

3. *Rely on others in your analysis.* You will likely work with colleagues who have quantitative analysis skills in certain disciplines and for certain types of business problems, and you can turn to them for technical help. Also, you can turn to others for analytical help, because when you analyze data in a group, you are less likely to inadvertently misinterpret the data.

4. *Stay focused on your business problem and look for the big picture.* Often, company databases or survey data contain so much information that you can easily be overwhelmed by the many ways to use it. As you discipline yourself to focus on your key research problems, you are less likely to get bogged down looking at tangential issues.

Communicate with Charts and Tables

Nearly all business activities and goals are measured and quantified: profit and loss, operating expenses, marketing expenditures, employee turnover, performance evaluations, market share, budgets, customer behavior, quality, and so on. Simply put, business executives and managers communicate with numbers. Some management experts even describe the ability to communicate numbers as a core managerial competency. Thus, in this section, we'll focus on using charts and tables to communicate numerical information.

After conducting survey research or other forms of business research, you typically have many statistics and figures that you could include in reports to decision makers. However, presenting this information effectively is challenging. In fact, most managers communicate numerical information poorly. Also, while business managers tend to like numbers, few listeners and readers can absorb a lot of them at one sitting. As one communication expert mentioned to managers, "The chances are good that you love numbers a lot more than most of your audience members do. . . . Overloading your audience members with data is a sure way to guarantee they'll forget almost everything you say."[2] Although most managers communicate with numbers with the intention of persuading and inspiring, they most often end up confusing or boring their audience.

The most fundamental mistake that executives and managers make when communicating with numbers is failing to focus on the main message, which tends to be nonnumerical. Phrases such as, "I'm going to spend a few minutes going through the numbers," or "Let me give you some background by running through the numbers" can cause your audience to tune out.[3] As you will learn in more detail in the next sections, your presentation's takeaway message should be your first and primary consideration when communicating with charts and tables. As you read through the next few pages, notice how Jeff designs charts and tables for his research about the Prestigio Hotel. In particular, pay attention to how these charts and tables are useful for Andrea, who is director of marketing and the primary decision maker.

Designing Effective Charts Charts can effectively convey complex numerical information in a simple, appealing format. A well-designed chart can express a strong message and leave a lasting visual impression on viewers and readers. Since many viewers and readers immediately gravitate to them, charts have the potential to draw readers into a document or presentation almost instantaneously.

Overall, the message of the chart is central. As Dona Wong, graphics director of *The Wall Street Journal* from 2001 to 2010, explained, "It is the content that makes graphics interesting. When a chart is presented properly, information just flows to the viewer in the clearest and most efficient way. There are no extra layers of colors, no enhancements to distract us from the clarity of the information."[4] As with other business messages, planning is the key component of developing charts.

Effective business communicators carefully select the few data relationships that most support their business messages. Top graphic designer Nigel Holmes, who is credited with coining the term *explanation graphics*, notes that charts must do more than describe or inform. They should explain important business ideas or relationships that support the key messages of a communication. Furthermore, charts should not require much mental effort for the reader. As Holmes points out, "Charts that don't explain themselves are worse than no charts."[5]

Throughout this chapter you'll find charts and tables that illustrate the strategic use of data to address the concerns of Andrea from the chapter case. While dozens of chart options are available, this section focuses on the three types used primarily within the workplace: line charts, pie charts, and bar charts. Several other chart and figure types are illustrated with less detail. Mastering the design principles of these most common and relevant charts will enable you to create other, less common types if you choose to do so.

Generally, **line charts** are useful for depicting events and trends over time. For example, stock prices over time would make the most sense when presented in the form of a line chart. **Pie charts** are useful for illustrating the pieces within a whole. Market share would be best illustrated with a pie chart. **Bar charts** are useful to compare amounts or quantities. The bar chart, with its many forms, is the most versatile of these charts since it can be used to compare many types of data.

Create Effective Charts

As you create charts, focus on the following criteria: (1) title descriptiveness, (2) focal points, (3) information sufficiency, (4) ease of processing, and, most important, (5) takeaway message. In the following pages, you will find a discussion of each of these criteria. Also, you will find less effective and more effective examples for each major type of chart. Each of the examples is supplemented with explanations about these five criteria.

Title Descriptiveness Most readers look first at the chart's title to grasp its message. Thus, the title should explain the primary point of the chart. However, it must be short enough for the reader to process quickly (generally less than ten words). In some cases you may add a subtitle if the short title is not sufficient.

Consider Figure 12.2, which illustrates identical information with a less effective and more effective line chart. In the less effective chart on the left, the chart title is a short and relatively unhelpful phrase, "Staff & Service Ratings." By contrast, the chart title in the more effective chart on the right uses a title and a subtitle. The main title, "Improvement in Staff & Service Ratings," uses the first word to immediately point out the main theme of the chart. The subtitle, in just seven words, accentuates the idea that the improvement was intentional or goal-based ("Raising Our Performance") and that the improvement far exceeded that of primary competitors.

LO12.4 Develop charts and tables to concisely display data and accentuate key messages.

Visit http://connect. mheducation.com for an exercise on this topic.

FIGURE 12.2

Less Effective and More Effective Line Charts

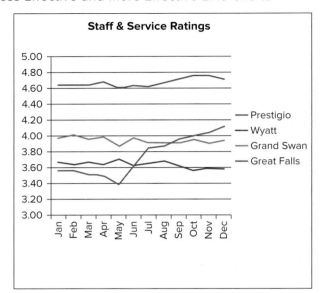

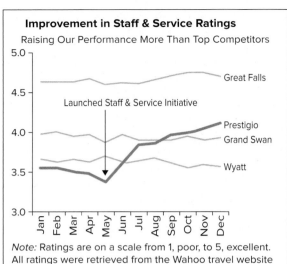

	Key Design and Formatting Problems in Less Effective Chart	Adjustments in More Effective Chart
Title descriptiveness	Nondescriptive, bland title. It does not tie into any primary message.	Title and subtitle focus on intentional improvement.
Focal points	Lacks focal points. All parts of the chart are treated equally—thus, there is no emphasis or indication of what should be the key points of comparison.	The callout box focuses attention on the staff and service initiative as the cause of rising customer satisfaction. A darker, thicker line with a bold label draws attention to the Prestigio data series.
Information sufficiency	Inadequate information about the rating scale. What do the numbers represent? What is the year for which data was gathered?	The note provides information about the rating scale.
Ease of processing	Legend placed on the right side. This forces the reader to move back and forth between the legend and the data series in the plot area. Further, the colors do not aid in the information presentation.	Instead of a legend, data labels are placed directly at the end of each data series (line) to make identification of each hotel's performance easier. Additionally, the color scheme is kept to a minimum, thereby prominently displaying the dramatic rise in ratings.
Takeaway message	Staff and service ratings have improved for the Prestigio over the past year. However, the message requires too much effort for the viewer and could easily be missed or forgotten quickly.	All elements of the chart capture the message that the Prestigio staff and service initiative has successfully improved customer satisfaction compared to competitors.

Focal Points   A chart should draw the reader's attention to the most-critical relationships and ideas. Much like unified paragraphs (Chapter 6), in which all sentences focus on one main idea, each of the chart's focal points should support one main idea. The focal points can be visually generated in many interesting ways—for example, font choices (**bold,** *italics*), color, size, and callout boxes.

In the more effective line chart in Figure 12.2, a variety of focal points highlight the improvement in staff and service ratings at the Prestigio. The callout box centered in the chart directs the reader to the point in time when the Prestigio launched its staff and service initiative, allowing the reader to trace the improvement in ratings since that time. The Prestigio data series is emphasized with a darker, thicker line that is placed on top of the other data series (for the other hotels).

Information Sufficiency   Just how much information should you include in your charts? Charts should contain enough information for the reader to quickly and reasonably understand the ideas that are being displayed. Clear labels and legends should demonstrate what is being measured and in what units. In some cases, readers will expect to know data values at each point within the chart.

Although the ineffective line chart in Figure 12.2 does contain a legend showing which lines correspond to which hotels, the meaning of the *y*-axis is not as clear. A reader may assume that the data comes from a survey, since *ratings* is in the title, but be unsure what the range or direction of the scale is. By contrast, the more effective line chart in Figure 12.2 contains a note indicating the range of the scale. Many charts place this information in a label along the *y*-axis.

Ease of Processing   Another basic purpose of a chart is to convey complicated information as quickly as possible. If your readers can't process the information rapidly, they will lose interest. To some degree, this requires a balancing act with information sufficiency. The more information you provide, the more difficult it may be for some readers to process the chart quickly. By selecting only the necessary information and placing labels and data at appropriate places, you enable your reader to process the information quickly and efficiently. Ideally, your reader should grasp the key ideas within 10 to 15 seconds.

The less effective line chart in Figure 12.2 reveals several processing problems. The most serious is that the legend forces the reader to glance back and forth between the lines and the legend to correctly link the data series. Another problem is that the Prestigio data series, which should be the center of attention, is placed underneath the other lines, with no special formatting features to make it stand out. The more effective chart is far easier to process. Data labels appear directly next to each line so that the reader does not have to glance back and forth between the legend and the plot area. Furthermore, the Prestigio line is bolder and thicker, and it is placed in front of the other lines to draw the intended attention.

Takeaway Message   An effective chart leaves a lasting impression about your key point. Will your readers remember your intended main message in two hours? If not, your chart had little impact. The takeaway is the essence of your chart—how the information, title, focal points, and other formatting combine to convey a lasting message. Overall, the ineffective line chart in Figure 12.2 leaves little lasting impression. The reader who studies the chart carefully might see that the Prestigio's staff and service ratings improved more than did those of competitors, but the reader has to get through a compilation of colored lines with little or no contextual reference. Furthermore, the chart offers no explanation for why this change in ratings may have occurred. By contrast, a reader can rapidly process the more effective line chart in Figure 12.2. The title, focal points, and simple design lead to one strong takeaway message: The Prestigio launched a staff and service initiative that has successfully improved customer satisfaction compared with its major competitors. Figures 12.3, 12.4, and 12.5 present other types of charts with less effective and more effective variations.

FIGURE 12.3

Less Effective and
More Effective Pie
Charts

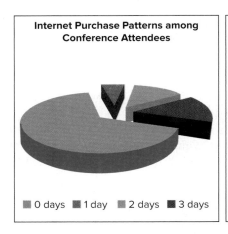

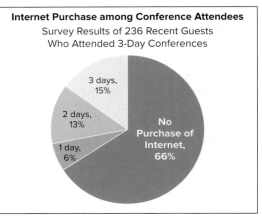

	Key Design and Formatting Problems in Less Effective Chart	Adjustments in More Effective Chart
Title	Descriptive but unexciting title.	Descriptive title focuses attention on the fact that these are 3-day conference attendees.
Focal points	The main focal point is the large pie slice. The colors used give a very dense and dark feeling to the visual.	The primary focal point is the slice highlighting those not purchasing any Internet service. It is labeled more effectively ("No Purchase of Internet" versus "0 days" in the less effective chart) and is written in bold text on a darker-colored background to draw attention to this key point.
Information sufficiency	Absence of data label on each slice makes this chart difficult to interpret.	Data labels are provided in percentages.
Ease of processing	Legend is placed on the bottom. This forces the reader to move back and forth between the legend and the pie slices in the plot area. Also, the breakaway, 3-D shape of the object skews the data. The pie slices are not arranged for fastest processing.	Data series names and data labels are placed together in the pie slices to foster easy processing. The largest pie slice is located at 12 o'clock for quick recognition (most people read pie charts beginning at 12 and continue to read in a clockwise direction).
Takeaway message	Most conference attendees do not purchase Internet services. However, getting the message requires a great deal of effort and could easily be missed or forgotten quickly.	All aspects of the chart collectively demonstrate that conference attendees are unlikely to purchase Internet services.

FIGURE 12.4

Less Effective and More Effective Bar Charts

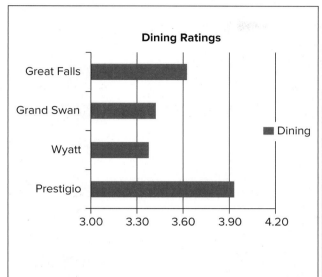

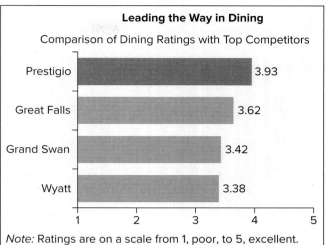

	Key Design and Formatting Problems in Less Effective Chart	Adjustments in More Effective Chart
Title descriptiveness	Nondescriptive, bland title.	Title immediately recognizes the Prestigio's leading position in dining ratings.
Focal points	Lacks focal points. All bars are treated equally.	Darker color of the Prestigio bar draws attention to it.
Information sufficiency	Inadequate information about the rating scale.	A note about the rating scale and inclusion of data labels provides sufficient information.
Ease of processing	The legend is unnecessary and distracting. The items are not ordered effectively (the order is neither alphabetical nor quantitative) to help draw rapid comparisons. The large gap size compared to bar width reduces quick processing. The axis increments are in rarely used units (generally, units in multiples of 2, 5, and 10 are more natural).	The chart is arranged in descending order by average ratings to make comparisons easier. Bar width in comparison to gap width is most conducive to rapid processing.
Takeaway message	The takeaway message is that the Prestigio has higher dining ratings. However, the message is weak and could easily be glossed over or forgotten.	The Prestigio occupies the proud position of leading its competitors in dining ratings. This is a strong, optimistic, and memorable message.

FIGURE 12.5

Ineffective Clustered-Column Chart and More Effective Panel of Charts

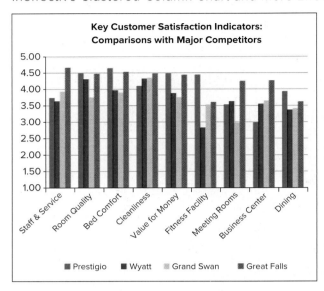

Key Customer Satisfaction Indicators: Comparisons with Major Competitors

(Legend: ■ Prestigio ■ Wyatt ▨ Grand Swan ■ Great Falls)

	Ineffective Clustered-Column Chart	Effective Alternative: Panel of Charts
Title descriptiveness	Descriptive but bland.	Curiosity-building ("How the Prestigio Stacks Up"); a call to action ("Room for Improvement in . . .").
Focal points	None. Too cluttered.	Prestigio rankings and position for each rating area. Red bars immediately reveal the weakest areas.
Information sufficiency	No data labels.	Data labels provided for each rating area.
Ease of processing	Nearly impossible. Too much information. Not sorted.	Simple and easy processing for each rating area. Charts are organized by relative performance (excellent performance on left side, needs improvement performance on right side).
Takeaway message	No key point related to the ratings.	The Prestigio is elite in various areas compared to its competitors, but is behind in other key areas.

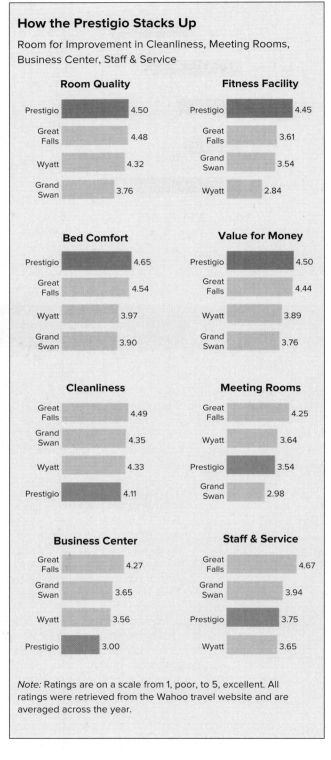

How the Prestigio Stacks Up

Room for Improvement in Cleanliness, Meeting Rooms, Business Center, Staff & Service

Room Quality

Prestigio	4.50
Great Falls	4.48
Wyatt	4.32
Grand Swan	3.76

Fitness Facility

Prestigio	4.45
Great Falls	3.61
Grand Swan	3.54
Wyatt	2.84

Bed Comfort

Prestigio	4.65
Great Falls	4.54
Wyatt	3.97
Grand Swan	3.90

Value for Money

Prestigio	4.50
Great Falls	4.44
Wyatt	3.89
Grand Swan	3.76

Cleanliness

Great Falls	4.49
Grand Swan	4.35
Wyatt	4.33
Prestigio	4.11

Meeting Rooms

Great Falls	4.25
Wyatt	3.64
Prestigio	3.54
Grand Swan	2.98

Business Center

Great Falls	4.27
Grand Swan	3.65
Wyatt	3.56
Prestigio	3.00

Staff & Service

Great Falls	4.67
Grand Swan	3.94
Prestigio	3.75
Wyatt	3.65

Note: Ratings are on a scale from 1, poor, to 5, excellent. All ratings were retrieved from the Wahoo travel website and are averaged across the year.

TABLE 12.6

Formatting Guidelines for Specific Chart Types

Chart Type	Formatting Guidelines
All charts	• Ensure that all data is appropriately labeled. • Avoid using too many bright colors; they can be distracting. • Use darker colors to represent your most important data series. • Avoid unusual fonts or too many special effects. • Avoid 3-D charts. • Ensure that all text is horizontal. • Avoid white type on dark backgrounds in most cases.
Line	• Scale should be about two-thirds of the range included in the chart. • Series names should be placed on or attached directly to lines. • Only four or fewer data series (lines) should be included.
Pie	• Largest slice should begin at 12 o'clock and go clockwise; second-largest slice should begin at 12 o'clock and go counterclockwise. • Exploding slices should be used sparingly. • Pie slices should complete a whole (add up to 100% of a data series).
Bar	• Bars should be about twice the width of the space in between bars. • Baseline should always be zero. • Bars should be arranged in ascending or descending order in most cases. • Legend should be used only if the chart has two or more data series.

General Rules of Chart Formatting

Although formatting a chart is secondary to creating a powerful takeaway message, it is by no means unimportant. Since visuals have an impact even before the reader begins reading, ineffective formatting can give the reader an impression of sloppy or imprecise work.

Generally, the formatting should be as simple as possible and should accentuate the key data relationships. If a formatting feature detracts from the key points, remove or improve it. Table 12.6 provides general formatting guidelines for charts.

Design Effective Tables

Generally, charts are the most effective way of quickly demonstrating a key point or relationship. However, charts are limited in the amount of information they can provide. Tables, by contrast, allow you to provide more data with additional precision. Because of this, charts are generally better for highlighting a key idea, and tables are generally better for comprehensiveness and precision.

Evaluating the Effectiveness of Tables Like charts, tables are typically more effective with simple formatting. In addition, the way a table presents data can affect the clarity of its message. Consider, for example, the tables in Figure 12.6, which are based on identical data. Place yourself in the position of the reader and assume you have the following question: "Does higher income level correspond with higher likelihood of purchasing Internet services?" It is difficult to answer this question quickly by looking at the less effective table. By contrast, glancing at the more effective table rapidly reveals that purchasing no Internet service (0 days) strongly correlates with the lowest income bracket (under $30,000/year).

The less effective table is cluttered due to excessive grid lines, poor labels, and non-indented items. By contrast, the more effective table limits the number of grid lines. Furthermore, each grid line serves a distinct purpose. The initial grid lines separate the

FIGURE 12.6

A Less Effective and More Effective Table

Less Effective Table

Survey Results

During the three days of the conference you attended at the Prestigio, how many days did you purchase Internet service?				
Days of Internet Service	0	1	2	3
All Respondents	154	15	31	36
Gender				
Male	82	8	15	22
Female	72	7	16	14
Income				
Under $30,000	15	0	1	2
$30,000–$39,999	41	4	3	7
$40,000–$49,999	48	3	11	12
$50,000–$74,999	33	6	7	8
$75,000–$100,000	12	2	4	4
Over $100,000	5	0	5	3

More Effective Table

Internet Service Purchases among Conference Guests

	Days of Internet Service Purchased (Number of Respondents in Parentheses)				
	0 Days	**1 Day**	**2 Days**	**3 Days**	**Total (#)**
All Respondents	65.5% (154)	6.4% (15)	13.2% (31)	15.3% (36)	236
Gender					
Male	64.6% (82)	6.3% (8)	11.8% (15)	17.3% (22)	127
Female	66.1% (72)	6.4% (7)	14.7% (16)	12.8% (14)	109
Income					
Under $30,000	83.3% (15)	0.0% (0)	5.6% (1)	11.1% (6)	18
$30,000–$39,999	74.5% (41)	7.3% (4)	5.5% (3)	12.7% (7)	55
$40,000–$49,999	64.9% (48)	4.1% (3)	14.9% (11)	16.2% (12)	74
$50,000–$74,999	61.1% (33)	11.1% (2)	13.0% (7)	14.8% (8)	54
$75,000–$100,000	54.5% (12)	9.1% (2)	18.2% (4)	18.2% (4)	22
Over $100,000	38.5% (5)	0.0% (0)	38.5% (5)	23.1% (3)	13

column labels from the survey data. Subsequent grid lines separate each category of data, including those for all respondents, gender, and income level. Indents of items within each category further accentuate the distinctions between categories.

The second table also is more effective because numerical adjustments have been made. The first table contains *counts* of respondents who responded in certain ways. Counts make it difficult for readers to make effective comparisons quickly. Yet, many readers are also interested in knowing how many people participated in a survey. By converting the counts into percentages, the more effective table enables readers to process the information more easily. Placing the counts in parentheses makes the data comprehensive.

General Rules of Table Formatting   Overall, more effective formatting and numerical conversion make a significant impact on the usefulness of a table. The general guidelines in Table 12.7 will help you create more effective tables.

Technology Tips

USING ONLINE SURVEY SOFTWARE

Conducting surveys has become increasingly easy with various software, such as SurveyMonkey, Qualtrics, Google Forms, and various add-ins for meeting and social software. The software, in many cases, helps you rapidly create survey questions. It often contains a pool of existing questions you can even select from.

In an online format, you can send the survey link to anyone in your contact list, including colleagues and customers. In other words, such software gives you greater access to survey respondents than was possible as recently as a few years ago. Furthermore, many companies specialize in helping you gain access to millions of potential respondents (called an *online panel*). When you conduct market or consumer research, these companies can help you get a large sample size for nearly any demographic of interest.

Another benefit of using online surveys is that the data is immediately dumped into a database or spreadsheet in a form you can quickly analyze. Some online survey software even provides immediate reports that include summary and crosstab statistics (although you'll often want to manipulate the data yourself to dig deeper and get answers to particular questions).

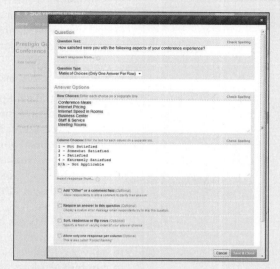

Source: SurveyMonkey.com

As you use online survey software, keep in mind the following tips:

Apply the same careful and thorough standards you would to any form of business research. The ease of creating online surveys often leads business professionals to use them carelessly, not putting enough time into designing the survey questions.

Avoid overusing online surveys. Again, because of the ease of administering online surveys, employees in many organizations are bombarded with surveys. As a result, employees often suffer respondent fatigue and respond to surveys less carefully. The results of the survey are only as good as the careful input of your respondents.

Your challenge: Create a simple but identical survey (3 or 4 questions; choose several question types such as multiple choice, ranking, and comments) in two different software platforms. Which features of each platform do you like best? Which platform do you prefer?

TABLE 12.7

Formatting Guidelines for Tables

Issue	Formatting Guidelines
Order	• Order your entries appropriately (alphabetical or numerical order of categories, or ascending/descending order of values of comparison).
Indentation	• Indent or otherwise set apart items within a category.
Data series	• Present comparative data series vertically.
Column/row labels	• Label columns and rows effectively.
Grid lines	• Use grid lines for every three to five rows at natural breaks (new categories); this simple design technique allows readers to easily scan rows. • Avoid grid lines on all borders; these tend to clutter the table. • Avoid alternating background colors on rows in most cases; this is also distracting and unnecessary.

Gathering Information through Secondary Research

In most cases, primary research is ideal. You can carefully tailor it to your specific business problems. Primary research, however, takes a lot of time and money. Even with sufficient resources, your organization may lack access to certain types of data. Generally, a far less expensive approach is secondary research. One advantage of nearly all secondary research is that someone else already spent the time to conduct and write it up.

Choose a Research Topic

Generally in the workplace, you'll conduct and write research as requested by your managers or clients. Many companies provide guidelines for how to approach secondary research. Even under an assignment from decision makers, you have some freedom to define the scope of your project. In some college courses, your instructors may give you a broad topic or you may have complete freedom to select your own topic. When you're in a position to choose your own research topics, you can follow several strategies to find a topic that is interesting and valuable to you and others.

Avoid Settling on Your Topic Too Quickly and Pace Your Research   Identifying your specific research topic takes time. Usually, you've got several months to deliver a final research report. Make sure to invest enough time early in the process to carefully explore your options. Ideally, you can spend four to five hours during the first two weeks of your project carefully weighing your options for a research topic. Figure 12.7 shows how you might approach a ten-week school research project.

Choose Your Topic Strategically   For school projects, consider choosing topics that will help you in your academic program and in your career. You can help identify topics of strategic interest by asking yourself questions such as the following: What do I know a lot about already? What would help me know more about my major or focus of study? What do I want to learn more about from a class I recently took? What do I need to learn more about to succeed in my first positions out of college? What kind of research paper could I envision talking about in a job interview? To help you think about some possible topics, consider some of the topics listed in Table 12.8 (this is a brief list of broad topics to get you started).

You might also consider writing down three to five research topics you're interested in. For each topic, answer questions such as the following: Who would be interested in this topic? (This helps you think about an audience.) What are some specific questions related to each topic? (This helps you think about the scope of your research—see the next paragraph.) How easily can I get information about this topic?

Define the Scope of Your Project   Early in your research project, you should take a somewhat broad or vague topic and make it specific and interesting. As you glance through Table 12.8, you'll notice these are quite general topics and serve only as starting points. Let's say you choose a topic such as *social media marketing*. This is so broad that you can't reasonably tackle the topic in a research paper. You can reduce the scope of your project in a variety of ways. First, try ways to narrow the topic itself: for example, you might focus the topic of social media marketing to something like developing customer relationships on Pinterest (in a few hours, you can find dozens of good options). Consider narrowing your project in terms of an organization or an industry (e.g., how Home Depot develops customer relationships on Pinterest). You might also confine

FIGURE 12.7

Sample Timeline for a Ten-Week Research Project

Weeks 1 and 2	Weeks 3 through 6	Weeks 7 and 8	Weeks 9 and 10
Choose Your Topic	Collect Research and Connect Ideas	Complete Solid Draft	Complete Research Report

Marketing	*Supply Chain Management/Operations*
Social media marketing	Enterprise resource planning systems
Brand management	Sourcing and supplier management
Marketing analytics	Production planning
Advertising	Quality management
Customer service	Inventory management
B2B (business-to-business) marketing	Resource forecasting
International marketing	
Sales	*Information Systems/Technology*
Product development	Big data/business analytics
	Cloud-based technologies
Finance/Accounting	Social media policies
Mergers and acquisitions	E-commerce
Auditing	Technology adoption
Risk management	
Banking and capital management	*Leadership/Management/Communication*
Corporate taxation	Business strategy
Financial planning	Leadership styles
International financial management	Personality
	Negotiation
Human Resources	Organizational change
Talent management	Conflict management
Performance management	Crisis management
Team development	
Salary and benefit plans	*Ethics and Corporate Social Responsibility*
Community management	Sustainability
Career paths	Diversity
Employee morale	Compliance and governance
Recruiting and hiring	Transparency
	Employee volunteering programs
	Corporate philanthropy

TABLE 12.8

Broad Research Topics by Business Discipline

your project by time (e.g., how Home Depot has developed customer relationships on Pinterest during the past year).

Find Ways to Make Your Research More Analytical Generally, you make your research more valuable (and challenging) as you examine relationships and integrate related information. You can examine causation or correlation (e.g., how corporate Pinterest pages impact purchasing decisions), comparisons or analogies (e.g., how Lowe's uses Pinterest pages to develop customer relationships), benchmarks (e.g., what experts say are best practices on Pinterest), or trends (e.g., how Pinterest users have changed expectations about content on corporate Pinterest pages over the past three years). Often, how you decide to approach or analyze your research will end up influencing your final topic.

Talk to Others Who Can Help You If you're not sure how to narrow your topic, you might consider talking with your instructor, a librarian, trusted classmates, or professionals you know. These conversations will often help you articulate your interests and refine your topics.

Evaluate Data Quality

As you collect secondary research, carefully evaluate it in terms of data quality. Concern yourself with the following issues:

- **Reliability** relates to how dependable the data is—how current and representative.
- **Relevance** of the data relates to how well it applies to your specific business problem.
- **Adaptability** relates to how well the research can be altered or revised to meet your specific business problem.

LO12.5 Evaluate the usefulness of data sources for business research.

TABLE 12.9

Strengths and Limitations of Data Quality for Primary and Secondary Research Sources

	Reliability	Relevance	Adaptability	Expert-Based	Bias
Primary research	✔ High	✔ High	✔ High	Medium ✔ – High	Goals and preexisting notions of the researcher
White papers	✘ Low ✔ – High	Medium ✔ – High	✘ Low	Medium ✔ – High	Organizational mission and objectives
Industry publications	Medium ✔ – High	Medium ✔ – High	✘ Low	Medium ✔ – High	Mission of the publication/editing team
Business periodicals	Medium ✔ – High	✘ Low – Medium	✘ Low	✘ Low ✔ – High	Mission of the publication/editing team
Scholarly journals	✔ High	✘ Low	✘ Low	✔ High	Theoretical significance
External blogs, wikis, and other websites	✘ Low ✔ – High	Medium ✔ – High	✘ Low	✘ Low ✔ – High	Writers' career objectives
Business books	Medium ✔ – High	✘ Low– ✔ High	✘ Low	Medium ✔ – High	The latest, greatest idea mentality; easy fixes

McGraw Hill connect

Visit http://connect. mheducation.com for an exercise on this topic.

- **Expertise** relates to the skill and background of the researchers to address your business problem.

- **Biases** are tendencies to see issues from particular perspectives. The possibility of biases does not necessarily imply that secondary research is unreliable; however, when using such research, view the data cautiously and keep in mind the ultimate objectives of the researchers.

Some secondary research reports cost thousands of dollars to purchase, whereas others are free. You have a variety of options to choose from with secondary research, including white papers, industry publications, business periodicals, scholarly journals, external blogs, and business books. Each of these types of secondary data has benefits and drawbacks (see Table 12.9). Thus, you will inevitably face trade-offs as you select secondary data.

White papers are reports or guides that generally describe research about solving a particular issue—perhaps one similar to the one you are encountering. They are issued by governments and organizations. White papers are readily available on many corporate and other organizational websites. However, they are often biased, since white papers are often produced by industry groups with an agenda or companies with specific marketing goals related to the white paper. Thus, when you rely on white papers, you should learn about the agendas of the sponsoring organizations.

Industry publications are written to cater to the specific interests of members in particular industries. These can include periodicals and reports. Industry reports often are highly reliable, relevant, and expert-based. However, industry reports are generally expensive, ranging from several hundred dollars to thousands of dollars. Typically, the more reliable the industry reports are, the more expensive they are. Fortunately, many business libraries carry a variety of expensive industry reports and publications that are free for you to use as long as you are enrolled at your university.

Business periodicals (magazines, newspapers) provide stories, information, and advice about contemporary business issues. They are often written by well-respected business journalists and experts. However, most articles in magazines and periodicals will have limited value in applying to your specific business problems and your organization. Furthermore, these articles often rely on anecdotal evidence rather than carefully controlled experiments and survey research. Periodicals that are industry publications are often far more relevant than general business magazines and articles.

Scholarly journals contain business research that is extremely reliable. The information comes from carefully controlled scientific research processes and has been reviewed by experts in the field. However, scholarly business articles rarely provide useful information for business problems that you will focus on in the workplace. Rather, scholarly articles focus on more theoretical and abstract issues. Furthermore, they are generally written with a level of statistical analysis and/or theoretical background that is difficult to understand.

External blogs and other online resources provide a plethora of information. Since most blogs are not formally edited or reviewed, the range in reliability is enormous. As you progress in your career, you will find those blogs that are reliable and relevant to the types of business problems you face. If you rely on blogs, make sure you carefully determine the expertise of the blog writer(s).

Business and management books range greatly in terms of their overall usefulness. Fortunately, you can usually better assess the usefulness of business and management books than other secondary sources because of the many online reviews available and the ability to preview sections of the books (online and in person at bookstores or libraries). Online reviews can help you gauge how useful various books can be for your particular business problems.

Conduct Library Research

Most university libraries have rich stores of information on business. Aside from a significant collection of books across a wide range of disciplines and topics, your library likely contains a wealth of digital resources. You likely also have access to thousands of company and industry reports (each of which cost hundreds and thousands of dollars to consumers); articles from hundreds of business periodicals, including *The Wall Street Journal*, *Forbes*, *Bloomberg Businessweek*, and many others; industry-specific periodicals and reports; scholarly journals; and many, many more avenues for research.

LO12.6 Conduct secondary research to address a business problem.

Most university libraries subscribe to dozens of online databases. Popular and useful ones with business research and articles include EBSCO Business Source Complete, ProQuest, IBISWorld, Hoover's, Global Financial Database, Conference Board, eMarketer, Mint Global, NetAdvantage by Standard & Poor's, Thomson One, and others. In Figure 12.8, you'll see a few examples of these databases and how they present information for your research. In the EBSCOhost window, you'll notice the many search options available. In the ProQuest window, you can see links to specialized reports on such topics as trends and forecasts, market research, or SWOT analyses. In the IBISWorld window, you can see the categories of information in a particular industry report. Working from this screen, Jeff can access reliable information about key success factors, cost structure benchmarks, technology, and many other topics about hotels in the United States.

Navigating the many resources in these databases and identifying the ones that will be most useful to you take time. You might consider spending several weeks browsing these various databases simply to become familiar with what's available. You should also seek a business librarian to help you identify those databases that best match your interests and needs.

FIGURE 12.8

Finding Valuable
Information with
Library Resources

Sources: (top) EBSCOhost; (bottom
left) ProQuest; (bottom right)
IBISWorld

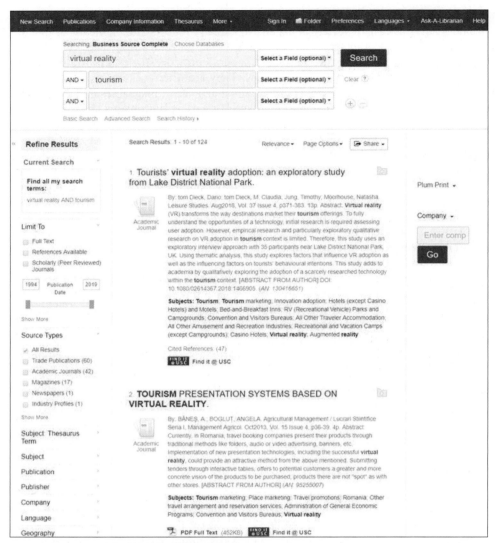

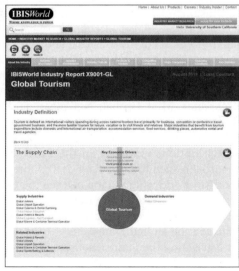

TABLE 12.10

Strategies for Using Search Terms Effectively

Strategy	Example	Number of Hits in ProQuest
Use Boolean operators.	"Virtual reality" and "Group tours" Virtual reality *and* Group tours Virtual reality *or* Group tours	328 145,822 7,928,251
Use alternative keywords.	"Augmented reality" *and* "Global tourism" "Emerging technologies" *and* "Historical tours" "VR headsets" *and* Tourism	62 8 305

Each of the databases contains search features, and several basic strategies will help you make the most of them. When you manually search, you can use Boolean operators *(and, or)* to widen your search. For example, when Jeff wants to find more information about virtual reality or group tours, his initial search of this phrase yields nearly 8,000,000 results. By looking for both words separately (using *and*) with quotation marks for each phrase, his search yields a more more manageable 328 results (see Table 12.10). Also, consider using alternative keywords and closely related ideas. Finding the right sources requires persistence. You might spend hours looking for useful information and then rapidly find dozens of relevant and useful sources.

Once you enter your terms, most online business databases provide a list of suggested topics based on commonly indexed terms. These can be very helpful. Notice, for example, Figure 12.9. You will see the many combinations of indexed terms (with the

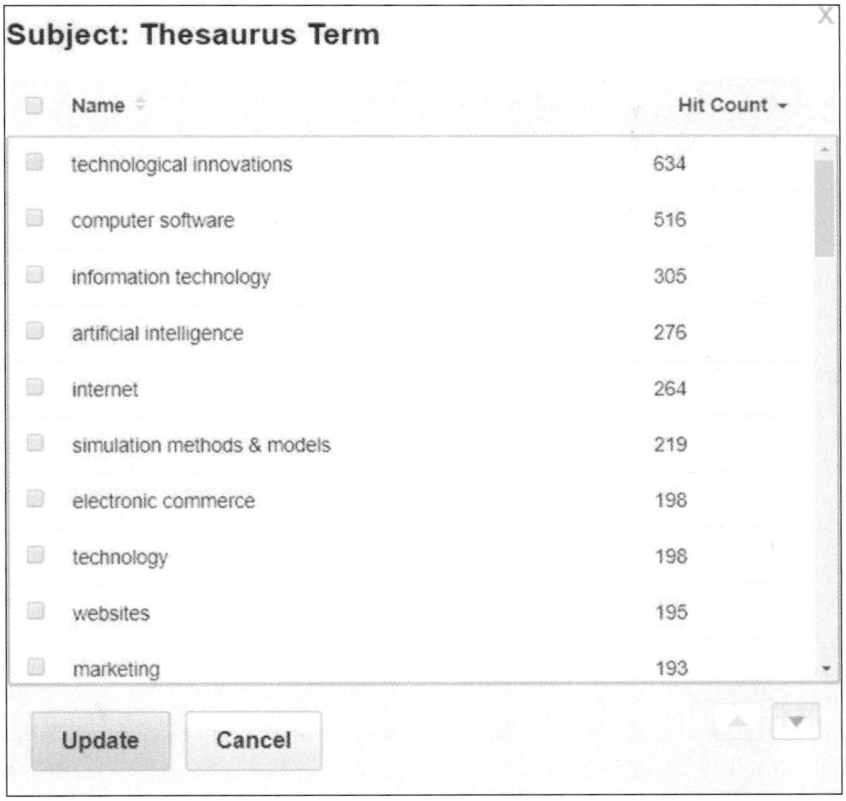

FIGURE 12.9

Using Suggested Terms in Online Business Databases

Source: EBESCOhost

thesaurus tool) that result from a manual search for virtual reality in EBESCOhost. By clicking on these various suggested searches, you can rapidly find which combinations of search terms yield the best results.

Document Your Research

As you collect secondary research, keeping track of the information sources is critical. Decision makers expect excellent documentation of your information because this helps them evaluate the credibility of your report. Since they often make high-stakes decisions based on reports, they expect to know *exactly* what the basis is for facts, conclusions, and recommendations you present.

When you keep track of your sources during the research stage, you can efficiently and accurately document your report. Many novice report writers waste time during the drafting stage trying to retrace their steps and find the sources for certain pieces of information. Worse, they may make errors in documentation by providing an incorrect source, casting doubt on the credibility of the report.

To avoid these problems, experienced writers have a system for recording all sources during the research stage. Not all report writers use the same system; some use word processing software, while others use spreadsheets or databases. The key is to create a system that allows you to accurately and efficiently record sources for your information. In Figure 12.10, you can see how Jeff combines taking notes with keeping track of his sources. This approach helps him organize his information and allows him to rapidly provide documentation once he begins drafting his report.

FIGURE 12.10

System for Recording Secondary Research Sources during Note Taking

Haugen, J. (2018, May 22). Virtual reality: Insights and opportunities in the travel industry. *Adventure Travel News*. Retrieved from https://www.adventuretravelnews.com/virtual-reality-insights-and-opportunities-in-the-travel-industry

- Many experts in the tourism industry wonder whether VR tools for travel are the next big thing or simply a fad.
- VR headsets are widely available and the technology is excellent; however, mainstream adoption and use are still low.
- Experts are not sure yet whether this is a marketing advantage or a deterrent. It could be a deterrent if it replaces the expensive experience of traveling.
- VR technologies can help travelers preview and sample various destinations.
- Examples include the following:
  - DiscoveryVR.com allows people to see many forms of wildlife and how people live their lives.
  - Navitaire is a booking tool. People can visit a destination and then book their travel all while in the VR experience.
  - Visit Sweden has three VR films.
  - Qantas has a variety of VR features about Australian locations.
  - Thomas Cook put VR headsets in many of its offices. Potential travelers could experience locations in Asia, Europe, and North America. Thomas Cook reported a 40 percent ROI. The most effective destination was New York.
  - Quark Expeditions allows customers to have a helicopter experience and cruise through icebergs.
- Hotels such as Marriott are offering VR. Cruise companies such as Royal Caribbean and Azamara Cruises have VR about entertainment and amenities. They report much better conversion rates.

Wu, S.-T., & Lee, B.-W. (2017). An innovative way of guided tour: A virtual experience of dark tourism. *Proceedings of the 2017 IEEE International Conference on Information, Communication and Engineering, IEEE-ICICE 2017*, 208–210.

- Examined dark tourism (sites involving massacre and/or war).
- Used VR headsets for 228 memorials and parks.
- The virtual tour included 360-degree panoramas, audio guides, various interactive features, and a self-paced format.
- Intended to help with tourism marketing and development.

Use Online Information for Business Research

For most business research, the information you can access through business databases and other sources at your library is generally the most reliable. However, you will also likely use Internet searches outside your library system to find relevant information on your topic. As you do so, keep in mind the following strategies:

- *Always evaluate data quality.* The range in quality on the web is immense. Make sure you're not using sources that are uninformed or inaccurate.

- *Do more than just "Google it."* You can employ many strategies for online research, including the following:

  - *Go to reputable business and industry websites and conduct searches.* For example, Jeff may go directly to general periodical or business news sites such as *Bloomberg Businessweek* or CNBC.com to do searches. Or he may go to industry sites. When he goes to the United States Tour Operators Association website, he finds a variety of sources that are not available at his library and that are more current than the information in business databases (see Figure 12.11).

  - *Find online discussions and forums about your selected topic.* You can learn what current professionals are saying about a topic by visiting online discussions and forums. For example, on LinkedIn, you can view the conversations of thousands of professionals on any given topic. Notice in Figure 12.12 the many options that Jeff has to choose from. Each of these groups holds dozens of ongoing conversations about current practices in the industry.

  - *Search beyond text-based information.* Increasingly, you can access a wealth of information in video and audio format. For example, when Jeff is seeking information about virtual reality and travel, a few simple searches yield thousands of online videos on YouTube. By viewing a few of these videos, he identifies many green meeting practices that hotels are using. He also gets information from speeches and presentations that he could not find elsewhere.

- *Be persistent.* In the age of the Internet, many of us are accustomed to quick answers. Getting solid business information, however, rarely involves quick answers. Try as many approaches as you can to find the data you need.

FIGURE 12.11

Using Industry Websites for Research

Source: USTOA

FIGURE 12.12

Using Online Groups and Discussion Forums for Research

Source: LinkedIn

Applying the FAIR Test to Your Research Data and Charts

LO12.7 Evaluate research data, charts, and tables for fairness and effectiveness.

As you conduct research for your reports, frequently evaluate whether you are being fair. For example, whether you are doing primary or secondary research, make sure you are examining all the available facts and interpreting them from various perspectives. A common problem is that business professionals may enter into research with preexisting assumptions or even conclusions. In primary research, such assumptions may lead you to ask the wrong questions or interpret the data incorrectly. In secondary research, they may lead you to gather only information that matches your assumptions and conclusions. For example, if Jeff already assumes that developing and marketing green meetings makes business sense for the Prestigio, he may inadvertently gravitate to information that supports his position and avoid information that does not, thus misleading his readers.

Another way you may unintentionally mislead a reader is with numerical data. However, you can take a few steps to ensure that you represent data fairly and avoid losing credibility. First, whenever you are unsure of a data relationship, discuss it with your colleagues. Collectively, you will often arrive at a fair way to represent the information. Also, ask yourself if you have provided enough information for your readers and audience members to make informed and accurate judgments.

Some business professionals show only the data that supports their points. In other words, they cherry-pick the data in their favor. This practice is deceptive. Furthermore, some business professionals distort information, even though it is technically correct.

TABLE 12.11

Creating Fair Charts

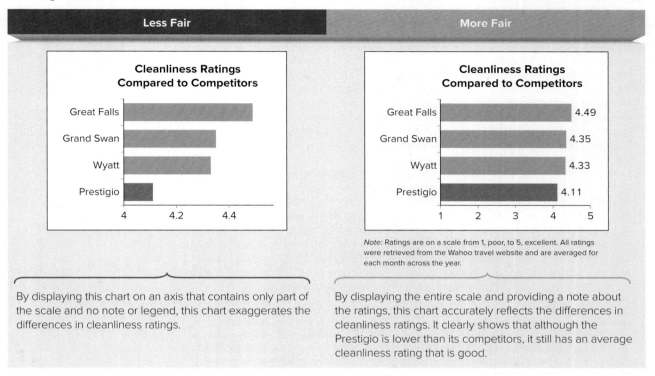

By displaying this chart on an axis that contains only part of the scale and no note or legend, this chart exaggerates the differences in cleanliness ratings.

By displaying the entire scale and providing a note about the ratings, this chart accurately reflects the differences in cleanliness ratings. It clearly shows that although the Prestigio is lower than its competitors, it still has an average cleanliness rating that is good.

Charts, for example, can be manipulated to exaggerate or misinform. Notice Table 12.11, which contains two versions of the same chart.

As you collect, analyze, and present data to others, ensure that you provide all the relevant *facts*, even if they don't fit into convenient conclusions. Grant *access* to your data. Your full disclosure of data to colleagues, clients, and others in your business dealings will pay long-term dividends in terms of credibility. Many businesses emphasize transparency on an institutional level. As an individual, when you make compelling numerical arguments through charts, tables, and other formats while also maintaining a level of personal transparency and full disclosure, you will gain many career opportunities. Also, remember the *impacts* of your data on others and present it with *respect*. For example, when you collect data on your colleagues' performance, how you present your information can impact career opportunities, team cohesion, and morale.

IDEAS IN ACTION

Learning from Books

Excellent business researchers read and study books to expose themselves to complex ideas. Oprah Winfrey is among the most popular people in the world due to her authentic and inspirational media presence, global philanthropic efforts, and immense business success. She believes books built the foundation for her career. In her 2004 Global Humanitarian Award acceptance speech at the United Nations, she explained, "Books allowed me to see a world beyond the front porch of my grandmother's shotgun house and gave me the power to see possibilities." Elsewhere, she has stated, "Books were my path to personal freedom." It's not surprising that one of her most influential efforts over the past few decades has been *Oprah's Book Club*.

CARL COURT/AFP/Getty Images

Like Winfrey, many business, nonprofit, government, and other leaders credit books with opening their eyes to new possibilities and sparking new ideas. In fact, many leaders read several hours each day to continue learning. Even as your career becomes busy and hectic, find ways to read every day and include book reading as part of your regimen. For instance, you might set aside 20 minutes a day when you can read without distraction. Consider carrying a book with you so you can read during "down times," such as while riding the bus or sitting in a waiting room. Read what interests you, and set goals for yourself, such as reading one new book each month. Developing a strong reading habit can keep you inquisitive and curious and help you develop meaningful approaches to business research.

Sources: Cowles, G. (2018). How to tap your inner reader. *The New York Times.* Retrieved from www.nytimes.com/guides/year-of-living-better/how-to-tap-your-inner-reader; Kniffel, L. (2011, May 25). Reading for life: Oprah Winfrey. *American Libraries Magazine.* Retrieved from americanlibrariesmagazine.org/2011/05/25/reading-for-life-oprah-winfrey/; Weller, C. (2017, July 20). 9 of the most successful people share their reading habits. *Business Insider.* Retrieved from www.businessinsider.com/what-successful-people-read-2017-7/#oprah-winfrey-4.

Chapter Takeaway for *Research and Business Proposals and Planning for Business Reports*

LO12.1 Explain how planning and conducting business research for reports impacts your credibility.

Planning and conducting research for business reports demonstrates **your personal credibility.**

It shows **competence** when you can collect, analyze, and present business research.	It shows **caring** when you collect business research that fills an unmet need for others.	It shows **character** when you collect, analyze, and report your research data fairly.

LO12.2 Create research objectives that are specific and achievable.

See *examples of research objectives* in Table 12.1.

LO12.3 Explain principles of effective design for survey questions and choices.

Principles for Survey Question Design	
• Simple to answer	• Exhaustive and unambiguous
• Non-leading	• Single idea

See *examples of survey question design* in Tables 12.2 through 12.5. See a *complete online survey* in Figure 12.1.

LO12.4 Develop charts and tables to concisely display data and accentuate key messages.

Criteria for Evaluating Charts	
• Title descriptiveness	• Ease of processing
• Focal points	• Takeaway message
• Information sufficiency	

See *examples of charts and tables* in Figures 12.2 through 12.6.

LO12.5 Evaluate the usefulness of data sources for business research.

Criteria for Evaluating Data Quality	
• Reliability	• Expertise
• Relevance	• Biases
• Adaptability	

LO12.6 Conduct secondary research to address a business problem.

Principles for Secondary Research
• Use business databases such as EBSCO, IBISWorld, and Hoover's.
• Document your research.
• Conduct online research carefully, strategically, and creatively.

See an *example of documenting research during the note-taking stage* in Figure 12.10.

LO12.7 Evaluate research data, charts, and tables for fairness and effectiveness.

Facts: Present all relevant facts, even when they don't fit nicely into convenient conclusions. Avoid exaggeration or any other distortion of the facts.
Access: Grant access to your data to decision makers and others affected by your report. Focus on transparency and disclosure.
Impacts: Consider how the data in your report will impact stakeholders.
Respect: Ensure that your presentation of the data demonstrates respect for stakeholders.

Key Terms

adaptability, 387

bar charts, 377

biases, 388

business and management books, 389

business periodicals, 389

closed questions, 371

exhaustive, 373

expertise, 388

external blogs, 389

industry publications, 388

line charts, 377

non-leading, 372

open-ended questions, 371

pie charts, 377

primary research, 371

relevance, 387

reliability, 387

scholarly journals, 389

secondary research, 371

unambiguous, 373

white papers, 388

Discussion Exercises

12.1 Chapter Review Questions (LO12.1, LO12.2, LO12.3, LO12.4, LO12.5)

A. Explain the features that distinguish reports from other types of business correspondence.

B. Describe ways in which you can enhance your credibility by creating reports.

C. Discuss the advantages and drawbacks of both primary and secondary business research.

D. Describe strategies for understanding the needs of your audience for reports.

E. Explain why developing clear research objectives is so crucial to business research.

F. Describe principles for effective survey questions.

G. Summarize the primary reasons for using charts and tables.

H. Explain at least three general design principles for charts.

I. Describe unique design and formatting principles that apply to line charts, pie charts, and bar charts.

J. Explain the criteria for judging the quality of research data.

12.2 Ideas in Action Discussion Questions (LO12.4, LO12.7)

In the Ideas in Action section, Oprah Winfrey is quoted as saying "Books allowed me to see a world beyond the front porch of my grandmother's shotgun house and gave me the power to see possibilities." Elsewhere, she has stated, "Books were my path to personal freedom."

A. Based on Winfrey's statements as well as your own experience, in what ways can books help you see new possibilities and personal freedom?

B. Based on Winfrey's statements as well as your own experience, in what ways can a habit of deep reading help you accomplish professional goals?

C. Develop a list of ten books you want to read next summer. Why did you choose these books?

12.3 Combining Quantitative and Communication Skills (LO12.1, LO12.4, LO12.5, LO12.6)

Lloyd C. Blankfein, chair and CEO of Goldman Sachs, was asked, "What would you like business schools to teach more of, or less of?" He responded:

> Look, I think it's very important to teach people to have a healthy respect for facts and information. And you know, to paraphrase Keynes, "to change minds when facts change." That's why I think certain careers—and maybe not intuitive careers—do very well. There's a lot of lawyers floating around Wall Street. There's a lot of engineers. A lot of people who deal in facts and have an appreciation for facts. A quantitative thing is very helpful. I was a social studies major, but you need to be numerate. If you have those good quantitative skills, it's very, very helpful.[6]

Based on Blankfein's comments and your own opinions, respond to the following questions:

A. Why are quantitative skills so highly valued in various business disciplines?

B. How important do you think quantitative skills will be to your career? In what ways?

C. What are your strongest areas in terms of quantitative skills? Weakest areas?

D. What are your strongest areas in terms of spreadsheet software? Weakest areas?

E. What are five goals you have for improving your quantitative skills?

Evaluation Exercises

12.4 Evaluating Charts and Tables in Annual Reports (LO12.4)

Choose an annual report from a company that interests you. Select several tables and graphs from the report. Evaluate each in terms of design. Describe at least three effective and less effective aspects

for each chart and graph. Also, make one recommendation for improving them.

12.5 Evaluating Charts about Exports (LO12.4)

Examine each of the following charts (Figures 12.13A, B, and C) and respond to the questions below:[7]

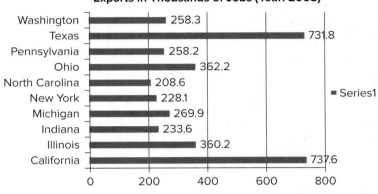

Ten States with Most Jobs Related to Manufacturing Exports in Thousands of Jobs (Year: 2008)

FIGURE 12.13A

Ineffective Bar Chart

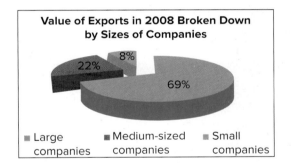

Value of Exports in 2008 Broken Down by Sizes of Companies

FIGURE 12.13B

Ineffective Pie Chart

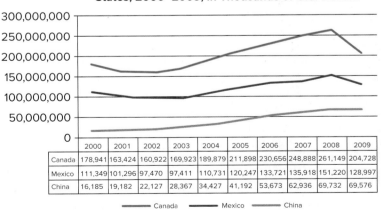

Value of Exports to Top Three Export Partners of the United States, 2000–2009, in Thousands of U.S. Dollars

FIGURE 12.13C

Ineffective Line Chart

	2000	2001	2002	2003	2004	2005	2006	2007	2008	2009
Canada	178,941	163,424	160,922	169,923	189,879	211,898	230,656	248,888	261,149	204,728
Mexico	111,349	101,296	97,470	97,411	110,731	120,247	133,721	135,918	151,220	128,997
China	16,185	19,182	22,127	28,367	34,427	41,192	53,673	62,936	69,732	69,576

For each of the above charts, describe their weaknesses in terms of the following: (a) title descriptiveness, (b) focal points, (c) information sufficiency, (d) ease of processing, and (e) takeaway message.

Application Exercises

12.6 Developing Research Objectives (LO12.2)

Choose three topics of interest that you could research. Write three specific research objectives that could provide a clear direction for you to collect primary data or gather secondary research.

12.7 Conducting Survey Research (LO12.3)

Individually or in groups, select a business problem that you can learn more about by conducting survey research. You will create an online survey for all of your classmates to take, so design your project around the assumption that you are finding out what university-aged students think or feel about the topic. Design the survey so that it can be completed in three to five minutes. Do the following:

A. Create the survey with between 5 and 15 survey questions.

B. Administer the survey.

C. Identify the major findings and conclusions.

D. State related recommendations.

E. Create two tables that summarize findings from the survey.

F. Create two charts that display key messages related to the data.

G. Write a report that includes your objectives, methodology, findings, conclusions, and recommendations.

12.8 Learning about Online Business Databases at Your Library (LO12.6)

Identify five online business databases available through your library. For each, explain what the key advantages are and provide one limitation. When you have written about each database, write a concluding statement that identifies which databases are most useful for your business interests.

12.9 Evaluating Data Quality (LO12.5)

Find five data sources related to a topic that interests you. Analyze reliability, relevance, adaptability, expertise, and biases.

12.10 Creating Charts from the Apple Annual Report[8] (LO12.4)

Assume you are working for Apple and are summarizing key sales data for presentation to an external audience, such as potential investors or media reporters. You would like to create charts to quickly summarize your performance and allow others to compare your performance across operating segments and product lines.

Use the two tables below to create the following charts. Remember to follow effective design principles.

A. Create a line chart to show net sales growth from 2014 to 2018.

B. Create a line chart to show unit sales of the top four product groups from 2014 to 2018.

C. Create a bar chart to show net sales for the five product groups in 2018.

D. Create a pie chart to show net sales for the product groups in 2018.

E. Create a bar chart to show unit sales by operating segments in 2018.

F. Identify two key relationships or comparisons from the table. Create charts that best illustrate these relationships or comparisons.

G. As directed by your instructor, exchange your charts with a partner from your class. Evaluate one another's chart designs in terms of title descriptiveness, focal points, information sufficiency, ease of processing, and takeaway message.

Table Net Sales, 2014–2018

	2018	2017	2016	2015	2014
Net Sales by Operating Segment:					
Americas	$ 112,093	$ 96,000	$ 86,613	$ 93,864	$ 80,095
Europe	62,240	54,938	49,952	50,337	44,285
Greater China*	51,942	44,764	48,492	58,715	31,853
Japan	21,733	17,733	16,928	15,706	15,314
Rest of Asia Pacific	17,407	17,407	18,828	17,407	14,127
Total net sales	$ 265,595	$ 265,595	$ 215,639	$ 233,715	$ 182,795
Net Sales by Product:					
iPhone	$ 166,699	$ 141,319	$ 136,700	$ 155,041	$ 101,991
iPhone	18,805	19,222	20,628	23,227	30,283
Mac	25,484	25,850	22,831	25,471	24,079
Services	37,190	29,980	24,348	19,909	18,063
Other products	17,417	12,863	11,132	10,067	8,379
Total net sales	$ 265,595	$ 265,595	$ 215,639	$ 233,715	$ 182,795
Unit Sales by Product:					
iPhone	217,722	216,756	211,884	231,218	169,219
iPad	43,535	43,753	45,590	54,856	67,977
Mac	18,209	19,251	18,484	20,587	18,906

Notes: Currency figures in millions of dollars and units in thousands.
*Greater China includes China, Hong Kong, and Taiwan.

12.11 Revising Charts about Exporting (LO12.4)

A. Revise the ineffective bar chart from Exercise 12.5.

B. Revise the ineffective pie chart from Exercise 12.5.

C. Revise the ineffective line chart from Exercise 12.5.

D. With your instructor's direction, consider evaluating your charts against those of your peers in the class. Decide which charts are most effective and share them with the class.

12.12 Evaluate Various Types of Secondary Research Data (LO12.5)

Based on a topic of interest, find at least one of each of the following types of sources: white paper, industry publication, business periodical, scholarly journal, external blog, and business book. Evaluate each of the sources in the following areas: reliability, relevance, adaptability, expertise, and bias.

12.13 Planning Research at the Prestigio (LO12.2, LO12.3, LO12.5, LO12.6)

A. Assume the role of Jeff Anderton and conduct research about green meetings. Specifically, your assignment is to identify best practices for green meetings from the perspective of vendors, compare marketing approaches, and evaluate the strategic and financial importance of offering green meetings. Do the following: Write three specific research objectives.

B. Explain strategies for collecting research for each objective.

C. Write three research questions that you could ask conference attendees that would help you understand what consumers think about green meetings.

D. Identify three online sources about green meetings. Evaluate each in terms of the following: reliability, relevance, adaptability, expertise, and biases.

Language Mechanics Check

12.14 Review all rules in Appendix A about punctuation, number usage, and grammar. Then, rewrite each sentence to make all needed corrections.

A. The majority of the marketing managers have argued for a strategy that differentiates the hotel from local, high end hotels.

B. These managers have focused on a strategy that positions the hotel as an eco friendly sustainable operation.

C. Other managers especially those in finance worries that this strategy will negatively effect profits.

D. In fact a few finance managers have all ready complained to the senior leadership team.

E. These managers say that the hotel needs to cautiously evaluate a variety of strategic options, before settling for a green strategy.

F. They also think the hotel faces more pressing threats such as employee moral union demands and outdated, in room technologies.

G. They say that the hotel should improve employee development programs and invest in inroom technologies not focus on unproven green strategies.

H. They also say that pay is an important issue and expect significant employee turnover unless the hotel increases compensation rates.

I. The senior leadership team seems to be taking their time as they consider how to resolve the differences between the marketing team and the finance team.

J. One board member said she will encourage the board to hold a meeting to weigh strategic options evaluate current plans and advice the senior leadership team.

Endnotes

1. Kintler, D., & Adams, B. (1998). *Independent consulting: A comprehensive guide to building your own consulting business.* Avon, MA: Streetwise.

2. Grimshaw, R. (2005). Communication by numbers. *Harvard Management Communication Letter, 8*(3), 3–4.

3. Grimshaw, R. (2005). Communication by numbers. *Harvard Management Communication Letter, 8*(3); Wong, D. M. (2010). *The Wall Street Journal guide to information graphics: The dos and don'ts of presenting data, facts, and figures.* New York: W. W. Norton & Company.

4. Wong, D. M. (2010). *The Wall Street Journal guide to information graphics: The dos and don'ts of presenting data, facts, and figures.* New York: W. W. Norton & Company, 13.

5. Sandberg, K. D. (2002). Easy on the eyes: A design legend tells how to turn complex "real world" information into clear visual messages. *Harvard Management Communication Letter, 5*(8), 3–5.

6. Bryant, A. (2009, September 1). Lessons learned at Goldman. *Corner Office* (blog), *The New York Times.* Retrieved from www.nytimes.com/2009/09/13/business/13corner.html.

7. Based on data retrieved June 15, 2010, from www.trade.gov/mas/ian/Jobs/Reports/2008/jobs_by_state_totals.html.

8. Based on 2018 and 2016 Apple annual reports. Available at www.apple.com/investor/.

Design elements: Set of universal icons for mobile app & web: ©Vitalex/Shutterstock; Learning Objective, Why Does This Matter?, Technology Tips, and Ideas in Action icons: ©McGraw-Hill

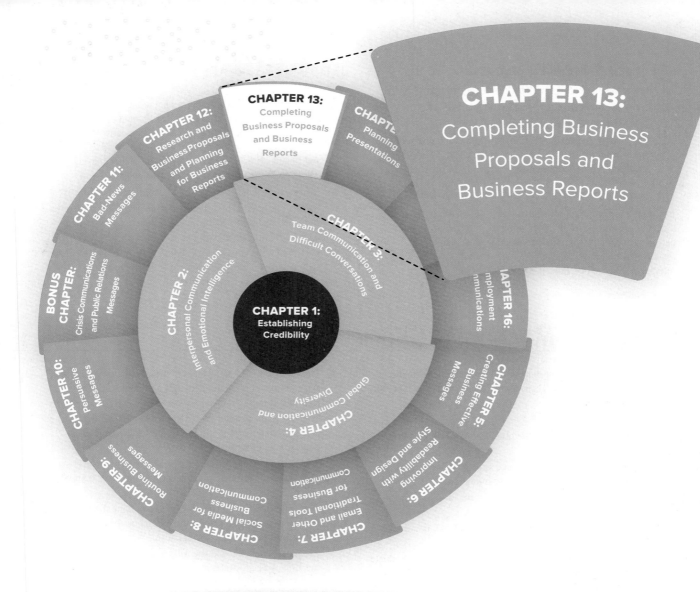

CHAPTER 13:
Completing Business
Proposals and
Business Reports

ESTABLISHING
CREDIBILITY

PRINCIPLES OF INTERPERSONAL
COMMUNICATION

PRINCIPLES FOR & TYPES OF
BUSINESS MESSAGES

LEARNING OBJECTIVES

After studying this chapter, you should be able to do the following:

LO13.1 Explain how completed reports affect your credibility.

LO13.2 Create specific and persuasive proposals.

LO13.3 Demonstrate excellent thinking by applying a precision-oriented style to reports.

LO13.4 Design your reports to aid in decision making.

LO13.5 Project objectivity in reports.

LO13.6 Review reports for effectiveness and fairness.

Your primary goal as you draft business reports is to improve decision making. More so than routine business correspondence, reports should be built on thorough, precise, and reliable information and analysis and should offer advice to help decision makers—typically middle-level and upper-level managers—make informed choices. As a report writer, your personal credibility is tied to how well you provide facts, conclusions, and positions that help decision making (competence), involve decision makers and address their needs (caring), and report information honestly and transparently (character).

Chapter 12 discussed collecting primary and secondary research for business reports and displaying the data in meaningful charts and tables. In this chapter, we focus on putting it all together. As you do with other written documents, when writing reports, you'll focus on achieving the right style, design, and tone. We focus first on style, emphasizing the importance of absolute precision. Next, we discuss design, which you can use to ensure that decision makers rapidly pull out the most important pieces of information. Finally, we focus on achieving an objective tone.

This chapter contains two sample reports: one based on primary research and one based on secondary research. There are far too many types of reports to display in this chapter. You can see more examples of business reports, including business plans, in the appendixes and in the online resources at www.mhhe.com/cardon.

The examples throughout this chapter are based on the continued case of the Prestigio Hotel. Read the chapter case to get reacquainted with the situation.

> **Hear Pete Cardon explain why this matters.**
> bit.ly/cardon13

LO13.1 Explain how completed reports affect your credibility.

CHAPTER CASE CONDUCTING RESEARCH AT AICASUS TOURS

WHO'S INVOLVED

Shania Baker

Jeff Anderton

Andrea Garcia

Owner of Baker Consulting

- Her business specializes in conducting market research and helping businesses develop plans to improve customer satisfaction and customer service
- Started her consulting business about one year after graduating with a major in statistics and a minor in finance

Market Research Associate

- Has worked at Aicasus Tours for three months
- Roles include conducting research about new markets and tracking customer satisfaction
- Graduated a year ago with a marketing major and statistics minor

Director of Marketing

- Has worked as director of marketing for one year
- Started at Aicasus Tours nearly nine years ago in a position similar to Jeff's market research associate position
- Expects well-analyzed, organized, polished reports

THE SITUATION

Aicasus Tours relies on a third party to annually conduct customer satisfaction research about its hotel properties so that the results are considered neutral and objective. In recent years, Shania Baker has conducted this research. Once again, Andrea has asked her to submit a proposal to conduct the annual survey. Andrea informed Shania that the marketing team would also seek other bids for this project.

Andrea has asked Jeff to write a report about the business opportunities associated with virtual reality (VR). She views this as an area of strategic concern. Jeff has collected secondary research and interviewed several VR developers who have successfully created VR content in the travel and tourism industry. Now, he needs to think about how to put all of the information together.

TASK **1**   **2**   **3**

| Shania will write a formal business proposal to Aicasus Tours. She knows that several other vendors are competing for this project. | Jeff will compose a report about the current use of VR in the travel and tourism industry and recommend courses of action for Aicasus Tours. | Shania will write a report about the results of the guest satisfaction survey and deliver it to the Aicasus Tours marketing team. She knows her future opportunities depend on the quality of this report. |

Developing Business Proposals

LO13.2 Create specific and persuasive proposals.

Components of a Business Proposal

- Cover Page
- Executive Summary
- Current Situation
- Specific Objectives
- Deliverables Overview
- Timeline
- Results Enhancers
- Pricing/Budget

Prior to examining reports in depth, we briefly discuss business proposals. Some proposals lead to business reports. For example, you'll notice that the proposal in Figure 13.1 leads to the report in Figure 13.7. You will likely have many opportunities to write proposals. If you're good at it, you gain resources—financial resources and organizational support—to follow through on your business goals and objectives.

Most proposals deal with decisions about allocating resources for various business activities. Proposals generally explain why business goals are beneficial and how you will use resources (people, time, partnerships, finances, etc.) to reach these goals. Proposals vary substantially in length and format. They range from a page or two to several hundred pages. Some proposals require a standard format, whereas others are more flexible.

Some of the most common elements of proposals, especially for consulting, include an explanation of the current situation (usually addressing an unresolved problem), specific objectives, a deliverables overview, a timeline, results enhancers (why you or your organization are positioned to add value), and pricing or budget (if appropriate). Most successful proposal writers speak to decision makers (supervisors, clients, or others) before submitting an official proposal. By negotiating some of the details ahead of time, proposal writers have a better sense of what decision makers want and expect. This helps proposal writers make decisions about how to structure the proposal to persuade decision makers. In Figure 13.1, you can see a simple proposal from Shania Baker for a relatively small project. As you view this proposal, notice the focus on action. One common mistake of proposal writers is to leave out details about deliverables and timelines.

FIGURE 13.1

Proposal to Conduct a Guest Satisfaction Survey

Proposal to Conduct Guest Satisfaction Survey for the Prestigio Hotel and Resort

Submitted by Shania Baker, Baker Consulting
October 1, 2019

Executive Summary

> The *Executive Summary* provides the most essential points from the proposal.

Baker Consulting proposes conducting a guest satisfaction analysis for the Prestigio Hotel and Resort. Baker Consulting will provide the following: (1) design and administration of a guest satisfaction survey; (2) a written guest satisfaction report; and (3) a guest satisfaction briefing to the marketing team. Prior to conducting the survey, the Prestigio Hotel and Resort will provide an email list of recent conference attendees and other requested information. The proposed price is $5,000, which includes a $2,000 up-front fee prior to conducting the guest satisfaction survey and a $3,000 final payment once the final guest satisfaction report is completed and delivered.

Current Situation

Guest satisfaction has always been the foundation for repeat business at the Prestigio. With so many online reviews of hotels readily available to meeting planners, the importance of achieving high guest satisfaction ratings is more important now than ever. Since 2013, the Prestigio has evaluated guest satisfaction and future intentions among conference attendees with an annual survey to help determine priorities in improving guest satisfaction. In the past four years, the Prestigio has evaluated conference attendees' views in the following areas: overall satisfaction, intent to return, intent to recommend, conference meals, meeting rooms, and staff and service.

Past surveys of guest satisfaction have not addressed several areas of interest to the Prestigio: (1) guests' views of Internet pricing and the business center and (2) guests' actual use of conference services and amenities. Also, prior analysis of guest satisfaction has not differentiated guest satisfaction by gender and income.

Specific Objectives

> The *Current Situation* section describes the basic challenges that need to be addressed and solved.

1. Conduct a survey of conference attendees in the following areas:

    A. Satisfaction with conference services and amenities
    B. Actual use of services and amenities by conference guests
    C. Repeat business indicators: overall satisfaction, intent to return, and intent to recommend

2. Complete a guest satisfaction report:

    A. Provide complete analysis of each survey area
    B. Analyze based on income level and gender
    C. Provide realistic recommendations

> The *Specific Objectives* section provides clear statements about outcomes of the proposed work.

3. Provide a guest satisfaction briefing to the marketing team

FIGURE 13.1

(Continued)

Deliverables Overview

Baker Consulting will provide the following deliverables:

> The *Deliverables section* describes the items and services that will be provided.

1. *A guest satisfaction briefing and discussion.* Baker Consulting will provide a written report, a 2-hour presentation and discussion, and a digital file with raw data from completed surveys.
2. *A written guest satisfaction analysis.* The report will include all survey findings. The report will be roughly ten pages.
3. *Raw data from the online survey.* Baker Consulting will provide a spreadsheet with all original survey responses.

The Prestigio Hotel and Resort will provide the following:

1. Two meetings between Baker Consulting and Prestigio Hotel and Resort to provide needed information for the research.
2. Email addresses to conference attendees during 2019.

Timeline

> The *Timeline* section clearly states when key activities will occur and when deliverables are due.

Date to Complete	Activity
November 15	Kick-off meeting at Baker Consulting office with the Prestigio marketing team (estimate: 1-1/2 hours).
December 15	Follow-up meeting to discuss survey design (estimate: 1 hour).
January 15	The Prestigio will provide all available email addresses of conference attendees during 2019.
February 1	Guest satisfaction report and raw data provided to the Prestigio.
February 15	Guest satisfaction briefing to the Prestigio marketing team.

Pricing and Payment Plan

The following table summarizes the price for this project based on my standard rates for soliciting survey responses and completing customer satisfaction reports.

Activity	Rate	Total
Survey design and administration	Standard rate for 10-item survey	$2,000
Data analysis	$150 per hour (10 hours)	$1,500
Guest satisfaction report	$150 per hour (10 hours)	$1,500
		$5,000

The total pricing for conducting the guest satisfaction research and creating a guest satisfaction report is $5,000. This includes two payments: an up-front fee of $2,000 and a final payment of $3,000 when the guest satisfaction report is delivered.

> The *Pricing and Payment Plan* section states the pricing for products and/or services and expectations for payment.

Demonstrating Excellent Thinking by Applying a Precision-Oriented Style

The most basic and critical component of any report is precision in thinking as reflected in style—meaning that it offers accurate, well-documented facts; good reasoning for conclusions; and a solid basis for recommendations (see Figure 13.2). The foundation for these facts, conclusions, and recommendations must be a well-stated business problem or challenge. In short, a report that facilitates effective decision making must demonstrate excellence in thinking.

In Jeff's case, he spends several months working from start to finish on his two research projects. After clearly articulating the business problem, he collects all the necessary information, carefully checks the reliability of each of his sources, examines the facts from many angles as he develops conclusions and recommendations, and asks various colleagues about their perspectives. His critical thinking skills allow him to apply a precision-oriented style to his reports.

Start with a Clear Statement of the Business Problem or Challenge

Placing a clear statement of the central business problem or challenge at the beginning helps establish the purpose and value of the report. Without such a statement, reports lack direction and may be perceived as unimportant. Also, without such a statement, decision makers may view the report writer as naive and excessively optimistic.

Problem statements are most effective when they provide the unique context of the problem for the organization and reflect an appropriate sense of urgency. Typically, such statements should be one to three paragraphs long. Notice how Jeff establishes the direction of the VR report in Table 13.1.

Use Fact-Based Language

Precision in reports relies on facts. You can raise the credibility of your report by (1) supplying the facts with precision, (2) providing supporting details for your conclusions, (3) carefully dealing with predictions and cause/effect statements (see Table 13.2), and (4) responsibly citing your research sources (see the next section about documenting secondary research).

Document Secondary Research and Avoid Plagiarism

By nature, decision makers adopt a methodical and skeptical approach to making investments, changing strategies, and making other substantial changes. They expect quality information to make these decisions. By documenting your sources, you allow decision makers to judge the quality of your data. Decision makers are also looking for signals that you have been methodical in collecting, analyzing, and reporting findings. By documenting your sources, you display your thorough, detail-oriented approach.

LO13.3 Demonstrate excellent thinking by applying a precision-oriented style to reports.

Mc Graw Hill connect

Visit http://connect. mheducation.com for an exercise on this topic.

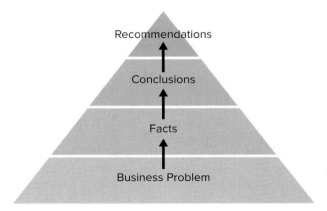

FIGURE 13.2

Excellence in Thinking for Reports

TABLE 13.1

Problem Statement or Business Challenge

Less Effective	More Effective
Virtual reality (VR) tools increasingly allow users to experience films and other content in more realistic, multisensory, and even adventurous ways. Many companies in the hospitality and tourism sector are exploring how to create new business opportunities with VR. Some companies have already succeeded in using VR content to market their sites and services as well as to enhance tour experiences. Therefore, we need to get in this space quickly.	Virtual reality (VR) tools increasingly allow users to experience films and other content in more realistic, multisensory, and even adventurous ways. One indicator of the growing demand for VR content is the demand for VR headsets. In 2018, global shipments of VR headsets amounted to 13.5 million. The demand for VR headsets is expected to more than double by 2023. Yet, a small overall percentage of consumers own VR headsets or regularly view VR content. Most experts suggest VR as a mainstream experience is still three to five years in the future (Hollander, 2018). Many companies in the hospitality and tourism sector are exploring how to create new business opportunities with VR. Some companies have already succeeded in using VR content to market their sites and services as well as to enhance tour experiences. Yet, while investments in VR may create competitive advantage, they involve significant risk and uncertainty. In this section, we describe two emerging functions of VR in our industry: (a) marketing sites and services and (b) enhancing the travel experience. Then, we describe the benefits and risks of developing and adopting VR content. Overall, the aim of our report is to evaluate the business opportunities of developing VR content for Aicasus Tours.
This brief statement focuses only on the opportunity. It doesn't draw any attention to the basic problem that needs to be solved. Most decision makers would increase their skepticism as a result.	This problem statement provides sufficient context to communicate the opportunities of developing VR. Yet, in each paragraph, it addresses the problems associated with developing VR content: uncertainty and risk because VR is not a mainstream experience yet.
Since 2013, we have evaluated guest satisfaction and future intentions among conference attendees with an annual survey. This report provides the results of this year's survey as well as year-to-year comparisons for the past five years.	Guest satisfaction has always been the foundation for repeat business. With so many online reviews of hotels readily available to meeting planners, achieving high guest satisfaction ratings is more important now than ever. Since 2013, we have used an annual survey to evaluate guest satisfaction, assess future intentions of conference attendees, and determine how we can improve guest satisfaction. This report provides the results of this year's survey as well as year-to-year comparisons for the past five years.
This statement fails to explain the basic purpose and value behind conducting the surveys.	By adding a few additional thoughts in just two sentences, this problem statement establishes the importance of using the survey to improve guest satisfaction and, consequently, repeat business. Furthermore, it explains the increased urgency of this effort.

Typically, you should provide a reference list at the end of the report that contains all your sources. Also, throughout your document, you should provide citations to indicate the information you have drawn from other sources. You can use a variety of *documentation* systems, including APA and MLA styles. You can see examples of these two styles in Table 13.3. You should, however, use an official style guide to document with precision. Style guides contain hundreds of rules for various types of sources. Additionally, many websites contain the most current documentation guidelines, including the APA style website (www.apastyle.org) and the Purdue Online Writing

TABLE 13.2

Using Fact-Based Language

Less Effective	More Effective
Nearly all of our respondents reported satisfaction with their conference experiences.	Overall, the vast majority (84 percent) of our respondents reported satisfaction with their conference experiences.
This fact is imprecise and open to interpretation.	By providing the exact percentage in parentheses, this fact is precise.
Many of our prior customers expressed interest in viewing VR content as they make tour decisions.	Many of our prior customers expressed interest in viewing VR content as they make tour decisions (see Table 1). Among customers who own tethered VR headsets, nearly three quarters (73%) expressed interest. For mobile VR headset owners and customers without VR headsets (in the survey, we suggested we would send them Google Cardboard headsets), roughly one-quarter (28%) expressed interest.
Without a supporting fact, this conclusion may be viewed as unsubstantiated or merely the writer's opinion.	This conclusion is immediately substantiated with supporting statistics (facts). It references a table with additional details.
In consultation with developers, each short VR film would cost only $5,500. At such a low cost, we're basically guaranteed a return on our investment.	In consultation with three VR developers, we estimate each short VR film of roughly two minutes can be produced for approximately $5,500 (includes equipment purchases). We could rely on our permanent tour guides at various locations to oversee the recording of the tour footage (J. Hardaway, personal communication, September 14, 2019; K. Cafferty, personal communication, September 15, 2019; M. Dipprey, personal communication, September 14, 2019).
This statement guarantees that the investment will bring a return. Many decision makers would view the statement as naïve. This statement lacks many details (i.e., type and number of developers who were consulted, length of videos) that can enhance credibility.	This set of more specific statements demonstrates a cautious but confident analysis of production costs. The citations bolster the credibility of the analysis.

Lab (http://owl.english.purdue.edu). Also, if you will spend a lot of time writing reports that need documentation, you might explore some of the available software to help in this process (see the Technology Tips box in the "Achieving Objectivity and Positivity through Tone" section in this chapter).

Although you will generally base your reports on secondary research, you must still demonstrate your originality in thought. That is, your goal is to combine information from your various sources in novel and insightful ways and thereby generate your own conclusions and recommendations.

To develop original reports, make sure that you avoid all forms of **plagiarism**. According to the *Merrian-Webster Online Dictionary*, to plagiarize is to "steal and pass off (the ideas of another) as one's own" and "to commit literary theft."[1] Thus, plagiarism is serious; it is literally stealing the ideas of others.

To avoid plagiarism on a sentence and paragraph level, document all references to the ideas of others, including (1) direct quotations, (2) paraphrases, and (3) other instances in which you borrow or reference the ideas of others. **Direct quotations** are verbatim restatements from another source. Use direct quotations only when the quotation

TABLE 13.3

References in APA and MLA Documentation Styles

	APA	MLA
Book	Rubin, P. (2018). *Future presence: How virtual reality is changing human connection, intimacy, and the limits of ordinary life*. San Francisco, CA: HarperOne.	Rubin, Peter. *Future Presence: How Virtual Reality Is Changing Human Connection, Intimacy, and the Limits of Ordinary Life*. HarperOne, 2018.
Report from an organization *(white paper)*	Resnick, M., & McGovern, J. (2018, December 4). *How architecting for next-generation experiences helps to deliver customer and business outcomes*. Stamford, CT: Gartner.	Resnick, Marty, and James McGovern. *How Architecting for Next-Generation Experiences Helps to Deliver Customer and Business Outcomes*. Gartner, 2018.
Scholarly or scientific journal	Wagler, A., & Hanus, M. D. (2018). Comparing virtual reality tourism to real-life experiences: Effects of presence and engagement on attitude and enjoyment. *Communication Research Reports, 35*(5), 456–464.	Wagler, Adam, and Michael D. Hanus. "Comparing Virtual Reality Tourism to Real-Life Experiences: Effects of Presence and Engagement on Attitude and Enjoyment." *Communication Research Reports,* vol. 35, no. 5, pp. 456-64.
Magazine/periodical	Porter, M. E., & Heppelmann, J. E. (2017, November/December). Why every organization needs an augmented reality strategy. *Harvard Business Review, 95*(6), 46–57.	Porter, Michael E., and James E. Heppelmann. "Why Every Organization Needs an Augmented Reality Strategy." *Harvard Business Review*, Nov.-Dec. 2017, pp. 46-57.
Conference paper	Jung, T., tom Dieck, M. C., Moorhouse, N., & tom Dieck, D. (2017, March 30). *Tourists' experiences of virtual reality applications*. Paper presented at the 2017 IEEE International Conference on Consumer Electronics (ICCE), Las Vegas, NV.	Jung, Timothy, M. Claudia tom Dieck, Natasha Moorhouse, and Dario tom Dieck. "Tourists' Experiences of Virtual Reality Applications." *2017 IEEE International Conference on Consumer Electronics (ICCE)*, 8 Jan 2017, Las Vegas, NV. Conference presentation.
Webpage (A variety of rules for online sources exist. Check a formatting guide to help you decide which information to provide.)	Hollander, R. (2018, March 27). When it comes to VR hardware, consumers are balancing price point and experience. *Business Insider*. Retrieved from www.businessinsider.com/the-vr-hardware-report-2018-3	Hollander, Rayna. "When It Comes to VR Hardware, Consumers Are Balancing Price Point and Experience." *Business Insider*, www.businessinsider.com/the-vr-hardware-report-2018-3. Accessed 3 April 2019.
Personal interviews	(J. Hardaway, personal communication, September 14, 2019)* *Not included in reference list; used as in-text citation only.	Hardaway, Jane. Personal interview. 14 September 2019.
In-text citations	(Wagler & Hanus, 2018)	(Wagler & Hanus)

contains a particularly compelling combination of words, flows effectively with your paper, and emphasizes the credibility of the original speaker or writer. In most situations, you should paraphrase rather than use direct quotations. **Paraphrasing** involves using your own words to express the meaning of the original speaker or writer. When you paraphrase, you significantly alter the original words and sentence structure, but you still need to give credit to the original speaker or writer for the idea. Notice Table 13.4 for examples of using direct quotations and paraphrasing in ways that avoid plagiarism.[2]

The best way to avoid plagiarism on a documentwide level is to demonstrate originality of thought—supplying your own ideas, conclusions, and recommendations that you support by weaving together information from a variety of sources. If the majority of ideas in your report are based on just one or two sources, your report is essentially plagiarized.

TABLE 13.4

Citing Secondary Sources of Information and Avoiding Plagiarism

Original Statement from Source	In July 2008, as the process became more involved, the committee began working with ASTM International, a voluntary standards-development organization. Through each stage, members of the ASTM community have read and voted on the evolving document, including people unfamiliar with the meetings industry. Spatrisano was hoping to submit the standards for the final balloting process at the end of September. "There have been some philosophical disagreements," notes Spatrisano, "such as how you determine what 'recycled' means, as in whether a recycled item contains preconsumed products or just postconsumed. That's one of the issues we are tied up in." *Source:* Braley, S. J. F. (2010, October). Guidelines for green meetings: M&C previews the forthcoming APEX Initiative. *Meetings & Conventions, 45*(10), 57.

Situation	Plagiarized Statement	Non-plagiarized Statement
Direct quotations	Spatrisano explained that there have been some philosophical disagreements such as how you determine what "recycled" means (Braley, 2010). Although this statement contains an in-text citation, it is plagiarized because it does not use quotation marks to indicate verbatim statements from Spatrisano.	As Spatrisano explained, "There have been some philosophical disagreements . . . such as how you determine what 'recycled' means" (Braley, 2010, p. 57). This statement correctly identifies the direct quotation with quotation marks and includes a source and page number.
	In July 2008, as the process became more involved, the committee began working with ASTM International, a voluntary standards-development organization. This statement is extremely deceptive; it presents verbatim text from another source without any documentation.	"In July 2008, as the process became more involved, the committee began working with ASTM International, a voluntary standards-development organization" (Braley, 2010, p. 57). This statement is technically not plagiarized. It uses quotation marks and indicates the source and page number of the original source. However, direct quotes should be used selectively, and this statement is unlikely to flow more smoothly than a simple paraphrase.
Paraphrasing	The ASTM/APEX process became more involved in July 2008, when ASTM International (a voluntary organization that develops standards) became involved. ASTM community members studied and voted on an evolving document at various stages. The final balloting will end around September after Spatrisano submits the standards (Braley, 2010). This statement is plagiarized because it retains essentially the same set of ideas with nearly identical phrases and sentence structures. Such minor alterations are not considered paraphrasing.	The Convention Industry Council has partnered with ASTM International to develop industry standards for green meetings. These evolving standards will go up for vote in September (Braley, 2010). This statement reflects the meaning of the original source but is reworded sufficiently. It correctly identifies the source of the information. It is effective to the degree it flows with the ideas before and after the paraphrasing.

TABLE 13.4

(Continued)

Situation	Plagiarized Statement	Non-plagiarized Statement
Other forms of borrowing the ideas of others	The process of developing industrywide standards is complicated. For example, even coming to agreement about the definition of a seemingly basic term such as *recycled* is a matter of contention. Currently, members are divided as to whether recycled items refer to those with *preconsumed* or *postconsumed* products (Braley, 2010).	The process of developing industrywide standards is complicated. For example, Amy Spatrisano, principal of MeetGreen, has indicated that even coming to agreement about the definition of a seemingly basic term such as *recycled* is a matter of contention. Currently, members are divided as to whether recycled items refer to those with *preconsumed* or *postconsumed* products (Braley, 2010).
	This statement partially identifies the source of this information. However, it can provide more complete accounting of where the information came from by identifying who originally stated these ideas.	By including a reference to the person who originally provided these ideas, this article provides more complete information about the original source of ideas.

Base Recommendations on Facts and Conclusions in the Report

One of the foremost goals of many reports is to give good advice, but business professionals often fail to sufficiently connect their recommendations to their facts and conclusions. If decision makers are to take your report seriously and feel comfortable acting on it, they must be able to see clear connections between the facts and conclusions you present and the related recommendations, as depicted in Figure 13.3.

FIGURE 13.3

Basing Recommendations on Facts and Conclusions

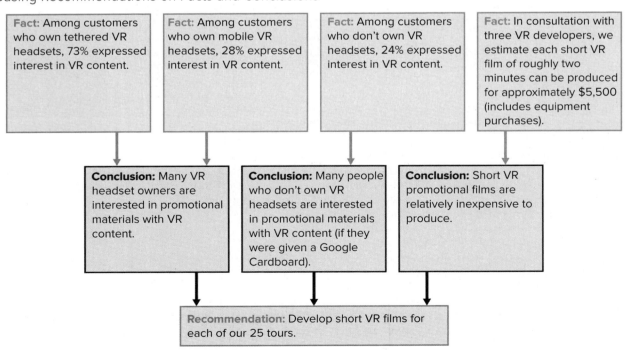

TABLE 13.5

Making Recommendations Specific and Actionable

Less Effective	More Effective
Send VR headsets to key customers.	*Send inexpensive mobile VR headsets to key customers.* At an estimated cost of $10,000 (1,000 Google Cardboard headsets with a cost of $10 per headset, including shipping), we can send mobile VR headsets to prior customers identified as most likely to purchase future tours. We recommend evaluating their purchase behavior to create an ROI analysis of the mobile VR headset strategy.
This recommendation is vague and lacks important details.	This recommendation contains a rationale as well as concrete details about the quantity and costs of VR headsets.
Place VR headsets at our major offices.	*Place high-quality VR headsets in our 10 major offices.* At an estimated cost of $40,000, we can market our tours with high-quality VR experiences at our major offices. We recommend tracking which tours our customers view and how that impacts their ultimate decision making.
This recommendation is vague. It indicates a superficial, nonthorough effort to provide advice.	This recommendation is specific and provides elaboration about a detail all decision makers are interested in: evaluating impact.

Provide Specific and Actionable Recommendations

In addition to being based on facts and conclusions in the report, recommendations must be specific and actionable. Many business professionals run out of steam by the end of the report or are reluctant to take a firm position, so they provide vague and sometimes superficial recommendations. Make sure you provide recommendations that are sufficiently detailed and realistic for decision makers (see Table 13.5). You can elaborate on your recommendations with a section on your rationale, the implications of your recommendations, and clear steps to take toward implementation.

Designing Your Reports to Help Decision Makers

Some decision makers will read your reports from start to end. Others will try to glean the key messages by first reading the summary and headings before reading the report completely. Other decision makers will skim the report due to time pressures. In any case, assume that decision makers may not read your report from start to end, and design it so they can navigate the information rapidly.

LO13.4 Design your reports to aid in decision making.

One way to make your report easy to navigate is to provide a structure that decision makers are familiar with. Figure 13.4 contains sample structures from common types of business reports. Some formal reports contain many additional components, as illustrated in Figure 13.5. These additional components can be classified as front matter, text, and back matter.

Tell the Story of Your Report with an Executive Summary

As you glance through Figure 13.4, you'll notice that one section common to all of these reports is the *executive summary*. Nearly all reports, especially those that are more than a few pages long, contain one at the beginning. The purpose is to summarize the most important contents, including key findings, conclusions, and

FIGURE 13.4

Common Structures for Business Reports[3]

Components of a Survey Report

Executive Summary
Introduction and
    Background
Methodology
Findings
Conclusions
Recommendations
References
Appendixes

Components of a Trend Report

Executive Summary
Introduction
Background
Trend Analysis
Recommendations
References
Appendixes

Components of a Business Proposal

Cover Page
Executive Summary
Current Situation
Specific Objectives
Deliverables Overview
Timeline
Results Enhancers
Pricing/Budget

Components of a Business Plan

Cover Page
Executive Summary
Business Description
    and Vision/General
    Company
Business Objectives
Description of the
    Market/Market
    Analysis
Description of the
    Products and
    Services
Organization and
    Management
Marketing and Sales
    Strategy
Financial Management
Appendixes

Components of a Strategic Plan

Cover Page
Executive Summary
SWOT Analysis
Vision, Mission, Values
Strategic Objectives
Action Items
Implementation
    Process
Evaluation

Components of a Progress Report

Executive Summary
Introduction
Background
Accomplishments
Problems
Future Plans/Timeline
Conclusion
References
Appendixes

Components of an Annual Report

Cover
Narrative Statements
    (letter to
    stockholders from
    the CEO—functions
    as executive
    summary, company
    overview, mission
    statement, history)
Financial Statements
    (income statement,
    balance sheet, cash
    flow, auditor's
    report)
References
Appendixes

Components of a SWOT Analysis

Executive Summary
Strengths
Weaknesses
Opportunities
Threats
Recommendations
References
Appendixes

Components of a Marketing Plan

Executive Summary
Market Research
Product
Competition
Mission Statement
Marketing Strategies
Pricing
Positioning/Branding
Budget
Marketing Goals/
    Objectives

FIGURE 13.5

Components of a Formal Report[4]

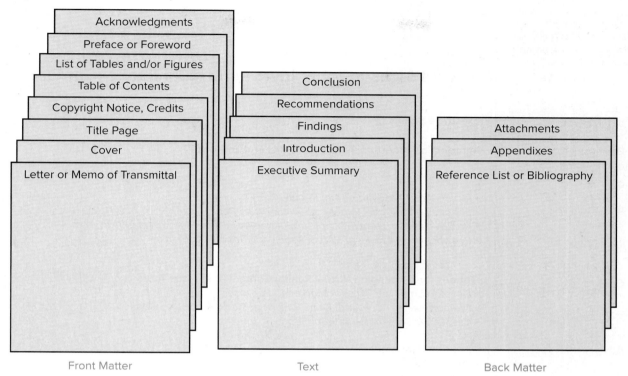

| Front Matter | Text | Back Matter |

recommendations, so that busy executives and other decision makers can quickly understand and act on the report.[5] A good executive summary "demonstrates that you can clearly focus on your goals and state, in no-nonsense fashion, who you are, what you want, and where you are going."[6] Generally, an executive summary should be about 1 page long for every 10 to 20 pages in the report. You can see two examples of executive summaries in the sample reports in the "Assessing Key Features of a Completed Report" section as well as an executive summary for the business plan in the Bonus Appendix.

Provide the Story Line with Descriptive Headings and Other Content Markers

Nearly all reports contain *headings* to help readers quickly navigate. Particularly with reports, decision makers often skim from section to section to find information. At a minimum, you will include first-level headings. For reports over five pages, you will likely use second-level headings and perhaps even third-level headings (see Table 13.6). In addition to accurately showing what is contained in each section, headings should also demonstrate the basic logic of a report. Notice in the left-hand column in Table 13.6 how Jeff uses headings to develop the basic story line of the report: business problem ⇒ opportunities and risks ⇒ options ⇒ advice.

Although your reports must generally follow a fairly standard order with regard to contents, you do have some flexibility in how you label your headings. Where possible, opt for descriptive titles and headings that help your readers quickly recognize the value and contents of any given section. Notice in Table 13.7 how minor changes can make headings more efficient and engaging.

TABLE 13.6

Providing Clear Headings That Support a Story Line

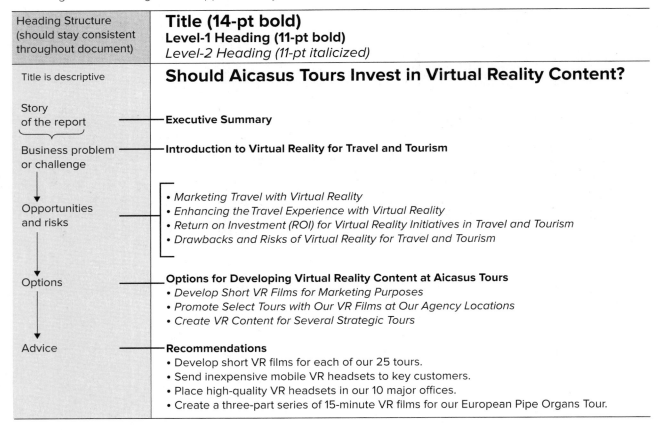

Heading Structure (should stay consistent throughout document)	**Title (14-pt bold)** **Level-1 Heading (11-pt bold)** *Level-2 Heading (11-pt italicized)*
Title is descriptive	**Should Aicasus Tours Invest in Virtual Reality Content?**
Story of the report	**Executive Summary**
Business problem or challenge	**Introduction to Virtual Reality for Travel and Tourism**
Opportunities and risks	• *Marketing Travel with Virtual Reality* • *Enhancing the Travel Experience with Virtual Reality* • *Return on Investment (ROI) for Virtual Reality Initiatives in Travel and Tourism* • *Drawbacks and Risks of Virtual Reality for Travel and Tourism*
Options	**Options for Developing Virtual Reality Content at Aicasus Tours** • *Develop Short VR Films for Marketing Purposes* • *Promote Select Tours with Our VR Films at Our Agency Locations* • *Create VR Content for Several Strategic Tours*
Advice	**Recommendations** • Develop short VR films for each of our 25 tours. • Send inexpensive mobile VR headsets to key customers. • Place high-quality VR headsets in our 10 major offices. • Create a three-part series of 15-minute VR films for our European Pipe Organs Tour.

TABLE 13.7

Creating Headings to Help Decision Makers Navigate the Document

Less Effective	More Effective
A Report on Virtual Reality Use in the Travel and Tourism Industry	Should Aicasus Tours Invest in Virtual Reality Content?
This title is difficult to process with a variety of noun clusters.	This title is more intriguing and signals to the decision maker the central direction of the report.
VR Options	Options for Developing Virtual Reality Content at Aicasus Tours
This brief heading in isolation tells little about the contents of the section.	The addition of just a few words clarifies what will be included in this section.

Use Preview Statements to Frame Your Messages and Accentuate Takeaway Messages

Reports are often lengthy and dense, so preview statements can help decision makers follow the direction of your text. Also, preview statements frame the message, allowing readers to create a mental map of your key takeaway messages (see Table 13.8).

TABLE 13.8

Providing Clear Preview Statements

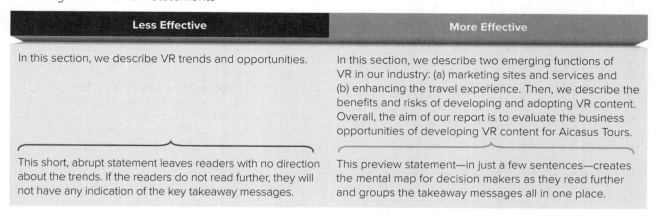

Less Effective	More Effective
In this section, we describe VR trends and opportunities.	In this section, we describe two emerging functions of VR in our industry: (a) marketing sites and services and (b) enhancing the travel experience. Then, we describe the benefits and risks of developing and adopting VR content. Overall, the aim of our report is to evaluate the business opportunities of developing VR content for Aicasus Tours.
This short, abrupt statement leaves readers with no direction about the trends. If the readers do not read further, they will not have any indication of the key takeaway messages.	This preview statement—in just a few sentences—creates the mental map for decision makers as they read further and groups the takeaway messages all in one place.

TABLE 13.9

Using Charts to Support the Story Line of the Report

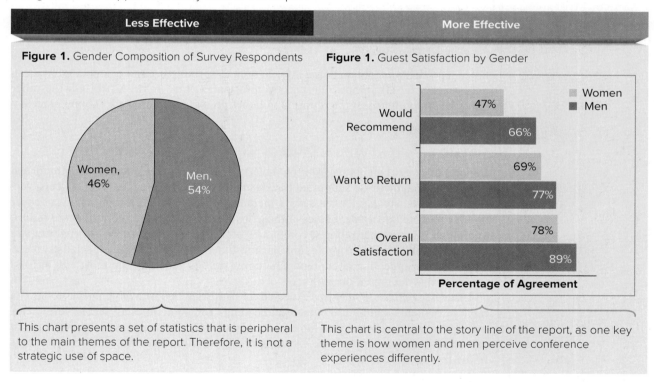

Less Effective	More Effective
Figure 1. Gender Composition of Survey Respondents	**Figure 1.** Guest Satisfaction by Gender
This chart presents a set of statistics that is peripheral to the main themes of the report. Therefore, it is not a strategic use of space.	This chart is central to the story line of the report, as one key theme is how women and men perceive conference experiences differently.

Insert Charts and Tables to Draw Attention to Your Key Points

Reports based on research data frequently include *tables* and *figures* (including charts) to supplement the text. You will apply principles for tables and charts that you learned in Chapter 12. Keep in mind that the purpose of tables and charts is first and foremost to fit into the story line you have established for your report. Also, tables and charts should simplify or clarify complicated numerical information that may bog down your reader in text (see Table 13.9).

TABLE 13.10

Applying Bulleting

Less Effective	More Effective
Based on the existing research about using VR content for promoting and enhancing tours and our own survey work, we recommend Aicasus Tours adopt a VR initiative that positions us as an early adopter of travel-enhancing technologies. Yet, we also recommend avoiding excessive risk. Specifically, we recommend the following: We should develop short VR films for each of our 25 tours; send inexpensive mobile VR headsets to key customers; place high-quality VR headsets in our 10 major offices; and create a three-part series of 15-minute VR films for our European Pipe Organs Tour.	Based on the existing research about using VR content for promoting and enhancing tours and our own survey work, we recommend Aicasus Tours adopt a VR initiative that positions us as an early adopter of travel-enhancing technologies. Yet, we also recommend avoiding excessive risk. Specifically, we recommend the following: 1. Develop short VR films for each of our 25 tours. 2. Send inexpensive mobile VR headsets to key customers. 3. Place high-quality VR headsets in our 10 major offices. 4. Create a three-part series of 15-minute VR films for our European Pipe Organs Tour.
This passage is too dense to read and process quickly.	By using bullets, readers can much more quickly digest the information.

Apply Bulleting and Enumerated Lists to Make Passages Easier to Process

Since reports often contain dense information, using bulleting and enumerated lists can help readers rapidly process and group information (see Table 13.10). On the other hand, when too much of the report is in bullet points, it can create a choppy, staccato-like effect.

Create a Cover Page, a Table of Contents, and Appendixes

Reports of more than ten pages often include a *cover page*. Regardless of length, formal reports—especially those submitted to external decision makers (i.e., loan officers, venture capitalists, stockholders)—always include a cover page. At a minimum, the cover page should include a title, names of those who wrote and/or are submitting the report, and a date. For formal reports, companies often rely on internal or external graphic designers, public relations professionals, and other document design specialists to create a visually appealing document. The cover page is generally the most emphasized aspect of this document design.

Likewise, a *table of contents* is expected for nearly any report over ten pages long. The table of contents contains all first-level headings and sometimes all second-level headings. Providing a well-designed table of contents immediately creates an impression that you are organized.[7] You can see an example of a business plan with a table of contents in the Bonus Appendix.

Reports also frequently include *appendixes* to provide reference materials. For example, common information in appendixes includes financial statements, marketing materials, detailed data tables, brochures, references, résumés, and biographies.

Achieving Objectivity and Positivity through Tone

LO13.5 Project objectivity in reports.

Achieving a positive, *can-do* tone in your communications is appropriate in nearly all business situations. In many business reports, projecting positivity is also important. However, more so than positivity, you should project objectivity—the sense that you are providing information, analysis, and advice that is sound, reliable, and unbiased. In

Technology Tips

USING SOFTWARE TO PROVIDE STRUCTURE AND DOCUMENTATION

Most word processing software packages—notably Microsoft Word—contain features to help you provide structure and documentation to your reports.

Using Word, you can accomplish some of the following tasks in your reports:

- Create a table of contents that can be automatically updated as you make revisions.

- Create your own styles that apply to headings (Title, Heading 1, Heading 2).

- Use captions for tables and figures that automatically update numbers as you work on the document.

- Use cross-referencing so that if you change the order of referenced objects, any references to objects in the text are updated with the new object reference number.

- Use co-authoring tools.

You can also use Word to help you document the information contained in your reports. Typically, you'll use the following sequence:

Create a source. You'll use a simple wizard that walks you through the information you need to provide. Word automatically generates the reference in APA or MLA style and places it in the reference list. Word also keeps track of sources you've used in any project. So, you have a library of sources to access any time in the future.

Create an in-text citation. Within your report where you want to insert a citation, simply use the Insert Citation feature, select the reference, and click OK: Word automatically inserts a properly formatted in-text citation.

Your challenge: Take a research paper you've done before. Re-create several paragraphs that contain in-text citations. Use these reference tools in Word. How well does it work? How can it help you work more efficiently?

Should Aicasus Tours Invest in Virtual Reality Content?

Contents

Microsoft Word

Microsoft Word

Microsoft Word

other words, project objectivity first and positivity second. Furthermore, ensure that your enthusiasm and strong positive emotion do not appear to cloud your judgment. In Table 13.11, notice the comparisons between two alternative approaches to writing an executive summary. As you read through these passages, consider how to strike the right balance between objectivity and positivity.

TABLE 13.11

Striking an Objective Tone while also Projecting Positivity

Less Effective	More Effective
Each of these use cases about VR to enhance tours shows tremendous potential. Research conclusively shows tourists enjoy these experiences and want to experience them again. Industry experts suggest these use cases can significantly enhance many tours, particularly those involving culture, history, and nature (Gerrity, 2018). These are exactly the types of tours we offer our sophisticated, educated customers. We definitely have a first-movers advantage to get into this space ahead of our competitors to gain a long-term advantage.	Each of these use cases about VR to enhance tours shows potential. Research shows tourists enjoy these experiences and want to experience them again. Still, most of these examples involve limited development and adoption. Industry experts suggest these use cases can significantly enhance many tours, particularly those involving culture, history, and nature. Further, experts suggest more sophisticated content that includes social content and gamification features can make tours more fun (Gerrity, 2018).
To assess interest in VR content as part of the tour experience, we surveyed former customers for the following three tours: (a) European Pipe Organs Tour, (b) Medieval Castles Tour, and (c) Redwood Forest Meditation Tour. Before answering survey items, customers watched a two-minute video explaining how VR headsets could be used in these tours. The short videos contained pictures and three sample video clips.	To assess interest in VR content as part of the tour experience, we surveyed former customers for the following three tours: (a) European Pipe Organs Tour, (b) Medieval Castles Tour, and (c) Redwood Forest Meditation Tour. Before answering survey items, customers watched a two-minute video explaining how VR headsets could be used in these tours. The short videos contained pictures and three sample video clips.
What is absolutely clear from the surveys is there is strong interest in VR content to enhance these tours (and think how much more interest they would show if they actually experienced VR rather than our explanation of what it's like). They were most interested in these tours in the following order: (1) European Pipe Organs Tour, (2) Medieval Castles Tour, and (3) Redwood Forest Meditation Tour. I strongly urge us to immediately begin production on VR content for these tours so we can reap the benefits and gain valuable strategic knowledge about how to enhance tours with VR. We anticipate explosive growth in this area, and we should certainly get on board before other companies do.	Prior customers of the Redwood Forest Meditation Tour were the least interested in VR content to enhance their experience (see Table 2). About one in five prior customers thought VR content could significantly enhance the tour, and just 3 percent thought this tour feature would increase the likelihood of selecting the tour. However, most prior customers of the European Pipe Organs Tour expressed interest in viewing VR content. About three-quarters of prior customers thought VR content could significantly enhance the tour, and about half thought this tour feature would increase the likelihood of selecting the tour. Since the European Pipe Organs Tour appears most promising, we recommend creating a three-part series of 15-minute VR films for this tour. This will serve as a pilot to determine whether we should continue developing VR content to enhance tours.
The tone of this passage projects excessive enthusiasm and perhaps a rush to action. Some of the adjectives are exaggerated, perhaps displaying an imprecise, unprofessional approach to the report.	The tone of this passage projects objectivity. The adjectives are businesslike and measured. A tempered *can-do* attitude emerges without sacrificing the sense that the research is methodical, thorough, and unrushed.

Assessing Key Features of a Completed Report

In the upcoming pages, you can see two examples of business reports. The first (Figure 13.6) is based on primary and secondary research. It can be classified as a *business trend* or *business issue* report. The second (Figure 13.7) is based on survey results, which is primary research. Although you will find that reports vary greatly in purpose and length, as you glance through these examples, consider the key features to strive for in all your reports: value to decision makers, precision, documentation, easy navigation, and objectivity. Also, notice how the report in Figure 13.7 is in slide deck format. Many reports, particularly survey reports, are increasingly created in slide deck format. This

FIGURE 13.6

Business Report with Secondary Research

Should Aicasus Tours Invest in Virtual Reality Content?

Prepared by Jeff Anderton and Barbara Brookshire
October 2019

iMoved Studio/Shutterstock; Cultura/Image Source

Executive Summary

The executive summary tells the story of the report so the busy reader can get the gist of the content.

Virtual reality (VR) tools increasingly allow users to experience films and other content in more realistic, multisensory, and even adventurous ways. Some companies in the hospitality and tourism sector are exploring ways to create business opportunities with VR by marketing tours and by enhancing tours.

The most common application of VR in hospitality and tourism is marketing. Marketing with VR helps promote lesser-known destinations and showcase the many available tour experiences in an area. Destination managers, tour companies, airlines, and hotels have successfully used VR content to market tourism sites. Many VR designers are in the early stages of creating content to enhance tours. Industry experts suggest tourists will enjoy certain types of tours—particularly those involving culture, history, and nature—much more with VR content. While cases of strongly positive ROI for applications of VR in marketing are well documented, much less is known about ROI for applications of VR to enhance tours.

Based on the existing research about using VR content for promoting and enhancing tours and our own survey work, we recommend Aicasus Tours adopt a VR initiative that positions us as an early adopter of travel-enhancing technologies. Yet, we also recommend avoiding excessive risk. Specifically, we recommend the following:

1. Develop short VR films for each of our 25 tours.
2. Send inexpensive mobile VR headsets to key customers.
3. Place high-quality VR headsets in our 10 major offices.
4. Create a three-part series of 15-minute VR films for our European Pipe Organs Tour.

The executive summary concludes with recommendations.

Introduction to Virtual Reality for Travel and Tourism

Introduction includes a problem statement.

Virtual reality (VR) tools increasingly allow users to experience films and other content in more realistic, multisensory, and even adventurous ways. One indicator of the growing demand for VR content is the demand for VR headsets. In 2018, global shipments of VR headsets amounted to 13.5 million. The demand for VR headsets is expected to more than double by 2023. Yet, a small overall percentage of

FIGURE 13.6

(Continued)

consumers own VR headsets or regularly view VR content. Most experts suggest VR as a mainstream experience is still three to five years in the future (Hollander, 2018).

Many companies in the hospitality and tourism sector are exploring how to create new business opportunities with VR. Some companies have already succeeded in using VR content to market their sites and services as well as to enhance tour experiences. Yet, while investments in VR may create competitive advantage, they involve significant risk and uncertainty. In this section, we describe two emerging functions of VR in our industry: (a) marketing sites and services and (b) enhancing the travel experience. Then, we describe the benefits and risks of developing and adopting VR content. Overall, the aim of our report is to evaluate the business opportunities of developing VR content for Aicasus Tours.

> *Headings clearly state section content.*

> *Introduction concludes with a preview of report contents.*

Marketing Travel with Virtual Reality

The most common application of VR in hospitality and tourism is marketing. More so than with brochures, still images, and even video, VR content can help prospective customers experience a hotel, catch a glimpse of a tour experience, and interact with tour sites in many ways. It provides a level of simulation not possible with traditional media.

> *In-text citations allow readers to know exactly where the information came from.*

Marketing with VR is particularly helpful for lesser-known destinations. For example, the Apulia region in Italy competes against dozens of better-known destinations in Italy. Tour planners created a VR app that allowed potential tourists to see the historical and cultural treasures in the area along with natural landscapes, local wildlife, and even a local bakery. This allows tourism planners to better market Apulia in a hypercompetitive destination country (Manghisi et al., 2017).

Marketing with VR also helps showcase the many available experiences in an area. For example, Visit Sweden has created many two-minute VR films that highlight the unique and lesser-known experiences of Sweden, such as enjoying the sounds of Sweden's forests, roaming through the countryside, swimming in lakes, and watching wildlife (available at visitsweden.com/sweden-vr-films/). Similarly, Visit Wales features two-to-three-minute VR films of zip lining, exploring caves, and participating in other exhilarating adventures (available at www.youtube.com/user/visitWales/videos).

Aside from destination managers, tour companies, airlines, and hotels use VR content to market destinations. Tour companies use VR films to feature niche elements of their tours. For example, Quark Expeditions, a company specializing in Antarctic tours, produces two-to-five-minute VR films with close-ups, aerials, and underwater views of icebergs, penguins, and other wonders of Antarctic explorations (see Figure 1; available at www.youtube.com/playlist?list=PLjqTuSPqDZUOz5-GZN8nX4Nxixie1xfWC). Airlines use VR films to highlight featured airline destinations. For example, Australian airline Qantas provides many two-to-eight-minute VR films of Australian destinations that focus on urban-centered and nature-focused vacations (available at www.

Hyoung Chang/The Denver Post/Getty Images

qantas.com/us/en/promotions/virtual-reality.html). Hotels and cruise lines also create VR films that display rooms and other amenities. Prominent examples include Marriott, Royal Caribbean, and Azamara Cruises (Haugen, 2018).

FIGURE 13.6

(Continued)

Enhancing the Travel Experience with Virtual Reality

Many VR designers are creating content to supplement and enhance tours. For example, VR designers created VR experiences for tourists at Kendal Calling, an annual music festival at the Lake District National Park in the United Kingdom. The VR experience included aerial footage of the lake and its wildlife filmed via drones (Jung, tom Dieck, Moorhouse, & tom Dieck, 2017). In an experiment of self-guided tours, VR designers created a VR tour of state capitol buildings to compare with audio tours. Tourists clearly preferred the VR experience (Wagler & Hanus, 2018). VR designers have also created content for castle tours in Finland that simulate medieval dining experiences (Qvist et al., 2016). Some destinations have even marketed VR experiences. For example, Legoland in Orlando promotes its VR roller coaster (Gerrity, 2018).

Samuel Borges Photography/Shutterstock

Each of these use cases shows potential for tours. Research shows tourists enjoy these experiences and want to experience them again. Still, most of these examples involve limited development and adoption. Industry experts suggest these use cases can significantly enhance many tours, particularly those involving culture, history, and nature. Further, experts suggest more sophisticated content that includes social content and gamification features can make tours more fun (Gerrity, 2018).

Return on Investment (ROI) for Virtual Reality Initiatives in Travel and Tourism

Reporting about VR tools for marketing suggests travel agencies gain significant returns on investment (Ghavri, 2018). For example, the travel agency Thomas Cook put VR headsets in many of its offices. Potential travelers could experience locations in Asia, Europe, and North America. Thomas Cook reported a 40 percent ROI. The most effective destination was New York (Haugen, 2018). Other research suggests using VR for marketing is particularly effective for younger consumers. For example, 73 percent of Gen Zers are interested in using VR for consumer decisions (Ghavri, 2018).

No known research provides reliable financial breakdowns of using VR tools to enhance tourist experiences. The examples we provided in the "Enhancing the Travel Experience with Virtual Reality" section are primarily proof-of-concept tests that are funded by governmental agencies and universities.

Drawbacks and Risks of Virtual Reality for Travel and Tourism

Developing VR content for marketing and tour enhancements presents several potential drawbacks and risks. On the marketing side, excellent VR content may deter some customers from purchasing tours. On the tour side, VR content is expensive to develop with unproven returns. Further, some experts wonder whether VR content for tours

FIGURE 13.6

(Continued)

is more of a fad than a trend (Haugen, 2018). For all VR content, no market research yet shows a significant demand for VR tools and content in travel and tourism.

Many experts wonder whether marketing with VR content is an advantage or a deterrent. While promotional materials have long relied on pictures and some video, they rarely simulate the travel experience as closely as well-produced VR content. As a result, VR experiences could serve as a deterrent if they replace the expensive experience of traveling (Haugen, 2018). For example, the Discovery VR app (available at www.discoveryvr.com) allows users to enjoy sky diving experiences, get close-up looks of giraffes or bears or dozens of animals, tour remote villages, and experience adventures across the world. Some experts wonder whether some potential customers will avoid travel if they can gain these experiences for little to no expense. While this is a reasonable risk, the research about marketing seems to suggest generally positive returns.

No market research yet shows a significant demand for VR tools and content to enhance travel and tourism. This may create an opportunity for early entrants in the industry, yet it may also result in wasted investments. We think mainstream adoption of these tools is likely given the broader VR trends. Most organizations are at the beginning stage of using VR tools to market to customers. Only about 12 percent of organizations are currently using VR. However, another 18 percent are evaluating VR options, and another 12 percent expect to evaluate or explore VR options soon (Resnick & McGovern, 2018). A survey of 595 VR and AR professionals found about 27 percent of these professionals believe VR will go mainstream within two years. Another 42 percent believe VR will go mainstream in roughly three to four years (Parrish, 2018).

> *Headings support common story lines and rationales in business decision making, including terms such as* benefits, risks, *and* best practices.

Options for Developing Virtual Reality Content at Aicasus Tours

Through our research (including conversations with VR developers), we suggest Aicasus Tours has the following reasonable options: (1) develop short VR films for marketing purposes; (2) promote select tours with our VR films at our agency locations (this will require the purchase of VR headsets); and (3) create VR content for several strategic tours. We describe each of the options in more detail along with related research and needed investments.

Develop Short VR Films for Marketing Purposes

Following the model set by tour companies such as Quark Expeditions, we can produce and develop 360 videos of our various tours, place them on YouTube, and link the videos to booking webpages (Tilly, 2017). Potential customers could watch the videos with or without VR headsets.

In consultation with three VR developers, we estimate each short VR film of roughly two minutes can be produced for approximately $5,500 (includes equipment purchases). We could rely on our permanent tour guides at various locations to oversee the recording of the tour footage (J. Hardaway, personal communication, September 14, 2019; K. Cafferty, personal communication, September 15, 2019; M. Dipprey, personal communication, September 14, 2019).

> *Report relies on firsthand interviews in addition to secondary research. The firsthand information addresses difficult-to-find secondary information.*

To assess interest in VR content to help make tour selections, we surveyed 515 former customers. We received responses from 217 of these customers. Each customer received a short online survey. Before answering survey items, customers watched a two-minute video explaining how VR headsets can be used to showcase tours. The short video contained pictures and three short sample video clips.

FIGURE 13.6

(Continued)

Many of our prior customers expressed interest in viewing VR content as they make tour decisions (see Table 1). Among customers who own tethered VR headsets, nearly three-quarters (73%) expressed interest. For mobile VR headset owners and customers without VR headsets (in the survey, we suggested we would send them Google Cardboard headsets), roughly one-quarter (28% and 24%, respectively) expressed interest. ◄———

Tables display survey statistics so busy readers can rapidly process them.

Table 1. Interest in Viewing VR Content to Evaluate Tours.

	Tethered VR Headset Owners[1] (*n* = 31; 14% of sample)	Mobile VR Headset Owners[2] (*n* = 45; 21% of sample)	Customers without VR Headsets[3] (*n* = 151; 70% of sample)	Customers Who Go to Our Offices[4] (*n* = 53; 24% of sample)
Interest in VR content to help you make tour decisions	73%	28%	24%	53%
Interest in sharing VR content with other group tour members	51%	25%	15%	14%

Note. Responses separated based on how they answered the following questions: 1. Do you own a tethered VR headset (i.e., Oculus Rift, HTC Vive, PlayStation VR)? 2. Do you own a mobile VR headset (i.e., Google Cardboard, Google Daydream View, Samsung Gear VR)? 3. If we sent you a Google Cardboard to watch VR videos of our tours, would you use it? 4. Have you visited an Aicasus Tours office? Some customers are included several times. For example, a customer may own a tethered headset, may own a mobile VR headset, *and* may have gone to one of our offices.

Promote Select Tours with Our VR Films at Our Agency Locations

Once we create 360 videos, we can allow customers who visit our offices to view the VR content on high-quality VR headsets. This option would require us to purchase roughly five VR headsets (about $800 per headset) for each of our 10 major offices. Among customers who go to our offices to book tours (see the final column in Table 1), over half expressed interest in viewing VR content.

Create VR Content for Several Strategic Tours

We can also create VR content to enhance our tours. This is clearly the most expensive and highest risk option. Content for these VR films would need to be higher quality, more sophisticated, more engaging, and more interactive than the short VR films used for promotion. In consultation with VR developers, creating a 15-minute VR film would cost between $25,000 and $50,000. We envision creating three VR films for tours of five to seven days.

To assess interest in VR content as part of the tour experience, we surveyed former customers for the following three tours: (a) European Pipe Organs Tour; (b) Medieval Castles Tour; and (c) Redwood Forest Meditation Tour. Before answering survey items, customers watched a two-minute video explaining how VR headsets could be used in these tours. The short videos contained pictures and three sample video clips.

Prior customers of the Redwood Forest Meditation Tour were the least interested in VR content to enhance their experience (see Table 2). About one in five prior customers thought VR content could significantly enhance the tour, and just 3 percent thought this tour feature would increase the likelihood of selecting the tour. However, most prior customers of the European Pipe Organs Tour expressed interest in viewing VR content. About three-quarters of prior customers thought VR content could significantly enhance the tour, and about half thought this tour feature would increase the likelihood of selecting the tour.

FIGURE 13.6

(Continued)

Table 2. Percentage of Customers Who Agree VR Experiences Could Enhance Select Tours.

	European Pipe Organs Tour (n = 73)	Medieval Castles Tour (n = 28)	Redwood Forest Meditation Tour (n = 82)
Do you believe the VR experiences would significantly enhance the tour?	73%	48%	18%
Would you be more likely to select this tour knowing it would have VR experiences?	45%	29%	3%

Recommendations

Based on the existing research about using VR content for promoting and enhancing tours and our own survey work, we recommend Aicasus Tours adopt a VR initiative that positions us as an early adopter of travel-enhancing technologies. Yet, we also recommend avoiding excessive risk. Specifically, we recommend the following:

1. *Develop short VR films for each of our 25 tours.* At an estimated cost of $137,500, we can immediately start promoting tours with these videos.
2. *Send inexpensive mobile VR headsets to key customers.* At an estimated cost of $10,000 (1,000 Google Cardboard headsets with a cost of $10 per headset, including shipping), we can send mobile VR headsets to prior customers identified as most likely to purchase future tours. We recommend evaluating their purchase behavior to create an ROI analysis of the mobile VR headset strategy.
3. *Place high-quality VR headsets in our 10 major offices.* At an estimated cost of $40,000, we can market our tours with VR experiences with high-quality VR experiences at our major offices. We recommend tracking which tours our customers view and how that impacts their ultimate decision making.
4. *Create a three-part series of 15-minute VR films for our European Pipe Organs Tour.* At an estimated cost of $137,000 ($105,000 of productions costs; $32,000 for 40 high-quality VR headsets for tour participants), we can test the value of developing VR content to enhance tours. ◄

At a total cost of $334,500, we anticipate the VR initiative will help us market our tours and strengthen our position as a distinctive provider of sophisticated tours.

Enumerated list contains recommendations. They are set apart in italics and followed by short rationale to allow decision makers to understand the ideas clearly.

Recommendations are specific and achievable. They are based on needs and opportunities described in the body of the paper.

FIGURE 13.6

(Continued)

References

Gerrity, C. (2018, October 30). How augmented reality travel will re-shape the tourism industry. *Mabu*. Retrieved from https://www.agencymabu.com/augmented-reality-travel-tourism/

Ghavri, S. (2018, June 1). VR in travel & tourism. *Code Brew Labs*. Retrieved from https://www.code-brew.com/blog/2018/06/01/virtual-reality-in-tourism/

Haugen, J. (2018, May 22). Virtual reality: Insights and opportunities in the travel industry. *Adventure Travel News*. Retrieved from https://www.adventuretravelnews.com/virtual-reality-insights-and-opportunities-in-the-travel-industry

Hollander, R. (2018, March 27). When it comes to VR hardware, consumers are balancing price point and experience. *Business Insider*. Retrieved from www.businessinsider.com/the-vr-hardware-report-2018-3

Jung, T., tom Dieck, M. C., Moorhouse, N., & tom Dieck, D. (2017, March 30). *Tourists' experiences of virtual reality applications*. Paper presented at the 2017 IEEE International Conference on Consumer Electronics (ICCE), Las Vegas, NV.

Manghisi, V. M., Fiorentino, M., Gattullo, M., Boccaccio, A., Bevilacqua, V., Cacella, G. L., Dassisti, M., & Uva, A. E. (2017, November/December). Experiencing the sights, smells, sounds, and climate of Southern Italy in VR. *IEEE Computer Graphics and Applications*, 19–25.

Parrish, K. (2018, August 13). Pricing and lack of content are still barriers against the adoption of VR. *Digital Trends*. Retrieved from www.digitaltrends.com/computing/vr-pros-see-pricing-and-content-as-mainstream-barriers/

Pettey, C. (2018, September 6). 3 reasons why VR and AR are slow to take off. *Smarter with Gartner*. Retrieved from www.gartner.com/smarterwithgartner/3-reasons-why-vr-and-ar-are-slow-to-take-off/

Qvist, P., Trygg, N. B., Luimula, M., Peltola, A., Suominen, T., Heikkinen, V., Tuominen, P., & Tuusvvuori, O. (2016, October 16). *Demo: Medieval gastro box–utilizing VR technologies in immersive tourism experiences*. Paper presented at the 7th IEEE International Conference on Cognitive Infocommunications (CogInfoCom 2016), Wroclaw, Poland.

Resnick, M., & McGovern, J. (2018, December 4). *How architecting for next-generation experiences helps to deliver customer and business outcomes*. Stamford, CT: Gartner.

Tilly, S. (2017, December 19). Advantages of virtual reality in the travel industry: How to integrate VR in your tours and activities. *Orioly*. Retrieved from https://www.orioly.com/advantages-of-virtual-reality-in-the-travel-industry/

Wagler, A., & Hanus, M. D. (2018). Comparing virtual reality tourism to real-life experiences: Effects of presence and engagement on attitude and enjoyment. *Communication Research Reports, 35*(5), 456–464.

FIGURE 13.7

Business Report with Primary Research in Slide Deck Format

**Guest Satisfaction among Conference Attendees
at the Prestigio Hotel and Resort**

baker consulting   •   *Prepared by Shania Baker*   •   February 2020

Andersen Ross/Blend Images LLC

The title page—visually and textually—rapidly shows the key theme: guest satisfaction among conference attendees.

In slide deck format for reports, analysts can focus slightly more on the visual and aesthetic nature of reports. However, the most important issues still relate to the strength of the research.

Executive Summary

Survey Details

Baker Consulting surveyed 236 conference attendees who participated in three- or four-day conferences between January and December 2019.

Key Findings

- Satisfaction ratings for key guest services and amenities: conference meals, 76 percent; meeting rooms, 75 percent; staff and service, 69 percent.
- Key indicators of repeat business: overall guest satisfaction, 84 percent; willingness to recommend the Prestigio, 57 percent.
- Overall satisfaction ratings by gender and income: women, 78 percent; men, 89 percent; higher-income, 66 percent; lower-income, 88 percent.
- Overall satisfaction in the past five years: 2015, 87 percent; 2016, 81 percent; 2017, 79 percent; 2018, 79 percent; 2019, 84 percent.

Key Conclusions

- The Prestigio fell short of 85 percent satisfaction targets in the following areas: conference meals, meeting rooms, and staff and service.
- The Prestigio received high ratings for its restaurants, which are the most popular guest service and amenity.

Key Conclusions (continued)

   Preferences for other guest services and amenities are highly variable based on gender and income.

- The Prestigio fell short of its goals for overall satisfaction and willingness to recommend.
- Women and higher-income guests tend to be less satisfied, less willing to return, and less willing to recommend the Prestigio. Similarly, women and higher-income guests are also less satisfied with conference meals and staff and service.
- The Prestigio has made significant improvement over the past year in nearly all satisfaction ratings following four years of declines.

Recommendations

- Examine ways to raise satisfaction among women and higher-income conference attendees.
- Adapt the marketing of meetings to the group composition of prospects.
- Continue customer service initiatives to improve staff and service ratings.
- Reexamine catering services to improve conference meals.

This executive summary is in *structured format* (compared to the narrative format of the executive summary in the prior report). The headings allow decision makers and other readers to easily distinguish among survey details, findings, conclusions, and recommendations.

FIGURE 13.7

(Continued)

Introduction

Guest satisfaction has always been the foundation for repeat business. With so many online reviews of hotels readily available to meeting planners, the importance of achieving high guest satisfaction ratings is more important now than ever. Since 2015, the Prestigio has evaluated guest satisfaction and future intentions among conference attendees with an annual survey to help determine priorities for improving guest satisfaction. This report provides the results of this year's survey as well as year-to-year comparisons for the past five years.

Survey Purpose and Administration

This guest satisfaction survey addressed the following broad questions:

- How satisfied are conference attendees with conference services and amenities?
- What hotel amenities do conference attendees use during their conference stays?
- How likely are our conference attendees to contribute to future business?

Most of the survey questions have remained identical since annual surveys were started in 2015. Some unique questions are inserted into the survey each year to address particular areas of strategic concern. Survey questions are provided in the Appendix of Survey Questions.

The survey was administered online. The survey link was sent to 534 guests who had participated in three- or four-day conferences between January and December 2019. Altogether, 236 respondents completed the survey, garnering a participation rate of roughly 44 percent.

Results from This Year's Survey

Findings and conclusions can be grouped into three broad areas: (1) satisfaction with conference services and amenities; (2) use of Prestigio guest services and amenities during conference stays; and (3) overall satisfaction and future intentions among conference attendees.

Satisfaction with Conference Services and Amenities

Between two-thirds (64%) and three-fourths (76%) of respondents expressed satisfaction with various conference services and amenities (see Table 1). These results indicate the following:

- *The Prestigio fell short of its goals in the following areas: conference meals, meeting rooms, and staff and service.* In January 2019, the Prestigio marketing team set goals to reach at least 85 percent satisfaction for these three key areas. Barbara Brookshire has indicated that 85 percent satisfaction in these areas would place the Prestigio in the elite category compared to our competitors. The Prestigio fell between 9 and 16 percent short of these goals.

- *Prestigio guests are most satisfied with conference meals and meeting rooms.* While the goal remains to reach 85 percent satisfaction for all conference services and amenities, the Prestigio marketing team generally views 75 percent satisfaction as good performance. Therefore, satisfaction with conference meals and meeting rooms is acceptable. However, the Prestigio may not have the unique competitive advantage in this area that it did five years ago.

- *Many of Prestigio guests are unhappy with Internet pricing and the business center.* Roughly one in three respondents was not satisfied with these services.

Headings and bulleted items allow readers to fairly rapidly read this report. This is particularly helpful for data-intensive reports such as this one.

Italicized conclusions help decision makers recognize what big ideas emerge from the report.

Table 1. Satisfaction with Conference Services and Amenities.

	Conference Meals	Meeting Rooms	Staff and Service	Internet Pricing	Business Center
All Respondents	76% (179)	75% (178)	69% (163)	66% (155)	64% (152)
Gender					
Male	85% (108)	76% (97)	72% (91)	73% (93)	56% (71)
Female	65% (71)	74% (81)	66% (72)	57% (62)	74% (81)
Income					
Under $40,000	73% (94)	77% (56)	78% (57)	38% (28)	64% (47)
$40,000–$75,000	62% (79)	76% (97)	68% (87)	76% (97)	66% (84)
Over $75,000	57% (20)	71% (25)	54% (19)	86% (30)	60% (21)

Note: Altogether, 236 respondents took the survey. Percentages and number of respondents (in parentheses) refer to those who responded *satisfied* or *extremely satisfied* on the survey.

Tables allow decision makers to examine the data themselves and make their own judgments.

Table 2. Use of Prestigio Guest Services and Amenities during Conference Stay.

	Prestigio Restaurants	Comedy Club	Fitness Center	Swimming Pool	Spa	Golf Course
All Respondents	53% (126)	39% (92)	35% (82)	31% (73)	19% (45)	8% (18)
Gender						
Male	46% (59)	53% (67)	38% (48)	29% (37)	2% (3)	11% (14)
Female	61% (67)	23% (25)	31% (34)	33% (36)	39% (42)	4% (4)
Income						
Under $40,000	33% (24)	22% (16)	18% (13)	33% (24)	1% (1)	3% (2)
$40,000–$75,000	62% (79)	50% (64)	39% (50)	30% (39)	17% (22)	7% (9)
Over $75,000	66% (23)	34% (12)	43% (15)	29% (10)	63% (22)	20% (7)

Note: Altogether, 236 respondents took the survey. Percentages and number of respondents (in parentheses) refer to those who responded *satisfied* or *extremely satisfied* on the survey.

Several pictures help readers visualize what survey respondents are providing feedback about.

Photos: (top) Monkey Business Images/Shutterstock; (bottom) Ingram Publishing/SuperStock

FIGURE 13.7

(Continued)

Use of Prestigio Guest Services and Amenities during Conference Stays

By far, the most used guest services and amenities by conference attendees are the Prestigio restaurants, with over half (53%) of our respondents stating they ate at Prestigio restaurants during their conference stays. Roughly 30 to 40 percent of respondents reported using the comedy club (39%), the fitness center (35%), or the swimming pool (31%). Relatively few of our conferences guests reported using the spa or golf course (see Table 2). These results indicate the following:

- *The restaurants are most convenient for use during conference stays.* Other internal surveys show that our non-conference guests tend to frequent the fitness center, the swimming pool, and the golf course more so than our restaurants. This implies that conference attendees most likely use the restaurants more than other services and amenities because of their busy conference schedules.

- *Use of guest services and amenities is highly variable based on gender and income.* This is discussed further in the *Differences by Gender and Income* section.

Overall Satisfaction and Future Intentions among Conference Attendees

Overall, the vast majority (84%) of respondents reported satisfaction with their conference experiences. Nearly three out of four (73%) respondents stated that they would want to attend another conference at the Prestigio, and nearly six in ten respondents (57%) said they would recommend the Prestigio as a good site for a business conference

(see Table 3). These results indicate the following:

- *The Prestigio fell short of its goals for guests' overall satisfaction and willingness to recommend the Prestigio.* In January 2019, the Prestigio marketing team set goals for overall satisfaction at 90 percent and willingness to recommend the Prestigio at 65 percent. The Prestigio fell short by 6 to 8 percentage points.

- *Overall satisfaction, desire to return to the Prestigio, and willingness to recommend the Prestigio are highly variable on gender and income.* This is discussed further in the *Differences by Gender and Income* section.

Table 3. Overall Satisfaction and Future Intentions among Conference Attendees.

	Overall Satisfaction	Want to Return	Would Recommend
All Respondents	84% (198)	73% (173)	57% (135)
Gender			
Male	89% (113)	77% (98)	66% (84)
Female	78% (85)	69% (75)	47% (51)
Income			
Under $40,000	88% (64)	81% (59)	67% (49)
$40,000–$75,000	87% (111)	74% (95)	57% (73)
Over $75,000	66% (23)	54% (19)	37% (13)

Note: Altogether, 236 respondents took the survey. Percentages and number of respondents (in parentheses) refer to those who responded *satisfied* or *extremely satisfied* on the survey. The full wording for survey items was as follows: Overall, I was satisfied with the conference experience; I would like to attend another business conference held at the Prestigio; I would recommend the Prestigio as a good site for a business conference.

Differences by Gender and Income

For the first time, this year's guest satisfaction survey includes breakdowns by gender and income. The results indicate the following:

- *Women and higher-income guests tend to be less satisfied, less willing to return, and less willing to recommend* (see Figures 1 and 2). A review of findings in Table 3 reveals that women and higher-income guests are far less likely to express satisfaction on those items that we consider barometers of future and repeat business. On the issue of willingness to recommend, roughly half (47%) of women reported that they are willing to recommend, whereas roughly two-thirds (67%) of men said they would recommend the Prestigio. The difference is even larger by income level. Just one-third (37%) of high-income respondents said that they would

recommend the Prestigio, whereas roughly two-thirds (67%) of lower-income respondents said that they would do so.

- *Women and higher-income guests are less satisfied with conference meals and staff and service.* A review of Table 1 reveals that women and higher-income guests are less satisfied with conference meals and staff and service. In past years, we have identified these as key factors leading to overall satisfaction. The gaps are especially wide for conference meals. Whereas the vast majority (85%) of men were satisfied with conference meals, just two-thirds (65%) of women were satisfied. The gap is wider when considering income level. Whereas nearly all (89%) lower-income respondents were satisfied with conference meals, just over half (57%) of higher-income respondents felt this way.

Figure 2. Guest Satisfaction by Income.

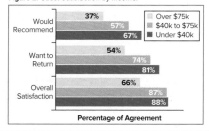

Figure 1. Guest Satisfaction by Gender.

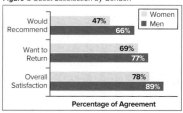

Formatting allows readers to quickly grasp the key ideas.

Table notes give additional information to decision makers to evaluate the data quality and relevance.

A section focused on gender and income emphasizes some of the key differences in satisfaction levels. These conclusions directly lead to some of the recommendations.

Charts reveal the key findings. Readers can rapidly see the differences by gender and income.

FIGURE 13.7

(Continued)

- *Women conference attendees tend to disproportionately choose Prestigio restaurants and the spa. Men conference attendees disproportionately choose the comedy club and the golf course.* Women attendees' top two choices of guest services and amenities are Prestigio restaurants (61%) and the spa (39%), whereas men attendees' top two choices are the comedy club (53%) and the Prestigio restaurants (46%). Men are roughly three times as likely to use the golf course (11% to 4%).

- *Higher-income guests tend to disproportionately choose the spa and the golf course; middle-income guests tend to disproportionately choose the comedy club; and lower-income guests tend to utilize all hotel services and amenities less with the exception of the swimming pool.* Higher-income guests are three to four times more likely to use the spa and golf course compared to middle-income guests. Lower-income guests rarely if ever use the spa and golf course.

These conclusions regarding the experiences of women and higher-income guests are quite concerning. The Prestigio deals mostly with meeting planners who are women, and our women respondents likely reflect the expectations of these meeting planners. Furthermore, the Prestigio brands itself as providing high-class conference experiences—those that would by assumption cater to the tastes of higher-income guests.

Comparison of Guest Satisfaction Rates over the Past Five Years

Comparisons of survey results over the past five years reveal several basic trends (see Table 4 for complete results):

- *Overall satisfaction and willingness to recommend have increased over the past year.* From 2015 to 2018, overall satisfaction and willingness to recommend fell 10 and 13 percentage points, respectively. However, in the past year (2018 to 2019), overall satisfaction and willingness to recommend improved 5 and 8 percentage points, respectively (see Figure 3).

Figure 3. Five-Year Trends in Indicators of Repeat Business.

The report provides perspective by comparing current satisfaction rates with those of past years.

A line chart rapidly allows readers to see a trend: slight declines over the 2015–2018 period and slight improvements during the past year.

- *Satisfaction with conference meals and staff and service has increased over the past year.* From 2015 to 2018, satisfaction with conference meals and staff and service decreased 19 and 3 percentage points, respectively. However, in the past year (2018 to 2019), satisfaction with conference meals and staff and service increased 8 and 7 percentage points, respectively.

- *Most indicators of satisfaction have returned to levels from five years ago.* In general, nearly all indicators of satisfaction showed steady deterioration from 2015 to 2018, with the past year showing improvement back to near-2003 levels of satisfaction.

Indicators of Repeat and Referral Business	2015	2016	2017	2018	2019
Overall Satisfaction	87%	81%	79%	79%	84%
Want to Return	72%	74%	71%	72%	73%
Would Recommend	62%	59%	55%	49%	57%
Conference					
Conference Meals	87%	76%	74%	68%	76%
Meeting Rooms	77%	71%	74%	76%	75%
Staff & Service	65%	64%	61%	62%	69%
Internet Pricing	-	-	-	-	66%
Business Center	-	-	-	-	64%

Note: Altogether, 236 respondents took the survey. Percentages and number of respondents (in parentheses) refer to those who responded *agree* or *strongly agree* on the survey. The items for Internet pricing and the business center were introduced for the first time in this year's survey.

Table with five years of data allows readers to quickly see the trend for all survey items.

FIGURE 13.7

(Continued)

Recommendations

1. *Examine ways to raise satisfaction among women and higher-income conference attendees.* Women and higher-income guests are particularly important to the Prestigio's brand and financial success. Most meeting planners the Prestigio works with are women and likely reflect the perspectives of female guests more so than our male guests. Furthermore, since the Prestigio brand stands for providing high-end conference services, the fact that higher-income guests are less satisfied is concerning. To better understand how to raise guest satisfaction among women and higher-income conference attendees, the Prestigio should take the following actions:

    a. Set up focus groups with women and higher-income guests to gain a more in-depth understanding of their concerns and suggestions for improvement.

    b. Informally talk to women and higher-income guests during conferences and catalog these guests' feedback in a lessons-learned database.

2. *Adapt the marketing of meetings to the group composition of prospects.* With a much better understanding of how the gender and income level of our guests impact which amenities and services they use, marketing materials can be developed to appeal more strongly to certain groups.

For example, each year the Prestigio hosts meetings for the Northern Hunters Association, with over 90 percent male membership, and the Farmers Healthcare Group, comprised mostly of female nurses.

3. *Continue customer service initiatives to improve staff and service ratings.* The recent initiatives to improve personalized guest service appear to have been successful. Given the emphasis on guest service as a foundation for all improvements, the Prestigio should maintain a high staff-to-guest ratio, provide incentives for exceptional guest service, and continue the intensive two-month mentoring and training program for new guest attendants.

4. *Reexamine catering services to improve conference meals.* Five years ago, Prestigio guests were overwhelmingly satisfied with conference meals. In fact, many guests recommended repeat business in large part due to the excellent meals. To cut costs, the Prestigio changed catering services over the past five years, and the result has been far lower guest satisfaction with meals. To strengthen or regain a reputation for high-end conference experiences, the Prestigio should identify ways to return to 2013-level guest satisfaction for conference meals.

Recommendations emerge directly from the survey findings and conclusions.

These recommendations serve as a good way to prioritize initiatives to improve guest satisfaction.

allows writers to create visually stronger and more creative reports. Yet, the same principles of strong report writing apply to this format. Notice that the report in slide deck format is for reading, not for a presentation. As you'll see in the upcoming chapters, your slides for presentations should contain far less content.

Reviewing Your Reports for Fairness and Effectiveness

LO13.6 Review reports for effectiveness and fairness.

As with other written documents, you will always review your reports to ensure that you have been fair to yourself and your readers. Also, you want to make sure the report is as effective as possible.

Since research-based reports are generally commissioned for high-stakes decisions, you have likely worked collaboratively with others. If you've developed the report by yourself, you should still try to get other perspectives before you officially submit it. When possible, discuss the report with the ultimate decision makers so that you can best tailor the final product to their needs.

As you review the report by yourself and with others, run through it numerous times, each time considering a different perspective. For example, review the entire document several times for accuracy and precision in logic. Review it at least once, imagining yourself in the position of decision makers to improve it based on what you perceive as their needs. Also, review it at least once for typos or mechanical errors. Make sure you review the report over several sittings and several days if possible, since you are unlikely to catch all of the changes you would ideally make in just one sitting.

💡 IDEAS IN ACTION

READING AND WRITING REPORTS

Jeff Bezos is one of the most successful businesspersons of our era. He started Amazon in 1993 and has turned it into one of the most important companies in the world.

Bezos leads and manages with a focus on effective decision making. As a result, he insists on carefully written reports. In fact, he bans PowerPoint slides in meetings. Prior to a meeting, someone on the team writes a six-page, carefully crafted report. At the beginning of meetings, the teams remain silent as they spend up to 30 minutes reading and evaluating the report. Then, they use the memo contents as the basis of their discussion. The report effectively serves as the agenda.

Franziska Krug/Getty Images

The Amazon approach is slightly unconventional. Yet, it's fundamentally no different than all high-performing companies in this sense: Decisions are made based on well-developed, data-driven reports.

Source: Bariso, J. (2018, April 30). Jeff Bezos knows how to run a meeting. Here's how he does it. *Inc.* Retrieved from www.inc.com/justin-bariso/jeff-bezos-knows-how-to-run-a-meeting-here-are-his-three-simple-rules.html.

Chapter Takeaway for *Completing Business Proposals and Business Reports*

LO13.1 Explain how completed reports affect your credibility.

It shows **competence** when you provide facts, conclusions, and positions that help decision making.	It shows **caring** when you involve decision makers and address their needs.	It shows **character** when you report all information honestly and provide access to your rationale.

LO13.2 Create specific and persuasive proposals. See *example of a proposal* in Figure 13.1.

LO13.3 Demonstrate excellent thinking by applying a precision-oriented style to reports.

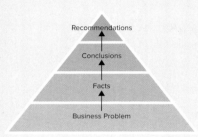

Style: Apply precision-oriented language and display excellence in thinking.

See *examples of a clear problem statement* (Table 13.1), *fact-based language* (Table 13.2), *citations to avoid plagiarism* (Table 13.4), *recommendations based on facts and conclusions* (Figure 13.3), and *specific and actionable recommendations* (Table 13.5).

LO13.4 Design your reports to aid in decision making.

Design: Provide easy navigation so that decision makers can quickly identify key points and themes.

See *examples of common headings/sections in reports* (Figure 13.4), *common components of formal reports* (Figure 13.5), *use of headings as a story line device* (Table 13.6), *wording for headings* (Table 13.7), *use of preview statements* (Table 13.8), *effective charts* (Table 13.9), and *bulleting and enumerated lists* (Table 13.10).

LO13.5 Project objectivity in reports.

Tone: Emphasize objectivity and project a tempered can-do attitude.

See *examples of objective tone* (Table 13.11).

LO13.6 Review reports for effectiveness and fairness.

Feedback: Involve as many trusted colleagues and partners as possible. Ideally, involve decision makers.

FAIR Test: Make sure facts, conclusions, and positions are as objective as possible. Make any of your biases apparent.

Proofreading: Check for precision and excellence in your thinking. Ensure your report is complete but easy to navigate.

Key Terms

direct quotations, 409   paraphrasing, 410   plagiarism, 409

Discussion Exercises

13.1 Chapter Review Questions (LO13.1, LO13.2, LO13.3, LO13.4)

For each of the following items, respond with one or two paragraphs.

A. Explain the significance of stating the business problem or challenge at the beginning of a report.

B. Discuss the various ways in which reports should be precise.

C. Describe the value of good documentation in your research reports.

D. Explain what it means for recommendations to be specific and actionable.

E. Discuss how charts should be used in reports.

F. Describe how you can strike a tone of objectivity in a report and also project positivity.

G. Explain various approaches for reviewing reports.

13.2 Ideas in Action Discussion Questions (LO13.1, LO13.2, LO13.3)

Read the Ideas in Action section with comments from Jeff Bezos. Respond to the following questions:

A. Why do you think Bezos bans PowerPoint slides in meetings?

B. What do you think the purpose is of team members silently reading reports together?

C. What do you think could be the major benefits of this approach to meetings? What do you think could be the major drawbacks?

13.3 Complete SBA Training for Business Plans (LO13.1, LO13.2, LO13.3)

Go to the Small Business Administration website (www.sba.gov) and complete the online training for "Starting a Business" (www.sba.gov/training/index.html), which takes about 30 minutes. In three to five paragraphs, describe the key points of developing a business plan that apply to writing effective reports.

Evaluation Exercises

13.4 Evaluating a Business Report (LO13.1, LO13.2, LO13.3, LO13.4)

Choose a business report to evaluate. Answer the following questions related to it:

A. How effectively does the report tell a story?

B. How effectively are headings used?

C. How effectively are charts, figures, and/or other graphics used?

D. How effectively are research results presented?

E. Overall, how reliable and useful is this report? Explain.

F. What three aspects of the report would you like to model in your report writing?

G. What three aspects of the report do you think should be improved?

You can find numerous reports online; often these are white papers. Ideally, search for a topic of interest. For example, if you are interested in the future of shopping malls, you could conduct an Internet search with a search phrase such as *future of shopping malls "white paper,"* and you will likely find dozens of options to choose from. Spend 10 to 15 minutes to find a report that is interesting to you.

Application Exercises

13.5 Writing a Survey Report and Marketing Plan for an Ice Cream Shop (LO13.1, LO13.2, LO13.3)

Assume you are planning to open an ice cream shop on campus. There are currently no ice cream shops within three miles of your campus. You are deciding between leasing space in the student center or opening a stand-alone shop on the outskirts of campus. You recently surveyed just over 400 university students to identify their preferences. The following table contains the results.

	Gender					
	Female		**Male**		**Total**	
	#	**%**	**#**	**%**	**#**	**%**
How often do you go to an ice cream parlor in a given month?						
0 times	26	14%	40	19%	66	16%
1 time	73	38	112	53	185	46
2 to 4 times	83	43	57	27	140	35
5 or more times	9	5	4	2	13	3
Would you prefer a drive-through versus sit-down?						
Drive-through	51	27	95	45	146	36
Sit-down	140	73	118	55	258	64
Which do you prefer?						
Ice cream	77	40	170	80	247	61
Frozen yogurt	102	53	43	20	145	36
Sherbet	12	6	0	0	12	3
How do you like your ice cream prepared?						
Sundae	57	30	38	18	95	24
Cone	47	25	40	19	87	22
Cup	64	34	67	31	131	32
Milkshake	23	12	68	32	91	23
What's your favorite condiment?						
Candy	35	18	93	44	128	32
Cookies	31	16	49	23	80	20
Flavored syrup	57	30	52	24	109	27
Nuts	45	24	19	9	64	16
Fruit	23	12	0	0	23	6
Have you bought store novelties in the past (i.e., shirts, hats, etc.)?						
Yes	111	58	178	84	289	72
No	80	42	35	16	115	28
How many scoops do you typically prefer?						
1	112	59	42	20	154	38
2	71	37	140	66	211	52
3	8	4	31	15	39	10
How much are you willing to pay for a one-scoop ice cream cone?						
$1.00–$1.50	67	35	45	21	112	28
$1.51–$2.00	105	55	64	30	169	42
$2.01–$2.50	13	7	62	29	75	19
$2.51 or more	6	3	42	20	48	12
How much are you willing to pay for a two-scoop ice cream cone?						
$1.51–$2.25	73	38	43	20	116	29
$2.26–$3.00	76	40	40	19	116	29
$3.01–$3.50	31	16	84	39	115	28
$3.51 or more	11	6	46	22	57	14
Would you prefer an all-you-can-eat ice cream shop?						
Yes	25	13	158	74	183	45
No	166	87	55	26	221	55

Write a marketing report that includes your survey objectives, methodology, findings, and conclusions. Also, provide your related marketing recommendations.

13.6 Writing a Proposal for a Student Club (LO13.1, LO13.2, LO13.3)

Assume your university has recently developed a grant program for student clubs. The goal of the program is to award between $5,000 and $10,000 per club for activities that promote academic research and/or travel to industry conferences.

Choose a student club of interest and write a proposal that describes the purpose of your club and a specific project that the grant money would support. Provide a rationale for how you will use the money, a timeline for completing your project (or travel), and a description of deliverables. (Look at the proposal in the Bonus Appendix as a guide.)

13.7 Writing a Survey Report about Mobile Phone Use in the Workplace (LO13.1, LO13.2, LO13.3)

Ashley Foxe works for Process Leadership, a large consulting group that advises companies in North America, Europe, and Asia. It typically works on one- to six-month projects with companies that are trying to develop more open and collaborative work environments. The Process slogan is *leading with culture*, implying that entire companies need to share work values to maximize their productivity.

Ashley's role with Process Leadership is to write research reports or white papers that are available free of charge. These research reports are distributed on the Process Leadership home page and are intended to reinforce the Process brand of improving corporate culture. Process generally disseminates press releases about the research. Often, the research is picked up in newspapers, business magazines, and other professional publications. Each time the research is mentioned, it serves as free marketing and advertising for Process Leadership.

Ashley recently conducted a survey project about mobile phone use in the workplace. She conducted a nationwide survey of full-time business professionals with annual salaries over $30,000. She compiled the following data tables from the survey.

TABLE A

Demographics of Survey Respondents

Gender	Count	Percentage
Male	186	53.1%
Female	164	46.9
Age Group		
21–30	35	10.0
31–40	95	27.1
41–50	87	24.9
51–65	133	38.0
Income		
$30,000 to $39,999	41	11.7
$40,000 to $49,999	46	13.1
$50,000 to $59,000	53	15.1
$60,000 to $69,999	31	8.9
$70,000 to $79,999	40	11.4
$80,000 to $89,999	33	9.4
$90,000 to $99,999	29	8.3
$100,000 to $149,999	50	14.3
$150,000 or more	27	7.7
Total	350	100

TABLE B

Appropriateness of Mobile Phone Use in Meetings by Gender

	Male		Female		Total	
	Rarely	Never	Rarely	Never	Rarely	Never
Bringing phone to meeting	34.5%	11.4%	33.7%	24.0%	34.0%	21.7%
Checking time with phone	26.9	30.6	27.4	30.5	27.1	30.6
Checking incoming calls	26.3	25.8	31.1	21.3	28.6	27.4
Checking text messages	30.1	41.4	30.5	50.6	30.3	45.7
Answering a call	35.5	41.3	25.6	64.0	30.9	56.3
Excusing self to answer call	36.0	18.8	30.5	23.8	33.4	21.1
Writing and sending texts	26.9	54.3	22.0	65.2	24.6	51.3
Browsing the Internet	28.5	43.5	26.8	53.0	27.7	48.0

TABLE C

Appropriateness of Mobile Phone Use in Meetings by Gender

	21–30		31–40		41–50		51–65	
	Rarely	**Never**	**Rarely**	**Never**	**Rarely**	**Never**	**Rarely**	**Never**
Bringing phone to meeting	20.0%	8.6%	28.4%	12.6%	35.6%	28.7%	40.6%	27.1%
Checking time with phone	37.1	2.9	22.1	26.3	28.7	34.5	27.1	38.3
Checking incoming calls	25.7	5.7	24.2	24.2	27.6	32.2	33.1	32.3
Checking text messages	28.6	20.0	30.5	37.9	32.2	50.6	21.3	54.9
Answering a call	22.9	42.9	36.8	42.1	34.5	51.4	26.3	67.7
Excusing self to answer call	31.4	11.4	23.2	16.8	313.1	25.3	37.6	24.1
Writing and sending texts	22.9	34.3	30.5	45.3	28.7	51.4	18.0	75.9
Browsing the Internet	28.6	20.0	32.6	32.6	24.1	57.5	26.3	60.2

TABLE D

Attitudes toward Texting and Making Calls with Mobile Phones

	Males	**Females**	**21–30**	**31–40**	**41–50**	**51–65**	**Total**
Overall, using mobile phones for *TEXTING* in the workplace . . .							
Reduces miscommunication.	37.6%	34.8%	54.3%	42.1%	33.3%	21.3%	36.3%
Makes communication more efficient.	41.4	45.7	71.4	55.8	41.3	34.6	47.7
Improves relations with colleagues.	32.3	21.3	60.0	37.9	28.7	11.4	30.9
Improves relations with clients.	36.6	26.8	54.3	34.7	31.0	24.8	32.0
Makes work easier.	43.5	40.2	65.7	56.8	35.6	21.3	42.0
Overall, using mobile phones for *CALLS* in the workplace . . .							
Reduces miscommunication.	64.0	53.7	77.1	74.7	55.2	45.9	51.3
Makes communication more efficient.	70.4	65.2	88.6	81.1	66.7	54.1	68.0
Improves relations with colleagues.	51.3	51.3	88.6	70.5	60.9	42.1	51.3
Improves relations with clients.	66.1	61.6	88.6	82.1	60.9	46.6	64.0
Makes work easier.	65.6	64.0	88.6	75.8	63.2	51.9	64.9

Take the role of Ashley and write a white paper on mobile phone use in the workplace. You can include any other information you find useful. Include sections for data collection, survey findings and conclusions, and recommendations. Make sure to include at least a few charts or figures that illustrate compelling points. Remember your corporate slogan as you develop the report.

13.8 Write a Business Plan for a Franchise (LO13.1, LO13.2, LO13.3)

Choose a franchise that interests you. Write a business plan for the franchise in your location (or location of your choice) that includes the following:

- Executive summary
- Introduction
- Management
- Marketing
- Financial projections
- Financial needs

Be creative with your management and marketing ideas. You may not be familiar with creating financial projections, but do your best and simplify this step if necessary. The point of this assignment is to practice writing the plan. Work with your instructor to decide what is acceptable.

You can find possible franchises for this project by searching online for franchising opportunities. Most franchisors supply plenty of information about requirements to open a franchise.

You may want to consult several online articles about writing business plans. You can find many good resources. For example, consider the following article: Jeff Elgin, "Writing the Franchise Business Plan," *Entrepreneur*, September 5, 2005, retrieved from www.entrepreneur.com/franchises/buyingafranchise/franchisecolumnistjeffelgin/article79626.html.

13.9 Conducting Survey Research (LO13.1, LO13.2, LO13.3)

Individually or in groups, select a business problem you can learn more about by conducting survey research. You will create an online survey for all of your classmates to take, so design your project around the assumption that you are finding out what university-aged students think or feel about the topic. Design the survey so that respondents can complete it in three to five minutes. Once you have conducted the survey, write a report that includes your objectives, methodology, findings, conclusions, and recommendations.

13.10 Write a Report about a Business Trend (LO13.1, LO13.2, LO13.3)

Using research from your university library, write a report in APA or MLA documentation style that accomplishes the following:

A. States a business problem or challenge (you might imagine yourself in a position within a company of interest).

B. Describes and substantiates a trend that impacts business.

C. Provides recommendations for how your company can respond to the trend to become more competitive.

Language Mechanics Check

13.11 Review all rules in Appendix A about punctuation, number usage, and grammar. Then, rewrite each sentence to make all needed corrections.

A. Frequent flier programs have traditionally awarded miles based on the number of miles in a flight not on the price of air tickets.

B. Some airlines are now changing these loyalty programs, to reward miles based on ticket prices which makes many bargain hunters upset.

C. These airlines say that dollars spent is a better indicator of loyalty than miles traveled but many long time loyalty program members disagree.

D. Some airlines have all ready expanded the options, for members to use their miles.

E. In addition to using miles to purchase flights they will now be able to purchase extra legroom, check in baggage and even in flight food and services.

F. Overall these policies are aimed at rewarding travelers who spend more money on flights and in flight services.

G. Most travelers, who purchase primarily based on ticket prices, are disappointed with the new changes, because they reduce the benefits of getting the best deal.

H. Many airlines now sell annual, checked baggage subscriptions for around 300 to 400 dollars.

I. Airlines brought in about forty billion dollars last year in baggage fees, most airlines are using these fees to significantly improve profitability.

J. Many budget airlines make more money from fees, than they do from ticket prices.

Endnotes

1. "Plagiarize," retrieved March 1, 2012, from *Merriam-Webster Online Dictionary* at www.merriam-webster.com/dictionary/plagiarize.

2. "What Is Citation?" retrieved March 1, 2012, from *Plagiarism.org* website at www.plagiarism.org/plag_article_what_is_citation.html; "Plagiarism FAQs," retrieved March 1, 2012, from *Plagiarism.org* website at www.plagiarism.org/plag_article_what_is_citation.html; "What Is Plagiarism?" retrieved March 1, 2012, from *Plagiarism.org* website at www.plagiarism.org/plag_article_what_is_citation.html.

3. Kintler, D., & Adams, B. (1998). *Independent consulting: A comprehensive guide to building your own consulting business.* Avon, MA: Streetwise; Ford, B. R., Bornstein, J. M., & Pruitt, P. T. (2007). *The Ernst & Young business plan guide.* Hoboken, NJ: Wiley; Small Business Administration. Write a business plan. Retrieved September 15, 2010, from splanner/plan/writeabusinessplan/index.html.

4. Moore, R., Seraydarian, P., & Fruehling, R. (2010). *Pearson business reference and writer's handbook.* Upper Saddle River, NJ: Pearson Education.

5. Roach, J., Tracy, D., & Durden, K. (2007). Integrating business core knowledge through upper division report composition. *Business Communication Quarterly, 70*(4), 431–449.

6. Covello, J., & Hazelgren, B. (2005). *Your first business plan,* 5th ed. Naperville, IL: Sourcebooks, 12.

7. Covello, J., & Hazelgren, B. (2005). *Your first business plan,* 5th ed. Naperville, IL: Sourcebooks.

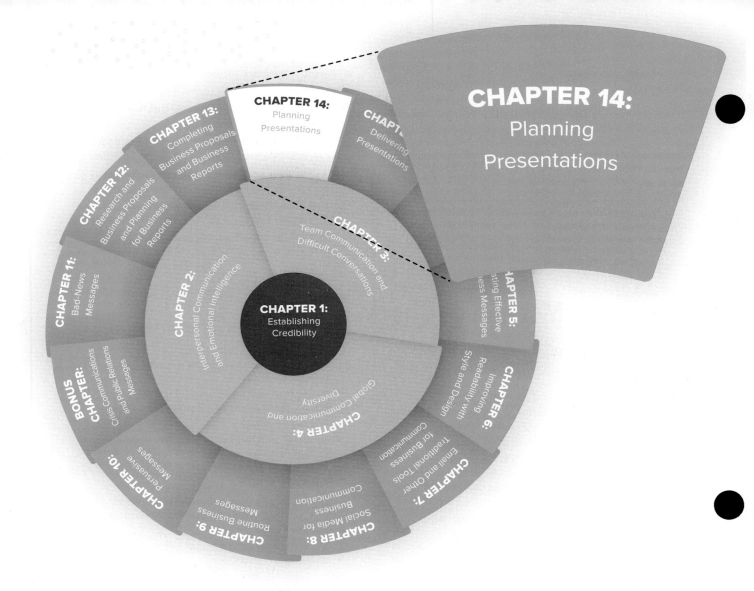

CHAPTER 14:
Planning
Presentations

ESTABLISHING
CREDIBILITY

PRINCIPLES OF INTERPERSONAL
COMMUNICATION

PRINCIPLES FOR & TYPES OF
BUSINESS MESSAGES

LEARNING OBJECTIVES

After studying this chapter, you should be able to do the following:

LO14.1 Describe how planning your presentations leads to credibility.

LO14.2 Analyze presentation audiences in terms of message benefits, learning styles, and communicator styles.

LO14.3 Organize and gather content for a preview, view, and review.

LO14.4 Develop effective slide presentations.

LO14.5 Use the story line approach to presentations.

LO14.6 Evaluate your presentations for fairness and effectiveness.

❓ WHY DOES THIS MATTER?

Presentations have many purposes, including promoting a new business or idea, reporting on the status of projects or product performance, helping management and employees stay informed about business policies, or selling a product or service. Presentations give you opportunities to connect deeply with your audiences and convey and control your messages carefully.

Presentations place a spotlight on you and allow you to maintain and even build your credibility. When you clearly know what you're talking about, audiences judge you as competent. When you show that you are interested in the needs of your audience, they judge you as caring. When you offer your views honestly and transparently, audiences judge you as having character.

Although speaking is a normal part of every day for you, making business presentations is not necessarily automatic or natural. As speech expert Thomas Leech explained, "Developing proficiency in oral communications doesn't occur automatically. The ability to speak may have come much as did walking and breathing, but speaking well to groups is another matter."[1] As you read this chapter, identify the areas that will help you most in developing your presentation skills. This chapter focuses on planning your content. The next one focuses on delivering that content effectively.

Read the chapter case about Latisha Jackson and her plans to develop a presentation about transitioning from annual performance reviews to continuous reviews.

> **Hear Pete Cardon explain why this matters.**
> **bit.ly/cardon14**

LO14.1 Describe how planning your presentations leads to credibility.

| **CHAPTER CASE** | PLANNING A PRESENTATION AT EASTMOND NETWORKING |

Latisha Jackson

Jeff Brody

WHO'S INVOLVED

HR Intern
- Hired for a summer internship to work on employee programs
- Double majoring in human resource management and health education

HR Director
- Worked as HR director at Eastmond Networking for the past five years

THE SITUATION

Eastmond Networking holds performance evaluations for employees once per year. Jeff sees the results of the company's internal, anonymous employee survey each year. Each year, he notices that employees do not like the performance

(Latisha Jackson character): LWA/Larry Williams/Blend Images LLC; (Jeff Brody character): Dougal Waters/Digital Vision/Getty Images evaluations. They think the evaluations are not fair and do not help them improve. Jeff has talked to several human resource (HR) directors and learned that many companies now use continuous performance reviews with a lot of success. To learn more about and help transition to continuous performance reviews, he asked Latisha Jackson to help formulate a plan for this transition.

Over an approximately six-week period, Latisha collected information about continuous reviews from other companies and software vendors. She also ran a few employee focus groups and helped conduct a detailed employee survey about performance reviews. Jeff has asked her to develop a presentation about continuous reviews to deliver at a senior management meeting. The meeting will include roughly 15 of the company's leaders, most of whom Latisha has not met in person. They expect a data-driven presentation. Jeff recently told Latisha that he was so impressed with her performance that he might be able to open a permanent position for her. Latisha hopes that a strong presentation will improve her chances of getting a permanent spot on the Eastmond team.

Jeff tells Latisha that the senior managers will most likely have the following major objections to continuous reviews: (1) they won't promote candid feedback, (2) they won't get support from managers, and (3) they will cost too much. Jeff believes that senior managers will support initiatives that improve employee engagement because a consulting firm recently surveyed employees and concluded that Eastmond's employees were below average in all measures of engagement.

Later, once the senior managers have approved the new review system, Jeff asks Latisha to deliver a presentation to the employees. This presentation should be less data-driven and more motivational.

TASK

1 Prepare the basic content of the presentation to explain the benefits of continuous reviews while also addressing concerns.

2 Develop slides to supplement the presentation and reinforce the key messages.

Applying the AIM Planning Process for Presentations

As you design your presentations and speeches, the AIM planning process will help you, just as it does in the writing process. You'll analyze your *audience* to make sure you're addressing audience members' needs and speaking to them in the way that is most appealing and easy to learn. You'll gather and develop your *information* and ideas by identifying the key facts and conclusions related to your topic. You'll also develop your *message* to focus on the key takeaway concepts and to provide supporting points throughout. In this chapter, we do not focus on developing your ideas, since this process is largely similar to that for writing. We instead discuss analyzing your audience and structuring your message since these processes have some unique features for presentations. Then, we discuss designing electronic slides since these are commonly included in many professional presentations.

Analyze Your Audience and Gather the Right Information

Understanding the needs of your audience is one of your first tasks as you develop your presentations. Of course, this is complicated by a variety of factors. Your audiences for presentations may differ in size and makeup, and in some cases, you won't know who they will be. As you do your homework about the audience, answer the following questions to the degree possible:

How Will Audience Members Benefit from the Product, Service, or Ideas I Am Proposing? This is the single most important question to guide you as you design your presentation. In particular, focus on benefits that fulfill an unmet need.[2]

In Latisha's case, she will focus primarily on improving employee engagement. Senior managers know this is a problem at Eastmond. She will explain that annual reviews lower engagement and continuous reviews improve engagement.

What Do the Audience Members Already Know about My Product, Service, or Ideas? Find out whatever you can about your audience members' knowledge level. If people know little about your product, you will need to spend a proportionately higher amount of your presentation time to inform them. Also, try to find out where they have gotten their information or how they have developed their perceptions about the topic. Knowing this allows you to more effectively deal with misinformation.

In Latisha's case, she thinks that senior managers don't know much about continuous performance reviews. She will need to explain the benefits clearly. Also, since continuous reviews depend on software platforms, she'll need to show the managers how these platforms operate. She assumes that these managers may not be able to visualize how the systems work unless she shows pictures or does a live demo.

What Are My Audience Members' Chief Concerns? Considering this question is particularly important for presentations. Whereas you can take time to gather your thoughts when responding in writing to someone's concerns, in presentations and other face-to-face communications you must respond immediately.

Latisha was wise to ask Jeff about the senior managers' chief concerns. Jeff told her they'd be worried about the candidness or accuracy of continuous reviews, support from managers, and cost.

Who Are the Key Decision Makers? Your presentation is generally intended to draw support from your whole audience. Typically, however, some people in your audience have more impact on your ability to achieve your work objectives than do others. These key decision makers are the ones you want to influence the most.

For internal presentations, think about those individuals who have the most influence and authority to act on your ideas. For presentations to clients, customers, and prospects, think about which individuals are the decision makers for their organizations or who you perceive as the most likely prospects for future business. Focus most of your attention on them.[3]

Once again, Latisha can rely on Jeff to identify which senior managers will have the most impact on whether continuous reviews get support. Latisha can think of ways to tailor her presentation to these individuals.

What Will Appeal to Your Audience? You can influence your audience by employing a combination of emotional and analytical appeals. Oral communications, especially speeches and presentations, are well suited to strong emotional appeal, as they create bonds between the speaker and the audience and emotional connections with products, services, and ideas. At the same time, your speeches and presentations will include a set of ideas that you want your audience to appreciate analytically. Plan to make both emotional and analytical connections with your audience.

LO14.2 Analyze presentation audiences in terms of message benefits, learning styles, and communicator styles.

 **connect**

Visit http://connect. mheducation.com for an exercise on this topic.

Principles of Audience Analysis

Identify the following:
- Audience benefits
- Existing knowledge
- Concerns
- Decision makers
- Appeals
- Communicator style
- Learning style

As you're thinking about emotional and analytical appeals, consider the motivational value systems (MVSs) of your audience members (see Chapter 2). Professionals with red MVSs will appreciate your ability to stay on point and discuss immediate goals. Emotionally and analytically, they are attracted to action-oriented and results-oriented language and logic. They generally think concise and confident presentations are more persuasive.

Professionals with blue MVSs will appreciate your ability to discuss business relationships—such as benefits to work teams and colleagues and loyalty to customers and clients. Emotionally, blues will connect to you with your use of "we" language and other relationship-centered terms. Analytically, blues will connect with your holistic approach to business benefits. They are attracted to business logic that includes more than just bottom-line measures of performance.

Professionals with green MVSs will appreciate your ability to provide all of the facts and avoid rushing to judgment about conclusions. Greens generally pride themselves on a dispassionate (nonemotional) approach to decision making and may be turned off by what they consider blatant and irrelevant appeals to emotion. However, this in no way implies that emotional appeal is unimportant to thinkers. Greens are often emotionally connected to precise language; well-designed and conceptualized charts, models, and other figures; and the ability to handle tough questions.

Professionals with hub MVSs are most common. Hubs are by nature pragmatic and flexible. They prefer a presentation that holds clear business logic with an emphasis on benefits to people—clients, customers, colleagues, and others. They prefer option-oriented language. Excessively confident language is often interpreted by hubs as arrogant or rigid.

What Is the Learning Style of Your Audience? As with motivational value systems, audience members have different learning styles. **Visual learners**, who make up about 40 percent of the population, learn best from illustrations and simple diagrams that show relationships and key ideas. They also enjoy gestures and metaphors. Ironically, text-based PowerPoint slides do not appeal to them much. On the other hand, PowerPoint slides rich in images and figures do help visual learners respond to your message. **Auditory learners**, who also comprise roughly 40 percent of the population, like loud, clear voices and believe emotion is best conveyed through voice. **Kinesthetic learners**, who make up about 20 percent of the population, need to participate to focus their attention on your message and learn best. They need group activities, hands-on activities, or breaks at least every 20 minutes.[4]

Learning about the needs, concerns, priorities, and learning styles of your audience members is a critical first step for an effective presentation.
Monkey Business Images/Shutterstock

Latisha can plan a presentation that appeals to all types of learners. She can use a variety of images and diagrams to appeal to visual learners, speak with energy and conviction to appeal to auditory learners, and provide handouts for participants to fill out to appeal to kinesthetic learners.

What Information Do I Need to Gather?   As you ask questions about your audience, you'll naturally create of list of information you need. As with other types of messages, make sure to also create a list of research questions that helps you develop the content of your presentation. As mentioned in the opening case to this chapter, Latisha spent about six weeks gathering information about annual performance reviews versus continuous reviews.

Develop Your Message

As with written reports, successful presentations rely on well-developed takeaway messages, supporting information, and structure. You'll get lots of advice during your career about how to deliver a successful presentation. Much of this advice is good because delivery is important. However, developing your content is still the most critical factor in presentation success, so prepare your content before you spend too much time on your delivery.[5]

Identify a Few Takeaway Messages   Your first task is to identify the two or three key messages you want to convey. Once you've developed these key messages, everything in the presentation should lead back to them.[6] Particularly for presenting to busy executives, summarize your key takeaway messages at the outset and reemphasize them several times.[7]

Overall, your presentation will be most effective if you focus on how your key messages relate to the common interests of your audience. At the same time, be cautious about trying to please everyone. Some presenters broaden their messages in an attempt to appeal to everyone in the audience. This approach is risky, however, since broadening the message so much may dilute its impact and power.[8]

In Latisha's case, she frames her message in the following way: Continuous reviews increase employee engagement. She has a few key takeaway messages to support this idea: Continuous reviews provide more accurate and more motivating feedback; continuous reviews make managers' jobs easier; and continuous reviews are relatively inexpensive.

Structure Your Presentation with a Clear Preview, View, and Review   Most audience members expect your presentation to include a **preview**, view, and review (analogous to the introduction, body, and conclusion in written documents). Typically, your preview occupies roughly 10 to 15 percent of your presentation time, your view takes up the vast majority (85 to 90 percent) of your time, and the review takes up the least time (5 percent).

Provide a Compelling Preview

The beginnings of your presentations and speeches are critical. Audience members who do not know you well often form quick impressions about you and your message. Even people who know you fairly well generally decide quickly if your message is important to them. Dana LaMon, who lost his sight at the age of four but went on to achieve a highly successful career as a judge and professional speaker, suggests that audiences make up their minds in the first minute or two of the presentation:

> As an administrative law judge for 26 years, I have heard and written decisions in about 6,400 cases. My unscientific estimate is that in about 95 percent of them, I knew what I would decide before the hearing was over. After 19 years in Toastmasters and 16 years as a professional speaker, I have learned that the audience, too, will make quick decisions. They will judge a speaker and his or her speech well before the presentation is done. That is why I have come to believe that the most important part of my speech is the opening.[9]

Components of Presentations

- Preview (10–15 percent of time)
  - Attention-getter
  - Positioning statement
  - Overview: Takeaway messages
- View (85–90 percent of time)
  - Takeaway message #1
  - Takeaway message #2
  - Takeaway message #3
- Review (5 percent of time)
  - Recap
  - Call to action

LO14.3   Organize and gather content for a preview, view, and review.

Visit http://connect. mheducation.com for an exercise on this topic.

In other words, during that first few minutes, audience members have their answers to the following questions: Am I going to listen? Am I going to benefit from what is said? Will it be valuable enough to take with me? Am I going to act on what I hear?

The *preview* should generally include an attention-getter, a positioning statement, and an overview. The preview should accomplish the following: create interest, show benefits, demonstrate value, and encourage action (all related to the four questions in the prior paragraph).

Choose an Effective Attention-Getter   In research among executives, the factors most likely to attract their attention were the following: The message was personalized, it evoked an emotional response, it came from a trustworthy source, and it was concise. In particular, personalized and emotion-evoking attention-getters led executives to pay close attention to presentations more than twice as often.[10]

Stephen Denning, one of the world's foremost authorities on leadership communication, spent decades working for the World Bank. While leading World Bank initiatives and meeting leaders throughout the world, he learned that influence in presentations depends heavily on first garnering attention. He explained:

> Successful leaders communicate very differently from the traditional, abstract approach to communication. In all kinds of settings, they communicate by following a hidden pattern: first, they get attention. Then they stimulate desire, and only then do they reinforce with reasons.[11]

The primary goals of attention-getters are to get your audience members emotionally invested in your presentation and engaged in thinking about your ideas. Table 14.1 focuses on seven types of attention-getters that Latisha could use in her presentation: rhetorical questions, vivid examples, dramatic demonstrations, testimonials or quotations, intriguing statistics, unexpected exercises, and challenges. This is not a comprehensive list; however, these strategies are among the most effective.[12] Think about how you might use each option in a presentation.

People enjoy humor in presentations. Generally, however, avoid opening with jokes. Few people do well when they open with jokes. Communication specialist Nick Morgan explains:

> You need to start with something clever enough to catch everyone's attention, but you're at your most nervous, and thus it's hard to shine like you want to. So how to get started? The traditional advice—still followed by many business speakers—is to begin with a joke. . . . For everyone except the professional comedian, this is bad counsel indeed. You're at your worst in terms of nerves. Don't compound the problem by setting for yourself one of the most difficult public speaking chores of all right off the bat: Delivering a punch line with brilliant comic timing. It's extremely difficult to do under the best of circumstances—even for seasoned professionals.[13]

Even if you're one of the rare breed of people who can consistently pull them off, opening jokes may have unintended consequences. Audience members may remember your jokes more than your key messages, so if you choose a humorous opening, tie it to your key messages.

Starting with an overwhelming set of facts and numbers or telling the story of your company may not be particularly effective either. If you choose to give background on your company, do so concisely, and make sure you connect the story of your company to the needs of your audience.[14]

Creating a Positioning Statement   A **positioning statement** frames your message in appealing terms to your audience members and demonstrates clear and valuable benefits to them. The positioning statement should be as concise as possible—ideally one to two sentences. With the attention-getter, you engage and capture interest. With the positioning statement, you demonstrate that your presentation is worth paying close attention to for its entirety.

TABLE 14.1

Types of Effective Attention-Getters

Attention-Getter	Example
Rhetorical question	Have any of you ever thought your performance review wasn't fair? Or, have you ever dreaded delivering a performance review? As we started looking at research about annual reviews, we found that most employees *and* managers don't think annual reviews improve performance.
	This attention-getter immediately evokes thinking about personal experiences for audience members. It focuses on an unmet need (using performance reviews to improve performance). It is also concise: It takes roughly 20 seconds to deliver (42 words).
Vivid example	We held two focus groups with employees about their views of annual reviews. Right at the start of the first focus group, one of the employees whom everyone recognizes as devoted, reliable, and friendly, simply said, "The reviews don't help us at all." Every person in the group nodded their heads. Nearly every comment I heard from employees came back to this simple theme: Annual reviews don't help the employees perform better, be more motivated, or be more invested in their work.
	This example captures the attention of the audience with its vivid, story-based description of what employees really think. Many audience members would take this example seriously. This example would take roughly 30 to 35 seconds to deliver (82 words).
Dramatic demonstration	(Live demo of the software) Some of you are probably wondering what makes continuous reviews possible. We can do it with a variety of software platforms. If you look at the screen, I'm going to take two to three minutes to demo how the platform works. You'll see how employees get immediate, helpful, and accurate feedback . . .
	This attention-getter gives the audience a tangible sense of how the platform can produce continuous, helpful feedback. This demonstration is delivered in a few minutes. Latisha should be prepared to demonstrate the technology rapidly or she'll lose the interest of audience members.
Testimonial or quotation	Managers at many companies say transitioning to continuous reviews has dramatically improved performance and morale. I talked to three HR directors who started using continuous review systems in the past few years. Janna Leahy, the HR director at Peakster Computing, told me that the company has increased billable hours in the consulting division by 35 percent. She attributes this to the coaching and motivating environment of continuous reviews. She said continuous reviews create an "enjoyable culture of performance."
	This short statement focuses on the testimonial of an HR manager who implemented a similar solution. The statement emphasizes a dramatic rise in profitability, which appeals to senior managers emotionally and rationally. It would take just 30 seconds to deliver (77 words). Ideally, a compelling video testimonial would be provided as well.
Intriguing statistic	It's no secret that employees don't think annual reviews are accurate indicators of their performance. In fact, roughly 50 to 75 percent of employees say this in various surveys. But, did you know that nearly 50 percent of HR managers don't even think annual reviews are accurate?
	This attention-getter focuses on a compelling but likely expected statistic about employees (50 to 75 percent don't think annual reviews are accurate indicators of their performance) and an unexpected statistic about HR managers (nearly 50 percent of HR managers don't even think annual reviews are accurate). These statistics rapidly create the message that annual reviews aren't considered reliable by all parties involved—the employees who receive them or managers who administer them. This concise statement takes roughly 20 seconds to deliver (47 words).
Unexpected exercise	As we get started, I'd like each of you to answer two questions with the person sitting next to you. First, ask your partner, "What was the worst experience you've had getting a performance review?" Then ask, "What was the best experience you've had getting a performance review?"
	This quick exercise gets participants talking right away about topics that are central to the presentation: performance, motivation, and management. This exercise may also get participants to open up and relax. Another benefit for Latisha is she can now adapt her presentation to the needs of her audience more effectively. This is a great approach for kinesthetic learners.

TABLE 14.1

(*Continued*)

Attention-Getter	Example
Challenge	Today I'm going to talk about transitioning from annual reviews to continuous reviews. I'm going to show you some new tools to provide feedback and coaching on a daily basis. Once I explain the tools, I'm going ask each of you to describe how you think this would impact your teams. This is a direct challenge to audience members to conceptualize and envision how the tools apply to their own teams. This approach will help many of the audience members become more engaged and active during the presentation. This is a concise opening at just 20 seconds or so (51 words).

In Latisha's case, she selects the following positioning statement: "Today I'm going to discuss how continuous reviews can significantly increase employee engagement. I'm also going to share our plan to implement continuous reviews throughout the company by January 2020." This positioning statement speaks directly to the needs of the senior managers. It employs positive and upbeat language.

Providing an Overview Statement   The final part of the preview is the overview. Ideally, you can state your overview in one to three sentences in simple, conversational language. Immediately after Latisha makes her positioning statement, she provides an overview: "We'll discuss how continuous reviews provide more accurate and more motivating feedback; how continuous reviews make managers' jobs easier; and how continuous reviews are relatively inexpensive." This overview segments the presentation in terms of three key benefits or takeaway messages. These benefits are easy to remember and help audience members think about the benefits to their units within the company.

Justify Your Views

The majority of your presentation will be devoted to expressing and supporting your **views**—your two, three, or four key messages. Recognize that many of your audience members are skeptical. After all, you will likely be asking them to commit to your products, services, or ideas at the expense of their time, money, or other resources. In other words, you are generally asking people to take some type of professional and/or personal risk. Make sure you can back up your main positions with strong support material, including specific cases or examples, stories and illustrations, analogies, statistics and facts, quotations, or your own professional experiences.[15]

Use support materials in moderation, however. You can easily overwhelm your audience. Furthermore, most audience members prefer certain types of supporting material during presentations. For example, personalized case studies are more likely to influence audience members than statistics. At the same time, avoid any weak evidence, since that will undermine your case, and be prepared with additional support material if audience members request it.[16] Furthermore, gain a sense of your audience members' preferences. For example, professionals with green MVSs are typically more influenced by quantitative information whereas professionals with blue MVSs are typically more influenced by personal experiences.

Executive communication coach Roly Grimshaw observes that the most serious mistake business managers make is to present the evidence (numbers, statistics, facts) first, or only the evidence, and leave out their primary conclusions or central positions.[17] A

Components of PREP Method

- Position
- Reasons
- Example
- Position

TABLE 14.2

The PREP Method

	Sample Statements
Step 1: **Position**	With annual reviews, our employees often get feedback when it's too late to make any changes. With continuous reviews from managers and peers, our employees will receive constant feedback—positive and negative—that will help them improve their performance right away.
Step 2: **Reasons**	Many HR professionals in recent years have found that the timing of feedback, the amount of positive feedback, and feedback from a variety of colleagues all contribute to better performance.
Step 3: **Example**	Let me give you a quick example at Peakster Computing. Janna Leahy, the HR director, estimated that productivity increased by 15 to 20 percent because of continuous reviews. After using continuous reviews for one year, Janna conducted a complete evaluation of the types of feedback that employees received. Here's what she found.
	First, employees said that feedback was "actionable." Before implementing continual reviews, employee surveys showed that only 23 percent of employees agreed with the statement *I've improved my performance due to performance reviews*. After a year of continuous reviews, employee surveys showed that 92 percent of employees agreed with the statement *I've improved my performance due to continuous reviews*. Clearly, the employees see value in this feedback.
	Janna estimates that employees now receive approximately 12 times more feedback throughout the course of a year! Of this feedback, roughly 80 percent is positive feedback and roughly 20 percent is negative or suggestion-based. She thinks that the positive feedback serves as motivation and confirmation of employee strengths. One concern many people have of continual feedback is that colleagues won't be candid about suggestions for one another's improvement. Janna has found this simply isn't the case. It's true most comments are positive. But, employees at her company regularly give tough love to each other. Janna estimates that the average employee last year received 31 clear recommendations about how to improve performance from fellow managers and employees. Now, compare that to an annual review from a single manager's viewpoint where an employee might get 5 to 6 suggestions.
	Finally, the amount of positive and negative feedback makes a huge difference. Janna estimates that employees now receive approximately 55 times more feedback throughout the course of a year! Of this feedback, roughly 80 percent is positive feedback and roughly 20 percent is negative or suggestion-based. She thinks that the positive feedback serves as motivation and confirmation of employee strengths.
	One concern many people have of continual feedback is that colleagues won't be candid about suggestions for one another's improvement. Janna has found this simply isn't the case. It's true most comments are positive. But, employees at her company regularly give tough love to each other. Janna estimates that the average employee last year received 22 clear recommendations about how to improve performance from fellow managers and employees. Now, compare that to an annual review from a single manager's viewpoint where an employee might get three to four suggestions.
Step 4: **Position**	So, we anticipate the same results here at Eastmond. Continuous reviews will ensure each employee gets more constructive feedback more often. We expect this helpful feedback will increase the performance level of our employees.

more successful approach is the **PREP method**, which involves stating your *position,* providing the *reasons,* giving an *example* or providing evidence, and then restating your *position*.[18] Table 14.2 provides an instance of the PREP method from Latisha's presentation. As you read through this example, think about what Latisha gains from starting and ending with her position.

Conclude with an Effective Review

The **review** comprises a small percentage of your presentation time. However, make sure to have a strong finish—this is the place where you are hoping to gain buy-in on specific actions. First, you will recap your message in just a few sentences. Then, you'll provide a call to action, where you'll ask the audience members to make specific commitments. For example, Latisha ends with the following call to action: "Thank you for your time and thoughts today. Jeff and I want to continue getting your feedback as we select a software vendor and start the pilot phase. We'll send updates and requests for feedback every few weeks. Please feel free to contact us with more of your ideas about making continuous reviews work effectively." This call to action is polite and sincere. It shows genuine interest in getting the input of others.

LO14.4 Develop effective slide presentations.

Mc Graw Hill connect

Visit http://connect. mheducation.com for an exercise on this topic.

Design Appealing Slides

Businesspeople frequently use PowerPoint or other electronic slide presentations as visual aids for their presentations (see the Technology Tips feature for alternatives to PowerPoint). The reason for doing so is compelling. Good visuals can increase communication effectiveness and persuasiveness by about 50 percent.[19] After all, about 75 percent of what people learn comes visually; 12 percent through hearing; and 12 percent through smell, taste, and touch.[20]

However, poorly designed or poorly selected visuals can actually detract from presentation effectiveness.[21] While the use of electronic slides is often effective and nearly ubiquitous for business presentations, take caution. People in the workplace sometimes mock poor electronic slide presentations as *suffering death by PowerPoint*. Consider some of the comments in Figure 14.1 from business leaders.[22]

While well-designed electronic slide presentations can dramatically increase audience learning, poorly designed ones can draw intense negative reactions, as evidenced by the quotations in Figure 14.1. Make sure your electronic slide presentations aid rather than detract from your presentation objectives. Consider the following advice as you design your slides:

You Are the Focus of Your Presentation

From the beginning of the design process, resist the urge to make your slides the primary focal point; they are just an aid. Ideally, audience members will focus their eyes on you for the majority of the presentation. Consider the comments of Judith Humphrey, a prominent executive trainer:

> Great leaders understand that they are the best visual. They instinctively know that their message will come through best if the audience looks at them and listens to them—with no distractions. Audiences that divide their attention will only be able to partially commit to you. PowerPoint slides are usually a dumbed-down version of the narrative script you are delivering. Visuals rely on bullet points; you speak in full sentences, with illustrations and stories. Slides are dispassionate; your voice and gestures provide passion and emphasis. So in deflecting the audience's attention away from you to the bullet points, you're reducing the quality of your material and its impact on the audience.[23]

Create a Storyboard with Your PowerPoint Slide Titles

Make sure that your presentations *tell a story* to your audience. To check whether your slides provide a flowing narrative rather than a disjointed set of ideas, line up your slide titles (see Table 14.3). Ask yourself whether the slide titles move naturally through the narrative of your presentation.[24]

Latisha sets up her slides in a pattern that is solution-oriented. The order of these slides includes the elements of a classic narrative of persuasion: attention, need and solution, rationale, counterpoints, and call to action (see Chapter 10). Also, notice how the slides position Latisha to tell the story of continuous reviews. Stories contain

FIGURE 14.1

Avoiding Death by
PowerPoint

I actively despise how people use PowerPoint as a crutch. I think PowerPoint can be a way to cover up sloppy thinking, which makes it hard to differentiate between good ideas and bad ideas. I would much rather have somebody write something longhand, send it in ahead of the meeting and then assume everybody's read it, and then you start talking, and let them defend it. The question from the beginning of the meeting to the end of the meeting is, "Have we added value: yes or no?" And I would say that if the meeting is mostly the presentation of a deck of PowerPoint slides, you conveyed information, but you didn't actually add value.

—Cristóbal Conde, former CEO of SunGard

I prefer that people not go through a slide deck. If you're working in an area, and you are running a business, you ought to be able to stand up there and tell me about your business without referring to a big slide deck. When you are speaking, people should focus on you and focus on the message. They can't walk away remembering a whole bunch of different things, so you have to have three or four really key messages that you take them through, and you remind them of what's important.

—James J. Schiro, director at PepsiCo

Death by PowerPoint occurs because of the bullet trap. Speakers and presenters often reduce their presentations to series of bullets and thoughts in outline form. As a result, they often bore their audiences and lose connection with their audiences.

—Ellen Finkelstein, communication specialist

TABLE 14.3

Setting Up Slide Titles to Help You Make a Smooth, Logical Presentation

Slide #	Title	Story Line
1	Improving Employee Engagement: Transitioning to Continuous Reviews and Recognition	*Positive overarching theme in the title slide:* higher employee engagement
2	Benefits of Employee Engagement	*Attention:* shows the benefits of increasing employee engagement
3	Problems with Annual Reviews	*Need:* shows how the current approach of annual reviews does not improve employee engagement
4	Our Employees' Views of Annual Reviews	*Need:* shows current disenchantment with annual reviews at this company
5	Benefits of Continuous Reviews	*Solution:* shows how continuous review systems overcome the problems of annual reviews and increase employee engagement
6	Our Employees' Views of Continuous Reviews	*Solution:* shows how continuous review systems have support from the employees
7	Positive, Helpful, and Candid Feedback	*Rationale/counterpoints:* describes the nature of feedback; addresses concerns that a new system won't promote candid feedback
8	Ease of Use for Managers	*Rationale/counterpoints:* describes how the system gets buy-in from managers; addresses concerns that a new system won't get support from managers
9	Cost-Effectiveness	*Rationale/counterpoints:* describes the costs of a system; addresses concerns that a new system costs too much
10	Proposed Implementation	*Call to action:* uses a timeline to identify implementation

answers to the questions *who? what? when? where?* and *why?* Latisha will engage her audience with responses to all these types of questions.

Setting out the titles in this storyboard approach helps you see which slides you really need. A common misperception of electronic slide presentations is that more is better. In fact, using fewer slides can help you tell the story more effectively. As one recruiter in a recent *Wall Street Journal* study stated, "Students seem to think a better grade is assigned based on the number of slides in a presentation. In real life, you have 10 minutes to present to management. If you can't get the whole story in that time on two or three slides, you're dead in your career."[25]

In Latisha's presentation (see Figure 14.2), she uses a total of ten slides—one slide for every two minutes or so of her 20-minute presentation. As a rule, avoid showing more than one slide for every minute to two minutes of a presentation.

Design Your Slides for Ease of Processing In relation to speeches and presentations, you have likely heard of the KISS method: *Keep it simple, stupid.* Creating simple presentations is a good strategy. However, a more overarching and effective strategy is to focus on ease of processing. Your goal is to take your often complex data, relationships, and ideas and illustrate and depict them in easy-to-learn ways. Consider the following approaches to facilitate ease of processing:[26]

- *Limit the amount of information on any given slide.* Readers should be able to grasp the content within 10 to 15 seconds. For text, rarely should you use more than ten words per line and more than five to six lines.
- *Use font sizes that all audience members can read easily.* For titles, use at least 24-point fonts; for body text, use at least 18-point fonts.
- *Focus on and highlight key information.* Use bold, italics, and other formatting features to make key phrases or key components in figures stand out.
- *Use plenty of white space.* White space is effective for borders and between items and text on slides; it provides an uncluttered appearance.
- *Use high-contrast backgrounds and colors.* Make sure backgrounds do not obscure text. For dark text, use light backgrounds. For light text, use dark backgrounds.
- *Use compelling images in moderation.* One of the basic reasons to use electronic slide presentations in the first place is to display images. You can use these images to convey powerful messages efficiently and with emotional power, especially for the visual learners in your audience. But make sure you are selective. Too many pictures, poor-quality pictures, or off-message pictures may detract from your message.
- *Develop simple charts and diagrams.* Charts and diagrams can be particularly helpful for simplifying complex data relationships. Make sure to use charts and figures that the audience can process in a matter of seconds. Otherwise, they have to spend an excessive amount of time trying to understand the chart or diagram and they're not paying attention to you. In some cases, they may give up and become annoyed.
- *Get professional design help when possible.* For high-stakes presentations, consider getting help from public relations or design specialists. If you are part of a large organization, you can often get this help internally. In many cases, well-designed templates may already exist. For smaller organizations, you may need to hire outside help.

Notice in Figure 14.3 how some of these principles are applied to the PREP example found in Table 14.2.

To this point, most of the tips are based on the creation of PowerPoint slides (PowerPoint is clearly the most used slide software). However, you have many other options (see the Technology Tip).

FIGURE 14.2

Less Effective and More Effective Slides for Presentation

Less Effective Slide #1

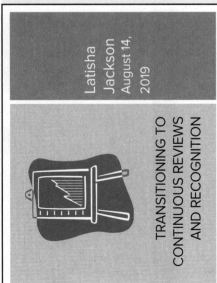

TRANSITIONING TO
CONTINUOUS REVIEWS
AND RECOGNITION

Latisha
Jackson
August 14,
2019

Key message
does not
stand out
clearly; most
prominent
text is the
presenter's
name.

Clip art on
title slide
does not
convey
professional
image.

Less Effective Slide #2

Research about Employee Engagement

- A 2013 meta-analysis of 263 studies of engagement
  involving 1.3 million employees found the following:
  - 47% fewer safety accidents
  - 21% higher productivity
  - 22% higher profitability
  - 41% higher quality
  - 37% reduced absenteeism

Source: Cameron, Yvette. (2013 December). *Social employee recognition
systems reward the business with results.* Stamford, CT: Gartner.

The key
messages of
this slide take
too long to
process
because of
cluttered text,
too much text
at the beginning
of the slide, and
too many
statistics.

More Effective Slide #1

Improving Employee Engagement
Transitioning to Continuous Reviews and Recognition

Latisha Jackson | HR Intern | August 14, 2019

Key message
(improving
employee
engagement
with continuous
reviews) stands
out clearly.

A professional
photograph
reinforces the
theme of
employee
engagement.

Digitalskillet/iSock/Getty Images

More Effective Slide #2

Benefits of Employee Engagement

- **21% higher productivity**
- **22% higher profitability**
- **37% reduced absenteeism**

Source and note: Cameron, Yvette. (2013 December). *Social employee
recognition systems reward the business with results.* Stamford, CT: Gartner.
These figures are based on the top quartile of employees in a 2013 *meta-analysis
of 263 studies involving 1.3 million employees.*

These statistics
tell the story of
benefits of
employee
engagement.
Most audience
members would
understand
these statistics
within seconds.
Because the
slide is so easy
to process, it
does not
distract
attention from
the presenter.

453

FIGURE 14.2

(Continued)

Less Effective Slide #3

Problems with Annual Reviews

- Most employees think annual reviews are not accurate.
- Most employees think the feedback is too late to make changes.
- Most employees think annual reviews feel like punishment.

Without any special formatting, audience members must work too hard to read each sentence. This will draw attention away from the presenter.

Less Effective Slide #4

Results of Our Employee Survey

Annual reviews are . . .	Strongly Disagree	Disagree	Neutral	Agree	Strongly Agree
accurate indicators of my performance.	12.6%	30.0%	14.8%	26.9%	15.7%
a productive experience.	21.5%	37.2%	9.4%	22.0%	9.9%
a forward-looking process.	21.1%	28.3%	14.3%	23.8%	12.6%
good recognition of my achievements.	25.6%	26.5%	19.3%	20.6%	8.1%
helpful in my career development.	18.4%	35.0%	10.8%	23.8%	12.1%
motivating.	22.9%	43.9%	12.6%	15.7%	4.9%

This table is accurate but difficult for audience members to process quickly. This much information would likely distract attention from the presenter.

More Effective Slide #3

Problems with Annual Reviews

- **Fairness:** most employees think annual reviews are not accurate.
- **Motivation:** most employees think the feedback is too late to make changes.
- **Morale:** most employees think annual reviews feel like punishment.

Key problems with annual reviews are recognizable within seconds.

The picture accentuates the message that annual reviews are dissatisfying to employees.

More Effective Slide #4

Our Employees' Views of Annual Reviews

Annual reviews are . . .

accurate indicators of my performance.	43%
helpful in my career development.	36%
a forward-looking process.	32%
a productive experience.	32%
good recognition of my achievements.	29%
motivating.	21%

Note: Percentages refer to number of employees who stated "agree" or "strongly agree" on our July 2019 survey of 223 Eastmond employees.

This chart is easier to process because it contains condensed information without sacrificing accuracy.

Racorn/123RF

FIGURE 14.2

(Continued)

Less Effective Slide #5

Continuous Reviews

- Peers and managers give daily feedback and recognition.
- Feedback and praise can be private or public.
- Features to improve rewards and recognition programs.
- Features for goal development and tracking.

Complete sentences without any special formatting require too much work for audience members.

Less Effective Slide #6

What Our Employees Are Saying

For performance reviews, I prefer . . .	Strongly Disagree	Disagree	Neutral	Agree	Strongly Agree
frequent feedback.	4.9%	14.3%	16.1%	40.8%	23.8%
more feedback from my supervisors.	7.2%	16.6%	17.0%	37.7%	21.5%
more feedback from my peers.	5.8%	8.1%	11.7%	46.6%	27.8%
more recognition from my supervisors.	3.1%	4.0%	6.3%	38.6%	48.0%
more recognition from my peers.	4.0%	6.3%	10.3%	35.4%	43.9%
crowdsourced input on my evaluations.	3.6%	9.4%	17.5%	43.9%	25.6%
more coaching from my supervisors.	4.0%	5.4%	9.4%	35.0%	46.2%
more coaching from my peers.	4.9%	4.9%	18.8%	36.3%	35.0%

This table provides far too much information for audience members to process. If the presenter wants the audience to see all this information, he or she can do it with a handout.

More Effective Slide #5

Benefits of Continuous Reviews

- **Multisource:** Peers and managers give daily feedback and recognition.
- **Private and public options:** Feedback and praise can be private or public.
- **Frequent recognition:** Features to improve rewards and recognition programs.
- **Goal-oriented:** Features for goal development and tracking.

Bolded keywords and phrases allow audience members to rapidly understand the key benefits.

Ariel Skelley/Getty Images

More Effective Slide #6

Our Employees' Views of Continuous Reviews

For performance reviews, I prefer . . .

more recognition from my supervisors. 87%
more coaching from my supervisors. 81%
more recognition from my peers. 79%
more feedback from my peers. 74%
more coaching from my peers. 71%
crowdsourced input on my evaluations. 70%

Note: Percentages refer to number of employees who stated "agree" or "strongly agree" on our July 2019 survey of 223 Eastmond employees.

This chart captures the key ideas from the survey fairly concisely. It still contains a lot of information, so the presenter needs to take time on this slide, put the information in context, and provide interesting commentary.

FIGURE 14.2

(Continued)

Less Effective Slide #7

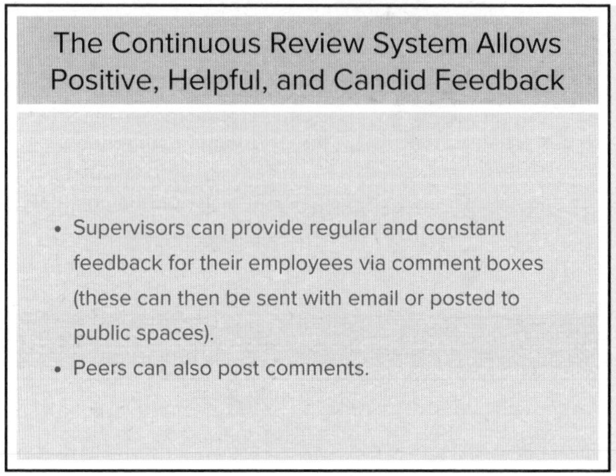

The Continuous Review System Allows Positive, Helpful, and Candid Feedback

- Supervisors can provide regular and constant feedback for their employees via comment boxes (these can then be sent with email or posted to public spaces).
- Peers can also post comments.

This slide contains far too much text. By this point in the presentation, audience members are tiring. Typically, the slides need to get simpler near the end of the presentation.

Less Effective Slide #8

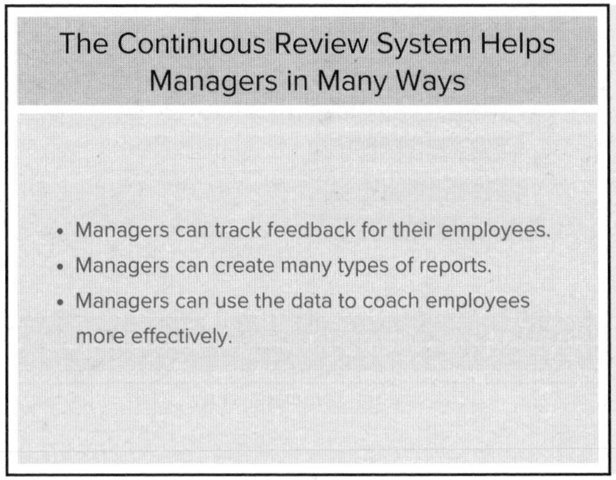

The Continuous Review System Helps Managers in Many Ways

- Managers can track feedback for their employees.
- Managers can create many types of reports.
- Managers can use the data to coach employees more effectively.

This slide contains far too much text. Audience members are getting more tired from trying to process this much text over the course of many slides.

More Effective Slide #7

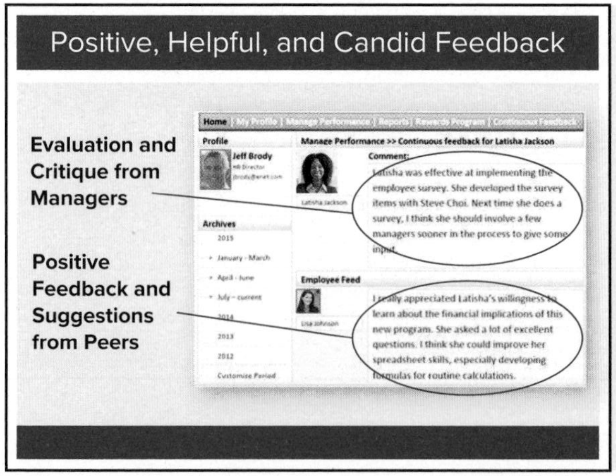

Positive, Helpful, and Candid Feedback

Evaluation and Critique from Managers

Positive Feedback and Suggestions from Peers

This slide is essentially a mock-up of the continuous review software. It allows audience members to visualize how the system works. It also positions the presenter to explain various functions depicted in the picture.

More Effective Slide #8

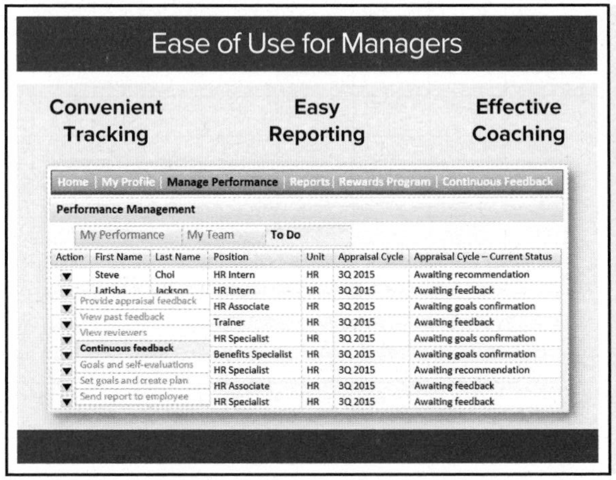

Ease of Use for Managers

Convenient Tracking   Easy Reporting   Effective Coaching

This slide provides simple statements about functions of the software. This positions the presenter to take center stage describing how managers accomplish these objectives.

Dougal Waters/Digital Vision/Getty Images; LWA/Larry Williams/Blend Images LLC; Polka Dot Images/Jupiterimages/Getty Images

FIGURE 14.2

(Continued)

Less Effective Slide #9

Costs of a Continuous Review System

- $10 to $20 per month per user (determined by the number of employees).
- Annual software administration fees of $1,600 to $2,100.
- Other indirect costs of around $2,000.
- Final costs will depend on the vendor we choose.

This slide provides a lot of data but almost no meaning or appropriate frame of reference. It mixes monthly and annual figures. It does not contain any summary totals to provide audience members with perspective.

More Effective Slide #9

Cost-Effectiveness (Annual Figures)

Item	Amount*
Software user costs	$2,750 to $5,500
Software administration fees	$1,600 to $2,100
Other indirect costs	$1,000 to $2,000
TOTAL	**$5,350 to $9,600**

*Variation in costs depend on the software vendoe we choose.

This slide includes summary totals on an annual basis. This provides decision makers with valuable and easy-to-process information.

Less Effective Slide #10

Implementation

- Phase I (August to September 2017)
  - Vendor selection
- Phase II (October to December 2017)
  - Pilot in the HR department
- Phase III (December 2015)
  - Companywide training
- Phase IV (January 2016)
  - Companywide adoption
- All activities conducted by HR department

This slide contains slightly too much text. It presents the timeline and related activities in vertical format. Most people can process timeline information more easily in a horizontal format.

More Effective Slide #10

Proposed Implementation

Time Frame	Activities
Aug to Sept 2019	Vendor selection
Oct to Dec 2019	Pilot in the HR dept
Dec 2019	Companywide training
Jan 2020	Companywide adoption

This slide allows readers to rapidly recognize key time frames and related activities.

Figure 14.3

Less Effective and More Effective Slides for a Presentation about Performance Reviews

Less Effective Slide #11

Our employees HATE annual performance reviews. By the time they receive the reviews, it's simply too late to make any significant changes.

This intro slide requires too much time to read. While it's a relatable point, an image in this case can much more powerfully show the exasperation of an employee.

Less Effective Comparison Slide #1

Study at Peakster Computing (according to Janna Leahy, HR Director)

- Each year, Janna conducted satisfaction surveys of employees.
- In the final year of annual reviews (2019), Janna said employee surveys showed that only 23 percent of employees agreed with the statement "I've improved my performance due to performance reviews."
- After a year of continuous reviews, employee surveys showed that 92 percent of employees agreed with the statement "I've improved my performance due to continuous reviews."

This slide relies on far too much text. The worst aspect of the slide is it doesn't make the clear distinctions between performance reviews and continuous reviews immediately apparent.

More Effective Slide #11

This intro slide uses a powerful image to show the exasperation of an employee. It invokes an emotional reaction and positions the presenter to fill in the exasperation many employees feel after an annual review.

More Effective Comparison Slide #1

With Annual Reviews (2019):

23% Say Feedback Is "Actionable"

With Continuous Reviews (2020):

92% Say Feedback Is "Actionable"

Source: Janna Leahy @ Peakster Computing

This slide—while relying only on text and an arrow—immediately shows the contrast between performance reviews and continuous reviews. It is a memorable distinction.

Antonio Guillem/Shutterstock

FIGURE 14.3

(Continued)

Less Effective Comparison Slide #1

Feedback Levels before and after the Implementation of the New Performance Review System

- Before the continuous review system was implemented, Janna estimates that most employees received documented feedback from one person and on rare occasions two people per year. This feedback was almost entirely from managers.

- With the new continuous review system, employees get feedback from an average of 15 colleagues per year.

The headline of this slide is neutral. The compelling distinctions are buried in the bulleted text. Many viewers will miss the strength of this contrast.

Less Effective Comparison Slide #2

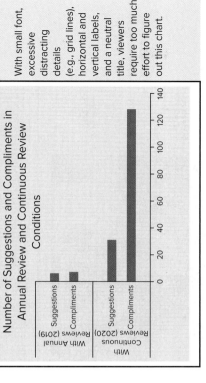

Number of Suggestions and Compliments in Annual Review and Continuous Review Conditions

With small font, excessive distracting details (e.g., grid lines), horizontal and vertical labels, and a neutral title, viewers require too much effort to figure out this chart.

More Effective Comparison Slide #1

Employees Hear from More People with Continuous Reviews (Annual Totals)

Annual Reviews

Continuous Reviews

The headline is clear about the impacts of continuous reviews. The visual element allows viewers to rapidly—within 1 to 2 seconds—grasp the dramatic difference in how many people employees get formal feedback from.

Source: Janna Leahy @ Peakster Computing

More Effective Comparison Slide #2

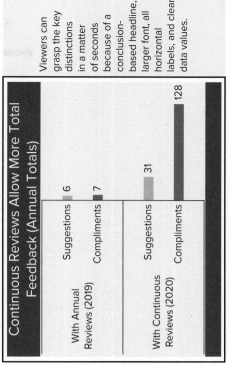

Continuous Reviews Allow More Total Feedback (Annual Totals)

With Annual Reviews (2019)
Suggestions 6
Compliments 7

With Continuous Reviews (2020)
Suggestions 31
Compliments 128

Viewers can grasp the key distinctions in a matter of seconds because of a conclusion-based headline, larger font, all horizontal labels, and clear data values.

FIGURE 14.3

(Continued)

Less Effective Concluding Slide

Ggstockstudio/123RF

The presenter has a good idea to conclude with a picture but misses an opportunity to emphasize the key impacts.

More Effective Concluding Slide

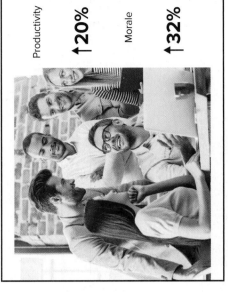

Ggstockstudio/123RF

Productivity

↑**20%**

Morale

↑**32%**

The picture highlights a more productive and enjoyable work environment, *and* the figures show rapidly show concrete results.

Technology Tips

ALTERNATIVES TO POWERPOINT

In many work environments, PowerPoint slides have become the standard visual aid for presentations and meetings. Even if you're great at using them, you might consider other types of visual aids and props to add impact, creativity, or simply variety to your presentations.

Try other electronic slide and presentation software. Consider trying Apple Keynote, Prezi, Google Slides, Canva, Zoho Show, Haiku Deck, or other software packages to see what you're most comfortable with. Many presenters find that presentation software such as Prezi does not box them into bullet-point-based, linear presentations and provides more flexibility.

Use smartboards, whiteboards, or chalkboards. The act of writing as you go with keyboards, markers, or chalk may allow you to engage your audience more effectively because you are presenting in the moment, avoiding the structure or order of electronic slides, and getting input from your audience as you go. Furthermore, you may find that drawing objects freehand allows you to depict ideas more accurately and forcefully than you can with the drawing tools in PowerPoint. Still, make sure you avoid spending too much time facing away from the audience.

Experiment with new presentation technologies. Hundreds of new and emerging presentation technologies are *social*. In other words, they allow you to get information and feedback from your audience that you can incorporate into your presentation. By experimenting with these technologies, you'll learn to tap into the incoming messages while also controlling your message or the conversation.

Your challenge: Take a slide deck you've already produced in PowerPoint and then convert it to two other presentation software programs. Try out the features of these other programs. Then, try out the presentation without slides but with a white board. What did you learn as you tried out these new tools and approaches?

Stockbyte/Getty Images

Applying the Story Line Approach to Your Presentations

Earlier in this chapter, you learned about the PREP method of providing rich examples to support your positions. You also learned that you should create electronic slides with a story line approach. This section explains how you can apply a story line approach to your entire presentation and enhance your ability to connect with and influence others.

The story line approach is useful for various types of presentations because it allows your listeners to engage on a deeper level emotionally and intellectually. Emotionally, they often feel a bond with you as a speaker. Furthermore, they tend to internalize stories, even developing their own parallel stories that evoke commitment, determination, sympathy, and other emotions. However, stories are far more than emotional tools. Research shows that people remember stories more easily than they do abstract information, and they are more likely to act on what they hear via stories.[27]

When James E. Rogers, president and CEO of Duke Energy, was asked "What would you like business schools to teach more of, or less of?" he had this to say:

> What I would really teach is how to write, and how to speak and make presentations. I've overused this term in this conversation, but *it's the ability to pull the salient facts together and tell a story, so that people feel it, sense it, they're convinced by it, and want to do something because of it.*

LO14.5 Use the story line approach to presentations.

Visit http://connect.mheducation.com for an exercise on this topic.

My first full-time job, I worked at night as a newspaper reporter, going to school during the day. So, I really started out covering police news, and then federal courts and political news. And I really kind of developed a sense of the importance of trying to find the essence of the story and trying to arrange the facts in some chronology to make sense out of it. In a sense, as a CEO, part of my job is not only to help develop direction but to teach the story-telling. Those early years as a reporter gave me a sense of that in terms of how to tell the story, how to communicate.[28]

Rogers is not the only business professional who emphasizes storytelling. Jathan Janove, who did extensive HR training about sexual harassment in the early to mid-1990s, described his transition to storytelling for presentations. Penalties to employers and employees had increased substantially, and his job was to explain new laws governing appropriate behavior. As he lectured employees, he found that they often resented the perceived intrusiveness of the new laws and the fear tactics of describing harsh penalties. And they found the lectures boring. Here is what Janove did:

It didn't take a great leap to realize that this training wasn't working, so I adopted a new approach, jettisoning scare-you-straight legal points. I substituted stories illustrating types of behaviors employees should avoid and how they unwittingly get themselves in trouble. Some-thing amazing happened: Suddenly, the rooms were full of bright eyes. Discovering that telling stories is an excellent way to train employees about workplace law, I began collecting parables.[29]

Janove further explained that once he adopted a story-based approach to business training, he became far more influential. Audiences listened more attentively, learned more, and changed their behaviors.

You can use stories in many kinds of business presentations. For example, Sally Herigstad, a CPA and consultant to *MSN Money*, spoke about using this strategy for delivering financial presentations:

Financial presentations tell a story. You're not just showing a collection of profit-and-loss statements and balance sheets—you're telling a story that your audience needs to hear. It may be a story of a new company with promising growth. Or maybe it's a story about meet-ing market challenges. Whatever your story is, stick to it: Toss everything that doesn't help you tell it in a compelling, easy-to-follow way. Tell your story with simplicity and clarity.[30]

Typically, stories for business connect facts with people and their business goals. Ide-ally, they are true, factual, and based on real events. In some cases, they may be hypo-thetical, but listeners still must find them realistic and relevant.[31] Generally, stories for business include the following components:[32]

- *Plot:* a business situation that involves challenges or tensions to overcome and a clear beginning and end.
- *Setting:* the time, place, characters, and context of the business situation.
- *Resolution:* a solution to the challenges or tensions.
- *Moral or lesson:* a point to the story.

In Figure 14.4, you'll find a story Latisha uses to explain how continuous review systems allow for better employee recognition and rewards. The story contains a plot, a setting, a resolution, and a moral. It speaks directly to a concern senior managers have—high employee turnover. This story is part of a larger story line that Latisha carries across her entire presentation.

Keep in mind that stories should be short. Even when audience members are engaged, their patience is limited. They expect to get the point quickly. Typically, stories should last 30 seconds to one minute. In some cases, a story can last two to three min-utes. Use your judgment and pay attention to your audiences. To help you identify how long a story is, time it while you rehearse. Or write it out and estimate how much time it will take to tell. Most people are comfortable with speaking at about 150 to 160 words per minute (this is the pace of most audio books). So, a 75-word story takes roughly 30 seconds, and a 150-word story takes about one minute.

FIGURE 14.4

Telling Stories to Connect with and Influence Audience Members

One of the pressing issues we're facing is high turnover among our employees. In the past three years, our annual turnover rate has been nearly 25 percent—nearly twice that of companies in our industry. As we've considered our strategies to address this problem, we've recognized that continuous review systems with frequent recognition and rewards are an effective way to reduce employee turnover.

Let me share with you what happened at Peakster Computing, a company that was in a similar situation five years ago. Its annual employee turnover was roughly 18 percent. It estimated that replacing each employee cost about $25,000. Across Peakster locations, it estimated excessive turnover was costing at least $35 million per year.

Janna, Peakster's HR director, tried a variety of approaches to learn about the high employee turnover. She used exit surveys and focus groups, and even contacted past employees. The message she kept getting from former employees was this: "No one appreciated us."

As a result, Peakster started instituting a variety of employee recognition programs. After several years of these programs, the company concluded the programs hadn't made any difference. Why? Because recognition and rewards still occurred only every six months or so. In other words, the recognition and rewards simply did not occur frequently enough.

Then, Janna adopted a continuous review system with the ability to give frequent recognition and rewards. Employees were getting highly visible compliments and kudos from managers and peers. Many employees got some type of recognition almost daily. Instead of employee recognition awards that arrived every six months, every year, or even every five years, employees were now getting smaller but more frequent rewards. Part of the rewards program involved receiving redeemable rewards points. On average employees were redeeming these points every five to six weeks for movie tickets, meals, other prizes, and even cash.

The results have been dramatic. Employee turnover is now around 11 percent. Janna says the drop in turnover alone accounts for millions of dollars in savings. She also says that improved morale is leading to far higher productivity. What Janna says makes all the difference is a "culture of appreciation."

What we've learned from Janna is that continuous review systems with options for frequent recognition and rewards lead to lower employee turnover. The main reason is that employees respond best to frequent recognition and small rewards more so than infrequent recognition and more prestigious rewards.

Plot: This plot is about how continuous review systems can lower employee turnover.

Setting: The setting focuses on Peakster Computing, where high employee turnover was costing the company millions of dollars. The company tried a variety of strategies to reduce employee turnover.

Resolution: By using continuous review systems, Peakster Computing was able to dramatically reduce employee turnover.

Moral or lesson: Frequent recognition and small rewards reduce employee turnover more effectively than infrequent recognition and large rewards.

At 399 words, this story would take roughly 2½ minutes.

It takes time to gather true stories for your presentations, so be alert for good ones. Remember, the purpose is always to make a point, not to entertain. If the stories have entertainment value, that's an added bonus.

Reviewing Your Presentations for Fairness and Effectiveness

LO14.6 Evaluate your presentations for fairness and effectiveness.

Review your presentations in the same way you review your written communications. In the first place, double-check every aspect of your supplementary materials as well as the technology you will use to ensure that it is perfect and working. Typos on electronic slides can be a glaring display of carelessness. Also, seek feedback from colleagues and clients before and after your presentations. Ask them how they would change the presentation to better meet their needs.

As with all of your communications, ask yourself how fair your business presentations are. Is the content based on *facts*? Have you granted others *access* to your real motives and reasoning? Have you been forthright about *impacts* on audience members and other stakeholders? Have you ensured that you show *respect* for audience members (see Figure 14.5)?

In Latisha's case, she evaluates her presentation in each regard. In particular, she has provided claims about the impacts of continuous review systems on employee engagement. Latisha is comfortable with these claims. She has researched these impacts carefully. She provides access to the sources of her information so senior managers can make judgments about the reliability of the information. She discusses impacts on stakeholders and explains that these changes require a new approach to managing employees. Finally, she should be respectful in every way as senior managers ask tough questions (you'll see some of these tough questions in Chapter 15).

FIGURE 14.5

Are Your Presentations FAIR?

Facts (How *factual* is your presentation?)
- Have you presented *all* the facts correctly?
- Have you presented information that allows colleagues, customers, and consumers to make informed decisions that are in their best interests?
- Have you carefully considered various interpretations of your data? Have you assessed the quality of your information?

Access (How *accessible* or *transparent* are your motives, reasoning, and information?)
- Are your motives clear, or will others think you have a hidden agenda? Have you made yourself accessible to others so that they can learn more about your viewpoints?
- Have you fully disclosed information that colleagues, customers, or consumers should expect to receive?
- Are you hiding any information to cast your recommendations in a better light or real reasons for making certain claims or recommendations?

Impacts (How does your communication *impact* stakeholders?)
- Have you carefully considered how your ideas, products, and services will impact colleagues, customers, and consumers?
- Have you made recommendations to colleagues, customers, and consumers that are in their best interests?

Respect (How *respectful* is your presentation?)
- Does the message offend or pressure in any way? Does it show that your colleagues' and customers' needs are important?
- Would a neutral observer consider your communication respectful?

💡 IDEA IN ACTION

IDENTIFY YOUR BIG IDEA

Screenshot from Nancy Duarte's firm's website.

Duarte.com

Nancy Duarte got a D in English and a C− in Speech Communication in college, yet she has risen to become among the most well-known and influential speech designers. She regularly coaches leaders and executives to deliver high-stakes speeches (she was the chief designer of Al Gore's Academy Award–wining documentary *An Inconvenient Truth*), speaks about how to influence others through presentations (her TED Talk "The Secret Structure of Great Talks" has been viewed more than 1.3 million times), and founded and leads one of the largest presentation-design firms in the country. Notice the screenshot above from Duarte's firm's website that shows its basic pitch to clients and its mantra of "ignite your ideas." Duarte's website layout is clean and simple, making it easy to read. The attractive design invites potential clients to contact Duarte to learn more about building persuasive presentations.

What's her secret? Providing value. She believes effective presentations must have a *big idea*, which means you take a position and explain why it matters (why it's valuable to your audience). No matter how well planned your presentation or how polished your delivery, the most important metric of success is whether your audience found value in the presentation. On an even broader level, providing value is the key to all work with clients. Duarte explains the success of her firm is measured by whether clients are successful when they deliver speeches and whether they are happy with her team's work.

So, as you're planning your presentations, never lose sight of developing a big idea that will influence your listeners.

Sources: Duarte, N. (2012). *HBR guide to persuasive presentations*. Boston, MA: Harvard Business Press; Cook, J. (n. d.). Nancy Duarte on failure, bootstrapping, and the power of better presentations. *99U*. Retrieved from http://99u.com/articles/28337/nancy-duarte-on-failure-bootstrapping-and-the-power-of-presenting-better.

Chapter Takeaway for *Planning Presentations*

LO14.1 Describe how planning your presentations leads to credibility.

Planning presentation content demonstrates **your personal credibility**.

It shows **competence** when you demonstrate that you know what you're talking about.	It shows **caring** when you provide content that meets the needs of others.	It shows **character** when you provide honest and transparent content.

LO14.2 Analyze presentation audiences in terms of message benefits, learning styles, and communicator styles.

Principles of Audience Analysis			Learner Types
Identify the following:			• Visual
• Audience benefits	• Decision makers	• Communicator style	• Auditory
• Existing knowledge	• Appeals	• Learning style	• Kinesthetic
• Concerns			

LO14.3 Organize and gather content for a preview, view, and review.

Audience   Information

Plan

Message

Audience: Identify how your message benefits your audience and make your message easy to understand.

Information: Gather the right information to support your key message.

Message: Give a preview of your message, justify your views, and end with a review.

Components of Presentations: Preview, view, review

Types of Attention-Getters: Rhetorical question, vivid example, dramatic demonstration, testimonial or quotation, intriguing statistic, unexpected exercise, challenge

See *examples of attention-getters* in Table 14.1.

PREP Method: Position, reasons, example, position

See an *example of a PREP statement* in Table 14.2.

LO14.4 Develop effective slide presentations.

Principles for Developing Slides	
• Create a storyboard with your PowerPoint slide titles.	• Use plenty of white space.
• Design your slides for ease of processing.	• Use high-contrast backgrounds and colors.
• Limit the amount of information on any given slide.	• Use compelling images, charts, and figures.
• Use font sizes that all audience members can read easily.	• Get professional design help when possible.
• Focus on and highlight key information.	

See *less effective and more effective examples of slides* in Figure 14.2 and Figure 14.3.

LO14.5 Use the story line approach to presentations.

Components of Effective Stories for Business
Plot, setting, resolution, moral or lesson

See an *example of a story for business* in Figure 14.4.

LO14.6 Evaluate your presentations for fairness and effectiveness.

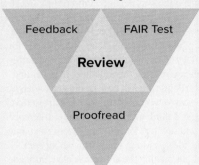

Feedback · FAIR Test · **Review** · Proofread

Feedback: Ask colleagues and clients what they would like you to change about your presentation.

FAIR Test: Focus on presenting factual information and being clear about impacts on others.

Proofreading: Make sure your slides, handouts, and other supplementry materials are attractive and error-free.

Key Terms

auditory learners, 444
kinesthetic learners, 444
positioning statement, 446

PREP method, 449
preview, 445
review, 450

view, 448
visual learners, 444

Discussion Exercises

14.1 Chapter Review Questions (LO14.1, LO14.2, LO14.3, LO14.4, LO14.5, LO14.6)

For each of the following items, respond with one or two paragraphs.

A. Explain why presenters must be aware of audience members' chief concerns.

B. Discuss the importance of knowing which people in an audience are decision makers.

C. Describe how presentations can be adapted to people of different communicator and learning styles.

D. Discuss the value of identifying just a few takeaway messages.

E. Explain the role of the preview, view, and review in presentations.

F. Describe common types of attention-getters. Explain the two types that you generally consider most effective.

G. Identify common types of support materials for presentations.

H. Explain principles of effective electronic slide use for presentations.

I. Describe the story line approach to presentations.

14.2 Ideas in Action Discussion Questions (LO14.2, LO14.4, LO14.5)

Read the Ideas in Action section featuring Nancy Duarte. Respond to the following questions about Duarte's comments as well as your own experiences:

A. What is the *big idea* according to Duarte? How can you stay focused on presenting a big idea?

B. What does it mean to provide value to your audience? What are some ways you can evaluate whether your audience found your presentation was valuable?

C. What are some ways you can ensure you're creating a high-value presentation? In other words, what are four or five ways you can learn whether your audiences will value your presentation before you deliver it?

14.3 Using Stories for Presentations (LO14.5)

Read the following quotation from Stephen Denning:

These days, command-and-control approaches are unlikely to generate positive responses in employees, let alone the marketplace. The era when top managers could simply give orders and expect their will to be done has long gone. As a result, leaders have turned to storytelling to overcome barriers to communication. Since time immemorial, human beings have used stories to spread religions, win support for political agendas or launch wars. And as we look around the business world, stories are everywhere. Managers think in stories, they remember in stories, they plan in stories, they express hopes and fears and dreams in stories, and they make decisions in stories. Storytelling is already part of our world.

Moreover, storytelling is not a rare skill possessed by a few people born with the gift of gab. All human beings start spontaneously telling stories at age 2 and go on doing it for the rest of their lives. They tell stories effortlessly in social settings. Leadership storytelling involves taking a capacity that people already have and applying it for constructive purposes. Anyone can master the discipline.[33]

Based on Denning's comments and your own experiences, respond to each of the following items:

A. Why are stories an effective communication tool compared to command-and-control approaches?

B. What are some steps people can take to become effective storytellers?

C. What are some of the risks of storytelling?

14.4 Overcoming "Death by PowerPoint" (LO14.4)

James E. Rogers of Duke Energy was asked, "What would you like business schools to teach more of, or less of?"

I believe there is such a thing as death by PowerPoint. Because I believe, and this is the storyteller in me and maybe the former newspaper reporter, that I'd much rather have someone write a two-page summary of what they're thinking. When you're forced to sit and write it, not only are you getting the subject, verb, predicates right, but you're tying the sentences together and ideas together. PowerPoints are just bullets, bullets, bullets, and when you actually have to write something, you start to develop a more cohesive logic. I think words really make a difference—what you say, how you say it. A lot of energy needs to go into how you present the idea. And I'm not talking about spin. I'm really talking about making the idea come alive through a story.[34]

Based on these comments, respond to each of the following items:

A. What are some specific ways in which you think PowerPoint lowers the level of effective business thinking?

B. What are some specific ways that you can alter the design of electronic slide presentations to bring out good business thinking?

C. What do you think is the difference between spin and story in a business presentation?

14.5 Avoiding Bad PowerPoint Presentations (LO14.4)

Read the various comments by business leaders in Figure 14.1. Respond to the following questions with one or two paragraphs each:

A. What are the key points that these leaders make about PowerPoints?

B. For each key theme or key point you've identified, make counterpoints. Explain another perspective on the issue and/or explain how to use PowerPoint slides without encountering this problem.

Evaluation Exercises

14.6 Evaluating an Electronic Slide Presentation (LO14.4)

Find an electronic slide presentation you are interested in on the SlideShare website (www.slideshare.net). In three to five paragraphs, describe the following:

A. The electronic slide presentation.

B. Use of white space.

C. Use of charts, diagrams, and other figures.

D. Use of pictures and other images.

E. Use of text.

F. Three recommendations to improve the electronic slide presentation.

14.7 Self-Assessment: Your Approach to Planning Presentations (LO14.2, LO14.3, LO14.4)

Evaluate yourself with regard to each of the practices listed in the following table. Circle the appropriate number for each.

Statement	1 – Rarely/Never	2 – Sometimes	3 – Usually	4 – Always
I carefully select two or three key messages that I want to get across for my presentations.	1	2	3	4
I design my presentations so that nearly every aspect leads back to one of my main points.	1	2	3	4
I repeat my main points at least several times during a presentation.	1	2	3	4
I provide an overview at the beginning of my presentations that includes my key messages.	1	2	3	4
I think carefully about how my key messages meet the needs of my audiences.	1	2	3	4
I think carefully about how to adapt my key messages to the preferred communicator styles of my audience members.	1	2	3	4
I think carefully about how to adapt my key messages to the preferred learning styles of my audience members.	1	2	3	4
I provide enough support materials to make my key messages convincing.	1	2	3	4
I speak with confidence about my key messages.	1	2	3	4
I conclude with a call to action that is built upon my key messages.	1	2	3	4

Add up your score and consider the following advice:

35–40: You are a *strategic, other-oriented presenter*. You think about how to prepare and deliver a presentation that meets the needs of others. Continue with such awareness of the impact of your written messages.

30–34: You are a *careful, considerate presenter*. You spend some time thinking about the content of your message and the needs of your audience members. Take time to think your message through even more carefully and pay close attention to the needs and potential responses to your written messages by audience members.

25–29: You are an *average* presenter. Sometimes you are careful about developing your message and considerate of the needs and reactions of others. Other times you are not. Get in the habit of taking time to carefully craft your message.

Under 25: You *need to improve* your approach to presenting. You likely don't spend enough time thinking through the key messages and their impacts on others. You will be far more influential if you spend more time preparing your messages and delivering them with your audience members in mind.

Once you complete the assessment, write three paragraphs about the three specific ways in which you can improve your ability to prepare and deliver your key messages in presentations.

14.8 Evaluating Learning and Communicator Styles (LO14.2)

Based on the descriptions of communicator styles (professionals with red, blue, green, and hub MVSs) and learning styles (visual, auditory, kinesthetic) described in the "Analyze Your Audience and Gather the Right Information" section of this chapter, do the following:

A. Describe your learning and communicator styles (you may consider yourself a combination of various styles).

B. Discuss how your learning and communicator styles may impact how you prefer to receive presentations.

C. Discuss how your learning and communicator styles may impact how you plan and deliver presentations.

D. Explain a few ways you can adapt your presentation style to learning and communicator styles other than your own.

14.9 Interviewing a Business Professional about Planning for Presentations (LO14.1, LO14.2, LO14.3, LO14.4)

Interview a business professional about best practices in planning business presentations. Write four to five paragraphs about the interview and address the following issues:

A. Planning themes and key points.

B. Adapting the presentation to the needs and preferences of the audience.

C. Using attention-getters or other strategies to engage the audience in the opening moments.

D. Preparing examples and support for key ideas.

E. Developing electronic slides and handouts.

F. Using technology.

14.10 Conducting a FAIR Test of a Recent Presentation (LO14.6)

Think about a presentation you made recently. Assess how you did in terms of the following:

A. Did you present the facts correctly?

B. Did you present all the relevant facts?

C. Did you present any information that would be considered misleading?

D. Did you make your motives clear, or will others perceive that you have a hidden agenda?

E. Did you hide any of the real reasons for making certain claims or recommendations?

F. Did you seek the opinions and ideas of those impacted by your communication?

G. Did you think about how your communication will help or even hurt others?

H. Would others consider your presentation respectful?

Application Exercises

14.11 Planning Attention-Getters (LO14.3)

Using Table 14.1 as a guide, do the following:

A. Identify a topic for a presentation.

B. Write how you could use each type of attention-getter: rhetorical question, vivid example, dramatic demonstration, testimonial or quotation, intriguing statistic, unexpected exercise, and challenge.

C. Explain the three approaches you believe would be most effective.

14.12 Creating Positioning and Preview Statements (LO14.3)

A. Identify a topic for a presentation.

B. Write a positioning statement.

C. Write a preview statement.

14.13 Employing the PREP Method to Take Positions (LO14.3)

Identify a key position that you intend to make during your presentation. Using Table 14.2 as a guide, write out how you could use the PREP (Position–Reasons–Example–Position) method to effectively convey this position to your audience.

14.14 Creating a Storyboard for Your Presentation (LO14.4)

Identify a topic of interest. Create a storyboard (similar to the one displayed in Table 14.3) to outline the titles, content, and related story line of your PowerPoint slides.

14.15 Creating Electronic Slides (LO14.4)

Create an electronic slide presentation for your topic of interest. Ensure that it conveys your key messages effectively.

14.16 Creating Electronic Slides from Reports (LO14.4)

Many times in the workplace, you will create a written report and provide an oral presentation as well. Select a written report and develop a set of electronic slides that could be used to present it. If you have not developed your own report, consider the following options:

- A report or other written message in the textbook. For example, you could consider the following: "Should Aicasus Tours Invest in Virtual Reality Content?" in Chapter 13 or "Guest Satisfaction among Conference Attendees" in Chapter 13.

- An annual report from a company of interest.

- A white paper from a company of interest.

Language Mechanics Check

14.17 Review all rules in Appendix A about punctuation, number usage, and grammar. Then, rewrite each sentence to make all needed corrections.

A. Jim I'm disappointed that many of our job candidates have rejected our high compensation attractive job offers during the past year.

B. I believe we're facing a crisis if we can't hire top tier candidates, soon we may face a major talent gap.

C. Job candidates may be dissatisfied with some of the following issues career path, office locations, perceived work hours, sign on bonus and/or benefits.

D. I think we should organize a committee which should include some of our more recent hires, to examine the reasons these job candidates are not accepting our offers.

E. I'd like you to give me some advice about the following (1) employees to place on this committee, (2) charges to give the committee, (3) information to give the committee and (4) timeline for the committee to complete their work.

F. Also I'd like you to send me your impressions of the last five job candidates, who declined our offers.

G. Since you got to know them so well perhaps you could contact them personally, and ask them directly why they chose not to accept our offers.

H. I think they will give you their candid views since you seemed to really connect with them.

I. I'm hoping that we make adjustments before our next recruiting season, because we can't afford to continue this hiring slump.

J. Thanks, Jim for your efforts on behalf of the firm, you make a tremendous difference for us.

Endnotes

1. Leech, T. (2004). *How to prepare, stage, and deliver winning presentations* (3rd ed.). New York: American Management Association, 9–10.

2. Grensing-Pophal, L. (2004, July 1). Presentations that sell without offending. Society for Human Resource Management website.

3. Mills, H. (2007). *Power Points! How to design and deliver presentations that sizzle and sell.* New York: AMACOM.

4. Morgan, N. (2002). Reach audience members where they learn. *Harvard Management Communication Letter, 9.*

5. Mills, H. (2007). *Power Points! How to design and deliver presentations that sizzle and sell.* New York: AMACOM.

6 Leech, T. (2004). *How to prepare, stage, and deliver winning presentations* (3rd ed.). New York: American Management Association.

7. Leech, T. (2004). *How to prepare, stage, and deliver winning presentations* (3rd ed.). New York: American Management Association.

8. Mills, H. (2007). *Power Points! How to design and deliver presentations that sizzle and sell.* New York: AMACOM.

9. LaMon, D. (2007, November). Making the moment meaningful. *Toastmaster.* Retrieved from www.toastmasters.org/ToastmastersMagazine/ToastmasterArchive/2007/November/MomentMeaningful.aspx.

10. Denning, S. (2007). *The secret language of leadership: How leaders inspire action through narrative.* New York: Wiley.

11. Denning, S. (2007). *The secret language of leadership: How leaders inspire action through narrative.* New York: Wiley.

12. Denning, S. (2007). *The secret language of leadership: How leaders inspire action through narrative.* New York: Wiley.

13. Morgan, N. (2003, June). Opening options: How to grab your audience's attention: Six great ways to begin a presentation. *Harvard Management Communication Letter, 3–4.*

14. Denning, S. (2007). *The secret language of leadership: How leaders inspire action through narrative.* New York: Wiley.

15. Leech, T. (2004). *How to prepare, stage, and deliver winning presentations* (3rd ed.). New York: American Management Association.

16. Mills, H. (2007). *Power Points! How to design and deliver presentations that sizzle and sell.* New York: AMACOM.

17. Grimshaw, R. (2005). Communication by numbers. *Harvard Management Communication Letter, 8*(3), 3–4.

18. Morgan, N. (2003, September). How to put together a great speech when you're under the gun. *Harvard Management Communication Letter, 3–4.*

19. Leech, T. (2004). *How to prepare, stage, and deliver winning presentations* (3rd ed.). New York: American Management Association; Mills, H. (2007). *Power Points! How to design and deliver presentations that sizzle and sell.* New York: AMACOM.

20. Mills, H. (2007). *Power Points! How to design and deliver presentations that sizzle and sell.* New York: AMACOM.

21. Leech, T. (2004). *How to prepare, stage, and deliver winning presentations* (3rd ed.). New York: American Management Association.

22. Bryant, A. (2010, January 16). Structure? The flatter, the better. *The New York Times.* Retrieved from www.nytimes.com/2010/01/17/business/17corner.html; Bryant, A. (2009, May 9). The C.E.O., now appearing on YouTube. *The New York Times.* Retrieved from www.nytimes.com/2009/05/10/business/10corner.html; Kosslyn, S. M. (2007). *Clear and to the point: 8 psychological principles for compelling PowerPoint presentations.* Oxford: Oxford University Press; Finkelstein, E. (2009, May). Sidestep the PowerPoint trap. *Toastmaster.* Retrieved from www.toastmasters.org/ToastmastersMagazine/ToastmasterArchive/2009/May/Sidestep-PowerPoint.aspx.

23. Humphrey, J. (2011). You are the best visual. *Harvard Management Communication Letter,* 10–11.

24. Grimshaw, R. (2005). Communication by numbers. *Harvard Management Communication Letter, 8*(3), 3–4.

25. Alsop, R. (2006, January 17). Poor writing skills top M.B.A. recruiter gripes. *The Wall Street Journal.*

26. Kosslyn, S. M. (2007). *Clear and to the point: 8 psychological principles for compelling PowerPoint presentations.* Oxford: Oxford University Press; Leech, T. (2004). *How to prepare, stage, and deliver winning presentations* (3rd ed.). New York: American Management Association; Herigstad, S. (2008, July). Giving effective financial presentations with PowerPoint. *Toastmaster.* Retrieved from www.toastmasters.org/ToastmastersMagazine/ToastmasterArchive/2008/July/PresentationswithPowerPoint.aspx; Mills, H. (2007). *Power Points! How to design and deliver presentations that sizzle and sell.* New York: AMACOM.

27. Brown, J. S., Denning, S., Groh, K., & Prusak, L. (2005). *Storytelling in organizations: Why storytelling is transforming 21st century organizations and management.* Burlington, MA: Elsevier Butterworth-Heinemann; Schank, R. C. (1990). *Tell me a story: A new look at real and artificial memoir.* New York: Charles Scribner's Sons; Swap, W., Leonard, D., Shields, M., & Abrams, L. (2001). Using mentoring and storytelling to transfer knowledge in the workplace. *Journal of Management Information System, 18*(1), 95–114; McLaughlin, M. W. (2010). Getting clout from speaking engagements. *Society for Human Resource Management* website.; Tingley, J. (2009, March). Walking a fine line: How much personal information should speakers share? *Toastmaster.* Retrieved from www.toastmasters.org/ToastmastersMagazine/ToastmasterArchive/2009/March/Walking-a-Fine-Line.aspx; Janove, J. (2009, July 1). A story is worth a thousand lectures. *HR Magazine, 54*(7); Mills, H. (2007). *Power Points! How to design and deliver presentations that sizzle and sell.* New York: AMACOM.

28. Bryant, A. (2009, October 10). The C.E.O. as general (and scout). *The New York Times.* Retrieved from www.nytimes.com/2009/10/11/business/11corner.html.

29. Janove, J. (2009). A story is worth a thousand lectures. Society for Human Resource Management.

30. Herigstad, S. (2008, July). Giving effective financial presentations with PowerPoint. *Toastmasters International, 74*(7), 19.

31. Armstrong, D. (1992). *Managing by storying around.* New York: Doubleday.

32. Adapted from Dennehy, R. F. (1999). The executive as storyteller. *Management Review, 88*(3), 40–43; Schank, R. C. (1990). *Tell me a story: A new look at real and artificial memoir.* New York: Charles Scribner's Sons.

33. Denning, S. (2008, October 1). Stories in the workplace. Society for Human Resource Management website.

34. Bryant, A. (2009, October 10). The C.E.O. as general (and scout). *The New York Times.*

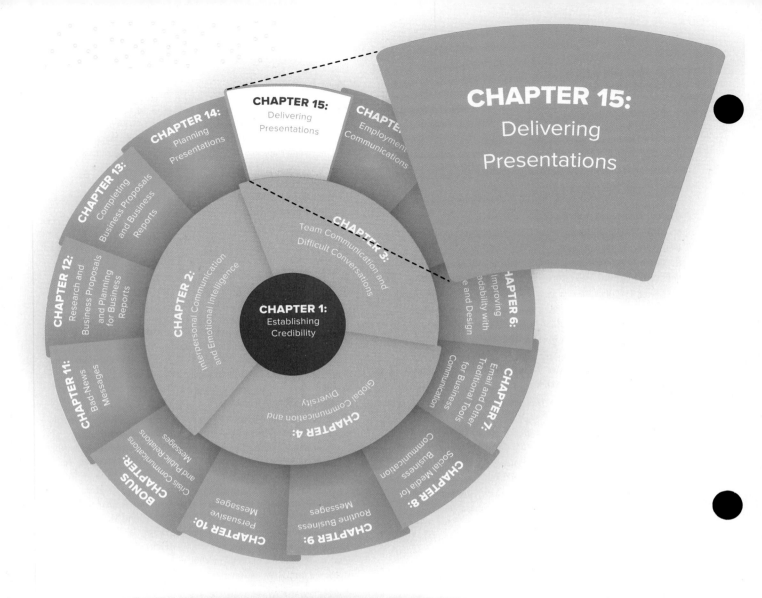

CHAPTER 15:
Delivering Presentations

CHAPTER 15:
Delivering
Presentations

 ESTABLISHING CREDIBILITY

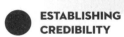 **PRINCIPLES OF INTERPERSONAL COMMUNICATION**

 PRINCIPLES FOR & TYPES OF BUSINESS MESSAGES

LEARNING OBJECTIVES

After studying this chapter, you should be able to do the following:

LO15.1 Describe how presentation delivery impacts your credibility.

LO15.2 Deliver presentations with authenticity, confidence, and influence.

LO15.3 Apply the SOFTEN model of nonverbal communication for presentations.

LO15.4 Use slides and handouts to supplement your presentation effectively.

LO15.5 Interact effectively with your audience.

LO15.6 Prepare to present effectively in teams.

Once you've settled on the content of your presentation, you turn to preparing for the delivery. Delivering great presentations involves art and skill. With each of your professional presentations, you'll fine-tune your abilities. In this chapter, we focus on making your delivery as smooth and engaging as possible so that you will successfully connect with your audiences. Read the chapter case, which is a continuation from Chapter 14 and is the basis for many examples in this chapter.

> **Hear Pete Cardon explain why this matters.**
>
> **bit.ly/cardon15**

CHAPTER CASE — DELIVERING A PRESENTATION AT EASTMOND NETWORKING

Latisha Jackson

WHO'S INVOLVED

Summer Intern

- Hired for a summer internship to work on employee programs
- Double majoring in human resource management and family development

Latisha has prepared a presentation to deliver to the senior management team about transitioning from annual performance reviews to continuous performance reviews. She hopes the presentation will provide her with more professional opportunities at Eastmond Networking. She's nervous, though, and uncertain of the outcome.

THE SITUATION

(Latisha Jackson character): LWA/Larry Williams/Blend Images LLC

TASK

1

Connect with the audience, gaining their trust and confidence.

2

Deliver a persuasive and memorable explanation of the benefits of continuous performance reviews.

Establishing Presence

LO15.1   Describe how presentation delivery impacts your credibility.

Visit http://connect. mheducation.com for an exercise on this topic.

Presenting gives you an excellent opportunity to connect deeply with your colleagues, your clients, and your other contacts. It allows you to express your views in a rich, two-way environment. As you do with your written communication, you will aim to strike the right style and tone in your presentations. Moreover, you will strive to establish a "presence," something great speakers and presenters are often described as doing. Having presence means commanding attention, garnering respect for your ideas, engaging your listeners, and even inspiring your audiences to action. In this section, we focus on strategies you can use to enhance your presence as you deliver your presentations.

Establish Credibility

For internal presentations, you often present to people who know you well and who have already formed opinions about your credibility; they have a sense of your competence, caring, and character. However, internal presentations still provide you the opportunity to change others' views of you. Without appearing self-serving, find ways to increase your perceived credibility. Use the presentation to show your thorough understanding of a business issue. Frame your ideas in ways that show clear benefits to your company, its employees, and its stakeholders. In every way, display honesty and openness.

For external presentations, you are often dealing with people who have superficial impressions of your credibility. You have opportunities before, during, and after your presentation to bolster your credibility. Before the presentation, you can make information about your background available or have someone introduce you with a brief statement.

During the presentation, you establish your competence by showing that you know the content well. You show your caring by connecting emotionally with audience members and adapting to their needs. You show your character by being open and honest. After your presentation, following up as appropriate with audience members shows your caring and character as well. Some audience members may raise issues for you to look into or ask for additional information. Comply with these requests promptly and you will establish a reputation for responsiveness.

LO15.2   Deliver presentations with authenticity, confidence, and influence.

Visit http://connect. mheducation.com for an exercise on this topic.

Maintain Authenticity

Standing in front of an audience feels anything but natural for many business professionals. Yet, nearly all audience members are making judgments about you and your message based on their perceptions of your authenticity. One of your primary goals as you develop your presentation skills is to find ways to present your real self to your audiences. Barbara De Angelis, a well-known communication specialist and speaker, explained the importance of maintaining authenticity:

> I often work with speakers who can't understand why they aren't more successful, or why they become so anxious in front of others. Often, they make the mistake of trying to imitate other speakers who they believe are more powerful or more skilled, or they mechanically follow learned formulas for successful public speaking. However, by doing this, they are unintentionally disconnecting from one of their greatest assets—and one of the secret ingredients for being successful: their authenticity. . . . People can sense when we are trying too hard, or faking confidence, or projecting an image that doesn't feel natural. When people see us appearing inauthentic, it makes them uneasy. And we actually appear awkward or nervous.[1]

As you read this chapter about presentation delivery, focus on making a few changes at a time. Attempting to alter too many of your presentation techniques at once may detract from your ability to speak naturally and genuinely. Add new presentation techniques to your repertoire constantly, but also make sure to draw on your natural strengths.

Principles for Establishing Presence

- Establish credibility.
- Maintain authenticity.
- Know your material.
- Speak with confidence.
- Focus on people.
- Stay flexible.
- Use the room to your advantage.
- Communicate nonverbally.
- Dress for success.

Know Your Material and Rehearse

By running through your presentations several times, you allow yourself to become more comfortable with the content, work out weakly connected areas, and identify parts that you want to emphasize through tone and nonverbal communication. Also, rehearsing allows you to time your presentation so you know if you need to add or remove content.

Far too many speakers and presenters avoid rehearsing. The presentation itself is often the first run-through. Executive speech coach Nick Morgan observed the following about this approach:

> The sad truth is that when you wing it, the performance is rarely as good in the audience's memory as it is in the speaker's. The reason is that your heightened adrenaline literally makes you feel better—more energy, more enthusiasm, more acuity—and so you rate your own performance better. What the audience all too often sees, on the other hand, is disorganization, fumbled examples, and the vagueness that comes from not knowing your material thoroughly.[2]

Rehearsing may involve running through the presentation in your mind or out loud. Ideally, you do it out loud. Consider videotaping your presentation so that you can get a sense of the overall impact of your ideas, the flow of your content, and the delivery of your presentation.

Many speakers and presenters use notes. Notes are not necessarily considered a weakness; however, use them sparingly or, ideally, not at all. Rehearsing will help you determine if you want or need notes. If you use them, rehearsing helps you choose which notes you need and allows you to become comfortable handling your notes in a nondistracting way.

Overcome Fear and Speak with Confidence

Nearly everyone gets nervous and even fearful of presenting in public, especially in unpredictable and high-stakes circumstances. Many polls show that adults fear public speaking more than death. Responding to these various polls, Jerry Seinfeld once joked, "At a funeral, the average person would rather be in the casket than giving the eulogy."[3] Other polls show that public speaking is among the most serious phobias among adults, with the fear of snakes and of heights the only phobias surpassing it (see Figure 15.1).[4]

FIGURE 15.1

Top Fears of American Adults

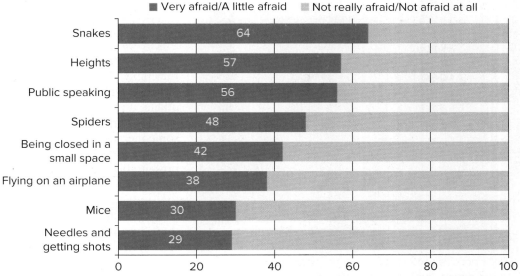

Source: YouGov. (2014, March 21–24). Afraid of...? YouGov.com. Retrieved from http://cdn.yougov.com/cumulus_uploads/document/zqmu1lifm8/tabs_OPI_fears_20140324.pdf.

Experiencing some nervousness as you speak and present is normal. Even experienced speakers get stage fright from time to time. Unexpected circumstances, for example, may cause unusual nervousness—unfamiliar or intimidating audience members, technology failure, pressure to perform with a skeptical audience, noticing the speech is being recorded, and many other reasons.[5]

Feeling some nerves is not necessarily bad. It shows you care about making an effective presentation. And feeling some nerves can heighten your ability to deliver forcefully and passionately. Nervousness is dysfunctional only when it impairs your ability to deliver your content. In most presentations, certain parts are the most critical—for example, a call to action (see Chapter 14)—and at the same time, they have the least-certain outcome. Sometimes, out of nervousness, presenters do not follow through completely at these moments. If nervousness means you shortchange yourself at those critical moments, use techniques to help you manage your nervousness.[6]

Consider some of the following recommendations:[7]

Engage in Relaxation Techniques   Consider some of the following options:

- Stretching.
- Meditating.
- Going hiking or exercising (a day or so before your presentation).
- Listening to music.
- Going to a movie.
- Watching a sunset.
- Thinking about the things in your life you are grateful for, such as your cherished relationships.
- Letting your mind go blank.
- Counting backward from 100.

Become Aware of Your Breathing   Taking several deep breaths is a great technique to quickly alleviate anxiety. Also, consistently taking full breaths leads to improved tone and timber of your voice as well as better, more confident posture.

Practice Visualization   Envision yourself speaking with confidence and ease. Imagine making nonverbal connections with your audience. Think about how you will respond to audience questions. In your mind, play out your presentation and see yourself succeeding.

Experiment with various relaxation techniques to find what prepares you mentally and emotionally for important presentations.
Racorn/123RF

Focus on Friendly Faces Initially to Gain Composure and Confidence   Inevitably, the presence of some audience members will make you more nervous than others. It may be a critical boss, a skeptical client, a person you disagree with often, or someone who intimidates you for other reasons. In the opening moments of your presentation, when you are most apt to suffer from nervousness, look at those in the audience with whom you are most friendly. This will help calm you during those ever-important first moments.

Watch Your Food and Beverage Intake   Pay attention to foods and beverages that impact your nervousness.

Some people avoid or minimize caffeine intake on speech days to avoid jitters. Others avoid dairy products since they can coat the mouth and throat and make speaking feel less smooth. Notice how various foods and beverages affect your body and adjust accordingly.

Get Comfortable with Audience Members before Starting Your Presentation   One of the best ways of relaxing immediately before your presentation is to speak with audience members. Greet them at the door, walk around the room, engage in small talk, and find other ways to break the ice and help you and your audience members warm up to each other.

Focus on People

If you make your speech about people, your audience members are more likely to trust your commitment to them and others: People like to hear about people. Also, a strong people-focus will allow you to liven up dry facts and statistics. Try the following methods of making your speech about people.[8]

Make People the Subject of Your Sentences   Especially when you present numerical information, using people as the subjects of your sentences humanizes your presentation. Notice how Latisha does this in Table 15.1.

Introduce Colleagues and Refer to Them by Name during Your Presentation   By naming members in your organization or other relevant people, you help your audience members feel they are getting to know these important individuals (see Table 15.2).

TABLE 15.1

Making People the Subject of Your Sentences

Less Effective	More Effective
The survey showed just 43 percent of respondents believe that annual reviews are accurate indicators of performance.	Jeff, Steve, and I developed the survey after holding focus groups with our employees to learn about their views of annual reviews. Of the 223 employees who took the survey, just 43 percent believed that annual reviews are accurate indicators of performance.
This statement is compelling but dry and impersonal to some audience members.	This statement is more compelling by introducing the people involved: the HR personnel who designed the survey based on what they heard from employees and the larger group of employees who ultimately took the survey.

TABLE 15.2

Introducing Colleagues by Name

Less Effective	More Effective
I'll be presenting research conducted by the HR team.	Our HR team, including Jeff Brody and Steve Choi, spent the last two months gathering information about annual reviews and continuous reviews. We've talked to HR directors at other companies, software vendors who provide new continuous review tools, and our own employees. Today we'll share this research with you.
This statement is good but could be improved by elaborating on who the members of the HR team are and why they're positioned to provide good advice.	This statement is stronger with its focus on the members of the HR team and why they are positioned to provide strong advice.

TABLE 15.3

Using Names of Audience Members

Less Effective	More Effective
It's common for managers to continue conducting annual performance reviews even though they think there should be better ways of evaluating and motivating performance.	Just before we started the meeting this morning, Cynthia, John, and I were chatting about annual performance reviews. They each mentioned great managers they knew here in this company who conduct annual performance reviews as a matter of routine but don't think they work. These managers think there should be better ways of evaluating and motivating performance.
This statement is good but is not personalized. It is essentially a "faceless" comment that may be less persuasive without talking about "real" people.	This statement makes the point in a personalized, relatable manner. It shows the presenter is connected to the experiences of the audience.

Use Names of Audience Members as Appropriate When you know the names of those in your audience, consider using their names from time to time to personalize your presentation (see Table 15.3).

Stay Flexible

Presentations rarely go as planned. Knowing your content perfectly will help you adapt to unexpected circumstances. Maintaining a flexible approach will help you think on your feet for unanticipated events. Consider the following ways of staying flexible.

Arrive Early Arriving early lets you notice if you have any surprises in terms of equipment, room layout, or people in attendance. If so, you may be able to make adjustments before the presentation begins. When presenting in a place you've never been before, arrive at least an hour or two early.

Focus on the Needs of Your Audience Some presentations can get off course when audience members raise questions or make comments. If you are preoccupied with your own agenda only, you can become flustered or disorganized if someone poses a question. Be ready to adapt to the immediate needs of your audience so you can quickly modify your presentation based on their requests. If you spend time anticipating possible questions, you will generally be prepared to answer them at any point in your presentation and segue back into the flow.

When You Lose Your Place, Don't Panic All presenters inevitably lose their train of thought from time to time. When this happens, you can try a few strategies. One is simply to pause until you regain your composure and your line of thinking. Within a few seconds, you will often get back on target. What seems like an eternity to you will be but a short pause to audience members. Many audience members will not even notice you lost your place. Another strategy is to repeat the last statement you made (five or six words). Doing so will help you regain your thought process.

Never Tell Your Audience Things Haven't Gone as Expected Many presenters instinctively tell the audience about problems that have disrupted the presentation (i.e., technology failures, misplaced handouts). Resist the urge to mention these mishaps. To many audience members, this sounds like excuse-making and detracts from your key messages and/or your credibility. Most audience members will never know that anything out of the ordinary happened if you simply proceed with slightly modified plans.

Always Have a Plan B If you have electronic slides to display, be prepared for a situation where the projector does not work and you need to speak without them. If you recognize factual problems in your handouts at the last moment, be prepared to present without them. Know ahead of time how you'll present under these situations.

Know What Your Key Messages Are You can often leave out parts of your presentations as necessary with little change in impact as long as you know your three or four key messages and accentuate them throughout your presentation.

Use the Room to Your Advantage

You will inevitably present in rooms of various sizes and layouts. Generally, you connect with your audiences best if you position yourself close to them and establish eye contact with them. Consider the following advice.

Position Yourself Where People Can See You Easily Walk around the room before your presentation to check the vantage points that various audience members will have. After you do this, you can generally determine where you can stand to get the most eye contact with your audience. Also, think about how you can be closest to them. If your audience members have taken all the back seats and left the front seats empty, move closer to them to reduce the spatial barrier. Or, politely ask your audience members to move forward to the front of the room.

Move Around but Avoid Distracting the Audience During presentations of more than five to ten minutes, you can keep the audience more engaged by moving around the room. This draws the focus to you and allows you to gain spatial proximity with most of your audience members at some point during your presentation. However, some movements can be distracting. For example, excessive pacing may show that you're nervous. Or, since you will likely be standing and your audience members will likely be seated, getting too close may make them feel that you are hovering over them.

Use Podiums and Tables Strategically Many rooms are set up with podiums or tables, where presenters can place notes and other materials. Standing behind a podium or table can help you project authority and add to the formality of the presentation. If you do use a podium to achieve these goals, make sure you stand upright. Avoid leaning on or gripping the podium, which indicates nervousness. Also, consider whether a podium, table, or other object placed between you and your audience creates a barrier to connection. If you stand in front of the podium or table, you can get closer to your audience physically. As a result, you may achieve a more friendly, accessible, and casual tone.

Communicate Nonverbally

Your audience members consciously and subconsciously make a variety of judgments about your credibility and your message based on your nonverbal behavior. Gary Genard, president of Public Speaking International, had this to say about nonverbal communication:

LO15.3 Apply the SOFTEN model of nonverbal communication for presentations.

> How comfortable a speaker is in his own skin, how he stands and moves, how he looks at others in the room, his tone of voice, even the clothes he wears—together, these variables constitute a constant flow of data running underneath whatever the speaker is saying . . . leaders know how to move boldly and decisively. There is nothing tentative about their movements and gestures—instead, they literally command the space through which they move.[9]

Consider the **SOFTEN model of nonverbal communication** in your presentations: *s*mile, *o*pen stance, *f*orward lean, *t*one, *e*ye contact, and *n*od. By focusing on these nonverbal behaviors, you can display confidence and strength while also showing warmth and concern.[10]

Smile Use your facial expressions to connect with your audience members and show your enthusiasm for your topic. Audience members are more likely to warm up to you when you put forth positive, can-do emotion.

You can use nonverbal communication to connect with your audiences, make them more comfortable, and build their trust in you.

Suedhang/Image Source/Getty Images

Open Stance Most people consider an open stance as warmer and more inviting. Excessively putting your hands on your hips, folding your arms, crossing your legs, and gripping a podium or other objects closes you off from some people and implies less warmth. Keeping your arms to your sides or gesturing with palms up is more inviting to the audience.

Forward Lean Facing your audience directly with a slight forward lean and upright posture shows confidence and interest. By contrast, leaning back, slouching, and lowering one's shoulders imply timidity and lack of confidence.

Tone Use your voice to express enthusiasm or other intended emotion. To make sure everyone in the room can hear the confidence of your message, project your voice adequately. Also, speak at a reasonable pace. Rushing your presentations is often a sign of nervousness. First impressions of self-confidence and empathy often come from a slower rate of speaking with fewer gestures.[11] On the other hand, many audience members tune out when you speak too slowly and may even think you are unprepared.

Evaluating your own voice is difficult, since the voice you hear is not what your listeners hear.[12] Consider recording your voice so you can evaluate your tone and pace. Also, ask people you trust to evaluate the tone, pace, and emotion conveyed by your voice during presentations.

Eye Contact Maintaining eye contact with your audience is among the most important forms of nonverbal communication. It creates an immediate sense of connection when you meet audience members eye to eye. The very act of keeping eye contact forces you to think about your listeners. It helps you evaluate and adjust your presentation as you observe your audience members' reactions. Perhaps most important, eye contact facilitates trust. Many people partially judge the truthfulness of a message from eye contact.[13]

Nod Use gestures that show affirmation and acceptance of your audience members. For example, nodding indicates that you agree or recognize the value of what others say. Gesture with your hands, arms, body, and head to achieve positive connections with your audience. Attempt to read your audience and get a sense for how much energy they have. Research shows that morning speakers should have medium energy and match most audiences' lower energy levels with a conversational tone. Afternoon and evening speakers can increase their expressiveness and energy.[14]

Remember to be natural. While you can improve your nonverbal communication to better connect with your audience, it takes time. Try out new forms of nonverbal communication incrementally. And be aware that people often misread body language. The more you pay attention to your audience's reactions, the more you will be able to identify how people respond to your nonverbal communication.[15]

Dress for Success

Business professionals are frequently advised to *dress for success,* especially for important events such as speeches and presentations. How you dress can make a big impact on how others perceive you. In a recent survey, 41 percent of employers stated that employees who dressed professionally were more likely to be promoted. This figure rises to 55 percent in certain industries, such as financial services.[16]

Most attire can be placed on a continuum from formal to casual. Common categories along this continuum are formal business, business casual, and casual. **Formal business dress**, at one end of the continuum, is intended to project executive presence and seriousness. It is distinguished by business suits, typically dark and conservative, accompanied by collared, button-down dress shirts. For men, neckties are essential.

Business casual dress is one step down in formality along the continuum. It is intended to project a more comfortable, relaxed feel while still maintaining a high standard of professionalism. Business casual dress is interpreted broadly and varies significantly by location and company. As a result, business casual can be divided into *high-level business casual* and *low-level business casual.* In Figure 15.2, you can see three

FIGURE 15.2

Formality of Workplace Attire

Formal Business

Men
Tailored business suits
Dress shirts
Neckties
Leather shoes

Women
Tailored business suit with pants or skirt
Dress shirts
Hosiery or socks
Leather shoes

Business Casual (high-level)

Men
Suit coats, sports coats, or blazers
Button-down collar shirts
Neckties optional
Leather shoes

Women
Pantsuits and tailored separates
Closed-toe or closed-heel shoes

Business Casual (low-level)

Men
Button-down collar shirts or polo-type shirts
Khakis or chinos
Leather belts and shoes
Conservative footwear

Women*
Dress shirt
Dress pants or skirt
Conservative footwear

*Standards for women vary more than for men.

Photos (left to right from top left): Justin Horrocks/Getty Images; Neustockimages/Getty Images; 4x6/Getty Images; drbimages/E+/Getty Images; g_studio/Getty Images; Ann Marie Kurtz/Getty Images

FIGURE 15.3

Messages Sent by Formality of Workplace Attire

Source: Cardon, P. W., & Okoro, E. A. (2009). Professional characteristics communicated by formal versus casual workplace attire. *Business Communication Quarterly, 72*(3), 355–360.

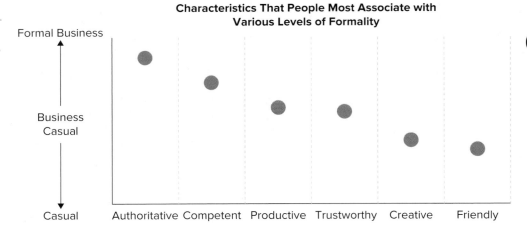

Characteristics That People Most Associate with Various Levels of Formality

levels of attire: formal business, high-level business casual, and low-level business casual. Business casual dress is the most common form of dress in the workplace today, but there continues to be wide variation based on geographic region, industry, company culture, and position.[17]

Casual dress is the least formal option. It is rare in a business-related setting, although there are notable exceptions in the tech industry.[18] While some companies have implemented casual Fridays, many executives and managers feel that employees dress too casually on these days. If your company allows casual Fridays, make sure your attire continues to project a professional image.

Your attire, and the level of formality you choose, projects a range of messages (see Figure 15.3). Generally, formal business attire projects authority and competence, high-level business casual is associated with productivity and trustworthiness, and low-level business casual is associated with creativity and friendliness.[19]

For business presentations, you should generally dress up slightly more formally than your audience. Also, consider the messages you intend to send. Younger professionals may not yet have established traits such as authority and competence, whereas they are often assumed to be friendly. So, younger professionals can gain significantly by dressing more formally.

Using Visual Aids and Handouts

LO15.4 Use slides and handouts to supplement your presentation effectively.

You can powerfully supplement your presentations with visual aids and handouts. In fact, many audiences expect both. In this section, we discuss how to use these items to increase your presentation effectiveness.

Use Visuals without Losing Focus on You

In Chapter 14, we discussed the design of electronic slides. Another option for presentations is the screencast video, described in the Technology Tips feature. Regardless of the technology you use, your goal is to keep yourself as the main focus of the presentation. Even with well-designed slides or videos, however, keeping the focus on you during the presentation can be challenging. Keep in mind the following tips as you present:

Avoid Turning Out the Lights in Most Cases Many presenters turn out the lights so that the audience can more easily view the slides. This makes the slides, rather than you, the focal point for the duration of the presentation. Some audience members may also get drowsy in low light. In some rooms, you can dim the lights next to the screen, but if you do, make sure that you are in full light to your audience.

ⓘ Technology Tips

CREATING SCREENCAST VIDEOS

Business professionals—especially executives, human resource professionals, and sales and marketing professionals—increasingly use screencast videos to reach audiences remotely. Many software packages, such as Camtasia, Adobe Captivate, and Jing, allow you to develop presentation videos that record the activity on your computer screen and combine it with video, audio, and other files. As you develop these screencast videos, keep in mind the following tips:

Plan your production and make several trial runs. A screencast video requires you to take the roles of producer, director, and actor all in one. You can choose elements to display on your screen, such as PowerPoint slides, spreadsheets, word processing documents, or other types of files. Simultaneously, you can narrate as you display the content and can even provide video of yourself. After recording, you have many tools available to edit your production.

Create short, concise videos. Most screencast videos are short. For example, most how-to videos created by companies and posted on YouTube or their own websites last one to five minutes.

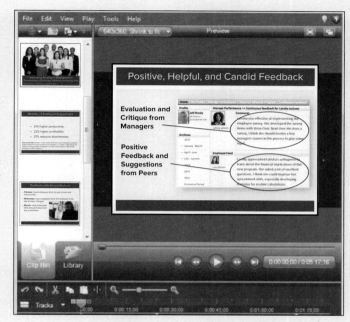

Source: Camtasia/TechSmith; Digitalskillet/iSock/Getty Images; Dougal Waters/Digital Vision/Getty Images; LWA/Larry Williams/Blend Images LLC; Polka Dot Images/Jupiterimages/Getty Images; Racorn/123RF

Use the right resources. You can use free screencast software and inexpensive video cameras and microphones to make screencasts; however, it's generally worth the investment to purchase state-of-the-art screencast software and the right cameras and microphones, especially if you intend to create professional-grade screencasts.

Your challenge: As a group of three to five people, choose a topic you could easily convert into a screencast video. Then, independently create the screencast videos. Next, get together and watch the videos together. What did you learn about how each of you approach messaging and presentation design? What features worked best? What caught attention? What was memorable and effective?

Don't Start Your Slides Right Away   The opening moments of your presentation are too valuable to devote to slides. Use at least the opening one to two minutes to make a personal connection with your audience. Then begin your slides.

Speak to Your Audience, Not the Screen   The single most important strategy is to face your audience. Presenters often spend too much time looking at their slides with their back or side to the audience.

Interpret, Don't Read Your Slides   When you simply read your slides, you reduce yourself to nothing but a narrator. Since audience members can read your slides more quickly than you can recite what they say, the slides become the primary source of information. When you explain and elaborate on the content in your slides, you draw your audience's attention to you as the primary source of information.

Preview the Slides before Showing Them   To keep the focus on you and more effectively control the timing of your message, introduce your slides before you show them.

Distribute your handouts strategically to maintain focus on you.

Fizkes/Shutterstock

When you move to a slide without any introduction, the audience automatically focuses on the slide more than on you.

Use a Remote Control to Advance Slides When Possible   Using a remote control to move from slide to slide allows you to move around as you talk and more effectively engage with your audience. It also allows you to maintain more eye contact, since using a keyboard requires glancing down.

Avoid Standing in Front of the Slide Projection   Make sure to stand to the side of the slide projection area. Standing in front of the projection causes two problems. It makes the slide more difficult to view. But, perhaps worse, it distorts your appearance.

Use Blank Slides Strategically   If you plan to speak for lengthy periods without referencing your slides, consider displaying a blank slide so that the screen does not become a distraction.

Use Handouts Effectively

Handouts generally make sense for detailed, numerical, and other information that is difficult to project adequately onto a screen. Also, you may want audience members to complete certain handouts during or after the presentation. For example, Shannon provides a handout on which seminar participants describe a manufacturing project they want to outsource.

However, handouts can distract your audience and take attention away from you. One primary advantage of presentations is that you have high control over what message your audience members hear, especially compared to written communications. As soon as you distribute handouts, you may lose this control since some audience members will immediately begin looking through the handouts and lose their focus on you.

If you can, wait until the end of your presentation to distribute handouts. This allows you to maintain more control over the message. If you need to use handouts during the presentation, consider how you might distribute them without losing control, especially during the opening one to two minutes of your presentation. Recall that audience members form many of their deepest impressions during this initial part of your presentation. Many presenters have lost the opportunity to connect effectively during their openings because of rustling handouts.

Interacting with Your Audience

LO15.5 Interact effectively with your audience.

Visit http://connect. mheducation.com for an exercise on this topic.

Good speakers involve the audience as much as possible without getting off message and taking too much time. A few ways to interact with your audience include fielding questions during the presentation as well as mingling and following up with audience members afterward.

Field Questions

Many of your presentations will involve a question-and-answer (Q&A) portion. You may ask for questions at the conclusion of your presentation or invite questions throughout.

When you take questions, you show you are interested in your listeners' real concerns and needs. You also have an opportunity to clarify points you may have misstated or omitted. Of course, fielding questions involves a number of risks: Your audience members may ask you difficult ones and may even get you off topic. The solution is to reinforce your key messages while also addressing the needs of your questioners. Practice the following strategies to make the Q&A go as smoothly and effectively as possible.[20]

Pause before Answering   This gives you time to reflect and quickly develop the best response. It also gives the impression that you are thoughtful. In some cases, you may feel under pressure during questioning. Pausing helps you stay calm and collected.

Be Honest   During questioning, many presenters are so committed to supporting their own positions that they respond with exaggeration or with excessive confidence. This is a mistake. Admit when you do not know the answer. Explain that you would like to get an answer to the question and seek an opportunity to continue the conversation later on. Notice in Table 15.4 how Latisha responds when she doesn't have a firm answer to a question.

Show Appreciation   Fielding questions allows you to develop an emotional bond with the questioner. You can do so by sincerely showing thanks, recognizing the importance of the question, and otherwise validating the questioner, as Latisha does in the more effective example in Table 15.5.

Be Concise   Short responses are effective for several reasons. First, the question may be of interest to just one or a few of your audience members. Second, the longer your response, the more likely you are to stray from your key messages or excessively repeat them. As a rule of thumb, keep most responses to between 20 and 45 seconds. Pay close attention to your audience members during Q&A to see if they are remaining interested and engaged. Table 15.6 compares Latisha's less and more concise responses.

TABLE 15.4

Be Honest

Less Effective	More Effective
Q. *I know you've said that managers will like this new system, but you haven't really talked about what managers wouldn't like about the system. For me, I'd worry about this system eroding my authority to ask for real changes, especially if other employees are giving so much positive feedback. So, don't you think this could actually upset some managers?*	
A. I guess that I haven't really heard that concern yet. I think that managers might have a concern like that initially, but as they continue using the system they'll notice they are actually empowered rather than having their authority eroded.	**A.** I'm not prepared to give a good answer to that question right now, but I think we certainly need to address it. Perhaps the HR team can ask some of our contacts at companies using continuous reviews to tell us their experiences with the challenges that managers face with these systems. If it's okay with you, the HR team and I will get some answers to your question and email the entire senior management team within a week.
Lathisha's response glosses over the fact that she is not informed enough to give an accurate answer. Although she attempts to put a positive spin on the problem, she may appear dismissive of some listeners' genuine concerns.	Latisha states that she is uncertain. However, she demonstrates a willingness to get the answer from reliable sources and promises to provide that information within a week. Overall, she gains credibility with her up-front, helpful response.

TABLE 15.5

Show Appreciation

Less Effective	More Effective
Q. Do you think there's a risk that because the feedback is public, managers and employees will avoid sharing their candid and real views of one another's performance?	
A. Actually, the system allows private feedback so that . . .	**A.** That's a good question. We talked to four or five HR directors who have implemented continuous reviews, and they each initially had this concern. In practice, employees and managers use the private feedback feature when they offer negative or sensitive feedback. . . .
This is a good, rational response but could be improved with additional validation of the questioner.	By briefly validating the importance of the question, Latisha is able to demonstrate that she relates directly to this concern and that Eastmond Networking is committed to facilitating this communication. The response is strong rationally and emotionally.

TABLE 15.6

Be Concise

Less Effective	More Effective
Q. You've mentioned a few success stories at Peakster Computing. Could you mention some examples at other companies you've talked to?	
A. Sure. I could give you lots of examples. Let me tell you about three other companies . . . (continues on for three to four minutes largely repeating the same key points).	**A.** Momentarily, I'll distribute a handout with more comprehensive information from our research. The handout provides cases for four companies we worked with, so you'll be able to see that the results at Peakster Computing are quite similar to those at the other three companies.
By providing such a lengthy answer, Latisha may inadvertently disengage some of her audience members who have already gotten her key points.	In this brief response (roughly 20 seconds), Latisha provides new information (that will be in a handout) and touches on but does not belabor key takeaway points. This response has broad appeal since it allows audience members to locate additional results from other companies.

Reframe the Question to Match Your Agenda   You should have fairly clear objectives for your presentation. When your listeners ask questions that could derail your agenda, find ways to tactfully reframe the conversation in favor of your objectives, as Latisha's does in the examples in Table 15.7.

Mingle and Follow Up

When you complete your presentation, your work is not complete. In most cases, this is a good opportunity to work the room, further connecting with your audience. You can get additional feedback and discuss future endeavors with your listeners.

Similarly, in the days following the event, you can reach out to your audience members. Follow up on any promises you made about providing additional information. If possible, send a quick email note to thank people for attending. Set in motion steps that turn a onetime presentation into an ongoing professional relationship.

TABLE 15.7

Reframe the Question to Match Your Agenda

Less Effective	More Effective

Q. *I'm quite skeptical that our company will get the dramatic results you've suggested. Do you really think a software program will help us reduce employee turnover?*

A. Well, actually, I can't guarantee anything. But, I can tell you with certainty that these types of software platforms have made dramatic differences in each company we've talked to. I think we'll have similar results here.	**A.** I think it's fair to say that we can reduce employee turnover by focusing on performance in a more positive and motivating way. What we've learned from these other companies is that they used the software successfully because they created a culture of performance where managers and employees are giving one another more frequent, more positive, and more candid feedback. This energizing environment is what reduced employee turnover. So, I'd say creating this culture with the help of these software tools will help us reduce employee turnover.
This question challenges the basic premise that technology (a software platform) can make a difference. It may raise this doubt among other audience members as well. While the response is true, it fails to reframe the question in a way that focuses on how managers and employees help each other.	This response reframes the conversation by emphasizing how managers and employees encouraging one another to improve is the key driver of lower employee turnover. This response is successfully reframed to address the questioner's real concern: Technology isn't the solution.

Present Effectively in Teams

You'll often have the opportunity to present in teams. Delivering an effective team presentation involves the same principles as an individual presentation with a few complications to address. The key is to plan for these issues well ahead of the presentation. Keep in mind these tips.

LO15.6 Prepare to present effectively in teams.

Be Clear with One Another about Your Objectives and Key Messages

The primary challenge for a team presentation is ensuring that it is cohesive. If you're united in your objectives and key messages, your team will present far more cohesively, smoothly, and influentially. As you prepare, make sure you and your team explicitly mention your key objectives and messages often.

Decide on Your Presentation Roles

Early in your planning, you should make decisions about how you and your team members will gather information, analyze it, and present it. Similarly, you should make decisions about which

Many of your most important business presentations will be accomplished as a team.
Hill Street Studios LLC

team members will deliver various portions of the presentation. Consider which team members are best suited to explain certain types of information and which team members should open and close the presentation. While roles are important, remember that you will need to hold team discussions and make team decisions during the entire process leading up to the presentation. One common mistake teams make is to assign information gathering to various team members early in the process and then work independently up until the presentation. This generally leads to disjointed, disorganized presentations. Also, an often overlooked issue for team presentations is assigning roles for responding to questions from the audience. Make sure you plan which team members will respond to various types of questions.

Stand Together and Present a United Front

Your team is far more effective when you maintain a united front. As much as possible, stand close to one another. Stay interested in your teammates as they present, nodding in agreement and interest periodically. Similarly, maintain eye contact with the audience to show your interest in them, even when you're not presenting. Coordinate with one another to make sure you all wear the same formality of attire.

Refer to One Another's Points

By referring to one another throughout the presentation, you make sure your comments connect with your teammates and you also show that your team is united. Phrases such as "As Latisha mentioned . . ." or "Jeff's point about . . ." are signals that your team has prepared its ideas carefully.

Transition Effectively

You and your team members should smoothly pass speaking roles from one to the next. Simple phrases such as the following allow effective transitions from one person to the next: "I've shared with you how employee engagement increases productivity and profitability. Now, Latisha will share some ways we can improve employee engagement." As you make transitions, however, be careful about taking opportunities away from your teammates to showcase their best points. For example, consider the following transition: "Now, Latisha will share how continuous reviews increase employee engagement. She will show you software tools that allow multi-source feedback and recognition. She'll even explain how for under $10,000 per year, we can substantially increase employee engagement with these tools." Notice how this transition doesn't allow Latisha to choose the timing of her key messages and key points. In short, use transitions that set your teammates up for success and avoid stealing their thunder.

Being a Supportive Audience Member

You will likely be an audience member more often than you are a presenter. Take this role seriously. Do all you can to support the presenter. Show interest by maintaining eye contact and sitting up straight. Avoid behaviors that may distract the presenter, such as glancing at your mobile phone or yawning. Make comments and ask questions that help the presenter stay on message. Publicly express appreciation for the merits of the presentation. Privately offer advice for making the presentation more useful.

Being a supportive audience member has many advantages. In most cases, you share professional interests with the presenter. As a result, the success of the presentation is a team effort. Furthermore, your reputation for being a supportive audience member may be reciprocated when you take the role of presenter.

IDEA IN ACTION

BE YOURSELF

Melinda Gates is the third most powerful woman in the world, according to the *Forbes World's 100 Most Powerful Women* list. After a successful business career, she has spent the last several decades as one of the most active philanthropists in the world. The co-chair of the Bill and Melinda Gates Foundation, she works tirelessly to fight disease, increase prosperity, and support opportunities for women in the most vulnerable communities across the globe. Her ability to prepare and deliver speeches on catchy topics is one key to her success at generating support for her causes. For example, her most-watched TED Talk is called "What Nonprofits Can Learn from Coca-Cola."

When Gates recently addressed college graduates, she said, "My best advice would be to be yourself." In the early 1980s, she was one of the only women at Microsoft with a technology background. She thought she had to adopt the "same style as all the men in the room." But she was so unhappy trying to mimic the behavior of others, she almost left the company. Ultimately, she pushed

Noam Galai/Contributor/Getty Images

through several years of discomfort and learned to be herself. In the process, she developed her own unique leadership style and gained much more satisfaction at work.

Gates's advice is important in many professional situations, especially in speech situations. Remember as you plan and develop presentations, your passion and authenticity are essential. Find ways to *be yourself* in this process, and you'll realize that your authenticity helps you connect with and influence others.

Sources: Pomerantz, D., Shaddock, S., & Howard, C. (2017). The world's 100 most powerful women. *Forbes.* Retrieved from www.forbes.com/power-women/#224262025e25 (the first and second most-powerful women on the list were Angela Merkel and Theresa May); Gates, M. (2010, September). What nonprofits can learn from Coca-Cola. *TED Talk.* Retrieved from ted.com/talks/melinda_french_gates_what_nonprofits_can_learn_from_coca_cola; Ward, M. (2017, May 17). 3 things we learned from Sheryl Sandberg's Facebook Live with Melinda Gates. *CNBC.* Retrieved from www.cnbc.com/2016/10/07/lessons-from-sheryl-sandberg-facebook-live-with-melinda-gates.html.

You can build important business relationships by sincerely serving as a supportive and helpful audience member.

Dmitriy Shironosov/Alamy Stock Photo

Chapter Takeaway for *Delivering Presentations*

LO15.1 Describe how presentation delivery impacts your credibility.
Delivering presentations demonstrates **your personal credibility**.

It shows **competence** when you know and provide valuable content.	It shows **caring** when you are responsive to the expectations of your audience.	It shows **character** when you display complete openness and honesty.

LO15.2 Deliver presentations with authenticity, confidence, and influence.

Principles for Establishing Presence		
• Establish credibility. • Maintain authenticity. • Know your material.	• Speak with confidence. • Focus on people. • Stay flexible.	• Use the room to your advantage. • Communicate nonverbally. • Dress for success.

Principles for Focusing on People	
• Make people the subject of your sentences. • Introduce colleagues by name.	• Use names of audience members.

See *examples of focusing on people* in Tables 15.1, 15.2, and 15.3.

Principles for Staying Flexible		
• Arrive early. • Focus on the needs of the audience.	• When you lose your place, don't panic. • Never tell your audience things haven't gone as expected.	• Always have a plan B. • Know what your key messages are.

LO15.3 Apply the SOFTEN model of nonverbal communication for presentations.

Principles of the SOFTEN Model		
• *S*mile • *O*pen stance	• *F*orward lean • *T*one	• *E*ye contact • *N*od

LO15.4 Use slides and handouts to supplement your presentation effectively.

Principles for Using Slides		
• Avoid turning out the lights in most cases. • Don't start the slides right away. • Speak to your audience, not the screen.	• Interpret, don't read your slides. • Preview the slides before showing them. • Use remotes to advance slides.	• Avoid standing in front of the slide projection. • Use blank slides strategically.

LO15.5 Interact effectively with your audience.

Principles for Fielding Questions		
• Pause before answering. • Be honest.	• Show appreciation. • Be concise.	• Reframe the question to match your agenda.

See *examples of fielding questions* in Tables 15.4, 15.5, 15.6, and 15.7.

LO15.6 Prepare to present effectively in teams.

• Be clear with one another about your objectives and key messages.	• Decide on your presentation roles. • Stand together and present a united front.	• Refer to one another's points. • Transition effectively.

Key Terms

business casual dress, 481

casual dress, 482

formal business dress, 481

SOFTEN model of nonverbal
communication, 479

Discussion Exercises

15.1 Chapter Review Questions (LO15.1, LO15.2, LO15.3, LO15.4, LO15.5)

For each of the following items, respond with one or two paragraphs.

A. Discuss how you can establish and build credibility before, during, and after your presentations.

B. Describe the importance of authenticity for presentations. Discuss how you can plan and rehearse for presentations and also maintain authenticity.

C. Discuss some strategies for overcoming nervousness and fear before and during presentations. Describe the three strategies you believe are most effective for you.

D. Describe strategies for making people the focus of your presentations.

E. Explain the SOFTEN model of nonverbal communication.

F. Describe strategies for using slides and handouts without distracting the audience from what you have to say.

G. Describe strategies for effectively fielding questions during or after your presentation.

15.2 Ideas in Action Discussion Questions (LO15.1, LO15.2, LO15.4, LO15.5)

Read the Ideas in Action section about Melinda Gates. Respond to the following questions based on Gates's experiences and your own experiences:

A. What are some of the negative consequences of trying to mimic the behaviors of others? How might this hurt you in presentation situations? How might it help you in presentation situations?

B. What do you think authenticity really means? In what ways is authenticity valuable for presenters? What are the risks of authenticity?

C. What do you think is the connection between experimenting with various presentation styles and authenticity? What are some ways you can experiment to raise your authenticity as a presenter?

Evaluation Exercises

15.3 Evaluating an Effective Presentation (LO15.2, LO15.3, LO15.4)

Think about a recent presentation you attended that you found effective. In three to five paragraphs, describe why it was effective. Include the following aspects in your analysis, referring to Chapter 14 if necessary for a refresher on preview-view-review:

A. Description of the presentation.

B. Key points.

C. Preview.

D. View.

E. Review.

F. Electronic slides or other visual aids.

G. Nonverbal behavior.

15.4 Evaluating a Corporate Presentation (LO15.2, LO15.3, LO15.4)

Go online and find a business presentation that interests you. You can generally find presentations easily on company websites (usually in the Media, Newsroom, or Investors sections), YouTube, or business websites (e.g., CNBC). Evaluate the presentation and in-

clude the following in your analysis, referring to Chapter 14 if necessary for a refresher on preview-view-review:

A. Description of the presentation.

B. Key points.

C. Preview.

D. View.

E. Review.

F. Electronic slides or other visual aids.

G. Nonverbal behavior.

15.5 Assessing One of Your Recent Presentations (LO15.1, LO15.2, LO15.3, LO15.4, LO15.5)

Think about a presentation you delivered recently. In three to five paragraphs, address the following issues, referring to Chapter 14 if necessary for a refresher on preview-view-review:

A. Description of the presentation.

B. Key points.

C. Preview.

D. View.

E. Review.

F. Electronic slides or other visual aids.

G. Nonverbal behavior.

H. Three improvements you would make if you did the presentation again.

15.6 Video Recording Your Presentation (LO15.1, LO15.2, LO15.3, LO15.4, LO15.5)

Record one of your presentations and then do the following:

A. Immediately following your presentation, draft your basic impressions of your performance.

B. Watch the video recording three times as follows:

- On the first viewing, observe the overall impact of your presentation.

- On the second viewing, turn the volume off and observe your nonverbal behaviors.

- On the third viewing, close your eyes and listen. Pay attention to the speed, volume, pitch, variety, and enthusiasm in your voice.

After completing steps A and B above, answer the following questions about your presentation:

C. How effective was your opening?

D. How effective was your nonverbal communication (e.g., voice quality, eye contact with audience)?

E. How effective was the content of your presentation (e.g., relevance to audience, logical order, impact)?

F. How persuasive was your presentation?

G. How well did you connect with your audience?

H. Overall, name two major strengths and two major weaknesses of your oral presentation.

I. If you were going to deliver this same presentation again, what three adjustments would you make?

J. What are the two presentation skills you believe you most need to improve? Explain.

Application Exercises

For Exercises 15.7 through 15.10, prepare five- to ten-minute presentations. Make sure you first identify your key messages and analyze your audience based on information in the textbook. Create a clear and compelling preview, view, and review (see Chapter 14). If directed by your instructor, create electronic slide presentations.

15.7 Presentation to the Executive Team at Better Horizons Credit Union (LO15.1, LO15.2, LO15.3, LO15.4, LO15.5)

Assume the role of Haniz Zogby (see Chapter 10). Based on the information in Chapter 10, create a presentation to the executive team on a marketing initiative about financial planning aimed at attracting new members. You could base a large part of the presentation on Figure 10.3.

15.8 Presentation to College Students about Joining Better Horizons Credit Union (LO15.1, LO15.2, LO15.3, LO15.4, LO15.5)

Assume the role of Haniz Zogby (see Chapter 10). Based on the information in Chapter 10, create a presentation to university students

to persuade them to join Better Horizons Credit Union. You could base part of the presentation on Figure 10.7.

15.9 Presentation Asking for Participation in the Hope Walk-athon (LO15.1, LO15.2, LO15.3, LO15.4, LO15.5)

Assume the role of Haniz Zogby (see Chapter 10). Based on the information in Chapter 10, create a presentation to encourage credit union members to participate in the Hope Walkathon. You could base part of the presentation on Figure 10.9.

15.10 Presentation about Changes at Marble Home Make-overs (LO15.1, LO15.2, LO15.3, LO15.4, LO15.5)

Assume the role of Juan Hernandez (see Chapter 11). Based on the information in Chapter 11, create a presentation to employees about temporary changes in work shifts. You could base the presentation on Figure 11.4.

Language Mechanics Check

15.11 Review all rules in Appendix A about punctuation, number usage, and grammar. Then, rewrite each sentence to make all needed corrections.

A. To gain experience as a public speaker, you can find many opportunities, to develop your abilities.

B. Many professionals join training groups or organizations such as Toastmasters, which focus on public speaking.

C. Once you're part of one of these groups you and the other members practice intensively, and give supportive and helpful feedback to one another.

D. Most of these organizations provide training materials, magazines, guidebooks and development plans.

E. You can also join organizations, which frequently hold public speeches that you can observe or even deliver.

F. Many civic organizations such as the Rotary Club hold weekly meetings, where community members are invited to speak.

G. You might consider volunteering to speak in classes, at clubs or at other events to increase your experience speaking, in uncomfortable and uncertain situations.

H. Many people, who aspire to develop public skills, regularly watch Ted Talks so they can see the delivery style of great speakers.

I. Surprisingly most expert public speakers get nervous nearly each time they speak.

J. Yet most audience members don't even notice these expert speakers are nervous, which shows how well these speakers have learned to control their emotions during public events.

Endnotes

1. De Angelis, B. (2007, June). Communicating with authenticity. *Toastmaster*. Retrieved from www.toastmasters.org/Toastmasters Magazine/ToastmasterArchive/2007/June/Authenticity.aspx.

2. Quoting Phillip Khan-Pami in Morgan, N. (2003, September). How to put together a great speech when you're under the gun. *Harvard Management Communication Letter, 3*.

3. Schulte, T. (2016, June 16). Why Jerry Seinfeld was right about public speaking. *Define Financial*. Retrieved from https://www.definefinancial.com/blog/jerry-seinfeld-public-speaking/.

4. Brewer, G. (2001, March 19). Snakes top list of Americans' fears: Public speaking, heights and being closed in small spaces also create fear in many Americans. Retrieved August 22, 2010, from Gallup, www.gallup.com/poll/1891/Snakes-Top-List-Americans-Fears.aspx.

5. Twichell, K. L. (2010, January). Stage fright—why now? *Toastmaster*. Retrieved from www.toastmasters.org/ToastmastersMagazine/ToastmasterArchive/2010/January/Stage-Fright.aspx.

6. Leech, T. (2004). *How to prepare, stage, and deliver winning presentations,* 3rd ed. New York: American Management Association.

7. Twichell, K. L. (2010, January). Stage fright—why now? *Toastmaster*. Retrieved from www.toastmasters.org/ToastmastersMagazine/Toastmaster Archive/2010/January/Stage-Fright.aspx; Bailey, J. (2007, December). Beauty and the beast: Changing your fear from fiend to friend. *Toastmaster*. Retrieved from www.toastmasters.org/ToastmastersMagazine/ToastmasterArchive/2007/December/BeautyandtheBeast.aspx; Dahms, G. B. (2008, June). Good posture = good breathing. *Toastmaster*. Retrieved from www.toastmasters.org/ToastmastersMagazine/ToastmasterArchive/2008/June/Departments/HowToPDF.aspx; Mills, H. (2007). *Power Points! How to design and deliver presentations that sizzle and sell*. New York: AMACOM.

8. Johnson, K., & Millo, T.-L. (2007, August). Put your audience in your speech. *Toastmaster*. Retrieved from www.toastmasters.org/ToastmastersMagazine/ToastmasterArchive/2007/August/Audience.aspx.

9. Genard, G. (2004). Leveraging the power of nonverbal communication. *Harvard Business Management Communication Letter, 3–4*.

10. Mills, H. (2007). *Power Points! How to design and deliver presentations that sizzle and sell*. New York: AMACOM.

11. Zielinski, D. (2007, September). Body language myths. *Toastmaster*. Retrieved from www.toastmasters.org/ToastmastersMagazine/ToastmasterArchive/2007/September/Myths.aspx.

12. Meyer, N. S. (2009, February). That's not my voice—is it? *Toastmaster*. Retrieved from www.toastmasters.org/Toastmasters Magazine/ToastmasterArchive/2009/February/Departments/Manner-of-Speaking.aspx.

13. Landrum, M. (2009). Speaking eye to eye: A meeting of the eyes denotes a meeting of the minds. *Toastmaster*. Retrieved from www.toastmasters.org/ToastmastersMagazine/Toastmaster Archive/2009/December/Articles/Speaking-Eye-to-Eye.aspx.

14. Zielinski, D. (2007, September). Body language myths. *Toastmaster*. Retrieved from www.toastmasters.org/Toastmasters Magazine/ToastmasterArchive/2007/September/Myths.aspx.

15. Zielinski, D. (2007, September). Body language myths. *Toastmaster*. Retrieved from www.toastmasters.org/ToastmastersMagazine/ToastmasterArchive/2007/September/Myths.aspx.

16. Haefner, R. (2008, July 30). How to dress for success for work. *CNN*. Retrieved from www.cnn.com/2008/LIVING/worklife/07/30/cb.dress.for.success/index.html.

17. Robert Half. (2017, June 19). Just how casual is the dress code becoming for accountants. *The Robert Half Blog*. Retrieved from https://www.roberthalf.com/blog/salaries-and-skills/just-how-casual-is-the-dress-code-becoming-for-accountants.

18. Olson, A. (2019, March 8). Wall Street's new dress code raises question: What to wear? *Star Tribune*. Retrieved from http://www.startribune.com/wall-street-s-new-dress-code-raises-question-what-to-wear/506866442/; Kiddie, T. (2009). Recent trends in business casual attire and their Effects on student job seekers. *Business Communication Quarterly*, 350–354; Langford, B. (2005). *The etiquette edge: The unspoken rules for business success*. New York: American Management Association.

19. Cardon, P. W., & Okoro, E. A. (2009). Professional characteristics communicated by formal versus casual workplace attire. *Business Communication Quarterly, 72*(3), 355–360.

20. Toogood, G. N. (2010). *The new articulate executive: Look, act, and sound like a leader*. New York: McGraw-Hill.

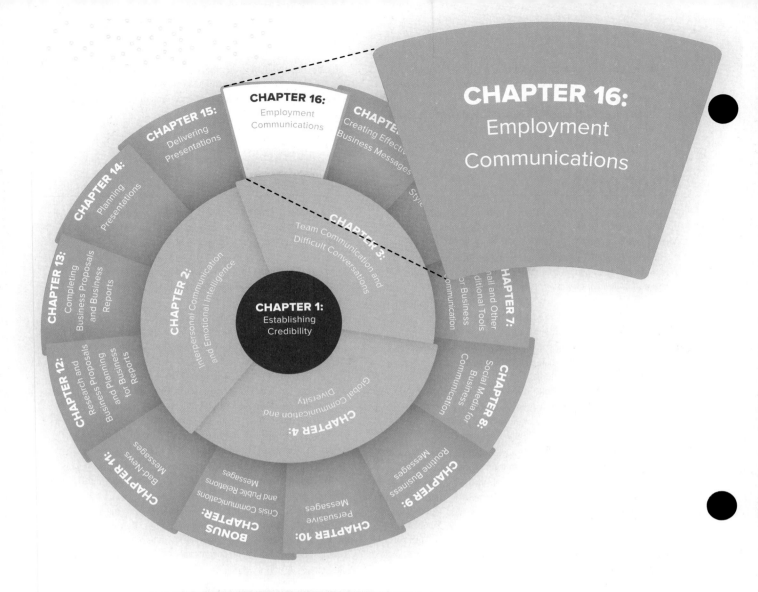

CHAPTER 16:
Employment
Communications

ESTABLISHING
CREDIBILITY

PRINCIPLES OF INTERPERSONAL
COMMUNICATION

PRINCIPLES FOR & TYPES OF
BUSINESS MESSAGES

LEARNING OBJECTIVES

After studying this chapter, you should be able to do the following:

LO16.1 Understand principles for professional networking.

LO16.2 Identify your key selling points for the job application process.

LO16.3 Evaluate the primary needs of employers for positions of interest.

LO16.4 Set up the message structure for résumés and cover letters.

LO16.5 Highlight your qualifications with effective tone, style, and design.

LO16.6 Create chronological and functional résumés to highlight your key selling points.

LO16.7 Use LinkedIn as part of the job search process and to network professionally.

LO16.8 Develop a list of references that will improve your employment prospects.

LO16.9 Compose effective cover letters that highlight your key selling points.

LO16.10 Review your job application documents for effectiveness and fairness.

LO16.11 Develop strategies for responding to common job interview questions.

LO16.12 Explain etiquette for following up after job interviews.

LO16.13 Explain etiquette for leaving an organization with grace and foresight.

? WHY DOES THIS MATTER?

Searching for jobs can be exhilarating. It involves hopes for new beginnings and possibilities! Many job applicants also find the process stressful, intimidating, and scary. In recent years due to the recession, one reality is that the number of applicants exceeds the number of positions. However, with determination, patience, and planning, you can land a job that will help you move forward in your career. In this chapter, you will focus on developing a job application package that allows you to identify and highlight your key selling points in a way that meets the needs of employers. Quickly read the following case that is the basis for examples you will see throughout the chapter.

Hear Pete Cardon explain why this matters.

bit.ly/cardon16

CHAPTER CASE HANIZ AND JACLYN APPLY FOR JOBS

WHO'S INVOLVED

Haniz Zogby

Marketing specialist and loan officer at Better Horizons Credit Union
Florida State University, Class of 2020
Major: **Finance;** *Minor:* **Event Management**

Jaclyn Peha

Technology intern at Better Horizons Credit Union
Major: **Business Information Systems**

THE SITUATION

Haniz Zogby will graduate soon. She has worked for Better Horizons Credit Union for five years and feels a high level of job security. At Better Horizons, she has been given many opportunities to assist and, in some cases, direct promotional campaigns. However, she typically spends less than half of her time involved in marketing. Haniz wants a job where she has more responsibility, spends more of her time on innovative marketing campaigns, and makes more money. Jaclyn is also applying for positions. Like Haniz, she is graduating soon. Unlike Haniz, she has less work experience.

(Haniz Zogby character): Ingram Publishing; (Jaclyn Peha character): Onoky/SuperStock

TASK

 1

Haniz and Jaclyn want to write résumés that effectively portray their selling points.

2

Haniz wants to write cover letters that introduce her to employers and explain her value to them.

3

Haniz wants to interview effectively and show she's ready for the job.

Networking for Professional Success

LO16.1   Understand principles for professional networking.

Networking can open many learning and professional opportunities. Some people think of networking as focused on selfish, short-term gains for the person building the network. A better view of **networking** sees it as a proactive approach to building professional relationships to achieve shared company, career, and professional development goals. The most effective networkers seek to help others in their networks in many ways, including providing advice, sharing information, giving referrals, and coaching and mentoring. They often receive professional opportunities in return but do not expect these to materialize at any given time. In other words, they view networking as relational but not as transactional.[1]

During school and early in your career, networking may seem challenging. Your network is generally smaller, and you often have less to offer people in your school and professional networks. Yet, you can still begin the process. As a student seeking new positions and opportunities, consider adding to your network by conducting informational interviews with people in your field of interest, attending campus job fairs and career networking events, joining clubs and other professional interest groups, attending campus speeches and other professional development events, and volunteering at a local nonprofit.

Conduct Informational Interviews

In an **informational interview**, you speak with a successful and accomplished professional to seek out career advice. It is an excellent opportunity to learn about career choices and career paths.

Most professionals are honored and flattered when asked to give career advice. So, aim to make conducting informational interviews a regular practice. Because your interviewees are granting you a favor, keep the conversation short—20 to 30 minutes is typical. Learn as much as you can about the person before meeting, and go prepared with questions such as the following:

- What are your daily activities in this position?
- What do you enjoy most about this position?
- How did you get this position? What are some of the qualifications for this position?
- What are typical career paths in your area of expertise? In your company? In your industry?
- How do you continue to grow and learn in your area of expertise? What sources of information do you use? Do you recommend any books?
- What advice would you give to someone like me who's just starting a career?

You can ask dozens of other questions. The key is to think about what you want to learn and then draft questions accordingly.

Avoid using informational interviews to directly ask for position openings or job leads. These interviews are intended for learning and growth only. However, if your interviewee offers some job leads without your asking, feel free to follow up.[2]

Attend Job Fairs and Other Career Networking Events

Make sure to go your school's career office or use other information sources to find out about various job fairs and career networking events on your campus. Even if you're not looking for opportunities for another year or two, go to these events to get accustomed to the way people interact and socialize. Even if a networking event is outside your professional interests (for example, you're a marketing student but you see a networking event for students interested in consulting), consider attending to meet others and practice holding conversations in these important situations.

Attend Campus Speeches and Other Professional Development Events

Be on the lookout for speeches by accomplished professionals and other professional development events. Not only can you learn a lot, but you'll often meet interesting people from inside and outside your school. You never know how showing interest in the speakers, trainers, and attendees at these events can lead to continued professional interactions over the years.

Join Clubs and Other Professional Interest Groups

By joining clubs, especially those in functional areas (data analytics club, developers club), you can learn a lot of skills that make you marketable. The networking aspects of joining clubs, however, is often even more important for your career. Many club members enjoy friendships and professional relationships that endure for years and decades. It's not uncommon for their interactions to result in job leads.

Volunteer at a Local Nonprofit

When you stretch yourself to volunteer in community organizations, you place yourself within a whole new network of people. In nonprofit organizations, you often meet many generous people. You shouldn't view these efforts as ways to get new professional opportunities, but you'll be surprised how often professional opportunities arise.

These networking activities require some initiative and persistence. You may need to get out of your comfort zone and be a bit more outgoing, but you'll be in good company: 40 to 50 percent of adults say they are shy.[3] By forcing yourself into these situations, you'll improve at small talk and quickly building rapport with others. Taking a sincere interest in others will also help you succeed.[4] Finally, remember networking takes time, often months or years.[5]

Applying the AIM Planning Process to Résumés and Cover Letters

Preparing for the job application process is similar to preparing for other forms of business communication: It involves analyzing your audience (meeting the needs of your employers), gathering the right information (identifying your key selling points), and developing your message. Your end products—cover letters and résumés—are persuasive messages that show how you meet the needs of your prospective employers.

Identify Your Key Selling Points

LO16.2 Identify your key selling points for the job application process.

To create résumés and cover letters that serve your long-term career interests, your first step should be to carefully evaluate your career ambitions and qualifications. In this process, you clarify your professional goals for the short term (one to two years) and long term (five to ten years), identify the skills you have developed at school and work, and sort out the attributes that define who you are as a professional. As with other business communications, you attempt to identify your most important and strongest features so you can develop a concise and compelling message about the value you will bring to your prospective employers.

To help you identify your interests, abilities, and attributes, you might consider completing a self-inventory (see Figure 16.1 with an example of Haniz's self-inventory). Start by writing your career goals. Even if you don't yet have clear ones in mind, do your best to imagine the type of work you would like to be doing in five and ten years. Allow yourself enough time to do some soul-searching and research about careers as you develop your goals.

FIGURE 16.1

Self-Inventory of Career Interests and Job-Related Abilities and Attributes

---

Haniz Zogby
April 1, 2019

My Career Goals
1.   To act in a leadership role to develop and market financial services for credit unions
2.   In five to ten years, to hold an influential marketing position within a credit union group

My Strongest Professional Abilities
1.   Developing strong professional relationships with clients and vendors
2.   Attracting new members to credit unions through referrals, seminars, mailings, and online social networking
3.   Organizing members to participate in credit union–sponsored financial workshops and community events

My Strongest Professional Attributes
1.   Trusted and reliable on important campaigns
2.   Innovative and creative in approach to marketing and promotions
3.   Passionate about the credit union industry

Areas Where I Need to Improve
1.   Conducting customer surveys, statistical analysis, and survey reporting
2.   Earning a reputation for excellence outside of my local community

---

Identifying your career goals helps you accomplish several things in the job search process. First, it helps you frame your résumé and cover letter to project your career hopes. Second, it helps you evaluate how well your abilities and attributes prepare you for your desired career. This process allows you to address those areas where you most need improvement. Finally, it shows employers that you are serious, as well-defined career goals imply seriousness in your approach to work.

Once you have written down your career goals, identify your abilities and attributes.[6] **Abilities** are skills and knowledge that can be applied to accomplishing work tasks. **Attributes** are personal traits or characteristics. In the job application process, employers are often looking for more than your abilities. They're trying to figure out the kind of person you are. These judgments often come in the form of adjectives, such as *reliable*, *analytical*, or *people-oriented*. These attributes are difficult to measure precisely, but they indicate how well you'll fit into the company culture, how much effort and commitment you'll put into your work, and how you'll impact the work of others.

Employers consider your mix of attributes as they try to determine if you have the right *chemistry*—an intangible that human resource professionals say they weigh heavily in the decision to hire. Fifteen percent of HR professionals say it accounts for 75 percent or more of the decision. Nearly four in ten (39 percent) say it accounts for about 50 percent of the decision.[7]

One useful way of analyzing your *abilities* and *attributes* is in terms of credibility. To do so, consider the features of competence (ability to accomplish work tasks), caring (ability to maintain effective workplace relationships), and character (ability to uphold corporate norms and standards). Competence focuses on the technical skills to achieve work tasks. In Table 16.1, you can see examples of abilities and attributes associated with competence, caring, and character.

LO16.3 Evaluate the primary needs of employers for positions of interest.

Understand the Needs of Your Potential Employers

When hiring you, employers are making a huge investment. They will make this investment only when you demonstrate that you meet *their* needs. You can learn how well you fit the needs of employers by conducting a thorough job search and carefully analyzing those positions that are most compatible with your abilities and attributes.

TABLE 16.1

Abilities and Attributes That Establish Credibility in the Job Application Process

	Abilities (*Skills and/or Knowledge*)	Attributes (*Enduring Approaches to Work*)		
Competence (*Task*)	Function-specific (e.g., marketing, finance) Company/industry Technology Analysis/research	Achievement-oriented Ambitious Analytical Assertive Creative Can-do attitude Curious	Decisive Detail-oriented Entrepreneurial Independent Inquisitive Passionate	Problem solver Resourceful Results-oriented Seeks challenges Takes initiative Visionary
Caring (*Relationships*)	Communication/interpersonal Teamwork Emotional intelligence Leadership Intercultural	Customer-oriented Diplomatic Empathetic Flexible Generous	Inspiring Loyal Motivational People-oriented Persuasive	Responsive Sensitive Supportive Team-oriented Tolerant
Character (*Values*)	Familiarity with corporate culture and values Dedication to the success of the company Knowledge of business ethics	Accountable Committed Constant Dedicated Dependable	Fair Hardworking Honest Open-minded Optimistic	Reliable Responsible Straightforward Trustworthy Unbiased

Complete a Thorough Job Search Process   Looking for jobs takes a lot of time. It's not uncommon for the process—from finding a position announcement to application to offer—to take three to six months (or even longer in some industries). Your thorough search for the best potential positions at the initial stages can save you a lot of time and increase the likelihood you'll get a position that is in your long-term interests.

Use all the resources available to learn about your options and ensure that you apply for the jobs that are good fits for you. You likely have a career center located in your college or university. Spend some time talking to experts there and make a plan for exhaustively searching for jobs that match your interests and qualifications. Where possible, contact and get involved with professional organizations and visit organizational websites to learn about options. Go to job fairs on and off campus to see what opportunities are open and to practice networking in a competitive environment.

Certainly you're aware of the many job websites to search for positions (e.g., indeed .com, monster.com, jobs.com, careerbuilder.com, collegerecruiter.com). Your college or university may even recommend particular websites. Use all the available online options, but also make sure you are networking in the traditional sense as well—talking to friends, relatives, and colleagues. Even in the Social Age, the most common forms of networking for employment opportunities remain people you know well.[8]

Analyze the Needs of Potential Employers   One of the best ways to understand an employer's needs is to carefully read and analyze the job position announcement. Then, group the requests in the announcement in terms of abilities and attributes (for an example, see Figure 16.2, where Haniz did this for a job announcement). Once you've done this, you're in a good position to decide whether you match these criteria and, if so, to frame your résumé and cover letter to highlight these abilities and attributes.

In addition to analyzing the job position announcements, consider other strategies to gain insight about what the company is seeking. Some job announcements include contact information for a company representative. You might call this person, express your interest, and find out more. By doing this, you connect with an influential company representative and gain insight not provided in the job announcement.

FIGURE 16.2

Analyzing a Job Posting for Key Needs

Job Summary	Credit Union Field Marketing Specialist
Location 84341 **Job Type** Full-time **Reference Code** 831481809	**Organization:** Anchor Federal Credit Union Network **Education Required:** College degree **Experience Required:** 1–3 years **Position Description:**

Works with managers throughout the Anchor Federal Credit Union network to develop local marketing events to promote Credit Union membership. Coordinates all activities for each event, including supply distribution, prizes, and duration of campaign, budget, marketing support, and staffing. Responsible for tracking results and providing recommendations for future events. Also is responsible for collecting and maintaining data related to market conditions of each proposed site. Performs various other marketing and support functions when not traveling including general promotional development, membership surveys, collateral production and tracking, retiree package mailings, and other projects as assigned by the VP of Marketing.

Position Requirements:

- Develops individual marketing activities to support branch growth and/or agency events.
- Travels to various locations throughout the country to organize events.
- Analyzes market conditions to ensure that the marketing activity is in line with the demographics of that particular region. Provides annual profile of demographics for each region.
- Oversees budget for each activity. Is responsible for reporting variances on a monthly basis.
- Works with outside vendors to solicit participation in marketing activities. Actively promotes the participation of both staff and monetary contributions from these outside sources.
- Works with VP and AVPs of branches to set priorities and establish goals for each event. Tracks results of each event and analyzes the success/shortfall of each. Distributes reports for review.
- Tracks marketing collateral inventory for branches and DMs. Ensures timely distribution and proper inventory controls.
- Develops mailings for account generation and retention.
- Develops ongoing mail programs to DMs and BCO managers for relationship development throughout the agency side of the business.
- Makes routine phone calls to HR managers, DMs, and BCO managers to establish event schedules, coordinate Financial Finesse seminars, and maintain relationships throughout the organization.
- Performs other duties as assigned.

Position Attributes:

- Candidate must be able to travel 25–30% domestically.
- A minimum of 2 years of field marketing and sales experience.
- Candidate must have presentation skills and experience.

Abilities wanted

Marketing: develop local marketing events, conduct market analysis, prepare marketing reports (written and oral), write sales letters and other mailings to generate membership, conduct seminars.
Relationship management: work with branch managers to organize local events and set marketing strategies; supervise staffing for events; maintain intra-organizational relationships and relationships with outside vendors.
Communication: supervise distribute event schedules, disseminate marketing reports, encourage participation, make sales presentations.

Attributes wanted

Ambitious: must be able to take initiative on organizing many events and meet deadlines.
Creative: must develop attractive and compelling marketing events and campaigns.
Organized: must be able to manage many simultaneous projects, events, and relationships.

Also, learn all you can about the company. Spend time researching its strategic goals. Find out about its unique challenges, and think about how you might fit into the company's plans to face these challenges. You can also see whether alumni from your school work there and are willing to do an informational interview. You can find alumni at companies of interest through your career center or LinkedIn. Also, online searches will often help you learn more. Consider using Glassdoor.com, a site that collects employee reviews of their companies, to learn about the culture and work environment of prospective employers.

Develop Your Message for Résumés and Cover Letters

LO16.4 Set up the message structure for résumés and cover letters.

Your résumé should tell a story of the value you can provide to a company. Like other persuasive messages, it is stronger if you have a central sales theme. By choosing two or three abilities and attributes to highlight, you can craft a compelling document that shows how you meet the needs of employers.

A mistake that many job applicants make is trying to display everything they do well. This approach often ends up sending a scattered message and diluting a central sales theme about your key abilities and attributes.

Historically, most employers have preferred one-page résumés. Recently, more employers consider two-page résumés. Two-page résumés become increasingly effective for positions of more responsibility and seniority.[9] As a university student, however, you should aim for a single page unless requested otherwise. If you find yourself using more than one page, you are likely weakening the message about your key selling points. Condensing all your experience may be painful, but keep in mind that executives are more than three times as likely to complain about résumés that contain too much information than they are about résumés that contain too little.[10] Typically, résumés contain the following major sections: name block, career summary or objective, education, and experience.

Name Block   Most résumés begin with your name and contact information. This section allows recruiters to easily find your contact information (i.e., address, phone, email). This section should not contain any distracting information, such as an unprofessional email address.

Summary or Objective (Optional)   Many professionals now create a short section just following the name block about their overall qualifications. They often label this section "Qualifications Summary," "Skills Summary," "Career Summary," or other similar phrases. In five to ten sentences, this section generally states the candidate's primary accomplishments, abilities, and attributes. This summary should stick to the central selling theme.

Instead of a summary, some professionals write a job objective in one to two sentences. Until about five to ten years ago, a job objective was expected by most HR professionals. Increasingly, however, a job objective statement is not expected. From a recent survey of HR professionals, just 7 percent of them said a job objective is important.[11]

Education   This section summarizes your experiences in higher education and professional training. Most university students place the education section before the work experience section, since it generally highlights studies in a discipline directly related to the jobs they are seeking.

Consider providing some information that distinguishes or explains the uniqueness and value of your education. For example, a short list of related coursework helps employers understand the content of your program. You might also include class projects, practicum, service learning projects, or other educational experiences that highlight your key abilities and attributes.

Include your GPA if it is high (3.5 or higher) or required. Also, if you have achieved any academic credentials or awards, mention them. For example, being on the dean's list or graduating summa cum laude are well-recognized honors. If you received scholarships or other academic awards that employers may not recognize, include a short note that explains why the awards are significant.

Generally, do not include information about your high school education. Employers are not interested. However, during your high school years, you may have been involved in work or other relevant activities that emphasize your key abilities and attributes. This type of information may be appropriate for the work experience or "additional information" sections of your résumé.

Work Experience   In this section, also called *employment history or experience*, list your accomplishments and responsibilities from prior jobs in chronological order beginning with your current or most recent one.

Some students wonder if they should include unpaid internships in this section. Typically, you should, since they are relevant and legitimate professional experiences. In fact, the abilities and attributes students gain from internships are often more relevant and transferable to sought-after positions than those from their previous paid positions.

If you have little or no work experience, you shouldn't panic. You can highlight your abilities and attributes by listing achievements and experiences in school and community activities. Later, in Figures 16.6 and 16.7, you can see ineffective and effective examples of résumés for Jaclyn Peha, who doesn't have a lot of work experience. You can see how she shows her strengths convincingly. Of course, you should make a priority of establishing a job history right away to bolster your credibility in the eyes of potential employers.

Additional Information   Education and work experience often account for the majority of your résumé content. You can provide a variety of other information, however, to accentuate your key abilities and attributes. In fact, some of the additional information may be critical to showing who you are as a person—your attributes. You have a great deal of flexibility with other information you display. You might consider including some of the following sections:

- Technology Skills
- Professional Associations
- School Clubs
- Honors and Awards
- Certifications and Licenses
- Community Activities
- Volunteer Work
- Training
- Language Abilities

As you think about additional information to provide, the standard is simple: *Does providing this information carry on a narrative of your key abilities and attributes?* Keep in mind that many employers are particularly looking for job candidates with strong technology and interpersonal skills.[12] You can highlight these skills when you showcase your community and volunteer work, professional and student affiliations, and computer skills. Do not include such personal information as marital status, age, religion, or sexual orientation because none of this is relevant.

Getting the Tone, Style, and Design Right for Résumés and Cover Letters

LO16.5 Highlight your qualifications with effective tone, style, and design.

Once you've analyzed your key abilities and attributes and gathered information to place in your résumé, you're ready to present the information in a compelling manner. The tone, style, and design must be perfect. Employers often skim your résumé on the first pass. Unless you can present your main credentials within 15 to 30 seconds, you may be eliminated from the job pool. Even if potential employers reward your well-designed résumé with a second look, they are unlikely to spend a lot of time. Most hiring managers will spend under two minutes per résumé.[13]

This section is about developing your résumé so that you can make the most of the small window you have with potential employers. What can you do to show your distinctive combination of abilities and attributes? What can you do to make your experience stand out? What can you do to persuade prospective employers that you will be a good investment for them? In short, how can you make sure that potential employers rapidly understand your story: the unique abilities and attributes that will deliver value to them?

Emphasize Accomplishments with Action Verbs

As you describe your accomplishments and experiences, begin your statements with action verbs (see Table 16.2 for a list). By doing so, you highlight your abilities and attributes in a way that emphasizes action and results.

Select your action words strategically. Without exaggerating, choose verbs that make your key abilities and attributes jump off the page. For example, if you want to show that you are a leader, a series of statements beginning with action verbs such as *guided, initiated,* and *led* paint a more vivid picture than the statement *I am a good leader.*

By the same token, avoid verbs that undersell your abilities and attributes. Many university students use weak verbs when describing their significant customer service and administrative experiences. Phrases such as *answered calls, entered information in the computer,* and *waited tables* do not emphasize transferable abilities and attributes. Rather, they focus on menial duties and do not focus on professional outcomes. Read through some of the less effective and more effective statements in Table 16.3 and notice how action verbs can bolster your credibility.

Quantify Accomplishments Where Possible

Your potential employers want to know how valuable your contributions have been in your prior jobs. So, where possible, describe key contributions and how they affected the bottom line. Often, even when you can't say for certain how much you affected financial results, you can provide numbers that show the significance of your work. Notice the contrasts between less effective and more effective examples in Table 16.4 and how quantification strengthens the more effective statements.

Position Your Most Important Contributions First

The order in which you place your accomplishments and other supporting details shows how you prioritize them. The supporting details you place first or second under each heading in your résumé form the deepest impressions about your abilities and attributes. Furthermore, because most potential employers skim, they may only see the first one or two supporting details for each heading. So, strategically arrange this information to highlight your best features (see Table 16.5).

Remove Irrelevant Details

Writing résumés and cover letters requires the discipline to tell a story of how your key abilities and attributes will provide value to an employer. You should generally avoid details about your personal life, especially those that some people may find objectionable or unprofessional (e.g., politics or religion). Other information—although technically okay on a résumé—should be provided only if it helps develop your narrative. Generally, avoid listing personal interests and hobbies unless this information takes up little space and accentuates your key abilities and attributes (see Table 16.6).

Avoid Clichés, Buzzwords, and Jargon

As you craft your job application, show enthusiasm for potential positions without resorting to clichés. Many clichés, such as *dream job* or *track record of success,* fail to highlight your abilities and attributes for a few reasons. First, they do not communicate your specific accomplishments. Second, many potential employers perceive these statements as showing unrealistic or naïve expectations about a job or inflated beliefs about abilities (see Table 16.7).

Be Exact and Avoid Errors

Potential employers examine your résumé with intense scrutiny. On the first pass, many discard it immediately if it contains typos or other careless errors. In one recent survey, roughly three out of four financial executives (76 percent) said they would eliminate job

---

Principles of Effective Résumés

- Emphasize accomplishments with action verbs.
- Quantify accomplishments where possible.
- Position your most important contributions first.
- Remove irrelevant details.
- Avoid buzzwords and jargon.
- Be exact and avoid any errors.
- Group and label information to improve ease of reading.
- Format to distinguish pieces of information.
- Select a simple yet visually appealing layout.

TABLE 16.2

Action Verbs for Résumés

Management/ Supervision	Finance/Accounting	Analysis/Research	Customer Service
Assigned	Contracted	Explained	Reorganized
Evaluated	Demonstrated	Informed	Reviewed
Executed	Developed	Mediated	Screened
Facilitated	Exceeded	Negotiated	Streamlined
Hired	Excelled	Persuaded	Systematized
Managed	Gained	Presented	Updated
Mentored	Generated	Promoted	
Monitored	Improved	Publicized	**Customer Service**
Motivated	Increased	Reported	Assisted
Organized	Launched	Specified	Clarified
Oversaw	Marketed	Summarized	Confronted
Planned	Proposed	Supported	Delivered
Scheduled	Raised	Teamed with	Greeted
Screened	Secured		Handled
Selected	Sold	**Analysis/Research**	Maximized
Strengthened		Analyzed	Met
Supervised	**Finance/Accounting**	Compiled	Minimized
Trained	Allotted	Conducted	Performed
	Appraised	Detected	Provided
Leadership	Assessed	Diagnosed	Resolved
Authorized	Audited	Explored	Responded
Decided	Averted	Gathered	Served
Delegated	Balanced	Identified	Settled
Directed	Budgeted	Inspected	Treated
Enabled	Controlled	Interpreted	Worked with
Encouraged	Corrected	Operated	**Innovation/Creativity**
Enlisted	Cut	Performed	Built
Executed	Earned	Proved	Completed
Formed	Estimated	Quantified	Conceptualized
Guided	Evaluated	Researched	Created
Implemented	Forecasted	Reviewed	Defined
Influenced	Interpreted	Solved	Designed
Initiated	Prepared	Studied	Developed
Instituted	Preserved	Surveyed	Devised
Led	Projected	Tested	Formulated
Set goals	Reconciled		Innovated
	Reduced	**Administration**	Invented
Marketing/Sales		Administered	Modernized
Accumulated	**Teamwork/ Communication**	Arranged	Ranked
Advertised	Coached	Edited	Received
Attained	Collaborated	Installed	Recognized
Boosted	Coordinated	Maintained	Revolutionized
Broadened	Described	Processed	
	Encouraged	Purchased	
		Recorded	

applicants with just one or two typos on their résumés (see Figure 16.3).[14] In other words, the standard is high, and few potential employers are forgiving. For an example of poor proofreading, see Table 16.8.

Throughout the job application process, potential employers will apply exacting attention to all of the information in your documents and interviews. Any inconsistency or questionable information may damage or disqualify your chances. Often, potential employers judge your character when they see seemingly contradictory information. So be accurate and precise in setting out dates of employment, job responsibilities and accomplishments, educational background, and all other aspects of the résumé and cover letter.

TABLE 16.3

Using Action Words to Emphasize Accomplishments

Less Effective	More Effective
Responsible for marketing efforts for younger members.	Developed and ran marketing campaigns targeting young professionals and university students that resulted in approximately 55 new members in the past year.
Without an action word, this statement sounds unnecessarily weak and passive.	By starting with strong action words, this statement illustrates a sense of goal setting and achievement.
Answered phones.	Greeted clients and scheduled appointments in person and by phone.
Although this statement starts with an action word, it emphasizes a menial, nonskilled effort.	This action word immediately draws attention to Haniz's focus on her customer orientation and value for a business.
Kept track of tanning products.	Took inventory of all items sold in the store.
This statement emphasizes a duty without any reference to the business importance of the task.	This statement illustrates a sense of purpose in accomplishing an important business task.

TABLE 16.4

Quantifying Accomplishments

Less Effective	More Effective
Supervised other tellers in the teller department.	Supervised six tellers—responsible for the overall direction, coordination, and evaluation of unit.
Without a quantity, potential employers might assume a rather inconsequential set of supervision duties.	With a number of tellers noted, potential employers see that the applicant has supervised a team.
In charge of effort to support local breast cancer awareness event.	Organized a group of 83 members to participate in a local breast cancer walkathon.
Without quantification and an action word to begin this statement, this phrase emphasizes responsibilities rather than accomplishments.	By quantifying the performance (recruiting 83 members), this accomplishment stands out as exceptional.

Group and Label Information to Improve Ease of Reading

When you have long lists of items, consider grouping the information to help recruiters quickly grasp your abilities (see Table 16.9). If you don't group lists of four or more items, recruiters will often skip or gloss over them. Furthermore, by grouping items on your résumé, you show your understanding of related skill sets.

Format to Distinguish Pieces of Information

As you format your résumé, focus on ease of processing and consistency. Imagine recruiters who are reviewing dozens if not hundreds of résumés in a day. They are likely

TABLE 16.5

Positioning Your Most Important Contributions First

Less Effective	More Effective
• Greeted clients and scheduled appointments in person and by phone. • Assisted with purchasing of medical supplies and processing of client orders. • Managed financial bookkeeping for the company using QuickBooks.	• Managed financial bookkeeping for the company using QuickBooks. • Assisted with purchasing of medical supplies and processing of client orders. • Greeted clients and scheduled appointments in person and by phone.
This list emphasizes customer skills and de-emphasizes financial bookkeeping skills. If the goal is to display financial abilities, then the list is not effective.	This list emphasizes financial abilities with less emphasis on purchasing and customer service.

TABLE 16.6

Removing Unnecessary Details

Less Effective	More Effective
Community Activities and Accomplishments Volunteer, VITA, Pescaloosa, FL (giving up my Saturdays in support of a good cause) Church Choir (my church choir contains professional-level talent and tours internationally) Member of the National Association of Federal Credit Unions Volunteer Gymnastics Coach, Columbia, SC Varsity Basketball Overall MVP (2012–2014), Team Captain (2013–2014)	**PROFESSIONAL ASSOCIATIONS AND COMMUNITY ACTIVITIES** **Member,** National Association of Federal Credit Unions, Arlington, VA, 2017 to present **Volunteer Tax Consultant,** Volunteer Tax Assistance Program (VITA), Pescaloosa, FL, 2015 to present **Volunteer Coach,** Elite Gymnastics Summer Camp, Columbia, SC, 2011 to 2014 (summers)
This list contains several unnecessary pieces of information. The references to the church choir and high school sports are interesting; however, in limited space, they do little to highlight Haniz's key abilities and attributes.	This condensed list better frames the activities in a professional light and in terms of Haniz's key abilities and attributes. She retains one sports item (gymnastics coach) to show her leadership abilities and commitment to the community.

TABLE 16.7

Avoiding Clichés

Less Effective	More Effective
The Credit Union Marketing Specialist position you posted is my dream job.	My successes in attracting new credit union members would translate well into the requirements of your Credit Union Marketing Specialist position. I am eager to speak with you by phone or in person to learn more about the position and explain how I can contribute.
This statement is inherently me-centered and naïve.	This statement projects credibility and shows an interest in dialogue about the position.

skimming on the first pass to see if your résumé deserves more attention. So make sure they can gather the most pertinent information quickly. By formatting your document effectively with bold, italics, spacing, and other features, you can help recruiters understand your primary abilities and attributes within 20 to 30 seconds (see Table 16.10).

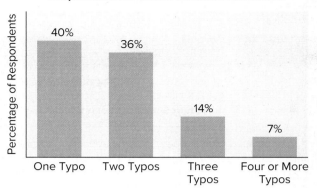

Responses from Senior Financial Executives

Percentage of Respondents

- One Typo: 40%
- Two Typos: 36%
- Three Typos: 14%
- Four or More Typos: 7%

Source: Accountemps. (2014, May 15). One or two resume mistakes enough for majority of managers to pass on a job candidate; still, managers more lenient than they were five years ago. Retrieved from http://accountemps. rhi.mediaroom.com/2014-05-15-Survey-One-or-Two-Resume-Mistakes-Enough-for-Majority-of-Managers-to-Pass-on-a-Job-Candidate-Still-Managers-More-Lenient-Than-They-Were-Five-Years-Ago.

FIGURE 16.3

How Many Typos in a Résumé Does It Take for You to Decide Not to Consider a Job Candidate for a Position in Your Company?

TABLE 16.8

Proofreading for Typos and Misspellings

Less Effective	More Effective
Increased the moral of the unit and gained incite into managing frontline employees.	Increased the morale of the unit and gained insight into managing frontline employees.
These spelling errors (moral, incite) would not be detected with spell-check software.	The spelling is correct in this case.

TABLE 16.9

Grouping and Labeling to Highlight the Employment Narrative

Less Effective	More Effective
Computer Skills: MS Word, MS Excel, MS Access, MS PowerPoint, Prezi, MS Publisher, MS Project, QuickBase, MS Outlook, QuickBooks, Powerscan Loan Display, WebEx	*Project Management/Scheduling:* MS Project, Zoho Projects *Finance/Accounting:* QuickBooks, Zoho Books *Spreadsheets and Analytics:* MS Excel, Google Data Studio, Python *Website Development/Publishing/Presentations:* Adobe Dreamweaver, Google Web Designer, MS Publisher, MS PowerPoint, Prezi
Since the list contains 12 items, recruiters are unlikely to read through it. Furthermore, they are unlikely to distinguish the various types of software skills.	Once the list is grouped, recruiters can quickly (within three or four seconds) recognize the types of software skills involved.
Major coursework: ECON 2013, 2023; ACG 2021, 2071, 3171, 3331; FIN 3244, 4424, 4324, 4329, 4453; MAN 3240, 4720	*Primary coursework:* bank administration, investments, marketing of financial services, event management
This list of major courses provides little meaningful information and does not feed into an employment narrative.	Because these courses are grouped into three or four areas that feed into an employment narrative, potential employers understand the gist of the academic program rapidly and see its place in Haniz's set of abilities and attributes.

TABLE 16.10

Formatting to Distinguish Key Pieces of Information

Less Effective	More Effective
Work Experience Better Horizons Credit Union, Pescaloosa, FL Marketing Specialist/Loan Officer July 2015 to present	**WORK EXPERIENCE** BETTER HORIZONS CREDIT UNION, Pescaloosa, FL **Marketing Specialist/Loan Officer July 2015 to present**
With formatting the same for company, position, and dates, this information is difficult to pick out quickly. This problem is amplified over an entire document.	With unique formatting applied to section headings (centered, capitalized, bolded), company (capitalized, left aligned), position (bolded, left aligned), and dates (bolded, right aligned), employers can pick out key pieces of information rapidly and within seconds gain a good sense of employment and education histories.

Select a Simple Yet Visually Appealing Layout

The last step in the résumé process is choosing a layout. Many job candidates instinctively worry about the appearance in the early stages of résumé writing, especially when they are working from model documents or templates. Resist this natural urge and focus on planning your message first and fine-tuning its tone and style. Then, select an appealing layout.

You can choose from dozens of layout options and even design your own. Generally, seek layouts with a lot of white space so that your résumé does not appear cluttered. Also, choose designs that contain a clear scheme for headings and formatting. Make sure that the content is balanced across the page rather than clustered on one side. Also, keep you mind you may need to use a template from your university if you are using career services.

Creating Chronological and Functional Résumés

LO16.6 Create chronological and functional résumés to highlight your key selling points.

One of your first choices as you assemble your résumé is the format. The two major options are **chronological résumés**, which present the information grouped by work and education over time, and **functional résumés**, which present the information in terms of key skills. The most common and generally preferred format, especially for young professionals, is the chronological résumé. One recent survey showed that 75 percent of hiring managers preferred them, whereas 17 percent preferred functional résumés, and 8 percent had no preference.[15]

Functional résumés draw special attention to your key skills. They are most often used by professionals with extensive (more than 15 years) experience and individuals with little or no work experience. Experienced professionals use them as a way to streamline a lengthy list of jobs, many of which involved similar accomplishments and experiences. Inexperienced individuals often use them to emphasize key skills developed through a combination of school, community, volunteer, and other types of activities while de-emphasizing a lack of work experience.

Components of Chronological Résumés

- Name block
- Summary of qualifications *or* Career objective (optional)
- Education
- Work experience
- Additional information

Components of Functional Résumés

- Name block
- Summary of qualifications *or* Career summary
- Skills
- Additional information

Consider creating both a chronological and a functional résumé to determine which format is more effective at selling your key abilities and attributes. The process of creating both types may even give you insight about how to present your selling points. So, even if you don't think you'll use a functional résumé, writing one will likely give you ideas to improve and refine your chronological résumé (or vice versa). Notice the ineffective chronological résumés in Figures 16.4 and 16.6 and the effective chronological résumés in Figures 16.5 and 16.7. Then, notice the example of an effective functional résumé in Figure 16.8.

FIGURE 16.4

An Ineffective Chronological Résumé

Haniz Zogby
164 Founders Ridge Court, Havana, FL 32333
Phone: 850-784-7391; email: hanizzogby@gmail.com

Education
Florida State University, Tallahassee, Florida, Graduation: May 2020, BS in Finance, Minor in
Event Management GPA: 3.714 (Magna Cum Laude)
Major coursework: ECON 2013, 2023; ACG 2021, 2071, 3171, 3331; FIN 3244, 4424, 4324, 4329,
4453; MAN 3240, 4720 3.924 GPA at Woodbridge High School (7th in Class), Palmetto Scholarship

Work Experience
Better Horizons Credit Union, Pescaloosa, FL
Marketing Specialist/Loan Officer, Oct 2018 to present
   • Extend business and personal loans to credit union members
   • Assist with promotional programs
   • Responsible for marketing efforts for younger members
   • In charge of effort to support local breast cancer awareness event
Teller Supervisor, Oct 2017 to Oct 2018
   • Responsible for all cash reserves at the credit union
   • Helped with referral and sales programs
   • Balanced monthly general ledgers
   • Supervised other tellers in the teller department
   • In charge of the entire unit and its activities
Teller, July 2015–Oct 2017
   • Managed banking transactions for members in a helpful and efficient manner
   • Recognized as the top referral getter among the tellers
Palmetto Home Medical, Columbia, SC
Receptionist/Billing Assistant, May 2012–May 2015 (summers)
   • Answered phones
   • Data entry into the computer
Ultra Tan, Blythewood, SC
Salon Attendant, September 2014 to May 2015
   • Cleaned the salon
   • Answered questions that customers had
   • Kept track of tanning products
Computer Skills
MS Excel, MS PowerPoint, Python, MS Project, QuickBooks, Zoho Projects Zoho Books Google
Data Studio, Adobe Dreamweaver, Google Web Designer, MS Publisher, Prezi

Community Activities and Accomplishments
Volunteer, VITA, Pescaloosa, FL (giving up my Saturdays in support of a good cause)
Church Choir
Member of the National Association of Federal Credit Unions
Volunteer Gymnastics Coach, Columbia, SC
Varsity Basketball Overall MVP (2010–2013), Team Captain (2012–2013)

Study Abroad
Cass Business School, Dubai, United Arab Emirates
   • Took business classes in a multicultural environment
   • Observed one of the most dynamic business environments in the world
   • Took Arabic language courses

The excessively plain appearance of this résumé does not create a positive initial impression.

Recruiters will have a challenging time identifying key attributes and abilities.

Text appears cluttered because it is mostly on the left-hand side of the page without space in between.

The lack of **bold,** *italics,* or other formatting features makes it difficult to rapidly identify key pieces of information.

The focus on responsibilities as opposed to accomplishments fails to sufficiently highlight abilities.

Weak verbs do not emphasize high-order thinking and transferable skills for business.

Sections with additional information do not effectively highlight key attributes and abilities.

FIGURE 16.5

An Effective Chronological Résumé

Haniz Zogby	164 Founders Ridge Court, Havana, FL 32333 • 850-784-7391 • hanizzogby@gmail.com *LinkedIn*: linkedin.com/in/hanizzogby • *Online Portfolio*: sites.google.com/site/hanizzogby

EDUCATION

FLORIDA STATE UNIVERSITY, Tallahassee, Florida
Bachelor of Science in Finance, Minor in Event Management   **Graduation: May 2020**
  • *Primary coursework*: bank administration, investments, marketing of financial services, event management
  • *Study abroad*: one semester at Cass Business School in Dubai focusing on international finance and marketing
  • *GPA*: 3.7; *Awards*: Magna Cum Laude

WORK EXPERIENCE

BETTER HORIZONS CREDIT UNION, Pescaloosa, FL
Marketing Specialist/Loan Officer   **October 2018 to present**
  • Developed and ran marketing campaigns targeting young professionals and university students that resulted in approximately 55 new members in the past year
  • Established a reward points program that was adopted by nearly 30 percent of members
  • Organized a group of 83 members to participate in a local breast cancer walkathon
  • Extend business and personal loans to credit union members

Teller Supervisor   **October 2017 to October 2018**
  • Implemented and tracked referral and sales programs in the teller department
  • Balanced monthly general ledgers, including branch and teller over/short
  • Managed all cash reserves at the credit union
  • Supervised six tellers; responsible for the overall direction, coordination, and evaluation of unit

Teller   **July 2015 to October 2017**
  • Handled banking transactions for members in a helpful and efficient manner
  • Obtained the most referrals in the teller unit during the entire year (2016)

PALMETTO HOME MEDICAL, Columbia, SC
Receptionist/Billing Assistant   **May 2012 to May 2015 (summers)**
  • Managed financial bookkeeping for the company using QuickBooks
  • Assisted with purchasing of medical supplies and processing of client orders
  • Greeted clients and scheduled appointments in person and by phone

ULTRA TAN, Blythewood, SC
Salon Attendant   **Sept 2014 to May 2015**
  • Sold tanning packages and tanning lotions
  • Took inventory of all items sold in the store
  • Resolved customer concerns related to products, billing, and scheduling

COMPUTER SKILLS

Project Management/Scheduling: MS Project, Zoho Projects
Finance/Accounting: QuickBooks, Zoho Books
Spreadsheets and Analytics: MS Excel, Google Data Studio, Python
Website Development/Publishing/Presentations: Adobe Dreamweaver,
Google Web Designer, MS Publisher, MS PowerPoint, Prezi

PROFESSIONAL ASSOCIATIONS AND COMMUNITY ACTIVITIES

Member, National Association of Federal Credit Unions, Arlington, VA, 2017 to present
Volunteer Tax Consultant, Volunteer Tax Assistance Program (VITA), Pescaloosa, FL, 2015 to present
Volunteer Coach, Elite Gymnastics Summer Camp, Columbia, SC, 2010 to 2014 (summers)

This simple but nicely formatted résumé allows recruiters to rapidly identify key abilities and attributes.

Distinctive and consistent formatting for headings (centered **BOLD CAPS**), organizations (CAPS), position (**bold**), and dates (right-aligned **bold**) make information easy to identify.

Specific accomplishments enhance credibility of claims.

Strong action verbs emphasize transferable management and marketing abilities.

Grouping helps rapidly display key computer skills.

Selective display of associations and community activities highlights key abilities and attributes.

FIGURE 16.6

Ineffective Chronological Résumé

Jaclyn Peha
1832 Weston Avenue, Pescaloosa, FL 32333
Email: jpeha@betterhorizons.net

Skills & Qualifications

Proven web developer with track record of success. Specialties in all areas of web development. Experience with many programming languages and web development tools. Strong communicator with excellent multitasking abilities.

Education and Coursework

Associate of Applied Science in Information Technology
Pescaloosa Community College, Pescaloosa, FL
April 2020

Classes

- Composition I & II
- Web & Multimedia Development
- Psychology
- Web Analytics & Search Engine Optimization
- Networking Basics
- Interactive Web Design
- Web Security
- Internet Commerce
- ActionScript Programming
- Introduction to Management
- Creative Writing
- College Algebra I

- Oral Communication
- Technical Communication
- Introduction to Databases
- Web Content Management
- Advanced Website Design
- Audio-Video Editing
- HTML Programming
- Web Scripting
- Server-Side Programming
- Microeconomics
- Macroeconomics
- College Algebra II

High School Degree
Joaquin Jacobi High School
May 2016, 3.69 GPA

Work Experience

IT Intern

Better Horizons Credit Union, Pescaloosa, FL
April 2020 to present

- Tech support
- Identify strategies for SEO
- Development of website

Personal Interests

Puzzles, video games, photography, hiking, camping, outdoor sports, hunting

---

Formatting does not allow recruiters to rapidly identify key abilities and attributes.

Words and phrases such as "proven," "track record of success," and "expertise in all areas of web development" are exaggerated and diminish credibility.

Jaclyn tends to provide too much information just for the sake of filling the page. For example, she lists nearly all courses she's taken as well as her high school degree. This strategy does not help sell her web development skills.

The most significant missed opportunities involve not emphasizing her web development experience. Jaclyn fails to provide enough detail about her activities at her current internship. She also fails to mention web development projects she's participated in.

FIGURE 16.7

Effective Chronological Résumé

Jaclyn Peha
1832 Weston Avenue, Pescaloosa, FL 32333
Email: jpeha@betterhorizons.net

WEB DEVELOPMENT SKILLS

Creative and talented web developer with skills in the following areas:
- *Web specialties*: Website design, web analytics, user interaction, search engine optimization
- *Programming languages*: JavaScript, Java, CSS, HTML, XHTML
- *Adobe Suite*: Dreamweaver, Muse, Fireworks, Flash Professional, Photoshop

EDUCATION AND COURSEWORK

Associate of Applied Science in Information Technology
Pescaloosa Community College, Pescaloosa, FL
September 2018 to April 2020

Web Development Coursework:

- Web & Multimedia Development
- Web Analytics & Search Engine Optimization
- Interactive Web Design
- Web Security
- Internet Commerce
- ActionScript Programming
- Web Content Management
- Advanced Website Design
- Audio-Video Editing
- HTML Programming
- Web Scripting
- Server-Side Programming

WORK EXPERIENCE

IT Intern
Better Horizons Credit Union, Pescaloosa, FL
April 2020 to present

- Assist in developing the branding and communication strategies for the website
- Develop multimedia content for the "Members" section of the website
- Identify strategies for search engine optimization
- Provide tech support for public relations events

PROJECTS

- Co-developed the "Career Resources" section on the Pescaloosa Community College website
- Developed the website of a local nonprofit (*Foundation for Consumer Fairness*)
- Created and maintained Joaquin Jacobi High School's Debate Club website for two years

PERSONAL INTERESTS

Sudoku and crossword puzzles, travel photography, travel documentaries, hiking

Formatting allows recruiters to rapidly identify key abilities and attributes. Recruiters can gather the main messages (Jaclyn's abilities and attributes) in each section in a matter of 10 to 15 seconds.

Despite relatively limited experience, Jaclyn portrays herself as skilled in many areas of web development. Her confident, but not exaggerated, language shows her strong potential.

Compared to the ineffective example, this résumé provides far more relevant details, particularly in the "Work Experience" and "Projects" sections

FIGURE 16.8

An Effective Functional Résumé

Haniz Zogby

164 Founders Ridge Court, Havana, FL 32333 • 850-784-7391 • hanizzogby@gmail.com
LinkedIn: www.linkedin.com/hanizzogby • *Online Résumé*: https://sites.google.com/site/hanizzogby

Qualifications Summary

Ambitious credit union professional with record of successful marketing through local events, seminars, mailings, online social networking, and referrals. Knowledgeable of best practices in marketing for credit unions and innovative financial services for credit unions. Committed to leading marketing efforts to increase credit union membership and empower those who use local credit unions.

Skills

Marketing for Credit Unions
- Developed and ran marketing campaigns targeting young professionals and university students that resulted in approximately 55 new members in the past year
- Established a reward points program that nearly 30 percent of members adopted
- Implemented and tracked referral and sales programs in the teller department

Event Management
- Organized a group of 83 members to participate in a local breast cancer walkathon
- Set up regular seminars about retirement plans, investing, and business loans for credit union members
- Minored in Event Management and completed team projects for a charity fund-raiser (organized a music concert), a sports event (set up a kids' night), and a wedding

Leadership
- Participated in all major decisions for Better Horizons Credit Union during the past year as assistant manager
- Supervised six tellers; responsible for the overall direction, coordination, and evaluation of entire teller unit
- Involved in leadership roles at work, school, and community for the past ten years

Technology
- Excel at using software to facilitate project management and scheduling (MS Project, Zoho Project, MS Teams, MS Outlook)
- Comfortable with a variety of online and face-to-face presentation software platforms (WebEx, MS PowerPoint, Prezi)
- Advanced-level use of a variety of finance, accounting, spreadsheet, and database software (QuickBooks, Zoho Books, MS Excel, Python, Google Data Studio)
- Expert at word processing and publishing software (MS Publisher, MS Word)

Employment History

07/2015–present	BETTER HORIZONS CREDIT UNION, Pescaloosa, FL *Marketing Specialist/Loan Officer* (10/2018–present), *Teller Supervisor* (10/2017–10/2018), *Teller* (07/2015–10/2017)
05/2012–05/2015 (summers)	PALMETTO HOME MEDICAL, Columbia, SC, *Receptionist/Billing Assistant*
09/2014–05/2015	ULTRA TAN, Blythewood, SC, *Salon Attendant*

Education

Bachelor of Science in Finance, Minor in Event Management, FLORIDA STATE UNIVERSITY, Tallahassee, FL, Graduation: 05/2020.

Study Abroad, one semester of business classes at CASS BUSINESS SCHOOL, Dubai, UAE

Community Involvement

Volunteer Tax Consultant, VOLUNTEER TAX ASSISTANCE PROGRAM (VITA), Pescaloosa, FL, 2015–present.

Volunteer Coach, ELITE GYMNASTICS SUMMER CAMP, Columbia, SC, 2010–2014 (summers).

This cleanly formatted résumé sends signals of professionalism and orderliness.

The "Qualifications Summary" section contains a concise statement that highlights key abilities and attributes.

By grouping skills, Haniz demonstrates what she has to offer in a matter of seconds.

A brief "Employment History" section helps recruiters judge the depth and consistency of her experience.

The "Education" and "Community Involvement" sections contain only a few strategically selected items that focus on her key messages.

Technology Tips

BUILDING YOUR RÉSUMÉ TO GET PAST APPLICANT TRACKING SYSTEMS

Many large organizations rely on applicant tracking systems (ATSs) to evaluate résumés, especially with positions with hundreds of applicants. These systems use AI-driven algorithms to help with screening. They may even eliminate some applicants from the pool.

When you apply to a large organization with many applicants, plan your résumé to get past the ATSs. Here are some of the important strategies:

1. *Use simple formatting.* These systems continue to get better but may still struggle to evaluate résumés with complex formatting.

2. *Apply the right keywords.* These systems often rely on the position announcements to help evaluate résumés. So, make sure to use keywords from the position announcement to show your skills and experiences align with it.

Rocketclips, Inc/Alamy Stock Photo

3. *Use action verbs.* Generally these systems positively evaluate action verbs that align with key skills.

4. *Be specific.* These systems respond negatively to generic résumés.

5. *Pay extra attention to spelling.* People often red flag poor spelling. Computers are even more effective at catching misspellings.

The good news is these recommendations mostly match best practices for creating any strong résumé. As you apply these changes, avoid excess. For example, you want to place the right keywords in your résumé but avoid going overboard.

Sources: Slack, M., & Bowitz, E. (2019, March 31). Beat the robots: How to get your resume past the system & into human hands. *The Muse.* Retrieved from www.themuse.com/advice/beat-the-robots-how-to-get-your-resume-past-the-system-into-human-hands; Jackson, A. E. (2018, April 25). Can your resume beat the bots? How to make it ATS-friendly. *Glassdoor.* Retrieved from www.glassdoor.com/glob/ats-friendly-resume/.

Using LinkedIn Strategically

LO16.7 Use LinkedIn as part of the job search process and to network professionally.

Social media platforms give you many opportunities to network and reach you professional goals. LinkedIn is the most popular professional networking platform. Approximately 87 percent of hiring managers use LinkedIn as they consider job applicants.[16]

A strong presence on LinkedIn can help you in a variety of ways in the job search process. Most often, your LinkedIn profile serves as a supplement to the materials you provide to a prospective employer. Many HR professionals will view your LinkedIn profile after seeing your cover letter or résumé. Just before a job interview, your interviewer may look at your profile to learn more about you. The company representative you met at a job fair may look at your profile to decide whether to follow up with you. In some cases, HR professionals may contact you after seeing that you match what they're looking for in certain positions.

You should consider using LinkedIn for many purposes, not just to find job opportunities. You can expect that many of your professional contacts—colleagues, partners, clients, customers, and others—will check your profile to learn more about you. Increasingly, LinkedIn is a professional learning platform. By following the posts of thought leaders, business leaders, companies of interest, and curated newsfeeds in specific topics, you can consistently learn and stay up to date with business and industry knowledge.

You should approach your LinkedIn profile in the same way you approach your résumé. By identifying a professional narrative of your key selling points, you're ready to set up a profile that is persuasive to your professional contacts. Typically, your LinkedIn profile is an elaborated version of your résumé. With fewer space constraints, you can provide additional types of information. Notice Haniz's LinkedIn profile in Figure 16.9. In addition to providing information about her education and work experience, she has dedicated space to list personal interests, languages, volunteer experience, certifications, courses, and other items. She also displays the people, organizations, and curated newsfeeds she follows. As long as these additional items reinforce her intended professional narrative, she should display them. Keep in mind these tips as you manage your LinkedIn presence.

Provide a professional photo. Unlike résumés, the first item most LinkedIn viewers see is your profile picture. Make sure you upload a high-resolution, warm, and professional photo.

Create a personalized URL. LinkedIn allows you to create a unique web address. Personalizing your link to include your name makes your profile more memorable and professional.

Complete the summary space. A common missed opportunity among LinkedIn users is failing to use the summary space. In one to three paragraphs, you can brand yourself with your key abilities and attributes and major accomplishments. Use concise, confident, natural, and cliché-free language.

Use multimedia. Increasingly, LinkedIn allows you to upload a variety of file types, including video and pictures. If you have appropriate multimedia to highlight your accomplishments, you can set yourself apart from others on LinkedIn.

Choose sections wisely. LinkedIn allows you to choose from well over 20 types of sections, including categories such as causes you care about, test scores, projects, honors and awards, publications, and so on. Choose to add information when these new sections add to your professional narrative. While you have more space than a résumé, you should still selectively choose content that highlights your key selling points.

Manage your recommendations and endorsements strategically. LinkedIn allows you to give and receive recommendations and endorsements. If you choose to display them, you should generally limit the number of recommendations to two or three per position or section. LinkedIn automatically gives your connections the option to endorse you for various skills. You can choose to display only those endorsements that are most accurate and align with your key selling points.

Build a network of important connections. LinkedIn prominently displays the number of connections you have in your network. As you build your LinkedIn connections, resist the urge to focus on the quantity of your connections. Rather, focus on the quality of your connections. Typically, connect with professionals and peers with whom you share professional interests. Make sure to personalize your invitations when you hope to connect with others. Notice Figure 16.10 in which the invitation is generic and nonpersonalized. By contrast, the invitation in Figure 16.11 is personalized. Taking 30 seconds to 1 minute to personalize the invitation shows your genuine interest in connecting with others.

Show some personality and be positive. While you should maintain professionalism on LinkedIn, you have more flexibility in how you portray yourself and interact with others than with résumés and cover letters. Find ways to show your personality in positive and warm ways.

FIGURE 16.9

An Example of a Well-Developed LinkedIn Profile

Haniz Zogby · 1st

Marketing Specialists/Loan Officer at Better Horizons Credit Union

Tallahassee, Florida Area

[Message] [More...]

 Better Horizons Credit Union

 Florida State University - College of Business

[A] See contact info

Ambitious credit union professional with record of successful marketing through local events, seminars, mailings, online social networking, and referrals. Knowledgeable of best practices in marketing for credit unions and innovative financial services for credit unions. Committed to leading marketing efforts to increase credit union membership and empowering those who use local credit unions.

Specialties:

Attracting new credit union members
Retaining credit union members with innovative financial services
Partnering with the local community in the fight against breast cancer

Experience

BH **Loan Officer/Assistant Manager**
Better Horizons Credit Union
Jul 2018 – Present · 9 mos
Pescaloosa, FL

- Developed and ran marketing campaigns targeting young professionals and university students that resulted in approximately 55 new members in the past year
- Established a reward points program that was adopted by nearly thirty percent of members
- Organized a group of 83 members to participate in a local breast cancer walkathon
- Extend business and personal loans to credit union members

BH **Better Horizons Credit Union**
2 yrs 7 mos

Teller Supervisor
Dec 2016 – Jan 2018 · 1 yr 2 mos
Pescaloosa, FL

- Implemented and tracked referral and sales programs in the teller department
- Balanced monthly general ledgers, including branch and teller over/short
- Managed all cash reserves at the credit union
- Supervised six tellers – responsible for the overall direction, coordination, and evaluati... See more

Teller
Jul 2015 – Dec 2016 · 1 yr 6 mos
Pescaloosa, FL

- Handled banking transactions for members in a helpful and efficient manner
- Obtained the most referrals in the teller unit during the entire year (2013)

 Receptionist/Billing Assistant
Palmetto Home Medical
May 2012 – Jul 2015 · 3 yrs 3 mos
Columbia, SC

Worked four summers here and did the following:
- Managed financial bookkeeping for the company using QuickBooks
- Assisted with purchasing of medical supplies and processing of client orders
- Greeted clients and scheduled appointments in person and by phone... See more

Salon Attendant
Ultra Tan
Sep 2014 – May 2015 · 9 mos
Blythewood, SC

- Sold tanning packages and tanning lotions
- Took inventory of all items sold in the store
- Resolved customer concerns related to products, billing, and scheduling

Education

FSU BIZ **Florida State University - College of Business**
BS, Finance, Event Management, GPA: 3.7: Awards: Magna Cum Laude
2015 – 2020

CASS **Cass Business School**
Study Abroad, Certificate in International Finance
2016 – 2016

Licenses & Certifications

 Certified Credit Union Lender
Credit Union National Association
Issued Mar 2019 · No Expiration Date

 Certified Personal Wealth Advisor
FINRA (Financial Industry Regulatory Authority)
Issued Mar 2019 · No Expiration Date

Volunteer Experience

VITA **Volunteer Tax Consultant**
Volunteer Income Tax Assistance
2015 – Present · 4 yrs
Economic Empowerment

High School Mentor
Junior Achievement USA
2018 – Present · 1 yr
Education

Volunteer Coach
Elite Gymnastics Summer Camp
2010 – 2014 · 4 yrs

Accomplishments

9 Courses
Advanced Spanish · Bank Administration · Business Communication · Event Management · Financial Accounting · International Finance · Investment Management · Managerial Accounting · Social Media Marketing

2 Languages
Arabic · Spanish

2 Organizations
Junior Achievement · National Association of Federal Credit Unions

Interests

 SunTrust
98,660 followers

 The Economist
7,497,303 followers

CASS **Cass Business School**
57,811 followers

TD Ameritrade
63,007 followers

Business Insider
6,252,965 followers

Bank of America
1,059,743 followers

See all

Source: LinkedIn; *photos: (left) Ingram Publishing RF*

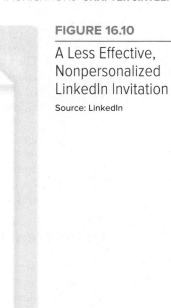

FIGURE 16.10

A Less Effective, Nonpersonalized LinkedIn Invitation

Source: LinkedIn

FIGURE 16.11

A More Effective, Personalized LinkedIn Invitation

Source: LinkedIn

Maintain a giver mentality. As discussed in Chapters 1 and 2, an important principle of networking is maintaining a giver mentality as opposed to adopting a taker mentality. The same principle applies to online networking. As you gain a reputation for helping and providing value to others, you will find many opportunities open up to you. LinkedIn allows you to provide others with recommendations, endorsements, likes, and lots of helpful information.

Stay active on LinkedIn. Make sure to consistently update your LinkedIn information. Use LinkedIn as a professional learning platform. Pay attention to the accomplishments of those in your network and congratulate them. Periodically share status updates. Join some communities and groups. As you invest an hour or two per week on LinkedIn, you'll find that professional opportunities will arise through your networking and learning.

Developing a Reference List

LO16.8 Develop a list of references that will improve your employment prospects.

You will need to provide a list of personal references as part of most job applications. Some job applicants put off this task until the last minute, often underestimating its significance. In fact, your references may be among the most important factors in gaining a new position. As you construct your list of references, consider these tips.

Develop Relationships with Potential References over Time

Well before you need to apply for a position, compile a list of people who can provide credible accounts of your qualifications. Consider people who work in fields and industries that interest you. Also consider professors with whom you have established a relationship over several semesters, ideally in classes directly related to your sought-after positions.

Contact Your References Ahead of Time

Before you place any names on your list, reach out to those individuals and, as a courtesy, ask permission to use their names. A short email may be enough to accomplish this request, but consider meeting in person or calling to explain the positions you are applying for and recent experiences you've had. These short conversations allow your references to speak about you with enthusiasm and up-to-date information. Also, these conversations give you a chance to seek advice about how to handle the job application process. Generally, also send these individuals your most updated résumé so they are aware of the information that potential employers have.

Some of your references will be former supervisors. Forward-thinking job applicants stay in touch with past supervisors from time to time to keep them updated with their career developments. Even small but sincere gestures such as sending yearly holiday cards can lead to favorable comments when these former supervisors speak with your potential employers.[17]

Think about whether you should include your current supervisor as a reference. In some cases, she or he will understand and even encourage your efforts to seek new positions and will serve as an excellent reference. In other cases, however, your supervisors may be unhappy that you want to leave your current position. For example, if your supervisor thinks your job search indicates a lack of dedication to your current job, you may find your professional opportunities diminishing. If you're uncomfortable telling your supervisor that you're searching for a new position, you likely should not provide him/her as a reference.

Thank Your References

Your references will undoubtedly wonder how your job search fares. Stay in touch with them about progress you've made. When your job search is over, thank them for their

FIGURE 16.12

References List

Haniz Zogby

164 Founders Ridge Court, Havana, FL 32333 • 850-784-7391 • hanizzogby@gmail.com
LinkedIn : linkedin.com/in/hanizzogby • *Online Résumé* : sites.google.com/site/hanizzogby

REFERENCE LIST

Christine Russo

CEO and President

BETTER HORIZONS CREDIT UNION

Address: 1488 Altura Dr.

Pescaloosa, FL 32315

Phone: 850-971-0234

Email: russo@betterhorizons.com

Relationship: Ms. Russo has been my supervisor for the past five years. She is intimately familiar with my work in the following positions: marketing specialist, loan officer, teller supervisor, and teller.

Jim Harrill, CPA

Owner

HARRILL TAX ASSOCIATES

Address: 3419 Main Street

Havana, FL 32333

Phone: 850-972-3188

Email: jamesharrilljr@harrilltax.com

Relationship: Mr. Harrill trained me and supervised my work as a volunteer tax consultant for the VITA program. He is familiar with my work ethic and commitment to the community.

Jamie McPherson, PhD

Associate Professor of Finance

FLORIDA STATE UNIVERSITY

Address: 719-C Thurmond Tower

Tallahassee, FL 32302

Phone: 850-777-1848

Email: mcpherson@fls.edu

Relationship: Dr. McPherson taught two of my courses and served as an advisor for my honors thesis about emerging financial services in credit unions.

Jack Gerardi

Owner and President

PALMETTO HOME MEDICAL

Address: 18 Foxborough Lane

Columbia, SC 29201

Phone: 803-798-1312

Email: jgerardi@palmettohomemed.com

Relationship: Mr. Gerardi supervised my work as a receptionist and billing assistant for 3-1/2 summers.

Consistent formatting allows recruiters to quickly gather key information.

Formatting that matches the résumé formatting shows attention to detail and a touch of class.

A brief statement about relationships with references demonstrates professionalism and helps recruiters make judgments about the value of each one.

participation in the process. These shows of goodwill may come in handy over the years as you ask these same individuals for assistance in future job searches.

Complete a Consistently Formatted, Well-Detailed Reference List

When you construct the list of references, check the job announcement to see how many references are required. If it does not provide a number, list three to five individuals. Make sure you provide current contact information. In addition, consider providing a brief (one or two sentences) description of your professional or school relationship to each reference. Finally, format the list of references to be compatible with your résumé (see Figure 16.12).

Constructing Cover Letters

Cover letters describe your interest in and qualifications for a position. Whereas you may have one, two, or at most three versions of your resume for various positions, you must uniquely tailor each cover letter to a particular position. No two cover letters should be the same.

LO16.9 Compose effective cover letters that highlight your key selling points.

Components of Cover Letters

- Interest in position.
- Match with position.
- Call to action.

The role of cover letters has changed in recent years. Some hiring managers no longer read or even expect them them. One recent survey showed 26 percent of recruiters still value them.[18] Yet, creating cover letters has distinct advantages. They potentially set you apart from other applicants who choose to only submit a résumé, especially with hiring managers who still value cover letters. They allow you to personalize your message to those who oversee your positions of interest. Finally, they help you articulate a narrative about your professional strengths and aspirations. The very act of writing a cover letter will help you field interview questions.

Your primary goal for cover letters is to sell your key abilities and attributes in a way that matches the needs of the employer for a particular position. As you do with sales letters, you build excitement and optimism that you can excel in the posted position. Unlike mass sales letters, however, cover letters deliver the message that you are writing to one particular employer, and only that employer.

Keep in mind the following advice.[19]

The Cover Letter Often Forms the First Impression

Since many potential employers read your cover letter (or a condensed version of it as an email) first, it forms the first impression of you. Therefore, it must be perfect. As an error-free message, the cover letter can immediately place you in the upper echelons. A New York tutoring company, Inspirica, recently sought out writing tutors. In 93 percent of the 220 cover letters, HR specialists found writing errors.[20]

Clearly Identify the Position You Are Applying For

Your potential employer is likely reviewing applications for many—sometimes hundreds or thousands—of positions at the same time. Many employers use electronic application systems to clearly identify the positions that applicants are seeking. In any case, clearly and prominently identify the position you are applying for in your cover letter. The subject line is often a good location for this information.

Be Focused and Concise

In recent years, potential employers have come to expect shorter, more concise cover letters. This is in part due to larger application pools for each position. Thus, you should generally aim for three to five targeted paragraphs.

In such limited space, focus on your main selling points—your key abilities and attributes—and how these selling points match the needs of your employer. By taking this focused approach, you create a prism from which the employer will interpret your résumé, thus strengthening the story you are telling of your qualifications.

Show a Confident and Enthusiastic Tone without Exaggerating or Displaying Arrogance

One of the most challenging aspects of the cover letter is getting the tone right. Employers are looking for employees who can contribute, so you should mention how your unique abilities can help the company. Yet, hiring managers may view excessive self-praise as arrogance.

Also, you should show your interest in the position and the company, as hiring managers will be trying to gauge your enthusiasm and commitment levels. At the same time, you will want to avoid flowery language, which hiring managers may find off-putting and not businesslike.

Tailor Your Cover Letter to the Job Posting and Needs of the Employer

By carefully reading the job announcement, you can prioritize your selling points so they are tailored to the position of interest. This approach not only accentuates your

FIGURE 16.13

An Ineffective Solicited Cover Letter

Haniz Zogby
164 Founders Ridge Court, Havana, FL 32333
850-784-7391
hanizzogby@gmail.com

May 15, 2020

Human Resources Department
Anchor Federal Credit Union Network
158 Anchor Loop
Raleigh, NC 27601

Hello Hiring Committee:

Please consider my application for the Credit Union Marketing Specialist position. I think you will find that I possess the skills that you are looking for.

My mother always has said, "The sky's the limit." I have always admired her sense of optimism. One reason I admire the credit union model is because of my mom. My mother was a teller for nearly 20 years, and I followed in her footsteps. She always felt that she was doing good for the community by working in a credit union, and I have gained this deep sense of commitment to the community through credit unions as well. In my current workplace, I have been promoted more quickly than any other employees. You will find that I am ambitious, organized, and I am passionate about marketing credit unions. My passion has driven me to success at Better Horizons Credit Union and will propel me to success at Anchor Federal Credit Unions if you give me a chance.

I want to illustrate to you the kind of abilities I can bring to Anchor Federal Credit Union Network by describing a recent marketing campaign that I ran. About one year ago, our CEO, Christine Russo, determined that we needed to gain younger members. She has relied on me often to help come up with ideas for important marketing campaigns, and she turned to me in this instance as well. After thoroughly examining best practices throughout the industry, we came up with a set of financial services and advertising ideas that resulted in approximately 55 new members. Our branch manager recognized this campaign as the most effective marketing effort during her 15 years at the credit union. I'm proud of this kind of effort and I can deliver this level of result at Anchor Federal Credit Union if you give me the chance.

The job you posted is my dream job. It combines my love of credit unions with my skills and interests in event management. You will notice on my résumé that not only do I have training in event management, but I also have experience using events as marketing tools for Better Horizons Credit Union. I thrive in these environments where I need to bring people together for fun and exciting events. Thank you for your attention to this letter. I hope that we can meet to further our discussions.

Sincerely,

Haniz Zogby

This letter contains too much text and long paragraphs. The body has 405 words and two long paragraphs of 138 and 143 words. Many busy recruiters will not read it carefully.

Because of excessive personal information and emotion, this cover letter lacks a professional and serious tone.

The use of clichés, such as "the sky's the limit" and "dream job," shows naïveté.

The closing does mention future contact but is vague.

ability to do the job, it also shows that you have researched the position and are responsive to the needs of the company. The Internet provides many avenues for job seekers to learn about companies.

Adapting for Unsolicited Letters

Most people gain their positions through formal job announcements—that is, jobs *solicited* by companies. When applying for these jobs, you will write a **solicited cover letter** since it is for an open position that a company advertises (see Figures 16.13 and 16.14 for examples of ineffective and effective solicited cover letters). In some cases,

FIGURE 16.14

An Effective Solicited Cover Letter

Haniz Zogby
164 Founders Ridge Court, Havana, FL 32333
850-784-7391
hanizzogby@gmail.com

May 15, 2020

Mr. Jacob Garcia, Director of Human Resources
Anchor Federal Credit Union Network
158 Anchor Loop
Raleigh, NC 27601

RE: Credit Union Marketing Specialist Position (Job Posting #831481809)

Dear Mr. Garcia:

My successes in attracting new credit union members would translate well into meeting the requirements of your Credit Union Marketing Specialist position. I am eager to speak with you by phone or in person to learn more about the position and explain how I can contribute.

During nearly five years at Better Horizons Credit Union, I have excelled at many of the responsibilities you are seeking, including marketing to increase membership, tracking the success of marketing activities, coordinating marketing events and efforts, and delivering presentations to partners and potential clients. I have helped gain new credit union members by developing marketing campaigns with many of the techniques you are seeking, including event marketing, mailings, referral programs, seminars, and online social networking.

One of my most successful marketing campaigns occurred last year when I was given the responsibility of increasing membership among young professionals and university students. I developed mailings, an online social networking campaign, and seminars that resulted in approximately 55 new members. Our president, Ms. Christine Russo, recognized this campaign as the most effective marketing effort during her 15 years at the credit union.

During my time working at Better Horizons Credit Union, I have been rapidly promoted and given critical marketing responsibilities due to my leadership, initiative, creativity, and performance. I can make these same contributions to the Anchor Credit Union Network.

Please call me at your convenience to arrange an interview. You can reach me at my mobile phone (850-784-7391) between 9 a.m. and 6 p.m. daily.

Sincerely,

Haniz Zogby

Haniz Zogby

This cover letter is brief but focused, stating key abilities and attributes in a professional and confident manner. The body contains 257 words. The longest paragraph is 75 words. Recruiters are far more likely to read this letter.

The letter demonstrates awareness of the needs of the employer and how her skills match those needs.

This letter conveys a professional and confident tone.

The closing statement is assertive and specific in requesting contact. Yet, it is not overbearing or pushy.

---

however, you may seek employment with a company that does not even have an open position. In these cases, you will submit an **unsolicited cover letter** since the company has not requested job applications.

When writing unsolicited cover letters, you make several modifications. You must first find out as much as possible about the employer so that you can explain how you fit the employer's needs. Also, you should open immediately with a proposition about how you can add value, and summarize your key abilities and attributes quickly, often in bulleted form (see Figure 16.15 for an example of an unsolicited cover letter in email form).[21]

FIGURE 16.15

An Unsolicited Referral Cover Letter

To:	Lucy Sharapova <l.sharapova@easterncu.org>
Subject:	Expansion Plans for the Eastern Credit Union Network

📎 Zogby_Haniz_Resume.docx (48.00

B *I* <u>U</u> F ᴛ**T** **T** ¹⁻²⁻₃⁻ ≡ ≡ ≡   <<**Plain Text**

Dear Ms. Sharapova:

After reading about your credit union network's expansion plans in the *Credit Union Leadership Journal*, I am eager to join your marketing team. My skills in attracting new credit union members through event marketing, mailings, referral programs, seminars, and online social networking could help you achieve your ambitious growth plans.

I am an experienced credit union professional with extensive marketing experience and financial background. My marketing successes include the following:

- Attracting 55 new members within one year in a marketing campaign targeting young professionals and university students
- Developing a reward points program that was adopted by nearly 30 percent of our members
- Establishing referral and sales programs in our teller department that significantly increased membership and member use of financial services

You can learn more about my qualifications by reading my attached résumé. Also, please see my online résumé and LinkedIn profile. My online résumé contains actual samples from marketing campaigns I have led. It contains mailings, content from the Better Horizons website, and video of two marketing seminars that I organized and presented.

I am seeking an entry-level marketing position in a credit union network with potential for advancement based on performance. As far as location, I am flexible and willing to relocate anywhere. I am seeking an opening salary range of $50,000 to $60,000.

Please give me a call at your convenience to arrange an interview. You can reach me on my mobile phone (850-784-7391) between 9 a.m. and 6 p.m. daily. Also, I plan to give you a call within the next two weeks to learn more about potential job openings and explore the possibility of a job interview.

Best regards,

Haniz Zogby

Mobile Phone: 850-784-7391
Email: hanizzogby@gmail.com
Online Résumé: linkedin.com/in/hanizzogby
LinkedIn Profile: sites.google.com/site/hanizzogby

The message is concise. The body has just 276 words. Further, the short paragraphs and bulleted items allow the recruiter to get the gist within 15 to 30 seconds.

The subject line focuses on the needs and ambitions of the employer.

Links to Haniz's online résumé and LinkedIn profile allow the recruiter to learn more if she is interested.

The tone is confident and assertive without being demanding.

As an unsolicited request for a job interview, this message is more up front about issues such as salary and promotional opportunities.

Reviewing Your Résumés and Cover Letters

Your job application must be perfect. Recruiters rarely have any tolerance for inaccuracies in a résumé. Furthermore, they won't hire you unless you present your selling points effectively.

On the most basic level, you should make sure every element of your job application correctly portrays your abilities and attributes, so you must avoid any urge to exaggerate. You should also review your documents over and over to ensure they emphasize your selling points in a compelling manner. Consider getting the opinions of many people about your résumé. You might start with some individuals in the career center and a few of your professors.

LO16.10 Review your job application documents for effectiveness and fairness.

Feedback · FAIR Test
Review
Proofread

Also, try to get the opinions of some people in positions that match your career interests. Since business professionals interpret résumés quite differently, you may get some conflicting advice. This is normal. Even all hiring managers won't agree about what makes the best résumé. However, by getting many opinions, you'll be able to make decisions about strategies that enhance your likelihood of success in the job search process.

Acing the Job Interview

Your cover letter, résumé, list of references, and other pieces in your job application package set the stage for the most consequential part of the process—the interview. When you have secured an interview, you have made the initial cut and are likely deemed a good candidate. You are now competing against the best candidates for the position.

Many job applicants spend little time preparing for the interview, essentially winging it. At this crucial stage—where hiring managers are making their decisions—preparation often sets apart those who receive offers and those who do not. In this section, we focus on a few parts of the job interview: dressing appropriately, using appropriate etiquette, responding to interview questions, and following up.

Dress for the Interview and Pay Attention to Etiquette

One of the first signals of professionalism you give at a job interview relates to your clothing choices.[22] Roughly 71 percent of HR managers say wearing inappropriate clothing to a job interview is a deal breaker.[23] As much as possible, gain a sense ahead of time about the dress standards at the company where you are interviewing. Generally, you should dress up, even when the company has a fairly casual environment. Typically, err on the side of conservative dress—that is, wear well-pressed, clean, and nicely fitted clothes. Hiring managers generally recommend "conservative" colors such as blue, black, gray, and brown. Avoid overaccessorizing with too much jewelry, flashy glasses, or other items. Consider a dress rehearsal at home to feel at ease in your chosen outfit.[24]

During your visit to the company—before, during, and after the formal interview—pay attention to appropriate etiquette. Most hiring managers expect you to maintain a certain level of formality. Greet those you meet with handshakes and enthusiasm.

Dressing professionally and conservatively is generally the right formula for first impressions during a job interview.
Andriy Popov/123RF

Respond Effectively to Interview Questions

The moment of truth for hiring managers generally occurs during the job interview. Many make fairly quick judgments about your abilities and attributes. In a recent survey of interviewers at university career fairs, one-third (35 percent) made their decisions within 5 minutes, and over half (52 percent) made that decision between 5 and 15 minutes.[25] Your window may be brief to make the case that you are a good fit for the company. To prepare for the questions you may be asked, consider the following tips.

Respond to Questions Strategically, Confidently, and Concisely As you crafted your cover letter and résumé, you identified those professional abilities and attributes that meet the needs of your employer. These are your selling points, and you should find ways throughout the interview to emphasize them. You are strategic to the degree that you find ways to bring up these selling points.

Also, show confidence. While you should avoid bragging, you need to emphasize your abilities and attributes. Some job applicants are uncomfortable doing this. Claim credit for work you have accomplished. Say "I" instead of "we" during the job interview more often than you would otherwise as you talk about accomplishments at work. Yet, at the same time, maintain a balance between taking credit for your individual accomplishments and demonstrating your team orientation.

Finally, give concise answers. Most responses should be between 30 seconds and two minutes. Briefer answers are generally too abrupt, and longer answers are often unfocused. Also, longer answers disrupt the conversational nature of the job interview.

In Table 16.11, you'll find many common types of interview questions. Be prepared to respond to any of them strategically, confidently, and concisely. In Table 16.12, you'll see some sample responses from Haniz. As you read these questions, think about how the hiring manager is likely responding.

LO16.11 Develop strategies for responding to common job interview questions.

Visit http://connect.
mheducation.com for an
exercise on this topic.

TABLE 16.11

Common Job Interview Questions for Entry-Level Business Positions

Type of Interview Question	Examples
Introduction questions	• Tell me about yourself. • How was your flight here? Did you find this office easily? • How was your flight here? How do you like living in _____?
Education and training	• Why did you choose your school? • Why did you choose your major? • What was your favorite part of your program? Least favorite?
Knowledge of company and industry	• What do you know about our company? • What do you think are some of our main business challenges? How can you help? • What trends do you see in this industry?
Work experience	• How did you get your last job? • Why did you leave your last job? Have you ever been fired? • What did you like least about your last job?
Approaches to work, goals, and successes	• Why did you apply for this job? • What are you looking for in a job? • How will you be successful in this position? • What were some tough decisions you had to make at your last job? • What are your biggest accomplishments? • Tell me about a project you worked on in your most recent job. How did you contribute to its success? • What do you wish you had accomplished but were unable to? • Can you tell me about a difficult situation you encountered at work? How did you respond? How did you get your team to work effectively? • Can you tell me about a situation where you had to work under pressure and deal with deadlines?

TABLE 16.11

(*Continued*)

Type of Interview Question	Examples
Personal attributes	• What are your strengths? Weaknesses? • What would your current boss say are your greatest strengths and weaknesses? • Are you creative? Hardworking? Ambitious? • What have you learned from your past jobs?
Interpersonal, team, management, and leadership skills	• What types of people do you like to work with? • What types of people do you think are most difficult to work with? • What is your leadership/management style? • Do you have top management potential? • How well do you work in teams? • What is your communication style when working with others? • Have you had to make an unpopular decision or announcement? How did you do it?

TABLE 16.12

Responses to Common Job Interview Questions

Less Effective	More Effective
Q. *Tell me about yourself.* **A.** Well, I'm a recent graduate with a degree in finance. I also minored in event management. I have worked for a credit union for the past five years. I started out as a teller and moved up from there. Prior to working at the credit union, I worked at a medical supplies company and a tanning salon. Outside of that, I've been heavily involved in sports my whole life. And, that brings me right up until now, ready to move into a new position.	**Q.** *Tell me about yourself.* **A.** About five years ago, I took a position as a teller at a credit union. I found that I really loved the credit union approach to providing financial services. Within months, I realized that this was a career direction for me. I was fairly quickly promoted into other positions—first as a teller supervisor and then as loan officer and marketing specialist. While working at the credit union, I also went to Florida State University, where I majored in finance and minored in event management. I focused all of my studies on my deep interest in marketing financial services for credit unions. One reason I'm so intrigued by the position is that it combines several of my key interests.
This response is factual but does not directly lead into a coherent, inspiring account of Haniz's selling points.	This statement captures Haniz's background, naturally describes several of her selling points, and ties her selling points to the needs of the position. At 115 words, this statement would take roughly 45 seconds to one minute to state.
Q. *It looks like you just graduated. Tell me about your university experience.* **A.** I had a great time in school. I had great professors all the way through my program in finance. I made great friends. One of the most exciting parts of my schooling was studying in Dubai for a semester, which really opened my eyes to the world. The only part I didn't like about school was the pressure of working full-time for most of my four years and also studying on the side. But, I think I grew a lot from the experience.	**Q.** *It looks like you just graduated. Tell me about your university experience.* **A.** Going to Florida State University was a great experience and helped me improve my skills in marketing financial services. Early on in my finance program, I took a variety of classes about banking and investments that helped me think about financial services we could offer at Better Horizons. Also, I used a lot of what I learned in my event management minor to think about events we could run at the credit union. I think my favorite semester was when I went abroad to Dubai. I was fascinated to see that the businesses in that country are using so many creative and innovative approaches to event marketing. I've tried to use some of those techniques I saw in Dubai at Better Horizons.
This response provides a general overview of Haniz's experience but fails to provide a sense that she was pursuing a set of goals. The response does not contain selling points.	This response ties Haniz's university experiences into her professional goals and accomplishments. It highlights her key selling points and shows her goal-directed approach to work.

TABLE 16.12

(*Continued*)

Less Effective	More Effective
Q. *Why do you want to leave your current job?* **A.** My job at Better Horizons Credit Union has given me many opportunities, but I am often frustrated with the conservative approach that our Board has taken to developing new services. My immediate supervisor usually agrees with my ideas, but she understands that the Board will not approve our most ambitious ideas. So, she falls in line. Better Horizons has been a great learning experience, but I'm simply ready to move on to a more ambitious work environment.	**Q.** *Why do you want to leave your current job?* **A.** Leaving Better Horizons Credit Union will not be easy for me. I've enjoyed working closely with so many of my colleagues, and getting to know the community has been wonderful. Last year, when I helped run our campaign that brought in so many younger members, I realized that I wanted to be part of a larger credit union network in a position where I could spend more of my time developing marketing events and facilitating coordination between branches. I think this is where my strengths lie, and as far as I can tell, would be a good match for your position.
By stating her displeasure with the Board and the less than ambitious work culture, Haniz makes a risky statement. Some hiring managers will worry that Haniz does not work well with others.	By focusing on the satisfying aspects of the position she intends to leave, Haniz is more likely to give the impression that she is a committed, team-oriented employee. She segues her response into the needs of the current position.
Q. *How well do you work in teams?* **A.** I take a win–win mentality into all team projects. I really believe that one plus one can make three if you work together as a team. I think if you ask anyone whom I've worked with, they'll tell you that I facilitate a productive work environment where we're feeding off one another's ideas and where the end result is a creative and effective solution.	**Q.** *How well do you work in teams?* **A.** I enjoy working in teams to meet marketing objectives. Last year's marketing campaign that resulted in 55 new members was the result of a five-member team at Better Horizons. I was asked to head up the team and focused on events and social media, while the other team members worked on their specialty areas, such as market research, print advertising, and radio spots. Even though we each had our specialties, we had to work together extensively to make sure we created a unified marketing message. We also pushed one another to come up with better ideas. I don't think we could have achieved such a successful campaign without one another.
This clichéd, vague response does little to convey Haniz's real ability to work in teams.	This response shows Haniz's ability to work in teams through a concrete example. It inspires confidence that Haniz is a team player and genuinely understands the economic value of working in teams.
Q. *Do you have management experience? What is your approach to managing others?* **A.** Yes. As a teller supervisor, I supervised a unit of six tellers. I was responsible for coordinating, scheduling, and supervising the overall performance of the group. I think the most important part of managing is being open. The tellers always knew where I was coming from and vice versa.	**Q.** *Do you have management experience? What is your approach to managing others?* **A.** Yes. At Better Horizons, I've managed the teller department and led a variety of marketing campaigns that required bringing together the ideas and resources of credit union employees and members. I have been most successful when I've followed several principles. First, I think it's important to set a vision and articulate the big goals. Second, I think it's critical to get everyone's ideas about how to achieve the goals. Finally, I think you have to find ways to gain buy-in and create incentives for others to engage in the goals. Here's how I did this with our mailing campaign to attract more members . . .
This response is too short. While the response is positive, it fails to lead into Haniz's selling points of developing marketing campaigns.	This response answers the question and also transitions to Haniz's selling points.

TABLE 16.12

(Continued)

Less Effective	More Effective
Q. *What are your weaknesses?* **A.** I can't really think of any weaknesses off the top of my head. Well, I guess one thing is that I never settle for anything less than excellence. Some people who accept mediocrity sometimes say I'm a control freak, but I get the job done. So, in one way you could view this as a weakness, but from the business viewpoint, it's a net plus.	**Q.** *What are your weaknesses?* **A.** One of the things I noticed in the job posting is that you are looking for someone with the ability to conduct member surveys. I wish I could say that I had experience doing surveys in my current job. I think it is critical to include surveys as part of market analysis. I took several courses about conducting surveys and statistical analysis, yet I haven't applied this knowledge to real business problems. I look forward to developing my abilities in this regard and would welcome any training or mentoring.
This question is common in job interviews. Many job candidates view it as a trick question and evade it or state a weakness that could really be viewed as a strength. This response does not show that Haniz is self-aware enough to improve quickly on the job.	This response shows that Haniz is self-aware. It also reveals her ambitious, goal-setting nature and recognition of what she needs to do to provide value for her potential employer.

Be Perceptive about What Hiring Managers Are Evaluating   Hiring managers ask most questions with specific goals in mind. They are trying to evaluate how well your abilities and attributes match the needs of the position and fit into the corporate culture. Thus, they will ask a variety of questions about your education, work experience, and knowledge of their company. In most questions, you can fairly easily discern what they are trying to find out about you.

Other interview questions, however, may be more difficult to "read." With such questions, think about what kinds of judgments the interviewer might make. For example, when hiring managers ask you to introduce yourself, they want to know how you see yourself; it gives them a glimpse into your sense of your life and career direction, your priorities, and your work values. When they ask you what your weaknesses are, they are generally less concerned about what you can't do now but rather what you can do later. They are trying to see how self-aware you are and if you are likely to improve over time. Even questions in small talk—such as how your flight was, how your hotel room is, or how your football team is doing—are asked by hiring managers to make judgments about your emotional intelligence.

Tell Success Stories   Throughout this book, we've discussed the importance of stories. During job interviews, telling stories about your successes can create a positive connection between you and your potential employers. By telling success stories, you provide specific and concrete examples as evidence of your abilities and attributes. Also, these stories often offer a glimpse into who you are as a person.

One approach to telling success stories is the **STAR method** (Situation–Tasks–Actions–Results). Table 16.13 shows how Haniz uses the STAR method to briefly but convincingly respond to the question *How well do you work with deadlines?* Read through this example and compare its specificity to an abstract, nonspecific response, such as "I work well under pressure and deadlines. In fact, I thrive under these conditions and often produce my best results."

As you tell success stories, make sure that they respond directly to interview questions and reveal your best selling points. Also, make sure your stories stay relatively brief. Generally, responses that are longer than one to two minutes are too long. You might consider writing out five or six success stories you could use in a job interview.

TABLE 16.13

The STAR Approach to Responding to Interview Questions

	Example Statements
Situation where you created a positive outcome **Tasks** you were assigned as part of a process **Actions** you took that led to outcome **Results** that occurred	**Q.** *How well do you work with deadlines?* **A.** I'm quite used to meeting deadlines, and actually, I've done some of my best work when I had to hit a deadline. One example occurred recently in organizing a group of credit union employees and members to participate in a local walkathon to support breast cancer. For over a decade, our credit union has been a prominent supporter of the event, but our participation has decreased almost every year. Last year, our group was comprised of just 15 people, most of whom were employees. Altogether, we raised only around $600. Two weeks before the deadline for signing up, our president approached me and asked me if I could head up a promotional effort to get a larger group from the credit union. She suggested that I aim for at least 30 people and focus on getting more of our members on the walkathon team, especially newer members. Within a few days, another marketing specialist and I had set up some incentives for members to participate, such as a free T-shirt and a water bottle. We developed promotional messages that we sent out by email and via our Facebook page and our website. I think what made the most difference is that we asked tellers to distribute flyers each time a member came in for a transaction. Ultimately, we recruited 83 walkers and raised nearly $10,000 for our local breast cancer center. We also were able to get a variety of new members to join our walkathon team and connect on a deeper level with our credit union community.

Avoid Criticizing Your Former Organizations, Supervisors, and Colleagues
About 49 percent of hiring managers say that talking negatively about previous bosses or supervisors is a "major problem/a deal-maker," and another 46 percent say it's "somewhat of a problem."[26] If you express negativity, hiring managers may wonder how well you get along with others and what attitude you bring to work. When you are asked questions such as *Why do you want to leave your current job* or *What is your least favorite part of your job*, be prepared with an honest response that is constructive, forward-looking, and complimentary if possible.

Ask Questions Generally, your interviewer will ask you what questions you have. Come prepared with some. When interviewees do not ask questions, hiring managers often view them as uninterested or inexperienced. In Table 16.14, you will notice several questions that are not effective and others that are generally effective.[27]

TABLE 16.14

Questions by Job Candidates in First Interviews

Less Effective	More Effective
• What kind of salary are you offering for this position? • How often can I work from home? • Is there a strong benefits package?	• Can you tell me about the company culture? • If there were any one thing you could change about the company culture, what would it be? • What are you looking for in the person who takes this position? • How do you evaluate employees' performance? • What are the next steps in the process? • Whom would I report to in this position? What management style does this person have? • Do you have any concerns about my ability to succeed in this position?

Typically, if you ask about salary, compensation, and other perks on the first interview, you may inadvertently send the meta message "this is all about me." One survey showed that less than one-third of hiring managers thought it was OK for interviewees to bring up salary on the first interview.[28] Of course, these are considered appropriate topics on second or third interviews when a potential employer is showing strong interest in you.

Succeed in Web Conference Interviews

Many companies are increasingly using web conferences for initial job interviews. Using Skype, Google Hangouts, or other platforms is far more convenient and less expensive—in time and money—than flying in job candidates for job interviews. Consider the following strategies for these types of job interviews.

Do Several Trial Runs   Make sure to do several mock job interviews via web conference. You'll notice that within 20 to 30 minutes, you'll learn a variety of ways to act professionally and feel natural. Consider asking a parent, a friend, or a professional to run the practice interview with you. As part of this process, test your equipment to make sure your video and audio work well.

Make Sure Your Profile for the Web Conference Software Creates the Right Impressions   The first thing that many recruiters will see is your profile on Skype or Google Hangouts. You can make a great first impression with a professional photograph and professional bio.

Look Professional   Some job candidates view web conference job interviews as less formal than in-person job interviews. That's simply not the case. Dress up in a suit or appropriate professional dress to show your interest in the job. Consider adjusting the temperature in your room to ensure you're comfortable with a suit on during the interview.

Tidy Your Room or Office   Many job interviewers form impressions of you based on the surroundings in your room or office. Make sure your room is clean, organized, and attractive.

Look Directly at the Camera   Holding an authentic conversation with your interviewer is one of your main goals. By looking straight into the camera, you allow eye contact to make the conversation more personable and real. To look straight into the camera and also position the web conference window so that you can see your interviewer may require several minutes of adjusting the location of your webcam.

Smile and Express Yourself Nonverbally   Many people find it challenging to express themselves nonverbally in web conferences. Initially, you may need to make conscious effort to smile more often and use gestures. Many people use gestures less because they rest their elbows on a desk or armchair, which hinders them from natural movements. You might consider not placing your hands or elbows on the desk in front of you to free up your hands and arms.

Make sure to look professional and generate enthusiasm for online job interviews.

Hero Images/Getty Images

Use Notes Strategically A major advantage of web conference interviews is you can have notes—on paper or in an open file on your computer—to give you cues during the interview. For example, you might have a list of points you want to emphasize or a few questions to ask. Use these notes sparingly, however, so that you can maintain eye contact with your interviewer and avoid the impression you're not prepared for the interview.

Avoid Distractions By removing clutter on your desk and closing all windows and unneeded files on your computer, you ensure you can focus completely during your interview. Similarly, make sure there aren't any interruptions during your interview. If you have roommates, make sure they know to be quiet during your interview. If you have a pet, make sure it's not close enough to your room or office that the interviewer might hear it. If you live where it's not uncommon to hear car honks, police sirens, or other distracting noises, consider finding a better location for your job interview.

Send a Thank-You Note As with any job interview, send a thank-you note soon after your interview (see the next section "Follow Up after the Job Interview").

Follow Up after the Job Interview

Sending a note of appreciation following an interview is a good strategy. In a poll of 300 hiring managers, 80 percent stated that sending a thank-you note could increase chances of employment. When asked how many job applicants actually did send thank-you notes, hiring managers said just 24 percent of candidates do so.[29]

LO16.12 Explain etiquette for following up after job interviews.

Within a few hours to one day after your interview, send a thank-you note. Your primary goal should be to express goodwill and confirm your interest in the position (see Figure 16.16). The note should be brief and genuine. Some job applicants wonder whether they should send a thank-you email or a handwritten thank-you note. Both methods are appropriate. In a recent survey, 94 percent of HR professionals said a thank-you email is appropriate and 86 percent said a handwritten note is appropriate.[30] Clearly, the only "right" answer is that you should send one.

FIGURE 16.16

Thank-You Note Following an Interview

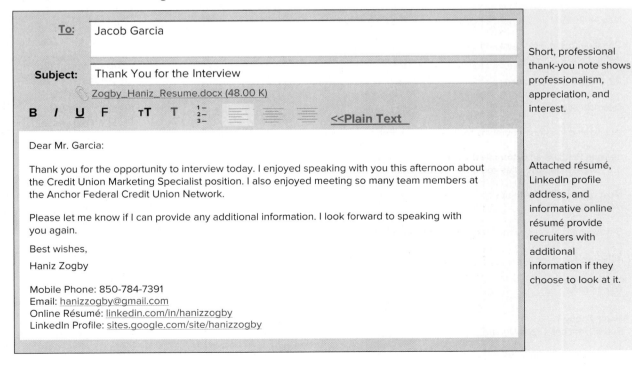

| To: | Jacob Garcia |
| Subject: | Thank You for the Interview |

Zogby_Haniz_Resume.docx (48.00 K)

B *I* <u>U</u> F ᴛT T 1—2—3— <<**Plain Text**

Dear Mr. Garcia:

Thank you for the opportunity to interview today. I enjoyed speaking with you this afternoon about the Credit Union Marketing Specialist position. I also enjoyed meeting so many team members at the Anchor Federal Credit Union Network.

Please let me know if I can provide any additional information. I look forward to speaking with you again.

Best wishes,

Haniz Zogby

Mobile Phone: 850-784-7391
Email: hanizzogby@gmail.com
Online Résumé: linkedin.com/in/hanizzogby
LinkedIn Profile: sites.google.com/site/hanizzogby

Short, professional thank-you note shows professionalism, appreciation, and interest.

Attached résumé, LinkedIn profile address, and informative online résumé provide recruiters with additional information if they choose to look at it.

Unless the interviewers tell you that you should wait until they contact you, feel free to follow up with their progress in making a selection. Many job applicants feel hesitant to follow up, assuming that they may annoy or nag hiring managers. The reality is far different. In a recent survey of HR professionals, 100 percent suggested job applicants should follow up! Roughly 29 percent said following up in less than one week is appropriate, 36 percent indicated one to two weeks is most appropriate, 25 percent suggest two to three weeks is most appropriate, and the remaining 10 percent encouraged applicants to wait three weeks or more to follow up. About 64 percent said the best way to follow up is by email, another 21 percent indicated phone is preferred, and 14 percent suggested in person is best.[31] Your polite follow-ups show that you want the position and that you are persistent.

Leaving an Organization

LO16.13 Explain etiquette for leaving an organization with grace and foresight.

When you accept a new position, you can extend several courtesies to your current employer and ensure that you leave on good terms so that your supervisors can provide a positive recommendation in the future if you need it. In the first place, you should inform your supervisor that you are leaving immediately, preferably in person. Show graciousness and appreciation for the professional opportunities you have been given. Be careful about bragging or boasting about your new position, which will imply to some of your colleagues that you do not appreciate the sacrifices that many of your supervisors and colleagues likely made for you.[32] In addition to telling your supervisor in person that you are leaving, you may be required to write a formal resignation. Write a brief, warm, and appreciative letter (see Figure 16.17).

FIGURE 16.17

Resignation Letter

BETTER HORIZONS CREDIT UNION
Est. 1937

May 14, 2020

Christine Russo, President and CEO
Better Horizons Loop, Pescaloosa, FL 91214

RE: Notice of Resignation

Dear Christine:

I am writing to inform you of my resignation from Better Horizons Credit Union effective May 31, 2020.

Leaving BHCU is an extremely difficult decision. Please accept my deep gratitude for the many professional opportunities you have provided me.

Most of all, I will miss the people of BHCU. When we say the "Better Horizons family," we are not exaggerating.

Best wishes to you and the credit union for continued growth and success!

Sincerely,

Haniz Zogby

Haniz Zogby
Better Horizons Credit Union

This concise letter provides all needed components: a resignation date and an expression of goodwill.

Expression of goodwill and gratitude is professional, warm, and sincere.

💡 IDEAS IN ACTION

Relying on Mentors

Geisha Williams has been CEO and president of Pacific Gas and Electricity (PG&E) for nearly the past decade. As a Cuban immigrant, she has relied on education, entrepreneurialism, preparation, and hard work to develop a satisfying and productive career. She's also depended on the advice and support of others.

Paul Morigi/Stringer/Getty Images

As an early-career professional in her early 20s, Williams made one of her best decisions: find a mentor. She explains, "My career aspirations were not very lofty. I thought, if I worked really hard, someday maybe I could be a manager. . . . Clark Cook [my mentor], looked at me, and said, 'Geisha, you know, someone has to run this place. Someone has to be in charge. Why not you?' What he meant was that I should aim for CEO or president of the company. I remember saying something like, are you kidding me?"

Cook became Williams's lifelong mentor. He believed in her potential, and he consistently shared ideas with her about how to move to the next stage of her career and develop her leadership skills. She explains, "[He] inspired me in a way that I had never been inspired before." Thirty years after Clark opened her eyes to her own potential, Williams became a company president. And she continues to go to lunch with Clark and discuss professional matters.

Like Williams, you should seek out people who can act as mentors, especially early in your career. Most companies now have formal mentoring programs. As you take new positions, make sure to inquire about options for new employees. Mentors can help you identify and pursue your interests, connect you with new opportunities, and guide you in career decisions.

Source: Caley, C. (2014, February 17). Geisha Williams: Set your sights high, take charge and keep the lights on. *Leadership California.*

Chapter Takeaway for *Employment Communications*

LO16.1 Understand principles for professional networking.

Principles for professional networking
• Conduct informational interviews. • Attend job fairs and other career networking events. • Attend campus speeches and other professional development events. • Join clubs and other professional interest groups. • Volunteer at a local nonprofit.

LO16.2 Identify your key selling points for the job application process.

Effective résumés, cover letters, and interviews enhance **your personal credibility.**

It shows **competence** when you demonstrate skills and/or knowledge to complete work tasks.	It shows **caring** when you demonstrate the ability to manage effective workplace relationships.	It shows **character** when you demonstrate that you uphold high professional norms and standards.

See *skills and attributes that reflect competence, caring, and character* in Table 16.1.
See an *example of a self-inventory* in Figure 16.1.

LO16.3 Evaluate the primary needs of employers for positions of interest.

See an *example of analyzing a job posting for key needs* in Figure 16.2.

LO16.4 Set up the message structure for résumés and cover letters.

Components of Chronological Résumés	
• Name block • Summary of qualifications *or* Career objective (optional)	• Education • Work experience • Additional information

Components of Functional Résumés	
• Name block • Summary of qualifications *or* Career summary	• Skills • Additional information

Audience   Information

Plan

Message

Audience: Identify the abilities and attributes that add value to employers.

Information: Identify your career interests and job-related abilities and attributes.

Message: Match your abilities and attributes to the needs of employers.

LO16.5 Highlight your qualifications with effective tone, style, and design.

Principles of Effective Résumés	
• Emphasize accomplishments with action verbs. • Quantify accomplishments where possible. • Position your most important contributions first. • Remove irrelevant details. • Avoid clichés, buzzwords, and jargon.	• Be exact and avoid any errors. • Group and label information to improve ease of reading. • Format to distinguish pieces of information. • Select a simple yet visually appealing layout.

See *examples of action words* in Tables 16.2 and 16.3; *quantifying accomplishments* in Table 16.4; *positioning contributions* in Table 16.5; *removing unnecessary details* in Table 16.6; *avoiding clichés* in Table 16.7; *proofreading for typos and misspellings* in Table 16.8; *grouping and labeling* in Table 16.9; and *formatting to distinguish key pieces of information* in Table 16.10.

Tone: Tell the story of your abilities and attributes with tempered enthusiasm and confidence. Avoid a me-first mentality.

Style: Display an action orientation and ensure consistency of facts throughout your employment application.

Design: Make sure that employers can pick out key pieces of information to understand your story quickly.

LO16.6 Create chronological and functional résumés to highlight your key selling points.

See *examples of ineffective and effective chronological résumés* in Figures 16.4, 16.5, 16.6, and 16.7.
See an *example of a functional résumé* in Figure 16.8.

LO16.7 Use LinkedIn as part of the job search process and to network professionally.

Tips for Using LinkedIn	
• Provide a professional photo. • Create a personalized URL. • Complete the summary space. • Use multimedia. • Choose sections wisely. • Manage your recommendations and endorsements strategically.	• Build a network of important connections • Show some personality and be positive. • Maintain a giver mentality. • Stay active on LinkedIn.

See an *example of a LinkedIn profile* in Figure 16.9.
See *examples of nonpersonalized and personalized LinkedIn Invitations* in Figures 16.10 and 16.11.

LO16.8 Develop a list of references that will improve your employment prospects.

See an *example of a reference list* in Figure 16.12.

LO16.9 Compose effective cover letters that highlight your key selling points.

Components of Cover Letters
• Interest in position. • Match with position. • Call to action.

See *examples of ineffective and effective solicited cover letters* in Figures 16.13 and 16.14.

See an *example of an unsolicited referral cover letter* in Figure 16.15.

LO16.10 Review your job application documents for effectiveness and fairness.

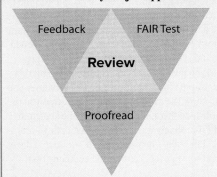

Feedback: Ask colleagues and clients what they would like you to change about your presentation.

FAIR Test: Focus on presenting factual information and being clear about impacts on others.

Proofreading: Make sure your slides, handouts, and other supplementary materials are attractive and error-free.

LO16.11 Develop strategies for responding to common job interview questions.

See *common interview questions* in Table 16.11.

See *ineffective and effective responses to interview questions* in Table 16.12.

Components of STAR Stories	
• Situation	• Actions
• Tasks	• Results

See *an example of a STAR story* in Table 16.13.

See *examples of ineffective and effective questions by job candidates* in Table 16.14.

LO16.12 Explain etiquette for following up after job interviews.

See *an example of a thank-you note following an interview* in Figure 16.16.

LO16.13 Explain etiquette for leaving an organization with grace and foresight.

See *an example of a resignation letter* in Figure 16.17.

Key Terms

abilities, 498

attributes, 498

chronological résumé, 508

functional résumé, 508

informational interview, 496

networking, 496

solicited cover letter, 521

STAR method, 528

unsolicited cover letter, 522

Discussion Exercises

16.1 Chapter Review Questions (LO16.1 to LO16.13)

A. What are informational interviews? How can you prepare to conduct an effective informational interview?

B. Aside from informational interviews, what other principles for professional networking are effective for university students?

C. How can identifying your job interests, abilities, and attributes help you develop an effective résumé?

D. In what ways can you categorize your key abilities and attributes to project credibility?

E. What are some ways of identifying the key abilities and attributes employers are seeking for unfilled positions?

F. What are the benefits and drawbacks of chronological and functional résumés?

G. What strategies can you use to project competence and confidence but not arrogance in your job application messages?

H. What is the underlying purpose of grouping and labeling data on your résumé?

I. What strategies can you use to develop a reliable reference list for your job searches?

J. What are the key factors in appropriate etiquette for your job interview?

K. Explain how the STAR approach to answering interview questions can help you display your key abilities and attributes.

L. What are some principles to abide by when leaving a position?

16.2 Using All Communication Channels in the Job Search Process (LO16.3)

Terry J. Lundgren, former CEO and president of Macy's, was asked, "[Do you have] any job-seeking advice for college grads?" Here's what he had to say:

Use whatever contact you have to try to get your résumé read. That's the most important thing—just to get it in front of people. Because we're all flooded with, of course, thousands and thousands of résumés in a company of our size, and getting your résumé read is not an automatic. And so do what you can do to get it in front of the people who matter who will read it. It's not the CEO typically, by the way; it's the HR person or the head of recruiting or head of training or whatever. Third, don't stop there. Don't just do it online, because it's easy to do it online. Do it online and then put it in an envelope and send it to the top company that you're interested in pursuing. And then follow up with a phone call, and talk to the assistant and say: "I just want to make sure that my résumé's getting read. I'm very interested in your company, and it's really important to me. And I just want to know—can you give me advice?—is there anything that I can do to get my résumé in front of your boss?" Whatever you have to say, just to show the most important thing—that you're hungry. And to convince them, maybe you use a little of your acting skills. And I'll probably relate it to college dating—you know, use a little, "I'm really interested in you"—to say: "This is the company I want to work for. Yours is the company that

I want to work for." And then once you get, hopefully, more than one opportunity, you're back in charge to say, "Where do I want to go and where do I want to work."[33]

Based on Lundgren's comments and your own perspectives, respond to the following questions:

A. Explain what Lundgren means by showing "you're hungry" for a position. Describe ways in which you can show hunger in a positive way.

B. What does he suggest about the effectiveness of relying exclusively on electronic means to submit job applications? What combination of communication channels do you consider optimal for gaining a job of interest?

C. He suggests that you should view the process like dating. In what ways does this analogy make sense to you? Explain.

16.3 Identifying What Employers Are Seeking (LO16.3)

Anne Berkowitch, co-founder and former chief executive of SelectMinds, discussed how her approach to hiring new employees has evolved:

I started out recruiting for skills that I knew I didn't have and I didn't understand intuitively. I was putting way too much emphasis on skills and background and what I could see on paper. I wasn't trusting myself to evaluate whether these were the right people. I'd say I went through a spate where I made the wrong hires. Then I said, "I have to do this differently, and I'm just going to trust my instinct about the right kind of person to bring onto this team." I had to hire people who had skills and

experience I needed, but who they were as a person played a much bigger role in what I looked for. The people I want to hire share a number of characteristics. They're smart. They're problem solvers. They're good at what they do. They are honest with themselves, which to me is extremely important. If you're not honest with yourself, then too much of your energy goes toward managing what you're saying to everybody else, rather than what you should be doing. They are curious and they want to do things outside their comfort zone. They're passionate—it doesn't matter about what. It could be about theater. It could be about your kids. The other quality is they're people who want to be part of a group to build something. They're not looking for title. They're really motivated by coming on board. At this point, I feel like I could talk to somebody for five minutes and have a good sense of whether they have those qualities, and I'll be right 85 percent of the time.[34]

A. Explain what you think Berkowitch means when she says she started prioritizing hiring employees for "who they were as a person" more so than by their skills and experience?

B. What attributes does she look for in particular when hiring new employees? Are these attributes that you can demonstrate on paper? Explain.

C. She says she can judge whether a person fits her company within five minutes. Do you believe that hiring managers can do this reliably? Assuming that you have only five minutes to demonstrate your value to a hiring manager, what would you want to stand out about yourself?

Evaluation Exercises

16.4 Interviewing with a Hiring Manager about Job Application Best Practices (LO16.2, LO16.3)

Contact a hiring manager (consider any person you know who is involved in the hiring process) and arrange a time to interview that person for 30 minutes to one hour. Ask the hiring manager about the following related to hiring new employees:

A. Most common mistakes on résumés and cover letters.

B. Aspects in résumés and cover letters that make successful job candidates stand out.

C. Keys to successful interviews.

D. Common mistakes at job interviews.

E. Appropriate ways to follow up after interviews.

After the interview, write a two-page report detailing best practices for successfully navigating the job application process and getting a job. Tailor your report to undergraduate students who are seeking entry-level professional positions.

16.5 Getting Feedback on Your Résumé and Cover Letter (LO16.4, LO16.5, LO16.6, LO16.9, LO16.10)

To determine how well you are promoting your selling points (your two or three key abilities and two or three key attributes), do the following in this order:

A. Write down your key selling points.

B. Create your résumé and cover letter to highlight these key selling points.

C. Without providing what you believe are your key selling points, ask a trusted classmate/colleague/professor to review your résumé and cover letter. Specifically, ask your peer to answer the following questions:

1. Based on these documents, what do you think my key selling points are? Ask your peer to mention abilities or skills and attributes or traits.

2. Do my key selling points stand out clearly? Do you think my résumé and cover letter provide a consistent message about my selling points?

3. What suggestions do you have for me to improve these documents?

After getting responses from your peer, answer the following questions:

A. What did your peer say were your key selling points? What did your peer say about how well your selling points stood out?

B. How closely aligned were your peer's observations with what you intended to be your key selling points?

C. Based on your peer's observations, what modifications should you make to your résumé and cover letter to better highlight your selling points?

16.6 Getting Feedback on Your Résumé from a Professional in Your Desired Discipline/Industry (LO16.4, LO16.5, LO16.6, LO16.10)

Find a professional in the discipline and/or industry that interests you. Ask this person to review your résumé and give you feedback about the following: (a) strength of your résumé in gaining the position you seek; (b) advice for improving the résumé; (c) areas of your résumé that may appear less credible or perhaps even exaggerated; and (d) advice for increasing career opportunities. Turn in the following:

A. Revised résumé.

B. Document detailing what you learned from the business professional and what changes you made to your résumé as a result.

16.7 Getting Feedback on Your Résumé from Classmates (LO16.4, LO16.5, LO16.6, LO16.10)

Form a group of three to four classmates. Read one another's résumés, spending three to five minutes per résumé. As you read, focus on how well the person communicates key abilities and attributes. Debrief by explaining the following:

A. Key abilities and attributes communicated by the résumé.

B. Two or three areas in which the résumé could be improved.

C. Any areas in the résumé that seem less substantiated than others.

Individually, write two to three paragraphs about the comments and advice you received from the other members in your group.

Application Exercises

16.8 Sharing Your Experiences from Informational Interviews (LO16.1)

You will conduct two or three informational interviews. Identify some professionals who work in positions you aspire to hold or who do work that you aspire to engage in. Set up 30-minute to 1-hour informational interviews with these individuals.

You should approach these informational interviews with real questions in mind—some issues you really want to understand better. You're strongly encouraged to reach out to people whom you don't know. Ideally, you'll meet in person. However, online video conversations work as well.

From your informational interviews, you'll develop a presentation to help your classmates understand professional opportunities and paths. Identify one or two interesting themes from your interviews to share in your presentation.

Ideally, you'll make your presentation story-based. Talk about the individuals you chose to interview (What are their areas of expertise? What are their accomplishments? Why do you admire or respect them? What are their personalities like? What drives them?). Spend most of your time providing key professional insights from your interviewees. Make sure to clearly identify the takeaway points while providing examples shared by your interviewees.

16.9 Evaluating Your Key Selling Points (LO16.2)

Using Table 16.1 and Figure 16.1 as guides, do the following:

A. State your career goals.

B. Describe the three or four abilities and three or four attributes that you want to stand out most prominently in your job application package. Why do you want these skills and attributes to stand out?

C. Name the two or three abilities and attributes you most want to develop.

16.10 Analyzing a Job Announcement of Interest to You (LO16.3)

Find a job announcement for a position of interest to you. Using Figure 16.2 as a guide, do the following:

A. Group and categorize the key abilities and attributes that are being sought.

B. Describe your fit with these abilities and attributes.

C. Explain how you can compensate for abilities or attributes that you have not yet fully developed.

16.11 Using Action Words (LO16.5)

Using Tables 16.2, 16.3, and 16.4 as guides, do the following:

A. Choose ten of the action words and create statements that you could use on your résumé with your accomplishments.

B. Make five statements of accomplishments that you could place on your résumé that include quantification (e.g., increased sales by 12 percent).

16.12 Creating a Résumé (LO16.4, LO16.5, LO16.6)

Create a perfectly polished résumé.

16.13 Creating Functional and Chronological Résumés (LO16.4, LO16.5, LO16.6)

Create two versions of your résumé—a chronological and a functional résumé. In addition to these two documents, create a separate document that describes the advantages and disadvantages of using each type.

16.14 Creating a Reference List (LO16.8)

Create a reference list with five individuals whom you could trust to provide good professional endorsements of your abilities. Provide all contact information and a brief statement about how each person knows you.

16.15 Creating a Cover Letter (LO16.9)

Choose a job announcement that interests you. Write a cover letter that is addressed to the contact person/organization in this announcement.

16.16 Telling Stories with the STAR Method (LO16.11)

Write down how you would answer one of the following interview questions using the STAR method: (a) Can you tell me about a challenge you overcame at work? (b) Can you give me an example of how you showed leadership at work? or (c) Can you tell me about one of your recent successes at work? You can substitute school experiences for work experiences if you'd like.

16.17 Writing a Thank-You Note (LO16.12)

Choose a job position that interests you. Assume you have just completed the job interview. Write a thank-you message that you think appropriately expresses gratitude and improves your chances in the hiring process.

16.18 Writing a Resignation Letter (LO16.13)

Assume that you will be resigning from a job (you can use a current/past position). Write a message that states when you will leave, shows your appreciation, and ensures goodwill with the employer in the future.

Language Mechanics Check

16.18 Review all rules in Appendix A about punctuation, number usage, and grammar. Then, rewrite each sentence to make all needed corrections.

A. Please except my application for the Web Developer position (Job ID#4392) on your companies website.

B. For the past 4 years I have helped develop and run several websites.

C. Before I describe some of my technical abilities I want to describe the success of these websites.

D. In my current position at Better Horizons Credit Union the marketing team and several web developers have worked on a web strategy, to attract younger members.

E. I've been a significant part of these efforts to match a strategy to a web design, improve the overall aesthetic appeal of the web page and identify strategies to improve our place in internet searches.

F. I was able to oversee some design changes on the *Members* section of the website

G. After applying these design changes the web traffic has grown by 18% in the last month.

H. In each of these web development projects, I've gathered input from all people who will use the websites; managers, colleagues, customers and prospects.

I. By getting this input, I can develop websites that are user-friendly, helpful and appealing.

J. I believe my primary strength as a web developer is to understand how the user experience impacts future use, of the website.

Endnotes

1. Chui, M., Manyika, J., Bughin, J., Dobbs, R., Roxburgh, C., Sarrazin, H., Sands, G., & Westergren, M. (2012, July). *The social economy: Unlocking value and productivity through social technologies.* McKinsey Global Institute.

2. Azua, M. (2010). *The social factor: Innovate, ignite, and win through mass collaboration and social networking.* Upper Saddle River, NJ: IBM Press.

3. Chui, M., Miller, A., & Roberts, R. P. (2010). Six ways to make Web 2.0 work. *McKinsey Quarterly.*

4. Wright, S., & Zdinak, J. (2008). *New communication behaviors in a Web 2.0 world–Changes, challenges and opportunities in the era of the Information Revolution.* Paris: Alcatel-Lucent, 10.

5. Henneman, T. (2010, March). At Lockheed Martin, social networking fills key workforce needs while improving efficiency and lowering costs. *Workforce Management.* Retrieved November 20, 2010, from www.workforce.com/section/software-technology/feature-lockheed-martin-social-networking-fills-key-workforce/index.html.

6. KSA (Knowledge, Skills, Abilities) approach for federal jobs.

7. Society for Human Resource Management. (2009, November 17). Final hiring decisions based on "chemistry" say HR managers. Society for Human Resource Management website. Retrieved from https://www.shrm.org/about-shrm/press-room/press-releases/pages/interviewdosanddonts.aspx.

8. Society for Human Resource Management. (2009, January 12). Networking professionally: Employee perspective. Society for Human Resource Management website. Retrieved from www.shrm.org/Research/SurveyFindings/Articles/Documents/OEnetworking.pdf.

9. Torres, M. (2018, November 21). New research says 2-page resumes are actually preferred by recruiters. *Ladders* website. Retrieved from www.theladders.com/career-advice/new-research-says-2-page-resumes-are-actually-preferred-by-recruiters.

10. Accountemps. (2005, March 31). The devil is in the "resume" details: Typos or grammatical errors most common resume mistake, survey shows. Retrieved from accountemps.rhi.mediaroom.com/index.php?s=189&item=250.

11. Society for Human Resource Management. (2014, April 28). *SHRM survey findings: Résumés, cover letters and interviews.* Alexandria, VA: Author.

12. Accountemps. (2009, October 29). Most wanted: "People" people: Survey shows interpersonal skills can trump technical knowledge in job search. Retrieved from http://accountemps.rhi.mediaroom.com/index.php?s=189&item=863.

13. Chung, D. (2017, October 2). 2 minutes. That's how long recruiters take to review your resume. Make it stand out. *Mission.* Retrieved from https://medium.com/the-mission/2-minutes-thats-how-long-recruiters-take-to-review-your-resum%C3%A9-make-it-stand-out-1634bc72bf7.

14. Accountemps. (2009, July 14). Have a keen eye for detail. Retrieved from www.accountemps.com/PressRoom?id=2491.

15. Robert Half. (2015, April 7). Which resume format is best for you? Retrieved from https://www.roberthalf.com/blog/writing-a-resume/which-resume-format-is-best-for-you.

16. Suder, R. (2019, March 31). How to use LinkedIn to get a job. *Top Resume.* Retrieved from https://www.topresume.com/career-advice/14-ways-to-leverage-your-linkedin-profile-during-your-job-search.

17. Shields, J. (2018, October 28). 3 things you need to know about cover letters. *Career Tool Belt*. Retrieved from www.careertoolbelt.com/3-things-you-need-to-know-about-cover-letters-for-2018/.

18. Shields, J. (2018, October 28). 3 things you need to know about cover letters. *Career Tool Belt*. Retrieved from www.careertoolbelt.com/3-things-you-need-to-know-about-cover-letters-for-2018/.

19. Lublin, J. S. (2010, July 6). The keys to unlocking your most successful career. *The Wall Street Journal Career Journal*.

20. Isaacs, K. Cold cover letters. Monster.com Advice blog. Retrieved January 20, 2011, from http://career-advice.monster.com/resumes-cover-letters/Cover-Letter-Tips/Cold-Cover-Letters/article.aspx.

21. Society for Human Resource Management. (2009, November 17). Final hiring decisions based on "chemistry" say HR managers. *SHRM* website. Retrieved from https://www.shrm.org/about-shrm/press-room/press-releases/pages/interviewdosanddonts.aspx

22. Gurchiek, K. (2010, November 1). Dress to impress, not stress, the hiring manager. *Society for Human Resource Management HR News* [online].

23. Spano, S. (2018, April 20). Survey says: Employee deal breakers to avoid. *Jazz HR Notes*. Retrieved from https://notes.jazzhr.com/2018/04/20/survey-says-employee-deal-breakers-avoid/.

24. Grasz, J. (2013, November 21). New CareerBuilder study looks at best and worst colors to wear in a job interview. *CareerBuilder*. Retrieved from https://www.careerbuilder.com/share/aboutus/pressreleasesdetail.aspx?sd=11/21/2013&id=pr791&ed=12/31/2013.

25. Workopolis. (2015, June 15). Study: How quickly do interviews really make decisions. Retrieved from https://careers.workopolis.com/advice/study-how-quickly-do-interviewers-really-make-decisions/.

26. Society for Human Resource Management. (2009, December 3). *SHRM poll: Interviewing do's and don'ts for job seekers*. Retrieved from https://www.slideshare.net/shrm/interviewing-dos-and-donts-for-job-seekers.

27. Accountemps. (2009, March 18). Most executives OK with applicants asking about compensation by second interview. Retrieved January 10, 2010, from http://accountemps.rhi.mediaroom.com/index.php?s=189&item=165.

28. Workopolis. (2017, March 17). When is the right time to ask about salary? Retrieved from https://careers.workopolis.com/advice/right-time-ask-salary/.

29. De Rose, B. (2017, November 20). Thank-you notes can tip scale in job candidates' favor, yet few write them. Retrieved from http://rh-us.mediaroom.com/2017-11-20-Thank-You-Notes-Can-Tip-Scale-in-Job-Candidates-Favor-Yet-Few-Write-Them.

30. De Rose, B. (2017, November 20). Thank-you notes can tip scale in job candidates' favor, yet few write them. Retrieved from http://rh-us.mediaroom.com/2017-11-20-Thank-You-Notes-Can-Tip-Scale-in-Job-Candidates-Favor-Yet-Few-Write-Them.

31. De Rose, B. (2017, September 17). The art of following up: 100 percent of hiring managers encourage checking up on job applications. Retrieved from http://rh-us.mediaroom.com/2017-09-19-The-Art-of-Following-Up.

32. Bryant, A. (2010, September 4). Learn to lead from the back of the boat. *The New York Times*. Retrieved from www.nytimes.com/2010/09/05/business/05corner.html.

33. As cited in Bryant, A. (2009, August 22). A C.E.O. must decide who swims. *The New York Times*. Retrieved from www.nytimes.com/2009/08/23/business/23corner.ready.html.

34. Bryant, A. (2010, September 5). Learn to lead from the back of the boat. *The New York Times*. Retrieved from www.nytimes.com/2010/09/05/business/05corner.html.

Punctuation, Number Usage, and Grammar

This appendix includes rules that cover many common writing issues. For a complete review of language mechanics guidelines, consult a comprehensive guidebook such as the *Gregg Reference Manual*. Also, use the online resources, including exercises and assessments.

Overview of Terms Used in This Appendix

Nouns are words or phrases that refer to persons, places, objects, qualities, or activities.

Subjects are nouns that are the primary topics of a sentence. The subject determines the verb form used in the sentence (see rule G2).

Verbs are words or phrases that express action or existence.

Predicates are verb phrases that in combination with a subject make a complete sentence.

Adjectives are words or phrases that modify nouns.

Adverbs are words or phrases that modify adjectives, verbs, or adverbs.

Prepositions are words that show the relationships between nouns (e.g., *at, in, by, from, with*).

Coordinating conjunctions connect words, phrases, or clauses; examples include *and, but, or,* and *nor*.

Clauses contain a subject and a predicate. **Independent clauses** express a complete thought and can stand alone, whereas **dependent clauses** cannot stand alone.

Participles are words that share characteristics of verbs and adjectives. *Present participles* end in *ing*; *past participles* end in *ed*; and *perfect participles* are a combination of a form of the verb "to have" and a past participle.

Punctuation and Formatting

Commas

Commas have two functions: (1) to set off nonessential expressions that break the flow of a sentence and (2) to separate items in a sentence so that their relationships to one another are clear. *Nonessential* expressions, if removed, do not alter the meaning of the sentence or make the sentence incomplete. Table A.1 lists ten key rules related to commas, with examples. Each rule in this section is identified by a letter (C, for comma) and a number.

TABLE A.1

Comma Rules

Rules	Examples
C1. Use commas to distinguish essential from nonessential information (essential expressions do not require commas; nonessential expressions do require commas).	✔ Sergey Brin and Larry Page, <u>who were attending Stanford at the time</u>, developed the initial technology for Google searches. ***Explanation:* The *who* clause is nonessential because a specific person is mentioned; the information does not narrow down who the people are.**
	✔ Graduate students <u>who were attending Stanford University at the time</u> developed the initial technology for Google searches. ***Explanation:* The *who* clause is essential because it further specifies, or narrows down, who the students are— students *at Stanford*.**
	✔ Google's initial public offering <u>occurred in 2004, the same year that</u> Google developed a multiyear alliance with AOL Europe. ***Explanation:* A comma is required after the year 2004 since the following expression does not further specify which year and is thus nonessential.**
	✔ Google's initial public offering <u>occurred in the same year that</u> Google developed a multiyear alliance with AOL Europe. ***Explanation:* A comma is not required because the that clause further specifies which year and is thus an essential expression.**
C2. Use commas to set off interrupting expressions.	✔ Larry, <u>rather than Sergey</u>, was listed as the inventor on the patent for Google's original search mechanism. ***Explanation:* The underlined expression interrupts the flow of the sentence from subject to verb.**
	✔ Eric Schmidt, <u>the CEO at Google since 2001</u>, was previously chairman of the board and CEO at Novell. ***Explanation:* The underlined expression is an appositive and interrupts the flow of the sentence from subject to verb.**
	✔ Google's largest market, <u>which accounts for 47 percent of revenues</u>, is the United States. ***Explanation:* The underlined expression provides further but nonessential information and interrupts the flow of the sentence from subject to verb.**
	✔ Google offers a variety of applications, <u>such as Google Docs and Google Calendar</u>. ***Explanation:* The underlined expression is additional and nonessential information.**
	✔ Google, <u>in my opinion</u>, is the best technology company to work for. ***Explanation:* Independent thoughts interrupt the flow of the sentence and require commas.**
	✔ Google Chrome, <u>if you're looking for an open-source web browser</u>, may be a fit for you. ***Explanation:* Dependent clauses in the middle of the sentence must be set off by commas.**
	✔ Double-digit annual sales growth at Google during the past three years, <u>in spite of the recession and increased competition</u>, demonstrates the strong demand for Google products and services. ***Explanation:* This nonessential prepositional phrase in the middle of the sentence interrupts the flow of the sentence.**
	Note: Many clauses that require commas in the beginning or middle of a sentence do not require one when they are at the end of the sentence.
	✔ Google Chrome may be a fit for you <u>if you're looking for an open-source web browser</u>. ***Explanation:* This dependent clause at the end of the sentence does not interrupt the flow of the sentence, so no comma is needed.**
	✔ Double-digit annual sales growth at Google during the past three years demonstrates the strong demand for Google products and services <u>in spite of the recession and increased competition</u>. ***Explanation:* This prepositional phrase at the end of the sentence does not interrupt the flow of the sentence, so no comma is needed.**

TABLE A.1

(Continued)

Rules	Examples
C3. Use a comma following a transitional expression.	✔ Also, Google's social networking website has gained little acceptance in the United States. ***Explanation:* Transitional expressions such *as also* help readers relate sentences to one another. Transitional expressions are followed by commas.**
	✔ As a result, Google purchased a new mobile display ad provider to increase its revenues in mobile advertising. ***Explanation:* Transitional expressions such as as *a result* help readers relate sentences to one another. Transitional expressions are followed by commas.**
C4. Use a comma between two independent clauses separated by *and*, *but*, *or*, or *nor*.	✔ Sergey Brin is currently the president of technology, and Larry Page is currently the president of products. ***Explanation:* Two independent clauses are separated by a comma and coordinating conjunction.**
	Exception: When an introductory expression applies to both independent clauses, a comma is not placed between the independent clauses.
	✔ Since Google's organizational restructuring in 2001, Sergey Brin has served as the president of technology and Larry Page has served as the president of products. ***Explanation:* A comma is not placed between the independent clauses because the introductory expression applies to both of them.**
	Exception: Short compound sentences often do not require a comma (generally less than 12 to 13 words).
	Sergey is in charge of technology and Larry is in charge of products. ***Explanation:* This sentence is short (13 words) and is understood easily without a comma separating the two independent clauses.**
C5. Use commas in a series with three or more items.	✔ Google's client services include Google Toolbar, Google Chrome, and Google Pack. ***Explanation:* Each of these three items in a series is separated from one another by a comma.**
	✔ Google has developed an innovative culture by setting up an informal work environment, providing the top incentives in the industry, and encouraging employees to spend 20 percent of their time on their own projects. ***Explanation:* Each of the three items in the series is separated from one another by a comma.**
	✔ Google spends far above industry averages in the following areas: marketing, training, and research and development. ***Explanation:* Each item in the series is separated by commas. Notice that *research and development* is a single item.**
C6. Use a comma between two independent adjectives preceding a noun.	✔ Google has long been recognized as an innovative, unconventional company. ***Explanation: Innovative* and *unconventional* each independently modifies *company.***
	Note: There are two quick ways to identify independent adjectives. First, if you can place the word *and* between the two adjectives without changing the meaning, then they are independent (innovative and unconventional). Second, if you can reverse the order of the adjectives without changing the meaning, then they are independent (unconventional, innovative).
C7. Use a comma after introductory expressions.	✔ After Google had installed solar panels at Googleplex, it continued its environmental efforts by placing herds of goats around the campus so that mowing the lawns was not necessary. ***Explanation:* Commas are always placed after introductory dependent clauses.**
	✔ By installing thousands of solar panels at Googleplex, Google showed its commitment to environmental causes. ***Explanation:* Commas are always placed after introductory participial phrases.**
	✔ To show its commitment to environmental causes, Google has installed thousands of solar panels at Googleplex. ***Explanation:* Commas are always placed after introductory infinitive phrases.**

TABLE A.1

(Continued)

Rules	Examples
	✔ <u>Under the new set of corporate policies</u>, Google will lease only LEED-certified buildings. ***Explanation:* Commas are placed after long (five or more words) introductory prepositional phrases.**
	Common Exceptions*
	Short introductory adverbs that explain *when* (e.g., next week), *how often* (e.g., frequently), *where* (e.g., at the office), *or why* (e.g., for this reason) do not require commas afterward.
	✔ <u>A few years ago</u> Google became part of the public debate over network neutrality. ***Explanation:* An introductory adverb that expresses *when* does not require a comma.**
	✔ <u>Often</u> the company issues public statements regarding its stand on this issue. ***Explanation:* An introductory adverb that expresses *how often* does not require a comma.**
	✔ <u>At Google</u> the leadership team believes that users should have complete control over the content they view. ***Explanation:* An introductory adverb that expresses *where* does not require a comma.**
	✔ <u>For this reason</u> Google supports network neutrality. ***Explanation:* An introductory adverb that expresses *why* does not require a comma.**
	Short (less than five words) introductory prepositional phrases that do not contain a verb, a transitional phrase, or an independent comment do not require commas.
	✔ <u>In the interview</u> Google's CEO emphasized the company's commitment to network neutrality. ***Explanation:* A comma is not required because the introductory prepositional phrase is short (three words) and does not contain a verb, a transitional phrase, or an independent thought.**
	✔ <u>In the interview with Google's CEO</u>, he emphasized the company's commitment to network neutrality. ***Explanation:* A comma is required because the introductory prepositional phrase is long (five or more words).**
	✔ <u>In the statement</u> he explained that broadband carriers should not be allowed to control content. ***Explanation:* A comma is not required because the introductory prepositional phrase is short (three words) and does not contain a verb, a transitional phrase, or an independent thought.**
	✔ <u>In making this statement</u>, he demonstrated Google's position that broadband carriers should not be allowed to control content. ***Explanation:* A comma is required. Though the introductory prepositional phrase is short (four words), it contains a verb.**
	*A lot of variation exists in how writers apply these exceptions. Many writers use commas after all introductory expressions to avoid analyzing each situation.
C8. Use commas in dates.	✔ Tuesday, May 10 ***Explanation:* A comma separates a day and a date.**
	✔ May 10, 2011 ***Explanation:* A comma separates a date and a year.**
	✔ May 2011 ***Explanation:* A comma does not separate a month and a year.**
	✔ Between May 10, 2011, and May 13, 2011, there were 13 billion Google searches. ***Explanation:* A comma follows a date-year combination in the middle of a sentence.**
C9. Use commas as needed for clarity.	✘ <u>At the Googleplex campus</u> building engineers have identified several approaches to reducing carbon emissions. ***Explanation:* Although technically correct (*At the Googleplex campus* is a short introductory adverb), many readers will wonder what the subject of the sentence is. Is it *building engineers* or just *engineers*?**

TABLE A.1

(Continued)

Rules	Examples
	✔ <u>At the Googleplex campus</u>, building engineers have identified several approaches to reducing carbon emissions. ***Explanation:*** **The comma between** *campus* **and** *building* **clearly shows that** *building* **modifies** *engineers.*
	✘ <u>In 2010</u> 37 of Google's top employees left and took positions at Facebook. ***Explanation:*** **Although technically correct (***In 2010*** is a short introductory adverb), readers may misunderstand or become momentarily confused with two sets of numbers placed next to one another.**
	✔ <u>In 2010</u>, 37 of Google's top employees left and took positions at Facebook. ***Explanation:*** **A comma between the two numbers clarifies that they do not belong together.**
	Alternatively: <u>In 2010 thirty-seven</u> of Google's top employees left and took positions at Facebook. ***Explanation:*** **Spelling out one of the numbers clarifies that the two numbers do not belong together.**
C10. Common misuses of commas.	✘ <u>Google, provides</u> a number of inexpensive enterprise products. ***Explanation:*** **Commas do not separate subjects from verbs.**
	✘ Google <u>provides, a number</u> of inexpensive enterprise products. ***Explanation:*** **Commas do not separate verbs from objects.**
	✘ Google provides a number of <u>free, services</u>. ***Explanation:*** **Commas do not separate adjectives from nouns.**
	✘ The <u>CEO, of Google</u> has prioritized the launch of enterprise products to compete directly with Microsoft. ***Explanation:*** **Commas do not separate related prepositional phrases.**
	✘ Sergey Brin <u>is currently the president of technology, and is a member of the board of directors</u>. ***Explanation:*** **Commas do not separate two predicates with a single subject.**
	✘ <u>Sergey Brin is currently the president of technology, Larry Page is currently the president of products</u>. ***Explanation:*** **Commas do not separate two independent clauses not connected with a coordinating conjunction (this is called a** *comma splice***).**
	✘ Google's stock price rose rapidly, <u>after it went public</u>. ***Explanation:*** **Commas do not separate a dependent clause at the end of a sentence.**
	✘ <u>To acquire On2 Technologies</u>, was a key move in improving Google's video compression capabilities. ***Explanation:*** **Commas do not separate infinitives that serve as subjects from verbs.**
	✘ <u>Acquiring On2Technologies</u>, was a key move in improving Google's video compression capabilities. ***Explanation:*** **Commas do not separate gerunds that serve as subjects from their related verbs.**
	✘ Google's <u>nearly, limitless</u> email service is free. ***Explanation:*** **Commas do not separate adverbs from adjectives.**

Semicolons

One major use for semicolons is to emphasize the relatedness between two independent clauses (see Table A.2). In a series, semicolons also separate items that contain internal commas or that are particularly long. Each rule in this section is identified with a letter (S, for semicolon) and a number.

TABLE A.2

Semicolon Rules

Rules	Examples
S1. Use a semicolon between two closely related independent clauses omitting *and*, *but*, *or*, or *nor*.	✔ Google's business model focuses on providing applications free of charge to users and receiving revenue through advertising; Microsoft's business model focuses on selling applications to users without the clutter of advertising. ***Explanation:*** **The semicolon separates two closely related independent clauses to emphasize their relatedness.**
	Alternatively: Google's business model focuses on providing applications free of charge to users and receiving revenue through advertising. Microsoft's business model focuses on selling applications to users without the clutter of advertising.
	Explanation: **A period separates two independent clauses.**
	✘ Google's business model focuses on providing applications free of charge to users and receiving revenue through advertising, Microsoft's business model focuses on selling applications to users without the clutter of advertising. ***Explanation:*** **A comma does not separate two independent clauses (unless connected by a coordinating conjunction). Using a comma in this way is called a comma splice.**
S2. Use a semicolon between two independent clauses separated by transitional expressions.	✔ Google's business model focuses on providing applications free of charge to users and receiving revenue through advertising; on the other hand, Microsoft's business model focuses on selling applications to users without the clutter of advertising. ***Explanation:*** **Semicolons separate two independent clauses separated by a transitional expression.**
	✔ Google offers more than 30 major products and services; however, Google derives 90 percent of its revenues through Google Web Search. ***Explanation:*** **Semicolons separate two independent clauses separated by a transitional expression.**
S3. Use semicolons between items in a series that contains internal commas.	✔ Google's major offices in the United States are in Mountain View, California; New York City; and Seattle, Washington. ***Explanation:*** **Semicolons separate items that contain internal commas in a series.**
	✔ The Google delegation includes Jeff Huber, senior vice president of engineering; Omid Kordestani, senior advisor in the Office of the CEO; and Rachel Whetstone, vice president of public policy and communications. ***Explanation:*** **Semicolons separate items that contain internal commas in a series.**
S4. Use semicolons in a series of long dependent clauses.	✔ Google's excellent brand recognition is due to a variety of factors, including that it accounts for 67 percent of the global search market; that it owns the popular online video service YouTube; and that, in spite of stiff competition, it maintains a dominant market share for webmail. ***Explanation:*** **Semicolons add clarity by separating long items in a series.**

Colons

Colons precede further explanations or elaborations. This rule is identified by letters (Co, for colon) and a number (see Table A.3).

Dashes and Hyphens

A dash is not the same as a hyphen; each has unique functions, and the two marks of punctuation should not be used in place of one another. A third, related mark is called an en dash. Table A.4 displays the widths and functions of hyphens, en dashes, and dashes.

The rules for dashes and hyphens are extensive, with many exceptions (see Table A.5). Consult a comprehensive style guidebook to ensure complete accuracy. Each rule in this table is identified with a letter (D, for dash; N, for en dash; and H, for hyphen) and a number.

TABLE A.3

Colons

Rule	Examples
Co1. Use a colon for further explanation or elaboration following an independent clause.	✔ Google faces <u>two major challenges</u>: It lacks product integration and its profitability is weakened by major currency fluctuations. ***Explanation:* The colon separates a complete thought with an elaboration of the *two major challenges*.**
	✔ Compared to other free webmail services, Gmail provides <u>several major benefits</u>: It provides more storage than any other major competitors, it contains a more efficient search-oriented interface, and it has a superior spam filter. ***Explanation:* The colon separates a complete thought with elaboration of the *several major benefits*.**
	✔ Google Sites has limited control of <u>various web design tools</u>: For example: you are restricted in using HTML, CSS, and JavaScript. ***Explanation:* Independent clauses and related series are often separated by a colon and phrases such as for *example, such as,* and *namely*.**
	✘ <u>Google's seven product groups are</u>: Google.com, applications, client, Google GEO, Android and Google Mobile, Google Checkout, and Google Labs. ***Explanation:* The underlined introductory expression is not an independent clause, so a colon is inappropriate. It separates the verb from the object of the sentence (see C10, above).**
	✔ <u>Google's seven product groups are the following</u>: Google.com, applications, client, Google GEO, Android and Google Mobile, Google Checkout, and Google Labs. ***Explanation:* The underlined introductory expression is an independent clause, so a colon is appropriate.**

TABLE A.4

Dashes and Hyphens

	Symbol	When to Use
Dash (also called em dash)	—	To take the place of commas, semicolons, colons, or parentheses to add emphasis. Should be used sparingly. Consists of two hyphens with no space on either side.
En dash (also called figure dash)	–	To separate a range of values, such as years or page numbers
Hyphen	-	To combine words (compound modifiers, some compounds)

TABLE A.5

Dash and Hyphen Rules

Rules	Examples
D1. Use dashes in place of commas for emphasis (often in pairs).	✔ Google Translate—which supports 59 languages—allows you to translate passages into nearly any language you can imagine. ***Explanation:* Using dashes instead of commas highlights the additional information in a much stronger way.**
D2. Use a dash in place of a semicolon for emphasis (but not between two independent clauses).	✔ Google Translate provides fairly good translation—that is, if you consider 70 to 75 percent accuracy as good. ***Explanation:* Substituting a semicolon with a dash emphasizes the closely related afterthought.**
D3. Use a dash in place of a colon for emphasis.	✔ Google Translate provides poor translation for most Asian languages—especially Chinese, Japanese, and Korean. ***Explanation:* Substituting a dash for a colon highlights the elaboration in a much stronger way.**

TABLE A.5

(Continued)

Rules	Examples
D4. Use dashes in place of parentheses for emphasis.	✔ WorldLingo—Google Translate's top competitor—provides the most accurate translation for most European languages. ***Explanation:*** **Substituting dashes for parentheses highlights the additional information in a much stronger way.**
D5. Use a dash to emphasize a single word.	✔ Innovation—that's what Google is all about. ***Explanation:*** **This dash draws sharp attention to the term *innovation* and defines it as a central feature of Google culture.**
D6. Use a dash for repetitions and restatements.	✔ Get a username now—before it's too late. ***Explanation:*** **The dash restates *now* to reinforce urgency.**
D7. Use a dash to summarize a preceding list.	✔ Brazil, Russia, India, China—these countries are the future for market growth. ***Explanation:*** **This dash separates a series of items with a summary of what they are.**
N1. Use an en dash to connect numbers or other items in a range.	✔ Google's headquarters are open for tours 10 a.m.–3:30 p.m. Monday–Friday. ***Explanation:*** **En dashes are used to separate a range of values, such as these ranges in hours and days.**
H1. Use a hyphen to connect adjectives that modify a noun.	✔ Computer programmers have <u>high-pressure jobs</u>. ***Explanation:*** **An adjective phrase or clause in front of a noun is hyphenated.**
	✘ Her computer programming job involves <u>high-pressure</u>. ***Explanation:*** **An adjective phrase or clause that does not precede a noun is not hyphenated.**
	✔ Her computer programming job involves <u>high pressure</u>. ***Explanation:*** **An adjective phrase or clause that does not precede a noun is not hyphenated.**
	✔ One of Google's <u>long-term objectives</u> is to rival Facebook with its social networking services. ***Explanation:*** **An adjective + noun combination in front of a noun is hyphenated.**
	✔ Over the <u>long term</u> Google seeks to rival Facebook in the area of social networking. ***Explanation:*** **An adjective + noun combination that does not precede a noun is not hyphenated.**
	✔ The <u>one-way road</u> in the Googleplex campus passes through three parks. ***Explanation:*** **A compound that includes a number or letter in front of a noun is hyphenated.**
	✔ The road that passes through the Googleplex is <u>one way</u>. ***Explanation:*** **A compound that includes a number or letter and does not precede a noun is not hyphenated.**
	✔ Larry Page is one of the most <u>well-known business executives</u> in the world. ***Explanation:*** **An adverb + participle combination in front of a noun is hyphenated.**
	✔ Larry Page is <u>well known</u> around the world for his leadership in the technology business. ***Explanation:*** **An adverb + participle combination that does not precede a noun is not hyphenated.**
	✔ Google Docs provides an <u>easier-than-ever approach</u> to team writing. ***Explanation:*** **A comparative phrase that includes the word *than* and that precedes a noun is hyphenated.**
	✔ Google Docs makes team writing <u>easier than ever</u>. ***Explanation:*** **A comparative phrase that includes the word *than* and that follows a noun is not hyphenated.**
	✔ Larry and Sergey's <u>agreed-upon plan</u> was to sell off Google so that they could focus on their academic studies. ***Explanation:*** **A participle + adverb combination in front of a noun is hyphenated.**
	✔ Larry and Sergey had <u>agreed upon</u> a plan that would allow them to sell Google and continue their academic studies. ***Explanation:*** **A participle + adverb combination that does not precede a noun is not hyphenated.**

TABLE A.5

(Continued)

Rules	Examples
	✔ Google executives have adopted a <u>wait-and-see mentality</u> as far as developing a new social networking platform. ***Explanation:* A verb + verb (often joined by *and* or *or*) combination in front of a noun is hyphenated.**
	✔ Google executives will <u>wait and see</u> how the market emerges before committing more resources to developing a new social networking platform. ***Explanation:* A verb + verb (often joined by *and* or *or*) combination that is not in front of a noun is not hyphenated.**
	✔ The <u>break-even point</u> is around sales of $4.3 billion. ***Explanation:* A verb + adverb combination in front of a noun is hyphenated.**
	✔ We will <u>break even</u> when we reach sales of $4.3 billion. ***Explanation:* A verb + adverb combination that does not precede a noun is not hyphenated.**
	✔ She sent a <u>thank-you note</u> to each of the board members for their time and contributions. ***Explanation:* A verb + noun combination in front of a noun is hyphenated.**
	✔ I want to <u>thank you</u> for your time and contributions. ***Explanation:* A verb + noun combination that does not precede a noun is not hyphenated.**
	✔ Google has made <u>across-the-board cuts</u>. ***Explanation:* Common phrases used to modify a noun are hyphenated.**
	✔ Google will make cuts <u>across the board</u>. ***Explanation:* Common phrases that do not precede a noun are not hyphenated.**
H2. Use hyphens for particular kinds of compound adjectives as described here.	✔ We take a <u>research-based approach</u> to marketing. ***Explanation:* A noun + participle combination is always hyphenated.**
	✔ Our approach to marketing is <u>research-based</u>. ***Explanation:* A noun + participle combination is always hyphenated.**
	✔ We have a <u>long-standing commitment</u> to net neutrality. ***Explanation:* An adjective + participle combination is always hyphenated.**
	✔ Our commitment to net neutrality is long-standing. ***Explanation:* An adjective + participle combination is always hyphenated.**
	✔ <u>High-priced products</u> are not part of Google's business model. ***Explanation:* An adjective + noun + *ed* combination is always hyphenated.**
	✔ Google's business model does not involve any products that are <u>high-priced</u>. ***Explanation:* An adjective + noun + *ed* combination is always hyphenated.**
	✔ <u>Price-conscious customers</u> tend to use Google Docs rather than Microsoft Office. ***Explanation:* A noun + adjective combination is always hyphenated.**
	✔ Most customers who choose Google Docs over Microsoft Office are <u>price-conscious</u>. ***Explanation:* A noun + adjective combination is always hyphenated.**

Quotation Marks

Quotation marks are used to display direct quotations, exact words, and some titles. Each rule in Table A.6 is identified by a letter (Q, for quotation) and a number.

Italics

Italics are used to emphasize words and phrases, highlight definitions, and set apart some titles. Alternatively, writers sometimes use underlining in place of italics. Each rule in Table A.7 is identified by a letter (I, for italic) and a number.

TABLE A.6

Quotation Mark Rules

Rules	Examples
Q1. Use quotation marks to enclose direct quotations.	✔ As Larry Page stated, "I'm excited about our opportunities to make a big difference in people's lives through technology." ***Explanation:*** **The quotation marks surround the *exact statement* made by Larry.**
	✘ Larry Page stated that "he's excited about opportunities to make a difference in people's lives through technology." ***Explanation:*** **Indirect statements typically begin with *that* and paraphrase a person's statements.**
Q2. Use quotation marks to indicate the exact words of a source or speaker.	✔ Larry Page said that Google's technologies "make a big difference in people's lives." ***Explanation:*** **The quotation marks indicate that these are exact words and not paraphrased.**
	✔ Larry and Sergey often say that their ultimate goal is to create the "perfect search engine." ***Explanation:*** **The quotation marks indicate that these are exact words and not paraphrased.**
Q3. Use quotation marks to enclose titles of articles, presentations, and speeches.	✔ Randall Stross discussed the culture of education at Google in his recent article "What Is Google's Secret Weapon? An Army of Ph.D.'s." ***Explanation:*** **Quotation marks surround the name of an article.**
	✔ Larry Page's speech, "Don't Be Evil," at the annual convention revealed his basic philosophy about developing products and services for customers. ***Explanation:*** **Quotation marks surround the name of a speech.**

TABLE A.7

Rules for Italics

Case	Examples
I1. Use italics to emphasize a word or phrase.	✔ The misspelled term *googol* became the name of the company. ***Explanation:*** **The word *googol* is emphasized by use of italics.**
	✔ *To google it* has become part of everyday language much the way *to xerox it* was an everyday phrase in the 1980s. ***Explanation:*** ***To google it* and *to xerox it* are italicized to highlight particular terms.**
I2. Use italics for formal definition.	✔ The term *cloud computing* refers to using remote servers hosted on the Internet, rather than local servers or personal computers, to manage and process data. ***Explanation:*** **Terms that are formally defined are typically italicized as is the case with *cloud computing*.**
I3. Use italics for titles of books, newspapers, and magazines.	✔ Larry and Sergey are featured nearly once each month in *The Wall Street Journal*. ***Explanation:*** ***The Wall Street Journal* is a newspaper, so it is italicized.**
	✘ Reports that Larry Page would replace Eric Schmidt as CEO first surfaced in "Bloomberg Businessweek." ***Explanation:*** ***Bloomberg Businessweek* is the name of a magazine and should be italicized.**

Parentheses

Although people sometimes use parentheses and dashes interchangeably, they have opposite purposes. Dashes are intended to emphasize and draw attention to the phrase they set off, whereas parentheses are used to set off nonessential elements and are thus intended to de-emphasize the phrase that is contained within them. Each of the rules in Table A.8 is labeled with a letter (P, for parentheses) and a number.

TABLE A.8

Rules for Parentheses

Rules	Examples
P1. Use parentheses to enclose details and explanation.	✔ All correspondence can be sent to the CEO (Eric Schmidt), the global sales director (Nikesh Arora), or the vice president of public policy and communications (Rachel Whetstone). ***Explanation:*** **By providing names in parentheses, additional details are provided for each position. The use of parentheses rather than dashes or commas emphasizes positions and de-emphasizes names.**
	✔ Google has been identified as the most recognized brand in the world for three of the past five years (2009, 2011, 2012). ***Explanation:*** **Provides additional information about the years.**
	✔ Google's recent acquisitions (AdMob, On2 Technologies, ZAO Begun) show that it is aggressively pursuing new technologies. ***Explanation:*** **Provides additional details about the acquisitions.**
	✔ Please send your comments to Google's cloud computing team within two weeks (by May 29). ***Explanation:*** **Clarifies the deadline.**
P2. Use parentheses to enclose references and directions.	✔ Please read my report (attached to this email) about opportunities for Google in emerging markets in Africa. ***Explanation:*** **Parentheses enclose directions to locate the report.**
	✔ My last email to Larry (dated July 15) outlined a plan for Google opportunities in emerging markets in Africa. ***Explanation:*** **Parentheses provide a date as a reference to a prior email.**

Numbers, Dates, and Currency

Multiple rules apply to the treatment of numbers in a text. The following ones—in Table A.9—are identified by a letter (N, for number) and a number.

TABLE A.9

Rules for Numbers

Case	Examples
N1. Spell out numbers one through ten.	✔ Google's <u>two largest markets</u> are the United States and the United Kingdom. ***Explanation:*** **The number is spelled out since it is ten or less.**
	Exceptions: When related numbers within a sentence or paragraph are above ten.
	✔ In Google's senior management team, <u>3 of the 15 members</u> are former Microsoft employees. ***Explanation:*** **Since a reference to 15 members is made, any other numbers referring to members should also be written in figure style.**
	When referring to figures.
	✔ You can see Google's sales projections in <u>Figure 3</u>. ***Explanation:*** **Any reference to a figure, table, or chart uses figure style.**
N2. Use numerals for numbers above ten.	✔ Google has <u>43 major product groups</u>. ***Explanation:*** **Numbers over ten are generally written in figure style.**
	✔ My Gmail account has <u>8,028 messages</u>. ***Explanation:*** **Numbers in thousands are generally written in numerals.**

TABLE A.9

(Continued)

Case	Examples
N3. Spell out numbers when they begin a sentence.	✔ <u>Eleven members</u> of Google's senior management team are former Microsoft employees. ***Explanation:* Since the first word is a number, it is spelled out.**
N4. Use a combination of numerals and words for large numbers (over a million).	✔ Revenues at Google topped <u>$2 billion</u> for the second consecutive year. ***Explanation:* Large numbers typically include figures and words to avoid displaying too many zeroes.** ✔ The mapping software project required nearly <u>3 million hours</u> of development. ***Explanation:* Large numbers typically include figures and words to avoid displaying too many zeroes.**
N5. Use numerals for dates.	✔ July 3, 2017 ***Explanation:* Most dates are written with the month in word form to avoid confusion since some countries use a day-month-year format.** **Alternatively:** 2017-07-03 ***Explanation:* The *International Organization for Standardization* has adopted the YYYY-MM-DD format.** **Avoid:** July 3rd, 2017 ***Explanation:* Endings to numbers such as *nd* and *rd* are avoided in most business communication.**
N6. Use numerals with currency symbols in text.	✔ On average Google software programmers make <u>$174 per hour</u>. ***Explanation:* Currency amounts are written in figure form preceded by currency symbols.** ✔ Many small businesses spend less than <u>$525 per month</u> on Google AdWords campaigns. ***Explanation:* Currency amounts are written in figure form preceded by currency symbols.**
N7. Spell out the word *percent* in text.	✔ The United States is Google's largest geographic market, accounting for approximately <u>47 percent of total revenues</u>. ***Explanation:* The word *percent* is typically spelled out within sentences.** **Exception:** Tables, forms, highly statistical documents.
N8. Use parentheses to indicate precise figures in text.	✔ Approximately half of Google's revenues (<u>47.3 percent</u>) came from the United States. ***Explanation:* Precise figures are often placed in parentheses so that readers can process the information more easily.** ✔ Nearly all of Google's revenues come from advertising (<u>$2.1 billion in advertising revenue out of $2.3 billion in total revenue</u>). ***Explanation:* Precise figures are often placed in parentheses in text so that readers can process the information more easily.**
N9. Spell out fractions in text.	✔ <u>One-fourth of all small businesses</u> in the United States use Google AdWords for advertising. ***Explanation:* Fractions are spelled out in text.** **Exception:** Mixed numbers (whole number plus fraction). ✔ Each year Google holds a <u>3½-day conference</u> for software developers. ***Explanation:* Since the number is mixed (whole number, 3, plus fraction, 1/2), the fraction is written in figure form.**
N10. Clearly differentiate adjacent numbers.	✔ In 2017, 89 percent of Gmail account holders accessed their email daily. ***Explanation:* A comma is used to help readers quickly identify that these are two separate numbers.** ✔ You can have up to twelve 100MB websites. ***Explanation:* One of the adjacent numbers may be spelled out to help readers see that they are two separate numbers.**

Grammar

Table A.10 presents only a few key rules of grammar among the many that guide written language. Each is identified with a letter (G, for grammar) and a number.

TABLE A.10

Grammar Rules

Case	Examples
G1. Ensure that pronouns agree with their antecedents in number, gender, and/or person.	✗ Google supports their employees by providing many professional development opportunities. ***Explanation:* The antecedent, *Google*, is a singular thing. It should not be referred to as *they*, implying a plural.** ✔ Google supports its employees by providing many professional development opportunities. ***Explanation:* The antecedent, *Google*, is a singular thing. Therefore, it is appropriately referred to as *it*.** ✗ Every employee at Google has their own health plan. ***Explanation:* The antecedent, *employee*, is a singular person. Therefore, it should not be referred to as *they*, implying a plural. Writers sometimes do this incorrectly to avoid using sexist language.** ✔ Every employee at Google has his/her own health plan. ***Explanation:* The antecedent, *employee*, is a singular person. Therefore, it is appropriately referred to as *he* or *she*.** **Alternatively:** Employees at Google have their own health plans. ***Explanation:* Changing the subject to a plural form avoids the necessity of using an awkward *he/she* expression.** ✗ Either Bill Gates or Satya Nadella will deliver their speech at the shareholders meeting. ***Explanation:* Two singular nouns connected by *or* or *nor* are treated with singular pronouns.** ✔ Either Bill Gates or Satya Nadella will deliver his speech at the shareholders meeting. ***Explanation:* Two singular nouns connected by *or* or *nor* are treated with singular pronouns.** ✗ I want to express our appreciation to you for your outstanding contributions over the past year. ***Explanation:* The singular pronoun, *I*, should not be the antecedent for a plural possessive pronoun, *our*.** ✔ I want to express my appreciation to you for your outstanding contributions over the past year. ***Explanation:* The singular pronoun, *I*, is an antecedent for the singular possessive pronoun, *my*.** **Alternatively:** On behalf of all members of the senior management team, I want to express our appreciation to you for your outstanding contributions over the past year. ***Explanation:* The antecedent for the plural possessive pronoun, *our*, is a plural noun, *members of the senior management team*.**
G2. Ensure that subjects are paired with the correct verb form to achieve subject-verb agreement.	✗ Microsoft and each of its partners in the delegation is providing reports about upcoming developments in cloud computing. ***Explanation:* The subject is plural (Microsoft and its partners), so the verb should not be in singular form (*is*).** ✔ Microsoft and each of its partners in the delegation are providing reports about upcoming developments in cloud computing. ***Explanation:* The subject is plural (Microsoft *and* its partners), so the verb should be in plural form (*are*).** ✗ The handbook of employee benefits are online. ***Explanation:* The subject is singular (*handbook*), so the verb should not be in plural form (*are*).** ✔ The handbook of employee benefits is online. ***Explanation:* The subject is singular (*handbook*), so the verb should be in singular form (*is*).**

TABLE A.10

(Continued)

Case	Examples
G3. Avoid comma splices.	✗ Sergey Brin is currently the president of technology, Larry Page is currently the president of products. ***Explanation:*** **Two independent clauses should be separated by a period or a semicolon. They should never be separated by a comma unless a coordinating conjunction is inserted.**
	✔ Sergey Brin is currently the president of technology. Larry Page is currently the president of products. ***Explanation:*** **A period separates two independent clauses that are not separated by a coordinating conjunction.**
	✔ Sergey Brin is currently the president of technology, and Larry Page is currently the president of products. ***Explanation:*** **A coordinating conjunction *and* a comma can separate two independent clauses.**
G4. Check for vague pronouns and replace them.	✗ Microsoft and Google are well known for attracting innovative, playful employees. They are also known for creating a work culture where playing practical jokes is common. They even play jokes on the public. ***Explanation:*** **Some readers will be confused whether the *they* pronoun refers to *Microsoft and Google* or the *employees.***
	✔ Microsoft and Google are well known for attracting innovative, playful employees. The work culture allows employees to play practical jokes on one another. Sometimes the employees even play jokes on the public. ***Explanation:*** **By removing so many references to *they*, the meaning becomes much clearer.**
G5. Check for dangling expressions and misplaced modifiers and rewrite to eliminate them.	✗ Bill Gates spoke about his experience taking his SAT examination at the local university. ***Explanation:*** **Dangling expressions create confusion because parts of the sentence are not in the correct order. In this sentence did Bill Gates talk at the local university or take the exam at the local university?**
	✔ Bill Gates spoke at the local university about his experience taking his SAT examination. ***Explanation:*** **This sentence is clear that Bill Gates spoke at the local university.**
	✗ Scoring 1590 out of a possible 1600, the SAT exam didn't seem difficult. ***Explanation:*** **Many dangling modifiers occur when an introductory participial phrase lacks a subject or does not clearly relate to the material that follows. This sentence is not clear because an SAT exam cannot score 1590 (rather, a person can score a 1590 on an SAT exam).**
	✔ Scoring 1590 out of a possible 1600, Bill Gates thought the SAT exam didn't seem difficult. ***Explanation:*** **This sentence is clearer—Bill Gates is the person who scored 1590 out of 1600.**
	Alternatively: Because he scored 1590 out of a possible 1600, Bill Gates thought the SAT exam didn't seem difficult.

Commonly Misspelled and Confused Words

Spell-checking software is a good tool for identifying most, but not all, spelling errors. Table A.11 lists some commonly misspelled words. Most of the misspellings that are identified as incorrect in this table would not be detected by spell-checking software. For a comprehensive list, consult a guidebook such as the *Gregg Reference Manual*. An ✗ precedes **incorrect** examples, and a ✔ precedes **correct** examples. Parts of speech are noted where the two cases differ.

TABLE A.11

Commonly Misspelled and Confused Words

Case	Examples	Case	Examples
Accept: to receive (verb) *Except:* apart from; without (preposition or conjunction)	✗ We <u>except</u> all forms of payment. ✔ We <u>accept</u> all forms of payment. ✗ We take all forms of payment <u>accept</u> debit cards. ✔ We take all forms of payment <u>except</u> debit cards.	*Apprise:* to inform *Appraise:* to assess	✗ You need to <u>appraise</u> him of the situation. ✔ You need to <u>apprise</u> him of the situation. ✗ You should <u>apprise</u> his performance. ✔ You should <u>appraise</u> his performance.
Advice: suggestions or recommendations (noun) *Advise:* to offer suggestions or to recommend (verb)	✗ Could you provide some <u>advise</u>? ✔ Could you provide some <u>advice</u>? ✗ Please <u>advice</u> whether to move forward with this plan. ✔ Please <u>advise</u> whether to move forward with this plan.	*Capital:* funds or resources; uppercase letters *Capitol:* a government building where the legislature meets	✗ We lack the <u>capitol</u> to make this investment. ✔ We lack the <u>capital</u> to make this investment. ✗ Our CEO testified at the <u>capital</u>. ✔ Our CEO testified at the <u>capitol</u>.
Affect: to influence (verb) *Effect:* a result (noun)	✗ This <u>effects</u> our business plan. ✔ This <u>affects</u> our business plan. ✗ This has an <u>affect</u> on our business plan. ✔ This has an <u>effect</u> on our business plan.	*Complementary:* something that fits well with or completes another person or object *Complimentary:* free (as in a product or service); giving praise	✗ We form teams with <u>complimentary</u> skill sets. ✔ We form teams with <u>complementary</u> skill sets. ✗ You will receive a <u>complementary</u> movie ticket as a show of thanks. ✔ You will receive a <u>complimentary</u> movie ticket as a show of thanks.
All ready: complete; finished *Already:* previously; by this time	✗ The business plan is <u>already</u>. ✔ The business plan is <u>all ready</u>. ✗ She <u>all ready</u> wrote the business plan. ✔ She <u>already</u> wrote the business plan.	*Council:* a group that provides advice or recommendations (noun) *Counsel:* to advise (verb), advice (noun), or legal representative(s) (noun)	✗ We will follow the recommendations of the <u>counsel</u>. ✔ We will follow the recommendations of the <u>council</u>. ✗ We received <u>council</u> not to provide this information publicly. ✔ We received <u>counsel</u> not to provide this information publicly.
Altogether: entirely *All together:* all in one place or in unison	✗ This report is <u>all together</u> confusing. ✔ This report is <u>altogether</u> confusing. ✗ We should work on the report <u>altogether</u>. ✔ We should work on the report <u>all together</u>.		

TABLE A.11

(*Continued*)

Case	Examples	Case	Examples
Elicit: to draw or bring out (verb) *Illicit:* illegal (adjective)	✘ We want to <u>illicit</u> their feedback. ✔ We want to <u>elicit</u> their feedback. ✘ We should avoid any <u>elicit</u> conduct. ✔ We should avoid any <u>illicit</u> conduct.	*Moral:* principles of rules of conduct *Morale:* cheerfulness, confidence, enthusiasm	✘ Our company abides by high <u>morale</u> and ethical standards. ✔ Our company abides by high <u>moral</u> and ethical standards. ✘ Our company enjoys high employee <u>moral</u>. ✔ Our company enjoys high employee <u>morale</u>.
Incite: cause, give rise to (verb) *Insight:* novel idea (noun)	✘ His decisions have <u>insighted</u> a minor revolt among employees. ✔ His decisions have <u>incited</u> a minor revolt among employees. ✘ The business plan contains many <u>incites</u>. ✔ The business plan contains many <u>insights</u>.	*Precede:* to come beforehand *Proceed:* continue or move forward	✘ Typically, the phone interview <u>proceeds</u> a face-to-face interview. ✔ Typically, the phone interview <u>precedes</u> a face-to-face interview. ✘ In some cases, you <u>precede</u> directly to a face-to-face interview. ✔ In some cases, you <u>proceed</u> directly to a face-to-face interview.
Insure: to provide compensation for damages *Ensure:* to make certain	✘ Let's <u>ensure</u> this against legal liabilities. ✔ Let's <u>insure</u> this against legal liabilities. ✘ Let's <u>insure</u> a smooth transition to the new executive team. ✔ Let's <u>ensure</u> a smooth transition to the new executive team.	*Principal:* primary; a person with authority *Principle:* a standard or guideline	✘ My <u>principle</u> place of work is in my home office. ✔ My <u>principal</u> place of work is in my home office. ✘ One <u>principal</u> for working effectively at home is to limit distractions. ✔ One <u>principle</u> for working effectively at home is to limit distractions.
Its: possessive for it *It's:* contraction for it is	✘ The beauty of this plan is <u>it's</u> simplicity. ✔ The beauty of this plan is <u>its</u> simplicity. ✘ <u>Its</u> rare to have such a detailed plan. ✔ <u>It's</u> rare to have such a detailed plan.	*Than:* used with comparisons *Then:* used to indicate a point in time	✘ Gold values have grown faster <u>then</u> stock prices. ✔ Gold values have grown faster <u>than</u> stock prices. ✘ When gold values start falling, <u>than</u> you should move your funds into stocks. ✔ When gold values start falling, <u>then</u> you should move your funds into stocks.
Lose: to lose or to misplace (verb) *Loose:* not tight (adjective)	✘ We'll <u>loose</u> this opportunity if we do not act immediately. ✔ We'll <u>lose</u> this opportunity if we do not act immediately. ✘ There is a <u>lose</u> connection between your ideas. ✔ There is a <u>loose</u> connection between your ideas.		

Capitalization

This is a short list of several important capitalization rules for business communication. See Table A.12 for these rules and several examples. Consult a comprehensive style guide for all capitalization rules.

TABLE A.12

Capitalization Rules

Rules	Examples
Ca1. Capitalize proper nouns, abbreviations and acronyms, and brand names.	✔ Sundar Pichai became CEO in 2015. ***Explanation:*** Sundar Pichai is a proper name. CEO is an acronym. ✘ The name of the company's headquarters is googleplex. ***Explanation:*** Googleplex is a proper noun and should be capitalized. ✔ The company's competitors include Apple and Microsoft. ***Explanation:*** Apple and Microsoft are brand names. ✘ The company is partnering with sprint. ***Explanation:*** Sprint is a brand name and should be capitalized.
Ca2. Capitalize a person's title when it appears before a proper noun but not when it is used alone.	✔ The company delegation visited President Obama. ***Explanation:*** The title precedes a proper noun. ✘ The company delegation visited professor Janikowski, an expert in artificial intelligence. ***Explanation:*** Professor should be capitalized since it precedes a proper noun. ✔ Our marketing director visited with Stephanie Larsen, operations manager at Google. ***Explanation:*** The two titles in this sentence, marketing director and operations manager, do not precede a proper noun. ✘ You should direct all questions to our Corporate Communication Officer. ***Explanation:*** This title should not be capitalized because it is not preceded by a proper noun.
Ca3. Capitalize names of areas and regions.	✔ Google's headquarters are in Northern California. ***Explanation:*** Northern California is capitalized because it is the name of a region. ✘ Google's headquarters are North of Los Angeles. ***Explanation:*** North should not be capitalized because it refers to a direction, not an area or region.
Ca4. Capitalize names of ethnic groups.	✔ The company is seeking to hire a higher percentage of African Americans for entry-level developer positions. ***Explanation:*** *African Americans* should be capitalized because the term refers to an ethnic group. ✘ The company has tried to attract hispanic americans without much success. ***Explanation:*** *Hispanic Americans* should be capitalized because the term refers to an ethnic group. Exceptions: The words *black* and *white* are usually not capitalized when referring to ethnic or racial groups.
Ca5. Capitalize titles of books, reports, chapters, and other named documents.	✔ Google has recently contributed to journal articles such as "Gender Differences in Factors Influencing Pursuit of Computer Science and Related Fields" and "Gender Differences in High School Students' Decisions to Study Computer Science and Related Fields." ***Explanation:*** These articles are appropriately capitalized. ✘ The company recently created a white paper called *data analytics in the era of artificial intelligence*. ***Explanation:*** The title of the white paper should be capitalized (with the exceptions of articles and prepositions).
Ca6. Capitalize the first word of a sentence, a quotation, and an independent clause after a colon.	✔ Sergey Brin stated, "We had a simple idea that not all pages are created equal." ***Explanation:*** *We* is capitalized because it is the first word in a quotation. ✔ Our company's current strategy is straightforward: We must integrate cognitive capabilities into all our products. ***Explanation:*** *We* is capitalized because it is the first word in an independent clause after a colon.

Application Exercises

Directions: Place commas and other punctuation marks throughout these passages wherever needed, and name the rule that applies.

Example: To develop supply chain software and services Microsoft partnered with Infosys.

Answer: To develop supply chain software and services, Microsoft partnered with Infosys. (C7)

Comma Exercises

1. Bill Gates and Paul Allen who were childhood friends founded Microsoft in 1975. Bill met Steve Ballmer who would later become the CEO of Microsoft at Stanford.

2. Bill Gates met the man who would later become the CEO of Microsoft at Stanford.

3. The two technology companies that consistently have the most brand value are Microsoft and Google.

4. In fact they consistently showed high profits during the recent recession.

5. Microsoft and Google the two companies that consistently have the most brand value showed high profits during the recession.

6. To hire Qi Lu as the new president of the Online Services Division was a masterful move by Microsoft.

7. Microsoft enjoys almost limitless advantages in terms of research and development budgets.

8. Steve Ballmer took a smooth methodical approach to developing the five-year strategy.

9. Microsoft from my perspective gained its market dominance through anti-competitive practices.

10. Microsoft Word if you're looking for maximum functionality in your word processing far outperforms Google Docs.

11. Microsoft Word far outperforms Google Docs if you're looking for maximum functionality in your word processing.

12. Steve Ballmer CEO from 2000 to 2014 was a college classmate of Bill Gates.

13. MS-DOS an operating system developed initially for IBM personal computers became Microsoft's first major success.

14. As a result Bill Gates moved the headquarters to Washington.

15. Bill Gates gave up the CEO position in 2000 but he remained active at Microsoft by taking a position as chief software architect.

16. In the early years of Microsoft Bill Gates spent most of his time conducting business but also stayed involved in programming.

17. Microsoft's product categories include operating systems, server applications, information worker productivity applications, business solution applications, high-performance computing applications and software development tools.

18. In 2008 Microsoft acquired Calista Technologies Kidaro Rapt Fast Search & Transfer Navic Networks and DATAllegro.

19. Most people who know Bill say that he is a stubborn determined executive.

20. After Bill moved to management roles he still read and approved most of the code developed for MS-DOS.

21. Under the new set of human resources guidelines all Microsoft employees must declare whether or not they are smokers.

22. Prior to joining the Microsoft team in 2009 Dr. Lu had worked at Yahoo! for 10 years.

23. By acquiring competitor companies Microsoft gains new customers new technology and new ideas.

24. Often Microsoft acquires competitor companies.

25. In July Bill Gates said that he would no longer focus on the day-to-day business activities at Microsoft.

26. In 1980 IBM agreed to let Microsoft develop an operating system for one of its lines of personal computers.

27. IBM agreed to let Microsoft starting in 1980 develop an operating system for one of its lines of personal computers.

28. The new Microsoft Office Suite will go on sale in July.

29. The new Microsoft Office Suite will go on sale in July 2015.

30. The new Microsoft Office Suite will go on sale on July 15 2015.

31. If you purchase the new Microsoft Office Suite between July 15 2015 and January 15 2016 you will receive a $100 rebate.

32. Microsoft employs more than 89000 employees.

33. The ED division develops and produces products such as the Xbox 360 third-party games and the Zune digital music and entertainment platform.

34. Steve Ballmer recently resigned as CEO of Microsoft, he is now the owner of the Los Angeles Clippers.

Semicolon, Colon, and Comma Exercises

35. Microsoft faces two major threats piracy and patent lawsuits.

36. Bill Gates focuses on product development and strategy Satya Nadella focuses on operations.

37. Bill Gates focuses on product development and strategy on the other hand Satya Nadella focuses on operations.

38. Microsoft's American offices are in Redmond Washington New York City San Francisco Birmingham Alabama and Phoenix Arizona.

39. Cloud computing involves three possible platforms software-as-a-service (SaaS) platform-as-a-service (PaaS) and infrastructure-as-a-service (IaaS).

Dash and Hyphen Exercises

40. Microsoft Office the leading business software for over two decades takes a research based approach to identifying new markets.

41. Microsoft's spreadsheet software Excel is preferred by engineers economists and statisticians due to the well known statistical functions.

42. Microsoft's strategy will likely produce positive results over the long term.

43. Managers say the break even point is around $50 million.

44. In the short run Microsoft would like to increase its market share in the search engine market.

45. Microsoft has a short run goal to increase its market share in the search engine market.

46. Microsoft's investment based approach to research and development ensures that it produces highly applied results.

47. Because Microsoft has adopted an approach to R&D that is investment based it tends to produce results that are highly applied.

Directions: For each set of choices below (separated by slashes), choose the correct answer and name the rule that applies.

Example: Microsoft has a presence in over one hundred/100 countries.

Answer: 100 (N2)

Italics and Quotation Mark Exercises

48. The recent story about Microsoft in *The Wall Street Journal*/"The Wall Street Journal" was called Microsoft's Gamble on Cloud Computing/"Microsoft's Gamble on Cloud Computing."

49. Bill Gates said that he'd like to see the phrase *go bing it*/"go bing it" replace the phrase *go google it*/"go google it."

50. At the luncheon, his speech, titled *The Road to the Future*/"The Road to the Future," laid out his vision for cloud computing over the next decade.

Number Exercises

51. In 2013, 3/three Microsoft business divisions were combined.

52. Revenues for the last fiscal year were $62,484 million/$62,484,000,000.

53. Revenues rose 28 percent/28% over the past year.

54. Microsoft employs over 89 thousand/89,000 employees.

55. Microsoft has five/5 business divisions.

56. 5/Five Microsoft divisions make up the Microsoft corporation.

57. Microsoft lost money in 3/three of the 17/seventeen product groups.

58. Microsoft's largest division, Microsoft Business, accounts for approximately 31%/31 percent of its revenues.

59. In the search engine market, Google holds 63%/63 percent of the market share, compared to just 13%/13 percent for Microsoft.

60. Microsoft was fined $388 million/388 million dollars for infringing on Uniloc's anti-piracy software.

61. The Washington home of Bill Gates is valued at approximately $125 million/$125,000,000, resulting in annual property taxes of roughly $990 thousand/$990,000.

Grammar Exercises

62. Microsoft joined with Accenture to create Avanade, an IT consultancy. They/It specialize/s in connecting to consumers through online platforms such as social networks.

63. Neither Yahoo! nor Microsoft has/have increased its/their market share in the search engine market for the past five years.

64. Microsoft hold/s its/their annual shareholders meeting at the corporate headquarters.

65. Every new Microsoft employee should provide copies of his/her/their Social Security card/s at the orientation.

66. The manual about computer programming tips are/is on reserve at the corporate reading room.

67. Microsoft and its competitors in the technology industry is/are constantly changing.

Misspelled Words Exercises

68. Many of Google's HR policies are aimed at eliciting/illiciting honest feedback.

69. The advice/advise on Microsoft's Help menu is not helpful.

70. All employees should ensure/insure that their LinkedIn pages do not contain any content contrary to the Code of Conduct.

71. This decision affects/effects every aspect of our marketing strategy.

72. Their next step is to identify how to raise enough capital/capitol for the venture.

73. She told me that the two products contain complementary/complimentary features.

74. This search engine is much more reliable than/then Google's.

Capitalization Exercises

75. Sundar Pichai, CEO/ceo of Google, says that Google is ahead of its competitors in the race to develop artificial intelligence capabilities.

76. We just hired her for a Senior Developer/senior developer position.

77. Google's headquarters are located in Silicon Valley/silicon valley.

78. The headquarters are located just West/west of Sunnyvale.

79. Please contact Eileen Chao, Communications Lead/communications lead, for additional press inquires.

80. Ms. Chao explained, "We/we will invest more than $50 million this year to research and develop artificial intelligence."

Formatting for Letters and Memos

Components of Memos

- To
- From
- Date
- Subject
- Body
- Notations (optional)

Although most written business correspondence is sent electronically, memos and letters continue to be used in various business situations. When you do use memos and letters, you should use professional, standard formatting. This appendix contains three examples. You can find additional examples in the online resources, including formats for letters that aren't on letterhead and that are more than one page long.

Memos are most often used for formal announcements within organizations (see Figure B.1 for a sample memo). In most cases today, memos are distributed as attachments (usually in .pdf format) by email or other forms of electronic messages. Regardless of how memos are distributed, they contain fairly standard components and formatting. They begin with *To*, *From*, *Date*, and *Subject* lines. Then, they move to the body or message, without a salutation or closing. They end with special notations (see below for common types of notations in memos and letters). In most organizations, you can use standard memo templates, which are often created in-house and stored on corporate intranets. If your organization does not have a standard template, you can choose from dozens of professional ones that come with word processing software.

Business letters are written far less today than a few decades ago; however, they are still appropriate for various business situations. When you write a letter on behalf of your organization, use official letterhead and find out if your organization employs a standard format. If it doesn't, you can choose from several options, including block format and modified block format (see examples in Figures B.2 and B.3). Block format is the most common because it is very clean, with flush-left margins for the entire letter.

Memos and letters may contain various notations, including the following:

Components of Letters

- Letterhead
- Date
- Inside address
- Salutation
- Body
- Closing/Signature
- Notations (optional)

- *Carbon copy* (indicated by *c:* or *cc:*). This allows primary message recipients to see all individuals who have received a copy of the memo or letter.
- *Distribution list* (indicated by *Distribution:*). When you send a memo or letter to many individuals, you can use a distribution list to ensure everyone knows who received the document.
- *Preparer's initials.* When someone has written the letter on behalf of the sender, the preparer places his/her initials in lowercase text.
- *Enclosure or attachments* (indicated by *Enclosure*, *Enc.*, *Attachment*, or *Att.*). When you are including additional documents or materials, make reference to them with a notation.

FIGURE B.1

Sample Memo

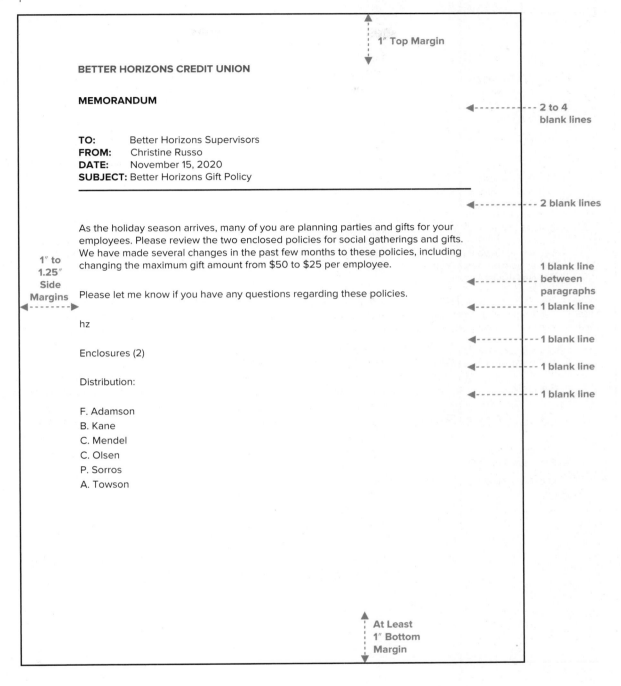

FIGURE B.2

Sample Letter in Block Format Style

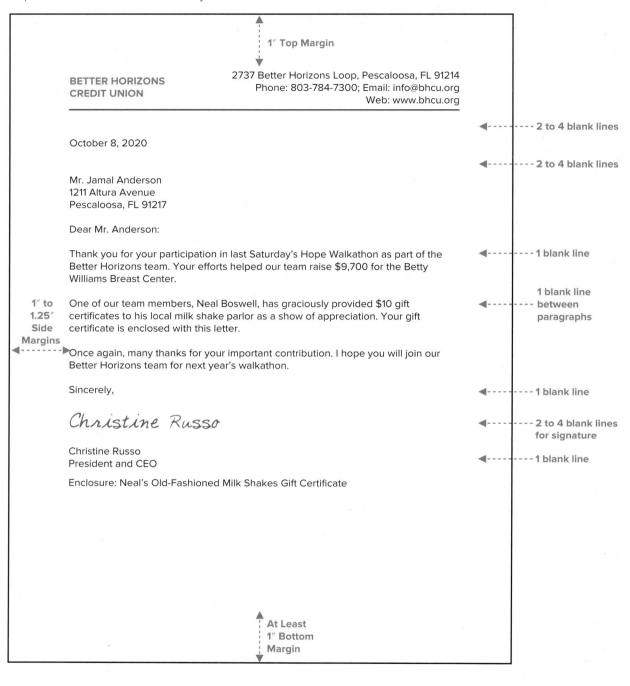

1″ Top Margin

**BETTER HORIZONS
CREDIT UNION**

2737 Better Horizons Loop, Pescaloosa, FL 91214
Phone: 803-784-7300; Email: info@bhcu.org
Web: www.bhcu.org

◄------- 2 to 4 blank lines

October 8, 2020

◄------- 2 to 4 blank lines

Mr. Jamal Anderson
1211 Altura Avenue
Pescaloosa, FL 91217

Dear Mr. Anderson:

Thank you for your participation in last Saturday's Hope Walkathon as part of the Better Horizons team. Your efforts helped our team raise $9,700 for the Betty Williams Breast Center.

◄------- 1 blank line

**1″ to
1.25″
Side
Margins**

One of our team members, Neal Boswell, has graciously provided $10 gift certificates to his local milk shake parlor as a show of appreciation. Your gift certificate is enclosed with this letter.

◄-------- 1 blank line between paragraphs

Once again, many thanks for your important contribution. I hope you will join our Better Horizons team for next year's walkathon.

Sincerely,

◄------- 1 blank line

Christine Russo

◄------- 2 to 4 blank lines for signature

Christine Russo
President and CEO

◄------- 1 blank line

Enclosure: Neal's Old-Fashioned Milk Shakes Gift Certificate

**At Least
1″ Bottom
Margin**

FIGURE B.3

Sample Letter in Modified Block Format Style

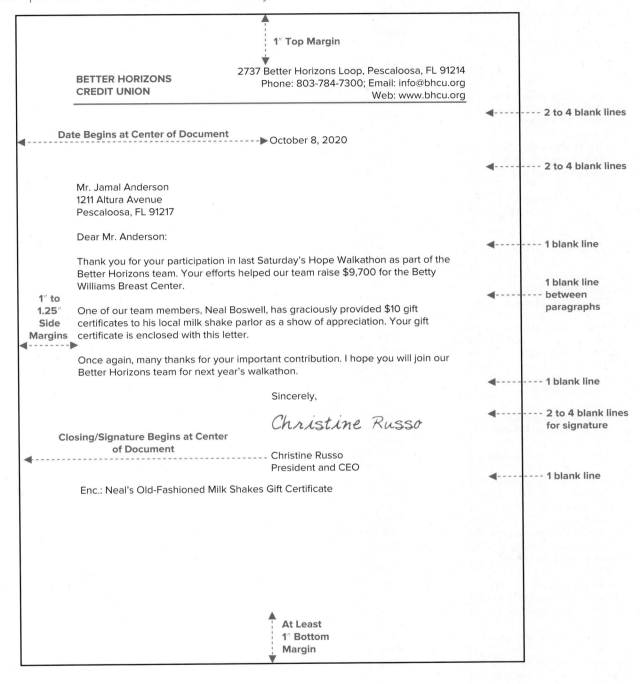

1″ Top Margin

2737 Better Horizons Loop, Pescaloosa, FL 91214
Phone: 803-784-7300; Email: info@bhcu.org
Web: www.bhcu.org

**BETTER HORIZONS
CREDIT UNION**

2 to 4 blank lines

Date Begins at Center of Document → October 8, 2020

2 to 4 blank lines

Mr. Jamal Anderson
1211 Altura Avenue
Pescaloosa, FL 91217

Dear Mr. Anderson:

1 blank line

Thank you for your participation in last Saturday's Hope Walkathon as part of the Better Horizons team. Your efforts helped our team raise $9,700 for the Betty Williams Breast Center.

1 blank line between paragraphs

**1″ to
1.25″
Side
Margins**

One of our team members, Neal Boswell, has graciously provided $10 gift certificates to his local milk shake parlor as a show of appreciation. Your gift certificate is enclosed with this letter.

Once again, many thanks for your important contribution. I hope you will join our Better Horizons team for next year's walkathon.

1 blank line

Sincerely,

2 to 4 blank lines for signature

Christine Russo

**Closing/Signature Begins at Center
of Document**

Christine Russo
President and CEO

1 blank line

Enc.: Neal's Old-Fashioned Milk Shakes Gift Certificate

At Least
1″ Bottom
Margin

Index

Note: Page numbers followed by f or t represent figures or tables, respectively.